THE MIXTECS
OF COLONIAL OAXACA

THE MIXTECS
OF COLONIAL OAXACA

Ñudzahui History,
Sixteenth through Eighteenth Centuries

KEVIN TERRACIANO

Stanford University Press
Stanford, California

Stanford University Press
Stanford, California

Published with the assistance of the Department of History and the Dean of Social Sciences
of the University of California at Los Angeles

Printed in the United States of America on acid-free, archival-quality paper

Library of Congress Cataloging-in-Publication Data

Terraciano, Kevin
    The Mixtecs of colonial Oaxaca: Nudzahui history, sixteenth through eighteenth
centuries / Kevin Terraciano.
        p.   cm.
    Includes bibliographical references and index.
    ISBN 0-8047-3756-8 (cl. : alk. paper) : ISBN 0-8047-5104-8 (pbk. : alk. paper)
        1. Mixtec Indians—History—Sources.   2. Mixtec language—Writing.   3. Mixtec
Indians—Social life and customs.   4. Indians, treatment of—Mexico—Oaxaca
Valley—History—Sources.   5. Manuscripts, Mixtec—Mexico—Oaxaca Valley.   6.
Mexico—History—Spanish colony, 1540–1810.   7. Oaxaca Valley—History—Sources.   8.
Oaxaca Valley—Social life and customs.   I. Title.
    F1219.8.M59 T47   2001
    972'.74—dc21

                                                                    2001020022

Typeset by Princeton Editorial Associates, Inc., Scottsdale, Arizona, in 10/13 New Baskerville

Original printing 2001

To Lisa

CONTENTS

ILLUSTRATIONS

FIGURES

MAPS

TABLES

ACKNOWLEDGMENTS

I am thankful for the opportunity to study Mixtec history. I have met many kind people in Oaxaca and in Mexico since I began this project in 1988. I am very grateful for their goodwill and friendship. I look forward to continuing my work in Oaxaca and to working with Oaxaqueños in California.

I am very fortunate to have learned from James Lockhart at the University of California, Los Angeles. Jim introduced me to the field, taught me Classical Nahuatl, and challenged me to do original research with native-language writings. Today, he continues to inspire me as a colleague and a friend.

Many colleagues have contributed their talents to this work. For reading and making extensive suggestions and comments on versions of the manuscript, I would like to thank John Chance, Maarten Jansen, Frances Karttunen, Cecelia Klein, James Lockhart, Pamela Munro, John Pohl, Mary Elizabeth Smith, Lisa Sousa, and Ronald Spores. Also, I have benefited from the assistance, encouragement, and good advice of William Autry, Elizabeth Boone, Woodrow Borah, Louise Burkhart, Nancy Farriss, Eulogio Guzmán Acevedo, Robinson Herrera, Barbara Hollenbach, Kathryn Josserand, Naomi Lamoreaux, Ubaldo López, John Monaghan, José Moya, H. B. Nicholson, Michel Oudijk, Aurora Pérez Jiménez, Jeanette Favrot Peterson, Armando Pimentel, Stafford Poole, Matthew Restall, Carlos Rincón Mautner, María de los Ángeles Romero Frizzi, Anita Sánchez de Downs, Susan Schroeder, Barry Sell, Jayne Spencer, Nancy Troike, and Bas van Doesburg.

In Oaxaca, I thank Gonzalo Rojo Martínez, former director of the Judicial Archive of Oaxaca, for his invaluable assistance. Gonzalo gave me full access to the documents and went out of his way to make my research possible. He has gone above and beyond his duty as an archivist in rescuing, preserving, organizing, and cataloging truckloads of documentation from local archives throughout the state of Oaxaca. I would also like to thank the director of the Archivo General de la Nación, Dra. Stella María González Cícero, and the dedicated staff in galería 4. I am grateful to the directors and staffs of the Biblioteca Nacional de Antropología e Historia in Mexico City, the

Archivo General de las Indias in Seville, and the Archivo del Estado de Oaxaca in Oaxaca City. I thank the authorities of Tlaxiaco and Teposcolula for giving me access to their municipal archives. I thank Dra. María Isabel Grañén Porrúa of the Biblioteca Francisco de Burgoa in Oaxaca, Laura Gutiérrez and Michael Hironymous of the Benson Library, and Bill Frank at the Huntington Library for allowing me to work with their priceless books and manuscripts.

My work has benefited from the study of multiple codices, maps, lienzos, and other sketches and paintings. I am grateful to the following institutions for granting me permission to publish photographs of the original images or of facsimile copies: the Akademische Druck-u. Verlagsanstalt in Graz, Austria; the Huntington Library in San Marino, California; the Middle American Research Institute at Tulane University in New Orleans, Louisiana; the Archivo del Museo Nacional de Antropología e Historia in Mexico City; the Benson Latin American Collection at the University of Texas, Austin; the Real Academia de la Historia in Madrid; the Bodleian Library at the University of Oxford; and the Archivo General de la Nación in Mexico City.

I am grateful for financial support provided by the National Endowment of the Humanities, the UCLA Latin American Studies Center, UCMexus, the UCLA International Studies Overseas Program, the Del Amo Endowment, and the UCLA Center for Medieval and Renaissance Studies. I would also like to thank the dean of Social Sciences, Scott Waugh, the vice chancellor of Research, Roberto Peccei, and the UCLA Department of History (especially chairperson Brenda Stevenson) for assistance with production costs. So many of my mentors, colleagues, and friends at UCLA have supported my work that I will thank them in person instead of filling up pages with their names. In spirit, I thank the late E. Bradford Burns, whose teaching inspired me to enter the field of Latin American history.

It has been a great pleasure and privilege to work with Norris Pope, director of Stanford University Press, and editor Anna Eberhard Friedlander. I would also like to thank Cyd Westmoreland of Princeton Editorial Associates for her patience and wisdom.

The love and encouragement of my mother and father in West Warwick, Rhode Island has been a constant source of inspiration and support. I can never thank them enough. Finally, I am truly grateful to Lisa Sousa, who has contributed to this project in countless ways, from researching in Mexico to reading versions of the manuscript. For this reason and for so many others, I thank Lisa with all my heart.

K. T.
Los Angeles, California

CHAPTER 1

Introduction

THE MIXTECA is a cultural and historical term for an area in southern Mexico named after its most prominent inhabitants, the Mixtecs. The Mixteca stretches west to east from the border area of the modern state of Guerrero to the Valley of Oaxaca, and north to south from southern Puebla to the Pacific Ocean. This area can be divided into four main geographical subregions: the Alta, the Baja, the Coast, and the Valley. The climatic and ecological diversity of the region is striking. The rugged mountains of the semiarid Alta descend to the hot and humid plains of the Pacific Coast to the south and to the fertile, temperate Valley to the east. Today, most Mixtecs live in the western part of the state of Oaxaca. *Mixteca* is actually a Nahuatl name meaning "people of the cloud place." In their own language, the so-called Mixtecs referred to themselves as *tay ñudzahui,* "people of the rain place" or "people from the place of Dzahui," the rain deity. When Spaniards arrived in the 1520s, they encountered hundreds of separate, autonomous states. These states were united by a shared culture and a common language, expressed in the ethnic term *Ñudzahui* (pronounced *nu sawi* or *nu dawi*).[1]

Three centuries of colonial rule mark the general temporal boundaries of this study, but the main focus is the especially well documented period between 1550 and 1750. This history is based primarily on Ñudzahui writings from the period, including pictorial texts and native-language alphabetic records. Pictographic writings date from the immediate preconquest period to the eighteenth century. Native-language writings in the Roman alphabet are dated from the late 1560s to the first decade of the nineteenth century, concentrated in the period between 1570 and 1770. I also use Nahuatl- and Spanish-language sources from the Mixteca, especially for the sixteenth century. The earliest colonial writings shed light on the period of initial contact between cultures and, by inference, are relevant for the study of preconquest indigenous society and culture. This study treats the entire cultural area in general terms, focusing especially on the Mixteca Alta.

After observing the repeated occurrence of the term *Ñudzahui* in the documentation, I have decided to adopt the word that people used in reference to themselves and continue to use in their own language today. I do not consider *Mixtec* to be a misnomer (I use the term in this work), but I think that *Ñudzahui* is an appropriate term, especially for this period. Whereas the indigenous term appears numerous times in native-language writings from the colonial period, I have never seen *Mixtec* used in the native-language record. I continue to refer to the entire region as the Mixteca, as it is called today, because there are many other peoples in the area who did not call themselves *tay ñudzahui*. The Mixteca was and continues to be a complex, multiethnic cultural area. In the colonial Teposcolula jurisdiction, the heart of the Alta region, where the term was used most frequently, three distinct variants of the Mixtec language and five separate native languages were spoken.

The Mixteca was one of the most densely populated cultural areas of Mesoamerica.[2] In the postclassic period (circa A.D. 1000–1500), Ñudzahui states attained unprecedented levels of artistic expression, demographic growth, and political expansion. By the last century of this period, groups from the Mixteca Alta exerted a powerful influence in the Valley of Oaxaca, burying their lords in richly decorated tombs at the monumental site of Monte Albán and forging marriage alliances with Zapotec states.[3] However, in the final decades before the Spanish invasion, much of the Mixteca Baja and Alta had been subjected by the Mexica, or "Aztecs," of central Mexico and their allies, between the reigns of Moteucçoma I and II, or from around 1440 onward. Some areas had come under Mexica influence only a few years before the Spanish arrival. Mexica tribute lists indicate that places in the Mixteca Alta such as Coixtlahuaca, Texupa, Tamasulapa, Yanhuitlan, Teposcolula, and Nochixtlan gave cloth, jade, green quetzal feathers, cochineal, gold dust, and warrior outfits to Tenochtitlan.[4] Despite giving tribute to a distant power, Ñudzahui states maintained their own rulers and forms of organization and did not become Mexica, culturally or politically. Nor did large contingents of Mexica move into the region. Cultural interaction with the Nahuas of central Mexico was more complex and reciprocal than the standard imperial narrative suggests. Royal marriage alliances, shared boundaries, interregional migration, long-distance trade, and many common Mesoamerican cultural attributes had brought groups from the two cultural regions into contact long before the Mexica rise to power.

By the end of 1520, Spaniards had entered and reconnoitered parts of the Mixteca before consolidating forces and attacking Tenochtitlan. Spanish expeditions passed through the Mixteca Alta in 1520 and 1521. When the Mexica submitted to a combined native and Spanish siege of their island *altepetl* (local Nahua state), Hernando Cortés sent Pedro de Alvarado with a group of Nahua "allies" to the coastal Mixtec area of Tututepec, which was renowned for its gold and other natural resources. The Spaniards used native aides and pictorial manuscripts to guide them to the most densely populated and wealthiest areas in the Mixteca. By 1523, the Spaniards had "pacified" much of the region. Most Ñudzahui lords must have realized that they had little chance of defeating a combined Spanish-native force coming from central Mexico, especially after hearing of Tenochtitlan's destruction. The Spaniards countered resistance with severe retaliation; flight from fully sedentary settlements was not a viable option. As representatives of local states that were not united politically or militarily, many native rulers were more inclined to negotiate with the newcomers than to fight and face the risk of annihilation. In any case, by the 1530s, Spanish rule in the Mixteca had been firmly established and was never seriously challenged during the colonial period, despite numerous local riots and rebellions.

Based on existing settlement patterns, *encomiendas* (grants of native tribute and labor) were assigned to the Spanish conquistadores between 1525 and 1530, and Nahua contingents were given some land to settle in the Valley of Oaxaca (a name derived from the Nahuatl place-name Huaxyacac). By 1530, Spanish *alcaldes mayores* (tribute collectors and first-instance judges) had begun to operate in the area.[5] Meanwhile, ecclesiastics followed in the footsteps of the conquerors. To the Spaniards, the Mixteca was one of the most attractive regions outside the densely populated Valley of Mexico. The Dominican order moved into and monopolized the Mixteca and the rest of Oaxaca soon after its rivals, the Franciscans, had occupied much of central Mexico. The Dominicans were forced to abandon Yanhuitlan, a major population center in the Mixteca Alta, in the face of continued "idolatries" and a conflict with the *encomendero* (holder of an encomienda grant). After a lengthy inquisitorial trial in the mid-1540s, the friars returned in force and founded multiple *conventos* (residences) and churches in the region by the end of the sixteenth century.

Europeans introduced deadly diseases into the Americas, which devastated the indigenous population. Epidemics pounded one generation after another for more than a century. Plagues were especially virulent in lowland areas, but people in highland regions were also vulnerable. Population estimates for the densely settled Mixteca Alta subregion at the time of the conquest place the total number of inhabitants at approximately 700,000.[6] This figure was reduced to about 57,000 by 1590, reaching its nadir toward the mid-seventeenth century and leveling off at about 30,000 by 1670. In the sixteenth century, Yanhuitlan had the largest population of any settlement in the Mixteca Alta, occupying the most expansive of many small valleys in the region (today called the Nochistlan Valley), measuring some fifteen by fifteen kilometers with numerous lateral extensions and rivers. Yanhuitlan's estimated preconquest population of 90,000 plummeted to about 10,000 in 1590 and had reached approximately 3,000 by 1680. After the mid-seventeenth century the population began a slow and steady climb until the present day, never coming close to the preconquest total.[7]

Despite its dense population and moderate climate, the Mixteca, and the region of Oaxaca in general, did not attract many Spanish settlers in the colonial period. To most Spaniards, Oaxaca was too distant from the center of Spanish economic activity. In particular, it was too far away from the commercial route that ran from the mining areas of north-central New Spain to Mexico City and from the capital to the Atlantic coast.[8] The movement of silver and goods and the provision of services along this trunkline did not reach southern Mexico in the colonial period. As a result, even by the end of the eighteenth century, only about three hundred non-native households, or less than 5 percent of the total population, lived in the colonial jurisdiction of Teposcolula

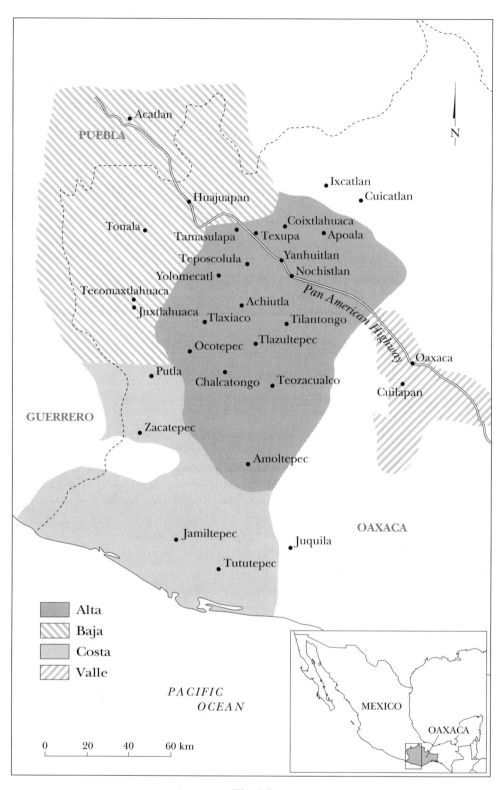

MAP 1. The Mixteca.

Alta
Baja
Costa
Valle

PUEBLA
GUERRERO
OAXACA

Acatlan
Ixcatlan
Cuicatlan
Huajuapan
Tonala
Coixtlahuaca
Tamasulapa Texupa Apoala
Teposcolula Yanhuitlan
Yolomecatl Nochistlan
Tecomaxtlahuaca
Achiutla
Juxtlahuaca Tlaxiaco Tilantongo
Ocotepec Tlazultepec
Putla
Chalcatongo Teozacualco
Oaxaca
Cuilapan
Zacatepec
Amoltepec
Jamiltepec Juquila
Tututepec

Pan American Highway

PACIFIC
OCEAN

0   20   40   60 km

N

MEXICO
OAXACA

in the Mixteca Alta. And this area contained the highest concentration of non-native residents in the Mixteca.[9] The census of 1746 shows that non-native families lived in only seven of the sixty-five Ñudzahui communities listed for that jurisdiction.[10] The strong indigenous presence in contemporary Oaxaca confirms the long-term consequences of relative isolation from Spanish contact.

As a well-defined and relatively isolated cultural area where the art of writing flourished before and after the conquest, the Mixteca offers a propitious convergence of circumstances for the study of indigenous lifeways in the colonial period. No native cultural group in the Americas possesses a comparable (extant) preconquest and postconquest pictorial record, a tradition that was complemented and then marginalized by native-language alphabetic writing. The magnificent Mixtec written record enables a diachronic and nearly continuous study of society and culture from the immediate preconquest period through the eighteenth century.

The interdisciplinary nature of this history requires an introduction to works in many related fields of study. The following section attempts to introduce some of the most relevant writings on the Mixtecs of Oaxaca and other Mesoamerican groups.

Historiography

The historical literature on the Indians of Mexico has been dominated by works on the Aztecs or Nahuas of central Mexico. The earliest works relied mainly on the most conspicuous sources generated by Spaniards, especially secular and ecclesiastical chronicles, royal decrees and laws, and official reports and correspondence. In these sources and histories based on them, native peoples were seen entirely through Spanish eyes. Spaniards tended to emphasize their own actions and introductions in "New Spain." Native survivals seemed minimal from this point of view. Charles Gibson was among the first historians to go beyond the "official story." In a history of the Nahua community of Tlaxcala in the sixteenth century, and then in a broader study of Spanish-native interaction in the Valley of Mexico, Gibson used archival sources from Mexico to demonstrate that Spanish introductions were based on existing indigenous mechanisms that continued to function in the sixteenth century and that native patterns of organization were more important than laws or Spanish institutions in shaping local realities.[11] Outside central Mexico, Nancy Farriss applied similar local sources to the study of Yucatan, extending her analysis into the late colonial period and showing how the Yucatecan Maya adopted active strategies for survival after the conquest.[12]

Several distinguished historians have applied similar sources and methods to the study of colonial Oaxaca. Woodrow Borah's book on the silk industry in the Mixteca Alta focused on native-Spanish relations within the context of this lucrative, introduced enterprise. Borah and Sherburne Cook produced a series of demographic studies, including a detailed work on the Mixteca Alta, that offered wider implications for the history of Mexico and Mesoamerica.[13] William Taylor's study of indigenous land tenure in the Valley of Oaxaca showed that the relative weakness of Spanish competition for land in this region enabled indigenous nobles and communities to maintain some of the largest landholdings in the Valley by the end of the colonial period. The growth of Spanish estates there was gradual and limited compared with that in central Mexico and northern Mexico.[14] Taylor followed this work with a comparative study of social patterns of drinking, homicide, and rebellion in the Mixteca Alta and the Valley of Mexico in the eighteenth century. John Chance's study of race and class in colonial Oaxaca city and his subsequent work on the Sierra Zapoteca and southern Puebla have made possible interregional and cross-cultural comparisons, particularly for the late colonial period.[15] Two Mexican historians, María de los Angeles Romero Frizzi and Rudolfo Pastor, have published complementary social and economic histories of the Mixteca Alta in the colonial period.[16] Romero Frizzi focuses on Spanish traders from the conquest to the early eighteenth century, but her work also contains valuable contributions on the topic of native-Spanish interaction. Pastor treats Mixtec society and the regional economy in the eighteenth century and early independence period. Both scholars have used local archival records from the Mixteca Alta as the basis of their findings. These histories of colonial Oaxaca are especially relevant to the present study.

Nobody has contributed more to our understanding of pre-Hispanic Mixtec culture than the eminent Mexican scholar Alfonso Caso, who began to publish his work in the late 1940s.[17] Among his many accomplishments, Caso correlated the genealogical portions of postconquest pictorial manuscripts from the Mixteca with several preconquest codices that had been attributed to central Mexico, demonstrating that an entire corpus of codices was Mixtec, not Aztec.[18] He showed how the Mixtec writing system, unlike any other in Mesoamerica, kept running histories (not just dated monuments) that covered the course of centuries. Caso proved that Mixtec cultural expression and interregional politics flourished at the time of the conquest and continued into the sixteenth century. His startling findings attracted a number of scholars to the Mixteca.

Bárbro Dahlgren, Ronald Spores, and Mary Elizabeth Smith followed Caso's work with broad, pioneering studies of Mixtec writing, society, and political organization. Dahlgren published a general survey of pre-Hispanic Mixtec society and culture only five years after Caso's breakthrough on the codices, based mainly on a synthesis of sixteenth-century Spanish-language sources, especially chronicles, the *Relaciones geográficas* of the late sixteenth century, and a limited corpus of archival records.[19] Ronald Spores combined archaeological fieldwork with archival investigations to map the preconquest settlement sites of the Mixteca Alta. In the second, historical half of his first book, Spores used colonial sources on dynastic succession in Yanhuitlan to illustrate Mixtec principles of hereditary rule in the sixteenth century, with great implications for the preconquest period. Spores followed this highly original work with several studies of Mixtec society and culture before and after the conquest.[20] Spores's basic mapping of sociopolitical units in the Mixteca Alta was indispensable to the present work. Mary Elizabeth Smith, an art historian, shed light on preconquest writing conventions by examining the entire range of colonial pictorial manuscripts, *lienzos* (paintings on cloth), and maps from the Mixteca.[21] Her work demonstrates the continued vitality of Mixtec writing in the colonial period. Most recently, Elizabeth Boone has compared Mixtec and Nahua pictorial writings from the immediate preconquest and early colonial periods.[22]

Recent interdisciplinary research has led to multiple breakthroughs in the interpretation of the preconquest-style Mixtec codices. Jill Furst wrote a detailed, insightful analysis of an extraordinary preconquest screenfold manuscript known as the *Codex Vindobonensis*.[23] Maarten Jansen set a new standard for studying the codices by consulting with Mixtecs who live in the same places that are featured in the writings, and by applying colonial data and the oral tradition to an interpretation of Vindobonensis and other codices.[24] In particular, Jansen and Aurora Pérez Jiménez have worked closely with people from the Nuundaya (Chalcatongo) area. Most recently, Jansen and Pérez have reproduced and analyzed several codices from the Mixteca, the Puebla-Tlaxcala region, and the Valley of Mexico, in collaboration with Luis Reyes García and Ferdinand Anders.[25] John Pohl's innovative study of the codices, including his recent work on "alliance corridors" within and beyond the Mixteca, sheds light on cross-cultural interactions and influences in Mesoamerica.[26] Several other scholars have made important contributions to our understanding of the codices, whose work I acknowledge in the chapter on writing.[27] Finally, a recent ethnography by John Monaghan is relevant to studies of the codices and so many other aspects of Mixtec ethnohistory.[28] Monaghan's concern with listening to how Mixtecs from Santiago Nuyoo refer to their *ñuu* (pueblo or community) has revealed an entire conceptual vocabulary. The attention to native concepts and terminology is relevant to a third major influence on the present work.

In the past half century, the translation and analysis of colonial native-language sources, written in the Roman alphabet, have become a major subdiscipline of ethnohistory. Most early indigenist philology focused on writings produced in the sixteenth century under the instruction and auspices of the religious orders. This type of work is exemplified by the collaboration of Arthur J. O. Anderson and Charles E. Dibble, who in 1950 published the first of twelve translated volumes of the *Florentine Codex*.[29] In addition to church-sponsored texts, native notaries throughout Mesoamerica generated countless unpublished records in their own languages from around the mid-sixteenth century onward. Only a small percentage of this documentation remains, yet it is a massive corpus expanding continuously with each archival investigation. In the 1970s, a small group of historians, anthropologists, and linguists began to work with archival documentation written in Nahuatl. In particular, Arthur J. O. Anderson, Frances Berdan, Pedro Carrasco, Frances Karttunen, Miguel León-Portilla, James Lockhart, and Luis Reyes García applied the high standards of Nahuatl-language studies to the translation and analysis of notarial sources.[30] The development of a historical approach based on native-language sources, called the "New Philology" by Lockhart and some of his colleagues, proceeds from social history in its concern with the behavior of groups and individuals. It also represents a shift of emphasis from institutional and career pattern history to the study of culture, modes of organization, and ways of thinking embedded in native concepts and terminology. Lockhart was the first to synthesize findings on the Nahuas of central Mexico, complemented by his own original research, in his recent book on the Nahuas.[31] Lockhart considers multiple aspects of Nahua society and culture in the colonial period from the perspective of Nahuatl-language sources; the work responds to many issues raised by Gibson and other studies based on Spanish-language records, but it also addresses several new areas of inquiry, accessible only through the use of Nahuatl writings. Other works associated with the New Philology have focused on collections of Nahuatl-language documents from particular areas of central Mexico, including Stephanie Wood on Toluca; S. L. Cline on Culhuacan and Morelos; Robert Haskett on Cuernavaca; Susan Schroeder on Chalco and the works of Chimalpahin; Susan Kellogg on Tenochtitlan; and Rebecca Horn on Coyoacan.[32] This philological tradition has had the most profound influence on the methodology and objectives of the present work.

The study of the Nahuas has contributed to the partial abandonment of the terms *Indian* and *Aztec,* forcing historians to acknowledge local differences and cultural complexities in Mesoamerica. In some respects, however, the quantity and quality of Nahuatl-language studies have reinforced a central Mexican version of indigenous history. The potential for comparison between Nahuas and other Mesoamerican language groups who wrote in their own languages is promising. Comparative studies are already fairly advanced for the Maya region. Ralph Roys and France Scholes pioneered the study of colonial Yucatec Maya in the 1930s and 1940s.[33] Roys produced a translated volume of land titles from Ebtun, for example. More recently, Philip Thompson and Matthew Restall have worked with Maya-language documents.[34] Restall's work is the first history based entirely on Maya-language sources. He analyzed hundreds of mainly late colonial notarial documents in the light of many issues addressed by Lockhart for the Nahuas and in the wake of Farriss's study based on Spanish-language sources.

The Mixtecs of Oaxaca also wrote in their own language during the colonial period. Almost as important for philological purposes, friars and bilingual native nobles produced native-language instructional materials in the sixteenth century. Very few scholars have studied the colonial Mixtec language or have worked with Mixtec-language documents from Oaxaca.[35] Two works from the 1960s opened the door for future studies of the colonial language. The first is Wigberto Jiménez Moreno's reprinting (with valuable commentary) of fray Francisco de Alvarado's Spanish-to-Mixtec *Vocabulario en lengua mixteca,* printed in 1593. The second work is a brief but useful dictionary based on the *Vocabulario* and other language texts, compiled by Evangelina Arana Osnaya and Mauricio Swadesh. In 1976, Ronald Spores made available a reprinted edition of fray Antonio de los Reyes's *Arte en lengua mixteca,* a basic grammar published in 1593. Finally, contemporary linguistic studies of Mixtecan languages are useful for the study of the colonial variants, despite significant change since the colonial period.[36]

In summary, this study has four direct intellectual influences and antecedents: history of the indigenous peoples of Mexico; native-language philological studies; Mixtec ethnohistory, including ethnography and the codices; and Mixtec (and Nahuatl) language studies. I have not mentioned the important influences of art history, women's studies, cultural and colonial studies, and comparative ethnohistory (including works on the Andes), which are addressed in different parts of the work.

Sources and Methods

This study is based primarily on native-language archival sources and published texts that I have located in Oaxacan archives, the national archive in Mexico City, and collections in the United States.[37] More than twenty types of archival documents are written entirely in the Mixtec language, including last wills and testaments (of nobles and commoners, men and women), inventories, personal letters, criminal records (reports, testimony, confessions), land transactions (transfers, sales, and lease agreements), sales of houses and businesses, personal business accounts and inventories, community fiscal accounts, election results, tribute records, petitions to Spanish authorities, official decrees, ecclesiastical records (marriages and baptisms), primordial titles or "false titles," and the proceedings of local *cabildos* (municipal councils) on internal civil matters. Finally, I make use of several native-language church-sponsored publications, including sixteenth-century language materials (especially the *Vocabulario* and *Arte*) and fray Benito Hernández's *Doctrina en lengua misteca,* a doctrinal book printed in 1567 and 1568.[38]

In all, there are some four hundred archival native-language documents for which a date and provenance are certain; the documents range in length from one side of a sheet to as many as seventy pages. Ranging in date from 1571 to 1807, the corpus is evenly spread across time; no five-year period is undocumented. More than eighty Mixtec ñuu are represented, from Cuilapa in the Valley of Oaxaca to Tonalá in the Baja, from Coixtlahuaca in the northern Alta to Chalcatongo in the south. Most of these ñuu are concentrated in the densely populated Mixteca Alta, in the colonial jurisdiction of Teposcolula and Yanhuitlan. The coast is the only area of the Mixteca not represented. Although the last extant record was written in 1807, native-language writing in the Mixteca was clearly on the decline in many places by the 1780s. In contrast, writing was widespread in the years between 1670 and 1730, and the preceding century (1570–1670) is well documented, despite continuous population decline throughout much of the period. No doubt, this collection is only a modest proportion of all that was written.[39]

The nature of the Mixtec-language corpus has influenced the direction of my study. Most of the surviving sources were used as evidence in local civil and criminal disputes adjudicated by the Spanish alcalde mayor in a given administrative and legal jurisdiction, or *alcaldía mayor.* Documents were stored in the judicial archives of each alcaldía mayor. Thus, the documents are not confined to one given place or period but are dispersed in provenance and date.[40] By far the largest surviving collection comes from the western half of the Mixteca Alta, from the alcaldía mayor of Teposcolula and Yanhuitlan. This one extensive jurisdiction included several dozen ñuu.[41] I have also located many documents in the national archive in Mexico City, especially cases involving land disputes decided by judges of the Audiencia, or high court. Native-language records in the national archive exist for all subregions of the Mixteca except the coast. Overall, the corpus lends itself to the study of general patterns in the Mixteca rather than the microhistory of a community. With some notable exceptions, centers of Spanish activity, especially the colonial *cabeceras* (head towns, or colonial administrative centers) of the Mixteca Alta, are much better represented than other, smaller communities.

The advantage of using Ñudzahui-language sources for a history of Ñudzahui people requires little explanation. I am concerned especially with listening to the categories that people used to describe themselves, other people, places, things, actions, ideas, and concepts. The language is crucial to understanding cultural categories. The original terminology is accessible only through the native language. Spanish translations avoided the use of native words. Fundamental indigenous categories and concepts are embedded in the language of each document, regardless of its specific content. For example, people referred to their place of origin with a set of terms and names that represented multiple levels of identity and sociopolitical affiliation. Since most notarial sources were produced primarily for an indigenous audience, the language is not contrived, and Spanish introductions were generally marked by a loanword. Another reason to use native-language records is that they register the impact of the Spanish language on native speakers.

In working with native-language sources, my initial concern was to observe the repeated usage of categories across time and region and to base each chapter on native categories, rather than colonial Spanish or contemporary scholarly constructions. Before long, I began to realize that native terminology for the communities in which people lived, the relations among people, land tenure, the household, kinship, and many other categories was consistent in each region, with some notable sub-regional differences. My observation of regional patterns has allowed me to generalize about the Mixteca as a whole, rather than focusing on one of its subregions or a given community, even though most of the sources were written in the western and central parts of the Mixteca Alta. The native-language corpus is diverse and yet manageable enough to observe patterns across the entire region throughout the colonial period. Despite my emphasis on the typical, I am careful to note the date and provenance of my data. Because this work is based primarily on sources generated by indigenous notaries, I provide multiple examples and native-language quotes for the benefit of those interested in the language.

For the crucial, understudied period between the 1520s and the beginning of Mixtec-language writings in the 1560s, I use a rich collection of postconquest pictorial records and Nahuatl-language writings. Preconquest-style writing, increasingly influenced by European art style and adapted to colonial legal demands, continued throughout the sixteenth century. In some places, pictorial and alphabetic forms complemented each other. The *Codex Sierra*, written in Texupa from 1550 to 1564, is an outstanding example of a Nahuatl-language alphabetic text with a parallel pictographic component based on Mixtec conventions. Nahuatl bridged the communication gap between Castilians and Mixtecs until Ñudzahui-language writing was developed in the second half of the sixteenth century.

In addition to Ñudzahui alphabetic and pictorial writings, I use Spanish-language records. In fact, most of the Ñudzahui-language sources in my collection were filed as evidence in legal cases; each Spanish-language dossier provides the context for the document. Sometimes, Spanish officials called a bilingual expert to translate the native-language document. These translations provide invaluable information on the language of the period. And there are many legal records that do not include native-language materials. Civil cases heard by alcaldes mayores and the Audiencia, landmark cases from the Mixteca that were sent to Seville, local judicial records, inquisitorial trial records, reports of the *Relaciones geográficas,* native complaints and petitions to the alcalde mayor—all are extremely valuable sources. Spanish-language sources provide unique types of information that are not found in native-language documentation and vice versa. For example, Inquisition records from the 1540s reveal a world of change and conflict years before indigenous notaries were trained to write in the alphabet. Even when Spanish- and native-language sources refer to the same issues, or when a native document was translated into Spanish, reading one source in relation to the other sheds light on the disjunction between native concepts and Spanish perceptions of those concepts.[42] Likewise, local trial records are filled with informative narratives and incidental references to everyday behavior.

In contrast to my interest in all archival sources, I have neglected the published writings of chroniclers and official historians, such as fray Francisco de Burgoa, fray Agustín Dávila Padilla, and Antonio de Herrera y Tordesillas. The first two wrote about earlier times in which they had not lived, and they were especially intent on glorifying the efforts of their Dominican predecessors to "civilize" the "barbarous" Indians. The third author, Herrera, dedicated several pages to the Mixtecs in his multi-volume work on the Indies, but I have no idea how he arrived at his information. In the historical tradition of their day, these writers rarely indicated their sources.[43] Thus, I use these types of writings sparingly and hesitate to draw conclusions based on their interpretations.

This history relies almost entirely on what was written in pictorial or alphabetic form. Most of the writings fulfilled a particular function of colonial administration. Indigenous writers in the Mixteca did not use the alphabet for literary expression in the manner of European poetry or literature, nor were diaries kept. The annals of central Mexico have no equivalent in the Mixteca, or at least none is preserved. So the types of questions addressed are limited. Native-language writings were not likely to expound on the general injustices of the colonial system but rather directed petitions to redress specific, local grievances.[44] Mundane native-language writing was an accepted form of agency within the colonial system, but it was restricted to certain forms and functions. Rapid and sustained population loss was surely a major shock, and yet it is mentioned only indirectly in the record. If it were not for the survival of an inquisitorial trial record from Yanhuitlan, one might be led to believe the ecclesiastical chronicles and conclude that everyone immediately embraced the Christian faith. The native-language record makes no mention of rebellion, and yet there were dozens of uprisings in this period. Thus, I am mindful of the written record's potential and limitations.

This book has two broad objectives. First, I intend to study Ñudzahui culture on its own terms, comparing findings with those of other Mesoamerican groups in this period, especially the Nahuas. The Mixtecs had much in common with the Nahuas of the Valley of Mexico, Tlaxcala, Puebla, Cholula, and Cuernavaca. I am also attentive to local and regional differences within the Mixteca itself. A second major concern is the impact of Spanish introductions and colonial changes, and the impact of interactions with Spanish-speaking people, on Ñudzahui culture during the colonial period, especially from the 1540s to the mid-eighteenth century. This concern follows the first objective in that it is necessary to identify cultural categories and modes of organization in order to understand the nature of colonial changes. However, I do not equate "Ñudzahui" with "preconquest," as if culture were a static category and Mixtecs lived in their own separate world before or after the conquest.

Each of the eight core chapters examines different aspects of Ñudzahui culture and traces patterns of change from the sixteenth century to the eighteenth. As the first work to use native-language records from Oaxaca for the study of colonial history, this study treats multiple, interrelated aspects of indigenous culture rather than focusing on one specific theme, question, theory, or model. Much of the historical literature on the Indians of colonial Mexico, and on native peoples everywhere who came into prolonged contact with Europeans, discusses introduced change in terms of a gradual process or a dramatic transformation. The two basic models attribute different degrees of conflict to the contact and ascribe relative types of agency to the colonized. I have adopted aspects of both perspectives in recognition of the complex, local dimensions of cultural interaction and its implications for loss and maintenance, adaptation and creation in the colonial period.

Overview of the Chapters

This book is designed to open many doors to a relatively new area of the field, using new types of sources and interdisciplinary approaches. It consists of eight substantive chapters that might be read independently, although chapters 4 through 9 build on and refer to previous discussions. The first two chapters are complementary studies of Mixtec writing and language. The first traces the development of writing from the early postconquest period until the late colonial period, examining the transition from pictorial to alphabetic text in the sixteenth century and the eventual dominance of Spanish-language writing by the late eighteenth century. Thus, chapter 2 views the full range of Mixtec written expression from preconquest times to the end of the colonial period, introducing some of the sources used in the following seven chapters.

Since much of this work is based on native-language documentation, chapter 3 introduces the language as it was represented in colonial writings. The first part of the chapter describes how priests worked with multilingual native nobles to produce an orthography and create instructional language materials. I use these materials and data from the native-language record to define basic phonetic characteristics, orthographic conventions, and language variants. The metaphorical, reverential speech of the nobility is also addressed in the first section of the chapter. The second part of chapter 3 traces the regional evolution of Mixtec in contact with Spanish. Language contact phenomena represent the extent of cultural contact between the two societies and indicate the timing of certain changes and adaptations. This study also provides evidence of language maintenance. The impact of Spanish on Mixtec is compared with similar processes documented for Nahuatl and, to a lesser extent, Yucatecan Maya.

Chapter 4 identifies the terminology that native speakers used to refer to the communities to which they belonged: the ñuu and its constituent parts, called *siqui, siña,* and *dzini,* depending on the subregion. Some ñuu were also called a *yuhuitayu,* referring to the marriage alliance of its male or female lord with the hereditary ruler of another ñuu. This sociopolitical arrangement is treated in detail in chapter 6. The second part of chapter 4 considers how the Spanish perception and reorganization of these structures and subsequent colonial changes affected the nature of sociopolitical organization in the Mixteca.

Chapter 5 is concerned with social relations within the yuhuitayu, ñuu, and siqui (and siña and dzini). The first section examines the full range of terminology, titles, and names that Mixtecs used in reference to social rank and status, from the most prestigious *yya toniñe* (lord ruler) to the humblest *ñandahi ñandahui* (poor commoner). This part contains a brief profile of men and women in each social category and considers how this terminology of social differentiation changed in response to changing social relations. The second part considers some aspects of social conflict in the colonial period. The final section of this chapter discusses indigenous naming patterns and, in particular, how the gradual adaptation of Spanish personal names and titles reflected social relations in the colonial period.

Chapter 6 analyzes forms of political government associated with the native nobility. The first part defines the concept of hereditary rule, called *toniñe*, and describes the royal palace, or the *aniñe*. A discussion of colonial ceremonies of palace possession reintroduces the yuhuitayu, which is discussed in detail. The second part of chapter 6 demonstrates how Spanish-style municipal government and Spanish laws, customs, ceremonies, and attitudes affected native systems of hereditary rule over the course of the colonial period. This section gives equal consideration to the changing roles of women and men in native government.

Chapter 7 considers topics related to land, the household, material culture, and work. It analyzes the categorization, possession, use, distribution, and transfer of land, houses, and other property in Ñudzahui society. The second part of this chapter complements the previous discussion on land and the household by examining local and regional trade and tribute. Certain categories of men's and women's work that were most affected by colonial changes, including long-distance trade and cloth production, are given special attention in this section. This chapter also considers conflicts over land and labor.

Chapter 8 examines local Ñudzahui religious beliefs and practices after the conquest. The first section uses preconquest codices and early colonial inquisition records, among other sources, to consider how the arrival of Christianity affected certain sacred practices and beliefs in the first half of the sixteenth century. The second section employs paintings, sketches, woodcuts, and a variety of native-language and Spanish-language texts to understand how local forms of Ñudzahui Christianity developed in the Mixteca.

Chapter 9 documents some of the many references to "Ñudzahui" ethnicity in the native-language record and considers how specific social and cultural circumstances influenced self-ascribed identity in the colonial period. After analyzing how people referred to other ethnic groups, I compare the construction and articulation of Ñudzahui identity with expressions of ethnicity among the Nahuas of central Mexico and the Maya of Yucatan. The second part of this chapter considers multiethnic interactions in the Valley of Oaxaca and in cabeceras of the Mixteca Alta, where expressions of ethnicity in the written record were most common. Finally, chapter 10 summarizes the two main objectives of the present work: the study of Ñudzahui culture in the context of Mesoamerican history and the overall impact of colonial changes and interactions with Spaniards and other ethnicities.

Since native-language writings are central to this work, I will explain my conventions for reproducing Ñudzahui words and passages. All passages are reproduced according to the original orthography, with spacing adjusted to grammatical norms established in the sixteenth century. Overbars and abbreviations are resolved, but no punctuation has been added to the original passages. In rewriting Ñudzahui words, I use the most common version of the word as it was written in the Teposcolula area of the Mixteca Alta, where the *Vocabulario* and the *Arte* of 1593 were produced. Conventional forms of words are italicized. In order to avoid italicizing Ñudzahui words each time, I reserve the use of italics for the first appearance of a term in each chapter (this is the case with all non-English terms). Nonconventional spellings or variations of a word outside the Teposcolula area are placed in quotes. When quoting Ñudzahui-language passages longer than a few words, I reproduce the original orthography of the passage and place it in brackets immediately following my translation. For longer passages, I use block quotations with the original text following my translation. In cases when quotes clutter the text, I have placed passages and examples in the notes.

I use Ñudzahui place-names, but in most cases I use the name that is used today. Sometimes, I provide both names, placing one or the other in parentheses. For example, the Ñudzahui community of Yodzocahi is better known by its modern name, Yanhuitlan, which was derived from Nahuatl. Likewise, Yucundaa is better known by its current name, Teposcolula. Every place with a Nahuatl-based name had a Ñudzahui counterpart. In their own native-language writings, people always referred to Yodzocahi and rarely wrote Yanhuitlan. Appendix A provides Ñudzahui equivalents of place-names derived from Nahuatl. Appendix B presents transcriptions and translations of Ñudzahui-language documents from the Mixteca Alta.

CHAPTER 2

Writing

THE MIXTECS PRACTICED a magnificent pictographic writing tradition in the post-classic and early colonial periods.[1] Ñudzahui writers continued to paint on deerskin, cloth, and paper in the early colonial period, but the Spanish administrative and legal system forced them to direct their images to colonial officials. In response, writers adopted multicultural forms and styles to communicate with both Spanish and indigenous audiences. By the second half of the sixteenth century, the Spanish preference for alphabetic script over pictorial and oral claims required native nobles to learn a new writing system. Writers used the new alphabet to convey many traditional types of information, especially the political claims of hereditary rulers and the autonomy of the communities to which they belonged. European priests taught alphabetic writing to the sons and grandsons of native nobles who had practiced the art of writing on deerskin. The existence of a close preconquest equivalent facilitated a rapid adoption of the new system.[2] A few decades after the conquest, when Nahuatl fulfilled a crucial role as the lingua franca of Mesoamerica, Ñudzahui-language alphabetic writing took root, spread rapidly, and eventually marginalized the pictorial tradition by the early 1600s. By the end of the seventeenth century, scribes in hundreds of communities throughout the Mixteca used the alphabet to write in their own language. Finally, in the late eighteenth century, Castilian became the dominant written language in the region.

This chapter examines the early and late colonial transformations of Ñudzahui writing, focusing on the florescence of native-language alphabetic writing between these two transitional periods, from the second half of the sixteenth century to the late colonial period. The native-language corpus, which spans more than two centuries, is an invaluable source of information for the following seven chapters of this work. At the same time, this study considers preconquest and colonial pictorial writings as informative, historical texts that complement the alphabetic corpus in function and content. The discussion begins with a concise introduction to preconquest pictographic writing.

Preconquest Writing in the Mixteca

Ñudzahui preconquest-style codices are painted on fig bark paper or strips of deer hide covered or sized with a gessolike layer of lime plaster and sewn together as a screenfold manuscript, so that each strip could be folded back upon the next and viewed individually. The whole work could also be stretched out so that one side could be viewed simultaneously in the manner of a lengthy foldout.[3] Codices relied on many formats to convey a narrative. On the obverse sides of the *Codex Nuttall* and *Codex Vindobonensis,* for example, the pictographic material is arranged to be viewed from right to left, in a meandering boustrophedon pattern. Direction is guided by incomplete vertical red guidelines that divide each page into two or more columns or sections; the reader follows the narrative in and out of each column through the breaks in the vertical guidelines (see fig. 2.1).[4] The strips, or "pages," are evenly sized, and the sequence of events, like the codex itself, is connected. In the *Nuttall* and *Vindobonensis,* the reverse sides are painted so that the unfolded screenfolds can be turned around and read in the other direction. Some of these extremely detailed painted works exceed ten meters in length when completely unfolded.[5] When folded, codices were as small and portable as a book.

Preconquest writing consisted of essentially three techniques: direct depiction by images; ideograms or logograms, conventional images that convey a word or idea without a reference to language; and phonetic transcription in which symbols are used to express the sound of words or roots of words.[6] Because Ñudzahui is a tonal language, the possibilities of logographic and phonetic expression were expanded through the use of "visual morphemes" or "tone puns."[7] All three techniques—pictographic, ideographic, and phonetic—could operate simultaneously in the same scene. In their direction (linear format) and epic length, codices approached an extended narrative form of expression, a dimension lacking in other Mesoamerican writing genres designed for more specific purposes.[8] In general, all codices employ the Mesoamerican calendar and vigesimal numbering system to refer to dates and named personages, and all contain numerous glyphs referring to specific places.

Writing and the oral tradition were intertwined in Mesoamerica.[9] The screenfolds were not read in our conventional manner of reading to oneself silently but were rendered in a more public setting as scores or scripts filled with performance guides and mnemonic devices for recitation.[10] As prompts for visual and verbal communication, the texts were unfolded and exhibited on the walls of lords' palaces.[11] The presentation may have included song, music, and dance, resembling the dramatic discourse of European theater.[12] The audience probably consisted of elite men and women who were conversant with the writing techniques and the reverential speech of the performance; on the other hand, nobles must have used the same type of language and gestures to address sacred and political matters before all members of the community.

FIGURE 2.1. Section of a preconquest-style "codex." *Codex Zouche-Nuttall,* p. 42. Codex-Zouche Nuttall, British Museum, London. Facsimile edition by Akademische Druck- u. Verlagsanstalt, Graz/Austria 1987.

Since memory and context guided a performer's reading of the codices, we will never know what the codices "say" because they invoked the subtleties of noble speech and local discourse, and passages were subject to elaboration with each recounting. A reading of the codices requires an understanding of semiotic conventions based on the language.[13] Thus contemporary interpretations are challenged by centuries of linguistic and cultural change; moreover, the texts evoked a metaphorical, honorific speech associated with the nobility, of which only traces remain. However, the general "Mixteca-Puebla" artistic style associated with the Mixtec codices was shared by multiple ethnic and cultural groups throughout much of central Mexico, Tlaxcala, Puebla, Cholula, and Oaxaca in the postclassic period.[14] This style relied on some conventions that transcended language differences or were based on common areal features and metaphors. Shared conventions and forms in Mesoamerica, including the calendar and vigesimal counting system, represented centuries of interaction, trade, intermarriage, and cultural influence. The Mixteca-Puebla style facilitated interregional communication among dynastic families in highland Mesoamerica. Writing assisted the propagation of certain Mesoamerican beliefs and practices beyond local cults.[15] Shared conventions reduced the need for language-specific content in the Mixtec codices.[16] Thus it is possible to make some sense of the codices without mastering the language and speech conventions of their authors.[17]

A primary function of Mesoamerican writing was to represent and communicate a vision of the past. Fray Francisco de Burgoa, a Dominican chronicler of Oaxaca who wrote in the mid-seventeenth century, recognized the historical content of native writing when he observed that "the children of lords, and those chosen for their priesthood, were taught and instructed from their childhood how to adorn the characters and to memorize the histories" of the codices.[18] Burgoa, who claimed to have held some of these codices in his own hands and to have heard their recitation among elders, described native "books" as: "folios or cloths made from the bark of a certain type of tree found in the hot lands, which [Mixtecs] cure and prepare in the manner of parchments." Each piece of the screenfold manuscripts was about twenty-five centimeters wide, and writers would sew together as many pieces as necessary to tell their histories. "They wrote," Burgoa observed, "with characters so abbreviated that one single page expressed the place, province, year, month, and day, in addition to the names of deities, ceremonies and sacrifices, or victories that were celebrated."[19] He saw Cuilapan's painted commemoration of victory over the Zapotecs during the feast of Santiago, when Mixtecs from Cuilapa "made songs of all their histories."[20]

Ñudzahui terminology for "history" makes associations between writing, verbal performance, and genealogical records.[21] Most codices record the genealogical history of particular dynasties from the Mixteca and adjacent cultural areas.[22] Some trace dynastic origins to the tenth century A.D., the beginning of the so-called postclassic period, after the fragmentation of many classic period sites throughout Mesoamerica. Writers invariably presented a local point of view, often revising the past in the light of the present by recopying and rewriting codices with each new generation of rulers.[23]

Codices were not only historical and genealogical sources. Even Burgoa was aware that the codices also presented religious and cosmological information, including origin myths, ceremonies, and "superstitions" passed along from one generation to the next.[24] The *Codex Vindobonensis,* in particular, articulates a worldview that encompasses the origins of life on earth, human and divine relations, cosmological and supernatural events, sacrifice and death, and much more. Codices link the genealogical histories of local dynasties with a primordial past filled with symbolic and sacred landmarks, personages, ceremonies, and events. In the case of the *Codex Vindobonensis,* this vision of the past extends to the beginning of life on earth. Commissioned by local elites, the artist-writers couched particular and collective ideologies in familiar cultural terms. Sacred knowledge explained and legitimated social relations.[25] At the time of the Spanish invasion, there must have been hundreds of manuscripts like the precious few known to us today. As elsewhere in Mesoamerica, friars recognized the sacred content of these writings and destroyed or confiscated as many as they could find.

Early Colonial Writing

Evidence of the preconquest pictorial writing tradition is better preserved in the Mixteca than in any other area of Mesoamerica. Extant manuscripts painted in a preconquest style include the codices *Zouche-Nuttall, Vindobonensis Mexicanus I* (also called *Vienna*), *Bodley, Colombino, Becker I* and *II, Selden,* and *Sánchez-Solís.*[26] Immediately after the conquest, the tradition of writing in the so-called preconquest style endured in the Mixteca with little apparent Spanish influence. The style persisted in some places for decades, virtually unaffected by European conventions or forms. In comparison, all extant pictorial writings from central Mexico were drawn or painted after the conquest and betray some European stylistic influence. In fact, many Nahua pictorial writings were done under Spanish auspices.

Early postconquest writings relied on the same conventions seen in the preconquest screenfolds, and they continued to document and legitimate claims of the hereditary nobility. But most extant colonial pictorial writings were directed to both native and Spanish audiences.[27] Native writers modified the form and content of their works and augmented their cultural conventions with European-style images to communicate their concerns to the colonizers. Artist-writers were forced into a conceptual and stylistic middle ground of expression and representation, employing conventions that made sense to them and, from their point of view, would also be understood by Spanish officials. This process was encouraged by friars who introduced and promoted a new art style and a new writing system. Since colonial officials were only interested in certain types of information and not the full discourse of codices, most postconquest pictorials were scaled down or simplified to make specific points and meet particular demands. This was a discourse in which native writers actively participated, but the rules and parameters of the exchange were increasingly dictated by Spanish authorities.

Lienzos served an important function in the sixteenth century. Lienzos are cloths featuring genealogical and place-name information painted or drawn across one side. Many lienzos are as large as tapestries, and most present historical narratives and genealogies related to the foundation, rulership, and geographical boundaries of a community. They resemble the codices but tend to convey information in a more dispersed and loosely arranged manner and rely less on a detailed, compartmentalized format and narrative structure; many were probably designed to address specific colonial concerns and thus were streamlined for Spanish eyes. In particular, lienzos attribute a demarcated territory to a community and its hereditary rulers. Most surviving lienzos date from the earlier part of the sixteenth century and contain relatively few distinctly European stylistic motifs. For example, the Lienzo of Zacatepec I, measuring 3.25 by 2.25 meters, is sketched with black ink on cloth (see fig. 2.2). As with the codices, the format follows a meandering pattern, directed by footprints and paths, and associates named ruling couples with specific places. The lienzo's seated figures, place signs, year glyphs, post-and-lintel buildings, and historical content represent a continuation of the codex tradition. But the integration of simple church structures into the narrative betrays an early colonial date of production, approximately between 1540 and 1560. The lienzo also functions as a map that delineates neighboring places and communities in the preconquest symbolic style, rather than the illusionistic European tradition.[28] A group of lienzos from the Coixtlahuaca Basin area display the same refined style and conventions of the Ñudzahui pictorial tradition, although most were produced by Chocho writers.[29] A cultural group in the northwestern section of the Mixteca, the Chocho shared numerous writing conventions associated with the Mixteca-Puebla tradition. In the area around Coixtlahuaca, Tamasulapa, and Texupa, Chocho and Ñudzahui groups lived closely among one another.

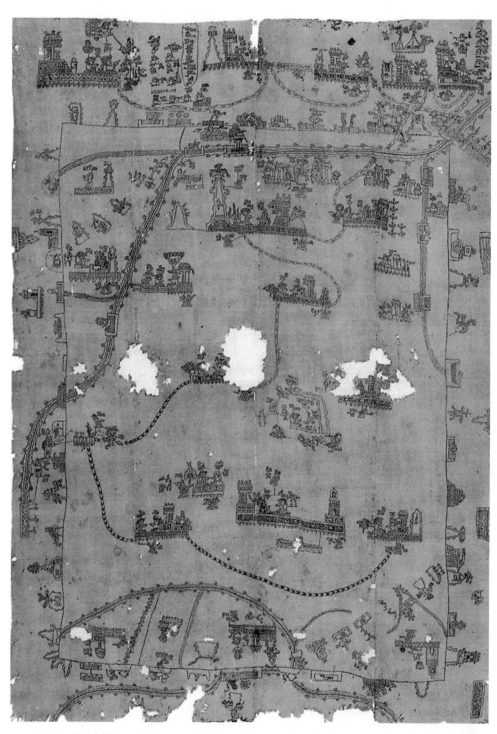

FIGURE 2.2. The Lienzo of Zacatepec (Yucusatuta). CNCA-INAH-MEX, Biblioteca Nacional de Antropología e Historia.

Representatives of communities also used *mapas,* usually drawn on paper in a "hybrid" native and European style, to present their particular and collective interests before Spanish authorities.[30] Hybrid style refers to a complex form of representation emerging from the multicultural demands of colonial discourse.[31] The typical native map of the sixteenth century located a community within a bounded rectangular or circular territory, surrounded by stylized glyphs for borders, natural features, and nearby communities.[32] Place-names were usually arranged in a series according to relative location rather than actual distance.[33] Similarly, codices contain highly stylized maplike portions in which place glyphs are ordered by the direction of the narrative. Native "maps" often attempted to relate a historical narrative, associating a particular ruling lineage with a place. In contrast, the European map of the early modern period focused on terrain, landscape, landmarks, and distance.

Maps were produced throughout the colonial period in the Mixteca, and they were especially common in the sixteenth century, when the native pictorial writing tradition continued to flourish. Many early colonial maps were produced in response to a project sponsored by King Philip II of Spain known as the *Relaciones geográficas.* In 1577 and 1578, questionnaires were distributed throughout New Spain, requesting towns to respond to fifty questions on numerous topics, from climate to culture and geography. Question number ten asked the respondents to describe "the site and location of the said town, if it is situated high or low or on a plain, with a picture of the layout and a design of the streets and plazas and other places indicated, including the monasteries, as well as can be sketched on paper, declaring which part of the town faces north and south."[34] Only sixty-nine maps from New Spain have survived from this project; maps are missing from many returned questionnaires, and it is likely that many more communities never fulfilled Philip's decree or even received the questionnaire.[35] I examine four of these maps from the Mixteca Alta as examples of the pictorial writing tradition around 1580.

The most famous map produced in response to the *relaciones* is the superb composition from Chiyocanu, better known as Teozacualco.[36] Alfonso Caso used this map in 1949 as a "Rosetta stone," proving that its genealogical portions corresponded with many codices that had been previously attributed to central Mexico. It is painted on dozens of sheets of paper that are glued together, measuring 1.4 by 1.75 meters altogether. The map applies a radial conception of bounded space to the landscape (see figs. 2.3 and 2.4).[37] The circle contains fourteen churches and a network of roads, rivers, hills, valleys, and other natural features, including flora and fauna. Inside the circle, space is represented more in the European tradition, giving some attention to approximate distance and the physical landscape. The main church and plaza left of center is Teozacualco, situated in the middle of a large hill glyph turned on its side, crowned by a cross.[38] Thirteen smaller churches represent separate settlements, which in the relación were called *estancias* (outlying settlements) of the *cabecera* (head town) of Teozacualco, representing Spanish designations for tributary and administrative purposes.[39] Thus the map was drawn to reflect the sociopolitical reorganization of the sixteenth century, which designated Teozacualco as the head of thirteen other communities. It is unclear whether this hierarchy existed before the conquest—a topic discussed in chapter 4. The perimeter of the circle features more than fifty place-names marking the borders of Teozacualco's extended jurisdiction, covering a geographical area of approximately thirty by seventy kilometers.[40] Hence the area represented by the circular map does not correspond at all to a circle. Space on the edge of the circle is ordered along traditional lines, with a string of consecutive place-name symbols that make no attempt at conveying distance; in contrast to an illusionistic landscape inside the circle, place glyphs on the edge present abundant topographic information in the symbolic style of the codices.

Left of the giant circle are two genealogies of hereditary rulers from Tilantongo (far left) and Teozacualco, respectively. The male and female ruler of each couple are seated together on a woven reed mat, facing each other; this political symbol represented a dynastic marriage as well as a political arrangement called the *yuhuitayu*, discussed in chapter 6. The vertical "ruler lists" that illustrate succession from one generation to the next, proceeding chronologically from the bottom, bring the viewer hundreds of years across time; the foundings of Tilantongo (called Ñuutnoo in Ñudzahui) and Teozacualco in the eleventh century are represented by two stylized palace structures.[41] Each of the rulers has a personal name glyph that allowed Caso to identify them in cognate genealogical narratives in the codices.[42] Footprints leading from the mat of a Tilantongo couple to the second generation of Teozacualco rulers indicate that a male heir from Tilantongo married a female ruler from Teozacualco. Apparently, they resided in the latter community. The codices confirm that the male heir was the son of the legendary lord, 8-Deer. A Spanish gloss informs us that in 1580 the rulers of Teozacualco, don Felipe de Santiago and his son don Francisco de Mendoza, were descendants of this historic alliance. The fact that Teozacualco already had a ruling couple before this advantageous marriage makes it clear that Tilantongo chose to affiliate itself with an existing royal house. This distinction was crucial from the point of view of Teozacualco.

Inside the circle is a third dynasty associated with Teozacualco's more recent history, beginning around the year 1321, and proceeding upward from the main palace structure adjacent to the church.[43] The founding couple of this dynastic line comprises two rulers who came from Tilantongo, an event depicted on the road that extends out of the circle, where seven warriors give the couple gifts of birds, feathers, and bundles of cloth.[44] The male ruler carries a bow and arrows, and the female ruler wears a serpent headdress. The same two rulers are shown seated inside the circle, right above the palace. This dynastic line continued to recruit marriage partners from Tilantongo and other places, surviving at least one case of failed succession when a male heir died without having married and, hence, without legitimate offspring. The lone male ruler seated at the top of this dynastic line is the bachelor don Francisco de Mendoza, the heir apparent of his father (seated below him), don Felipe de Santiago, who ruled in Teozacualco when the map was painted in 1580. The fact that the son is not seated on a reed mat throne indicates that he will not inherit the yuhuitayu until his father is deceased and until he is married. The woman who is seated alone at the top of the vertical ruler list of Tilantongo (far left of map), doña Francisca de Mendoza, is don Francisco's cousin. She was the chosen ruler of Tilantongo until her premature death in 1576.[45]

Teozacualco attempted to validate its own lineage through a long-standing association with Tilantongo, one of the most prestigious dynastic lines in the Mixteca Alta. Although codices such as the *Nuttall, Vindobonensis,* and *Bodley* illustrate Teozacualco's alliances with Zaachila, Tlaxiaco, Achiutla, and other places, the map focused on only one dimension of Teozacualco's dynastic past.[46] It is a pity that a map does not survive from the relación of Tilantongo, completed in 1579, as well, which states that native nobles used *pinturas* (paintings) to convey their responses to the questionnaire.[47]

The map of Teozacualco reveals how native artists used both old and new criteria in constructing their case for autonomy and high status in the colonial order. The map represents Teozacualco's authority in both native terms and Spanish terms, as yuhuitayu and cabecera. In their multicultural presentation of complex information, maps relied on traditional conventions while incorporating certain aspects of the new art style. The shaded hills and leafy trees, the countenance of the sun, and many new church buildings made the composition more familiar to a Spanish audience. Nonetheless, the map's style, presentation, and pictorial conventions spoke to a native audience. Significantly, when writers from Chiyocanu set out to make a geographical map of their community based loosely on the questionnaire's specifications, they included

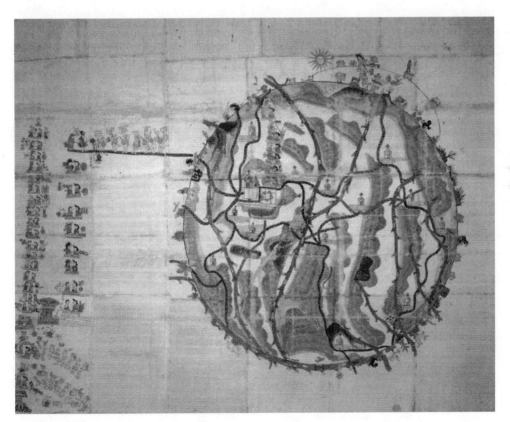

FIGURE 2.3. Map of Teozacualco (Chiyocanu), drawn in response to the *Relaciones geográficas* of 1579–81. Benson Latin American Collection, University of Texas at Austin.

its ruling representatives. They did not think of "maps" and "genealogies" as discrete categories, as did Europeans of the early modern period. The map's vertical alignment of ruling couples, the men and women who represented numerous people and places, associated the landscape with centuries of human occupation and history, combining representations of space and time in the same composition.[48] The prominence of place-names and human figures on the "mapa" invokes the Ñudzahui term for "world," *ñuu ñayehui*—literally "communities" or "places" (*ñuu*) and "people" (*ñayehui*). From a local point of view, this map represents Teozacualco's world.[49]

Another map solicited for the *Relaciones geográficas,* from a small community in the jurisdiction of Teozacualco named Amoltepec, employed a similar radial design to demarcate its perceived territory; the artist aligned nineteen preconquest-style place glyphs on the perimeter of the circle, all to the left of the rushing preconquest-style river (see fig. 2.5).[50] The Nahua name Amoltepec is synonymous with its Ñudzahui name, Yucunama, which means "soap herb" or "hill of soap" (*yucu* is "hill" or "herb," depending on tone, and *nama* is a plant used for cleansing); nama plants sprout from the stylized boot-shaped hill at the center of the composition.[51] To the left of the place glyph for Yucunama stands the colonial church, above the ruling couple's palace, where a male and female ruler (the yuhuitayu) are seated, facing each other. Water flows from another hill glyph beside the palace, a Nahua pictorial convention for the *altepetl,* or local ethnic state (*atl* is "water," and *tepetl* is "hill"). Thus the author(s) of this map drew a cluster of familiar images proclaiming Yucunama's autonomous status with its own political and religious institutions that would be recognizable to a Ñudzahui, Nahua, and Spanish audience. The border that frames the map reinforces Yucunama's claim to autonomy; the circle encloses six place-name glyphs that represent the community's named constituent parts. Five of the six glyphs contain the *yodzo,* or "plain" symbol, typical of many place-names, which consists of the stylistic depiction of feathers (yodzo can mean "feather" or "plain," depending on tone). The map relied on preconquest-style conventions to proclaim autonomy, but the anonymous couple in the temple betrays its weak claim. In reality, Yucunama, struggling to maintain independent status after the conquest, succumbed to major population loss from disease in the sixteenth century. By the time of the relación, Spanish officials had designated it as a distant *sujeto* (subject town) to the cabecera of Teozacualco.[52]

Whereas the maps of Teozacualco and Yucunama relied principally on native conventions to order the landscape, a map from Texupa (Ñundaa, or "blue place" in Ñudzahui), drawn in 1579, juxtaposes a new section of the community alongside the old one. The bottom, western half of the map is dominated by a representation of the colonial *traza,* a gridwork layout of streets, blocks, and buildings characteristic of Spanish American cities and towns (see fig. 2.6). Houses, patios, and lots are aligned in an orderly fashion, eight to each block.[53] All roads lead to the new church and its orchard. The top, eastern half of the map reveals the native identity and history of old Ñundaa. At the center of the composition a preconquest-style temple stands in profile at the base of a hill, crowned by the ancient place glyph of Ñundaa. The native temple marked the original site of the community; less than a decade before the relación, Dominicans and Spanish officials had congregated and moved the decimated population to the valley floor, about a kilometer from the old settlement.[54] Space is

FIGURE 2.4. Detail of map of Teozacualco. The dynasty proceeds upward, from the fourteenth century to the unmarried heir apparent in 1580 (lone figure at top). The royal palace is adjacent to the church. Benson Latin American Collection, University of Texas at Austin.

FIGURE 2.5. Map of Amoltepec (Yucunama), 1580. Benson Latin American Collection, University of Texas at Austin.

distorted so that the stylized temple marks the boundaries of the new and old sites. To the left (north), a large hill buttressed with stone walls is pierced with five arrows, a reference to some historic conflict.[55] The individual, carefully outlined, bell-shaped hills are reminiscent of the symbolic pictographic tradition of the codices, but the use of shading and grouping creates a spatially ordered landscape, complete with trees and a variety of plants, in the illusionistic tradition of the European Renaissance. Fish swim in the simple wavy lines that denote streams. Roads to nearby communities in the Mixteca Alta are marked by footprints, in the traditional manner, as well as hoofprints. Although the layout of streets on the map corresponds rather closely with the town's actual urban layout, as verified by modern aerial photographs, the credibility of the plan is compromised by the fact that many roads and streams pass straight through houses and lots.[56] By all appearances, Texupa looks like a well-ordered colonial town surrounded by a lush, green landscape. On closer examination, the division into eastern and western halves represents a tension between the old temple and the new monastery, the sacred mountains and the secular grid, the historical narrative on the hill and the colonial plan on the valley floor—in other words, a tension between the past and the present. In presenting the two faces of Texupa-Ñundaa, the author betrayed a certain ambivalence toward the new arrangement.[57]

A fourth map, produced by Nochixtlan (called Atoco in Ñudzahui), is a barren and colorless production in comparison with the ornate and detailed maps from Teozacualco, Amoltepec, and Texupa, although it features the familiar, homogeneous grid pattern of the Texupa map. In fact, the map of Nochixtlan is a skeletal outline of the traza (see fig. 2.7). The discrepancy between spacious layout and sparse occupation leaves the impression of an incomplete model or a colonial ghost town. But there is evidence of life here: footprints follow paths aligned to the four directions and converge on the plaza and marketplace of this colonial cabecera.[58] Preconquest-style Nahua and Mixtec codices depicted markets as bounded spaces (usually circular) filled with footprints, and in the colonial period the Spanish word "plaza" was associated with the native term for market—*yahui.*[59] The map's focus on the plaza/marketplace corresponds with Nochixtlan's response to the questionnaire, which pays considerable attention to the types of goods sold in the marketplace. The church is a simple building adorned with a *tablero* facade, topped by a bell and a cross. Whereas the artists of Teozacualco identified the lords' palace with the church, here the humble palace structure, identifiable by the circular motif on its facade, is off to the far left. Aside from the use of native conventions to locate certain buildings and arenas of activity in the new Nochixtlan, this European-style "mapa" is nothing more than thin lines and empty squares. The colonization of space and centralization of activity according to a "logic of the grid" represent new relations of power in Nochixtlan, as they did in Texupa.[60]

In addition to maps and lienzos, native writers adapted their skills to a variety of genres to address Spanish legal or administrative requirements. For example, a sketch from Tlazultepec, submitted in a legal case to support the inheritance claims of doña Juana de Rojas, was designed to associate particular rulers with various places in the Mixteca, represented by the familiar hill glyphs (see fig. 2.8).[61] Drawn in 1597, the document demonstrates that in some places native writers continued to rely on preconquest conventions by the end of the century. The format of the document confines all images to the space of two legal-size pages, however, while Spanish-language alphabetic text facilitates its presentation to colonial officials. Seated male and female rulers associated with place glyphs are linked by footprints indicating lines of succession. Spanish surnames are given in lieu of calendrical names, reflecting changing naming patterns among native nobles in this period. In addition to the introduction of pictorial documentation, a native-language last will and testament was used as supporting evidence in the case. The "Genealogy of Tlazultepec," as it is called, is one of many examples of how native writers were able to communicate with a Spanish legal audience. By the end of the sixteenth century, their stylized conventions were usually confined to legal-sized pages and were often supplemented by alphabetic writing.

Early postconquest pictorial writings influenced by European art style reflect patterns of cultural transformation, maintenance, adaptation, and creation. Despite the guidelines specified by question number ten of the relaciones, it is clear that each community had its own idea of a map. That the maps of Teozacualco, Amoltepec, Texupa,

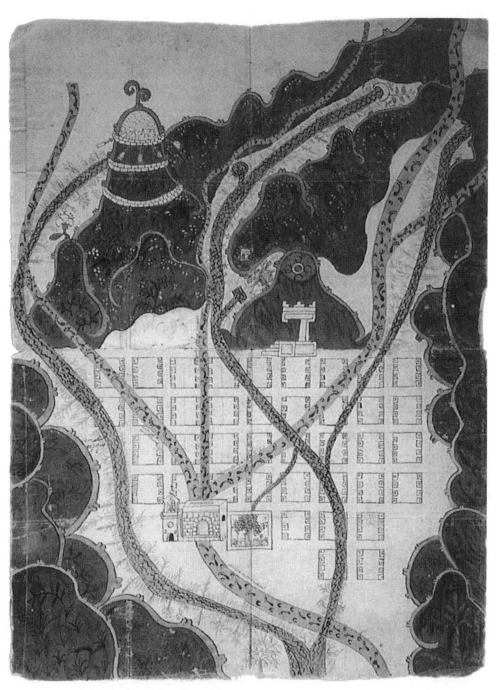

FIGURE 2.6. Map of Texupa (Ñundaa), 1579. Real Academia de la Historia, Madrid.

FIGURE 2.7. Map of Nochixtlan (Atoco), 1579. Real Academia de la Historia, Madrid.

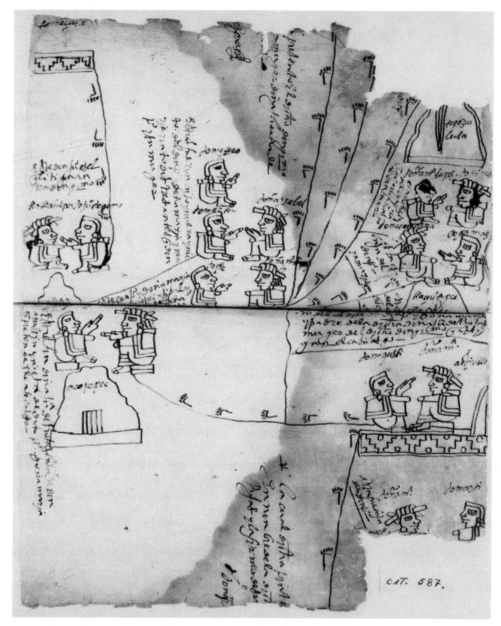

FIGURE 2.8. Genealogy of Tlazultepec (Yucucuihi), 1597. The order of the two pages should be reversed. AGN-T, 59:2.

and Nochixtlan were executed within the same two-year period indicates a considerable degree of variation in the timing of these changes. The diffusion of European style in Ñudzahui pictorial manuscripts, beginning as early as the mid-sixteenth century, was geographically and temporally uneven.[62] Texupa had been exposed to European artistic conventions since at least the *Codex Sierra* (beginning in 1550, as discussed below), but more inaccessible places such as Zacatepec, Tlazultepec, Ocotepec, and Nativitas continued to employ preconquest-style forms throughout the sixteenth century. Writers in remote communities such as Teozacualco and Amoltepec relied far more on traditional conventions in their maps than did Nochixtlan, which is located along the main highway that links the Valleys of Oaxaca and Mexico. European forms of graphic representation, like the diffusion of alphabetic writing and the Spanish language, as we shall see, were propagated from colonial administrative and religious centers in the region. Although it is not possible to date this process precisely, regional patterns are observable.

Despite European influence, these culturally mixed or "hybrid" compositions are still native productions in that they were drawn or painted by native artists.[63] Drawing a sharp line between "European" and "Indian" style fails to recognize that native artists were active participants in the creation of hybrid images, not passive recipients of introduced phenomena. Images need not be preconquest in appearance to be attributed to native artists, nor do skilled or unskilled native adaptations to European introductions make the images less indigenous. Hybrid cultural production functioned to communicate with internal and external audiences; artists transmitted signs that were intelligible to both native nobles and colonial authorities. In this sense, the products are multicultural and constantly changing, as the social context of their production changed. The hybrid maps of Teozacualco and Texupa, for instance, contain as much information for a native audience as they do for Spaniards. The juxtaposition of the native palace and the church in many maps was a compromise acceptable to both sides. If the act of mapping territories signified their control and administration, some communities played an active role in this process, using a combination of native and European symbols and styles to assert their claims to authority. However, in contrast to the many hybrid images produced by native artists in the colonial period, Spanish artists and cartographers did not adopt a hybrid style.[64] This simple fact reminds us that the colonial discourse to which Ñudzahui artists-writers responded reflected relations of domination.

A collection of sketches from Yanhuitlan exemplifies the use of culturally hybrid images in the sixteenth century. The *Codex Yanhuitlan* has attracted relatively little attention from scholars working on the codices, in part because it appears to deviate from the preconquest style. The sketches are particularly valuable for their depiction of Spaniards and introduced objects, a rarity in native manuscripts from the Mixteca. Just as European images of Indians in the sixteenth century inform us about European points of view, indigenous images of Spaniards in the *Codex Yanhuitlan* shed light on Ñudzahui practices of representation in these unstable times. A semiotic reading of the ambivalent and multivalent images shows how native artist-writers retained many of their own symbolic conventions while adapting or mimicking European forms to interpret cultural and social changes.[65] Let us turn to these colonial images to consider Ñudzahui artists and writers as seeing subjects.

The Codex Yanhuitlan

Sometime between the 1540s and 1560s, Mixtec artists drew images of people and objects in a collection of papers known as the *Codex Yanhuitlan*. As a major yuhuitayu in the Mixteca Alta, Yanhuitlan became a center of Spanish activity and administration in the colonial period. The *Codex Yanhuitlan* is not a native codex in terms of the deerskin codices described above but rather a number of sketches drawn in ink on Spanish paper.[66] The order of the sketches is unknown; many pages seem to represent a framed passage of postconquest life, perhaps influenced by European models in books, paintings, or woodcuts. Images of a Spaniard wearing a turban, a friar writing at a desk, and native men sporting European haircuts suggest the use of models from European illustrated books and engraved images. Some sketches contain idealized features, while others resemble portraits. The convergence or juxtaposition of native and European conventions in the same scene often creates an unusual and unexpected perspective. Many human figures are portrayed in semiprofile, in a compromised pose somewhere between preconquest-style two-dimensional depiction and three-dimensional European drawing. Frontal portraits are rare in the preconquest-style codices, but they are common here. The representation of two churches, analyzed in chapter 8, confirms the simultaneous transformation of art and architectural style in this period. Some pages contain well-ordered rows of place glyphs arranged in the manner of a preconquest map, but on most pages, native conventions, including stylized glyphs and dates, share space with new subjects and objects. The prominent role assigned to friars in the sketches and the notable impact of European art style and form suggest that native artists were trained in church workshops. The *Codex Sierra*, a contemporary text from nearby Texupa (discussed below), makes references to native painters who worked in the church. Some scenes suggest that Nahua aides may have played a role in training Yanhuitlan artists in the new art style.[67]

We may assume that the content of the sketches is historical. In their attention to dates and events, they are comparable to the codices. A key scene in the *Codex Yanhuitlan* portrays a meeting between a native lord of Yanhuitlan and an ecclesiastical official, flanked by two other men (see fig. 2.9).[68] The man standing in front of the seated Spaniard (facing him) is the *yya toniñe*, or ruler, of Yanhuitlan, don Domingo de Guzmán, identified by the calendrical name below his feet (7-Monkey, or *sañuu*, in the calendrical vocabulary). He is dressed in a European shirt tapered at the neck and wrists and an indigenous cape; the fall and fold of his sleeved shirt are reminiscent of sketches in the Nahua *Florentine Codex*. The friar holds a giant rosary that spills to the ground and flows over onto the following page; in fact, the rosary takes up the entire next page (plate XV, not shown here), depicted in enlarged detail, as if it were an object worthy of close inspection. The two central figures are flanked by translators, perhaps one who spoke Spanish and Nahuatl and another who spoke Nahuatl and Ñudzahui, a typical method of translation in the Mixteca during the early sixteenth century. The hand gestures, always a prominent feature in preconquest codices, signify multiple possibilities, from discussion and negotiation to command and agreement. The artist relied on a mimetic representation of verbal discourse. Hand gestures facilitated communication across three languages and served as markers of status and rank.[69] The images convey negotiation and discussion, but only the Spanish official is seated, and he is larger than the others.

As in the codices, seated figures play a powerful role in the manuscript. In one scene, two seated Spaniards (judging by their clothes and European chairs) face and

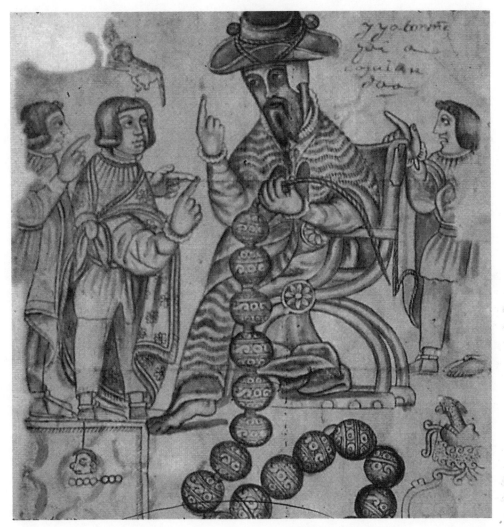

FIGURE 2.9. The yya toniñe and cacique of Yanhuitlan (Yodzocahi), don Domingo, converses with a seated ecclesiastical official who holds rosary beads in his hand. *Codex Yanhuitlan,* plate XVI.

gesture toward each other (see fig. 2.10). In the codices, seated figures (usually on reed mats) symbolized positions of authority; in this case, the man on the left is seated on the traditional place sign for Yanhuitlan, representing his authority in that community. Yanhuitlan was called Yodzocahi by Ñudzahui speakers, meaning "extended plain or valley," signified by an empty, rectangular glyph. The year symbol to the man's left, 11-Rabbit, corresponds to the Christian year 1530 in the Mixtec calendar. In this year, Yanhuitlan came under crown control as a *corregimiento* (before the return of the *encomendero,* Francisco de las Casas).[70]

A separate fragment of the codex, bearing a calendrical glyph corresponding to the Christian year of 1524, is highly symbolic. A Spaniard sits in a chair atop the place glyph of Yanhuitlan, looking down on a smaller cacique who is seated on a reed mat

FIGURE 2.10. Two seated Spaniards engaged in a discussion. The man on the left, presumably the encomendero, is seated on the place glyph of Yanhuitlan. *Codex Yanhuitlan,* plate VIII.

(see fig. 2.11).[71] The female member of the yuhuitayu is "out of the picture," so to speak. The indigenous ruler sports a European hat and full beard but wears a stylized native cape. Native writing portrayed the act of conquest by showing the place glyph of a defeated community as pierced with an arrow; in similar fashion, the seated Spaniard rests the point of his sword on the glyph of Yanhuitlan, symbolizing his conquest of this place.[72] Smaller in stature, the native ruler appears demoted, if not deposed. As in the last image of seated persons, feathers adorn the headgear of the

FIGURE 2.11. Indigenous artist's depiction of the cacique, seated on a reed mat to the right, and the Spanish encomendero of Yanhuitlan. AGN-V, 272:3.

encomendero. In native society and iconography, feathers were symbols of power.[73] Native persons wear no feathers in the codex.

The act of writing with feather quill pens is conspicuous in the *Codex Yanhuitlan*. The native artists associated alphabetic writing with priests, the only people who are depicted holding quill pens in these drawings. In one scene, a Dominican is seated at a desk, preparing to write on a blank sheet of paper (see fig. 2.12).[74] The writer looms large next to the two native men who stand at his side. Shaded surfaces suggest an attempt to model the forms, as in the European tradition. Another scene depicts two ecclesiastics engaged in the unlikely act of simultaneously writing on the same page. A still-life passage of writing equipment—an inkpot and a pen pouch—seems to hover

FIGURE 2.12. Depiction of a friar writing in the presence of two indigenous men. *Codex Yanhuitlan*, plate XIX.

FIGURE 2.13. Depiction of two ecclesiastics writing. *Codex Yanhuitlan*, plate XIV.

between the two writers (see fig. 2.13).[75] The native artist's conception of space and depth lends an original, hybrid appearance to the composition.

The *Codex Yanhuitlan* represents a time when native pictorial representation, although clearly affected by European style and form of presentation, continued to employ native conventions and symbols. Some drawings contain glosses in alphabetic text, but they are never substantial enough to be more than complementary. Plates X and XI of the Jiménez Moreno and Mateos Higuera edition of the *Codex Yanhuitlan*, for example, portray stylized fields (or storage structures) of staple crops accompanied by descriptive glosses such as "ytu yaha si yya toniñe" [the chili field of the lord ruler], "ytu nduchi tnuu" [field of black beans], and "ytu huiyo" [maize field]. Plate II (see fig. 6.1) features the word "aniñee" (usually written as *aniñe*) written on the palace of the hereditary lords, the equivalent of the Nahuatl *tecpan*. Although occasional glosses add little to our understanding of the drawings, some of the images are telling. Two scenes depict the violence of the conquest: Spaniards fire muskets and cannon at native warriors, and armed Spaniards force native men and women to mine gold in streams (see fig. 7.2).[76] The illustration of coins and numerous locked, wooden chests signifies a recognition of the value of money, probably in reference to tribute. Many of the images portray new actors who sit in new types of seats and hold powerful objects, such as swords, pens, and rosary beads. Whereas native lords are named with the familiar dot-and-symbol notation of the ancient calendar, none of the Spaniards is named. Some of the sketches convey negotiation and discourse, but they also invoke representations of conquest, power, and unmistakable change. While the feathered foreigner, the encomendero, sits atop the place glyph of Yanhuitlan, most natives stand or work in the codex, symbolizing their subservient or secondary status. In fact, nearly all Spaniards are shown as seated figures of authority. A semiotic reading of the surface meaning and "deep structure" of the images, informed by native conventions and symbols, reflects the realities of colonial rule in Yanhuitlan.[77]

Unlike the maps, legal documents, and lienzos generated by native artists in this period, it is unknown what function or objective the *Codex Yanhuitlan* may have served. What were the artists' intentions or goals? We know that parts of the codex were used to verify historical claims. In 1707, eight pages were furnished in a legal dispute by the cacique of Teposcolula and Tututepec, don Agustín Pimentel y Guzmán y Alvarado, who inherited the papers from his father, don Francisco Pimentel y Guzmán, the former cacique of Yanhuitlan. But the legal proceedings do not shed light on how the sketches (including fig. 2.11) preserved in the case were intended to support his claim to hereditary authority.[78] The sketches may have fulfilled a familiar native strategy of presenting Yanhuitlan in a favorable light. As in the Lienzo of Tlaxcala and similar postconquest writings, native representatives are shown negotiating and cooperating with Spanish secular and ecclesiastical authorities. The seated encomendero and cacique represent an alliance, however unequal, of Spanish and Mixtec rulers.

The prominent presence of the church in the codex is no coincidence. From 1544 to 1546, the Inquisition investigated accusations of idolatry and resistance to Christianity in Yanhuitlan (discussed in chapter 8). Spanish inquisitors imprisoned and interrogated three lords and several native priests for their alleged participation in idolatrous acts, including human sacrifice. One of these lords, don Domingo, was the same 7-Monkey who is shown in figure 2.9 standing before the friar with the rosary beads, presumably only a few years before or after the trial. Dozens of people from the surrounding region were implicated in the proceedings. Thereafter, Yanhuitlan became a center of ecclesiastical activity in the Mixteca. From this perspective, the overbearing, almost menacing appearance of the friars confirms the colonial context of the drawings.

The Act of Writing

Perhaps the artists of the *Codex Yanhuitlan* were fascinated by the act of writing at desks because they understood the basic principle of applying ink to paper. Like the Nahuas of central Mexico, the Mixtecs possessed an extensive terminology to describe the act and instruments of writing. The adaptation of native-language terminology to the introduced practice and paraphernalia of alphabetic writing demonstrates how natives interpreted the new writing system in terms of the old.[79] For example, a quill pen is listed in Alvarado's *Vocabulario*, on the Castilian side, as "writing feather/quill," but the entry is translated as *yeque taa tutu,* or "bone that writes on paper," referring to the preconquest tradition of painting with finely carved and ornamented bones.[80] The Ñudzahui word for feather, *yodzo*, does not appear. Similarly, a "writing box" (*caja de escrivanias*) is called *sasacuino yeque taa tutu*, or "place where the writing bone is kept."[81] Like *tlilli* in Nahuatl, "ink" is simply "black," *tnoo*, or "black water (liquid)," *duta tnoo*. A "book" is likened to a "painting," *tacu*, and there appears to be a relation between "the paper on which the ancient Indians wrote," *ñee tutu* (literally "skin paper," that is, deer hide), and "white paper," *tutu* or *tutu cuisi*.[82] Native fig-bark *amatl* paper is referred to as "papel de estraça, o de la tierra" [coarse paper or native paper] and is defined as *tutu ñuhu* (literally a translation of "papel de la tierra") but also as *tutu ñudzavui* and *tutu ñuu dzúma*, ethnic terms applied to the Ñudzahui and Nahuas, respectively, in reference to specific types of paper and perhaps even types of manuscripts.[83]

The Ñudzahui nobles who contributed to the *Vocabulario en lengua mixteca* (1593) apparently drew little distinction between writing and painting. The verb "to write" is defined as *yotaandi tutu* and *yotaandi tacu;* the verb *taa* has multiple meanings: "to write," "to place," "to apply," and "to arrange."[84] But *tutu* and *tacu* refer to the object of the verb *taa*, as in "paper" and "painting," respectively. There seems to be little clear difference when a "writing" (*escriptura*) is defined as a *tacu*, not a *tutu*. In the colonial period, a notary was usually referred to as *tay taa tutu*, "person who writes [on] paper," or *tay yondaa tutu*, "person who applies [something to] paper," until the Spanish loanword *escrivano* was adopted in the late colonial period. However, it seems as if painting was not viewed as entirely the same as writing; a "painter" was called *tay huisi tacu*, "master of painted works," and "to paint" was *yodzatacundi*, "to make painted works," using the causative prefix *dza* to create a verb based on a noun, *tacu*.[85] Thus, the Ñudzahui verbs "to write" and "to paint" approach the same meaning but do not come as close as the Nahuatl *icuiloa*, the verb used for the act of both painting and writing. Whereas the act of writing was likened to painting, the Mixtec *Vocabulario* distinguished painting from alphabetic writing (see fig. 2.14). Finally, the verb "to read" suggests a link with the preconquest oral and visual tradition of codices: *yonacahuindi tutu* and *yositondaandi tutu* mean, respectively, "to count or relate things [on] paper" (like *pohua* in Nahuatl) and "to see designs or writing on paper."[86]

Convergent terminology for writing with pictorial and alphabetic text suggests a basic functional association between the two systems of communication.[87] In the sixteenth century alphabetic writing in the form of glosses complemented images; glosses were applied to maps, codices, lienzos, and sketches but were largely confined to identifying persons, places, and objects for colonial authorities.[88] Of the eight preconquest-style codices attributed to the Mixteca, three contain native-language glosses.[89] The *Codex Colombino*, for example, was used by the rulers of Tututepec to advance land claims in the colonial period; glosses were added later to convince Spanish officials that the codex corroborated their claims.[90] Many colonial pictorial writings, such as the *Codex Tulane, Codex Muro*, Lienzo of Xicayan, and *Codex Yanhuitlan*, contain alphabetic glosses.[91] Several genealogies and lienzos end two or three generations after the conquest, indicating the date and transitional function of these writings in the sixteenth century. Designed as legal claims to land and succession in Spanish courts, some types of pictorial writings were eventually superseded in function by the testamentary genre of alphabetic writing.

FIGURE 2.14. 9-Wind, the Mixtec prototype of Quetzalcoatl, depicted as a writer (tay huisi tacu). *Codex Vindobonensis*, obverse 48. Codex Vindobonensis Mexicanus I, Österr. Nationalbibliothek, Wien, Vienna. Facsimile edition by Akademische Druck- u. Verlagsanstalt, Graz/Austria 1961.

One Mixtec text, in particular, exemplifies the convergence of pictorial and alphabetic writing in the sixteenth century: the *Codex Sierra*.

The Codex Sierra

The *Codex Sierra* illustrates the transition from pictorial to alphabetic text in the Mixteca. Written from 1550 to 1564, this "codex" is actually a book of accounts from Santa Catalina Texupa with pictographic and alphabetic components in which the former is as informative as the latter. The pictorial portion is arranged on the left side of the page, with separate space for alphabetic commentary in the middle column and numerical accounts on the far right.[92] The alphabetic text is written in Nahuatl, but the manuscript comes from Texupa, a Ñudzahui-Chocho community in the Mixteca Alta. In fact, the first and only full-length study of the manuscript claims that it owes more to the Chocho of Texupa than to the Mixtecs.[93] However, the manuscript betrays a definite Ñudzahui presence. In addition to the interlocking "A-O" year sign, the Ñudzahui words for "year" (*cuiya*) and the corresponding number and sign of the calendrical vocabulary appear eighteen times in the manuscript, attached to the Christian date and the Nahuatl word for "year" (*xihuitl*). A typical reference to the date is written "1551 xiuitl cuyya ñuhuiyo," designating the year 6-Reed, whereby *ñu* is "six" and *huiyo* is "reed." (see fig. 2.15).[94] The calendar employed a separate lexicon for day signs and numbers that was probably based on an archaic, honorific register.[95] For example, "reed" was known conventionally as *ndoo*, and the number six was normally written as *iño*. References to the Ñudzahui cuiya, preceded by the Christian date and Nahuatl *xihuitl*, reveal the manuscript's multicultural nature. Since Nahuas had no reason to record Ñudzahui years, it is likely that the text was produced by Ñudzahui writers who were fluent in the Nahuatl language. Had Nahuatl-language alphabetic writing not been more developed than Ñudzahui at this time, the authors would have produced the text in their first language. Or perhaps the choice of Nahuatl reflects a desire to communicate with a multilingual audience. Nahuatl was a lingua franca in this Mixtec-Chocho region. The language of the text is not so different from Nahuatl in central Mexico, and it may be that Nahuas were involved at some level as intermediaries in promoting the Roman alphabet.

There is further evidence that the *Codex Sierra* is a Ñudzahui text, this time from the pictographic side. The depiction of a hand to portray the giving of tribute appears to be a Ñudzahui convention based on a tone pun, since *daha* can signify either "tribute" or "hand," depending on tone. Each time a hand appears in the text, it is accompanied by a Nahuatl word for "tribute," *tlacalaquilli* or *tequitl*, and is usually pointing to money. The meaning of this convention is especially clear when the hand emerges from a wooden chest, representing the treasury, and points to the quantity of coins being paid (see fig. 2.16).[96] The manuscript refers to the chest as *caxaco* (literally "in the chest"), using the Spanish loanword *caxa* and the Nahua locative suffix *-co*. It is also called *caxaco de comunidad*, in reference to the colonial introduction described in chapter 6 of this work. One entry combines three pictorial conventions based on the language. The first is the place glyph for Mexico, which was called Ñucoyo in Ñudzahui, whereby *ñu* is "place of" and *coyo* is "reeds." The glyph consists of the ñuu place symbol (with the *greca* motif, as in the codices), from which bunches of reeds protrude. The second convention is the hand for tribute (daha). The third convention is the familiar footprints along a road; *saha* means both "foot" and "to go" in Ñudzahui. Thus the three conventions are combined to represent tribute paid to sponsor a delegation that traveled to the capital, an action confirmed in the Nahuatl alphabetic text to the right (see fig. 2.17). The manuscript depicts several journeys to Mexico in this manner.

The importance of writing is illustrated by periodic entries recording the purchase of books, paper, and ink. When the Spanish *alcalde mayor* appears, flanked by a

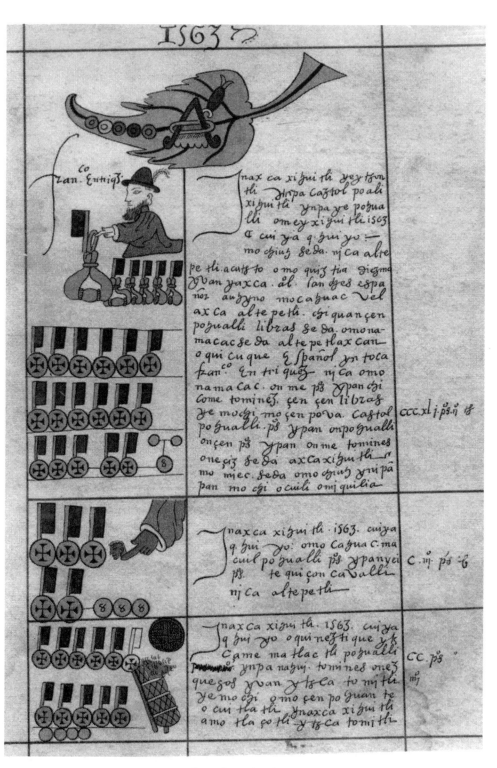

FIGURE 2.15. Page from the *Codex Sierra*, p. 55.

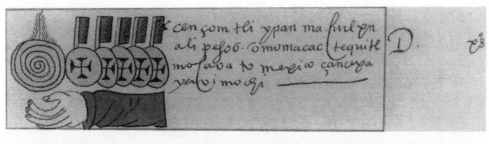

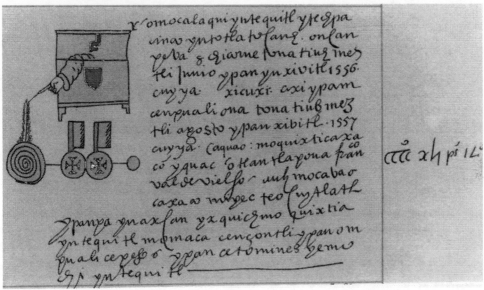

FIGURE 2.16. Illustration of tribute payments based on a Ñudzahui tone pun involving *daha*, "hand" or "tribute." *Codex Sierra*, pp. 19, 42.

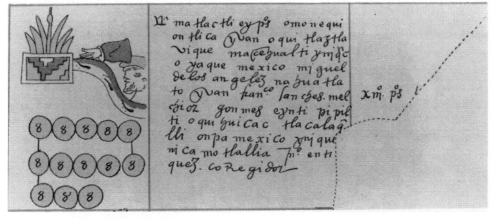

FIGURE 2.17. Representation of the act of bringing tribute money to Mexico City, based on three pictorial conventions. *Codex Sierra*, p. 59.

notary and an interpreter, he is usually engaged in the act of writing and counting. The codex also depicts a *tlacuylo,* or artist, who paints a *manta* (cloth, perhaps canvas in this context) for the church, purchasing his colors and materials with community funds.[97] In keeping with its multicultural nature, the codex utilized a combination of native, Arabic, and Roman numbers. The Mesoamerican vigesimal system of circles (1), banners (20), and bundles of feathers (400) was used to count Spanish coins (reals), each of which was represented by the number eight or a cross. Alphabetic text spelled out the corresponding number in Nahuatl, leaving little room for error or doubt. The measurement of a pound was represented by a neatly twisted bundle tied at the top. Twenty pounds was conveyed by a bundle combined with a banner.

The text uses a variety of symbols to denote familiar and introduced objects, actions, and events. For example, a metate (grinding stone) stacked with tortillas and a cup brimming with cacao or pulque symbolize food and drink in general. The inclusion of other items, such as turkeys and wine skins, indicated a feast. Individual saints are represented by objects and attributes associated with them in Christian iconography. Saints Peter and Paul, for example, are represented by a crowned key and a sword. A lienzo of Saint Peter is depicted as a cloth with a hand holding a large key. The Holy Spirit appears as an ascending dove, and Santiago is represented by a lance, a cross, and a banner.[98] Prominent persons are featured in profile and identified by name scrolls, one of the rare cases in which alphabetic writing intrudes on the pictorial portion of the text. Thus, the use of phonetic components for names, as seen in some Nahua manuscripts, was unnecessary here. All people—except the alcalde mayor—are portrayed in profile; the venerable Spanish official appears four times in a frontal position.[99]

The range of items introduced by Spaniards in the codex is extensive; some objects were so unusual that they were best represented by images combined with words. For example, the "tepuztli tornos seda" makes little sense until one sees the six iron instruments to the left of the page, which include spools and cranks.[100] Very few items described in the Nahuatl alphabetic portion were neither painted nor depicted on the left. The commissioning of a painting for Holy Week, however, seems to have eluded pictorial representation, if only because the work of art had not yet been painted. Alphabetic writings such as official decrees are portrayed on the pictorial side as sheets of paper marked "nnnnnnnn." Toward the end of the document, when different hands were involved in the writing, seven entries contain no accompanying pictorial script on the left.[101] It is likely that the alphabetic part became easier to render than the pictorial part, that the former was done first and the author(s) never got around to completing the latter. This is especially the case when the list of goods and moneys became too lengthy to illustrate easily. Perhaps, in the later period, more of those involved with the manuscript were trained in alphabetic writing, although it is uncertain whether the same author was responsible for both the pictorial and the alphabetic portions of entries.

The Texupa manuscript records the convergence of pictorial and alphabetic text and demonstrates the transitional role of Nahuatl in a multilingual area, before alphabetic writing was under way in other languages. In the *Codex Sierra,* native writers used images and words in complementary ways so that the two forms of communication shared a common space. Although Ñudzahui (and Chocho) scribes were able to write Nahuatl in alphabetic letters, they also used pictorial conventions that made sense primarily in their own language. The *Codex Sierra* leads us to consider the importance of Nahuatl for communication among various native groups and Spaniards in the early colonial period and the influence of this language on the development of Ñudzahui alphabetic writing.

Nahuatl as Lingua Franca

The ancient interaction of Nahuatl- and Ñudzahui-speaking peoples continued after the conquest. In the first two-thirds of the sixteenth century, Nahuatl was a lingua franca in the Mixteca, a language that facilitated communication between Spaniards, Nahuas, and other native groups. As intermediaries, Nahua nobles played a crucial role in the introduction of European art style and alphabetic writing in the region. A study of the translators on whom Spanish officials relied sheds light on this process. As discussed in reference to a scene in the *Codex Yanhuitlan*, Spanish officials frequently relied on two "interpreters," one who knew Castilian and Nahuatl, and the other who spoke Nahuatl and Mixtec.[102] The former was either a Spaniard (sometimes with a Nahua aide) or a Nahua, and the latter was always a Ñudzahui male. A typical pair who went around the Mixteca Alta in the early 1560s was the Spaniard Pedro Salazar, translator of Nahuatl and Castilian, and Andrés Jusepe, translator of Nahuatl and Mixtec. Eventually Ñudzahui interpreters (called *tay caha dzaha,* "those who speak languages"), who began their careers knowing only their own language and Nahuatl, would acquire Castilian and simplify the process, as Andrés Jusepe did by the end of the 1560s.[103] Friars were often involved in the translation process; three friars served as translators during the Inquisition trial of Yanhuitlan in the 1540s.[104] Fray Antonio de Larralde of Tamasulapa, with the assistance of fray Pascual de la Anunciación, arranged the commission of artist Andrés de Concha to paint a *retablo* (altarpiece) in the church in 1586. They introduced the painter to the *cabildo* (the Spanish-style municipal council staffed by native nobles) and negotiated a deal with governor don Fernando de Andrada.[105]

Nahuatl played such a prominent role in this interim period that the interpreter, even when he translated Mixtec directly into Spanish, was generically called the *nahuatlato.* In 1541, a case from Tlaxiaco introduced Laçaro de Aunxal as a "naguatato de lengua española y misteca," as well as three other "naguatatos" from Teposcolula and Tlaxiaco.[106] The encomendero of Yanhuitlan had his own personal "nahuatlato" in the 1540s. Etymologically, a "nahuatlato" in Nahuatl merely meant a "clear speaker," regardless of the language spoken. The use of the term throughout New Spain for "translator" suggests that Spaniards consciously adapted the Nahuatl meaning of the word. In the *Codex Sierra,* the Spanish alcalde mayor was always accompanied by a nahuatlato and a notary (see fig. 2.18).[107]

Just as Spanish translators acquired a knowledge of Nahuatl in the early period, many Spaniards who lived in the Mixteca became familiar with the Ñudzahui language. When a legal dispute in Yanhuitlan called five Spaniards to testify as witnesses in 1584, three claimed to know Mixtec, and one said he knew Nahuatl and Mixtec. This last witness, Damián de Torres Corilla, a resident of the Mixteca Alta for some forty years, testified that he "understood, spoke, and read Mixtec."[108] A prominent

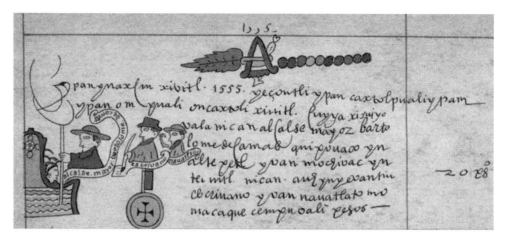

FIGURE 2.18. A Spanish official, a notary, and a "nahuatlato" in the *Codex Sierra,* p. 15.

Spanish scribe (*escribano publico*) in Teposcolula, Juan de Medina, was said to have spoken and understood Ñudzahui perfectly well in the 1620s.[109] Similarly, many Mixtecs, especially nobles and merchants, knew Nahuatl and Spanish. More than half of the Ñudzahui nobles who appeared in Yanhuitlan as witnesses in the hearings of 1584 knew Nahuatl, for example. Even on the coast, in Tututepec, many cabildo officers and nobles spoke "Mixteco and Mexicano" in 1598. The translator at that time, Sebastián Jusepe (perhaps a descendant of Andrés Jusepe, mentioned above), knew Mixtec, Nahuatl, and Spanish.[110] Mestizos were prime candidates for bilingualism, a topic discussed further in the chapter on ethnicity.

Several Nahuatl-language archival documents from the Mixteca confirm the use of Nahuatl as an intermediary language (see table 2.1). A case from Texupa, home of the *Codex Sierra,* characterizes the timing of this process. A land dispute in Astatla elicited multiple documents: the first was a Nahuatl-language title from 1551 (contemporaneous with the *Codex Sierra*) accompanied by a rudimentary pictorial representation of the land; next was a title in the Ñudzahui language transferring the same plot of land in 1579; last, a Chocho-language testament referred to the land and its owner in 1684. Significantly, the earliest document was written in Nahuatl and contained a pictorial element, followed by Mixtec and later Chocho.[111] A related case from Coixtlahuaca brought forward three testaments from cacique don Domingo de Mendoza to support his claims: the first is from 1597 and is in Nahuatl, whereas the others are dated 1615 and 1633 and were written in Chocho.[112] This sequence suggests that Chocho speakers also wrote Nahuatl before writing in their own language.[113] A multilingual document from Tonalá, in the Mixteca Baja, typifies the intermediary role played by Nahuatl. In 1584, the Spanish alcalde mayor of Tonalá ordered interpreters to translate a Spanish decree into Nahuatl, and he sent it to Atoyac.[114] The Ñudzahui officials of Atoyac responded to the Nahuatl decree by writing on the back of the original letter in Mixtec and then returned it to Tonalá. The alcalde mayor received the Ñudzahui response and had it translated into Nahuatl "so that it could be better understood." This last Nahuatl version of the Ñudzahui letter was never officially translated into Spanish,

TABLE 2.1
Extant Nahuatl-Language Documents from the Mixteca

Provenance	Date	Languages Spoken by Population
Texupa (Astatla)	1551	Ñudzahui, Chocho
Zapotitlan	1561–73	Nahuatl, Chocho, Ñudzahui
Ixcatlan	1568	Ixcatec
Chicahuastla	1575	Ñudzahui, Trique
Coixtlahuaca	1578	Chocho, Ñudzahui
Teposcolula	1580	Ñudzahui
Tonalá	1584	Ñudzahui, Nahuatl
Achiutla	1590	Ñudzahui
Istepec	1594	Ñudzahui
Coixtlahuaca	1601	Chocho, Ñudzahui
Acatlan	1601	Ñudzahui, Nahuatl
Ocotepec	1612	Nahuatl, Amuzgo, Trique, Ñudzahui
Cuicatlan	1623	Cuicatec
Xicayan	1636	Chatina

as if Nahuatl were good enough for Spaniards. Thus, the process of three-way translation practiced by interpreters was adapted to writing. These cases indicate that Nahuatl was a useful intermediary language in Oaxaca, not just a "prestige language" employed by nobles.

The nature of Nahuatl documentation in the Mixteca can be characterized by two distinct features. First, most of it is early in date; all but five examples are from the sixteenth century (and two of these five are dated 1601). Second, fourteen of the seventeen documents either refer specifically to non-Ñudzahui-speaking groups—including Nahua, Chocho, Trique, Cuicatec, Ixcatec, Chatino, Mazatec, and Tepeneme—or were written in areas peripheral to the Mixteca Alta. Nahuatl prevailed in areas where lesser-known, minority languages were spoken and where there were Nahuatl-speaking minorities (especially in the Mixteca Baja and the northern perimeter of the region). All five of the Nahuatl documents from the seventeenth century were written in non-Ñudzahui-speaking areas. Only one Nahuatl document has appeared from the Teposcolula area, a rudimentary receipt from the sale of a musket.[115] The written Nahuatl ranges from an elegant letter composed in Coixtlahuaca in 1578 to tiny slips of election papers from coastal Xicayan in 1636.[116] Most are typical Nahuatl writings from the fringe; some betray a labored attempt to communicate. Once Mixtecs began to learn Spanish after prolonged contact, Spaniards disappeared from the position of translator, and Nahuatl was no longer needed. This process was just about complete by the time of the *Relaciones geográficas* (1577–80), when native nobles had become capable of translating directly from Ñudzahui to Spanish.[117] A few Mixtecs had learned how to speak and even write Spanish by the last quarter of the sixteenth century; for example, don Gabriel de Guzmán, cacique and governor of Yanhuitlan, claimed that he was *ladino* (conversant) in the Castilian language, which he "understood, spoke and wrote well."[118]

Although it is true that many nobles were well versed in the imperial language, it appears that people chose to write in their own language whenever possible. Once

Ñudzahui-language alphabetic writing took root, it rapidly displaced Nahuatl in all but the most peripheral areas of the Mixteca. Nahuatl continued as a lingua franca along the non-Ñudzahui-speaking fringes of the Mixteca, especially among the Trique, Chatino, Cuicatec, and Ixcatec groups. It is possible that some of these languages were never written in the colonial period.[119]

Ñudzahui-Language Alphabetic Writing

The eventual spread of native-language alphabetic writing resulted from a prolonged, intensive dialogue between members of the Dominican order and native nobles. This dialogue required the active participation of both sides in that Ñudzahui nobles and Dominicans trained each other in their native tongues. The dialogue did not produce immediate results, however. It took decades to develop an orthography and to assemble instructional materials on the language. Although the Roman alphabet failed to record tone and certain phonological features, priests and native nobles managed to develop a fairly standardized orthography in the Mixteca Alta by the 1550s and 1560s. The first published text, the *Doctrina en lengua misteca,* was printed in November 1567. Fray Benito Hernández produced the *Doctrina* in the variant of the Achiutla area; two months later it was reprinted in the Teposcolula area variant, using the same font, basic format, and many of the same illustrations. The *Doctrina* represents the first extant example of alphabetic text written entirely in the Ñudzahui language (the book contains only a few lines of Spanish and Latin). The first copy consists of 197 folios, or 394 pages, and is certain proof that Ñudzahui alphabetic writing was fully developed by the 1560s.[120]

The publication of church-sponsored texts coincided with the appearance of notarial records produced by indigenous escribanos, noble scribes who were trained to record mundane affairs in their own communities. The *Doctrina* predates the earliest extant Ñudzahui-language notarial document by only four years. The document is a last will and testament, written in 1571 on behalf of the *cacica* doña María López of Yucucuihi (Tlazultepec).[121] Among her collection of books, she possessed a "tutu dotrina" [doctrina book], probably a copy of Hernández's *Doctrina* of 1567. Both writings are from the same general area. In her will she asked fray Antonio de los Reyes, who published a grammar titled *Arte en lengua mixteca* in 1593, to say masses on her behalf. Doña María personally associated with the friars, the "zutu mani" [precious fathers] who played a prominent role in the development of writing in the area. By the last quarter of the sixteenth century, native scribes in cabeceras had mastered the art of alphabetic writing. From that time onward, the basic phonetic transcription and orthography that emerged from the sixteenth-century dialogue between Dominicans and Ñudzahui nobles persisted throughout much of the colonial period with minimal revision. Early colonial commentaries and studies of the *dzaha ñudzahui* (Ñudzahui speech) and its distinct variants are examined in the following chapter on language.

The Spanish administrative and legal system required municipal record keeping. Native notaries of cabildos recorded local transactions involving properties, accounts, and other official business in their communities. Native officials handled many conflicts according to local custom unless a Spaniard was involved or the aggrieved party approached the Spanish alcalde mayor with his or her complaint. In handling a legal

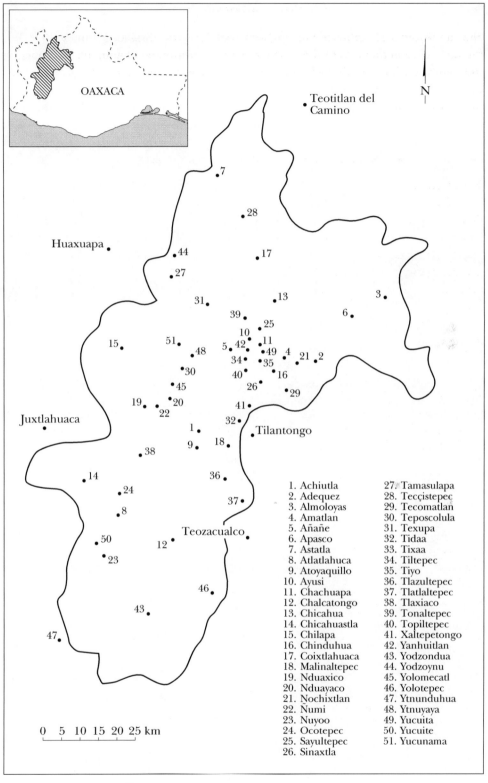

OAXACA

N

Teotitlan del Camino

•7

•28

Huaxuapa •

•44

•27

•31

•39   •13

•25   6•   3•

10   •
•   •42 •11
15•   51•   5• •49 4• 21• 2•
     48• 34•   •35
       •30   40• •16
      •45   26•
19• •20   •29
  22•   41•
Juxtlahuaca   32•
        1•   Tilantongo
      9• 18•

•38

•14   36•

•24   37•

8•

•50   12•   Teozacualco•
•23

46•

43•

47•

1. Achiutla	27. Tamasulapa
2. Adequez	28. Tecçistepec
3. Almoloyas	29. Tecomatlan
4. Amatlan	30. Teposcolula
5. Añañe	31. Texupa
6. Apasco	32. Tidaa
7. Astatla	33. Tixaa
8. Atlatlahuca	34. Tiltepec
9. Atoyaquillo	35. Tiyo
10. Ayusi	36. Tlazultepec
11. Chachuapa	37. Tlatlaltepec
12. Chalcatongo	38. Tlaxiaco
13. Chicahua	39. Tonaltepec
14. Chicahuastla	40. Topiltepec
15. Chilapa	41. Xaltepetongo
16. Chinduhua	42. Yanhuitlan
17. Coixtlahuaca	43. Yodzondua
18. Malinaltepec	44. Yodzoynu
19. Nduaxico	45. Yolomecatl
20. Nduayaco	46. Yolotepec
21. Nochixtlan	47. Ytnunduhua
22. Ñumi	48. Ytnuyaya
23. Nuyoo	49. Yucuita
24. Ocotepec	50. Yucuite
25. Sayultepec	51. Yucunama
26. Sinaxtla	

0   5 10 15 20 25 km

MAP 2. Provenance of Ñudzahui-language documentation from the colonial jurisdiction (alcaldía mayor) of Teposcolula.

dispute, whether civil or criminal in nature, the alcalde mayor and his staff began a formal investigation by assembling evidence and obtaining preliminary declarations from the parties involved, making arrests, if necessary, and scheduling a hearing with witnesses.[122] The entire proceedings were recorded in Spanish with the aid of translators.[123] Thus, most surviving sources in judicial archives involving native communities were written in Spanish by notaries attached to the staff of the alcalde mayor. However, many records of civil disputes contain native-language writings as evidence produced by plaintiffs and defendants to document succession or property rights. Usually, the evidence submitted was in the form of a last will and testament. In their dual role of distributing property and serving as de facto titles for native heirs, testaments were valuable, multifunctional legal documents. Some judicial cases include four or five testaments, extending across multiple generations, as evidence of continual possession.

The last will and testament was the first genre of alphabetic writing to be practiced within the indigenous community (see appendix B, section III for examples). Priests promoted the writing of testaments for obvious reasons: to account for one's body and soul, to settle matters of debt and inheritance, and to leave money or land to the church.[124] The convergence in function of European testaments and indigenous traditions explains the early proliferation of testaments in native society.[125] The testament fulfilled a basic function of preconquest-style codices and lienzos in confirming kinship ties, hereditary rights, and property entitlement. Appropriately, the earliest extant Ñudzahui-language testament appears in a legal dispute with a preconquest-style pictographic text (the Genealogy of Tlazultepec, discussed above and shown in fig. 2.8). In this period, alphabetic writing served as a complement to the native pictorial tradition. Although nobles continued to use pictorial records to document their patrimonial claims before Spanish officials, they came to rely increasingly on the genre of the testament for these purposes.[126] In fact, the succession of rulers in many pictorial genealogies from the sixteenth century ends about two or three generations after the conquest, when the first extant native-language testaments were written.[127] Many caciques must have recognized that wills were more effective claims to lands and succession in the Spanish legal system than pictorial records. The importance of dynastic lineages and the occasion for inheritance and property disputes made the writing of testaments indispensable. The cabildo of Yanhuitlan made this fact clear in 1591 when it actively encouraged the writing of testaments and inventories (*memorias*) with native escribanos and witnesses to facilitate property transactions and to mitigate the frequency of property disputes, especially among nobles, merchants, and traders.[128]

If the introduced testamentary genre fulfilled a function of preconquest-style pictorial writing, it was also adapted to a strong oral tradition. The native testament consisted of a speech to a group of relatives and friends and was more of a statement before a gathering of witnesses than the typical private European testament.[129] For most indigenous wills, the audience played an important role in the proceedings; many men and women, sometimes the entire cabildo, attended the event.[130] The testaments of high nobles occasioned large gatherings. For example, more than sixty men and women witnessed the testament of don Pedro Osorio, the ruler of Teposcolula, in 1566.[131] Nahua informants in the *Florentine Codex* suggest a preconquest precedent for the testament by attributing to the Mixtecs an ancient tradition of summoning a diviner when someone was about to die, whereupon the sick person would generally confess his or her faults and settle matters of earthly debts and possessions. The informants wrote: "It is said of the Mixtecs, that in the time of their idolatry, when one was about to die, he/she summoned the diviner, the advised one. Before him/her one told all, before him/her one placed all that one had done, all that one had performed—one's faults, one's good to others, one's harming of others. Perhaps one had stolen, perhaps one had taken something from someone. One told all, concealed nothing, hid nothing. And the diviner or the healer commanded the sick one to make restitution to people, to return property and belongings to people."[132] Similarly, the native Christian testament entitled a sick person to settle accounts on earth and to make a final pronouncement of faith on his or her deathbed. It is unclear why Nahua nobles who contributed to the *Florentine Codex* singled out the Mixtecs for such a ritual. Their reference is part of a larger discussion of confession and penitence involving ancient deities and diviners in highland Mexico. But it is clear that the resemblance of this pre-conquest practice to the nature and function of the colonial last will and testament (not to mention the Catholic sacrament of confession) provided grounds for association.

A fine example of an early Ñudzahui-language testament was written in Tlaxiaco in 1573. Don Felipe de Saavedra may have written his own will before a noble audience; the testament bears no signature other than his own and those of the witnesses who were able to sign their names.[133] The neat document was written in a reverential vocabulary befitting don Felipe's high rank; its language and orthography correspond with the *Doctrina* from nearby Achiutla. The three-page document comprises almost ninety lines of neat writing, with an extensive religious formula and a long list of lands and place-names associated with his patrimony. Among his numerous possessions are items associated with alphabetic writing, including five books ("hoho tutu libronde"), a writing box ("hatnu escrivania"), and a pair of eyeglasses ("antojos"). Judging by this sample, the native-language testamentary genre was well established in this area by the 1570s; its style and format remained essentially the same for more than two centuries.

The testament was one of several native-language writing genres established by the last quarter of the sixteenth century. Another category of mundane writing was criminal records. Criminal investigations often originated at the level of the local cabildo and proceeded to the alcalde mayor in the form of a written record. When a serious crime such as homicide was committed in a community, the nearest cabildo officials investigated the crime, made arrests, and sent the Spanish alcalde mayor a brief written report of the crime. Sometimes the native officials recorded confessions or statements from victims and suspects. For example, one case from San Andrés Chalcatongo elicited three testimonies about an attempted homicide involving two men and a woman in 1581 (see appendix B, section II, for a transcription and translation of this document).[134] The text amounts to a fascinating "archival narrative" of adultery and sexuality, as told by commoners in their own words.

Even Spanish officials came to rely on native-language writing for their daily business. For example, alcaldes mayores commissioned numerous native-language *mandamientos* to be distributed and read aloud in the major communities of the Mixteca Alta. One of these decrees, written in Teposcolula in 1616, called for the provision of labor to build a military fort in the port of Acapulco.[135] Spanish officials also relied on native-language correspondence with cabildos. For example, in 1579, the Spanish alcalde mayor of Teposcolula sent a letter to the cabildo of Achiutla about a thief who had looted the church sacristy. The terse, plain language of the letter bears little resemblance to the reverential, refined language of the reply from Ñudzahui nobles in Achiutla.

Once the new legal system and local cabildos were established in the 1550s and 1560s, native-language writing took root by the last quarter of the sixteenth century in and around the *cabeceras* and Dominican *conventos* of the region, where Ñudzahui and Spanish contact was most intensive. By 1600, native-language writing extended to encompass a wide range of genres and functions, from the sale of properties to marriage arrangements. For example, Juana de Zárate produced a bill of sale documenting her late husband's purchase in 1618 of a blacksmith's shop in the plaza of Teposcolula, with an attached inventory of the forge. The bill is essentially an informal written agreement between two nobles; in 1658, the document was translated for the alcalde mayor by the cacique of Teposcolula, don Francisco Pimentel y Guzmán, who could read and write Spanish and Mixtec.[136] In contrast to such mundane matters, a gathering of prestigious nobles from Chalcatongo and Miltepec came to Teposcolula in 1622 to arrange a marriage by church dispensation between don Diego de Velasco y Arellano and his cousin doña Micaela de la Cueva. The meeting generated a lengthy text on the qualifications of the caciques and a discourse on marriage written in the form of a narrative and dialogue.[137] Priests presided over the ceremony while a native noble drew up the document inside the entrance to the church (see fig. 2.19).

From the 1670s to the mid-eighteenth century, the volume of extant native-language documentation increases dramatically. The general proliferation of alphabetic writing in the region reflects two developments: first, many former sujetos achieved independence from nearby cabeceras in this period and began to produce their own corporate writings; second, demographic renewal and increasing demand for land generated more legal documentation in the form of civil disputes. The increase in native-language writing after 1670 is represented by a series of civil proceedings in Yanhuitlan. In 1681, an entire case involving a barrio (*siña*) of Yanhuitlan against a cacique over disputed lands was recorded in the Ñudzahui language.[138] This one document includes twelve pages of presentation, petition, notification of parties, and so forth, with a supporting native-language testament from 1642 (see appendix B, section IV, for a transcription and translation of this case). In similar manner, another twenty pages of proceedings were recorded in a separate case the following year.[139] Such documentation from Yanhuitlan indicates an ability to apply Ñudzahui writing to a specific Spanish model, even replacing Castilian as the official legal language of the proceedings when the indigenous cabildo attempted to resolve its own disputes involving corporate landholdings.[140]

Native writers put the alphabet to multiple uses by the latter part of the seventeenth century. As an extreme example of its utility, a man from Yanhuitlan killed his wife and pinned a murder note to her body before fleeing from the community in 1684.[141] The murderer was a noble who possessed pen and paper and the ability to write a three-page letter, complete with reverential language, addressed to both Ñudzahui and Spanish officials. Testimony from the murder investigation alleged that the victim, a mestiza, had written letters to her lover, a sacristan of the church. A more benign type of informal

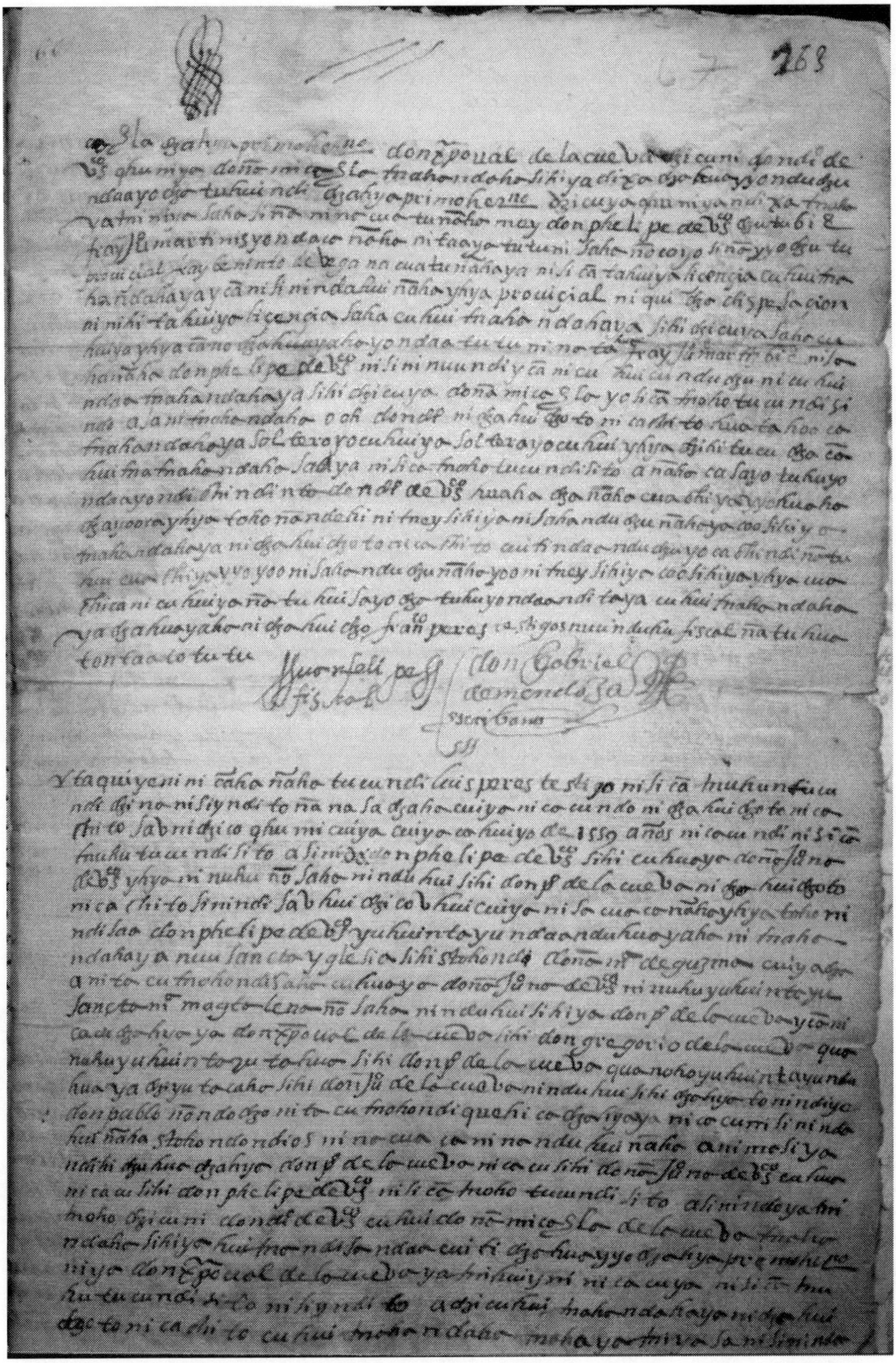

FIGURE 2.19. Page from an ecclesiastical dispensation for marriage granted to don Diego de Velasco y Arellano and doña Micaela de la Cueva in 1622. AGN-T, 637:1.

writing was the personal letter. One such letter, written in 1572, appears to us today only because it concerned the possession of a contested plot of land. The lord of San Juan Bautista Tiyta (Atoyaquillo), don Diego de Guzmán, wrote a letter to nobles in Tlaxiaco in response to a verbal or written message they had sent him about some land named "Yucundjeñu" (see fig. 2.20).[142] This practice may have been fairly common among the literate nobility, but the letters rarely appear in archives. Usually, one sees only oblique references to the practice: for example, in 1622, a noble named Francisco Pérez mentioned that he customarily delivered letters written by don Felipe de Velasco of Chalcatongo to his nephew in Miltepec, don Cristóbal de la Cueva.[143] Some letters were written on behalf of the community. In 1671, an alcalde of Santa Cruz Chalcatongo wrote to the alcalde mayor in Teposcolula that his community had just received a letter in Spanish from Mexico City that nobody could understand. He informed the Spanish official that his cabildo intended to send a delegation to Teposcolula, bearing presents for him and the notary. They had planned to come on Monday, the letter stated, but someone remembered that it was market day in Teposcolula, and they knew that his house "would be very full" on that day. Thus, they informed him in the letter that they would come to Teposcolula on the following day. These letters and notes demonstrate that literacy often spread beyond the official business of trained notaries to serve multiple functions in native society.[144]

By the eighteenth century, many smaller places had begun to generate extensive written records. In 1704, for example, the community of Santiago Yolomecatl produced a seventy-page account of expenses.[145] This document served the same function as the *Codex Sierra* (written from 1550 to 1564), but it was written entirely in Mixtec and contains no pictorial portion. Similar types of accounts exist for Topiltepec, Tiyacu, and Yanhuitlan.[146]

Literacy

The geographical range of Ñudzahui-language writing marks the general boundaries of this cultural area in the colonial period. Although no documentation is known to exist from the coastal region, glosses on pictorial writings and Reyes's commentary on orthographic conventions in the coastal area confirm that the language was also written in that subregion.[147] The spread of writing across the cultural area raises the question of the extent of literacy.

Literacy cannot be measured precisely, but it is safe to say that reading and writing were limited to nobles and notaries in the colonial period. Among the nobility, there were exceptional writers who achieved a reputation for their works. Fray Francisco de Burgoa, the Dominican chronicler, referred to prolific Ñudzahui authors such as Diego Osorio, a cacique in the Achiutla area, "who left translated into his language many prayers of saints and hymns." He also mentioned a certain Gabriel de Valdivieso, cacique in the valley of Yanhuitlan, whom he called "an Indian of such capacity, and so given to reading books, that by his hand he put into his language and composed from prayers and spiritual tracts twenty-seven books, large and small, of great erudition in wording and phrasing, of which many ministers have made use."[148] Some of the church-sponsored manuscripts were written by Mixtec men, such as a handwritten

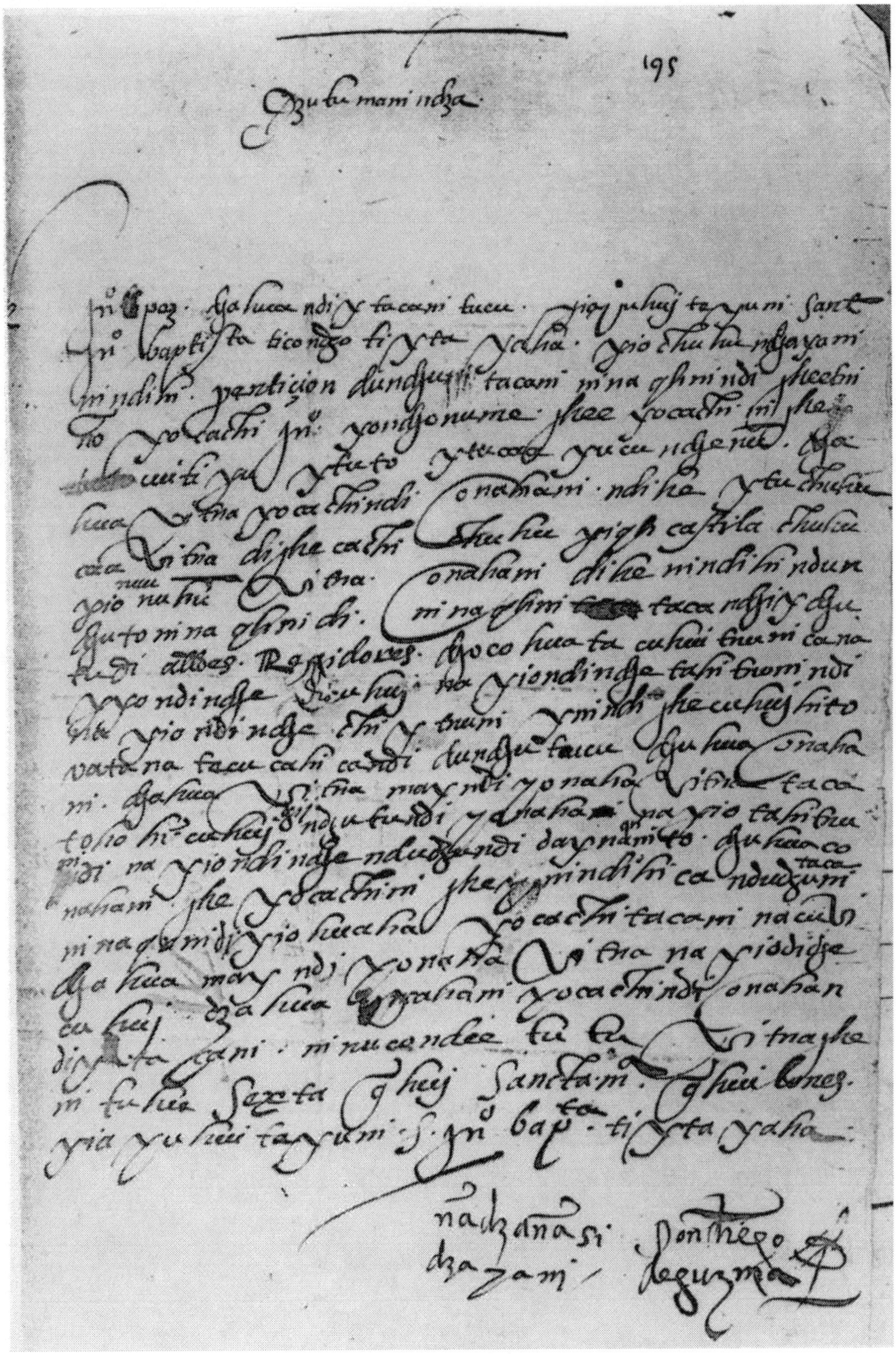

FIGURE 2.20. Letter written by don Diego de Guzmán to nobles of Tlaxiaco (Disinuu), 1572. AGN-T, 57:2, f. 194. See appendix B, section I for a transcription and translation of the letter.

catechism of 1584 based on the work of the Dominican Gerónimo Taix.[149] Works in the native language circulated throughout the period. Don Nicolás de Santiago, a noble of Yolomecatl, possessed a chest of documents and several books, including a *Doctrina en lengua mixteca* and a "libro de historia en lengua mixteca" [a history book in the Mixtec language].[150]

The testaments and inventories of lords and nobles contain numerous references to the possession of writing instruments such as quill pens, paper, writing boxes, desks, and printed books. For example, the lengthy testament of don Diego de Velasco provides an inventory of his goods and properties. Among his many possessions in 1627 were three inscribed writing boxes with locks, at least ten gold and silver gilded books ("hoho libros siñuu cuisi . . . hoho libros tutu siñuu quaa"), three "vocabularios de lengua mixteca," a desk with all the colors that he used "to paint," several legal documents, and many papers and books given to him by various friars.[151] Native nobles also possessed books in the Castilian or Latin languages. In 1591, the hereditary lord of Yanhuitlan, don Francisco de Guzmán, owned books with Latin titles, such as *Flor Sanctorum* and *Contemptus Mundi*.[152] Traders kept books and sold books; Juan Ramírez kept a book of accounts from 1740 to 1758 that totaled sixty-eight pages. His trade in and around Yanhuitlan included books such as the "libro coronica Burgoa" [chronicle book of Burgoa] and the "libro nani Palestra de Burgoa" [book by Burgoa titled Palestra], in reference to *Palestra historial de virtudes y ejemplares apostólicos*.[153] Even lowly Martín Vásquez of Tlaxiaco, who was imprisoned for biting an official in 1601, owned two books among his modest possessions.[154]

There was in colonial times a continued and heightened awareness of the importance of safeguarding papers and titles. In 1669, the cabildo of Teposcolula ordered everyone—married couples, widows and widowers, and unmarried adults—to assemble and bring forward all the testaments in their possession, suggesting that these documents were kept by all the community's households.[155] In 1636, the cacique of Chalcatongo, don Diego de Velasco, guarded the papers documenting his patrimony.[156] In 1678, don Felipe de la Cruz of Topiltepec referred to his favorite desk and a locked chest containing many writings, including records of community tribute and expenses, as well as two books of accounts.[157] Diego Jiménez of Yanhuitlan submitted a list of property stolen from his house in 1686, which included a chest containing Spanish feathers (pens) and "all of [his] papers and titles to lands and possessions that [he had] owned, which cost [him] eighty-four pesos."[158] Don Raymundo de Santiago y Guzmán, the cacique of San Bartolomé Coculco in 1676, referred to his "testamendo dzaño pintura" [testament [and] border painting].[159] Don Juan Agustín, the cacique of Acaquisapa, Huaxuapa, in 1642, spoke of "all the titles that he guarded in his palace" [niycutu títulos yonehy hua aniy] and "a lienzo of all the land borders" [naa niy cutu terminos ñuhu dayu].[160] Repeated references to valuable documents demonstrate a recognition, especially among the nobility, that writing and literacy were crucial to protecting property and status in colonial society.

It is unclear how many nobles could read and write. In certain places, the literacy rate among members of the cabildo appears to have been relatively high. When the cabildo of Teposcolula and nobles from all its outlying subject settlements convened in 1583 to ratify an agreement with the Spanish alcalde mayor, 15 of 17 cabildo members from Teposcolula and 26 of 31 nobles from the sujetos and estancias signed their names to the document.[161] A signature indicates only the probability of literacy, but it is true that the cabildo was the main site of reading and writing.[162] Since women were excluded from the all-male Spanish-style municipal council, they were not trained to write in the colonial period. Whereas noble boys learned how to write at an early age when they were schooled in Christian doctrine and groomed to serve as church and cabildo officials, girls received no such training.[163] Circumstantial evidence suggests, nonetheless, that some women knew how to read and write. Noble women owned and bequeathed books and desks and writing equipment to their daughters and other women kin. Like men, women safeguarded written records: Petrona de Osorio of Yolomecatl had a "chest of land documents and other papers" [satnu ñuhu ndihi taca tutu], and doña Josefa de Salazar of Chilapa owned a "small locked chest containing all the testaments of her ancestors" [satno duchi yondey ndaha caá sihi ndihi taca testamento sanaha].[164] And a few women signed their names to documents.[165] On the other hand, there is plenty of evidence that women did not write, even when the occasion demanded it. For example, there were 11 women among the group of 104 people who gathered in the marketplace of Suchitepec in 1587 to protest excessive taxation on goods sold in the market; none of the women present joined the 25 men who signed their names to the petition drawn up on their behalf.[166] Although there is some evidence for literacy among a limited group of women in the Mixteca, it is clear that Ñudzahui women rarely wrote in the colonial period.[167]

The Decline of Pictorial Writing

The spread of alphabetic writing in the Mixteca contributed to the decline and eventual displacement of pictographic modes of communication and expression. In the sixteenth century, alphabetic text complemented and then competed with pictorial writing in serving the dual functions of record keeping and political representation. As alphabetic writing spread throughout the Mixteca, Spanish officials discouraged communities and individuals from using pictorial evidence as proof of possession. For example, in 1569, one Spanish lawyer argued that native pinturas did not portray the truth but only a community's "private and particular will, based on no authority." The lawyer claimed that "Indians just paint what they want" and dismissed native writing as "a tradition from heathen times, when they did not know the truth and were easily deceived by the devil."[168] This sweeping condemnation of native writing represents a general attitude among Spaniards that pictographic text was inferior to the alphabet.[169] Faced with colonial realities, native nobles must have recognized the need to learn the new method, although they did not abandon the use of pictorial writings. In fact, many communities kept both pictorial and alphabetic writings to support their claims. In 1707, officials in Topiltepec safeguarded a map of the "community and pueblo" in the "community archive," along with papers documenting their recent separation from the cabecera of Yanhuitlan."[170] In this case, pictorial records continued to serve the important function of marking borders. By the seventeenth century, however, pictographic writing had become a complementary, mainly secondary form of communication that rarely went unaccompanied by explanatory alphabetic text or other legal documentation.

The drawing and painting of maps continued throughout the colonial period, in part because this genre conformed to Spanish expectations of supporting land documentation. In contrast to the elaborate maps executed for the *Relaciones geográficas*, the map presented in a land dispute between the communities of San Andrés Sinastla and San Juan Sayultepec in 1690 served a more limited objective (see fig. 2.21).[171] Actually, the document demonstrates a greater understanding of the type of information required by Spanish officials and thus a reduction of extraneous detail. Indicative of its later date, it is less dependent on pictorialism; place-names are represented by means of the alphabet instead of glyphs, and the cardinal directions are rendered in Spanish (*oriente* at the top is spelled "oriende"). Although the six stylized hill glyphs and the river are reminiscent of earlier conventions, especially in the Amoltepec (Yucunama) map, they have been reduced to a bare minimum. The relative location of communities is marked by stylized churches and crosses instead of a European illusionistic landscape. The depiction of Sinastla and its neighboring communities conforms to the radial orientation of the maps of Teozacualco and Yucunama, but this map lacks the ornate, informative detail of the earlier works and does not refer to any people.

Similarly, a genealogy from the Teposcolula area, dated around 1600, is a rudimentary sketch on native paper that depicts a family's lineage by way of a European-style tree (see fig. 2.22). As in the codices, married couples face each other in profile; the figures are portrayed with their eyes closed or open, indicating whether they were alive or deceased at the time of the drawing. First-generation individuals, depicted at the bottom, retain their calendrical names instead of adopting Spanish names, but these names are expressed with the alphabet rather than the traditional dot-and-symbol notation of pictorial writing, discussed in chapter 5.[172] Although it retains a pictorial element, this genealogy relies entirely on the alphabet to convey information.

Even though distinctive traits and conventions of the preconquest style were drawn as late as the end of the eighteenth century, as in the map of Xoxocotlan, the transformation of pictorial writing reflected its gradual decline.[173] As we have seen, a hybrid indigenous style flourished only a couple of decades after the conquest. Despite the influence and incorporation of European stylistic forms and techniques, it was nonetheless indigenous in that its practitioners were native artists who sought to communicate valuable information to a mixed audience.

A genre of writing typical of the later colonial period is the *título primordial*, or the so-called false title. In the last quarter of the seventeenth century and beyond, anonymous indigenous writers produced what they considered to be approximations of early colonial Spanish land titles and maps in order to maintain or extend claims to landholdings on behalf of a community or a particular group. The titles were produced in response to legal and commercial demands on native lands. The authors typically dated the manuscripts to around the time of the Spanish conquest in order to demonstrate continuous possession since that significant event. The documents were usually dismissed as fraudulent by Spanish authorities. Títulos primordiales, especially those associated with the Techialoyan Codices, are most common in central Mexico, but they were also produced in other parts of Mesoamerica.[174] Many titles contain pictorial portions that manifest a collective memory of the ancient writing tradition that is inseparable from the hybrid tradition of colonial maps. The pictorial writing represents how local

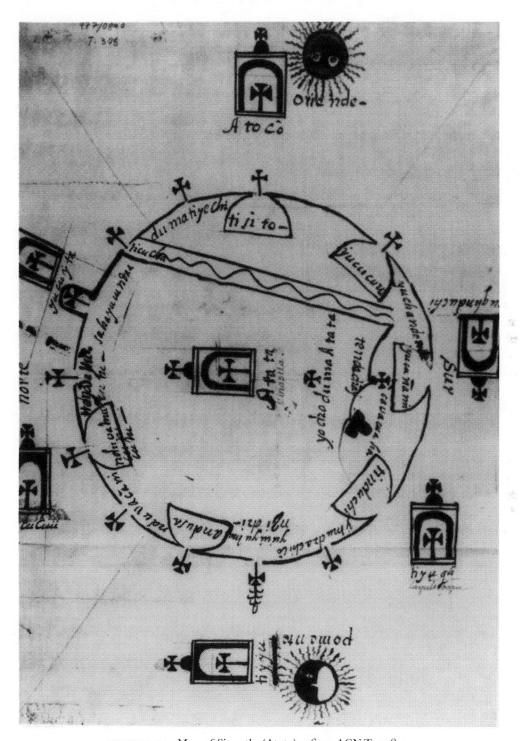

FIGURE 2.21. Map of Sinaxtla (Atata), 1690. AGN-T, 308:4.

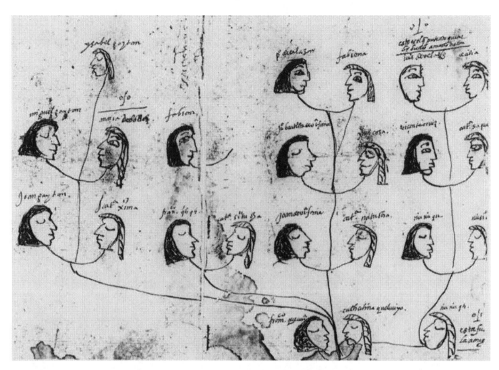

FIGURE 2.22. Anonymous genealogy from the Teposcolula area, n.d. AJT-C, 4:467.

native authors in the late seventeenth century remembered and imagined ancient writing, particularly its style and content. The titles drew on a local oral tradition and popular consciousness rarely seen in other forms of native writing. Although considerable attention is given to pictorial text, alphabetic writing is the primary medium of expression in these archaistic documents.

One Ñudzahui false title from the Valley of Oaxaca consists of eleven pages of text and a painting in a contrived early colonial style (see fig. 2.23).[175] A group from San Juan Chapultepec claimed that they had found the ancient document, which was dated 1523. Actually, this group produced the document in 1696 in response to a Nahuatl-language title that had been presented to Spanish officials by the neighboring community of San Martín Mexicapan, whose "title" was dated 1525. The "pintura y mapa" was designed, in the words of the presenters, "to be viewed as one speaks with the said title."[176] That is, the eleven pages of alphabetic text were designed to complement the pictorial writing. The map's principal function is to delineate borders and major landmarks, but it also contains genealogical information and references to symbolic, historic events. Chapultepec is featured just left of center on the map; in the top portion, the cacique, don Diego Cortés Dzahui Yuchi, defends the community against a bellicose Mexica contingent. A brief text beneath don Diego's coat of arms announces that the map and title belong to San Juan Chapultepec and that the borders have been verified by the people of Mexicapan, a satellite group from central Mexico who apparently settled in the Valley of Oaxaca when they accompanied the Spaniards as allies in the 1520s. Chapultpec's title attempted to demonstrate that the two communities had

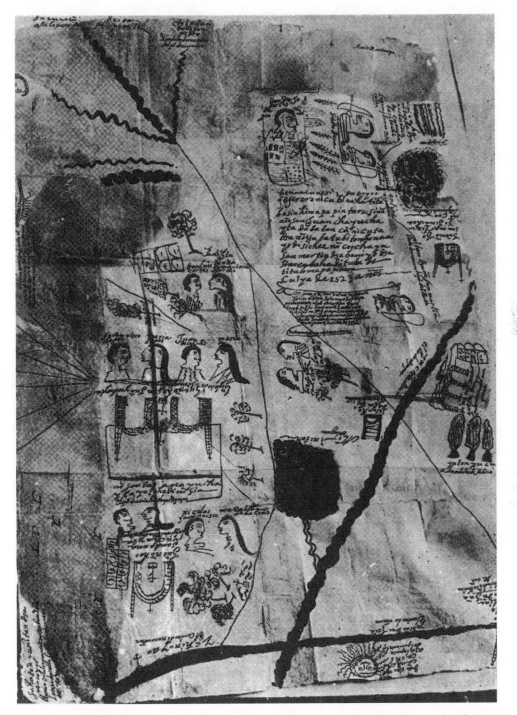

FIGURE 2.23. The pictorial portion of a primordial title from the Valley of Oaxaca, dated 1523 but written around 1696. AGN-T, 236:6.

forged a historic agreement in 1523, on which Mexicapan had reneged. This strategy explains Chapultepec's desire to surpass its neighbor's claim to antiquity by two years. Of course, these dates are impossible; if the document were from 1523, it would pre-date the earliest extant example of Ñudzahui writing by nearly half a century. The paper was purposely aged by either burial, smoke, or water stain, and the handwriting attempts to imitate sixteenth-century script. The use of many Spanish loanwords betrays its late-seventeenth-century origins. The map seems like a poorly executed imitation of the older style.[177]

There is little doubt that the Mixtec "pintura y mapa" was drawn in the seventeenth century. It is a product of the hybrid indigenous map tradition, vaguely reminiscent of the *Relaciones geográficas* maps of the late 1570s. By this time, European introductions had clearly influenced indigenous forms of expression. Unlike their ancestors, men have mustaches and women wear their hair unbraided. They lack the detail, elaborate clothing, and regalia of preconquest-style figures. Besieged by Mexica warriors, don Diego de Cortés Dzahui Yuchi defends himself with a phony coat of arms instead of a Mixtec *yusa* (hand-held shield) and brandishes a lance rather than an obsidian-blade club.[178] Hills bordering maps are a familiar sight in preconquest and early colonial manuscripts, but these shaded blotches bear little resemblance to the stylized glyphs of the earlier period. A smiling sun, leafy trees, and an attempt to draw perspective reflect European influences. Alphabetic glosses identify place-name glyphs located on the edges of the map. Other features of the map are plainly anachronistic; the four churches could not have been built in 1523, within two years of the conquest. The church is a prominent, symbolic structure in colonial pictorials from the Mixteca, including those drawn for the *Relaciones Geográficas* of 1579–81. The map's local perspective or bias is betrayed by the relative size of Chapultepec's church.

Despite its late colonial style, the Mixtec map evokes remnants of the form and function of preconquest-style writing. A principal function of codices and lienzos was to link the genealogies of indigenous rulers to sacred events and personages from the past. Likewise, titles connected communities or members of political factions to ancestors who negotiated agreements with Spanish authorities at the time of the conquest, such as Hernando Cortés. In form and style, the pictorial portion of the Mixtec title reveals a conscious attempt to imitate earlier writing. For example, the map portrays couples in profile, who face each other, reminiscent of ruling couples in preconquest-style codices and early colonial pictorial writings. Here, the couples appear before churches, just as the codices depicted couples seated by or inside temples. The author(s) used ancient images to legitimate their claims, even though the precise relation of the couples to those claims is unclear. In general terms, the author(s) asserted their autonomy by representing Chapultepec as a yuhuitayu with its own hereditary rulers.

The function and style of the title extend beyond land documentation to encompass a much broader spectrum of indigenous writing and expression. The false title was a creative, hybrid form of writing more than a Spanish land title. Primordial titles are visual testimony to the faded but not entirely forgotten art of using images to communicate in the late seventeenth century. The writing style, language, and content of the title convey a sense of how some people imagined writing nearly two hundred years earlier and how they adapted and reconstituted images from the past to serve present concerns. Chapultepec's strategy of transmitting a historical narrative through images and alphabetic text reveals the extent of change and continuity in Ñudzahui writing and culture by the end of the seventeenth century. More will be said about this document in chapter 9.

Late Colonial Writing

Ironically, once the practice of alphabetic writing was widespread enough to extend across the entire region, some indigenous elites had already begun to write in Spanish. Many lords and nobles spoke, wrote, and dressed like Spaniards by the beginning of the eighteenth century, a cultural behavior described as *ladino*.[179] Some caciques and cacicas made their wills in Spanish as early as the late sixteenth century. Don Gabriel de Guzmán, cacique of Yanhuitlan, gave his testament in Spanish in 1591. Doña María de Paredes, a widowed noblewoman from Teposcolula who claimed to know Spanish, made her testament in that language with the assistance of a translator in 1585.[180] Some people preferred to have their will written in Spanish even when they did not know the language; doña Micaela de la Cruz, cacica of Teposcolula in 1738, had her testament made by the Spanish notary through the translator Juan Carrillo.[181] This phenomenon was common only by the late colonial period, but it reached beyond lords and nobles. In 1788, for example, a humble soul named Mateo Barrios gave his own testament in Castilian, even though eight other testaments from Atlatlahuca that year were written in the Ñudzahui language, including his father's. The Spanish was so awkward that it needed to be translated when presented as evidence in a land dispute.[182] Likewise, Matías Bautista of Tamasulapa made his testament in Spanish in 1721, whereas all five of his relatives had made theirs in Mixtec.[183] In 1784, María López of Santa Catarina Adequez had the luxury of making her will in Ñudzahui and then again a few days later in Castilian.[184]

The choice of writing in Castilian or Mixtec reflected increasing bilingualism by the later period. Documents written in Spanish by native hands often betray the first language of their authors in their appearance and language. Many are written in a carefully etched style characteristic of native calligraphy, and some contain numerous clues that the writer was a native speaker. When a native notary of Yanhuitlan wrote the testament of Juan de la Cruz in the Castilian language, he continued to use Ñudzahui place-names; for example, he referred to Coixtlahuaca as Yodzocoo.[185] When two noblewomen from Yanhuitlan initiated a suit in 1674, the resulting proceedings alternated between Ñudzahui and Castilian; much of the documentation was written by the same notary.[186] Juan Ramírez, a bilingual nobleman and itinerant trader from Yanhuitlan who kept a book of his accounts from 1740 to 1758, wrote in both languages, depending on the language of his clients.[187] Even the author of the native-language murder note from Yanhuitlan, discussed above, attempted to close his letter with three lines of garbled Spanish. As native-language writing became more widespread, Spanish came to be a viable second language of communication in places where there was a distinct mestizo and Spanish presence, such as Yanhuitlan. To some extent, nobles and commoners who preferred Spanish writing also responded to prejudices against native-language writing. At the same time that don Agustín Carlos Pimentel y Guzmán, cacique of Teposcolula, wrote and signed a document in Spanish concerning his title to a piece of land, Juan de la Cruz and María de Osorio of Yolomecatl presented a document that they avowed was legitimate "even though it [was] written in the Ñudzahui language."[188] Legal writings in Spanish became more expedient in the late colonial period. The function and content of the writing remained essentially the same, but switching to the official language was a matter of prestige and security.

In the mid-eighteenth century, some Spanish officials questioned the validity of using testaments as legal instruments for documenting property possession. In a lengthy dispute between the native cabildo of Yanhuitlan and its caciques over possession of the royal palace, the Audiencia expressed doubt as to whether testaments, submitted by the caciques to document continuous possession, represented valid legal instruments in lieu of official titles, even though earlier titles were based mainly on testaments.[189] The Audiencia ruled in 1759 against the caciques, despite their impressive collection of testaments dating from the mid-sixteenth century. The ruling reflected changing Spanish attitudes toward native-language writings as legal documents.

Nonetheless, if the testament was the first genre of alphabetic writing to be employed within the indigenous community, it was also the most conservative and durable. More than three-fourths of all documents in the present collection dated after 1700 are testaments, whereas testaments for the entire colonial period represent about half of all documentation. In the later period, native-language testaments were usually written in areas not represented in the earlier period, on behalf of a broad segment of society; these documents tend to focus simply on what goes to whom and do not follow an elaborate formula. The testament was a genre of writing not directly associated with the corporate community by this time. Whereas all sources generated by the native cabildo were eventually superseded by Spanish, the testament became more of a private document, often written outside the cabildo's purview. Most late colonial documents typically bear the signatures of only one or two witnesses, unlike the lists of names attached to testaments of the early period. The immediate audience was personal, conforming more to the Spanish model.[190]

On the other hand, some Ñudzahui testaments from the late colonial period are beautifully written texts signed by members of the entire cabildo; such documents usually come from remote, smaller communities where the nobility was actively involved in native-language writing. In general, the language itself betrays less Spanish influence.[191] In those areas more influenced by Spanish and mestizo contact, the tradition evolved more along a Spanish model until Spanish eventually took over as the language of legal discourse, while those areas more removed from Spanish influence continued writing in their own language, according to custom. Spanish-language writing gradually supplanted native-language writing in the more prominent cabeceras, where writing first appeared, and where contact with Spanish speakers was greatest. Accordingly, smaller, more peripheral communities practiced Ñudzahui writing later and continued the tradition longer, so that most documentation from the late eighteenth century is from more isolated places such as Atlatlahuca and Adequez. Such is the case with the testament of Casimiro de los Santos from Tonaltepec. Drawn up in 1807, this neatly written document abounds with reverential vocabulary reminiscent of the early period and is duly signed by the entire cabildo. Although it is the latest extant sample of Ñudzahui-language writing, its polished prose defies a dying tradition.[192]

Today, Mixtec is not even spoken in many of the communities where writing flourished in the colonial period. Many of these pueblos are situated along the highway from Mexico City to Oaxaca, the road running through the Mixteca that slowly integrated much of the region into the Spanish-speaking sphere. On the other hand, colonial documentation exists for many Ñudzahui communities where the language is still spoken today, places that were latecomers in the documentary record. In areas of intensive cultural contact, writing in Spanish became more expedient for legal purposes, much as native-language alphabetic writing had proved more suitable than a painting two centuries earlier. Ñudzahui communities and individuals innovated and adapted by necessity in order to defend and promote their restricted rights within the Spanish legal system; the adoption of Castilian writing reflects greater changes within the indigenous community, in the presence of an ever-growing mestizo and ladino population. The decline and eventual loss of Ñudzahui-language writing marked the end of an era.

The native-language sources introduced in this chapter represent only a tiny fraction of all the writings that were safeguarded in wooden chests and archives. Nonetheless, this collection of documentation is representative of writing in the Ñudzahui language and, as such, is a running record of that language. It follows, then, that language is the subject of the next chapter and a major concern throughout the book.

CHAPTER 3

Language

MIXTECAN IS ONE OF EIGHT BRANCHES of the Otomanguean family of languages, a family accounting for about a third of all indigenous-language speakers in Mexico today. Mixtecan and Zapotecan are two of the largest and most internally diversified branches of this family. At the time of the Spanish conquest, the Mixtec language group was one of the largest in Mesoamerica, with well over a million speakers.[1] A few decades later, many native nobles learned how to write their languages with the Roman alphabet. Their writings and a few church-sponsored texts are the only sources for language-based studies in the historical period. These texts are useful for what they say as well as how they say it. Native-language writings from the Mixteca preserve many aspects of ordinary speech for a period of nearly 250 years.

This chapter consists of two broad parts. The first examines how friars and native aides produced language instructional materials in the early colonial period, a process as relevant to a study of the language in this period as it is to the beginnings of alphabetic writing. I use these instructional materials in conjunction with other sources to highlight basic phonetic characteristics of variants of the language in the colonial period. I also analyze the reverential, metaphorical lexicon and compare this "lordly speech" with Nahuatl honorific speech. The second and most substantive part of this chapter examines changes in the Ñudzahui language as native speakers came into contact with Castilian and compares the timing, circumstances, and limits of this process with similar studies for Nahuatl and Yucatec Maya. The documentation records linguistic change and maintenance, from the initial second and third generations of contact with Europeans to the last decades of the colonial period. A basic premise of this study is that linguistic change and maintenance reflect broader patterns of general social and cultural change and continuity.

Few studies have focused on the colonial language, or what might be called the "Classical Mixtec" of the early postconquest period.[2] Native-language sources from the colonial period provide useful data for modern linguistic studies; in turn, my analysis of the colonial language has benefited from studies of contemporary Mixtec languages.[3] Before examining the written words of native scribes, let us listen to what observers had to say about the language.

Early Colonial Observations

The Dominicans spearheaded the Spanish attempt to learn and document native languages in the Mixteca. The only information from the early period of language contact comes from their publications and the writings of native nobles whom they trained. In order to convert the indigenous to Christianity, to convey their message from the pulpit, friars realized that they needed to learn native languages, dialects, and idioms. There was no alternative in New Spain, where few natives could be expected to learn Spanish in the early period. Ecclesiastical orders, including Franciscans and Dominicans, were the European groups most likely to study native languages. Language training was a cornerstone of the scholastic tradition; in Spain, the University of Salamanca was a thriving center for the study of philosophy, theology, law, and language in the fifteenth century. The Mediterranean intellectual world was a multilingual milieu; scholars read and translated works in Greek, Latin, Arabic, Chaldean, Hebrew, and many other languages. By the mid-thirteenth century, the Dominican Thomas Aquinas used recent translations of Aristotle to write his *Summa Contra Gentiles,* designed to aid friars in the conversion of heretics and infidels. In the fifteenth century, the use of Latin for this purpose was giving way to many vernaculars. In the prologue to his Castilian grammar of 1492, the first of its kind in Europe, Antonio de Nebrija proclaimed from Salamanca that "language was always the instrument of empire" and that Castilian would eventually be accepted by the conquered "barbarous peoples and nations of foreign tongues."[4]

In the meantime, the orders promoted the learning of foreign tongues among their own brethren in New Spain. The Dominican Actas of the 1550s demanded that friars master at least one indigenous language and prohibited them from preaching and hearing confession before demonstrating proficiency.[5] Examinations were conducted in the major languages of each province, and promotions depended, at least in theory, on an understanding of the language spoken in the parish. The Dominican Actas distinguished language skills at two levels: the ability to preach and the ability to hear confession.[6] The Dominicans boasted that their members knew a total of thirteen distinct languages within the province that included Oaxaca.[7] Many of the Dominicans who first learned Ñudzahui had also studied Nahuatl and were no doubt familiar with some of the many church imprints from central Mexico. The study of Nahuatl among Dominicans was actively encouraged in the early sixteenth century.[8] Fray Antonio de los Reyes incorporated Nahuatl vocabulary in his *Arte en lengua mixteca* and used Nahuatl for examples when Castilian or Latin would not suffice, just as fray Francisco de Alvarado's *Vocabulario en lengua misteca* contains several Nahuatl-based entries on the Spanish side.[9] A list of Dominicans from the province of San Hipólito who knew indigenous languages in 1703 contained nearly as many friars who knew Nahuatl (sixteen) as those who knew Ñudzahui (nineteen), and seven claimed to know both.[10] Some friars, such as fray don Domingo de Josef Pérez y Sánchez, a resident of Chicahuastla in 1754, possessed *vocabularios* in both Nahuatl and Mixtec.[11]

Little is known about how the first generation of Dominicans in the Mixteca learned native languages. Fray Agustín Dávila Padilla wrote in the early 1590s that one pioneer, fray Francisco Marín, studied Mixtec and Chocho for thirty years and was able to give half-hour sermons in both languages. However, many early attempts at preaching failed miserably because few friars knew the indigenous languages well enough to communicate effectively. As a result, priests employed interpreters, including native boys, to preach in the early period.[12] Surely, this was not the most desirable method of communicating the faith. Fray Gonzalo Lucero was one of the first friars to attain fluency in the language and to be considered expert by his peers. Fray Gonzalo's peripatetic preaching career highlights some of the difficulties faced by the first friars who sought to publish native-language texts comparable to those produced in central Mexico. He began his study as early as 1529 by "writing the words and sounds of the language" in the Valley of Oaxaca.[13] He spent a year in Cuilapa before he was recalled to Mexico, where he studied Nahuatl for four years. Returning to Oaxaca in 1534, he resided in Chila for three years until the Dominicans abandoned their *convento* in the face of open hostility. They attributed their failure to an inability to communicate with indigenous rulers. Fray Gonzalo then went back to central Mexico, this time to Coyoacan, for ten years. Finally, he returned to Oaxaca in 1548 and relieved a secular cleric in Tlaxiaco who had failed to learn the language. By the time he died in 1562, he had lived in Tlaxiaco, Achiutla, Tamasulapa, Yanhuitlan, and Teposcolula—five places in the Mixteca Alta where at least four variants of the language were spoken.[14] In fact, his first three assignments in Oaxaca were in three distinct subregions of the Mixteca, including the Valley of Oaxaca, the Baja, and the Alta. It is said that he "knew the language of the Indians [well enough] to be able to confess them."[15]

The circle of ecclesiastics who produced native-language instructional materials and publications in the Mixteca was so small that it is possible to know all the key Spanish participants. Although it is unlikely that Lucero published anything, he did leave his successors many notes and manuscripts.[16] Both fray Benito Hernández and fray Domingo de Santa María served as Lucero's apprentices. Santa María is credited with the first publication of a *doctrina* in the 1540s, but these references come from later chronicles.[17] In any case, something was printed. The cacique of Yanhuitlan, don Domingo, testified in 1545 that he had learned the Christian doctrine, including many prayers, "in the form and manner in which it [was] printed in the Mixtec language."[18] In 1561, Hernández and fray Juan Cabrera were instructed to begin a Mixtec *vocabulario* and, with the help of two assistants, to "examine the Mixtec primer and to add what was lacking."[19] This "primer" consisted of papers handed down from Lucero and his generation. Cabrera studied with Lucero and fray Antonio de los Reyes in Teposcolula. He was compiling a dictionary when he died in 1563, but his notes were passed along to fray Francisco de Alvarado, via Hernández and Reyes. Hernández, another graduate of the University of Salamanca, learned the language spoken in the Achiutla-Chalcatongo area while working with Lucero. It was said that fray Benito was fluent in the language, conversant with the speech of nobles and commoners alike.[20] In November 1567, Hernández published *Doctrina en la lengua misteca* in the dialect of Achiutla, followed two months later by a translation of this work into the dialect of Teposcolula, printed in 1568. The role of Ñudzahui participants in the production of these works was crucial. Dominicans designed the *Doctrina,* supervised its production, and printed the books, but only the participation of Ñudzahui speakers who had learned Castilian (and perhaps Latin) made the work possible. Hernández died three years after the book's publication.

Another alumnus of the University of Salamanca, fray Antonio de los Reyes, was assigned in 1558 to Teposcolula, where he studied the language with Cabrera and Hernández. After serving as vicar of Teposcolula and Tlaxiaco, he was appointed to produce a vocabulary and grammar in 1587.[21] Reyes compiled a grammatical sketch of the language and described a few phonological characteristics of Ñudzahui variants. Published in 1593, the *Arte en lengua mixteca* is the most complete commentary on the language in the sixteenth century.[22] The author was undoubtedly influenced by Hernández's *Doctrina* of 1567, judging by his many references to that work. In the preamble, Reyes addressed orthography and pronunciation, or "the ways of speaking and writing the language." He delineated the various geographical areas of the Mixteca, summarized the phonetic differences of each region, and noted the ways different variants were written. Reyes was able to describe how the language was both spoken and written because his work was not printed until at least three decades after native-language alphabetic writing had begun in the area. As early as 1571, fray Antonio appeared as a witness to a last will and testament that was written in the Ñudzahui language. Doña María López, the cacica of Tlazultepec, requested him to say masses on her behalf.[23] Because he had worked in various areas of the Mixteca, Reyes was very attentive to recording regional and local differences. He considered the Teposcolula area variant to be most perfect in that "one could write more fully with all the letters." [24] Thus Reyes's *Arte* was composed with writing and reading the language in mind, and it was published in conjunction with a Spanish-to-Mixtec vocabulary, also written in the Teposcolula area variant.

When Reyes was instructed to produce both a vocabulary and grammar in 1587, he may have requested the assistance of fray Francisco de Alvarado. Born in New Spain, Alvarado probably began learning the Ñudzahui language around 1580, before he was thirty years old. Alvarado studied with Reyes in Teposcolula before becoming vicar of Tamasulapa; they signed their names to many legal documents in Teposcolula in the late 1580s and early 1590s.[25] In 1589, Alvarado was assigned to compile a vocabulario by using his predecessors' materials. In the dedication and prologue of his work, Alvarado humbly acknowledged his elders who had kept notebooks and working dictionaries on the language.[26] The provincial had instructed him to collect and incorporate these works into his own vocabulary. Thus the final product is a complex source, containing expressions from an earlier time and from various regions, converted to the Teposcolula area variant. After four years, Alvarado and his assistants had packed

more than ten thousand entries into 204 folios. The work is based on a Latin/Spanish
model and contains many Spanish entries (words and phrases) that elicited multiple
native-language responses, not all of which were precise semantic equivalents. Unfortunately, the work presents only native responses to Spanish entries, comparable to the
first edition of Molina's Nahuatl *Vocabulario,* printed in 1555. Whereas Molina's version
was complemented in 1571 by a full Nahuatl-to-Spanish side, the Mixtec *Vocabulario* was
never reversed.[27] Reyes oversaw Alvarado's work and checked the final product with
several native-language speakers and other friars before recommending it for publication. Alvarado concluded that his work would be very useful for preaching in the
Mixteca.

In the prologue, Alvarado affirmed that although the principal debt for the conception and compilation of the publication was owed to the friars, much of the work
was actually done by unnamed "Indians, who [were] the best teachers and thus were
the authors."[28] Despite the fact that colonial native-language texts are associated with
the names of Spanish ecclesiastics, indigenous nobles obviously played a crucial role
in the compilation and production of these books. Spaniards determined the nature
of the dictionary's Spanish-to-Mixtec entries, based loosely on a format derived from
Latin vocabularies adopted by fray Alonso de Molina for Nahuatl and Antonio de
Nebrija for Castilian. But Ñudzahui participants composed, verified, and edited the
final version. The compilations of Reyes and Alvarado, published in 1593, were the
only instructional Ñudzahui-language texts published in the colonial period.

As a source on the language, the *Vocabulario* must be used cautiously, for several
reasons. First, a Ñudzahui translation of a Spanish term or concept does not necessarily prove the existence of a true equivalent but merely indicates its potential use in
daily speech. Spaniards determined the entries and then prompted native-language
speakers to provide equivalents, which were sometimes literal translations of the foreign concepts. One can imagine the following scenario: a friar who sought the translation of a word taken from a model Latin or Castilian vocabulary was confronted with
the question "What's that?" He then elicited a native response by describing the Castilian word and recorded a literal translation of the description, regardless of whether
the concept itself existed in the indigenous vocabulary, or whether it was a close equivalent. An obvious example is the entry *nariz Roma,* "Roman nose," which was hardly a
Mixtec concept.[29] Clearly, religious phenomena and more abstract concepts were subject to a dialogue. Thus, we cannot assume that an entry was commonly used or that
it accurately described a native concept until it is attested elsewhere. Second, many
Spanish words have multiple Ñudzahui entries, with no indication of what each of the
entries signifies. Is the first entry the primary equivalent, and are the other entries
merely different ways of saying something? Some verbs have ten or more separate
Ñudzahui listings, often indicating examples of usage. Third, previous studies have
suggested that some "words" in Ñudzahui can have several different meanings and are
thus inherently related. However, because the colonial orthography did not mark tone,
some words that are written the same are not related in meaning. Tone differences
distinguish one "word" from another with the same consonants and vowels. Thus, the
fact that "deity," "fire," and "earth" are all translated as *ñuhu* does not mean that these
are semantically related concepts. In terms of pictorial writing techniques, tone was

manipulated to suggest near homonyms or tone puns in relation to images, thereby conveying multiple meanings. Despite these cautions, the *Vocabulario* is an excellent resource for the sixteenth-century language but must be handled like any other historical source, checked against other sources, especially writings by native authors.

The task of compiling instructional manuscripts and publishing native-language texts took much longer than anticipated. The difficulty of representing Mixtec phonology and tones with the Roman alphabet and the need to distinguish among significant regional differences precluded rapid advances. By comparison, aside from marking glottal stop and vowel length, the study of Nahuatl had no such obstacles. Nahuatl dictionaries and grammars were written as early as the 1540s, when the Dominicans had only begun to establish a presence in the Mixteca. The Franciscan Alonso de Molina had published his second dictionary by 1571, twenty-two years before the first and only colonial Ñudzahui vocabulario appeared. But it was not a Franciscan propensity for language that distinguished early works in Nahuatl from the delay in Dominican publications in the Mixteca. In comparison with the many men who learned Nahuatl, few friars studied Mixtec. In addition, Mixtec was a more difficult language for Europeans. Both Reyes and Alvarado confessed to having struggled with the language for some time. As fray Francisco de Burgoa observed, these early efforts "to write the words, and to learn how to pronounce them," were characterized by "serious difficulty and error."[30] These difficulties were surely related to tone and significant regional differences in the language.

Regional Variants

In his *Arte,* Reyes commented on the various "mixtures in the language" and "great differences and distinct ways of speaking," which he attributed to the interaction of many communities through wars and intermarriage. He distinguished at least six Mixtec "lenguas": that of Teposcolula, associated with major communities such as Tamazulapa, Tilantongo, Texupa, and Mitlatongo; that of Yanhuitlan, associated with Coixtlahuaca, Xaltepec, and Nochixtlan; that of Tlaxiaco and Achiutla; that of the Mixteca Baja; that of Cuilapa and Guaxolotitlan in the Valley of Oaxaca; and that of the Mixteca Costa.[31] Reyes used the word *lengua* in reference to the one Mixtec lengua as well as several lenguas of Mixtec. This ambivalence reflects significant phonetic variation in the language or languages. In addition to regional variation, Reyes indicated two other variants: a reverential court language and a commercial standard.[32] The former is discussed below, but I have found no trace of the latter in the written record.

Reyes searched for the most intelligible lengua in order to preach to the greatest number of people. He outlined the basic characteristics of each variant and singled out the Teposcolula area version as a prestige or canonical dialect, the "most universal and clear, and the best understood in all the Mixteca."[33] In his experience, the speech of Teposcolula was more complete in pronunciation and the easiest version to write.[34] In contrast, the versions of Yanhuitlan, Tlaxiaco, and Achiutla presented certain difficulties that made them less comprehensible to outsiders, nobles and commoners included.[35] Teposcolula's location must have influenced Reyes's assessment. Situated at the crossroads of three distinct variants in the Mixteca Alta, the Teposcolula area is considered to have been the center of innovations for most phonological changes affecting Ñudzahui speech communities.[36] In the documentary record, however, there is little evidence that it was perceived as more standard or refined than any of the other dialects. Of course, Reyes's judgment contains a certain personal bias; having lived most of his life in the Teposcolula area, he naturally considered that variant to be the most accessible. Similarly, Hernández favored that of the Achiutla area, where he compiled the *Doctrina* of 1567.

Despite recognizing various distinct versions of the "lengua mixteca," the friars concluded that they were dealing with one language. The Dominican chronicler fray Francisco de Burgoa wrote: "Although the language is generally the same to everyone, in many parts the syllables are made differently, and the manner of pronouncing them is different, but all communicate and understand one another to the extent that the language expands across more than 100 leagues, from the Chocho nation to the greater coast of the South Sea [Pacific Ocean]."[37] Several decades earlier, in the response of Cuilapa to the *Relaciones geográficas* questionnaire, fray Agustín de Salazar concluded his discussion of speech differences between the Mixteca Alta and Baja with the qualification "but it is all one Mixtec language."[38] Reyes observed that the language often differed in nuance not only from one community to the next but also within the same pueblo and from one barrio to another. Despite these qualifications, he concluded that all the variations constituted "one single Mixtec language" covering a large area. Unfortunately, these judgments do not include the opinions of native speakers on the question of mutual intelligibility.[39] However, chapter 9 shows that native speakers in the Mixteca Alta referred to a *dzaha ñudzahui,* or a Ñudzahui language.

Although the friars' application of the Roman alphabet and Spanish orthographic conventions failed to record tonal and other phonological differences in Ñudzahui speech, writers in each of the major areas delineated by Reyes adopted somewhat predictable conventions to represent aspects of variation. The documentation suggests that the differences did not make communication impossible, at least not between contiguous areas. A prominent example of cross-variant communication is the *Doctrina,* which was first printed in the language of the Achiutla/Tlaxiaco area and then reprinted less than two months later in the variant of the Teposcolula area. A comparison of the two imprints reveals the nature of differences perceived by friars and their indigenous collaborators. The second work consistently and predictably converts the orthography of the first; the differences are restricted to a select group of sound segments. Furthermore, a copy of the Achiutla version in the Huntington Library contains marginalia and endnotes in the Yanhuitlan area variant, indicating that Ñudzahui speakers from one area of the Mixteca Alta used a text written in another, noncontiguous area. The orthography of the marginalia, especially the added syllable-initial nasals in loan-words, suggests a native authorship. Furthermore, correspondence sent from one region to another suggests that native-language writing traversed speech communities without presenting insurmountable translation difficulties. Several documents contain responses or addenda from different regions. Despite the friars' reassurances and my own observations of how letters and books circulated across the region, it is unclear whether documentation was mutually intelligible in all the regions. Comparisons between Baja, Alta, and Oaxaca Valley writings indicate significant phonological and lexical differences.

Over the course of the colonial period, writing itself probably had a standardizing effect on certain Ñudzahui vocabulary domains, especially among educated nobles who wrote standardized genres within official circles. Writing offered the possibility to reflect on the meaning of statements, to read selectively, and to mull over the meaning of written words. For translation purposes, the context and content of colonial legal genres reduced the potential semantic range of a given written word; on the other hand, a document that offers little context is often very difficult to decipher. Since tone was one aspect of local and regional differentiation, the reduction or exclusion of this feature in writing may have facilitated communication among literate people. Nonetheless, the same word can appear in many different but still recognizable forms in a given document. For example, I have seen *huahi* (house) written as "huay," "huehe," "huehi," "huey," "vehe," "vahi," and "uagy." The differences could be orthographic, or more likely they could represent different pronunciation. Individual license complicated matters; the same word was often spelled differently even within a document or series of documents written by the same author.[40]

The study of colonial native-language writings from the Mixteca Alta seems to confirm Reyes's observation that Mixtec was a language with distinct regional differences. However, it is impossible to conclude from the documentation that all dialects were mutually intelligible. Bárbro Dahlgren mapped the dialects of the Mixteca based on Reyes's observations, designating six separate areas, with Cuilapa as a distinct dialect.[41] Wigberto Jiménez Moreno elaborated his own map of seven "dialect complexes," synthesizing many of the earlier attempts with modern linguistic data and adding Guerrero and an enclave in the northeastern Cuicatec area. However, it is unclear whether he meant to draw a map for the sixteenth century or for the modern period, since data from both periods are used in the final estimation.[42] Most scholars have reiterated Reyes's remarks on the various "lenguas," but only one study has tested or elaborated his classifications by examining colonial Ñudzahui-language materials. Kathryn Josserand, Maarten Jansen, and María de los Ángeles Romero Frizzi published a preliminary analysis of colonial documentation, including a comparative lexicon of twenty words. The results of this comparison reflected expected regional variations, based on Reyes's analysis and modern data.[43] In her dissertation, Josserand mapped regional phonetic differences by reconstructing a proto-Mixtecan model from modern Mixtecan languages.[44] Her work has demonstrated the potential for using colonial native-language sources to reconstruct the timing of phonological innovations.[45]

Mundane archival records written by native speakers confirm the existence of multiple dialects or variants. The documentation reveals five areas in which orthographic variation, corresponding to phonetic and morphological distinctions, was consistent and somewhat predictable: (1) the Baja area around Huajuapan; (2) the Oaxaca Valley around Cuilapan; (3) the Alta around the Valley of Nochixtlan, including Yanhuitlan and Coixtlahuaca; (4) the Alta around the Valleys of Teposcolula and Tamasulapa; (5) and the Alta around the Valley of Tlaxiaco, Achiutla, and Chalcatongo. These five areas correspond roughly with Reyes's observations in the late sixteenth century

and are confirmed by Josserand's modern data. The last three areas correspond with
a division of the Alta into northeastern, eastern, and western sections, respectively.
However, Josserand further divided the Baja into multiple sections and associated
Cuilapan with the northeastern Alta. The documentation can shed light on variant
boundaries in the absence of modern data. For example, four native-language documents from Coixtlahuaca, dated as early as 1596 and as late as 1669, indicate that this
community belongs in the northeastern Alta on Josserand's map. And in Cuilapan and
nearby San Juan Chapultepec, the colonial language shares certain phonetic characteristics with that of the Yanhuitlan area, but it also contains significant differences, as
Reyes indicated.

I will provide a few examples of differences in the Alta. The two editions of the
Doctrina compiled by Hernández, and marginalia contained in one of the copies,
demonstrate variation within three major areas of the Mixteca Alta. Both editions are
identical in content, but the first (1567) corresponds to the variant of Achiutla while
the second (1568) conforms to that of Teposcolula. The Achiutla edition consistently
represents the *s* of the Teposcolula edition as *h* or *jh*, so that *saa, sitoniñe,* and *yosini*
are written as "jhaa," "hitoniñe," and "yohini."[46] The *dz* of Teposcolula, described
below, was written in Achiutla as *ç* or *z,* as in "çutu," "çaya," "ñazaña," and "çaâ." It also
appears in the 1567 edition as *dç,* as in "dçehe," for *dzehe.* In the 1567 edition, word
final [i] after a vowel is often written as *y,* as in "andehuy," "ñuçahuy," and "huay."
These variations presumably correspond to speech rather than simple convention.
As an example of distinctions based on convention, the first edition from Achiutla
employed a circumflex accent over the second like vowel instead of an *h,* as in "caâ,"
"ñuû," and "tnaâ," to indicate glottal stop or a rearticulation of the second vowel. The
second edition from Teposcolula employed an *h* instead of a circumflex accent for the
same words. Conforming to the precedent set by the *Doctrina* of 1567, notarial documents from the Achiutla/Tlaxiaco area used acute accents instead of *h* to represent
glottal stop or aspiration. The avoidance of *h* was probably related to the frequent use
of *h* and *jh* in this area. In the 1567 edition, marginalia in the Yanhuitlan area dialect
also exhibit orthographic traits corroborated in notarial records.

The major dialect groupings presented by Reyes corresponded roughly to regional
divisions of the Mixteca (Baja, Valle, Alta, and Costa) and to valley and river systems
within each region.[47] The central and eastern parts of the Mixteca Alta comprise the
Valleys of Nochixtlan, Teposcolula, Coixtlahuaca, and Tamasulapa. In the western
Mixteca Alta, south and west of the Yanhuitlan-Nochixtlan Valley system and south of
Teposcolula, a long chain of mountains converges around Tlaxiaco and Achiutla, continuing farther to the south and cutting off Chalcatongo and San Miguel el Grande
from the Pacific coastal region. Many narrow valleys and winding rivers draining to the
Pacific Ocean divide the entire region; modern linguistic language boundaries corre-
spond to the mountainous terrain. Settlement patterns constitute a second condition
of variation. The Mixteca Alta was the most complex subregion, suggesting that
Ñudzahui-speaking populations have inhabited the Alta longer than any other region.[48]
The Mixteca Baja (around Huaxuapa) diverges most from the other regions in its
phonetic and lexical written form.[49] Whereas lexical variation among the three main
Alta variants has not been attested, I have observed lexical differences between the

Baja and the Alta. Language differences support archaeological evidence of a distinctive late classic "Nuiñe" culture in the Baja.[50] The coastal variants are relatively uniform, suggesting recent migrations to the coastal region and reflecting their isolated location.[51]

Today, most linguists agree that there are multiple, mutually unintelligible Mixtecan languages, some with their own dialects.[52] Josserand sampled 120 Mixtec-speaking villages and found that "the speech of any one village never coincided in all its details with that of any other."[53] Dialect and language differentiation is intensified by the existence of contrasting tonal systems in different communities. This extreme local and regional variation has evolved over the course of at least two millennia and has accelerated since the Spanish conquest. As groups and native speech communities were reduced in size and became increasingly isolated by the growth of Spanish-speaking administrative and commercial centers throughout the colonial and postcolonial periods, many variants evolved into distinct languages. Another possibility is that two or more Mixtec languages, such as those of the Baja and Alta, continued to evolve into multiple languages.

Let us continue our general discussion of language and orthography by turning to phonology.

Mixtec Phonology

Ñudzahui roots (or stems) are characteristically bisyllabic, and stress invariably falls on the first of these two syllables. The bisyllabic root is a nucleus to which other syllables can be added, without disturbing stress placement, and is the basis for all word and phonological phrase constructions.[54] Mixtecan languages have multiple tones, glottal stops, and both oral and nasalized vowels. Lexical tones and tones affected by sandhi rules were not represented in colonial transcriptions using the Roman alphabet, nor were devices established to mark tone consistently with diacritics.[55] For these reasons, friars who sought to speak and write the native language often complained that the alphabet was deficient for the purposes of phonetic transcription. In particular, both Reyes and Alvarado acknowledged the problems presented by tone, and they recognized that the meaning of many written words depended on their pronunciation. In the prologue to the *Vocabulario* Alvarado referred to the importance of nasalization and tone: "In their accent many words vary in meaning, some in having or not having an accent mark, others in pronouncing with softness or full voice. Not being content with what nature gave us, this language is pronounced through the nose, and this [the nose] is so important in certain pronunciations that mistakes occur without its assistance."[56] Dávila Padilla also observed that "the entire pronunciation is sometimes made by use of the nose, and has many nuances or ambiguities that are made with great difficulty."[57] Fray Antonio de Remesal was particularly baffled by vowels, which were articulated by "sound from the nose and inhalation of breath."[58]

Aside from relying on the usual phonetic meaning assigned to Roman alphabetical characters, the friars adapted some standard conventions to represent sounds. Alvarado usually marked the glottal stop with the letter *h*, especially between identical vowels, to indicate a reenunciation of the second vowel rather than a simple lengthening (e.g., *ñuhu* as opposed to *ñuu*).[59] But this convention was not always used for other occurrences of the glottal stop, between unlike vowels or preceding consonants. As discussed above, in Hernández's *Doctrina* of 1567, compiled in Achiutla, acute accents (or circumflexes) were placed over the second vowel (e.g., *ñuú* or *ñuû*) to indicate the presence of a glottal stop before the vowel on which the accent or circumflex was placed, instead of the *h* employed between vowels in the Teposcolula area and elsewhere (including the *Doctrina* of 1568).[60] These different ways of marking glottal stop were reflected in notarial writings from the two regions, though there was considerable variation. It is unclear whether both the orthographic *h* and the acute accent were operating simultaneously as conventions for marking the glottal stop. Reyes also registered glottal stops between vowels by the use of the letter *h.*[61]

Tone is a feature of all vowels that usually went unmarked. The inability of the friars to mark tone is understandable; even today different analysts interpret and transcribe tone differently. Tonal variation among Ñudzahui languages or dialects is so great that it is often the first feature distinguishing the speech of one community from that of others.[62] In the *Vocabulario,* Alvarado did not consistently use diacritics or other devices to mark tone. Some entries are marked, but the meaning or purpose of the diacritics is unclear.[63] The *Arte* sheds some light on this matter. Reyes attempted to promote a standard pronunciation and orthography in his *Arte* by using accents, noting in one section that the absence of accents indicated a plain or even pronunciation, which could have represented midtone.[64] He suggested that the *Vocabulario* and the *Arte* attempted to coordinate these conventions.[65] However, he did not explain the meaning of accents (both grave and acute) and circumflex marks in the course of his work.

Drawing on the work of his predecessors, Reyes used some digraphs or syllable sequences that combined conventional consonants to represent sounds not found in Spanish, such as *dz* and *nd.* Of *dz* he wrote, "In the pronunciation of the dz we strike softly on the d and more strongly on the z."[66] In the Teposcolula area, this *dz* seems to represent [đ], a voiced interdental fricative or a voiced counterpart of theta (eth). Josserand suggested that *dz* was a "fricative đ" or a "voiced theta," based on the interpretation of [z] in terms of contemporary Castilian pronunciation as theta.[67] The writing of Spanish loanwords in the Teposcolula area seems to confirm this observation. For example, in Yolomecatl, one writer used "pedzaso" more than once for the loan noun *pedaso.*[68] The fact that Reyes emphasized "striking" the *z* in *dz* seems to suggest how the *dz* of Teposcolula may have represented a voiced dental affricate, or a [dz]. As noted above, *dz* was also written in the Achiutla area as *ç* or *z,* or even *dç,* suggesting that *dz* represented [z], a voiced dental fricative. Likewise, in the Inquisition proceedings of the 1540s, *dzavui* was written as "çaagui" and "zahui."[69] In the Yanhuitlan area, *dz* was often written as simply *d,* especially in the late colonial period. For example, *dzehe* appears as "dehe." For the value of *dz* in the Mixteca Alta, the ambiguity between [đ] or [d] and [s] is related to regional difference; *dz* as [đ] was more prominent in the northeastern Alta around Yanhuitlan, while *dz* as [s] was more typical of the western Alta area around Tlaxiaco, Achiutla, and Chalcatongo. In between these two dialectal areas, in the eastern Alta area around Teposcolula, *dz* represented [đ]. These differences are reflected in contemporary languages and even in the writing of place-names.

Compare the *yodzo* of Yosonotnu and Yosondúa in the Chalcatongo area, for example, with the *dzahui* of Yucunudahui in the Yanhuitlan area.[70] Writers from the Teposcolula area continued to write "dzehe" throughout the colonial period.

To indicate a prenasalized stop, Reyes used *nd,* as in *ndehe;* for [t] followed by a nasal vowel, he used *tn* (plus the vowel), as in *tnaha.*[71] Reyes described the pronunciation of *vu* as "striking both the letters vu so that only one is heard clearly and distinctly."[72] This sound approximates [w]. According to this scheme, *vu* plus a vowel was distinguished from *hu* plus a vowel in that the latter marked a medial glottal before [w].[73] In reality, more often than not, the distinction between *hu* and *vu* made by Reyes and Alvarado was either unknown or ignored by native writers (and by Hernández's *Doctrina*). The words *dzavui* and *yuvui,* for example, were often written as "yuhui" and "dzahui." Likewise, for the syllable-initial glide [w], *huitna* was often written as "vuitna." The writing of loanwords such as "eschrihuano" for *escribano,* "natihuidad" for *natividad,* "huixilia" for *vigilia,* and "cahuildo" for *cabildo* suggests that the pronunciation of *hu* was somewhere between [w] and [v] or that this was a nonstandard way of substituting [w] for [b].[74] In the Teposcolula area, *hu* and *vu* occurred only before [a] and [i], whereas *hu* also preceded [e] in the Yanhuitlan and Tlaxiaco areas.

Mixtec had no equivalents of sounds corresponding to the following Spanish letters in the sixteenth century: *b, f, g, l, p, r, rr,* or *v.*[75] Table 3.1 matches the phonetic inventory of the Teposcolula-area variant with corresponding characters of the Roman alphabet. It is important to note that some of these phonetic values were subject to significant regional variation, some of which has been discussed above in reference to the *Doctrinas* from Achiutla and Teposcolula. For example, in Yanhuitlan *t* followed by *a* and *i* was replaced by *ch,* so that *tay* in Teposcolula was *chay* in Yanhuitlan. The use of *ch* before *a* and *i* instead of *t* was typical of the Mixteca Baja and the Valley of Oaxaca, too. I will not address all the differences here. Suffice it to say that these differences are not simply orthographic conventions.

Reverential Speech

The record contains evidence of the so-called seignorial vocabulary used by and for elites, the form of Ñudzahui honorific speech known as the "*yya* vocabulary." The term *yya* or "iya" signifies a person of high social rank, a "lord."[76] This rhetorical register reinforced distinctions between nobles and commoners, but it is unlikely that it was entirely unintelligible to commoners. As in Nahuatl, the honorific register was more a manner of speaking properly and respectfully than a separate language or vocabulary.[77] Many of the reverential expressions and words were probably more archaic forms associated with a tradition of nobility and rulership. The vocabulary consisted primarily of reverential nouns and verbs referring to parts of the body (including relational terms based on body parts, such as "head" to signify "above"), possessions, or actions of the elite. In the colonial period, a common convention involved the use of the humble *ñadzaña* as a first-person subject and possessive pronoun and the -*ya* pronoun suffix for third-person pronouns.[78] These pronouns were also employed by lords when speaking to lesser nobles, or by nobles when speaking to commoners, as a form

TABLE 3.1

Teposcolula-Area Ñudzahui Phonetic Inventory and Standard
Orthography in Colonial Writings from Teposcolula

Inventory	*Orthography, (Comments), Explanation*
[k]	*c* (before [a] and [o]); *qu* (before [e] and [i]); *qh* or *c* (before [u]) voiceless velar stop
[ch]	*ch* (only before [i]) voiceless alveopalatal affricate
[kw]	*cu* (before [a] or [i]) labialized voiceless velar stop
[d]	*d* voiced dental stop
[d]	*dz* voiced interdental fricative (see discussion in text)
[m]	*m* labial nasal
[n]	*n* dental nasal
[nd]	*nd* prenasalized voiced dental stop
[ñ]	*ñ* (not before [i]) alveopalatal nasal
[s]	*s* (only before [a] or [i]) voiceless dental fricative
[sh]	*x* voiceless alveopalatal fricative
[t]	*t* voiceless dental stop
[w]	*vu* (before [a] or [i]) labial glide (see discussion in text)
['w]	*hu* (before [a] or [i]) medial glottal and labial glide (see discussion in text)
[y]	*y* (*ll* in the later period) palatal glide
[a]	*a* low central unrounded vowel
[e]	*e* (sometimes *i*) midfront rounded vowel
[i]	*i* (often *y* in initial position) high front rounded vowel
[i]	*i* (sometimes *e*) high back unrounded nonfront vowel
[o]	*o* (sometimes *u*) midback rounded vowel
[u]	*u* (sometimes *o*) high back rounded vowel
[']	*h* glottal stop
[nV]	*n* (+ vowel) nasal vowels

NOTE: Brackets [] indicate conventional phonetic forms.

of social inversion. The honorific register provided nobles with a functional, shared lexicon that transcended regional speech conventions.

In the sixteenth century, the friars were well aware of this yya speech. Supposedly, Hernández had mastered the "metaphorical ways of speaking" and used words, phrases, and idioms of high speech to preach to the nobility. Burgoa thought that this speech was cultivated by priests who were responsible for speaking to the ancient deities and performing special rituals.[79] Reyes recorded remnants of a reverential "language" associated with the nobility and employed by commoners when speaking to or about lords and nobles. The *Arte* lists more than a hundred examples of this vocabulary, which are probably a mere sampling of terms from a much more extensive lexicon.[80] Apparently, this prestigious, flowery speech of the nobility had begun to wilt by the end of the sixteenth century.

Traces of honorific terminology appear in both printed texts and handwritten testaments of the sixteenth century. Nowhere is it more apparent than in the *Doctrina*, which employs this reverential vocabulary in reference to any Christian personage. For example, "Christmas day" was referred to as "the day our precious lord ruler Jesus Christ revealed his face" [quevui nituvuinanaya stohondo mani yya toniñe Jesus Christo], using a metaphor for birth, the -*ya* subject pronoun, and the most reverential titles of *stoho* and *yya toniñe*. The phrase may be analyzed as:

quevui	*ni-*	*tuvui*	*nana*	-*ya*	*stoho*	-*ndo*	*mani*	*yya toniñe*
day, when	past tense	to reveal	face	he	lord	our	precious	lord ruler

Don Felipe de Saavedra used the same metaphor to refer to the Christian year (since the birth of Christ) in his testament of 1573.[81] Many people used the polite word *nana* for "face," instead of the customary *nuu* to denote "in the presence of" or "before." In the presence of an assembly of nobles, a speaker referred to himself or herself as *ñadzaña* instead of *nduhu* or *njuhu*. Some of this "metaphorical" speech employed simple semantic extensions. The use of *yuchi*, "flint," to denote "teeth" in the honorific vocabulary makes an association based on function or appearance: that is, something that is sharp and pierces.[82] Other terms appear to be laden with meaning: a lord's tomb was called *dzoco ñuhu*, "earth" or "sacred womb." A dowry or marriage gift is called *yno dzehua*, "tobacco cacao." In the preconquest-style codices, marriage partners are depicted holding these precious items in their hands. Appropriately, several entries on the native-language side of the *Vocabulario* are followed by the explanation in Spanish "it is all by metaphor."[83] The euphemistic, metaphorical nature of the vocabulary is illustrated by the terminology of selected verbs and nouns (see tables 3.2 and 3.3).[84]

The Ñudzahui reverential vocabulary is comparable to Nahuatl high speech, or *huehuetlatolli*, preserved in the many "high Nahuatl" or "classical Nahuatl" texts from

TABLE 3.2
Reverential Vocabulary for Some Verbs and Literal Meaning

to speak reverently	*yosaidzaha*, "to obey the rules"; *yocahaquai*, "to speak calmly, agreeably"; *yocahayeheñuhuhuij*, "to speak beautifully and gracefully"
to speak gracefully	*yocahatnuhu*, "to sing a song"; *yosaicaini*, "to tell a tale"; *yocahadzaha*, "to speak knowingly"; *yocahayaa*, "to speak of stories, lineages"
to speak elegantly	*yocahatoho*, "to speak nobly"; *yocahahuij huayu*, "to speak beautifully and courteously"
to be born	*quevui*, "to enter"; *ndacu*, "to descend"; *yotuvuiyuhunuu*, "to reveal one's mouth and eyes"; *yosiñenánaya*, "the lord's face falls"; *yotuvuinanàya*, "the lord reveals his or her face"; *yocôôcoodzicaya*, "the lord arrives in his or her dwelling place"
to marry	*yocuvui huico yuvuiya*, "to celebrate a feast of the mat"; *yotnahandáyaya*, "to join hands"; *yondoosiñaya nisiñesahaya*, "to drink pulque"
to divorce	*yonandasidaha*, "to separate hands"
to drink water	*yodzasaaya nduta*, "to refresh oneself with water"
to drink pulque	*yosaisahaya nduzi*, "to drink honey, nectar"
to weep	*yocaindutaya*, "to let water fall"
to urinate	*yodzayuyuya*, "to sprinkle"

SOURCES: Reyes, pp. 74–81, and Alvarado.

TABLE 3.3
*Reverential Terminology Related
to Body Parts and Nouns*

English	Ñudzahui	Literal Meaning
teeth	*yuchi*	"flint"
eyes	*duchiya*	"beans"
brains	*yusayaya*	"*masa* of the head"
shoulder	*yusa*	"shield"
stomach	*ñono*	"net"
fingernail	*teyusiya*	"turquoise"
foot	*nduhua*	"arrow"

SOURCES: Reyes, pp. 74–81, and Alvarado.

the sixteenth century, such as the Bancroft Dialogues or the speech of Sahagún's Nahua aides (especially book 4 of the *Florentine Codex,* on rhetoric).[85] Nahuatl reverential conventions included the use of applicative and causative affixes inserted within the verb phrase and the addition of the diminutive -*tzin* to nouns. Reverential pronouns simply appended this suffix, as in *tehuatzin* (from *tehuatl*) and *yehuatzin* (from *yehuatl*). Nahuatl also contained countless metaphorical expressions, many of which combined two separate nouns or verbs imparting a particular meaning when joined as a pair. For example: *cuitlapilli* (tail) and *atlapalli* (wing) indicated a "commoner"; *atl* (water) and *tepetl* (hill) referred to the local Nahua state when paired together or combined as *altepetl*. To be in "someone's lapfolds," -*cuexanco,* and "someone's backpack," -*mamalhuazco,* meant "to be the responsibility of, or to be governed by, someone."[86] Mixtec also combined words to create specific metaphors, such as *yuhui,* "reed mat," and *tayu,* "seat" or "couple" (depending on tone), to denote the most complex sociopolitical entity. Semantic couplets or pairings are very common in the two languages, especially in formulaic statements. For example, similar to Nahuatl, the Ñudzahui expression "our fathers and mothers," *taando dzehendo,* was a polite way of referring to ancestors.

The shared honorific grammatical conventions and metaphors in the Nahuatl and Ñudzahui languages may be considered a Mesoamerican areal feature.[87] Even though the languages are unrelated, body parts are used for an extensive list of relational words in both languages (as in Yucatec Maya). Many verb phrases and idioms for certain actions are semantically related. Many compounds to express emotion in both languages are based on the word "heart" or "insides" (*yollo* in Nahuatl and *ini* in Mixtec).[88] Third person is morphologically unmarked in both, and there is no overt marking of plurality for nouns (in Nahuatl, inanimate plural nouns are unmarked).[89] Overall, there are many similarities, from the use of metaphorical couplets to the manner in which cardinal directions are expressed.[90] These shared linguistic features reflect centuries of cultural interaction and contact within the broader Mesoamerican cultural area.[91] Shared linguistic conventions and a common calendar facilitated the evolution of a pictographic-phonetic writing system in central Mexico, the Puebla-Tlaxcala area, and Oaxaca. The distinctive style of this writing is often called "Mixteca-Puebla." And yet, despite these shared characteristics and the proximity of the two speech communities, the two languages apparently had minimal lexical influence on each other. In this period, whereas even Spaniards borrowed Nahuatl words, Ñudzahui writers rarely introduced Nahuatl loanwords into their texts.[92] In contrast, Yucatec Maya in the colonial period contains clear lexical influence from Nahuatl.[93] Ñudzahui-language speakers did borrow from Spanish, however. These borrowings are the subject of the following section.

Language Contact and Change

Language contact phenomena provide a useful context for the study of the nature, extent, and effect of contact between Ñudzahui and Spanish speakers. Evidence of language contact phenomena is best observed in archival documents produced by native writers within their communities for mundane purposes, because these scribes made little apparent effort to preserve archaic forms of the language.[94] Each document contains data on the lexical, phonological, and morphological effect of contact with Spanish.

For Nahuatl, Frances Karttunen and James Lockhart have proposed a model consisting of three stages for the evolution of Nahuatl in contact with Spanish, which Lockhart then applied to social and cultural changes.[95] This chapter makes preliminary comparisons, based on the same types of sources, between the evolution of Ñudzahui and the stages outlined for Nahuatl, conscious of both the potential and limitations of this model for another Mesoamerican language. Attention is given to both similarities and differences, especially in the nature and timing of change and maintenance.

The three stages correspond to the increasing frequency and intensity of contact between Nahuatl and Spanish speakers, leading to the creation of diglossic speech communities. The beginning of stages is defined more by the extent and nature of contact than the actual date of conquest. The first stage proceeds from the arrival of the Spaniards (1519–21) to a time between 1540 and 1550. This period was characterized by virtually no change in the language itself; new things were expressed fully within Nahuatl conventions. The only exception to this rule was that proper and personal (baptismal) names were adopted by those who came into contact with Spaniards. Stage two extends from the mid-sixteenth century until around the mid-seventeenth and is characterized by the massive borrowing of Spanish nouns, but the language remained little altered in other respects. A third stage can be traced from about 1640–50, with some indications as early as the beginning of the seventeenth century, and involves a deeper and broader Spanish influence.

If the rate of linguistic change in a population that comes into contact with another is a function of the extent and type of contact between the two, then change would have occurred first where the greatest numbers of Spanish and indigenous groups and individuals interacted, and it would have spread from there to the rest of the indigenous-speaking community or region.[96] Hispanic centers of activity were obviously the greatest areas of contact. In the Nahua cultural area of central Mexico, however, various subregions were unified to the extent that linguistic change generally occurred within a decade or two, so that the entire evolution has been treated as a single process. As Karttunen and Lockhart have demonstrated, regional and subregional variation was not unimportant, and variation has been observed, but the relative and consistent contemporaneity of linguistic change across central Mexico makes it difficult to discern varying patterns of contact. Even outside central Mexico, peripheral Nahuatl exhibited many of the same contact phenomena as central Mexican Nahuatl and seems to have kept pace with changes in the central areas.[97] Of course some conventions of the language differ. Innovations at the center took time to reach distant places. The center of any given extended speech community is characteristically the origin of phonological and lexical innovation. Nahuatl at a distance from the center tended to adhere to expressions and conventions in the colonial period that were no longer used in central Mexico and that would have been considered unusual in the Valley of Mexico. However, most of the archaic features are related to the language itself. In terms of Spanish contact phenomena, many of the same changes seem to have occurred rather simultaneously in Tlaxcalan and Oaxacan Nahuatl, for example.

In the Mixteca, linguistic change occurred neither as rapidly nor as evenly as in central Mexico. Distinct patterns can be discerned for the regional and subregional development of Mixtec in contact with Spanish. These regional patterns are difficult to detail in this limited context; nevertheless, this chapter presents some general patterns for the regional variation of linguistic change in the Mixteca.[98]

The Early Period of Language Contact

In stage one of the evolution of Nahuatl in contact with Spanish, normal, daily interaction was minimal.[99] Communication fell to a small group of intermediaries and was limited to servants of Spaniards, aides to friars, interpreters, and the highest nobles. In this setting, linguistic adaptation was minimal; new concepts and objects were merely seen or heard of. Widespread use of alphabetic writing had not been developed in this period; the writing of notarial alphabetic documents in Nahuatl did not begin until around 1545. The most useful language resource for this early period is Molina's *Vocabulario*, which, despite reaching its final edition by 1571, already contained an impressive range of vocabulary in the first version of 1555. In fact, the work of translation, interpretation, and compiling had been under way for many years before the 1550s. Thus, some entries contain both early (stage-one) and later (stage-two) versions of words.

The general scenario proposed for stage-one Nahuatl can also be applied to the Mixteca, with one important difference: Nahuas served as intermediaries between Ñudzahui nobles and Spaniards in the early colonial period, especially in the first half century after contact. The Nahua presence was an additional factor influencing the nature of Ñudzahui responses to Spanish introductions. The degree of this influence is nearly impossible to measure, however, because it is difficult to discern whether shared Nahua and Ñudzahui responses to introduced phenomena represent Nahua influence or independent but similar responses. There are enough similarities and differences to suggest both possibilities.

The best sources for stage-one phenomena are the vocabularios that bridged the first two stages in their conception and production. The intention of the vocabularies was not to define terms but to produce an equivalent of the Spanish term or phrase. Consequently, some entries in the works attributed to Molina and Alvarado represent impromptu interpretations of an indigenous aide or clever renderings of Spanish descriptions; many equivalents were little more than literal descriptions of the original Spanish term, similar to definitions in a modern-day, monolingual dictionary.[100] As farfetched as some of these terms may seem, however, most were not arbitrary inventions of native assistants but rather represented learned attempts at applying a very extensive native vocabulary to unfamiliar cultural concepts and objects (see table 3.4).

During the first decades after the arrival of the Spaniards, native people came to terms in their own language with many introduced phenomena. Linguistic innovation was limited to a novelty that they considered so new and different that no existing indigenous word or expression seemed appropriate. The solution to introduced phenomena in Nahuatl and Mixtec was usually the extension of an existing etymon to the new concept. This usually resulted, in the early period of Spanish contact, in semantic adjustments for new distinctions in meaning. Certain vocabulary domains were likely to incorporate Spanish loans, such as the introduced civil-religious hierarchy, material culture, and the ideological lexicon. In this initial phase, basic categories were not changed; introduced objects and actions prompted possibilities for new expressions. In some cases the differences were ignored or subsumed under the generic aspect of indigenous terminology; in others new expressions were invented, old words were invested with a different meaning, or meaning was extended by metaphor or identification.[101] The practice of extension based on a perceived resemblance of function or appearance was already a common convention of the Ñudzahui language, such as the extension of *yuchi* (flint) to anything sharp, or of *tachi* (wind) to human breath. When identity with an existing Nahuatl or Ñudzahui word seemed inadequate, the initial

TABLE 3.4
Early Ñudzahui Descriptions of Some Spanish Introductions and Concepts

English	Ñudzahui	Literal Meaning
musket	*yutnu tehui*	"blow stick"
key	*daha caa*	"metal hand"
clock	*caa cánda maa*	"metal that divides from the middle"
hour	*cuhua ndicandij*	"sun measure"
reliquary	*sañoho yeque sanctos*	"container of saint's bones"
bell	*caa yocanda*	"ringing metal"
sword	*tatnu caa*	"metal staff"
horseshoe	*disa caa*	"metal shoe"
to print	*sadzi dusa caa*	"to strike metal bumps"
stamp	*caa sadzi tutu*	"metal that strikes paper"
hat	*cate dzini*	"head shade"
tongue of fire	*yaa ñuhu*	"fire tongue"
chessboard	*yutnu catni*	"square wood"
vinegar	*duta yya*	"sour water"
hairshirt	*dzono daye*	"rough shirt"
roman nose	*dzitni tnama*	"wide nose"

SOURCES: Alvarado, ff. 25, 140v, 181, 158v, 163, 181, 43, 103, 124, 131, 188, 191, 154v, 140v, 193, and Smith 1973a, 209.

response was a descriptive term for the new phenomenon. The resulting neologism was based mostly on function.[102] Another response to introduced items was the qualified identification—that is, an identification plus a second word modifying it.[103] For example, the general term for *huahi* (house) was extended with a qualifying term to describe variations on a familiar theme (see table 3.5).

Once a new expression became common, its usage and application underwent little innovation. In Mixtec and in Nahuatl, a complex arose around the new term that was extended and modified to encompass a whole range of activities and objects associated with the new item. Some of these complexes were outdated by the appearance of actual Spanish loanwords in Nahuatl-language documents before 1571 (the publication date of Molina's second edition of the Nahuatl *Vocabulario*) and by Ñudzahui-language notarial sources before 1593 (Alvarado's Mixtec *Vocabulario*). Much of the material in these two texts was cumulative and reflects earlier periods of language contact. Although a few neologisms were used for quite some time, most eventually yielded to a Spanish loan. The expressions that lasted throughout the colonial period (and in some cases beyond) usually involved a close indigenous equivalent that was likely viewed as more of a continuance than an actual introduction, such as *huahi ñuhu* (sacred house) for the church, *yuchi* for knife, and much of the terminology associated with *caa* for iron, such as bells, coins, and metallic objects in general. As late as the mid-eighteenth century, the following neologisms were still being used: *yutnutehui* (blow stick) for musket; *ydzundiqui* (horned deer) for oxen; *caayondaa* (fastening metal) for lock; and *ndahacaa* (metal hand) for key. Some of this terminology is still used today.[104]

Of the new phenomena introduced in the first generation after the conquest, perhaps the most ubiquitous were the horse (along with other European domesticated animals) and iron. Both introductions had an immediate effect on material culture and are referred to repeatedly in the historical record. Nahua and Ñudzahui speakers referred to iron and horses and a whole complex of related terms in their own languages.[105] Metaphorical extensions expanded the meaning to include additional

TABLE 3.5
Qualified Identifications Based on huahi *(house)*

English	Ñudzahui	Literal Meaning
church	*huahi ñuhu*	"sacred house"
jail	*huahi caa*	"metal house"
forge	*huahi tihuicaa*	"metalworking house"
purgatory	*huahi caa purgatorio*	"metal house of purgatory"
chimney	*nama huahi ñuma*	"smoke house wall/enclosure"
sepulcher	*huahi yeque*	"bone house"
store	*huahi yocuvui yahui*	"market house"
tower	*huahi dzuq cuiñe*	"tall, narrow house"
shed, shack	*huahi cate*	"shade house"
horse stable	*huahi idzu*	"deer house"
tavern	*huahi sadzico dedzi*	"house where pulque is sold"

SOURCES: Alvarado, ff. 129v, 44v, AJT-C, 6:575, AJT-C, 3:295; Alvarado, ff. 46v, 64, 188v, 196, 45v, 197, 178, 193v.

things related to the original, much like simple identifications. Thus, the horse was equated with the deer, and iron was likened to copper. Vocabulary for the horse and iron and associated terminology were two of the great complexes of stage-one identifications and extensions.

Both the Nahuatl and Ñudzahui speakers distinguished precious metals such as gold and silver from others, and after contact they used copper as a generic word for metal to describe iron and steel, frequently employing the qualification that it was black instead of red. Copper was the hardest metal known in Mesoamerica before iron was introduced and was used for axes, knives, and similar objects. Thus, *tepoztli* in Nahuatl and *caa* in Ñudzahui are frequently mentioned words in colonial texts.[106] The color designation of metals was important. For example, in Nahuatl, *teocuitlatl* meant precious metal in general, but when modified by *iztac* (white), it specified silver, and when modified by *coztic* (yellow), it referred to gold. Likewise, in Mixtec *dziñuhu quaa* (yellow precious metal) was gold, and *dziñuhu cuisi* (white precious metal) was silver. For iron, *tepoztli* was first used in Nahuatl with a color designation as *tliltic tepoztli* (black metal). In the same manner, Ñudzahui-language speakers wrote *caa tnoo*. In both languages, the complex surrounding the terms *tepoztli* and *caa* was the largest of any known and served as a type of general qualifier, prefixing *tepoz-* or using *caa* as a qualifying, second noun to a wide range of instruments and metal artifacts. The influence of iron was so important in every aspect of daily life that the complex persisted well after stage one.[107]

In Mixtec, the complex of native-language terminology referring to a wide range of metal objects, based on *caa,* was reduced by the gradual incorporation of Spanish loanwords. But use of the term persisted in many forms throughout the colonial period. In fact, Ñudzahui speakers still use *caa* today as a general term qualifying metal objects. An interesting use of *caa* is its pairing with the loanword *horas* to tell time, based on an association with the tolling of metal bells or the metal hands of a clock.[108] For Nahuatl, when the increase in Spanish loanwords began in stage two, *tepoztli* words were also affected; most of the terms were out of use by the end of the sixteenth century, though *tepoztli* itself survived in reference to "metal" and "iron."[109]

A similar complex formed around the deer to describe the introduction of the horse. The deer, *ydzu* in Mixtec and *maçatl* in Nahuatl, was the only large, grazing quadruped known to the area.[110] An identification was made based on the similarity of the two animals, regardless of obvious differences. Similarly, in Yucatan, Maya speakers referred to horses as tapirs, which were unique to that area, and used *tzimin* instead of the Spanish loan *caballo.*[111] The prominence of the horse (and mule) in early post-conquest life led to the development of an extensive complex of related terminology surrounding *ydzu.* Despite the fact that the Spanish loan for horse, *caballo,* became current by the time of Molina's *Vocabulario,* one still finds a large number of deer compounds for objects and actions associated with the horse.[112] In the *Vocabulario,* however, "horse" does not appear in the entry for *maçatl,* and there is no entry for "horse," despite the frequent mention of *cavallo* on the Nahuatl side; for "stable" Molina only gave *maçacalli,* "deer house."[113] This fact suggests that by the time of the second version of the *Vocabulario* in 1571, which included a Nahuatl-to-Spanish section, the term was no longer being applied directly for horse. In the Mixteca, the loanword *caballo* had already entered the Nahuatl language by 1558, as it appears in the *Codex Sierra.*[114] Two

documents dated 1601 suggest the extent to which Nahuatl had come into greater contact with Spanish by this time. Two small communities near Coixtlahuaca reported a
horse theft; one letter was written in Nahuatl and the other in Ñudzahui. The Nahuatl
letter called the horses "cavalu," employing a version of the Spanish loanword *caballo*,
while the Ñudzahui letter employed the native term *idzu*, "deer."[115] Even on the Nahua
periphery, Nahua speakers employed the loanword, whereas Ñudzahui speakers
retained the extension of a native word. In 1593, Alvarado's *Vocabulario* listed *idzu*
under the Spanish *caballo* and most terms related to the complex; on the other hand,
a few entries on the Mixtec side employed the loanword instead of the native word.[116]
In general, most Ñudzahui speakers continued to use the word *idzu* for horse in the
seventeenth century.

   In addition to neologisms and extensions, there were some Spanish loanwords
in stage one, limited primarily to Spanish proper names and titles. In both Mixtec and
Nahuatl, Spanish (Christian) names assigned at baptism were assimilated to indigenous pronunciation and were usually followed by an indigenous name. The titles don
and doña were also adopted in this early period, confined to a few select nobles.

   An exceptional, commonly used proper loan noun in the early period was *Castilla*
(Castile). Nahuatl and Mixtec used a form of this loanword to qualify native terms that
referred to introduced animals, foods, and artifacts and other things associated with
the newcomers. Both Nahuatl and Ñudzahui grammar allowed one noun to modify
another. Many objects were modified by *castilla* in Ñudzahui, illustrated by examples
in table 3.6. In the Nahuatl case, however, *caxtillan* was used as a locative, as denoted
by the combining form of the locative suffix *-tlan*, indicating that the noun was located
in or came from that place.[117] For example, Nahuas called a European domesticated
chicken *caxtillan totolin*, "Castile turkey hen," and the Spanish language was known as
caxtillan tlatolli, "Castile speech." In Ñudzahui, these were known as *tiñoo castilla* and
dzaha castilla, respectively, using equivalent loans but placing the loan noun in each
case after the modified noun (in its usual position as modifier). In Nahuatl, many of
these expressions gave way to Spanish loanwords early in stage two; even when the
original Nahuatl was retained, the *caxtillan* was dropped and usually limited to direct
references to Spain. Later, from the seventeenth century onward, modifiers such as
castilla were reduced considerably in Mixtec. Ñudzahui writers never adopted the term
castellano, as did Yucatec Maya.[118]

   Introduced items that were associated with other places were coupled with those
place-names as well, such as *coho china* for plates from China, or *dzoo bretaña* for linen
from Great Britain or Britany.[119] A consequence of such usage was the inclusion of references to the indigenous item with the self-ascribed term *ñudzahui* for things such as a
turkey (*tiñoo ñudzahui*), amatl paper (*tutu ñudzahui*), and cotton cloth (*dzoo ñudzahui*).
But the usage of such terminology was typical of a later period and is discussed in detail
in chapter 9.

   Animal names reflect the characteristic techniques of stage one. In Mixtec, a descriptive association *ydzundeque*, "horned deer," was applied to oxen and *ydzu* in general to mules and bulls, usually qualified by a Spanish loanword, such as *ydzu toro*. The
term for "cow," *ydzu dzehe*, was modified by *dzehe*, "female." In addition, *cachi*, "cotton,"
and *ticachi* (literally "cotton animal" with the *ti-* animal prefix) were used in reference

TABLE 3.6
Use of "Castilla" as Modifier for Introduced Items

English	Ñudzahui	Literal Meaning
almond	*dzehua castilla*	"Castile shelled nut"
wheat	*nuni castilla*	"Castile maize"
chicken	*tiñoo castilla*	"Castile turkey"
bread	*dzita castilla*	"Castile tortilla"
watermelon	*yeqh castilla*	"Castile melon"
saffron	*dzaha castilla*	"Castile flower"
pen	*llodzo castilla*	"Castile feather"
tallow wax	*ñuma castilla*	"Castile beeswax"
olive	*tecahua castilla*	"Castile plum"
mint	*mino castilla*	"Castile epazote"
carrot	*ñami quaa castilla*	"Castile orange sweet potato"
walnut	*ticaha castilla*	"Castile nut"
Spanish	*dzaha castilla*	"Castile language"

SOURCES: Alvarado, various documents.

to sheep, associating the cloth fiber with the animal's fleece.[120] The Ñudzahui word for "sheep" based on "cotton" persists in many places today.[121] In Nahuatl, *quaquahue*, literally "head-tree (horn) possessor," was used for "bovine animal" (as well as "goat"), based on a description of the animal's horns. The term for antlers is *quaquahuitl*, or literally "head-tree." Likewise, in Nahuatl *ichcatl*, "cotton," was extended to "sheep."

Another device to handle new terms and concepts was a verbal substantive (impersonal agentive), which in Nahuatl was usually recognizable in the form of the *-loni* or *-oni* suffix that designated something as an instrument for performing a certain function.[122] In Mixtec, a similar use of the impersonal agentive was applied (though not as an instrumental), using *sa*, "thing" or "that which," or "where." Thus, *sa caa yondaa*, "metal thing that fastens," was used for "lock"; *sasinindisa*, "that which is known as true," was used for "faith"; and *sa yyo ticachi*, "where the sheep are," was used for "estancia." This procedure was already quite common in the language: "food" was called *sacasi*, or "that which is eaten," and the term "bad" was *sa ñahuaha*, or "that which is not good" (like *amo qualli* in Nahuatl). An appropriate term for the plaza was *sa caa yahui*, or "where the market is."[123] The personal agentive was also extended to new actions and behavior by the use of *tai* or *tay*, "person" (usually a male) or "one who." A "sinner" was called *tai dzatevui*, or literally "person who causes harm"; an *alguacil* (Spanish-style constable) was called *tai tatnu*, or "person of the staff."[124] These types of constructions were common features of the language.

The identifications, extensions, and descriptions of the early period demonstrate how fully Nahuatl and Ñudzahui speakers continued to rely on their own established lexical resources and existing mechanisms to deal with new objects, introduced actions, and foreign concepts. Many of these constructions survived through the mid-seventeenth century, despite the existence of directly competing Spanish loanwords. But Spanish influences and words gathered momentum in the seventeenth century.

Mixtec in the Middle Years

Nahuas were writing alphabetic texts in their own language by the second half of the sixteenth century, as a new postconquest generation came to terms with the new medium of communication. In *cabeceras* of the Mixteca, such as Yanhuitlan and Teposcolula, a corresponding process occurred around a generation or so later. The publication of church-sponsored texts indicates the relative timing of these developments in central Mexico and Oaxaca. The *Doctrinas* attributed to Hernández appeared in 1567 and 1568, about a quarter of a century after comparable works in Nahuatl by fray Pedro de Gante, fray Alonso de Molina, and fray Bernardino de Sahagún. The Ñudzahui *Arte* and *Vocabulario* were published in the early 1590s, two to four decades after corresponding works were printed in Nahuatl. The timing of Ñudzahui church-sponsored materials is somewhat comparable to those produced for Yucatec Maya; the manuscript Motul dictionary dates from the 1580s, and Juan Coronel's grammar was not published until 1620.[125] The relative timing of such publications in Ñudzahui and Maya reflects a later development of indigenous writing in these two areas and a less pronounced degree of language contact in the sixteenth century and beyond.

Stage two is characterized by the full borrowing of Spanish nouns. By the midsixteenth century, as Nahuas began to produce alphabetic writings in their own language, they also began to borrow hundreds of basic Spanish nouns on a regular basis.[126] Ñudzahui speakers also borrowed many Spanish nouns after the 1570s, though the people of this southern region generally had less contact with Spaniards, their ideas, and their goods. The fact that Ñudzahui borrowed so freely and copiously from Spanish is somewhat surprising, considering how uncommon loans from non-Ñudzahui languages were in pre-Spanish times.[127]

Spanish loans reflect the impact of Spanish culture on the indigenous world, pinpointing that part of Hispanic society and culture that Nahuas and Ñudzahui came to understand and incorporate. Loans were used for those items, actions, and concepts that had become familiar and for which new terms were considered necessary. The borrowed nouns reflect, above all, introduced religious and civil terminology and names for European objects, units of measurement, plants, animals, and food. At first, the new vocabulary did not displace as much as augment the native lexicon, though replacement becomes increasingly evident. After a while, these words were no longer considered "new" or foreign; they were adopted by many people across a large area, incorporated into the indigenous lexicon, and assimilated to indigenous phonology. It is a matter of chance whether a specific loan appears in a given document, and some loans have more occasion to appear in the written record than others, depending on the nature of the source. Words for artifacts and introduced objects that had no ready indigenous equivalent stand out in most texts. Most sources contain an obvious bias in representing specific vocabulary domains; ecclesiastical texts, for example, were usually conservative in their use of loans and continued to employ archaic native terms long after they had gone out of use.[128] In both Ñudzahui and Nahuatl, a loanword could have made its first appearance in texts decades or centuries after it actually entered or became common in speech.

When a loan was appropriated into the Nahuatl or Ñudzahui language, or when it was still new to a particular speaker, it was paired with a semantic equivalent in the native language. This transitional device was usually an identification or description, such as *huahi tihuicaa fragua,* "metal-working house forge," in which case the final word is the loan. At other times the indigenous expression was modified by the Spanish loan, as if the loan were a qualifier.[129] For example, common Ñudzahui constructions with accompanying loanwords included *nuni trigo* (wheat maize) for wheat, *tayu silla* (chair stool) for the European-style chair, *ydzu mula* (mule deer) for mule; *caa hacha* (ax metal) for metal ax, and *yuchi tijeras* (scissors flint) for a pair of scissors.[130] As in Spanish, Mixtec places a modifier after the noun to which it refers. The first word in the pair is the Ñudzahui word; the translation refers to the Spanish loanword and then the native word, because the native noun is modified by a loanword, as if the loan were an adjective. A few loans diverged semantically from the original Spanish meaning, though some relation always remained. For example, both Nahuatl and Ñudzahui speakers used *tomin* for "money" in general, even though it referred to a specific coin. As in the early period, when complexes formed around important neologisms to reduce the necessity of further innovation, elaborate complexes formed around important Spanish loanwords in stage two.[131] The fact that Ñudzahui and Nahua writers interpreted many Spanish loans in the same manner points to another possible Nahua influence on Ñudzahui borrowing strategies.

Loans other than nouns were minimal during this period in both Nahuatl and Ñudzahui, and in most cases verbal constructions involving a loan can be interpreted as nouns rather than verbs. Such constructions are verbs in the infinitive form, functioning as a noun and usually acting as the object of a verb. In Nahuatl and Ñudzahui, loan phrases providing equivalents for verbs in this period usually consisted of a native verb and a Spanish noun. For example, Ñudzahui combined *quidza* (to make, do, or perform) with a Spanish noun such as *firma* (signature) for verbal constructions beginning in the first half of the seventeenth century and lasting throughout the colonial period. Thus, *yoquidzafirmandi* was employed to convey the introduced act of signing one's name to a document:

yo-	quidza	firma	-ndi
indicative	make	signature (Sp. loan)	I (Teposcolula variant)
I make a signature.			

Employing the loan noun *firma,* Nahuatl used *firmayotia,* "to make a signature," based on a noun, rather than directly borrowing the verb *firmar,* "to sign." The Nahuatl *chihua* (to make, do, or perform) was used occasionally with the infinitive of a Spanish verb.[132] In both Nahuatl and Ñudzahui, borrowing the infinitive form of the Spanish verb as a noun was rather uncommon in the sixteenth and early seventeenth centuries; incorporating a Spanish noun into a native verb phrase was much more common.[133]

Pronunciation

In both Nahuatl and Ñudzahui, Christian names and loan nouns of the first two stages accepted indigenous affixes and were assimilated to native pronunciation and morphological interpretation. In other words, despite obvious lexical augmentation, Nahuas and Mixtecs made few or no changes in their usual pronunciation. Common loanwords from Spanish were spelled standardly if they conformed to indigenous phonology; when they did not conform, the loanwords were often modified to approximate the closest familiar sound.[134] As a result, some loanwords in documents appear unrecognizable at first sight and must be deciphered within the context of indigenous orthography and phonology. Letter substitution and hypercorrection were common. The following section presents a preliminary comparison of how Nahuatl and Ñudzahui phonetic inventories responded to Spanish sounds.[135]

To summarize, Ñudzahui had no equivalents of sounds corresponding to the following Spanish letters: *b, f, g, l, p, r, rr,* and *v.* In comparison, Nahuatl had no equivalents for Spanish orthographic *b, d, f, g, j, ll, ñ, r,* or *rr.* In Nahuatl, the liquid [r] and [rr] were often replaced by [l]; [d] was replaced by [t] and sometimes [l]. In typical cases of orthographic hypercorrection, *l* was replaced by *r,* and *t* by *d.* Ñudzahui also underdifferentiated [r] and [l]. For example, Baltasar was often written "Bartasar," *arcabuz* appeared as "alcabus," and *alguacil* was "aguacir."[136] In Nahuatl, little distinction was made between palatal consonants [rr], [ll], and [ñ] and alveolar [l] and [n]; [n] was often geminated as [nn]. In the eighteenth century *ll* sometimes came to represent [y] in both Nahuatl and Mixtec, a development related to changes in Mexican Spanish pronunciation. This change in Mixtec was not prominent until after 1750.[137]

Nahuatl speakers devoiced the voiced stops [b],[d], and [g] to [p], [t], and [c], respectively. Ñudzahui speakers also pronounced [g] as [c], as shown in the following examples: "cofornador" for *gobernador;* "procatorio" and "purcatorio" for *purgatorio;* "yclecia" for *yglesia;* and "Acustina Comes" for Agustina Gómez. Some hypercorrection was common, as *c* was replaced by *g* in "artigulos" for *artículos* and "gorregidor" for *corregidor;* sometimes both were used, as in "artigucolos."[138] Ñudzahui speakers had no equivalent for either [p] or [b] and wrote *p* for *b,* as in "sapado" for *sábado* and "jonpon" for *jubón;* they also wrote *b* for *p,* as in "san bablo" for San Pablo.[139] Sometimes, *b/v/u* was written and pronounced as *hu* before a vowel, as in "eschrihuano" for *escrivano,* "natihuidad" for *natividad,* "huixilia" for *vigilia,* and "cahuildo" for *cabildo.*[140] On occasion, [d] was replaced by *t,* as in "sabato" for *sabado* and "cotraticio" for *contradicción.* There was a rough equivalent for [d], though it was usually written either *nd* or *dz;* at times, *d* was substituted for [t], as in "candores" and "cadorres" for *cantores.*[141]

Mixtec exhibited a strong preference for [n] instead of [m], evidenced in such words as "testinonino" for *testimonio,* "neenoria" for *memoria,* and "testaneto" for *testamento.* Many times the [m] was simply omitted, as in "sobrero" for *sombrero.* A telling indication of Ñudzahui authorship in the writing of Spanish loanwords was the alternate omission and inclusion of the nasal [n]. This practice resulted from the fact that the Ñudzahui language had very few consonant-final words or morphemes and many nasal-initial utterances. Ñudzahui speakers consistently omitted [n], especially in syllable-final position, as in the following cases: "yformaçio" and "yfromacio" for *información;* "peticio" for *petición;* "coceptio" for *concepción;* "cruzmaga" for *cruz manga;* "sa migel" for San Miguel; and "testameto" for *testamento.* Many times, the nasal was metathesized to initial position: "ndo njua" for don Juan; "naudieçia" for *audiencia;* and "niformacio" for *información.*[142] There is a strong case here, however, for prenasalization, which is very common among Ñudzahui-language speakers. Nasal omission and intrusion were also very common in Nahuatl. In Nahuatl the site for both omission and intrusion of nasals is in syllable-final position, whereas in Mixtec the usual site for intrusion is syllable-initial, and omission is syllable-final. Karttunen has affirmed the constant omission of word-final [n] in modern spoken Nahuatl.[143]

Vowel substitution was common in both Mixtec and Nahuatl. Nahuatl had only [o] but wrote both *u* and *o* for this vowel; it had distinct [e] and [i] vowels, but Nahuas tended to interpret unstressed Spanish [e] as [i]. Likewise, Mixtec had a high, back unrounded vowel [i] for which Spanish orthography provided no symbol. Some attempt seems to have been made to designate one of the vowels *y* and the other *i*, but this was not a consistent designation. In the Mixteca, the vowels [e] and [i], and to a lesser extent [a], were subject to regional differences. In Tlaxiaco, for example, *e* often replaced the *a* and sometimes the *i* of the Teposcolula area. Ñudzahui has distinct [u] and [o] vowels, but they were also subject to significant regional difference; in the Mixteca Baja and Valley of Oaxaca, the *o* of the Teposcolula area variant was often substituted for *u*.

Adapted to Ñudzahui phonology, the Spanish loanword was used exactly like any indigenous noun. A noteworthy feature of contemporary Mixtec languages is that the last syllable of Spanish loanwords has high pitch, similar to the addition of the glottal stop to vowel-final Spanish loan nouns in Nahuatl.[144] Nahuas rarely applied absolutive suffixes to unpossessed Spanish nouns but consistently used possessive prefixes with possessed Spanish nouns (and the plural possessed suffix), just as Mixtec attached possessive suffixes (and additionally prefixes in the Yanhuitlan area) to possessed loan nouns (there was no absolutive in Mixtec). In Mixtec, for example, nouns such as *ánima,* "soul, spirit," were usually possessed, so that *animandi,* "my soul" (Teposcolula area), *coanimanju,* "my soul" (Yanhuitlan area), or *animañadzaña,* "my soul" (reverential possessed form of noun), were more common forms than the bare loanword. Finally, Spanish plurals caused confusion or were ignored in both native languages, since only animate nouns were pluralized in Nahuatl and neither animate nor inanimate nouns had marked plural indicators in Mixtec. Thus, native writers used Spanish plurals for nouns almost indiscriminately in this period, often adding them when they did not belong and omitting them when they belonged.

Late Colonial Changes

Stage two was a long period in which loans were virtually all nouns and indigenous pronunciation and grammar were little affected. However, increasing bilingualism had a definite impact on native speech communities. The uneven geographical distribution of bilingual population centers contributed to the more sporadic nature and gradual timing of a third stage in the Mixteca than in central Mexico. For Nahuatl, distinct characteristics of a third stage were incipient as early as the end of the sixteenth century but only fully manifest by around 1650. In particular, borrowing was not as selective as it once was. Nahuas went beyond borrowing nouns to the use of loan verbs, prepositions, adverbs, and conjunctions. In addition, idiomatic expressions were translated, and Spanish principles of pluralization were adopted. By this stage, many Nahuatl speakers had become familiar with Spanish phonology.

In the Mixteca, the transition to a third stage corresponding to the process outlined for Nahuatl was very gradual. But the process was not merely slower. Change and transformation were subject to considerable regional variation and were in many ways much less extensive than in central Mexico and surrounding Nahuatl-speaking areas. In the period under study, some of the more remote monolingual areas of the Mixteca appear to have been largely unaffected by most third-stage characteristics identified for Nahuatl. Unlike Nahuatl (including peripheral Nahuatl written as far away as the Valley of Oaxaca), Mixtec did not borrow prepositions or idioms by the end of the colonial period, with a few notable exceptions, and took an intermediary approach to verb borrowing. This fact is significant in that it indicates a different rate and degree of language change and maintenance in the Mixteca, in comparison with the pattern detailed for the Nahuas and, to a lesser extent, for the Yucatec Maya.

An aspect of the language that underwent gradual change in the later period involved the formation of equivalents for Spanish verbs. As discussed above, the Ñudzahui convention, employed as early as the beginning of the seventeenth century, for achieving an equivalent to a Spanish verb was to borrow a cognate noun, used as the object of a common Ñudzahui verb such as *quidza*, "to do or make," an equivalent of the Nahuatl *chihua*. A typical case was *niquidzandi firmandi*, analyzed as follows:

ni-	*quidza*	*-ndi*	*firma*	*-ndi*
past tense	make	I	signature (loan)	my

I made my signature, or I signed.[145]

Other Ñudzahui verbs were paired with Spanish nouns to describe an action associated with the European context. For example, the following verbs were used with the Spanish loan noun *firma* (signature): *taa*, "to write"; *tniño*, "to perform a task" or "to work"; *ndaa*, "to be applied or placed"; *quidza*, "to do or make"; and *saha*, "to give." The native verbs *cachi*, "to speak," and *cuhui*, "to be," were also modified by Spanish nouns for a wide range of activities from alleging something to contradicting someone. *Firma* was the most common loan noun used with these native verbs, and *quidza* was the most commonly used native verb. There was no need to invent an expression by borrowing a Spanish loan for "writing," but there was little preconquest precedent for signing one's name, an action that occasioned the use of a loan verb. Throughout the colonial period, Mixtec retained the strategy of borrowing nouns to complement native verbs as a way of describing new actions and never adopted a verb-borrowing convention that used the Spanish verb in a manner other than the infinitive, and it therefore treated the verb as if it were a noun.

In Nahuatl, the method for incorporating loan verbs continued to be based on the Spanish infinitive, but in stage three it was affixed to the native verbal element *-oa*, one of the most common suffixes attached to Nahuatl verbs.[146] Verbalizing suffixes were added to Spanish loan nouns in order to create verbs from nouns. This was a common feature of the Nahuatl language: for example, one could say "to make tamales" by adding an *-oa* suffix to the noun *tamalli* and arrive at the verb *tamaloa*. The same effect could be achieved through the use of a noun as an object in combination with *chihua* "to do or make." For example, *tamalchihua* is "to make tamales," and *huenchihua* means "to make an offering," based on *huentli*, "offering."

Ñudzahui speakers used only the second strategy discussed above, employing a noun as the object of a common verb to denote a particular type of action; for example, the verb *quidzatniño* (to work) combines *quidza* (to do) and *tniño* (labor).[147] Certain nouns modified a verb to signify an action distinct from the meaning of the original verb.[148] For example, the verb *sicatahui* (to request something) is a combined form of *sica* (to ask for) and *tahui* (gift or favor).[149] The verb *tasitnuni* (to bequeath) combines *tasi* (to leave behind or to give) and *tnuni* (agreement or command). The verb "to love" is *sinimani*, consisting of *sini* (to know) and *mani* (preciousness).[150] The term *mani* could also be interpreted as an adverb. Similarly, the term *huaha* (good) is often used as a modifying noun in many verb phrases (especially with *quidza*), appearing more or less as an adverb but perhaps signifying the completion of the verb.[151]

Mixtec seems to have employed the same convention of using nouns to modify verbs in order to incorporate Spanish verbs from the early seventeenth century onward. Inflected native verbs were combined with Spanish nouns to represent an introduced action. The noun, either possessed or unpossessed, served as the object of the action and was at first postposed to the inflected verb. Later, the infinitive of the Spanish verb was used instead of the noun, but the native verb remained, and so the infinitive was used as if it were a noun, or it functioned as a complement of the native verb. Finally, the infinitive of the Spanish verb was compounded with the native verb, representing a type of verb incorporation, perhaps, but differing in retaining an entire native verb in the new construct rather than a verbalizing element, as in Nahuatl. The hypothetical sequence is described in table 3.7.

The two examples in the first step of the sequence, 1(a,b), represent a variation of the same convention, using a borrowed noun, first unpossessed and then possessed, with a native verb: "I made a signature [on] the paper" and "I made my signature [on] the paper." These two examples do not represent verb borrowing but rather use a noun as the object of a native verb. The second step represents a Spanish (verb) infinitive being treated as if it were a noun outside the verb phrase, which is usually defined by the tense marker (to the left of verb stem) and subject indicator (to the right of verb stem). The absence of a subject pronoun suffix in step 2(a) leaves some doubt as to the loan verb's inclusion in the verb phrase, which is often the case when there is an unmarked third-person subject (unless it is the honorific *-ya*). The third step in the sequence places the infinitive of the loan verb in the position of an incorporated object within the verb phrase, as if it were a noun. Although it is positioned in relation to the verb stem as a noun, it is unclear whether it functioned syntactically as a noun.[152] In this case the subject pronoun *-ndi* is positioned after both *quidza* and *firmar* and acts as a subject pronoun for the entire construction. One might write *niquidzafirmarndi tutu*, since it seems that *-ndi* is placed after the whole verb word. Rather than "I make my signature," this could conceivably be interpreted as "I sign the paper."

Nahuatl's definitive verb-borrowing strategy also used the uninflected infinitive as an incorporated stem, but it completed the construction with a verbalizing suffix *-oa* rather than with an entire recognizable native verb as Mixtec did. It is tempting to think that the Ñudzahui *quidza* compounds may have been evolving toward some

TABLE 3.7

Hypothetical Sequence of Verb Borrowing Strategies Using the Native Verb quidza
(to do or make) and the Loanwords firma *(signature) and* firmar *(to sign)*

1. (a) *niquidzandi firma tutu*

ni-	quidza	-ndi	firma	tutu
preterit	to make	I	signature	paper

I made a signature [on] the paper.

1. (b) *niquidzandi firmandi tutu*

ni-	quidza	-ndi	firma-ndi	tutu
preterit	to make	I	signature-my	paper

I made my signature [on] the paper.

2. (a) *niquidzafirmar tutu*

ni-	quidza	firmar	tutu
preterit	to make	to sign	paper

He or she signed the paper.

2. (b) *niquidzandi firmar tutu*

ni-	quidza	-ndi	firmar	tutu
preterit	to make	I	to sign	paper

I signed the paper.

3. *niquidzafirmarndi tutu*

ni-	quidza	firmar	-ndi	tutu
preterit	to make	to sign	I/my	paper

I signed the paper.

equivalent of the Nahuatl -*oa* construction. After all, the verbalizing Nahuatl -*oa* suffix can impart the meaning "to make" or "activate" something when attached to a noun, as discussed above. Table 3.8 provides examples of this sequence of noun- and verb-borrowing strategies, or what may be called verb-as-noun– or verb-as-complement–borrowing strategies, attested in colonial texts.

The sequence in table 3.8 is a selective but representative sample, drawn from more than two hundred attestations of loan verbs, or loan nouns used in connection with native verbs, in colonial archival sources. In general, the infinitive Spanish verbs appear to be treated as nouns or as complements to native verbs, whether freestanding or incorporated into the verb phrase. There is some question as to how they were perceived, given the increasing use of the infinitive in the later period, which could represent a recognition that Spanish loan verbs were being borrowed, if not exactly used as verbs. No examples of loan nouns used in connection with native verbs have been found in Ñudzahui-language records dating from the sixteenth century; the first cases appear in the central areas of the Mixteca Alta, in and around Yanhuitlan and Teposcolula, and are essentially confined to the noun *firma*. By the end of the seventeenth century, Ñudzahui speakers had adopted more direct methods of borrowing by using the infinitive, and they were using a variety of Spanish verbs (though still mostly of a legal nature) in conjunction with a handful of basic native verbs but also continued to employ older strategies based on a noun. For example, in 1738, a writer from Tonaltepec used the loan noun *gasto* (expenditure) for the act of spending money; he wrote "niquidzagastodza" [I made an expenditure] and "nicuhuigasto" [he had an

TABLE 3.8

Examples of Noun and Verb-as-Noun Borrowing in Ñudzahui Texts,
with Provenance and Date of Attestation

Examples of 1(a) in sequence:
  niquidzandi prenda, "I made a pledge" (Tamasulapa, 1680)
  yoquidzañadzaña contadiçion, "I make a contradiction" (Yanhuitlan, 1681)[a]
  yoquidzanju cargo, "I charge somebody" (Yanhuitlan, 1689)
  niquidzandi rendado, "I rented" (Ytnoyaya, 1692)
  yoquidza guramento, "he makes an oath" (Yanhuitlan, 1705)

Examples of 1(b) in sequence:
  yondeefirmaata, "he writes his signature" (Achiutla, 1577)[b]
  nitaata firmata, "he wrote his signature" (Teposcolula, 1601)
  yochaamainju cofirmanju, "I write my own signature" (Topiltepec, 1610)[c]
  nitaandi firmandi, "I wrote my signature" (Teposcolula, 1623)
  yotniñonju firmanju, "I make my signature" (Yanhuitlan, 1681)

Examples of 2(a) in sequence:
  niquidza presendar, "he presented" (Teposcolula, 1622)
  cadza presentar, "he will present" (Yanhuitlan, 1681)
  niquidza notificar, "he notified" (Yolomecatl, 1730)
  cadza estorbar, "they will obstruct" (Nduayaco, 1757)
  niquida recibir, "he received" (Añañi, 1777)

Examples of 2(b) in sequence:
  cadzañadzaña falçear, "I will falsify" (Yanhuitlan, 1681)
  yoquidzanju sitar, "I cite" (Yanhuitlan, 1681)
  cadza ñadzaña alegar, "I will allege" (Yanhuitlan, 1699)
  yoquidzaya renunsiar, "he renounces" (Yolomecatl, 1708)
  yosayya arrentar, "he rents" (Tlaxiaco, 1713)

Examples of 3 in sequence:
  niquidza liar ñahata, "he tied them up" (Chalcatongo, 1681)
  yoquidza mandar ñadzaña, "I order" (Yanhuitlan, 1756)
  yochidzo firmar nju, "I sign" (Amatlan, 1777)
  yoquidza testar dza, "I make a will" (Yucunama, 1785)
  yoquida firmar ndehe taca ñadzaña, "we all sign" (Tonaltepec, 1708)

SOURCES: AJT-C, 11:938; AJT-C, 4:467; AJT-C, 5:535; AJT-C, 6:575; AJT-C, 5:506;
AJT-C, 1:54; AJT-CR, 1:150; AJT-C, 8:705; AJT-C, 4:400; AGN-T, 637:1;
AJT-C, 4:467; AGN-CR, 630:4; AJT-C, 17:1467; AJT-C, 18:1524; AJT-C, 4:467; AJT-C,
4:467; AJT-C, 5:535; AJT-C, 8:724; AJT-C, 6:624; AJT-CR, 5:550; AJT-C, 15:1232;
AJT-C, 18:1578; AJT-C, 15:1251; AJT-C, 18:1578.

NOTE: Based on sequence in table 3.7.

[a] *Ñadzaña* is a reverential first-person subject and possessive pronoun. In 1776, a notary
in Adequez used a similar construction when he wrote, "Ña hoo cada contra" [nobody
is to make a contradiction], reducing *contradicción* to "contra" and using the future
tense of the verb *quidza* (*cadza*, written here as "cada"). AJT-C 18:1516.

[b] The verb *taa,* "to write," was pronounced and written as *dee* in Achiutla. In Yanhuitlan,
taa was pronounced as *chaa.*

[c] In the Yanhuitlan dialect area, *-nju* or *-nchu* is the first-person subject and possessive
suffix, equivalent to *-ndi* in the Teposcolula dialect area. Speakers from the Yanhuitlan
area attached a *co* to the front of the possessed noun, in addition to possessive pronoun
suffixes. "Own" is expressed by *mai.*

expenditure] in reference to moneys paid.[153] On rare occasions, the Spanish infinitive was unaccompanied by a native verb; for example, one document from 1643 referred to a don Fernando Salazar who "rented cultivable lands which are in back of San Andrés" [do fernando y salasar arrendar ñoho situyo ñoho yata san adres], using the infinitive of the Spanish verb *arrendar* without a native verb.[154] Inflected Spanish verbs in Ñudzahui texts are seen only within bilingual portions of documents. Some loan verbs were used with Mixtec equivalents; for example, in the case of *yosaha dar poder,* "he gives power [of attorney]," the Mixtec *saha,* "to give," is the equivalent of the Spanish verb *dar.*[155] Such phrases inclined toward bilingualism or might be considered unanalyzed phrases that had entered into Ñudzahui legal talk.

Most important, Ñudzahui writers seldom borrowed a Spanish verb without a native verb. The native verb in these complex verb constructions is not simply an auxiliary; semantically, native verbs possessed an auxiliary function, but syntactically (especially if paired with nouns) they did not. Thus, even though Ñudzahui developed a capacity to borrow Spanish nouns and verb infinitives in connection with inflected native verbs and incorporated them into Ñudzahui morphology, the nouns and infinitives never displaced native verbs in the process.

Thus, in a sense, the Ñudzahui equivalent of the Nahuatl adoption of Spanish loan verbs did not go beyond the use of a native verb and a Spanish noun, or a native verb and a Spanish infinitive, somewhat analogous to the earlier use of *chihua* and an infinitive in Nahuatl. Essentially, a handful of other native verbs were paired with loan nouns to describe an introduced action. The use of the infinitive Spanish verb as if it were an object of the inflected Ñudzahui verb may have represented a more direct verb-as-noun–borrowing strategy and a familiarity with Spanish verbs as such. Even this convention did not appear until the 1670s and 1680s, or the last quarter of the seventeenth century.[156] This period reflects an increase in the number of loan nouns entering the language and changes in Ñudzahui writing discussed in the preceding chapter. Most of this loan borrowing, as modest as it was in comparison with that of central Mexico, was centered around Yanhuitlan and Teposcolula, and Hispanic influence in general proceeded from administrative and ecclesiastical centers to contiguous communities, especially by the eighteenth century. Loan verbs became somewhat commonplace after the mid-seventeenth century but were always few in number compared with nouns.[157] Although loan verbs never represented more than a small proportion of the overall lexicon, some verbs are attested very frequently and must have constituted part of the accepted vocabulary of ordinary people.

Perhaps the most significant indication of a third stage for Nahuatl, in addition to the direct borrowing of Spanish verbs as verbs, involved the borrowing of prepositions, conjunctions, and adverbs. The appearance of Spanish *para, por,* and *hasta* in Nahuatl-language texts represented increased contact with Spanish in stage three, the borrowing of grammatical function words in addition to content words, and a corresponding effect of Spanish on Nahuatl syntax. Although Nahuatl relational words differed from freestanding Spanish prepositions and relationships among clauses were indicated with adverbs and relational nouns rather than by means of conjunctions and relative pronouns, Spanish prepositions and conjunctions conveyed little that could not already be expressed in Nahuatl. Bilingualism was the reason for the loans.[158]

Whereas Nahuatl borrowed prepositions and conjunctions quite freely after 1650, Mixtec did not do so even by the end of the eighteenth century. Ñudzahui had a number of prepositions and conjunctions that native speakers continued to use throughout the period, including the following: *nuu,* "on, over, toward"; *dzini,* "on top of"; *sihi,* "for"; *taca,* "with"; *ndehe,* "and"; and *nani,* "until." The borrowing of prepositions that were associated with specific European-style contexts was limited; for example, the Spanish preposition *a* (to) was used in the address of letters and other documents, such as "a stoho cuihi mani ñadzaña" [to my precious, true lord].[159] And the words *de* and *en* were common within formulaic statements. But the occasional appearance of these prepositions in frozen expressions bears little resemblance to important functional prepositions, such as *para* and *hasta,* which entered the Nahuatl language by the mid-seventeenth century.[160]

Many Spanish prepositions and articles were apparently unrecognized as independent words. In Nahuatl, the phrase *a la huerta,* "to the orchard," was a stage-two loan used as a noun. That is to say, *alahuerta* was used for "orchard" or an intensely cultivated plot in general. This type of underanalysis persisted in the same form throughout the colonial period, suggesting that Nahuas originated such loans, since a Spaniard would not have treated a prepositional phrase as a noun.[161] The same unanalyzed phrase has been attested in four separate Ñudzahui-language texts, as early as 1573 and as late as 1682. Finally, in 1752, the word *huerta* was used in a document from Texupa, marking the late adoption of the actual Spanish noun.[162] The use of this phrase as a noun in Mixtec seems to indicate a shared or coincidental strategy for borrowing in central Mexico and the Mixteca. Perhaps Mixtec was even directly affected by the Nahuatl pattern during the formative but transitory period of Nahuatl as a lingua franca in the Mixteca proper. Even if Nahuas did influence Ñudzahui strategies of adaptation to Spanish, their presence did not preclude innovation. Regardless of the circumstances, in the case of *alahuerta,* both Ñudzahui and Nahua speakers failed to distinguish the noun from the preposition and article. Confusion also arose when indigenous particles resembled parts of Spanish words, such as the Nahuatl *in* and the Ñudzahui *co-* (Yanhuitlan area).[163]

In Mixtec, one identifiable loanword based on a Spanish noun, *cuenta* (account), was used much like a preposition or a dative. The term, often spelled "quenta," has been attested several times in documentation of the later colonial period. The loan was used as an equivalent of the Spanish *para,* "for, to, in order to," perhaps because of its occurrence in the Spanish phrase *a cuenta de,* "on account of," or *por cuenta de,* "on behalf of." The term *cuenta* was a loan noun from the earliest period and accords well with Mixtec pronunciation, sounding like a typical bisyllabic root ending in a vowel.[164] The term appears several times in Santa Catarina Adequez in the years 1798 to 1800, for example, and was used in many different ways to approximate the meaning of *para* (see table 3.9).[165] Spanish translations of the two testaments from Adequez, and similar texts that feature the use of this loanword, glossed it consistently as *para* or *por.*

Again, the use of *cuenta* is characteristic of the very late colonial period. Its use has also been noted in contemporary Ñudzahui-speaking communities, in Ocotepec ("kwénda"), Yodzondua ("kwénta"), Diuxi-Tilantongo, Chalcatongo, and Silacayoapan.[166] In the first two places, it has been defined as the equivalent of Spanish *para;*

TABLE 3.9
Examples of the Spanish Loanword cuenta *Used as a Preposition in Colonial Texts*

- "ñuhu yucuticoo *quenta* Petronilla sihi *quenta* Tomasa"
  The land [named] yucuticoo is *for* Petronilla and *for* Tomasa.
- "nihuanina Pasqual Miguel sihi Frcacica *quenta* ñuhu yucha 3 peso"
  Pascual Miguel and Francisca received three pesos *in exchange for* the river land.
- "ñuhu ytnuniquaha nandosi *quenta* vicoñadaña Andrea Hernandez"
  The land [named] Ytnuniquaha will be left *for* my niece Andrea Hernández.
- "ticachi ndidyu *quenta* caniy hoho dico te nacuhui si Dominga"
  One hundred sheep and goats will be *for* my sister Dominga.
- "ñuhu ytnuayuu *quenta* Dominga"
  The land [named] Ytnuayuu is *for* Dominga.
- "ñuhu ytnuhu Achatiñu *quenta* cuhuiñadaña micayla lopes sihi cadañadaña Vicente de la Cruz"
  The slope land [named] Achatiñu is *for* my sister Micaela López and my brother-in-law Vicente de la Cruz.

---

in the remaining three places, its meaning varies from "how" to "on account of" and "on behalf of." Thus, the interpretation of *cuenta* in modern transcriptions corresponds with its meaning in late colonial documents.

The Ñudzahui use of *cuenta* was not nearly as widespread as was the adaptation of *para, por,* and *hasta* in Nahuatl. Nahuatl seemed to borrow prepositions that had no ready native equivalents, until later when loans flowed almost indiscriminately into the language. It is not clear, in this context, how *cuenta* would have fulfilled a need not already covered by Ñudzahui words such as *sihi,* "for," and *saha,* "in order to." It was used in testaments as a convention to denote possession or entitlement to lands or properties and therefore functions like *para* or *por* in only a limited sense, not as a general preposition. In any case, *cuenta* seems to have functioned differently than its original meaning in Spanish, an observation made by Karttunen in reference to the use of Spanish prepositions in Maya and Nahuatl.[167]

Another possible sign of Spanish influence on Mixtec was the appearance of entire Spanish phrases in Ñudzahui-language texts. For example, in the 1680s, Yanhuitlan produced Ñudzahui-language documentation riddled with loanwords and Spanish phrases, such as "asi ndeclaramos legua misteca" [thus we declare in the Mixtec language]; "penas e docenas asotes" [penalties and dozens of lashes]; and "alabado seya el santissimo sacramacto" [praised be the Holy Sacrament].[168] These Spanish phrases were dropped in the middle of native-language texts. Some phrases combined Spanish and Ñudzahui words, as in the following opening formula of a testament: "all the mysteries of our most holy trinity and that which is called faith, hope, and charity" [ndee cutu misterio santissima trinidad sihi sanani fee, esperanza, y caridad].[169] All the Spanish loans in this phrase were used to express novel concepts, except for the Spanish conjunction *y,* which was part of the frozen expression "fee, esperanza, y caridad." Most of the time, however, Ñudzahui speakers joined native and Spanish nouns with native conjunctions, even in formulaic statements. Perhaps the most obvious example was the common phrase in the opening line of testaments "God the Father and God the Son and God the Holy Spirit" [dzutu ndios ndehe dzaya ndios ndehe espiritu santo ndios], whereby *ndehe* is a conjunction joining the three persons but one true God ("ndios") of the Holy Trinity.

A certain number of late colonial loans in Ñudzahui and Nahuatl belong to categories with no earlier loans, such as words for directions. The first known use of Spanish cardinal directions as loans in Mixtec was in 1726; thereafter, the usage of loanwords for directions was attested several times.[170] For example, in Yanhuitlan, the dimensions of a plot of land were described in whole Spanish phrases, "de norte a sur" [from north to south] and "de oriente a poniente" [from east to west].[171] Both Nahuatl and Ñudzahui retained use of the older native expressions for the cardinal directions throughout the colonial period, but borrowing was nonetheless evident in the eighteenth century.[172]

By the late seventeenth century, the phenomenon of "code switching," when both Ñudzahui and Spanish were used within the same phrase, was fairly common in cabeceras such as Yanhuitlan and Teposcolula. For example, one testament written in 1686 concluded with the statement "ago firma nuu tutu testamento" [I make a signature on the testament], where "[h]ago" is the inflected Spanish verb, and "nuu tutu" is the native term for "on the paper/document."[173] In this case, it seems as if the writer actually knew some Spanish grammar, not just loanwords. Similarly, a bilingual Ñudzahui merchant from Yanhuitlan chose freely between Ñudzahui and Spanish, alternately writing native verbs such as "nidziconju" [I purchased] and "yocuviquentacha" [he/she has an account], as well as Spanish verbs such as "dio" [he/she gave] and "pagó" [he/she paid].[174] This behavior may be considered active, conscious choice rather than passive acculturation, though the ultimate outcome of such a capacity for bilingual choice tended to favor the dominant language in the long run. On the other hand, code switching as discourse by bilinguals may not have affected Mixtec much at all. Writers simply may have had a command of some Spanish phrases that were associated with specific contexts.

Finally, an important characteristic of stage-three Nahuatl was the use of calques. By the eighteenth century, Nahuas had adopted word-for-word translations of normal Spanish expressions using native vocabulary, whether the expression made immediate sense in the Nahuatl language or not.[175] This phenomenon signifies advanced structural change in the native language. Calques have not been observed in colonial Ñudzahui texts.

Local Variation

Whereas Nahuatl speakers as a group, from one region to the next and from both the center and the periphery of the language area, responded quite uniformly as they came into increasing contact with Spanish, there was less temporal and regional unity in the Mixteca. Language contact and acculturation have had a more significant impact in the more nucleated population centers and irrigated valleys of the Mixteca, especially along the Pan American Highway, which cuts across the northern Baja and runs by Acatlán, Huaxuapa, Tamasulapa, Texupa, Teposcolula, Yanhuitlan, Nochixtlan, and many adjacent communities. The highway was founded upon preconquest roads and footpaths that linked Mexico City and Puebla with Oaxaca and Guatemala. Many of these communities were designated administrative centers in the colonial period, in part because of their favorable and easily accessible location. It is no coincidence that documents from this region often refer to the "yaya cano camino real," or "the great royal road," combining Spanish loanwords with *yaya*, "road," and *cano*, "great." The road brought dozens of communities into contact with Spanish speakers. Another ancient road branches off from the Pan American Highway and runs through the Teposcolula Valley, past Tlaxiaco, and down to the coast.

The intrusion of Spanish speakers into communities located along major roads has had a profound impact on languages in the region. The major concentrations of native population prior to the Spanish conquest, the communities designated cabeceras in the sixteenth century, no longer speak Mixtec languages.[176] Regions where Mixtec languages are currently being lost show the most Spanish influence and interference in native phonology and lexicon. Of course, no language in Mexico does not have some such influence and interference. Migration to Mexico City and the United States has forced many people to adopt Spanish and English. Meanwhile, social, economic, political, and educational prejudices and pressures to assimilate to the dominant language continue to threaten native languages. Native vocabulary comes into constant competition with Spanish loanwords. Monolingual Mixtecan speakers live at a distinct disadvantage in Mexico. On the other hand, along parts of the coastal plain and mountainous, interior areas of the Mixteca Alta, Mixtec languages are still spoken. To this day, much of this area is accessible by dirt roads, by mule or horse, or on foot. Most Mixtec-speaking places are isolated from one another and interspersed among neighboring communities of Spanish speakers; linguistic variation is accentuated by the relative separation and local orientation of each community.

Patterns of language change are discernible by the latter part of the sixteenth century. Not surprisingly, the greatest evidence of change comes from ecclesiastical, administrative, and commercial centers where native-language writing began in the sixteenth century and where the Spanish presence was most concentrated. Ñudzahui-language writings from these colonial centers document an increasing use of Spanish loan vocabulary and bilingual influences. Ñudzahui and Spanish speakers lived among one another in about a dozen centers of cultural and commercial contact in the colonial period. In these cabeceras where Ñudzahui-language writing originated, places such as Yanhuitlan and Teposcolula, many native scribes could write in Spanish by the second half of the eighteenth century.[177] Meanwhile, individuals from San Esteban Atlatlahuca continued to produce Ñudzahui prose with only a minimum of Spanish loan nouns. In the period when notaries on the *cabildo* of Yanhuitlan wrote bilingual phrases fraught with Spanish loans, their counterparts from the remote *ñuu* of Santiago Nuyoo wrote brief documents that relied on few loanwords. Even the calligraphy of the two documents suggests the difference between a polished hand in the administrative center and an unpracticed one in the hinterland. At the same time, dozens of small communities generated few or no records in the colonial period; people from these places came into limited contact with Spanish speakers and continued to rely primarily on their own languages.

In general, a given community's proximity to the highway, what I have termed the "southern trunkline," and its location in respect to Hispanic administrative and residence centers conditioned its adaptation to Spanish. I have located Ñudzahui-language documentation from the colonial period for fourteen communities where a Mixtecan language is spoken today, including Achiutla, Adequez, Atlatlahuca, Chalcatongo, Nduayaco, Nuyoo, Soyaltepec, Tlatlaltepec, Tidaa, Tlazultepec, Xaltepetongo, Yodzondua, Yucuiti, and Yucunama. Appropriately, writings from these fourteen pueblos contain relatively little evidence of Spanish language contact phenomena. In contrast, Mixtecan languages are spoken in none of the more central communities where writing began, in places such as Yanhuitlan, Teposcolula, Texupa, Tamasulapa, Huaxuapa, and Tlaxiaco. Together, these communities generated more than half of all extant colonial Ñudzahui-language documentation. All these communities were colonial administrative centers.[178] Ironically, the development and practice of alphabetic writing did not contribute to language preservation.

Ñudzahui speakers made a series of adjustments and adaptations to Spanish across the colonial period. Linguistic data reflect the increasing interaction of native-language speakers with Spanish-speaking members of colonial society. The sources also reveal a selective retention of native conventions alongside Spanish intrusion. This gradual, complex process of change and continuity resonates with historical processes examined in other chapters of this work. The focus of this study now turns to the specific content of native-language writings, beginning with a discussion of Ñudzahui communities.

CHAPTER 4

Communities

IN THEIR OWN LANGUAGE AND WRITINGS, Ñudzahui people did not use Spanish terms such as *ciudad, pueblo, cabecera, sujeto, rancho, estancia,* or *barrio* to describe the places where they lived and worked in the sixteenth century, places that are known today in the most general sense as "communities." In fact, most of these terms never appear in native-language sources from the colonial period. Spanish sources and translations of native-language texts reduced complex native terminology to Spanish equivalents, giving the impression that "pueblos de indios" were simple, undifferentiated structures. These impressions have been reinforced by modern studies of the Mesoamerican corporate community.[1]

The translation and analysis of native-language writings have enabled historians to identify and detail the nature and evolution of Nahua and Maya sociopolitical organization.[2] I have adopted a similar approach and methodology by using Ñudzahui-language and Spanish-language sources in conjunction, reading the two types of texts against each other. Repeated references to native-language sociopolitical terminology make a detailed study of categories and names possible across the entire region. Whereas native-language sources reveal how Ñudzahui writers referred to their own communities, Spanish sources indicate how colonial officials interpreted and redefined these places in their own terms. Native entities and sociopolitical relations were affected by the external perception and redefinition but were not transformed beyond recognition. The survival of many communities to the present day, despite severe population decline and sociopolitical reorganization, confirms the integrity and resilience of these structures.[3]

This chapter has four main objectives: first, to identify and describe native sociopolitical organization at the time of contact by analyzing how native people referred to and affiliated themselves with the places where they lived and how they recognized different types of relations among various places; second, to understand how Spaniards perceived this organization and attempted to reorganize it to fit their colonial interests; third, to show how native rulers and communities responded to this reorganization; and fourth, to consider the long-term effects of this process. This analysis considers both general cultural patterns and regional differences. I begin with the most visible of all sociopolitical structures, the *ñuu*.

Ñuu and Yuhuitayu

Ñudzahui-language sources show that all settled places were called *ñuu*. The term conveyed "place" in the broad sense of the word, as a settlement or even a region. The Mixteca, for example, was known as the *ñuu dzahui*, "the place of rain." Every settlement was inherently or potentially a ñuu; many place-names contain *ñuu* as a prefix, often reduced to *ñu*, such as Ñunduhua (Oaxaca), Ñundaa (Texupa), and Ñundecu (Achiutla). Tenochtitlan and the region of central Mexico in general were called Ñucoyo and the nearby Chocho region Ñutocuiy. Ñudzahui people called the world in which they lived *ñuu ñayehui*, or "places and people," referring to all the people collectively in their innumerable ñuu.[4]

The *Vocabulario en lengua mixteca*, published in 1593, employs "ñuu" alone or modified to define such terms as "pueblo," "territory," "villa," "place for a pueblo," and "site of a pueblo."[5] The mundane question in Spanish "De que pueblo eres?" (From which pueblo are you?) was given as *Nandaa ñuundo* and *nañuu yehe tnahando*, literally "To which ñuu do you belong?"[6] To settle a site was literally "to make a ñuu," *yoquidza ñuundi*.[7] A city was simply a *ñuu cánu*, "large ñuu," and Castile (Spain) was listed as *ñuu sata duta*, or the "ñuu beyond the waters."[8] In reference to "all the pueblos of the Mixteca," Reyes's *Arte en lengua mixteca* used *ñuu* twice: *neecutundu ñuu ñudzavui*, "all the Ñudzahui ñuu."[9] The term *ñuu* is still used today as the equivalent of the Spanish word "pueblo."

The ñuu was as central to local indigenous organization as the *altepetl* in central Mexico and the *cah* in Yucatan. Ñudzahui individuals were usually identified in terms of their affiliation with a specific ñuu. A person was typically called, for example, *tay ñuu Yucunduchi*, "person from the ñuu of Etlantongo," or simply *tay ñuu*, "person from a ñuu."[10] Ñudzahui-language documentation abounds with references to the ñuu. Polities as large as Yodzocahi (Yanhuitlan), Yucundaa (Teposcolula), and Yodzocoo (Coixtlahuaca) were referred to as ñuu, as were relatively small places such as Tiñuhu and Tiyacu.[11]

Prominent places such as Yodzocahi (known to Spaniards as Yanhuitlan), Yucundaa (Teposcolula), Disinuu (Tlaxiaco), and Yodzocoo (Coixtlahuaca) were called ñuu only in the most general sense, however. In 1573, don Felipe de Saavedra referred to his wife, doña María, as *yya ñuu yaá*, or "ruler of this ñuu," in reference to Disinuu (Tlaxiaco), but he and other writers also referred to Disinuu and other populous ñuu as *yuhuitayu*.[12] In fact, Ñudzahui writers referred to the most populous political centers in the Mixteca as yuhuitayu and only referred to them as ñuu in the most general sense of the word, as physical settlements divided further into complex subunits. The term *yuhuitayu* is a metaphorical doublet: *yuhui* is "reed mat," and *tayu* is "seat" or "pair" (depending on tonal pronunciation). Tayu is a tone pun or metaphor for both the seat of rulership and the married, ruling couple. A yuhuitayu resulted from the marriage of a male and female lord, each of whom represented the ruling lineage of a respective ñuu. In the abovementioned case of 1573, doña María represented Ñundecu (Achiutla), and don Felipe represented Disinuu (Tlaxiaco). The yuhuitayu resulting from their marriage joined the resources of both ñuu until both rulers died. In his testament, don Felipe referred to the "yuhuitayu of Tlaxiaco and Achiutla" [yuhuitayu dihinuu hiy ñondecu] that his wife would rule upon his death.[13] In turn, when she died, their eldest daughter would inherit his part belonging to Disinuu, as he wished in his last will.

Illustrations in chapters 2 and 6 show how Ñudzahui codices, *lienzos,* and maps from the preconquest and postconquest periods represented the yuhuitayu as a royal couple facing each other, seated together on a reed mat (for examples, see figs. 2.4, 2.5, 2.8, 6.3, 6.4, 6.7, 6.8, 8.4, and 8.8).[14] The prominence of the term *yuhuitayu* in colonial documentation, represented by a metaphor rooted in the reality of local rule and applied to specific places, confirms its indigenous origins.[15] As a metaphorical doublet representing an actual place, the yuhuitayu is comparable to the Nahuatl term for the local ethnic state, *altepetl,* a combining form of *atl,* "water," and *tepetl,* "hill." The symbol of the yuhuitayu represented an institution that joined the resources and rulerships of two ñuu without compromising their autonomy and separateness. The yuhuitayu survived the conquest and persisted throughout the colonial period. In Alvarado's *Vocabulario* the yuhuitayu, or tayu for short, is associated with a number of Spanish terms: "ciudad" is defined as "large tayu" (*tayu cánu*) and *yuyuitayu* [*sic*]; "provincia" is equated with *tayu;* "cabecera del pueblo" is translated as *sacaa tayu,* "where there's a tayu"; the Spanish *assiento,* "site," is defined as tayu; *comunidad* and pueblo are also called "yuvuitayu."[16] The term is used in the earliest postconquest writings, including the religious texts of the 1560s.

The terms *ñuu* and *yuhuitayu* were used consistently in all parts of the Mixteca represented by colonial documentation—the Valley of Oaxaca, the Alta, and the Baja. Hardly a document can be found that does not use one or the other term. But if all yuhuitayu were also considered ñuu, not all ñuu were yuhuitayu. People often distinguished between the two. Don Domingo de Celís, who came from San Pedro Mártir Yucunama to give his testament in San Pedro y San Pablo Yucundaa (Teposcolula), consistently called Yucundaa a yuhuitayu and Yucunama a ñuu.[17] Only ñuu that were represented by a royal couple were also called a yuhuitayu. In general, the term *yuhuitayu* was not used in reference to smaller settlements that lacked a lordly establishment.

Sometimes, the terms *ñuu* and *tayu* were used in conjunction, as when a native lord proclaimed his origin in 1642: "I am called don Gerónimo de Guzmán of my ñuu yuhuitayu of San Bartolomé Coculco" [yuhu naniyu ndo geronimo de gusman ñuuyu yuhuitayu sa baltolomen ñucucu].[18] At times, the two terms were combined as "ñuu tayu" in phrases such as "person from this ñuu tayu of Santo Domingo Yanhuitlan" [chay ñuu chayu Santo Domingo Yodzocahi yaha], a common practice in the Yanhuitlan area.[19] It is unclear whether these terms had a separate meaning or referred to the same types of structures. Judging by context, it seems as if *tayu* is simply an abbreviated version of *yuhuitayu.* Perhaps this range of terms explains the variation in depictions of the couple and reed mat motif in codices, and why the yuhui was depicted more prominently in some pictorial manuscripts than in others. A royal couple seated on a raised platform or ñuu (*tablero*) frieze could represent the ñuu tayu. If the yuhui or reed mat was omitted in some cases, however, the emphasis always remained on the ruling couple. Since chapter 6 focuses on the yuhuitayu, let us consider additional terminology.

Another term that appears in the *Vocabulario* of 1593 under the Spanish words *pueblo*, "town," and *çiudad*, "city," is *yucunduta*, which means "hill" and "water" and is the semantic equivalent of the Nahuatl *altepetl*, a combining form of "water" and "hill."[20] Its appearance in the dictionary suggests convergent Nahua and Ñudzahui sociopolitical structures, or at least terminologies. The term also appears in the documentary record. For example, in 1584, a Spanish decree was translated into Nahuatl and sent by the Spanish *alcalde mayor* in Tonalá to Atoyac.[21] The native alcaldes of Atoyac responded to the decree by writing in Ñudzahui on the back of the paper and returned it to Tonalá. The altepetl of Atoyac (called Yutacano in Ñudzahui), mentioned in the original Nahuatl version, was written as "yucuduta yutacano" in the subsequent Ñudzahui letter. The writer's choice of *yucuduta* over *yuhuitayu* or *ñuu* seems to represent a literal translation of the Nahuatl word. In 1623, the cacique don Miguel de Guzmán used the words *yuhuitayu* and *yucunduta* interchangeably in references to Ñoniy (called Tonalá in Nahuatl).[22] He bequeathed lands and tribute laborers associated with the yucunduta and commoners belonging to an *estancia* of his yuhuitayu.[23] In Tequistepec, don Jorge de la Cruz Alvarado made his testament in 1678 and referred to "the labor duty of the yucunduta of Tequistepec" [chiño yucunduta yucundahi yoho].[24] Despite the clear reference to Tequistepec as a yucunduta, he called it a yuhuitayu throughout most of the text. As a final example, don Gerónimo de Guzmán made an oblique reference in 1642 to *yucunduta* as a general term for places where he had claims to land.[25] But this statement does not preclude the constant references to "my ñuu, the yuhuitayu of San Bartolomé Coculco" [ñuuyu yuhuitayu sa baltolomen ñucucu].

In summary, the term *yucunduta* has been attested in only four Ñudzahui-language documents from the Mixteca Baja region. Records from this subregion of the Mixteca indicate a high degree of cultural contact with Nahuas. Some testaments from the Baja, from places such as Coculco and Tequistepec, use both Nahuatl and Ñudzahui placenames when enumerating local borders and lands.[26] Despite the suggestion of convergent Nahua-Ñudzahui terminology and regional difference by the use of the term *yucunduta* in the Mixteca Baja, the terms *ñuu* and *yuhuitayu* were used throughout the Mixteca, including the Baja and the Valley of Oaxaca.[27]

Subentities of the Ñuu

Each ñuu and yuhuitayu consisted of constituent parts. The terminology for these units differed in three major regions. In the Teposcolula Valley, Tamasulapa, and Tlaxiaco areas, the word for the smallest identifiable unit of corporate organization was *siqui*. In Yanhuitlan and vicinity (including Yucucata), *siña* was the term for the constituent subunit. In the Mixteca Baja (around Huaxuapa and including Coculco, Tequistepec, and Acaquisapa), *dzini* was the operative term. The differences between these three terms, apart from their regional usage, are unclear. They may be somewhat analogous to Nahua terms commonly accepted for the subentity of the altepetl: *calpolli, tlaxilacalli,* and *chinamitl.* Beyond regional usage, distinctions among the three Nahua terms are still unclear.[28] The Nahua annalist Chimalpahin tended to associate tlaxilacalli with subdivisions of an established altepetl, and calpolli with subdivisions of wandering ethnic groups.

Native-language documentation refers to named subdivisions of the ñuu that the Spaniards called barrios. The term *barrio* is defined in the *Vocabulario* simply as "siqui."[29] Other entries reveal additional terms. The Spanish *collacion* (territory or neighborhood) reads "see barrio"; *a cada barrio* (each barrio) is listed as *ee siqui ee siqui* (each siqui) and the Spanish *a cada collacion* (each territory) is listed as *ee siña ee siña, ee dzini ee dzini* (each siña, each dzini).[30] Thus, siqui, siña, and dzini are indirectly equated in the text. Although the *Vocabulario* is most representative of the Teposcolula-area variant of the Ñudzahui language, notes were compiled by many friars who had lived and worked throughout the region. Neither *dzini* nor *siña* has been attested in documents written in Teposcolula. In fact, each of the three terms has not been found in documentation outside its specific area of reference. The term *siña* appears in several other entries of the *Vocabulario.* The entry "vezino del barrio" (resident of a neighborhood) appears as *tai yehe tnaha ñuundi siñandi siquindi,* or "person who belongs to a ñuu, a siña, a siqui."[31] *Siña* is associated with a "a gang or group of people" (*cuadrilla de gente*), which appears as *ee siña ee sichi,* "one siña one section."[32] The "parish" also involves the use of *siña* and *siqui,* defined as "a church for each siña and siqui, each section, each ñuu" [huahi ñuhu ee siña & siqui, ee sichi ee ñuu]. One is reminded of the fact that fray Alonso de Molina, author of the Nahuatl *Vocabulario* (1571) and the Nahuatl *Confesionario* (1569), used the Spanish word *perrochia* (parish) in his model testament where we would expect to find a reference to tlaxilacalli or calpolli, Nahuatl terms for the subunit of the central Mexican altepetl.[33] Interestingly, Alvarado's *Vocabulario* lists the "corte de Papa" (Pope's court) as a "sacred siña" (*siña ñuhu*) and the "King's court" as a "royal siña" (*siña tayu and siña toniñe*).[34]

The precise meanings of *siqui, siña,* and *dzini* are unclear. First, *siqui* appears to signify a corner, a square, or something quartered, perhaps in reference to the four cardinal directions. Alvarado gives *cuadrar,* "to square," as *yoquidzahuahandi siqui,* literally "to make a siqui," and a definition for the Spanish *cuadrada cosa,* "something quartered," is *sacaa siqui,* or "where there is a siqui."[35] If we interpret the initial morpheme *si* as an inalienable possessor, like *-yotl* in Nahuatl, then perhaps *qui* is a reduction of *qhmi,* "four."[36] This interpretation emphasizes the Mesoamerican number of four and resembles an established Nahua pattern of organization based on the numbers two, four, and eight. The term *siña* is somewhat clearer: *ña* is "person" or "people" derived, perhaps, from the word *ñayevui.* Thus, *siña* may be defined as "belonging to people."[37] Finally, *dzini* means "head" and possibly "bunch."[38]

The specific meaning of these three terms aside, their consistent usage in colonial documentation leaves little doubt as to the existence of distinctly defined and named subentities. I interpret the siqui as a corporate group unified by ethnic and kinship ties, common origin, and political and economic relations.[39] Ethnicity was one organizing principle of the siqui, but it was not a thoroughly endogamous kin group.[40] The

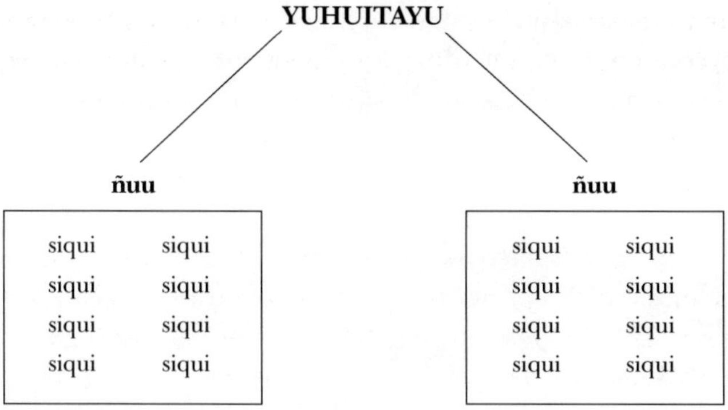

YUHUITAYU

FIGURE 4.1. Hypothetical diagram of yuhuitayu-ñuu-siqui configuration.

fact that entities called siqui, siña, and dzini had indigenous names, like all ñuu, indicates that they were not based on Spanish units. The terms are especially evident in documentation from Tamasulapa, Teposcolula, Yanhuitlan, and Huaxuapa (see fig. 4.1). Like Nahua calpolli and tlaxilacalli, Ñudzahui subunits also had specific names that were usually based on diverse geographical features such as *ytnu* (slope) or *yuta* (river) and one or two more qualifying elements. Many are named after a particular animal or insect (bearing the *ti-* prefix). Whereas so many ñuu and yuhuitayu names begin with *yucu*, "hill," very few of the siqui do.[41]

The following sections illustrate how these terms were used relative to one another in postconquest texts produced by Ñudzahui writers.

Siña of Yodzocahi

The Ñudzahui-language documentary record for Yodzocahi (Yanhuitlan) provides the most information on subdivisions of the ñuu and yuhuitayu. Appropriately, the picture is complex. The term *siña* is ubiquitous in Yodzocahi. Unlike anywhere else (to my knowledge), Ñudzahui-language testaments written in Yanhuitlan customarily included a notation in the upper left-hand corner bearing the testator's name, the name of the siña to which he or she belonged, and the usual reference to the yuhuichayu of Yodzocahi (the *t* of the Teposcolula area was pronounced and written as *ch* in the Yanhuitlan area). Consequently, there are many references to siña affiliation in the sources. Repeated references to the various siña of Yanhuitlan and aberrant spellings make it difficult to discern whether some names are one and the same siña or different entities. The following siña are probably variant spellings of the same entity: Yuyuyucha; Yoyucha; Yuyusha; Yuhuyucha; and Yuuyucha. The same can be said for Yuchayoyo; Yuchayoo; and Yuchayoho. To complicate matters, Yuhuyucha was often called Analco, its Nahuatl equivalent, in translations. More similar-sounding versions of siña featuring a use of the word *yucha*, "river or stream," include Yuchacoyo; Yuchaychi; Yuchandodzo; Yuchaxitu; Yuchacano; Yuchasitu; Yuchasichi; Yuchasihi; Yushacoyoyo. Some of these differences can be attributed to predictable orthographic variations.

Obviously, Yanhuitlan contained many siña that were located or had been located along the Yanhuitlan River and its tributaries, since these names are presumably as old as the groupings themselves. Indeed, an archaeological survey of this area performed by Ronald Spores revealed a number of settlement clusters for the postclassic period (Natividad phase, ca. A.D. 1000–1520) that were located by the course of the main river and within the river valleys.[42] A map of this survey shows approximately ten settlements located along a river, perhaps corresponding to the nine or ten separate yucha-based siña mentioned above. Data from hundreds of documents reveal as many as twelve to sixteen siña of Yanhuitlan containing the word *yucha*. In addition, four so-called estancias included yucha in their title (see map 3).

In a dispute between Yanhuitlan and Tecomatlan that generated hundreds of pages of testimony, Yanhuitlan was said to consist of twenty-three "barrios" and twenty-six "estancias" in 1584.[43] The proceedings imposed Spanish categories on the indigenous units. In separate documentation from 1580, fourteen barrios were listed as serving the cacique don Gabriel de Guzmán.[44] Of the fourteen barrios from 1580, six (possibly seven) do not appear in the list of barrios of 1584. And of the twenty-four barrios from 1584, fifteen (possibly sixteen) do not appear in the list of 1580. Among those that are not included in the *cacicazgo* is the siña of Ayusi—a prominent siña of the colonial period. Several estancias are also listed in the report of 1584 that do not appear in the list of 1580. Based on these two documents, then, Yanhuitlan contained at least thirty and possibly as many as thirty-two siña in the 1580s. They are listed as follows, in alphabetical order: Atucu; Ayuxi; Chiyoniñe; Danacodzo; Dzaynu (Dayno); Itnuñute; Ñondoco; Nunaui; Nusaa; Ñuyahui; Sahayuqhu; Ticuaa; Tindee; Tindua; Tinducha; Tinduchi; Tiquihui; Titee; Tiyusi; Yodzoconuu; Yoyucha; Yuchacano; Yuchachaco; Yuchacoyo; Yuchandodzo; Yuchasitu; Yuchaychi; Yuchayocoo; Yuqhcava; Yuyayy. Potential alternate spellings are placed in parentheses in table 4.1.

However, there are additional references to siña of Yanhuitlan in the record that are not included in the two lists of the 1580s. A systematic survey of Ñudzahui-language documents from 1575 to 1783, including the 1580s data, reveals that Yanhuitlan consisted of at least thirty-nine discernible siña and as many as forty-six if seven can be interpreted as not already represented in the original thirty-nine (see table 4.1). None of these siña or barrio names correspond to any of the estancia names listed in the 1580s, so it is not the mistaking of estancias for siña that accounts for the increase in the overall number of siña names. The estancias listed in the 1580s include Ama; Anañe (Anane); Andua; Anduto; Atat; Ayna; Chinduhua (Chindua); Chiu; Donuuno; Duxa; Nunaa; Ñutuui; Sachio; Suchitepeque; Teaxila; Teyo; Tia; Tiaco; Tiyaha; Tiyuqh (Tiuquo); Tnuñuu; Xiñoo; Yocuntatne; Yodzoñuhu; Yoquoqui; Ytuyua; Yuchandeye (Yuchandei); Yuchanicana; Yuchañunda; Yuchañunduu; and Yucucata (Yucuncata).[45]

The data leave many questions unresolved. It is unknown whether all of these numerous entities were siña, whether some siña were organized into larger ñuu, or exactly how they were related to this complex yuhuitayu.[46] It is also unknown whether the reports of the 1580s omitted some siña from the count, or if some of the units had divided into additional entities. The references currently available are too scattered in time to draw any firm conclusions. There may have been even more subentities in the preconquest period, considering the effects of depopulation by the 1570s, the period

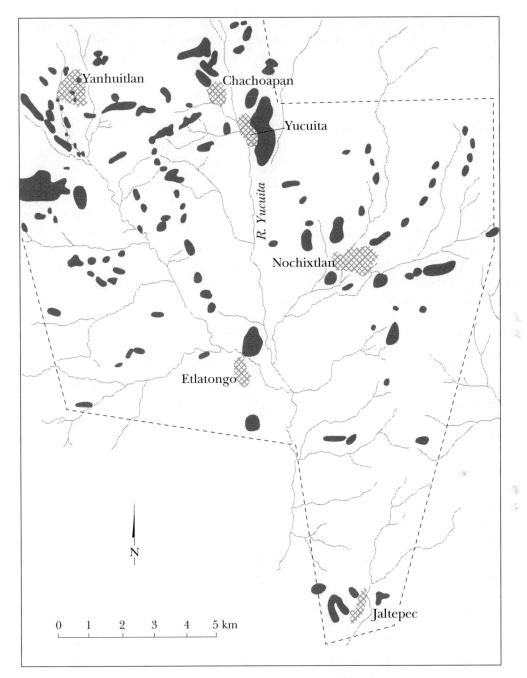

MAP 3. Postclassic settlement pattern of Nochixtlan Valley. Based on Spores 1983d, 246. Shaded areas indicate occupied sites during this period (c. 1000–1520 A.D.); grids mark the approximate sites of colonial town centers.

TABLE 4.1
Siña of Yanhuitlan in the Documentary Record (1575–1783)

Atucu (Atocho)	Tiquehui (Tiqueui, Tiquihui)
Ayuçi (Ayusi, Ayuxi, also called Ziquitongo)	Titee
Chaini	Tiyusi (Tiuxi, Tiusi)
Chiyoniñe (Chioneni)	Yayadza
Danacodzo	Yodzoconuu (Yodoconuu)
Dicoo	Yoyucha [?] (Yuchayoo)
Dzanaha (Danaa, Danaha, Dzanaa)	Yuchacano
Dzaynu (Dzaino, Dayno)	Yuchachaco
Dzoconuu	Yuchacoyo
Itnuñute	Yuchandodzo
Ñondoco	Yuchasichi
Ñucaa	Yuchasihi
Nunaui [?] (Ñuyahui)	Yuchasitu (Yuchaxitu)
Nusaa (Ñusa)	Yuchaychi
Nuyachee	Yuchayocoo
Ñuyahui	Yuchayoho (Yuchayoo)
Sahayuqhu (Sayu, Sayuqu, Çaayugu)	Yuchayoyo [?] (Yuchayoho)
Tiaso	Yuchayuchi
Ticoho (Ticoo)	Yuhuyucha (Yuuyucha, Yuyusha, also called Analco)
Ticuaa (Tiquaa, Tigua)	Yuqhcava
Tindehe (Tindee)	Yushacohoyo [?] (Yuchayocoo)
Tindoo [?] (Tindua)	Yuyayy
Tinducha [?] (Tinduchi)	Yuyuyucha [?] (Yuhuyucha)

NOTE: Variant spellings are noted in parentheses. Repeating references are omitted if already obviously represented on the list. Those that may or may not represent alternate spellings of names already listed are followed by [?] and their possible equivalent in parentheses.

when the data begin. It is also possible that people had different names for the same siña. One thing is certain: the fact that Yanhuitlan contained about forty siña in the sixteenth century demonstrates a more complex and dispersed settlement pattern than the postconquest scenario suggests. Many siña did not disappear after the conquest, despite the major epidemics of the sixteenth century. As late as 1783, at least eight siña were still intact: Ticoho; Yuyusha; Ayushi; Sahayuqhu; Danaha; Tindehe; Yushacohoyo; and Yuchayoho.[47] And yet, one is left wondering what happened to the others: did some siña simply disappear from the record, or were they eventually ignored, or did they become untenable after population loss and combine to create larger entities, or did some assert themselves as independent ñuu? In reality, it is likely that all four possibilities occurred at some point during the colonial period.

Expressions of siña affiliation abound in documentation from the Yanhuitlan area. In 1598, a petition was brought before the *cabildo* by two siña of the "yuhuichayu" of Yodzocahi—Chaini and Yayadza—against the nobles of the siña of Yuyuyucha (called Analco in the Spanish-language section of the document), who were accused of having five *saquiñehe* (*tequitlatos*, or "tribute overseers") when they traditionally only had four.[48] The governor, don Francisco de Guzmán, and alcaldes presided over this dispute in the *huahi tniño*, or the "duty house," in reference to the municipal council meeting place. The five tax collectors in question—Esteban García, Andrés Sichi, Juan Sacussi, Juan Siyo, and Juan Dzayo—claimed that their accusers were from another siña and were motivated only by traditional rivalries and resentments. It is possible that Yuhuyucha, or Analco, was a Nahua barrio, given the popularity of that name among Nahua immigrants in their new settlements, and that perhaps ethnic rivalry was behind the inter-siña animosity. With four tribute collectors in 1598, Yuhuyucha must have been a sizable siña. Some evidence suggests that siña acted as corporate landholding units.[49] In 1681, six nobles of the siña of Ayusi filed a petition against the *yya toniñe* (cacique) of Mascaltepec, don Domingo de San Pablo y Alvarado, and against another siña Yuhuyucha (Analco) for encroaching upon the lands that belonged to their siña. They complained: "The natives of the siña of Yuhuyucha have entered the lands which belong to us, the people of the siña of Ayusi, in order to cultivate them; they have always belonged to our ancestors and are still today lands of the siña of Ayusi. Thus, they belong to all who pay tribute to the siña of Ayusi and perform the labor duty [*tniño*] of the ñuu tayu" [Chay nicacu siña yuhuyucha saha niyehui huidzana cha yosinicha ñuhu chay siña ayusi si sa naha saya tasitaa si dzehe taca ñadzaña chay yyo huitna tucu ñuhu njacu ytu siña ayusi yca yocuvui sasi may taca chay yocuvui tributario siña ayusi sihi yoquidza tniño ñuu chayu].[50] The "lands of Ayusi called Yuhuicani" [ytu ayusi sanani yuhuicani] were repeatedly referred to as "land of our fathers and mothers" [simayndo ytu taa dzehendo], namely, our ancestors. The nobles of Yuhuyucha called themselves "we the people who were born in the siña of Yuhuyucha" [ñadzaña chay nicacu siña yuhuyucha]. The case was dropped when the cacique of Mascaltepec, who also served as governor of Yanhuitlan, furnished proof that it was part of his patrimony. The representatives of Ayusi were forced to acknowledge that certain lands and commoners (*dzaya dzana*) of the siña of Ayusi belonged to don Diego the cacique (yya toniñe). As we shall see in chapter 7, the crucial question was whether the land was controlled by a lord or the siña; in this case, the siña of Ayusi was forced to recognize the patrimonial right of a cacique. In the 1540s, Mascaltepec was called an estancia of Yanhuitlan and tried to gain autonomy from the cabecera as early as 1552.[51] The fact that the cacique of a sujeto had risen to become governor of the cabecera indicates the complexity of social and political organization within the simplified cabecera-sujeto scheme. The cacique of Yanhuitlan in the 1680s, don Francisco Pimentel y Guzmán, was also resident cacique and governor of Teposcolula, explaining in part how a cacique from Mascaltepec came to be governor in Yanhuitlan. The fact that nearly all Yanhuitlan's multiple sujetos had caciques with very prestigious names and titles in 1587, discussed below, suggests the high social status of lords in some of these so-called sujetos.

Another case involving Ayusi illustrates the nature of siña organization. In 1711, the electors of Ayusi chose a *mayordomo* (municipal official assigned with a specific secular or ecclesiastical task) and presented him before the officials of the yuhuitayu of Yodzocahi: "Domingo Juan will swear the oath as mayordomo of the barrio of Xiquitongo, the ñuu siña of Ayusi, by the law of our lord King, it is done [before] all of us officials of the tayu of Santo Domingo Yanhuitlan" [Juramento si domingo juan saha cocuhuicha mayodomo barrio xiquitogo ñuu siña ayusi saha dzaha costohondo Rei yocuhui tacanju justicias chayu santo domingo yodzocahi].[52] Shortly thereafter, Felipe Ortiz, a *regidor* (municipal council member) of both Yanhuitlan and the siña of Ayusi,

appeared with thirteen other nobles of Ayusi before the Spanish alcalde mayor to
present a petition occasioned by the sudden death of Domingo Juan. They explained
how Ayusi kept an image of Christ that was brought out each year for the Holy Week
procession, "just like the other barrios that constituted the pueblo of Yanhuitlan."
They recounted how they customarily chose from among their group, the nobles of
the barrio, a mayordomo in charge of the offerings and goods for the dressing and
procession of the sacred image. A procession and feast were organized for each day
according to the ordering of the various siña. This testimony suggests that siña organization in Yanhuitlan extended to political and religious matters. In Ayusi a large body
of nobles reserved the right to elect their own officials, one who was also a regidor of
the larger yuhuitayu, and the right to hold their own religious ceremonies with their
own images. Even these ceremonies were subject to some larger organizational, perhaps rotational, scheme in which Ayusi naturally claimed to be the first and foremost
siña. Judging by the prominence of Ayusi in the record, their claim may have been
valid.

   The siña was central to an individual's or a household's identity. In 1699, Juan
Domingo appeared before the alcalde mayor and summarized his affiliations in the
following terms: "Juan Domingo, a Ñudzahui person from this ñuu tayu of Yodzocahi,
a tributary of our Lord King, in the barrio siña of Ticoho" [juan domingo chay ñudzahui ñuu chayu yodzocahi yaha tributario costohondo Rey barrio siña ticoho].[53] In one
concise phrase, Juan referred to his ethnic identity, his subject status, his yuhuitayu,
and finally his siña. The last constitutes the most specific category of identification
beyond the level of the household.

   Finally, even a Nahuatl-language testament of 1595 from the Yanhuitlan area,
from Santiago Istepec, makes a reference to the siña.[54] Martín Cortés alternately called
his ñuu of Istepec "nochinamil yeztepel" [my chinamitl of Iztepec] and "noycha yetztepel" [my residence of Iztepec], using the Nahuatl terms *chinamitl* (literally "fence" but
often the rough equivalent of calpolli in the southern Nahua-speaking region) and
chantli (home, dwelling place); the term *altepetl* is not used.[55] Most interestingly, the
writer called his subdivision of Istepec "siña titnee" (the siña of Titnee), subsequently
translated as "barrio de tinee." Even though the testament was written in Nahuatl, the
writer used the Ñudzahui term for "barrio" instead of its Nahuatl equivalent, *tlaxilacalli*.
The use of *siña* for a subunit of the chinamitl of Istepec is curious, when *chinamitl* is
usually reserved for a barrio in Nahuatl.[56] Martín Cortés's barrio Titnee may be included
in the list of barrios compiled for Yanhuitlan, which includes Tindehe, Tindee, and
Titee. If this is the case, Istepec itself was considered a chinamitl of Yanhuitlan and
consisted of subunits that were called siña. Such possibilities are discussed below.

Siqui of Yucundaa and Tiquehui

The term *siqui* was a common designation for the subunit of the ñuu in Yucundaa
(called Teposcolula by Spaniards). The multiple siqui of Yucundaa include Dzumañuu,
Dzitinama, Ñuniñe, Ticuhu, Dziqui Tiyeye, Saha Tiyeye, Yaaçahi, and Dzayata.[57] It appears as if the two Tiyeye represented an upper and lower type of organization of the
type common in central Mexico—*dziqui* means "head" and by normal extension "top"

or "upper," and *saha* means "foot" or "below."[58] The name Ñuniñe is the same for Tonalá and was used in reference to the Mixteca Baja in general, so this siqui might represent an ethnic grouping. Such ethnic barrios were apparently common; according to Reyes, Teposcolula had been populated by lords of Tilantongo, who established barrios of people there.[59]

Scattered references to siqui are found in different types of native-language records. In 1623, Lucía de la Anunciación of San Pedro and San Pablo Teposcolula introduced herself as "here in my ñuu, the siqui of Ñuniñe" [yaha ñuundi siqui ñuniñe]. Petronilla de la Cruz hailed from "San Pedro and San Pablo, here in my ñuu, the siqui of Ticuhu" [san pedro san bablo yaha ñuundi siqui ticuhu].[60] In 1672 don Gerónimo García y Guzmán came from "the siqui Yaasahi of this yuhuitayu of San Pedro and San Pablo Teposcolula" [siqui yaaçahi yaha yuhuitayu san pedro san pablo yucundaa]. When his widowed wife, the cacica doña Lázara de Guzmán, made her testament nineteen years later, she stated that she was also from the "siqui barrio Yaasahi" [siqui bario yaasayhe], conflating the native and Spanish terms.[61] The richest and most complex source for references to the siqui is a collection of Ñudzahui-language baptismal registers from Teposcolula, beginning in 1646.[62] The siqui of each baptized child was recorded in the margin of the book. I counted more than twenty siqui for Teposcolula, which is called the "ñuu yuhuitayu San Pedro y San Pablo Yucundaa." Three siqui—Dzumañuu, Yaaçahi, and Ticuhu—have been observed in other sources and were especially prominent in the baptismal register. One of the siqui was called "Yucundaa," the same name given to the larger ñuu. During the same period, births were recorded for the ñuu of San Juan Teposcolula, a sujeto of the cabecera, which contained at least eight distinct siqui.[63] References to siqui in the Teposcolula area continued until at least the first half of the eighteenth century.[64]

Siqui also appears as a term for subentities in Tiquehui, called Tamasulapa by Spaniards. An inspection of documents from the years 1585 until 1726 has revealed fourteen siqui, named: Nduhua; Yuhuitandiqui; Chiyo; Miniqui; Yayanino; Ytandique; Tiyahua; Ñundee; Nduvuadzuma; Tisica; Ñundecu; Ñuhuico; Tnundoco; and Ytnunama.[65] A typical reference to siqui in Tamasulapa is the sort Luis de Mora made in 1679, when he began his testament: "I am called Luis de Mora, from this siqui Tiyahua, of this yuhuitayu Santa María Natividad Tamasulapa" [nduhu nani luis de mora yaha siquindi tiyahua yaha yuhuitayu santa maria ñatihuita tiquihui].[66] In 1608, Diego Siquaha came from "this siqui Yuhuitandiqui of this yuhuitayu Santa María Tamasulapa" [yaha siqui yuhuitandiqui yaha yuhuitayu santa maria tiquivi yaha].[67] Similarly, in 1665, a woman proclaimed: "I am the woman named Inés Juárez from my siqui Ytandiqui of my ñuu the yuhuitayu of Santa María de la Natividad Tamasulapa [nduhu ñaha nani ynes xuares yaha siquindi ytandiqui yaha ñuundi yuhuitayu santa maria nativita ñuu tiquihui].[68] The term *siqui* is used more than twenty times in a lengthy testament of 1687, referring to nine distinct subunits while describing the extended boundaries of scattered lands.[69] One siqui mentioned repeatedly in the document was called Tiahua, a name shared with a hill in the ñuu; Juan Castilla owned a "field named Quindaha at the foot of the hill Tiahua" [ytu nani quindaha saha yucu tiahua]. This reference suggests that one of these subdivisions was apparently named after a local toponym (or vice versa), a prominent hill that was considered part of the ñuu territory. This document shows that by 1687, *barrio* and *siqui* could be used inter-changeably and were considered synonymous terms, since more than one siqui is also called a barrio in the course of the document.

Dzini of the Ñuuniñe

The third term for a subunit of the ñuu or yuhuitayu, *dzini*, was found exclusively in Ñudzahui-language writings from the Mixteca Baja, called Ñuuniñe in the Ñudzahui language. In and around Huaxuapa, the *alcaldía mayor* (the jurisdiction or office of an alcalde mayor) of most of the Mixteca Baja, the term *dzini* was used in reference to subentities of yuhuitayu. The term has been attested in documentation from Huaxuapa (Ñuudzay), Coculco (Ñucucu), Tequistepec (Yucundahi), and Acaquisapa. The extant Ñudzahui-language documentation from the Baja is not sufficiently extensive in any one place to compile lists of dzini names. Nevertheless, basic patterns emerge by ana-lyzing sources from various yuhuitayu.

In 1611, doña Juana Beatriz, cacica of Acaquisapa and other places, associated dzini with her royal patrimony. She stated in her testament: "I declare concerning the lands, dzini, and commoners which belong to me—I bequeath everything to my son don Juan Agustín" [yodasitnonitucuyu saha ytu ndayu dzini tuta sihi ñadehi siyu niy-cutu yonacuhuayu dzayayu do juan acosti].[70] In her testament of 1633, doña María de Velasco of Coculco (Ñucucu) introduced herself thus: "I, doña María de Velasco, of my ñuu yuhuitayu San Bartolomé Coculco here in this yuhuitayu San Pedro and San Pablo [Tequistepec]" [yuhu ndoña maria nde velasco ñuuyu yuhuitayu sa patolome ñocucu yoho yuhuitayu san pedro san pablo]. After paying tribute to the saints and images of the church, she proceeded to earthly matters and referred to eight dzini of Coculco:

> I declare concerning my yuhuitayu San Bartolomé Ñoñaña Yucuihi Ñocucu, all my palaces in the yuhuitayu, all the lands and hill lands of the tayu, and all the dzini to which all the lords and elders belonged: one dzini is Noyahui Ñocucu; the second dzini [contains the border] Sahayoo; the third dzini is Yucuñoma [which was a part of the] dzini named Duta; the fourth dzini is Ñodzami; the fifth dzini is Dzoco Dzahui, which borders Yuhuitiyoco at the field guarded by Inés San[tiago]; the sixth dzini is Ytnotaa; the seventh dzini is Yucuñoyuu; the eighth dzini is Saha Yucutandiqui [which was two parts]. It was passed on to me by all my ancestors, all my grandfathers and grandmothers. Now, if God should wish that I die, all the dzini and lands of the tayu, the hill lands and the patrimonial lands with all the commoners of mine . . . I give to my child don Raimundo de Santiago.

> Yotasitnonitucuyu saha yuhuitayu siyu sa poltolome ñoñana yucuyhy ñocucu niy cutu yuhuitayu siyu aniy siy niy cutu ñoho tayu yucu ytu siyu niy cutu dzini dza tnaha nisiyo taca yya nisano–i dzini noyahui ñocucu nicuhui uhui [ ]ninodzaño sahayoo nicuhui uni dzini yucuñoma tandisi si dzaa ca[a] dzini nduta nicuhui qhmi dzini ñodzami nicuhui hoho dzini[ ]dzoco dzahui nisatnaha yuhuitiyoco siña caa ytu ninatasi ynes san[ ] nicuhui yño dzini ytnotaa nicuhui usa dzini yucuñoyuu nic[uhui] una dzini saha yucutandiqui uhui ca ta sadota ta nisiyo nicutu dzoho[ ]yu taca sihy sitnayu sañaha ta huichi nicuhui yni ndios nindiy to[ ]ninaata ndiy ndzoho dzini ñoho tayu yucu ytu chiyu dzaa dzito ndzin[i] ñandey ñatahui siyu ndiy ndzoho yonacuhuayu ndzayayu ndo r[emu]ndu de sandiago.[71]

The eight dzini appear to have been part of the lord's patrimony, with lands and dependent laborers attached. The first dzini was named after the yuhuitayu Ñocucu; one wonders what the specific relation is between this first named dzini and its parent tayu. It is unclear whether the yuhuitayu of San Bartolomé Ñoñaña Yucuihi Ñocucu consists of three separate yuhuitayu or three parts of the same, or merely one entity with three names. Nevertheless, doña María does specifically refer to eight dzini, a pattern based on multiples of four seen elsewhere in the Baja.

Another document from the Mixteca Baja refers specifically to dzini as parts of a yuhuitayu. The hereditary ruler don Juan Agustín began his testament in 1642: "I, don Juan Agustín, of my pueblo yuhuitayu San Juan Bautista Ynicuaa [Cosoltepec] and this yuhuitayu of Santa María Asunción Yucuyuta [Yquisapa] and all the dzini and the tayu of San Joseph Ytnunyuudoo and a dzini of the yuhuitayu of San Francisco Yuhuhuitu [Huepanapa] called Cahuadzadaha and all the many dzini that our lord God has granted me" [Yuhu naniyu do juan agusti ñuuyu yuhuitayu san juan baptista ynicuaa sihy yucudzoco sihy yoho yuhuitayu santa maria assopcio yucuyuta sihy niy cutu dzini sihy tayu san joseph ytnunyuudoo sihi i dzini yuhuitayu san francisco yuhuhuitu nani cahua dza daha niy cutu hui dzini si nidahuiñaha stohodo dios].[72] Here the phrase "all the dzini and the tayu" [niy cutu dzini sihy tayu] seems to suggest that these units were separate entities. The fact that he claimed one dzini in another yuhuitayu (named Cahuadzadaha) also suggests that some of these units were tied to specific royal lineages and inherited as if they were separate entities with laborers attached. Perhaps the tayu or *aniñe*, "palace," was based in one of these dzini.

A legal case from Tecomaxtlahuaca generated a stack of paperwork illustrating the internal organization of this yuhuitayu.[73] In 1578, the cacique don Francisco de Arellano explained that Tecomaxtlahuaca was a polity divided into four parts: Tecomaxtlahuaca la vieja; Tlahixtlahuacan; Yoçochiyo; and Chapolixtlahuacan. The lord's *terrazgueros* (Spanish term for dependent laborers in the personal service of a native lord) are subsequently listed according to the four barrios: Tecomaxtlahuaca la vieja; Tlauyxtlahuacan; Yoçochio; and Yoçondica. The last of the four in each listing appears to be a Nahuatl and Ñudzahui version of the same entity, since both can be defined as "grasshopper plain."[74] All four probably had recognized Ñudzahui names; documents translated into Spanish in the sixteenth century typically reflected the presence of Nahuatl-speaking translators. The four-part arrangement of barrios is comparable to Nahua altepetl organization, which often involves division into four constituent entities. Several ñuu seem to have been divided into four or eight parts, including Coculco, Coixtlahuaca, and Achiutla; others, such as Tlaxiaco, Texupa, Nochixtlan, and Sayultepec, had five or six.[75] Also comparable to central Mexico, the name of the larger unit is based on the first division and is perhaps the origin of the ruling line and thus was called "la vieja."[76] I suspect these entities were called either dzini or ñuu in the Ñudzahui language.

Finally, one document from the Mixteca Baja refers to the dzini as a political entity. In 1674, Huaxuapa's elections assembled the officials who called themselves "we the lords, nobles, and people from the dzini, the elders of this yuhuitayu of Huaxuapa and all its jurisdiction of tribute ñuu and cabeceras: Yucundayy; Tnohuitu; Ayuu; Daaduhua; Yucuytayno; Ñoñaña; Ñuchihi; Yuhuacuchi; Ñunya; Ñuhuiyo; Ytanoni;

Dzomayodzo" [duhu yya toho taa dzini taa nisano yuhuitayu ñudzey yoho sihi nee cutu jurisdiccion daha ñoo cabesera – yucundayy – tnohuitu – ayuu – daaduhua – yucuytayno – ñoñaña – ñuchihi – yuhuacuchi – ñunya – ñuhuiyo – ytanoni – dzomayodzo].[77]

The reference to "people from the dzini" after lords and nobles seems to represent the third position in the customary listing of social groups, ordinarily reserved for a term designating "commoners" (*ñadey* in the Baja) and sometimes followed by a reference to elders. This statement identifies commoners with the dzini, associating social groups with particular structures. If lords were associated with leadership at the level of the yuhuitayu and the ñuu, the dzini was the domain of the commoner. In other words, structures were created by the organization of social relations. This conception of the dzini brings to mind the potential literal meaning of *siña*—"belonging to people."

Ñudzahui writers used the Spanish term *barrio* in reference to subunits of the ñuu as early as 1579, but the word does not appear consistently in the written record until the eighteenth century.[78] In some of the examples listed above, the term was paired with siqui, siña and dzini for the sake of clarity. The usage of the loanword *barrio* in native-language texts, often in conjunction with the native equivalent, suggests that the two terms overlapped to some degree in meaning or that the native concept was extended in meaning to include the new concept. In contrast, sociopolitical terms such as *ñuu* and *yuhuitayu* were never abandoned in the colonial period, nor were the Spanish terms *pueblo* or *ciudad* ever adopted in native-language writings.[79] The eventual use of *barrio* would seem to represent a departure from the pattern of borrowing Spanish terms only when there was no native equivalent. Perhaps the fluid and dynamic structure of the entities invited overlap and borrowing.

Convergent Terminology

The relationship between ñuu and smaller subunits may have been flexible and ambiguous. Phrases that combine references to the ñuu and the siña, siqui, or dzini were not uncommon. Even Alvarado's *Vocabulario* includes a few ambiguous equivalences. In response to the everyday query "which pueblo are you from?" the given phrases are *na ñuu yehe tnahando,* "to which ñuu do you belong?" and *na siña yehe tnahando,* "to which siña do you belong?"[80] And again, "resident of a barrio" is listed as "person who belongs to a ñuu, a siña, a siqui" [tai yehe tnaha ñuundi siñandi, siquindi].[81] These examples might be considered as unrepresentative entries in the *Vocabulario* if mundane documentation did not contain similar usage. Several writers used the words *ñuu* and *siqui* in conjunction, comparable to the frequent pairing of *ñuu* and *tayu* discussed above. In effect, each siqui was a potential ñuu and each ñuu a potential yuhuitayu, a possibility accounting for the ambivalence of intermediary terms such as *ñuu siqui.*

Let us turn to a few examples in the written record. Inés Rodríguez and Ana Jacinta of Yanhuitlan referred to a ñuu siña when they appeared before the Audiencia in 1674 to present the "testament of our deceased mother María Méndez, from the ñuu siña Yuchayoyo" [testamento ndeye ñu María Mente codzehende ñaha ñuu siña yuchayoyo].[82] The most famous ñuu siña associated with Yanhuitlan was named Ayusi. Located well within Yanhuitlan's sphere of influence, Ayusi was a prominent site that defied subordinate subunit status by its repeated appearances in the documentary record. Ayusi was customarily referred to as a ñuu siña. Residents of Ayusi filed a petition in 1681, calling themselves "we the commoners of the ñuu siña Ayusi" [ñadzaña ñanjahi ñuu siña ayusi].[83] In 1711, the election of an official in Ayusi described the new member as "mayordomo of the barrio of Xiquitongo, the ñuu siña of Ayusi" [mayodomo barrio xiquitogo ñuu siña ayusi].[84] In Teposcolula, Lucía Hernández made her last will and testament in 1633 and introduced herself thus: "I, the woman named Lucía Hernández 5-Alligator, of this ñuu siqui Dzumañuu, my ñuu siqui" [nduhu ñaha nani lucia hernandez ñuquihui yaha ñuu siqui dzumañuu ñuu siquindi]. In closing, she reiterated her affiliation with the "ñuu siqui Dzumañuu attached to this yuhuitayu San Pedro and San Pablo" [ñuu siqui dzumañuu yehe ndahui tnahandi yaha yuhuiytayu san pedro y san pablo].[85]

Spanish-language translations of Ñudzahui-language documents often obscure matters. Consider the language of a testament in 1621 that began: "I, the person named Domingo Siyo, here in my siqui Chiyo, in this yuhuitayu of mine [called] Santa María Tamasulapa" [nduhu tay nani ndgo siyo yaha siquindi chiyo yaha yuviteyundi sacta maria tiqui yaha]. This one line was translated in 1779 as "I am called Diego de la Cruz and I am a native in this, my pueblo of Santa María Natividad Tamasulapa" [yo que me llamo Diego de la Cruz y soi natibo en este mi pueblo de Santa María Natividad Thamasulapa].[86] Thus, the translator edited the original by changing his baptismal name from Domingo to Diego, inserting a Spanish surname (de la Cruz) in place of a native calendrical name (Siyo), omitting any reference to his siqui named Chiyo, reducing yuhuitayu to "pueblo," and calling Tiquihui by its Nahuatl-Spanish name (Tamasulapa). One small line contains five alterations. Sometimes these omissions or mistakes reveal a failure to recognize native categories, which is a significant fact in itself. In 1741, Juan Joseph Carrillo translated a collection of documents ranging in date from 1648 to 1687 and consistently failed to acknowledge the siqui names in the translation; rather, he attached the name of the siqui to the person as if it were a second surname. In 1687, the words *barrio* and *siqui* were used interchangeably, but he never translated the latter as "barrio," even when the two were clearly synonymous.[87] Could it be that the *ladino* Juan Joseph Carrillo was out of step with the older Ñudzahui terminology? This possibility is especially apparent when reading eighteenth-century translations of sixteenth-century records, which are characteristically half the size of the original Ñudzahui writing and frequently rely on formulaic statements of the later period that misrepresent the language of the original documents.

Postconquest Reorganization

This chapter has identified the observable structures of Ñudzahui sociopolitical organization as they appear in early colonial Ñudzahui-language alphabetic and pictorial writings. Each of the entities has its origins in the preconquest period. Since the language was not transformed in the early colonial period, people continued to refer to named sociopolitical institutions and cultural categories in their own terms. After the conquest, Ñudzahui structures were reorganized to accommodate colonial demands, but they were not altered beyond recognition. Native principles continued to organize structures, despite the degree to which Spanish perceptions reconstituted the inter-relation of various units and subunits. Let us consider the many dimensions of this reconstitution, beginning with the institutionalization of colonial jurisdictions.

The first colonial jurisdiction established in the sixteenth century, the *encomienda*, was based on native sociopolitical units. The encomienda was a grant issued to a Spaniard that entitled him to receive labor and tribute from a specified native socio-political unit, represented by one or more caciques, or native rulers. As elsewhere in New Spain, the encomienda was assigned on the basis of preexisting indigenous entities and, in the Mixteca, combinations of sociopolitical units. Thus the Ñudzahui encom-ienda was based on at least one yuhuitayu and multiple ñuu and siqui. Encomiendas were assigned as soon as the Mixteca was controlled and surveyed. Hernando Cortés handed out grants during the 1520s, and his cousin Francisco de las Casas received Yanhuitlan and several surrounding sites; it was revoked in 1529 and placed under crown jurisdiction, but he regained title in 1537, and his heirs controlled it until 1622.[88] Other encomiendas ranged from the nine cabeceras given to don Francisco Maldonado, to the grant of Atoyaquillo to a Greek conquistador named Juan Griego. Many of the major encomiendas became *corregimientos* (jurisdictions under royal authority) within a few decades. Several epidemics of the sixteenth century made the encomienda impractical in many areas by 1600. A wave of epidemics in the 1540s and another in the 1570s may have halved the population each time.[89] The encomienda was based on existing ñuu and relied on its authorities and mechanisms of labor and tribute for its support. Characteristic of a region with a relatively weak Spanish presence and a large number of small units, the encomienda was based on multiple units and, as an institution, lasted longer than it did in central Mexico.

Likewise, *doctrinas,* or indigenous parishes, were based on existing ñuu. There were more encomiendas than parishes in the Mixteca. Whereas *encomenderos* relied entirely on native mechanisms for the payment of tribute and did not need to reside in the area of their encomiendas, parishes required the presence of priests. In the sixteenth century, a single friar was responsible for administering the doctrine in many churches representing multiple ñuu. One priest was responsible for churches in fourteen sepa-rate ñuu in the area of Teozacualco at the time of the *Relaciones geográficas* of 1580.[90] There were twenty-one parishes in the Mixteca by 1600 (twelve *conventos* before 1560, most of them in the Alta), compared with twenty-nine encomiendas in the Mixteca Alta alone.[91] Spaniards attempted to retain and in some cases create the largest viable indigenous units, but competition and pressures worked against such a strategy in central Mexico. In central Mexico, large altepetl were divided according to their inter-nal structure, and several were so large that they were never put into encomiendas, or rapidly fell under direct crown jurisdiction. In the Mixteca, larger units were often cre-ated by combining several yuhuitayu that were located in the same area. Tribute and labor for the encomienda were channeled through the recognized hereditary rulers or caciques of those areas.

Political jurisdictions generally followed the outline of churches and encomiendas, based on the location of prominent yuhuitayu in larger valleys. Teposcolula (Yucundaa) and Yanhuitlan (Yodzocahi), and later Nochixtlan (Atoco), became dominant centers of colonial activity by the mid-sixteenth century; Huaxuapa (Ñudzahi) and Tonalá

(Ñuniñe) were the major centers of the Mixteca Baja, and Cuilapa (Yutaticaha) predominated in the Valley of Oaxaca. Places along the southern trunk line—the highway that connected Mexico City and Puebla with Oaxaca City and Guatemala—such
as Tamasulapa (Tiquevui) and Texupa (Ñundaa) were rapidly drawn into the Spanish
orbit of activity. Other clusters of Spanish administrative and ecclesiastical activity
formed around sites that had been garrisons of the Triple Alliance led by Tenochtitlan,
such as Tlaxiaco (Disinuu) and Coixtlahuaca (Yodzocoo), as well as fairly densely populated areas around Juxtlahuaca and Achiutla (Ñundecu). Teposcolula became the
first alcaldía mayor in 1531.[92] By 1552, it had jurisdiction over eighteen major crown
and encomienda communities.[93] Two years later, the alcaldía mayor of Tonaltepec-
Sayultepec was absorbed into that of Yanhuitlan, with a jurisdiction comprising
Yanhuitlan and its numerous subject settlements, including Nochixtlan; Chachoapa;
Etlatongo; Tiltepec; Xaltepec; Coixtlahuaca; Chicahua; Iztactepec; Guautla; Tecçistepec; Xaltepetongo; Xocotipac; and Tecomatlan. For still unknown reasons, Yanhuitlan
lost its separate status as an alcaldía mayor and was "aggregated" to Teposcolula
around 1595. Separate judicial and notarial registries were kept in Yanhuitlan, but
records were stored in the archive of Teposcolula. Criminal and civil cases were heard
in Yanhuitlan and Teposcolula, and jails and offices of the crown were maintained in
both places. Similar arrangements existed in other centers by the second half of the
sixteenth century.

Physical Resettlement

When the Spaniards arrived in the Mixteca, they envisioned a mountainous landscape
of dominant centers, or cabeceras, with nearby barrios and more dispersed estancias
or sujetos. They intended to create more manageable units by collapsing some of the
outlying units upon the center, moving settlements from hilltops and slopes down to
level valleys and plains, and re-creating the semblance of a Mediterranean city with
its rural hamlets. The general term for coerced resettlement was *congregación*. Despite
rhetoric and terminology suggesting considerable movement and change, congregación
generally began late and was confined to just a few areas in the Mixteca.[94] Yuhuitayu
and their constituent entities were scattered over a fairly dispersed area, and congregation was limited to the removal of a few yuhuitayu from hilltop sites to the valley
floor (a process that already was advanced in the late postclassic period) and the collapsing of some structures upon themselves. For example, according to Woodrow Borah
and Sherburne Cooke, the core settlement of Texupa was relocated from the foothills
to the eastern Tamazulapan valley floor, about a kilometer away.[95] The movement
was facilitated by the fact that defensive protection was no longer necessary (and was
discouraged) under Spanish rule; in addition, decades of depopulation had made
settlement on fertile valley lands an option because much of the land was not under
intensive cultivation. But by all indications, ñuu were not moved very far, and the great
majority retained their separate identities, names, and lands. Descriptions of movement are often characterized as *a un tiro de piedra* (at a stone's throw) or *a un tiro de
arcabuz* (at a musket's shot). The siña or ñuu siña of Ayusi, one of the forty-odd barrios that constituted the yuhuitayu of Yanhuitlan, was still located about two to three

kilometers from the colonial plaza of the cabecera after congregation. Some of the so-called estancias were more than five kilometers distant from the center. Yucundaa (Teposcolula) was moved to the foot of the hill, but its former site was still partially settled and referred to in some documents as "Teposcolula la vieja." Teposcolula had six barrios and thirteen estancias in 1548; a congregation was proposed to consolidate the estancias into six places in 1603, but it obviously failed, because the thirteen survived throughout the eighteenth century.[96] Another wave of congregations took place in the early seventeenth century, after nearly a century of dramatic population decline, when some of the separate, subordinate siqui had become too small to be viable and were collapsed upon the ñuu of which they were a part.[97] In other words, people from outlying areas were moved toward the center. But most of the constituent structures remained intact. By the second half of the seventeenth century, the new alignment did lead to increasing concentration within the cabecera, but not to the extent Spanish officials had planned.

The purpose of this congregation was to shape the cabecera into a city; existing clusters of siqui were reorganized according to the *traza* layout with important civil and ecclesiastical buildings arranged around a central plaza.[98] In many places, however, the traza layout took different forms. The maps of Texupa and Nochixtlan from the *Relaciones geográficas* illustrate two versions of the model (see figs. 2.6 and 2.7). In Texupa, despite the creation of a grid pattern after relocation, there is really no plaza or center in this map. On the other hand, the vacant map of Nochixtlan seems to portray an ideal that is still in the planning stages; there is a center, but it is practically empty. The central plaza complex of the type depicted in the map of Nochixtlan came to be called the *yahui*, a Ñudzahui term for "market" applied to the Spanish *plaza* presumably because of an association based on the market's location within the colonial ñuu. In the preconquest arrangement, the market area may have served as the modest basis for a center. The church and municipal government building were built in the plaza, and the lord's palace was usually not too far away. Smaller churches built away from the center represented former temple sites of constituent siqui. Many settlements remained a good distance from the plaza, spread out evenly across the land, and most people probably went to the colonial center only during market days and feasts. The palace-market complex of the ñuu did tend toward nucleation, but not to the degree of a European (especially Mediterranean) city with its surrounding countryside.

The type of center imagined for the traza layout had little basis in ancient settlement patterns. A nucleated center was not really a pivotal component of the preconquest yuhuitayu, primarily because the constituent parts did not revolve around one center.[99] In fact, a dominant center controlling the hinterland was incompatible with the internal organization of the yuhuitayu.[100] The yuhuitayu functioned as a constituency of parts and may or may not have maintained—but did not require—an urban nucleus or dominant center. The Spanish municipality, on the other hand, was based on a dominant urban center surrounded by scattered subordinate settlements—an urban head and its rural dependencies. Spaniards tried to mold the yuhuitayu into a hierarchically ordered municipality, as the basis of the encomienda and the parish, distinct from the original arrangement of constituent siqui. In the preconquest period, each constituent part may have had a ruler or ruling couple and a palace, but only one was recognized after the conquest.[101] Thus, the vision of a permanent kingdom with subordinate satellite settlements was based on Spanish perceptions, not indigenous realities. The nature of the yuhuitayu and dynastic succession patterns also undermined the existence of a center ruled by one autocratic king. The hierarchy of cabeceras, barrios, and sujetos was a model that required a considerable degree of reorientation and adjustment in some places.

The process of designating cabeceras was not entirely arbitrary, and the larger yuhuitayu must have been recognizable from the beginning. The presence of dynastic rulers was the initial criterion for cabecera status. Every yuhuitayu had a ruler and a palace, but only one yuhuitayu in a given area was chosen. Other nearby yuhuitayu and ñuu were designated sujetos and subordinated to the center. The densely populated valleys (such as the Tamazulapa, Coixtlahuaca, Nochixtlan, and Tlaxiaco Valleys) consisted of multiple yuhuitayu. The Nochixtlan Valley had the highest concentration of yuhuitayu in the Mixteca; some places that were located within a few kilometers from Yanhuitlan, such as Chachoapa and Yucuita, were reduced to mere sujetos. Since a yuhuitayu was not based on a geographical jurisdiction, nearby entities were not necessarily subject to larger yuhuitayu. In less populated places, singling out one cabecera might have been less difficult and may not have misrepresented the local situation. Spaniards may not have been blind to all the complexities, either. The location of the settlement along roads and the acquiescence of individual lords were undoubtedly important factors of consideration. Previous arrangements with the Mexica and their allies must have influenced the reorganization, especially since Nahuas played an active role in mediating between Spaniards and Ñudzahui in the early sixteenth century. Spaniards tried to reshape the yuhuitayu into a hierarchically ordered municipal center, as the basis of political and religious jurisdictions.

A nucleated center was not a defining characteristic even of the densely populated central Mexican altepetl. Robert Haskett observed a more dispersed and scattered settlement pattern in Cuernavaca than the postconquest scenario would indicate. Cuernavaca was divided into four major tlaxilacalli, which in turn were subdivided into twenty-eight to thirty smaller units.[102] Perhaps the four tlaxilacalli were analogous to the Nahuatl term *tlayacatl altepetl*, discussed by the Nahua historian Chimalpahin.[103] Similarly, Rebecca Horn found that Coyoacan consisted of five altepetl, which contained as many as one hundred constituent tlaxilacalli.[104] In both cases, however, only one cabecera was created, singling out one of the parts among the rest.

Cabecera and Sujeto Status

Upon their arrival in the Mixteca, the Spaniards immediately sought the largest entities and attempted to deal with their leaders. They recognized the most prominent yuhuitayu in a given area and perceived all smaller yuhuitayu, ñuu, and siqui (and their lords and nobles) to be subordinate to the larger "kingdom." They thought of geographical territories ruled by a governing center with one native cacique. Some of the less prominent yuhuitayu and semiautonomous ñuu were not distinguished from constituent parts of the recognized yuhuitayu and were relegated to subject status—whether barrio, estancia, rancho, or pueblo. But the subdivisions of the yuhuitayu did not

constitute a nucleated settlement with a center. Yuhuitayu were not evenly distributed
geographically, nor were their lands contiguous. Two or more yuhuitayu could occupy
a relatively small area depending only on the number of ruling couples and lordly
establishments. Since the Spaniards could only create so many encomiendas, parishes,
and cabeceras in a given area, many of the separate units were lumped together based
on their appearance or other criteria. Thus, not all yuhuitayu became cabeceras.
Those that became cabeceras were considered administrative units with jurisdiction
over potentially numerous surrounding places that were formerly either autonomous
or associated with the larger unit in a more reciprocal fashion. Sometimes, even the
larger unit was more a group of constituents than a single body with a single rulership.
The nature of dynastic rule did not necessarily subordinate ñuu to their proximate
yuhuitayu, a fact that the Spaniards tended to ignore when assigning encomiendas
and regional jurisdictions. The new configuration simplified and consolidated sociopolitical organization and set the stage for the eventual splitting-off of smaller units
from the "head" municipality.

More than any scholar, Ronald Spores has addressed issues of settlement patterns
and sociopolitical relations in his interdisciplinary studies of the Mixteca Alta. He used
terminology from a selection of sixteenth-century Spanish-language sources to describe
the physical and sociopolitical structure of the "kingdom-cacicazgo," in conjunction
with archaeological evidence, especially from the Valley of Nochixtlan. He characterized the Mixtec community in the sixteenth century as a "center with its barrios and
more sparsely occupied and dispersed ranchos."[105] He described barrios as "probably
more or less contiguous districts comprising the compact pueblo center" that were
"associated with certain agricultural lands in the vicinity of the center." Hamlets, ranchos, and estancias were outlying dependencies of larger units and were all known as
sujetos. Communities were normally composed of a cabecera with a central core or
"tecpan" precinct and one to several barrios situated near the main settlement. Most
core communities contained one to several outlying dependencies.[106] Spores acknowledged that postconquest change must have significantly altered the preconquest configuration and that there was an increased concentration of settlement in the center
as a result of a new postconquest alignment.[107] But he suspected that archaeological
data "would verify the existence of this pattern of relationships for many years before
the conquest."[108]

Excavation data from the Nochixtlan Valley for the postclassic period both confirmed and contradicted sixteenth-century reports.[109] Most noticeably, Yanhuitlan resembled a cluster of multiple sites, but none was significantly larger or contained more
impressive remains than the others.[110] Spanish sources portrayed an extensive "kingdom-
cacicazgo" with a centralized rulership that subjugated and appointed nobles in all the
surrounding hamlets, and yet the archaeological record indicated no center. In fact,
the site most likely to be considered a center or capital of the kingdom of Yanhuitlan
was Ayusi—a siña in the colonial period. Ayusi, a site located more than a mile from
the plaza of the colonial cabecera, had the highest concentration of "multi-component
dwelling complexes," or noble residences.[111] Based on the center-hamlet model, this
apparent contradiction seemed to suggest that the population lived in "resident
estancias" and "outlying hamlets," not in the center. As Spores observed, some settle-

ments were "widely spread over a community territory of forty to sixty square kilome-ters."[112] The paradox was that those ruling centers with the most barrios had the least concentrated settlement patterns. The image of Yanhuitlan that the Spanish-language sources presented in the 1580s, of a highly nucleated settlement with multiple inner barrios and outer estancias, had little basis in the preconquest archaeological record. Even if congregation had been administered effectively, the nucleated center did not exist before the conquest.[113]

Spanish-language documentation often blurred distinctions between barrios and other structures, sometimes representing new relationships imposed by the colonial reorganization and other times reflecting ambiguities inherent in native entities. In Coixtlahuaca, one writer referred to an "estancia of San Gerónimo" but later called it the "estancia and barrio of San Gerónimo."[114] Texupa was said to have six barrios as sujetos.[115] One document reveals that residents of San Pedro Yodzotatnu repeatedly called their community "our barrio and pueblo." Once, it was described as the "barrio of San Pedro, sujeto of our cabecera Santa María Ocotepec."[116] Use of this terminol-ogy calls into question the nature of these entities and the distance between them. The estancia has been traditionally defined as a distant, constituent part and the barrio as a subdivision of the nucleated center.[117] This distinction did not correspond to the dispersed settlement pattern of the Mixteca, however. To say that a barrio was a sujeto of a cabecera suggests that it was more of an outlying settlement than an included entity attached to a core or center. The Spanish cabecera-sujeto-barrio system not only obscured the nature of sociopolitical relations among yuhuitayu, ñuu, and siqui but also did not accurately represent colonial settlement patterns.

Native Terminology for New Sociopolitical Entities

Although congregation and reorganization did not significantly alter settlement pat-terns, the redefinition of entities and the concentration of status and power in the center reinforced the Spanish conception of the cabecera as a head town.[118] Ñudzahui writers continued to use their own terms for yuhuitayu and ñuu throughout the period, but the concentration of authority demanded some terminology that distinguished a nucleus from its outlying parts. Thus Ñudzahui speakers developed a terminology to accommodate the meaning of cabecera and sujeto and occasionally used the loanword *jurisdicción* to provide the context of their relation. Translations of documents usually called the ñuu "pueblo" or "sujeto" and the yuhuitayu "cabecera." But some people were cognizant that the yuhuitayu and ñuu were not quite the same as the cabecera and sujeto. "Cabecera" was called *dzini ñuu*, "head pueblo," and sujeto was *daha ñuu*, "trib-ute pueblo."[119] Such terms appeared only in particular contexts, however, and arose from specific Spanish genres of legal documentation. They appear especially in late colonial election documents and legal petitions presented before the Audiencia. A typical election document from Teposcolula recorded an assembly of nobles in 1707 from "eleven tribute ñuu and the head ñuu of this community palace yuhuitayu San Pedro and San Pablo Teposcolula" [usi ee ndaha ñuu sihi maa dzini ñuu yaha aniñe comonidad yuhuitayu santo san pedro san pablo yucundaa].[120] In 1699, a writer called Yanhuitlan "this head ñuu yuhuitayu Santo Domingo Yanhuitlan" [dzini ñuu yuhuichayu santo domingo yodzocahi yaha].[121] A year later the whole was referred to as "this great head ñuu tayu Santo Domingo and all the tribute ñuu and neighboring ñuu" [dzini ñuu chayu canu sancto domingo yaha sihi nee cutu ndaha ñuu besino ñuu].[122] By 1750, a writer from Chilapa used the new term *dzini ñuu* with the loanword *cabecera*. Tlaxiaco was called "his ñuu, the head ñuu cabecera of Tlaxiaco" [ñuuya dzini ñuu cabesera ndisinuu], and another time it was simply called "ñuu tayu cabesera ndisinuu."[123] It is possible, however, that use of the word *dzini* in the Mixteca Baja as an equivalent for "barrio" precluded use of the term *dzini ñuu* for "cabecera." The term does not appear in the record from 1584 until 1678, suggesting that such terminology was very selective and that speakers and writers consciously avoided competing and obfuscating terms.

Nahuatl employed a similar term to refer to the cabecera as a head town. Chimalpahin resorted to *tzontecomatl* and neologisms such as *tlahuilanal* and *tlatititzal* for "dependency" or "subject town."[124] Such terms were used primarily to describe the situation after congregation and constitute the exceptional case in which a central part of the altepetl is distinguished from outlying parts in Chimalpahin's writings. It is unclear whether the terms to approximate *sujeto* referred to actual constituent parts or to other subordinate units—or even to other altepetl paying tribute to a dominant one.

Thus, the new terminology recognized another level of political relationships among entities that was quite separate from the preconquest order of yuhuitayu, ñuu, and siqui. The Spaniards reshaped sociopolitical relations among the various entities without displacing the original indigenous terminology or fundamentally altering the actual physical structures and area settlement pattern. The discrepancy between the Spanish articulation of this reordering and the actual settlement pattern in the sixteenth century (and immediate precontact period) betrays the inaccuracy of the perceived model based on Spanish terminology. In addition to misrepresenting the existing order, the reorganization suppressed an inherent tendency of Ñudzahui sociopolitical organization, founded on the respect of smaller, segmentary units that constituted the whole. Colonial attempts to establish permanent relations between sociopolitical structures had frozen a dynamic system based on shifting and realigning alliances and associations. Many communities rejected the new arrangement.

Indigenous Responses to Reorganization

Indigenous responses to the imposition of a static, hierarchical model of sociopolitical organization began as soon as the real nature of the Spanish reordering became apparent. Many sujetos and estancias sought autonomy from their cabeceras as early as the 1550s and continued to struggle against the colonial hierarchy throughout the sixteenth and seventeenth centuries. Legal cases typically refer to estancias that attempted to *sustraerse* (withdraw) from the cabecera. In 1608, the estancias of San Pedro, San Miguel, San Antonio, and Santiago tried once again to break away from Tamasulapa.[125] In 1616, people from the ñuu of Nuyoo refused to recognize the authority of its cabecera, Ocotepec, and its cacique.[126] Several pueblos sought autonomy from Yanhuitlan as early as 1552, and more followed in subsequent decades.[127] The venerable cacique and governor of Yanhuitlan, don Gabriel de Guzmán, was challenged in 1558, 1580, and 1582 by caciques in subject estancias.[128] His uncle, don Domingo, was denounced before the Inquisition by a parade of lords from Etlantongo, Nochixtlan, Teposcolula, and other neighboring places. Several lords testified against don Domingo on charges of idolatry, polygyny, and human sacrifice. The witnesses must have realized the consequences of such testimony. Don Domingo acknowledged the implications of the accusations and speculated aloud as to why he was being attacked. He said very clearly that "Etlantongo and their allies [did] not want to serve the cabecera . . . they want[ed] to be cabeceras."[129] Although Etlantongo and its allies (especially Nochixtlan and Jaltepec) did not succeed in stripping don Domingo of his powers or Yanhuitlan of its status, the accused cacique spent at least a year in prison and was forced to fight for his life.[130] Despite these challenges, the leaders of Yanhuitlan did not renounce their status as one of the most powerful cabeceras in the Mixteca Alta. On the contrary, they claimed to have ruled over their "kingdom" since time immemorial and dismissed the enmity of other yuhuitayu as nothing more than petty jealousies. Similar claims were reiterated in a suit against Tecomatlan in the 1580s, discussed below.

What came to be known as the cabecera of Yanhuitlan after the conquest had encompassed a complex cluster of settlements stretching within an area of a few kilometers along the narrow alluvial plains of the Yanhuitlan River, in northwestern Nochixtlan Valley. The recognition of one part as a center and the others as barrios or estancias simplified a complex, dynamic situation and uplifted one royal line of a yuhuitayu to a commanding position above all equals, factions, or otherwise disempowered constituencies. A number of siña were considered undifferentiated barrios of the center, barely distinguished in rank from estancias that were located a little farther away, or more distant "sujetos" that might have been formerly independent ñuu. Yanhuitlan had almost thirty estancias in the 1580s, most of which were probably former ñuu. Perhaps some ñuu even became barrios and thus blurred the distinction between siña and ñuu in the sixteenth century. Even the barrios were dispersed. For the colonial cabecera of Yanhuitlan, which continued to be known as Yodzocahi by Ñudzahui speakers, the "center" was created on the site of the new church and royal palace, adjacent to the main highway. Its rulers were recognized above other dynasties, and all other nearby units were relegated to secondary status. Even Yanhuitlan's yuhuitayu ally after the conquest, Tamazola-Chachoapa, was considered a sujeto, despite the fact that the ruling couple of the yuhuitayu, don Diego Nuqh and doña María Coquahu, had resided there instead of Yanhuitlan. Indeed, it is likely that constituent siña and nearby ñuu possessed more autonomy from the yuhuitayu of Yodzocahi than was recognized in the postconquest period; as constituent parts, certain high-ranking siña or ñuu may have had a stake in the local dynastic rulership. One document recording the assembly of the Spanish-style municipal council, or cabildo, of Yanhuitlan and all its sujetos and estancias in 1587 corroborates this scenario.[131] The municipal council included representatives from seventeen sujetos and estancias of Yanhuitlan—all called "caciques." The caciques of these so-called sujetos possessed the noble title *don* and distinguished noble names such as Guzmán and Mendoza. Clearly, these men were *yya* (high lords) who were eligible members of a yuhuitayu. As noted above, a lord from Mascaltepec occupied the governorship of Yanhuitlan in 1681, indicating the importance of yya in these so-called subordinate parts.[132]

The definition of "cabecera del pueblo" in the *Vocabulario* as "sacaa tayu" or "where there's a tayu" is a revealing association of the yuhuitayu with the cabecera.[133] The presence of a ruling couple was an important symbol and proof of high status in the preconquest period. In several sixteenth-century maps, many yuhuitayu included images of their ruling couples as proof of autonomy and status (see figs. 2.4 and 2.5, for example). In the colonial period, members of a yuhuitayu expected their ñuu to be recognized as cabeceras. Witnesses in one case articulated this expectation very clearly. In 1583, officials from Santiago Yolomecatl, a sujeto and estancia of Teposcolula, argued for independence from the cabecera on the grounds that they had their own ruling couple. Juan Bautista Contuta told Spanish officials through an appointed translator that his ñuu refused to pay tribute to the cabecera because "we have our own caciques, don Pedro and doña Juana." Unfortunately, this assertion of yuhuitayu status, significant as it was to native concepts of sociopolitical organization, had little meaning within the Spanish cabecera-sujeto scheme.[134] Yolomecatl's appeal was denied, but its officials continued to demand autonomy from the cabecera until finally gaining it in the late seventeenth century.

The Case of Yanhuitlan versus Tecomatlan

A landmark sixteenth-century legal dispute, appealed before the Audiencia of Mexico, highlights many aspects of the sixteenth-century reorganization of yuhuitayu, ñuu, and siqui into cabeceras and sujetos.[135] The case attempted to establish grounds for resolving community conflicts in the Mixteca and was eventually deposited in the Archive of the Indies in Seville. In the 1580s, Tecomatlan attempted to secede from the cabecera of Yanhuitlan, claiming that it had been an independent "pueblo y cabecera" before the conquest but was unfairly reduced and placed into a large encomienda with Yanhuitlan by Cortés. Since that time it had been subject to the cabecera, forced to bring tribute there and to receive the sacraments in its church. Tecomatlan's efforts to achieve autonomy were spearheaded by its own "cacique" named don Diego de Guzmán, called in Nahuatl Matlactl çe (Miqu)Yztli, son of Nahui Caltzin, who claimed to descend from a dynastic line that had ruled in the Mixteca Alta and Baja for more than four hundred years.[136] On the other side, witnesses for Yanhuitlan testified that Tecomatlan, located about two leagues to the south, always had been their subordinate "estancia y sujeto" and that their own eminent cacique, don Gabriel de Guzmán, had "appointed" his brother, don Diego de Guzmán, as "principal" in Tecomatlan about a decade ago. According to witnesses from Yanhuitlan, don Diego de Guzmán was to administer the collection of tribute there and to tend to other matters on behalf of Yanhuitlan—with no title to rule.

The sixteenth-century reorganization had far-reaching economic implications for all ñuu. Part of Tecomatlan's refusal to pay tribute and perform services stemmed from a recent demand to grow and process silk for the cabecera, a profitable and labor-intensive industry that would have benefited Yanhuitlan's *caja de comunidad* (community treasury) at the expense of its sujeto's land and labor. Significantly, four friars, an encomendero, and a Spanish merchant testified on Yanhuitlan's behalf when the proceedings addressed the question of whether it was customary for sujetos to provide the cabecera with personal services.[137] Clearly, additional parties stood to gain from this new demand. In addition, the people of Tecomatlan clearly resented the fact that they were forced to receive the sacraments in the church of Yanhuitlan and had been forced to help build the church.[138] The case expanded beyond these immediate matters, however, to encompass a broad range of fundamental issues concerning preconquest precedents of dynastic rulership, community status, and territorial jurisdiction in the Mixteca. The case elicited testimonies of nobles from various parts of the Mixteca Alta, responding to questions of social and political organization both before and after the Spaniards' arrival. A principal concern of this case was that don Diego attempted to assert his autonomy from Yanhuitlan by creating his own yuhuitayu. Appeals for autonomy based on the existence of a local yuhuitayu made sense to a native audience and were typical of the early period, as discussed above in the case of Yolomecatl. From don Diego's point of view, as a son of a yya (male lord) and *yya dzehe* (female lord), he had every right to assert his freedom from giving tribute to the yuhuitayu of Yanhuitlan. How such an assertion was customarily verified and acknowledged is unknown, but it is likely that codices and the testimony of nobles were used to legitimate claims. His assertion of autonomy would have resulted in a schism, warfare, strategic marriage, or some form of compromise. In the new order, however, only one yuhuitayu was recognized as cabecera. Legal action before the Audiencia was the only recourse.

Legal conflicts between sujetos and cabeceras often focused on the status of the lords and nobles who represented those communities within the Spanish legal system. Before the conquest, Tecomatlan's status as a yuhuitayu entitled to autonomy, or conversely as a subordinate ñuu, depended on whether don Diego de Guzmán was born of a lordly mother and father and whether he married a noblewoman who was born of lordly parents. Ideally, lesser nobles were descendants of only one lord and exercised limited positions of authority at the level of the siqui, whereas lords who descended directly from two royal parents ruled yuhuitayu. The proceedings indicated that don Diego de Guzmán had been recently married to the daughter of don Antonio de Velasco, "cacique and governor" of Malinaltepec. Thus don Diego married a royal lady and could succeed as ruler (in association with his wife) of a new yuhuitayu based on the principle of direct descent from two royal parents. Only one of the witnesses testifying on Yanhuitlan's behalf—a Spaniard from Antequera—suggested that don Diego of Tecomatlan was a "bastard" or half brother of don Gabriel and was therefore ineligible to rule.[139] The majority of witnesses on both sides referred to the two as simply brothers. Earlier in the proceedings, don Diego of Tecomatlan was identified as the brother of don Gaspar (no surname is given), cacique of Mitlantongo, but don Gaspar was not a brother of don Gabriel. Thus, don Diego shared one parent with don Gabriel and one with don Gaspar. Their elder brother, don Matías de Velasco, had ruled in Tamazola. If both of his parents were lords, don Diego would have been entitled to rule when he took a royal bride. Alternatively, don Diego de Guzmán may have been a lesser noble or an unlucky, disfranchised lord who had been relegated to a subservient position in relation to his brother, the chosen ruler of Yanhuitlan. In either case, his main recourse was the Spanish legal system. Don Diego did, in fact, admit that he moved to Tecomatlan to get away from his brother, don Gabriel of Yanhuitlan.

In the case between Yanhuitlan and Tecomatlan, each side offered completely contradictory testimony to support its claims. Yanhuitlan declared that there had never been a *senorío* or cacicazgo in Tecomatlan and that don Diego was neither a "cacique" nor a "principal." To prove this first assertion, it presented an ancient painting that was kept locked in a chest in the archive of the lord's palace, which listed all the subject communities and estancias within the cabecera, and displayed twenty-four consecutive "caciques y señores." The painting, ending with the present ruler of don Gabriel, represented more than five hundred years of dynastic rule and demonstrated Tecomatlan's subject status. Witnesses on Yanhuitlan's side referred to this ancient painting as irrefutable evidence. Yanhuitlan relied on several prominent Spanish witnesses and Ñudzahui nobles from various parts, especially Soyaltepec and Tonaltepec. Tecomatlan countered that don Gabriel had bribed all of them to appear on his behalf. Witnesses on Tecomatlan's side included a few Spaniards and Ñudzahui nobles from Mitlantongo, Xaltepec, and Malinaltepec. Not denying the power of Yanhuitlan, they all insisted that Tecomatlan had never paid tribute to anyone and had always been an independent entity with its own cacique. Two witnesses admitted that they used to bring tribute to Moteucçoma's representatives in Coixtlahuaca, however. The Yanhuitlan side dismissed the testimony of the Spaniards, who, it alleged, all had something to gain from Tecomatlan's independence because they lived in that area; as for the indigenous witnesses, they either were related to don Diego or were from places such as Xaltepec, which were rivals of Yanhuitlan. On both sides, communities lined up to support one or another claim, and some witnesses from more distant places such as Tlaxiaco, Tilantongo, and Nochixtlan, summoned by the alcalde mayor, presented more impartial and unpredictable testimony.

The conflict between Yanhuitlan and Tecomatlan represented inherent tensions between yuhuitayu and ñuu, and between lords and nobles, which were complicated by the postconquest reorganization. Indeed, several witnesses claimed that many communities were not satisfied with the new hierarchy created by Cortés, which gave undue privileges to Yanhuitlan. One is reminded of how some altepetl in central Mexico, such as Xochimilco and Huexotzinco, resented Tlaxcala's privileges under Spanish rule. In response, authorities from Yanhuitlan dismissed the testimony of Ñudzahui witnesses from five separate, neighboring communities with which Yanhuitlan had "ancient rivalries." Some witnesses asserted that these problems were not confined to the Yanhuitlan area but also existed in many other parts of the Mixteca. Sebastián de Mendoza of Tilantongo and Juan Pérez and Mateo Durán of Nochixtlan spoke of *vexaciones* (troubles) and *agravios* (insults) resulting from the new order.[140] The existing arrangement under the Spanish cabecera-sujeto system gave undue advantage and privilege to a few yuhuitayu and their rulers at the expense of other yuhuitayu and ñuu with resident nobles or disfranchised lords. Indigenous sociopolitical relations between entities such as Yanhuitlan and Tecomatlan were based on a more reciprocal arrangement than the colonial scheme allowed. The reorganization and redefinition of sociopolitical relations simplified an extremely complex scenario, the nuances of which did not concern most Spaniards. Although the Spanish legal system provided a form of recourse and redress for smaller units, officials were more interested in maintaining larger structures and working with a manageable number of caciques than in preserving the dynamic preconquest situation.

On the other hand, even when Spanish officials attempted to define the "traditional" arrangement, they stepped into a swamp of rivalries and contentions that were typical of local ethnic states in postclassic Mesoamerica. When officials sought to inquire about the way things had been arranged in ancient times, they often elicited two completely contradictory responses. Pictorial writings did not necessarily resolve matters, not only because officials could not decipher them but also because each place might have its own version of who was entitled to what. One lawyer raised this possibility in 1566 when he argued that paintings do not constitute reliable evidence because "Indians just paint what they want on them."[141] Of course, this remark betrays a typical ethnocentric attitude toward other cultures' writing systems. But it is possible and even probable that the ancient paintings that allegedly proved Tecomatlan's subject status might have been little more than a pictorial version of Yanhuitlan's side of the story. Another important issue raised in this case was the question of how "community" borders were "measured." The question elicited the ambiguous reply that there were many different ways of demarcating borders and that each community kept its own reckoning. This explanation baffled Spanish officials, who thought of land measurements in their own cultural terms.

Moreover, the questions posed to witnesses in legal proceedings were phrased within the terminology and framework of Spanish sociopolitical organization. Inquiry about the nature of traditional relations between cabeceras and sujetos was anachronistic and confusing. The vagueness and inconsistency of Spanish terms in the documentation betray their inappropriateness. For example, in the dispute between Yanhuitlan and Tecomatlan, every witness from Yanhuitlan claimed that Tecomatlan was nothing but another "sujeto y estancia" from which it had always received tribute, whereas every one of the witnesses from Tecomatlan claimed that they had always been a "pueblo y cabecera."[142] This was not simply the case of a smaller unit stubbornly rebelling against a larger one. The real issue at hand was that don Diego de Guzmán, cacique of Tecomatlan and brother of the cacique of Yanhuitlan, was asserting his perceived right to establish a yuhuitayu that was independent of Yanhuitlan, a right that went unrecognized in the new order. Confronted with such colossal contradiction, Spanish authorities tended to favor the existing arrangement that they had established. Although Yanhuitlan won this legal battle with its prominent witnesses and paintings, Tecomatlan won the war a century later when it achieved permanent autonomy from the cabecera.

Disputed successions and claims of yuhuitayu status undoubtedly existed before the conquest, but the new order gave undue advantage to a few prominent places to the exclusion of others. As a center of local government, administration, writing, economic enterprise, tribute collection, and religious authority, the cabecera became more powerful than any of its parts. Tecomatlan was forced to grow silk for the cabecera of Yanhuitlan and to provide other personal services for its cacique. One case illustrates the tensions between cabeceras and sujetos when it came to the provision of labor:

when the Spanish alcalde mayor presented a decree to all the major yuhuitayu calling for *repartimiento* labor (rotary labor service) from the Mixteca Alta to build a fortress in Acapulco, the cacique of Yanhuitlan complained that it was too far away and insisted that the sujetos should be made to provide the labor, not the cabecera.[143]

The case of Yanhuitlan versus Tecomatlan illustrates how the colonial sociopolitical hierarchy fomented inequalities between ruling centers and subordinate satellites and fueled local campaigns for autonomy, especially in the second half of the colonial period.

Late Colonial Changes

Ñudzahui writers continued to use native sociopolitical terminology, including terms for subunits of the ñuu, into the eighteenth century. One also finds *barrio* in this period as a common loanword. Because both kinds of words were sometimes used in the same document in reference to the same entity, it is difficult to detect any conceptual change in the introduction of the Spanish term. The words were often interchanged for the same units in the course of a single document.[144] Thus, siqui were maintained as identifiable units into the eighteenth century, and references to siña are found as late as 1787 in Yanhuitlan. These results contradict the notion that barrios had lost their identity, function, and character by the end of the sixteenth century.[145]

In Spanish terminology of the later period, the "pueblo" was an undifferentiated cluster of people, regardless of status or structure; differences between sujeto and cabecera diminished, just as differences between ñuu, tayu, and ñuu tayu were not as salient as in the sixteenth century. Speakers did not use the word *pueblo* in native-language writings from the period, however. The terms *ñuu* and *tayu* or *yuhuitayu* were never abandoned in the colonial period. As a reference to place, the term *yuhuitayu* appears in the latest extant native-language archival source, dated 1807.[146] In general, however, less attention was given to specific corporate terminology in the writings of the later period, especially to the smaller subunits. By the late colonial period, most people simply referred to their ñuu, with its saint's name and a Ñudzahui name. In the native-language record, even by the early nineteenth century, people did not adopt place-names derived from Nahuatl, such as Yanhuitlan, Teposcolula, or Oaxaca.

From the late seventeenth century to the end of the colonial period, many sujetos gained autonomy from their cabeceras. The entities most affected were those estancias or ñuu located at a considerable distance from the cabecera center. Campaigns to achieve corporate autonomy represented the inherent capability of ñuu to separate from larger conglomerations, spurred by inequalities resulting from the hierarchical ordering of cabeceras and sujetos. The movements were also encouraged by colonial legislation. The title verification program, carried out by Spanish officials from 1696 to 1718, was designed to establish the limits of corporate holdings and to raise revenue by the granting of titles to land called *títulos de composición*. Indian "pueblos" were entitled to possess an area of six hundred varas in diameter from the center, measured from the church, as the minimal extension of an indigenous community's property, known as the *fundo legal*.[147] However, this law did not make clear what exactly constituted a pueblo, reflecting the ambiguity of Spanish settlement terminology.[148] Thus, any place that could establish pueblo status would be eligible for the six hundred varas. In effect, Spanish officials began to recognize only pueblos by the later period, whether or not they contained complex, constituent parts. Some barrios were able to acquire pueblo status under these circumstances, especially those that were distant from the center.[149]

In the Mixteca, the policy of assigning and formally recognizing the six-hundred-vara entitlement of all pueblos coincided with a revival of demographic growth. By the early 1700s a number of autonomous communities appeared in the native-language written record. For example, in 1707, the governor of Topiltepec referred to papers in the "community archive" that documented the separation of his ñuu from the cabecera of Yanhuitlan.[150] In the last quarter of the seventeenth century, various pueblos had attained partial autonomy in that they were entitled to elect alcaldes and to manage their own resources. Several "pueblos" broke away from Yanhuitlan in this period, including Tecomatlan and Suchitepec in 1688. Whereas Achiutla had four barrios in 1548 within an area of three to four leagues, it had divided into three separate pueblos and the original cabecera by the eighteenth century; each of the former barrios had achieved autonomy.[151]

The case of Yanhuitlan illustrates how the desire for local autonomy gathered momentum over time. As early as 1552, seven estancias sought independence from the cabecera of Yanhuitlan, and at least two more tried to secede by the 1580s. In 1587, cabildo records show that Yanhuitlan had sixteen sujetos.[152] In 1679, a cabildo record referred to Yodzocahi (Yanhuitlan) as a "chayu" (Yanhuitlan-area equivalent of *tayu*) with jurisdiction over the following nine places: chayu San Mateo Yucucuiy; ñuu Santiago Tiyyu; ñuu San Andres Anduhua; ñuu San Francisco Chinduhua; ñuu San Juan Tiyuqh; ñuu San Juan Yucuyta; ñuu San Andrés Atata; ñuu San Mateo Chayo; ñuu Santa Maria Chiyo.[153] Even by this later date, officials of Yanhuitlan acknowledged that one of their nine sujetos, Yucucuiy, was a yuhuitayu. As noted above, many sujetos of Yanhuitlan had attempted to secede from the cabecera as early as 1552. The cabildo records indicate that seven sujetos achieved autonomy between 1587 and 1679. From 1690 to 1779, the number of cabeceras with full cabildos (including a governor) expanded from twenty-one to thirty-seven in the Mixteca Alta, and from thirty-seven to eighty in the last two decades of the eighteenth century. Limited autonomy was achieved by many ñuu at the end of the seventeenth century, with the addition of partial cabildos headed by an alcalde. The last quarter of the eighteenth century was a watershed for settlements seeking autonomy from cabeceras.[154]

Political change did not fundamentally alter the main lines of regional organization. By 1746, the communities of the Mixteca Alta were grouped into four political-administrative units. The largest in territory and population was the jurisdiction of Yanhuitlan-Teposcolula; it remained intact when the area was converted in 1786–87 into *subdelegaciones* of the Intendancy of Oaxaca. Thus, there was little change in regional political organization, administration, or judicial function after the mid-sixteenth century, when the main framework of local government and ecclesiastical jurisdictions was established. After independence, the more nucleated population centers became *municipios* in charge of a given area, following the main outline of colonial cabeceras. In this period, municipal status was actually a burden for communities, as they were responsible for administrative tasks without the benefits of the former tribute system.[155]

The right to control local labor and tribute and to sponsor a cabildo with local leaders was great incentive for seeking autonomy.

In terms of sociopolitical organization, the late colonial period should not be characterized as a time of chaos or collapse. Autonomous ñuu were pulling away from cabecera arrangements as early as the mid-sixteenth century.[156] Campaigns for autonomy represented active responses to the Spanish reorganization of the sixteenth century, which had relegated smaller units to subordinate status. The indigenous tendency to rely on separate, equal entities was another reason for the campaigns of autonomy. In the resulting process of fragmentation, most of the original units remained intact. The most basic units, ñuu and their constituent siqui, were inherently capable of collapsing or combining in response to internal and external demands. However, the ability of ñuu to incorporate smaller units (siqui) and to align with other ñuu (yuhuitayu) was restricted by the eighteenth century. Ultimately, sociopolitical organization was simplified.

The configuration of centers with outlying hamlets portrayed by Spanish-language sources represents postconquest conceptual changes that were reinforced over time by congregation attempts and population loss. The Spanish reorganization did not radically transform settlement patterns in the Mixteca, but it did alter the nature of relations among yuhuitayu and ñuu and their constituent parts. This reorganization simplified and misrepresented sociopolitical relations, a process that was bound to affect indigenous structures. The retention and organization of subordinate units as constituent parts of a greater whole made autonomy a constant possibility, however, and many sought independence as soon as the consequences of the new order became apparent. The long-term result of resistance and adaptation to the Spanish colonial reorganization was autonomy, a possibility inherent in the indigenous structures.[157] Autonomy based on a minimal number of units allowed settlements to survive congregation, depopulation, and political reorientation. The viability and adaptability of the smaller units is confirmed by the high number of municipios that have persisted to the present. As Borah and Cook noted in the 1960s, the Mixteca is an area of Mexico with one of the greatest concentrations of communities per square kilometer.[158]

This chapter has focused on a defining characteristic of Ñudzahui organization and culture—where Ñudzahui people lived and how they organized themselves both before and after the conquest. The term *community* falls short of representing the complex, multilevel, and dynamic sociopolitical structures that survived the conquest. Yet these entities were more than simply territorial settlements; they were groups of households bound together by political, economic, and social arrangements. Let us consider the relationship between structures and social relations by reading how writers referred to the people in their ñuu.

CHAPTER 5

✤ Nuttal

Social Relations

IN THE SIXTEENTH CENTURY, Ñudzahui society consisted of two hereditary categories, nobles and commoners.[1] The first was headed by lords according to principles of dynastic rule and included a lesser nobility, who performed leading roles in the administration of local resources, trade, and religious ceremony. The second group was a much larger body of common people who constituted the great majority of the population. Commoners performed agricultural labor, worked various crafts and textiles, and provided tribute in goods and labor to their *ñuu*. Members from both groups participated in local markets. Notable gradations in wealth and status among members of the two hereditary groups created a continuum of classes rather than distinct castes. Society was neither egalitarian nor rigidly stratified. In many ways, Ñudzahui society was not unlike Nahua, Spanish, or most fully sedentary agricultural societies in the early modern period. But in some ways, it was unique.

The first section of this chapter introduces social categories by examining the full range of terminology that Ñudzahui people used to distinguish status and rank among themselves and by observing the context of its usage in native-language records. The second section considers the mutual obligations and expectations of each social group from the point of view of colonial petitions and complaints. The third and final part identifies preconquest naming patterns and outlines how Spanish names and titles were adopted over the course of the colonial period. The selective adaptation of Spanish personal names reflected Ñudzahui social distinctions while distinguishing most natives from Spaniards.

Spanish sources speak of three basic social categories or classes in Mesoamerica: *caciques y señores* (native rulers and lords); *principales* (lesser nobles); and *macehuales* (commoners). Other lower-ranked categories included dependent agricultural laborers (*terrazgueros*) and domestic servants (*naborías* or *criados*). Two of these terms were adopted in the Caribbean (*cacique* and *naboría*), and one was borrowed from the Nahuas (from *macehualli*). Although Spaniards recognized a fundamental distinction between hereditary nobles and commoners, typical of European society, Ñudzahui society was more complex and dynamic than this classic three-tiered model would suggest. Early colonial Ñudzahui-language writings make repeated references to social categories that are valid for the immediate preconquest and postconquest periods. Inventing new categories after the arrival of Spaniards was unlikely and, if Spanish-influenced, would have taken a loanword.[2] Native scribes continued to refer to fundamental concepts when they wrote documents and letters intended primarily for other native speakers. Some categories faded or disappeared by the time native-language writing was fully developed, such as slaves taken in warfare, but new or totally transformed categories did not appear. Writings from different areas of the Mixteca refer to basic categories of social organization and demonstrate consistent patterns of change throughout the colonial period, despite local variation. Let us begin with the most prominent group in the record.

Yya and Toho

Native hereditary rulers were called *caciques* in Spanish, based on an Arawak word and applied to all native rulers in the Spanish Indies. Spaniards used the term *cacica* to designate the wife of a cacique or a female hereditary ruler. In the Ñudzahui language, rulers of the *yuhuitayu* were called *yya toniñe*, "lord ruler" and *yya dzehe toniñe*, "lady ruler." High status applied to both male lords (*yya* or "iya") and female lords (*yya dzehe*). The term *yya* was reserved for the highest lords who descended directly from parents of the same high status. The word itself conveyed sacredness.[3] Another term for "lord," *stoho*, had the same connotation.

Yya and yya dzehe commanded the highest positions of political and religious authority in Ñudzahui ñuu. They embodied prestige, sophistication, and elegance. The polite and flowery speech of the lords was so elaborate that the meaning of its complex metaphors and conventions often eluded commoners. Yya and yya dzehe commanded local audiences with speeches about morality and maintained the oral traditions and histories of their communities. They understood the complex conventions of the pictographic writing system and commissioned trained nobles to write on deerskin and cloth. In the codices, yya and yya dzehe associated themselves with sacred events, ancestors, and deities from the primordial past. Clothing further distinguished yya and yya dzehe from other members of society. They wore finely woven garments of cotton, feathered headdresses, animal skins and furs, and footwear. They sported ornamental plugs in their pierced noses and ears and wore necklaces, armbands, bracelets, rings, and pendants of precious metals and stones. They collected prestige items such as bright green quetzal feathers, pieces of turquoise, gold, and jade. They feasted on delicacies such as quail, turkey, and deer and drank chocolate and pulque whenever they pleased. They handled and used sacred substances such as tobacco and copal incense, hallucinogenic mushrooms, and medicinal herbs.

Throughout much of the colonial period, yya and yya dzehe continued to control multiple tracts of patrimonial lands and relied on the services of agricultural laborers. They lived in large palaces of stone or adobe, built on raised platforms with constructed floors and sunken patios. The interiors of their palaces were decorated with mats, weavings, and animal skins.[4] They counted on multiple servants to prepare food, fetch wood and water, and weave textiles for them. From their dependent laborers, they received tribute in raw materials and finished goods. They sponsored traders or engaged in the local market system to acquire various necessities and prestige items. Spaniards recognized yya as high-ranking lords who were entitled to certain rights and privileges. Many yya interacted closely with Spaniards, spoke some Castilian, and made use of the Spanish legal system in order to advance local and family interests. As privileged lords, they obtained special permits to own horses, livestock, swords, and even muskets. They were the first to adopt European architectural features and to modify their residences with doors and windows. Many yya sought to acquire Spanish prestige items from fine clothing and furniture to books, African slaves, and Christian images.

Yya and yya dzehe were in many respects inseparable from *toho* and *toho dzehe* (noblemen and noblewomen). The *Vocabulario* defined *toho* in terms of "good lineage" and equated this Spanish phrase with *dzaya yya*, "children of yya."[5] The *tay toho* (noble person/people) was also equated with the Spanish *hidalgo*.[6] Native-language sources speak of yya and toho in the same breath. The earliest extant Ñudzahui-language notarial document refers repeatedly to "taca yya toho" [all the yya, the toho] who assembled to hear the last will and testament of a prominent yya dzehe in Yucucuihi (Tlazultepec). Doña María López closed her testament by addressing the witnesses as "my yya, toho of my yuhuitayu of Yucucuihi" [yya tohondi teyudi yucucuihi yaha].[7] In 1579, when *cabildo* members from Achiutla responded to a letter sent by the Spanish *alcalde mayor*, they referred to themselves in honorific terms as "we the yya, toho of this yuhuitayu of Ñundecu" [ñadzaña yya thoó yuhuitayu ñundicu yaá].[8] And in 1622, when many people gathered in Teposcolula to witness the arrangement of a royal marriage, the Ñudzahui *fiscal* (church steward) referred to the various social groups in attendance, including the "yhya toniñe" [male yya], "ñaha toniñe" [female yya], "tay toho" [male toho], "ñaha toho" [female toho], "toho nisano" [elder toho], and all the "ñandehi" [commoners].[9] Records from the Baja also refer to yya and toho as two entities within the same hereditary group. In 1678, don Jorge de la Cruz Alvarado of Huaxuapa referred to "all the yya, the toho of the ñuu tayu" [taca yya toho ñutayu] and "all the yya, together with all the toho" [taca yya dihi taca toho]. He also invoked "all the toho fathers, mothers and grandfathers, grandmothers" [taca yuhua dzihiyu sihi siy sitna toho] as a metaphor for his noble ancestors, which was later translated as "all my parents, the nobles [*principales*]."[10] In 1705, the "female yya toho" [yia toho dzehe] of Yolomecatl were in charge of cloth production.[11] The conception of yya and toho as one group is analogous to the Nahua practice of calling everyone who was not a macehualli a *pilli*, "noble."[12]

One of the categories introduced in 1622 by the fiscal of Teposcolula, *toho nisano*, or "elder toho," bears closer examination. The term was probably an honorary title, similar perhaps to the Nahua *huehuetque*, a group of elders who often appeared in Nahua election documents.[13] Like the fiscal, many people referred to tay nisano as if they were a separate social group. For example, in San Felipe, a *sujeto* of Teposcolula, a testament of 1729 refers to "all the yya, toho, commoners, elder nobles" [taca yia toho dzaya dzana toho nisano].[14] The title was invariably associated with toho and yya, even though high social status was not necessarily tied to age or seniority. Doña María de Velasco of Huaxuapa referred to "all the yya elders" [taca yya nisano] who were present when she gave her testament in 1633.[15] In 1693, María de la Cruz Avendaño of Yucucata was called a "toho elder witness" [testigo toho nisanu].[16] In typical recognition of women's membership in the group, a church record from San Juan Teposcolula referred to "all the male elders and female elders" [taca tey nisano sihi ñaha nisano].[17] If preconquest tradition assigned special status to elders, regardless of social rank, yya and toho nisano were nonetheless the most prominent elders in the record.

Every yya and yya dzehe was a leading member and representative of an *aniñe*, or lordly establishment, that is, the buildings, lands, relatives, and dependent laborers associated with a particular yya lineage. As mediators between yya and all non-nobles, toho channeled goods and services to the aniñe and, in turn, derived certain benefits and privileges from their service. Whereas yya descended directly from two parents of the same lordly status, a toho descended from only one yya parent, presumably a male lord and a secondary wife or woman of lower rank. But it is not likely that all toho were born from yya. As in the Nahua relationship of *pipiltin* (nobles) to *teteuctin* (lords), collateral relatives must have maintained toho status over generations.[18] At present, it is unclear exactly how toho were recognized as members of particular lordly establishments and what privileges their membership may have entailed. However noble status was defined and recognized, it seems that each toho was affiliated with a particular aniñe and exercised an important role in a *siqui* or equivalent subunit of the ñuu. Toho were probably not appointed by yya to positions of authority in their siqui. More likely, each separate entity had its own lordly or noble lineage that was recognized by and subject to influence from the dominant establishment of the ñuu and yuhuitayu.[19] Normally, toho could not aspire to the rulership of a ñuu or yuhuitayu because they could not claim direct descent from a ruling couple. It is conceivable that a toho lineage could achieve yya status through successful intermarriage, political intrigue, or warfare or by gaining the approval of other lordly establishments. On the other hand, lordly houses could fail. The dynamic and contested nature of sociopolitical organization, with its transitional and ambiguous categories such as *ñuu siña* (discussed in chapter 4), was related to dynamic social relations and, in particular, the controversial relationship between noble lineages and sociopolitical structures. I elaborate on many of these issues in the following chapter on the yuhuitayu and in the discussion of land tenure in chapter 7.

Before the conquest, toho paid tribute in goods (*daha*) but not in physical labor (*tniño*), comparable to the obligations of Nahua pipiltin.[20] However, toho performed a wide range of administrative functions that were considered a type of tniño. This term *tniño* may be defined in broad terms as duty, labor, or responsibility. The *Vocabulario* defined the term *oficio*, or "occupation," as tniño.[21] Tniño referred to community labor, akin to the *cargo* or *tequio* in contemporary Mixtec communities, as well as individual responsibility or household labor.[22] In the colonial period, yya toho occupied the offices of the local cabildo, whose members were called the *tay natnay tniño*, "those who arrange the tniño."[23] The tniño of yya and toho was to organize the general tniño of the ñuu.

As we shall see in the following chapter, the periodic assembly of yya and toho of the cabildo (Spanish-style municipal council) for the purposes of ordering the tniño surely drew on preconquest precedent; women were excluded from the colonial institution, however. The service-oriented nature of organizing the tniño qualifies the premise that an elite group ruled over and dominated a subject class. Yya and toho may have enriched their own households by organizing and allocating the resources of their ñuu, but their positions involved a range of responsibilities and reciprocal obligations that were not to be taken lightly.

Aside from the duties of local government and administration, toho in the six-teenth century performed a range of specialized tasks from metalworking to long-distance trade; toho dzehe managed craft production and traded a wide variety of goods in local and distant markets. Many noblemen and noblewomen, particularly in the Yanhuitlan area, were actively involved in long-distance trade and the production and management of textiles. Most of these traders also controlled multiple tracts of land. Some toho stood to profit from the money economy of the colonial period, an abundance of land (especially in the late sixteenth and seventeenth centuries), and the possibility of investing in new enterprises, such as livestock raising. The roles of yya and toho in agriculture, long-distance trade, and cloth production are addressed in chapter 7 of this work.

Although references to individual yya and toho became less frequent by the begin-ning of the eighteenth century, the categories of yya and toho persisted in many places throughout the colonial period.[24] In 1705, community accounts from Yolomecatl referred repeatedly to the "yia toho" of the ñuu.[25] In 1709 and again in 1713, don Agustín Carlos Pimentel y Guzmán, the cacique of Teposcolula, was called a yya toniñe and recognized as a dynastic ruler.[26] In 1717, a toho named Domingo de Celís referred to the cabildo members of Teposcolula as "yya toho" and referred to the scribe as a "yya escrivano."[27] In 1726, Francisco Avendaño was proud to call himself a toho from the *siña* of Yuchayoho in Yodzocahi (Yanhuitlan), indicating the continuity of both sociopolitical and social terminology in the eighteenth century.[28] The latest Ñudzahui-language document that I have seen, written in 1807, refers to both yya and toho.[29] In the later period, translations defined yya and toho in general terms as simply *principales* (important people) or *caciques y principales*. For example, in 1652, doña Francisca Pet-ronilla referred more than once to "all the yya, toho, humble commoners" [niy cutu yhya toho ñandehy ñandahui] of Tequistepec. A late-eighteenth-century translation of the document reduced this phrase to "all the important people and natives" [todos los principales y naturales], suggesting how the social content of these terms had been simplified, at least in the eyes of the bilingual translator, in the century since doña Francisca made her testament.[30]

Terminology for lords and nobles was frequently juxtaposed with references to commoners and dependents.

Ñandahi and Dzaya Dzana

When people referred to Ñudzahui society as a whole, yya and toho were joined by another major group, called *ñandahi*. The term *ñandahi* corresponded in meaning with the Nahua macehualli (plural, *macehualtin*). A bilingual Ñudzahui and Nahuatl document from Tonalá and Atoyac, written in 1584, equates "maçehualtin" with "ñadey" (Mixteca Baja version of ñandahi).[31] The Mixtec *Vocabulario* gives "maçegual" as "ñanday" and also as "tay ñuu" (person from a ñuu).[32] Similarly, "vassal" (*vasallo*) is listed as "ñandahi," "tay ndahi," and "tay ñuu."[33] Defined as a person from a ñuu, *ñandahi* represents a label that might apply to anybody. In fact, the entry "people or multitude" is assigned the same three Ñudzahui terms associated with "vassal," suggesting how this group of people represented the vast majority.[34] Similarly, Molina listed "macehualli" under the entry of "people" (*gente*) in his Nahuatl *Vocabulario*.[35] Finally, "man of low lineage" is called ñandahi or *tai ndahi*.[36] The word *ndahi* has a semantic range from "strong" to "lowly."

The term *ñandahi* was the most frequently used term in the record for a common Ñudzahui person. In Yodzocoo (Coixtlahuaca), the commoners who worked the "rotary labor community fields" [ytu comonidad chiño] in 1596 were called "ñanchahi" and "ñanchay" (Yanhuitlan-area version of *ñandahi*).[37] When Ana Bautista Qhuañe went before the cabildo of Tlaxiaco in 1602, the lords and nobles addressed her in the reverential, familiar form "you female commoner" [ña ñanday ni].[38] In 1701, when the commoners of San Bartolomé Tiyacu appeared before the Spanish lieutenant of the alcalde mayor, they referred to themselves as "we humble ñandahi of the ñuu Tiyacu" [taca ñadzaña ñandahi ñuu tiyacu], "we humble poor people" [taca ñadzaña chai dahui], and "we humble, poor children" [taca ñadzaña dzaya dahui].[39] The association of *ñandahi* with poverty and humility was typical of the Nahua macehualli, too. In Nahuatl, the addition of the normally reverential element -*tzin* to macehualli (*macehualtzintli*) imparted the meaning of poverty or pitifulness to the term.[40] In Mixtec, one's use of the reverential subject pronoun *ñadzaña* in reference to self (singular or plural) was a similar, honorific convention reserved for polite speech. In 1681, a group from Ayusi, Yanhuitlan, combined the term "ñadzaña" with "ñandahi" when they called themselves "we ñandahi of the ñuu siña of Ayusi" [taca ñadzaña ñanjahi ñuu siña Ayusi].[41] They humbly referred to themselves as "we the poor ñandahi of the lord God and commoners of our lord King" [ñadzaña chay ndahui ñanjahi stoho ndios sihi ñanjahi stohondo Rey]. This entire phrase was translated as simply "poor vassals." Some of these individuals may have been toho who submitted themselves to the higher authority of the cabildo. A more neutral form of identification used in this document was the term "one who was born" in a given place [chay nicacu . . .], an equivalent of the Spanish "natural."

Despite an association with poverty and humility, the term *ñandahi* did not necessarily have a pejorative connotation. On the other hand, many nobles clearly saw themselves as superior to commoners. One criminal record makes this assumption all too explicit. In 1637, when two nobles from sujetos of Achiutla were riding horses along a river, one knocked the other off his horse, dismounted, and began to beat him. Two women who were going to bathe in the river saw the incident and attempted to break up the fight. According to the testimony, the assailant angrily confronted one of the women, saying: "Who are you, commoner, to come between nobles?"[42]

Another term used for commoners was *dzaya dzana*. The meaning of the term is somewhat obscure: *dzaya* is simply "child," but it is unclear whether *dzana* is postplaced as a qualifier or part of a semantic doublet. By itself, *dzana* refers to an unrooted or adopted person.[43] The term is also applied to "servant born in the house" (*siervo nacido en casa*), as a type of dependent.[44] Dzaya dzana has been attested numerous times in the record. In Yolomecatl, an alcalde referred to the social hierarchy with the phrase "all the yya, toho, and all their dzaya dzana" [taca yia toho sihi ndihi taca maa dzaya dzana].[45] In 1690, a letter from Sinaxtla called the commoners of the yuhuitayu "all the dzaya dzana of the tayu of San Andrés Sinaxtla" [taca dzaya dzana chayu San Andres Atata].[46] Two records from Teposcolula, written in the 1720s, refer to community members as "all the yya, toho, dzaya dzana" [taca yia toho dzaya dzana].[47] As a final example, a primordial title from the Valley of Oaxaca, written in the 1690s, referred to the commoners of Yuchaticaha (Cuilapa), Ñuyoo (Xoxocotlan), and Yuchayta (Chapultepec) as dzaya dzana. But the title also employed the valley variant of ñandahi ("ñanchehe") in describing how Hernando Cortés baptized the people of Yuchayta in 1523: "[First] the yya don Diego Cortés was baptized; second, all the toho were baptized; third, all the ñandahi were baptized" [niseenducha yya don Diego Cortés sihi nicuhui uhui niseenducha ndihi taca toho sihi nicuhui uni ñanchehe niseenducha].[48] The difference between ñandahi and dzaya dzana, if any, is unclear. Perhaps the latter term is associated more with dependents of yya, a possibility discussed below.

The *Vocabulario* of 1593 contains additional entries associated with "commoner." For example, *campesino* is equated with *tay yucu* (hill or forest person) and *tay ñuuyucu* (person from a hill or forest place).[49] The term appears only rarely in the record, especially in writings from the Tlaxiaco area, and it is often used in conjunction with ñandahi. In a testament of 1571, for example, doña María López referred to her "toho, ñayucu, ñandahi of the yuhuitayu of Yucucuihi" [toho ñayuqh ñadehi yuhuiteyu Yucucuihi].[50] Similarly, don Felipe de Saavedra referred to the "ñandehi" (commoners) and the "tóo ñajuqu" (toho, ñayucu) of Tlaxiaco.[51]

Ñandahi and dzaya dzana constituted a diverse category of men and women. Many ñandahi held and worked modest amounts of land associated with a particular household and gave daha (tribute in kind) to the ñuu based on their landholdings, textile production, and other resources. They were also subject to the tniño or draft rotary labor of the ñuu. Like the Nahua macehualtin, the ñandahi group was not sharply divided into categories of skilled or unskilled laborers; agriculturalists were generally not distinguished from artisans or local traders. This fact does not deny the existence of specialization. In general, work was gendered in colonial Ñudzahui society, but the gendered division of labor was not so strict as to prohibit men and women from performing a variety of duties that did not conform to an idealized division or specialization. Typical of most ñandahi, Inés Cahuiya of Teposcolula was associated with the "occupation of weaving *mantas*," whereas Juan Nahuaco "had no occupation other than his work in the fields."[52] These two occupations represent the basic gendered division of labor, reflecting the bare minimum of ideal responsibilities. These roles were so basic that Spanish officials described the oficio of some people in generic terms, as *trabajo de indio*, or "Indian work."[53] However, many ñandahi performed multiple types of work for the benefit of their households and communities. The typical male ñandahi worked on the land and gave his labor to communal projects such as building, clearing fields, chopping wood, working a mill or furnace, and transporting goods. Ñandahi women mastered spinning and weaving and performed a number of

tasks around the household and patio complex, which often extended to local marketplaces and fields.[54] Women prepared and cooked food and procured drink on a
daily basis. At times, women helped out in the harvesting of certain crops and gathered alimentary and medicinal plants. Certain places were known for particular trades
or goods because they had special access to the necessary raw materials.

Some male and female ñandahi served in the palaces and on the lands of yya,
either permanently or on a rotational basis. A category of commoners associated with
ñandahi and dzaya dzana were the so-called dependents of yya and toho.

Dependent Laborers

Dependent laborers did not hold lands directly from the ñuu but rather worked on
designated tracts of land or in the households of yya or toho. The *Vocabulario* lists "ter-
rasguero," a Spanish term for dependent agricultural laborer, as simply "tay situndayu,"
literally "one who works the land."[55] The equivalent of "work land" (*labrar tierra*) is the
verb *situ*.[56] The term *ndayu* means "mud" or "black" and was often used in conjunction
with *ñuhu* (land) in reference to fertile, valley lands.[57] Thus the term *tay situndayu*
suggests that agricultural dependents of yya worked the best, alluvial or irrigated
lands of valley floors. This social category is considered to represent a special class of
"servants-renters-tributaries" without land.[58] There are two important reservations to
the application of this term *tay situndayu* to the category of dependents. First, the word
has not been attested in the Nudzahui-language documentary record, despite many
clear references to dependent laborers in the service of lords. Second, this term refers
to only one type of labor—the agricultural work of men. Women also worked cloth
and prepared food for yya, and yet they would not have been called tay situndayu,
which refers explicitly to working lands. Since dependents and servants usually appear
in the record as married couples, this term would only apply to the males, if it was used
at all.

With few exceptions, native-language sources reveal that the terms *ñandahi* or *dzaya
dzana* were used in reference to dependents. The "tay situndayu" of the *Vocabulario*
may have represented a literal response to the Spanish word *terrazguero*. The fact that
there was not a separate term for dependents suggests that they were not clearly distinguishable from other ñandahi. The extension of the general term for "commoner"
to dependents is analogous to the use of *macehualli* in Nahuatl-language sources. In
the sixteenth century, the Spanish official Alonso de Zorita was among the first to consider the *mayeque* to be serflike and lower in status than the macehualtin, constituting
a separate category of Nahua society designated by a separate term. In reality, dependent persons did work the lands of nobles, but the terminology for them varied, and
they were most often called macehualtin.[59]

Yya often associated dependent laborers with their patrimonial lands. Sources from
the Mixteca Baja are especially rich in references to dependents. In her last will and
testament of 1611, the cacica doña Juana Beatriz consistently referred to the many
"ñadehi" (Baja equivalent of *ñandahi*, also spelled as "ñadey" and "ñadehy") who worked
her alluvial lands ("ñoho dayu").[60] Translators of the document consistently rendered
"ñadehi" as *terrazgueros*. In 1623, don Miguel de Guzmán mentioned the ñadehi who

worked the lands of his "large house palace" [huehi aniy canu]; he also referred to all the people of his yuhuitayu as "yia toho ñadehi."[61] In 1642, don Juan Agustín described "all the poor commoners of the yuhuitayu" in terms of "ñadey" [taca ñadey ñadahui yuhuitayu].[62] In the same year, don Gerónimo de Guzmán bequeathed Tisacu with its three *dzini* (subunits of the ñuu in the Baja area) and dependent laborers to his son don Domingo. Included in his bequest were "all my houses of the yuhuitayu of Santa Catarina Tisacu . . . and all my poor ñadey of Tisacu" [niy cutu huehy yu yuhuitayu santa caterina tisacu . . . sihy niy cutu ñadey ñandahui tisacu].[63] He continued to associate "all the poor ñadehy" [niy cutu ñadehy ñandahui] with "all the alluvial lands" [niy cutu ñuhu ndayu]. The translator once defined this latter statement as "all the male and female Indians along with all the lands of the cacicazgo."[64] Similarly, the cacique of Tonalá and Etla bequeathed lands, livestock, and dependents to his wife in 1643. He called the latter group "the poor ñadehi of the ñuu tayu" [taca ñadehi dahui ñuu tayu] and entrusted "my dzaya dzana" [dzaya dzanayu] to his wife.[65] Later he combined all the terms in one phrase: "all my dzaya dzana, the poor ñandahi from this ñuu tayu" [taca dzaya dzanayu ñadehi dahui saha ñuu tayu]. Perhaps the possessed form of the term accentuated the fact that the commoners were dependents.[66]

The frequent use of the term *ñandehy ñandahui* (commoner, poor person) in the Mixteca Baja reinforces the idea that dependents were marginal, humble people who derived their sustenance primarily from the lordly establishment. It is possible that the phrase "commoner, poor person," constituted a recognized metaphorical couplet for a dependent, that the qualifying term *ndahui* (poor, humble) distinguished dependents from ordinary ñandahi. In 1633, doña María de Velasco made frequent references to the "humble ñanday of mine" [ñanday ñatahui siyu], a phrase that was translated as "my terrazguero children" [mis hijos terrasgueros].[67] In 1652, the cacica doña Francisca Petronila seems to have drawn a distinction between "ñandehy" and "poor ñandehy" (ñandehy ñandahui) when she mentioned her patrimony of Tequistepec in terms of "all the yya, toho, ñandehy, ñandehy ñandahui, [and] all the cultivated lands" [niy cutu yhya toho ñandehy ñandehy ñandahui niy cutu ytu ñohodayu].[68] In 1676, when don Raimundo de Santiago y Guzmán bequeathed his "alluvial lands and poor commoners" [ñoho dayu ñadehi ñadahui] to his wife, the statement was translated simply as "lands of my cacicazgo," as if the dependent laborers were attached to the lands.[69]

Extant native-language testaments of prominent yya and yya dzehe from the Mixteca Baja seldom failed to refer to dependents who worked on their lands and provided various services to the aniñe. The preconquest arrangement of commoners in the personal service of the lord survived into the eighteenth century. Dependent commoners are most conspicuous in records from the Baja, because of the strength of its lordly establishments relative to the corporate structure of the ñuu, as discussed in the following two chapters. But dependent ñandahi appear in other parts of the Mixteca, too. One of the best examples comes from sixteenth-century Yanhuitlan, where don Gabriel de Guzmán claimed to possess several hundred dependents in the 1580s, scattered throughout fourteen siña of the yuhuitayu.[70] In 1704, don Agustín Carlos Pimentel y Guzmán y Alvarado traveled from Yucundaa (Teposcolula) to Yniyoho Yuchiquaa (Yolomecatl) "to see the people who periodically sowed his lands" [nindicotoya ñayehui yositu nino ñuhudeyuya].[71] This phrase "people who sow the lord's lands periodically" [ñayehui yositu nino ñuhudeyuya] is perhaps the nearest equivalent to "tay situndayu" that I have seen in the record.[72]

The precise labor and living arrangements that existed between yya and dependent ñandahi probably varied considerably from one time and place to the next. Although testaments from the Mixteca Baja refer to their agricultural dependents in terms of property, dependent agricultural laborers may have retained as much as half of the produce of the fields they worked. The *Vocabulario* defined the phrase "to work a field in order to collect half" with the verb *situ* (to cultivate) and the noun *ndayu*, replicating the term associated with terrazguero.[73] This phrase and associated terminology may shed light on a decree of 1567 issued by the Spanish alcalde mayor of Teposcolula, ordering that those who engaged in cultivating lands on behalf of the cacique should receive one-half of the harvest as compensation.[74] It is uncertain whether this percentage represents a colonial innovation or a preconquest arrangement; the decree attempted to standardize and limit caciques' traditional rights. In any case, this was a favorable arrangement for dependents by modern standards. It is also unclear whether some ñandahi may have served as part-time dependents. Some sources, including the abovementioned case from Yolomecatl, suggest that ñandahi were obligated to sow tracts of land and to perform services for yya on a temporary, rotational basis.

The most humble dependents were orphans or destitute people who lived and worked in others' households. Most yya and toho had live-in dependents, called *criados* (servants) or *huérfanos* (orphans) in Spanish. These men and women were usually called *dzaya*, or "children," often qualified by expressions to the effect that they had raised them as their own children. For example, in 1623, Lucía de la Anunciación of Teposcolula had two female dependents living with her. She referred to an orphan woman named Juana as "a child whom I raised myself" [dzaya nidzaquanomayndi]. Because she had no children of her own, she "took care of the child as if I gave birth to her myself" [dzahua tnaha dzaya nidzacacumayndi yotadziynindi]. Lucía referred to her other live-in dependent, named Ana, "as if she were my own child" [dzahua tnaha dzaya-mayndi].[75] Similarly, in 1726, Petronilla Calderón, a widow of Teposcolula, referred to two orphan women ("dzayandahui," or literally "poor children") who had been like daughters to her.[76] I have not come across references to these people as "dzaya dzana," but one entry in the *Vocabulario* suggests such a connection: "to have someone in place of a child" is given as "yoquidza dzaya dzana ñahandi," or literally "I make someone my dzaya dzana."[77] This sense of the term *dzaya dzana* may explain why some yya in the Mixteca Baja referred to "my dzaya dzana" in the same manner as "my lands and houses." In other words, they were part of a lordly establishment. These surrogate dzaya lived with yya and toho as contributors to the productive capacity of the household or patrimony. Sometimes, live-in dependents acquired property from testators who made provisions for them in their wills. Chapter 7 provides examples of dependents who inherited substantial properties in the absence of eligible heirs.

Many live-in dependents came from outside the ñuu and thus had no household or land of their own. The record provides many glimpses of these humble folk. In 1701, several people from the Coixtlahuaca area had become dependents in Tlaxiaco (and other places in the Mixteca) because of a "drought and a great hunger" in their home-land.[78] In 1685, Pablo de la Cruz, who was married to a woman named Juana López, came to Yanhuitlan from a sujeto of Tamasulapa (Santiago Tiñuu) in search of work. He became a dependent in the household of an elderly widow in Yanhuitlan named Catalina Gómez.[79] Catalina recalled how Pablo had proven to be very respectful and resourceful, a good person to have around "in place of her son and husband." He ended up working in the household of the cacique and cacica of Yanhuitlan, tending to magueyes. In fact, he became a *topile* (mid-level constable) by virtue of his middling noble status and his new connections in Yanhuitlan. All was well until he drunkenly offended the cacica and was forced to flee to Teposcolula. Let us consider a few more examples of live-in dependents. In 1681, a woman named Dominga Lucía came to Teposcolula from Las Minas de Silacoyoapan, in the Mixteca Baja, and found work in the house of the cacica of Teposcolula, doña Lucía de Orozco.[80] In 1605, a native tai-lor from Texupa, Luis Camani, served in the house of a merchant couple from Yan-huitlan, who made him perform agricultural labor and tend to mules in addition to making European-style clothing.[81] Sometimes, married couples served as dependents. In 1608, Juan Cunchi and his wife, María Hernández, who came from Topiltepec, grew wheat for a woman named Inés López in Yanhuitlan.[82] Many of these examples correspond with a pattern observed among the Nahuas: lords and nobles took in mar-ginal or desperate people who had recently arrived from other regions.[83]

Some dependents relocated to serve a lord's household or lands. For example, the yya of Tilantongo brought a group of people to Teposcolula, who settled into *barrios* there, when he married the yya dzehe of that yuhuitayu.[84] The relocation of dependents was part of a normal sociopolitical arrangement based on the residence patterns of yuhuitayu alliances. Yya or yya dzehe who moved to reside in a spouse's palace were accompanied by people, including toho and ñandahi, who might constitute the basis of another siqui (siña or dzini) in the new place of residence. Once again, dependents were outsiders or newcomers in these arrangements. The list of "macehuales terras-gueros" from Tecomaxtlahuaca referred to people who had come from outside the ñuu.[85] Sometimes, yya or yya dzehe sent a group of dependents to establish a settle-ment on distant patrimonial lands. For example, the cacique of Tlaxiaco founded a "barrio" called Ñuyucu, near the ñuu of Malinaltepec, when he sent ten married couples to work and live on ("poblar y guardar") his lands at the end of the sixteenth century.[86] In 1613, a representative of the group, Gaspar Juárez, recalled how the cacique of Tlaxiaco had ordered his parents twenty years earlier to settle there. These dependents were considered ñandahi by the officials of Malinaltepec, who refused to acknowledge claims by the cacique of Tlaxiaco and who demanded tribute from the barrio.

In summary, the group known as dependents did not constitute a separate, totally marginalized class. Previous studies have characterized this group in terms of lowly people who lived outside the social order.[87] The fact that the term *ñandahi* was employed for commoners as well as dependents suggests the lack of a fixed distinction between the two categories and the possibility of movement from one status to another. Instead of a rigidly stratified classification, the dependent laborer was merely a type of ñandahi whose position within a particular household and community depended on numerous factors. Far from being a homogeneous group, there were many different levels and types of dependents. In the colonial period, many dependents were outsiders who sold their labor to a household in return for food and shelter. Often, they ended up in the households of yya or toho, those who were most likely to possess the resources to put them up and to put them to work. In many ways, they were simply laborers in an economy with little money. Others were attached as a group to a lordly establishment and were considered part of a lord's patrimony. The two types of status are variations on the same theme; both were marginal types who lacked resources of their own and made arrangements to work for a lord.

As Lockhart noted for the Nahuas, the ambiguous distinction between dependents of noblemen and ordinary commoners is also due in part to the dynamic position of the lordly establishment in a given community or subregion.[88] The unclear distinction was also reinforced by colonial conditions, including Spanish pressures to reduce the number of lordly dependents and the desire of dependents to work lands of their own, especially when so much land fell out of use by the end of the sixteenth century. As pressure on the cultivable land supply declined in relation to the population throughout the first half of the colonial period, yya could no longer count on large numbers of dependents who had no access to lands. And by the late colonial period, Spaniards competed for the labor of marginal people in the Mixteca. Nevertheless, as we shall see in chapter 7, many yya and toho managed to retain many lands and a steady supply of labor throughout this period. In some parts of the Mixteca, the lord-dependent structure persisted well into the eighteenth century.[89]

The most humble dependents who came from outside the community performed many of the same functions as native slaves. The native-language archival record does not refer to indigenous slavery in the Mixteca because its practice and its principal source, warfare, had been abolished by the time native-language writing was fully developed. One term in the *Vocabulario* hints at the ambiguous distinction between slaves and dependents: the entry "slave born in one's house" is listed as *dzaya dzana*, one of two terms for a commoner (or a dependent).[90] The term "siervo" (servant, slave) is listed as *daha saha* (hands, feet) and *tay noho yahui* (person who is sold).[91] The Inquisition trials of the 1540s reveal several native slaves who served in the households of yya in Yanhuitlan.[92] All the slaves who appeared in the proceedings came from other communities. Native witnesses testified that slaves were bought and sold in Suchitepec, the most prominent marketplace in the Yanhuitlan area.[93] Thus, it is clear that a form of slavery existed in the Mixteca, but the actual terminology used to describe this category is attested only in the *Vocabulario*.

In reality, a form of native slavery persisted in the colonial period, although it was very limited. First, in the early sixteenth century, some *encomenderos* possessed native slaves who had been captured in "just wars." Second, the labor of convicted criminals was sold in public auctions.[94] These "slaves," as they were called in Spanish documents, were bound to serve their buyers for a designated number of years. In 1579, the cacique of Yanhuitlan, don Gabriel de Guzmán, bought a native slave for a period of six years.[95] The slave, Mateo López, had been caught stealing silver, and his labor for the six-year term was sold for thirty-six pesos. In 1596, the agent of a Spaniard in Antequera bought the labor of a Ñudzahui man from Tilantongo at the low price of ten and a half tomines

TABLE 5.1
Some Ñudzahui Social Categories

Term	Translation
yya toniñe	lord ruler
yya, stoho	lord
toho	noble
ñandahi	commoner or dependent
dzaya dzana	commoner or dependent
ñandahi ñandahui	poor commoner or dependent
dzaya (ndahui)	orphan, household dependent
daha saha	slave (attested only in *Vocabulario*)

NOTE: Females in each category are identified by the qualifying term *dzehe*, "woman."

for five years.[96] Essentially, male and female slaves who were sold to Spaniards, *obrajes*, and native nobles became lowly dependent laborers. Normally, convicted persons were threatened with additional penalties if they attempted to flee from an obraje. Whereas normal dependents presumably had some discretion in choosing where to live and work, these slaves had no choice. If punishment for criminal activity was a source of slavery in preconquest times, as some sources suggest, this form of colonial slavery would have continued a native practice.

Social Obligations

The discussion of social categories leads us to consider in more detail the overlapping obligations that bound members of each group to one another. Conflict among social groups in the colonial record, and between Spanish officials and representatives of the ñuu, usually concerned the performance of labor (tniño) and the giving of tribute (daha). Colonial petitions and complaints, despite a tendency toward partisan exaggeration inherent in the genre, shed light on social relations by revealing the expectations of each group. Like moral speeches, petitions invoke the unwritten and contested social contract that governed relations among yya, toho, and ñandahi. Conflict makes the distribution of power and status more visible within the ñuu.[97] Discrepancies between ideal and actual relations that involve Spaniards or Spanish introductions suggest how colonial changes affected social relations. Clearly, the practice of airing grievances was not unprecedented. When redress could not be found within the ñuu, Spanish authorities were a potential recourse. Native officials and individuals rapidly learned how to file petitions in the Spanish legal system and overwhelmed administrators in the early period with complaints against both Spaniards and other indigenous people.[98] Once again, we begin with the most active and vocal group in the record—the nobility.

After the conquest, yya and yya dzehe continued to receive numerous services and goods, but colonial changes increasingly reduced these privileges to a minimum. For example, in 1558, don Domingo de Guzmán, yya toniñe of Yanhuitlan, was entitled by

Spanish law to receive one turkey and the labor of ten native men and women who served in his palace or aniñe each day. The *Codex Yanhuitlan* depicts men and women who provided goods and services as couples (see fig. 5.1). Every six months, he also received two large containers (*xiquipiles*) of cacao and seven *cargas* of cotton. He was entitled to the yield of at least four fields of maize (ranging in size from 200 × 200 brazas to 800 × 800) and one fruit orchard (300 × 300 brazas). In reality, the patrimonial land-holdings of the aniñe were extensive and included many tracts of land in other communities.[99] In response to a declining population, colonial authorities restricted the number of dependents in the service of lordly establishments, who were not required to pay tribute to the ñuu, in order to increase the number of native tributaries whose labor and wealth supported the encomendero, the church, Spanish officials, and the crown. In other words, Spaniards competed with yya for access to the tniño and daha of commoners and dependents.

FIGURE 5.1. A couple provides food and household labor. *Codex Yanhuitlan*, plate XII.

In 1573, when the number of servants working in the palace of Yanhuitlan had been reduced to six men and women, don Gabriel de Guzmán (don Domingo's successor) objected on the grounds that he possessed certain traditional obligations that required many more servants and dependents, including the provision of food and drink for nobles, who assembled and stayed in his palace.[100] To assist him in this obligation, he insisted that he needed twelve men to fetch wood and water and twelve women (the marriage partners of the twelve men) to make tortillas and prepare food, in addition to those dependents who cultivated his lands and who provided tribute items, such as food and cloth. He reciprocated their service in the palace by feeding them and by giving them a daily quantity of cacao (chocolate beans).[101] His request was denied. When don Gabriel's son inherited the position of cacique and the palace of Yanhuitlan in 1591, he immediately complained that he spent an inordinate part of his estate fulfilling the obligations of his position as cacique and governor. Don Francisco argued that while his salary and servants were increasingly limited by Spanish law, his traditional obligations as yya remained the same.[102] Witnesses testified that he spent considerable sums of money regaling the yya and toho who visited him and stayed in his palace, and he redistributed part of his wealth to commoners who worked for him. He was also obligated to sponsor feasts, and, in fact, his palace or aniñe was the site of most community feasts.

Conspicuous consumption was a strategy of social distinction among elites in Mesoamerica, as it was in Europe during this period. At the same time, the emphasis on feeding and sheltering people evoked the ideal of redistribution.[103] The yya couched his complaint in the language of reciprocity and ancient custom. Yya and yya dzehe received goods and services from the community and, in turn, redistributed a part of their resources to nobles. In the Ñudzahui system, high status was validated by the ability to feed people and to sponsor feasts, among other symbolic and material acts. Nancy Farriss has observed similar references to the significance of *convites* or banquets among the Maya *batabs* of colonial Yucatan.[104] As Spaniards placed restrictions on traditional rights and privileges, yya complained that they could no longer fulfill the social responsibilities that represented and sustained their authority.

The yya of Yanhuitlan were not alone in their complaints to Spanish authorities about declining privileges. Don Francisco de Arellano, cacique and governor of Tecomaxtlahuaca, stated that in ancient times there were eight hundred "maceguales terrazgueros" [commoners dependent laborers] who lived on his patrimonial lands and served his palace. He complained that this number had dwindled to sixty-five couples by 1578.[105] In don Francisco's defense, numerous witnesses testified to the many traditional rights associated with the palace named Caltitlan. The case is accompanied by a pictorial manuscript that illustrates the declining amount of tribute received by eight successive generations of ruling couples, proceeding from the earliest rulers at the bottom of the manuscript to don Francisco and his wife at the top.[106] Don Francisco's petition for access to more labor, in the midst of another major epidemic (1576–81), gained little sympathy from Spanish authorities. Social relations between yya, toho, and ñandahi were profoundly altered by the recurring diseases that decimated the native population. Don Francisco's complaints reflected a bitter realization that Spanish law continued to restrict his patrimonial privileges while his base of support declined with each decade. The situation worsened over time. Thirteen years after his protest, in 1591, another virulent epidemic swept through the Mixteca.[107]

As some yya complained of their diminished access to labor and tribute, factions within some ñuu accused yya of abusing their traditional rights. These factions, often led by "macehuales," as ñandahi were called in Spanish legal cases, refused to pay for the maintenance of their caciques' estates. After failing to find recourse at the local level, they brought their petition to the Spanish alcalde mayor, thus expanding the arena of conflict. For example, in 1598, "macehuales" from Chicahuastla accused their cacique, don Martín de Fonseca Pimentel, of overstepping his authority.[108] In 1600, the "macehuales of the cabecera, estancias, and barrios" of Chalcatongo filed a complaint against the cacique, don Antonio de Arellano, for excessive labor and tribute demands.[109] The men and women complained that for the past twenty years they had provided the services of five women and two men to the palace, without compensation. For the past ten years, they had tended to his cows, pigs, sheep, and goats, they had spun great quantities of cotton, and they had woven many bundles of cloth. Each person had paid the yearly tribute of six reals, in addition to a tomín to feed the bishop, even when he never came to the community. A lawsuit against Tecomastlahuaca had sapped another two reals apiece. Several trips to Mexico to dispute the *congregación* and other legal matters had amounted to additional costs. The members of the *cabecera* and nine sujetos and *estancias* demanded a financial compensation of three hundred pesos, salaries in return for service, and a prohibition of increased tribute and periodic *derramas,* or levies. A similar complaint was filed in 1625, when the commoners of the cabecera and sujetos objected once more to the taxation and tribute levied on them by the nobles.[110]

Some social conflicts stemmed from the sixteenth-century sociopolitical reorganization. For example, in 1612 and again in 1616, Santiago Nuyoo refused to recognize the cacique of the cabecera of Ocotepec, don Pedro de Sotomayor, who demanded the harvest of several plots of land and a quantity of cloth, among other goods and services. [111] He also required three married couples to serve in his palace. People from Nuyoo complained that in order to travel from Nuyoo to Ocotepec the couples were forced to walk as far as six leagues; women carried grinding stones on their back to serve for periods of eight days without compensation. Before 1616, Nuyoo was instructed to fulfill its tribute obligations to the cacique on five separate occasions; each time it did not comply. Toho from Nuyoo defended their resistance by claiming that the ñandahi refused to give their labor or goods to him. A young noble of Nuyoo, don Tomás de Rojas, a cousin of the cacique of Ocotepec, said in plain terms: "The macehuales refuse to comply." He confirmed that commoners had approved of using *cofradía* (lay sodality) funds to offset community expenses in lawsuits against Ocotepec. In addition, many people had paid two or three tomines apiece for the suit. By 1616, community officials had been jailed three times on account of the conflict in Nuyoo, indicating how nobles assumed the responsibility and blame for a community's actions in the colonial order. "The macehuales have done this on their own," Marcos de la Cueva replied to questions about leadership. Although the ñandahi were obviously involved in this dispute over local resources, it is likely that the strategy of blaming commoners was designed to deflect liability from the cabildo and to diffuse accountability within the community.

After all, Spanish officials could not jail the entire community. This pragmatic strategy helps explain why so many community rebellions in the colonial record seemed so leaderless and spontaneous. The fact that the officials immediately escaped from jail by "tricking" the jailer suggests that the entire community supported the resistance. In any case, it is clear that ñandahi could exercise a vocal, active role when their collective livelihood was threatened, whether they supported or opposed the local yya and toho. Of course, another form of collective action was the *tumulto*, or riot, documented for the Mixteca Alta by William Taylor. Appropriately, Taylor found that many civil disturbances of the late colonial period began with an attack on the local jail where the officials were being detained.[112]

Toho who benefited from their positions as mediators between ñandahi and yya were often drawn into disputes over social obligations. For example, confrontation between the ñandahi and yya of Chicahuastla spread to the nobles in 1625, when they were accused of benefiting from their control of the cabildo and close relations with the cacique.[113] In Teposcolula, several yya and toho on the cabildo were accused of abusing their positions of authority in 1648.[114] The governor, *alguacil mayor* (constable) of the church, interpreter, and notary were accused of demanding uncompensated personal services. For example, the alguacil mayor allegedly forced other church officials (*cantores*) to work his lands, while the notary allegedly forced men and women to serve in his house. In Coixtlahuaca, a group of ñandahi opposed the toho who made them work on an estancia of the local friars in 1628.[115] Representatives of eight sujetos of Coixtlahuaca complained that the Spanish *mayordomo* of the estancia mistreated the fifteen men (and one woman who cooked for them) who went to work on the estancia every week.

A final example from Achiutla illustrates how ñandahi in sujetos could come to resent the uncompensated labor they gave to yya and toho in the cabecera.[116] In 1601, a group of macehuales from the cabecera and three "estancias" refused to serve the nobles any longer. Their uncompensated burdens included working silk, cultivating lands, giving chickens in tribute, providing food for feasts, spinning cotton and weaving, working as carpenters, tending to sheep and cattle, and providing domestic service. One pound of cotton (to be spun and woven) was distributed to every four tributaries, and one of every four tributaries was obligated to provide a chicken. They also alleged that a group of nobles sold surplus community maize for their own profit instead of redistributing it according to custom. Moreover, they accused nobles of collaborating with the Spanish alcalde mayor, especially in the production of cloth for profit. The group managed to win a settlement of 101 pesos from the nobles, who paid the fine according to their resources (ranging from 15 pesos to 3 tomines per person). This case demonstrates how commoners resisted the consequences of the colonial reorganization by refusing to provide goods and services to those who stood to benefit from the new system.

The Spanish legal system required caciques to maintain a local consensus and heard complaints from factions who contradicted their authority. When internal conflicts over tniño reached the boiling point, factions called on Spanish officials to limit caciques' privileges. In response, caciques called on Spanish judges to enforce their perceived rightful due. By the eighteenth century, conflicts between factions and caciques over tniño made the status of dependents and tribute labor subject to the legal rulings of Spanish judges. The following two chapters address this aspect of changing social relations from the perspective of political authority and property rights.

Internal discord tends to conceal the structural conditions of conflict. The colonial system placed multiple demands on the tniño of yya, toho, and ñandahi. When necessary, cabildo officials took an active role in countering these demands with petitions, protests, or violence on behalf of the entire ñuu. For example, in the year of 1647, the cabildo of Yanhuitlan demanded that the Spanish alcalde mayor obey the labor laws regarding "indios de servicio" that he was appointed to protect. They accused him of using native men and women for personal services, from the spinning and weaving of cotton to the care of his stable and the provision of food and drink.[117] Soyaltepec and Coixtlahuaca made the same complaints that year. In the same year, native nobles from Achiutla and its three sujetos complained of abuses by the Spanish alcalde mayor and other Spanish residents. They were compelled to perform many personal services, tend cattle, provide food, spin great quantities of cotton, collect cochineal, and serve in the houses of Spaniards. They were forced to fulfill these obligations in addition to their usual *repartimiento* duties, they claimed.[118] In the same year, 1647, the communities of Chalcatongo, Iscatlan, Yolotepec, Atlatlahuca, Atoyaque, Tlaxiaco, Cuquila, Chicahuastla, and Ocotepec joined the protest.[119] Teposcolula lodged a similar complaint with Spanish authorities the following year.[120]

The complaints and conflicts presented in this section demonstrate the contested nature of social relations in the colonial period. Often, grievances were expressed in terms of a breakdown in the idealized, reciprocal obligations of yya, toho and ñandahi. Although similar types of conflict over rights and obligations must have existed before the conquest, colonial changes and institutions threatened to widen the gap between cultural expectations and social realities. Most grievances revolved around the issues of tniño and daha, as the colonial system placed increased demands on local resources for labor and goods. Some elites benefited from their roles as mediators and their relatively favorable position in the local economy, but they were still obligated to fulfill their tniño. The discussion of social conflict and change is continued in the following two chapters.

The next section addresses the topic of social relations from the perspective of naming patterns. The selective adaptation of Spanish personal names and titles reflected Ñudzahui social distinctions and revealed one's position within colonial society.

Ñudzahui Personal Names

Preconquest-style pictorial writings identify individuals with calendrical names based on the Ñudzahui version of the ancient Mesoamerican calendar. Diviners who kept track of the calendar and its associated rituals assigned names to newborn children based on their day of birth or birth naming ceremony. The 260-day ritual calendar consisted of 20 day names and thirteen numbers; each day name was identified by a sign, and each of the numbers was represented by a large dot. In pictorial writings, names appear as stylized glyphs of day signs, connected to a string of dots from one to thirteen. The words for each day sign and numeral differed from conventional vocabulary for these numbers and nouns. For example, "deer" was *cuaa* instead of the conventional word for the animal, *idzu*, and "twelve" was *ca* instead of the usual term for the number, *usi uvui*. Thus someone named 12-Deer, according to the calendrical day on which he or she was born, was called Cacuaa, and not "usi uvui idzu." The famous warrior *yya* of the codices, 8-Deer, was known as Nacuaa. A few of the terms bear a resemblance to the conventional vocabulary. For example, "eight" is ordinarily *una* but is *na* in the calendrical vocabulary, whereas "wind" or *tachi* is reduced to *chi*. Other calendrical names and numbers do not resemble conventional terms, however. Perhaps this terminology is part of the honorific register or noble speech discussed in chapter 3. Some ambiguity between certain numbers exists, probably because the orthography does not mark tone; for example, *si* could indicate 10 or 13, while *ca* could be interpreted as 1, 2, or 12. Table 5.2 lists calendrical terminology for day signs and numerals, based on Dahlgren's and Smith's observations of codices containing alphabetic glosses, including the *Codex Sánchez-Solís* and the Lienzo of Nativitas.[121]

Early colonial records show that every Ñudzahui man and woman possessed a calendrical name.[122] Pictorial writings reveal that noblemen and noblewomen also possessed personal names, represented by additional stylized glyphs. It is unclear whether commoners possessed personal names or nicknames. Personal Ñudzahui names were not maintained in the colonial period, at least not in writing.[123] In the Nahua area, in the early postconquest years, the majority of women and girls had a second name that indicated birth order, a gender-specific method of naming rarely observed among males.[124] Nahua names tended to limit women's names to a small repertoire.[125] Ñudzahui naming patterns, on the surface at least, applied to women and men equally. Names for men and women were both derived from the calendar and were not restricted by gender or status. Distinctions of rank and status may have been built into the calendrical system, based on the specific meaning inherent in each number or sign, or even the connotation associated with each combination or permutation. And in the case of nobles, personal names may have conveyed a measure of social status and prestige. It is possible that some personal names were associated with particular lordly establishments, since palaces were assigned names, too.

Adoption of Spanish Names

In the colonial period, one's name reflected his or her social status and cultural standing vis-à-vis Spaniards. Yya and toho were the first to be baptized and the first to adopt Spanish names after the conquest. By 1550, most yya and toho had a Christian baptismal name and a calendrical last name. Baptismal names were derived from saints' names, which were normally chosen by a child's parents or assigned by a priest. Often, but not always, the sex of the saint corresponded with that of the named person.[126] Baptismal names and calendrical names were combined so that the latter served as a surname, and two names became the norm. By the 1560s and 1570s, most nobles had acquired both baptismal and Spanish surnames, judging by the signatures of those who witnessed the testaments of yya and toho. For example, everyone who attended the writing of doña María López's last will and testament, done in 1571, had Spanish surnames, but the testator also referred to some people with native calendrical names, such as

TABLE 5.2
Ñudzahui Calendrical Vocabulary

Day Signs	Conventional Term	Calendrical Equivalent
Alligator (crocodile)	coo yechi	quevui
Wind	tachi	chi
House	huahi	cuau; mau
Lizard	tiyechi	que
Serpent	coo	yo
Death	ndeye	mahu
Deer	idzu	cuaa
Rabbit	idzo	sayu
Water	nduta	tuta
Dog	ina	hua
Monkey	codzo	ñuu
Grass	yucu	cuañe
Reed	ndoo	huiyo
Ocelot	cuiñe	huidzu
Eagle	yaha	sa
Vulture	tisii	cuii
Movement (earthquake)	tnaa/nehe	qhi
Flint	yuchi	cusi
Rain	dzavui	co
Flower	ita	huaco

	Conventional Numeral	Calendrical Equivalent
1	ee	ca, co
2	uvui	ca, cu
3	uni	co
4	qhmi	qui
5	hoho	q
6	iño	ñu
7	usa	sa
8	una	na
9	ee	q
10	usi	si
11	usi ee	si i
12	usi uvui	ca
13	usi uni	si

SOURCES: Dahlgren 1954 and Smith 1973a.

Mateo Cahua (1- or 12-Dog) and Catalina Qhuañe (5-Grass), who owed her money.[127] The last witness to sign the testament of the yya toniñe of Tlaxiaco, don Felipe de Saavedra, wrote a simple "nju°" (abbreviated Juan) with rubrics.[128] The other witnesses who signed the document included their Spanish surnames, however. In contrast to these noble gatherings, when Diego de la Cruz of Tamasulapa made his testament in 1621, many of the witnesses possessed calendrical surnames, including Diego Siqhu (10- or 13-Lizard), Juan Siquaha (10- or 13-Deer), Gabriel Sicuii (10- or 13-Vulture),

Gaspar Qhuii (5- or 9-Vulture), Juan Quicuii (4-Vulture), María Qhuqhu (5- or 9-Lizard), and Catalina Qhcuii (5- or 9-Vulture).[129] Similarly, in San Bartolomé Ñucucu (Coculco), a testament of 1633 referred to several people who had retained their calendrical names: María Sacuaa (7-Deer); Domingo Sicuey (10- or 13-Vulture); Pedro Coquihui (1-Crocodile); Domingo Camahu (12-Death); Baltasar Qhñoo (5-Monkey).[130]

Unlike yya and toho, many ñandahi continued to bear calendrical names throughout the seventeenth century. The appearance of indigenous surnames is especially common in criminal records referring to a cross section of social types. For example, a ñuu near Coixtlahuaca generated a record of tribute money paid to a native *regidor* who was accused of abusing his authority.[131] The complaint contained the names of "ñanchahy" (*ñandahi*) who had given the native official money. Table 5.3 lists the names and amounts paid. The first line of the list features the only person without a calendrical name, "Juan García, also known as 8-Ocelot" [juan garcia naqh may navidzu].[132] Even though he possessed a Spanish name, the writer felt it necessary to provide his native name, too. This Juan García 8-Ocelot, who represented the group in legal proceedings against the regidor, was probably a toho. Only one person from this remote ñuu had a Spanish surname in 1596, but he was not the greatest contributor to the collection. A woman named "Anasayu," or Ana 8-Rabbit (*na* is "eight," and *sayu* is "rabbit"), gave the most. She effectively combined Spanish (Ana) and Ñudzahui (nasayu) names by reducing the redundant *na*. We would expect her new name to be pronounced much the same as her old one.

Double names such as Juan García 8-Ocelot were common in the transitional period between calendrical and Spanish surnames, especially in the late sixteenth and

TABLE 5.3
List of Tribute Payers from a Ñuu near Coixtlahuaca, 1596

Juan García[a]	3 pesos	Francisco Qhuvidzo	4 tomines
Juan Sichi	1 peso, 4 tomines	Martín Coco	4 tomines
Pedro Namañi	2 pesos	Juan Qhucusi	1 peso
Anasayu	7 pesos	Domingo Qhucuaha	4 tomines
Catalina Cacuii	5 pesos	Diego Cocuaa	5 tomines, medio
Maria Qhqhehui	5 pesos	Diego Qhcusi	3 tomines
Domingo Nuqhuu	1 peso	Martín Siquehui	6 tomines
Martín Siquehui	2 pesos	Juan Sicuii	2 tomines
Juan Sicuiy	4 tomines	Pedro Qhcuañe	3 tomines
Pedro Qhcuañi	4 tomines	Domingo Cacuaa	6 tomines
Domingo Cacuaa	1 peso, 4 tomines	Domingo Nachi	7 tomines
Domingo Nachi	1 peso	Juan Sichi	2 tomines
Cristóbal Namao	1 peso	Juan Qhucusi	3 tomines
Vicente Coqhoo	4 tomines	Domingo Cocosi	1 tomín
Diego Qhcusi	1 peso	Juan Nuviyu	2 tomines
Diego Cocuaa	1 peso, 4 tomines	Josef Siqhii	2 tomines

SOURCE: AJT-CR, 1:52.

NOTE: Written at the top of the list: "memoria pesos nisica francisco ximinez regidores sa geronimo" [Account of the pesos given to the regidor of San Gerónimo, Francisco Jiménez]

[a] "naqh may Navidzu nitasicha" [also known as 8-Ocelot, gave him . . .]

early seventeenth centuries. In Teposcolula, the noblewoman Lucía de la Anunciación was also called Lucía Siqhu (10-Lizard) in supporting documentation, although she used only the Spanish name in her testament of 1623.[133] Lucía Hernández Ñuquihui (6-Crocodile) was called Lucía Hernández de Ñuquihui in supporting Spanish documentation, as if her calendrical name were a place-name or a Spanish surname.[134] Likewise, Ana García of Tlaxiaco kept her calendrical name Qhuañe (9-Grass) and thus had two surnames; to make matters even more confusing, she was also called Ana Bautista in Spanish documentation.[135] In Topiltepec, Juan Pérez Siquidzu (10-Ocelot) and Andrés Pérez Sicuañe (10-Grass) were present when Gonzalo López made his last will and testament in 1610; Juana Qhchi (5- Wind), Francisco Cacuahu (12-House), and Marcos Siquahu (10-House) also attended the solemn ceremony.[136] In 1618, Juan López of Tlaxiaco was also called Juan Ñucuii (6-Vulture), and, curiously, María Ñututa (6-Water) was also called María Xita, perhaps a name derived from another language, such as Chocho.[137]

By the second half of the seventeenth century, Ñudzahui calendrical names were being replaced by Spanish surnames in most of the major cabeceras of the region. This pattern was not observed everywhere, however. In 1704, many people in Yolomecatl entered the record with familiar names, including María Siquaa (10- or 13-Deer), Rosaria Saquaa (7-Deer), Pedro Osorio Dzahuiyo (7-Reed), Pedro de la Cruz Sichi (10- or 13-Wind), and Pedro de la Cruz Siquaa (10- or 13-Deer).[138] The use of indigenous names alongside Spanish names would give way to full Spanish names in the course of the eighteenth century, or at least they no longer appear in the documentary record. In more remote places where there was little need or pressure to adopt a Spanish surname, the use of indigenous names and nicknames probably endured throughout the colonial period. One has the impression that Spanish surnames were of limited value in familiar circles, where kinship, reverential, and informal nicknames were commonly used.[139] Many people testified in the criminal record that they did not know their neighbors' Spanish surnames. In 1662, for example, Melchor de Morales could not remember the surname of his niece, Catalina, even though he frequently went to her house.[140]

Ñudzahui calendrical names bore no relation to family or lineage.[141] Perhaps for this reason, many children had Spanish surnames that were unrelated to those of their parents or siblings. A typical naming scenario can be observed in Huaxuapa, in the year 1642.[142] The yya toniñe don Juan Agustín was married to doña Francisca Petronilla; he was the son of doña Juana Beatriz and the father of don Rafael de la Cruz and don Baltasar de los Reyes. Thus, even though Spanish surnames eventually replaced calendrical names, they were still thought of in terms of variable names. For nobles, the choice of prestigious surnames was more tied up with *compadrazgo* (ritual co-parenthood) than with lineage. However, some of the more illustrious Ñudzahui families guarded and maintained their patronymics, including names such as Guzmán, Alvarado, Maldonado, Pimentel, Mendoza, and Saavedra. Indeed, don Agustín Carlos Pimentel y Guzmán y Alvarado, cacique of Teposcolula in the first quarter of the eighteenth century, was very proud of his title *don*, his two first names, and his three distinguished surnames. To these he added the titles of yya toniñe and cacique.

Names and Social Status

In the early period, having a Spanish or indigenous surname indicated one's social status within colonial society. Later, when most people had a Spanish surname, the name itself distinguished degrees of social differentiation.[143] A distinguished Spanish surname indicated high status for both men and women. The highest names were those of famous conquerors, encomenderos, or well-to-do Spaniards. In some cases, a local Spaniard consented to lending his name to a native lord and served as *padrino* (ritual godparent). Below these distinguished names, Spanish patronymics bearing the -*ez* suffix were generally more plebeian unless accompanied by a second surname. Toho were most likely to adopt these more homogeneous Spanish surnames, including Hernández, Sánchez, López, Pérez, and García. It was not uncommon for yya from relatively minor ñuu to adopt such names, also. Saints' names could also be used as surnames, especially by commoners, in the absence of Spanish sponsors. Apparently, the names of friars served as the model for such a practice.[144] Friars often assumed the names of specific saints, in place of their own surnames, when they took their vows. For example, Juan García might call himself Juan de Santo Domingo. A native commoner might receive his or her baptismal name and second name at the same time. Eventually, the repetitive "de san" or "de santo" was omitted, leaving Juan Domingo. Two first names were typical of indigenous commoners but rare among Spaniards.

It is no coincidence that most Ñudzahui names looked alike. The naming system maintained distinctions between indigenous people and Spaniards; even after native surnames had gone out of (public) use, one could usually tell a Ñudzahui man or woman from a Spaniard by his or her name. A typical native person's name was usually recognizable as the double first name of a ñandahi, or one first name with a predictable surname. Moreover, Spanish names were adapted to Ñudzahui phonetics. For example, don Felipe de Saavedra of Tlaxiaco was also called Sahabedra, inserting a glottal stop between the like vowels; similarly, a woman from Yolomecatl named María Sánchez was called Sahanchez, mistaking a stressed vowel for a glottal stop.[145] In remote Santiago Nuyoo, a document dated 1699 listed its cabildo members in unmistakably native terms: "ndo yose carçias" [don Josef García]; "tomas nde çatiago alcandes" [Tomás de Santiago, alcalde]; "ndego çarapia regindo" [Diego Sarabia, regidor]; and "pedro spaña escrivanos" [Pedro de España, escribano].[146]

Names also reflected, to a certain extent, one's place of residence and its position within the sociopolitical order. For example, when the tribute collectors of the siña of Yuhuyucha appeared in Yanhuitlan in 1598, all but one of them had indigenous surnames, including Andrés Sichi (10-Wind), Juan Sacussi (7-Flint), Juan Siyo (10-Serpent), and Juan Dzayo (7-Serpent). The one with a Spanish second name was Estevan García, a typical name for a toho in this period.[147] In contrast, all the cabildo officials from Yanhuitlan had prestigious Spanish surnames (Guzmán, Zárate, Torres), and two (the governor and an alcalde) bore the title *don*. The tribute collectors from this outlying siña were toho who had not attained Spanish surnames by this period.

In general, the names of yya and toho who lived in cabeceras stood out from those who lived in sujetos. A legal dispute between Yanhuitlan and Tecomatlan in 1584 illustrates the difference. Witnesses testifying on behalf of the so-called estancia of Tecomatlan included several men with middling Spanish names such as Ramírez, López, García, and Hernández. Also included on Tecomatlan's side were men with combined Spanish and Ñudzahui names, such as Domingo García Sacui, Luis Carlos Simaa, Mateo Camaa, Miguel Gerónimo Cavico, Juan López Sico, Juan García Nisayo, Domingo Hernández Sichi, and Joseph Hernández Siviyo. In contrast, Yanhuitlan's side featured many prominent Ñudzahui lords and Spanish residents who testified on their behalf.[148] Not one of Yanhuitlan's witnesses had an indigenous surname.

An important aspect of the relationship between naming patterns and social status was the use of titles *don* (sir, lord) and *doña* (madam, lady). Only the very highest Spanish nobles possessed the title *don* or *doña* in the sixteenth century. Accordingly, the title was reserved for the most elite members of Ñudzahui society. Thus, when forty prominent witnesses from Yanhuitlan testified in the case against Tecomatlan, only two had the title *don*.[149] In Teposcolula, don Felipe de Santiago was governor in 1586, while don Andrés de Tapia and Gaspar de Palmas were alcaldes; nobody on the municipal council below these men possessed the title *don*.[150] Earlier, in 1564, five dons had graced the cabildo with their presence, led by the yya toniñe don Felipe de Austria, who was bold enough to name himself after the reigning Hapsburg king.[151] Don and doña were practically synonymous with yya and yya dzehe, though not every yya and yya dzehe became a don or doña.[152] Whereas the title lost its luster among Spaniards by the late colonial period, in part because it was used in a more liberal manner, Ñudzahui society continued to hold the titles in high regard and continued to limit their use to a few men and women. Repeated epidemics reduced the pool of candidates who were eligible to bear the high title.

A preliminary review of Chocho-language records indicates that Ñudzahui naming patterns may also apply to patterns among their prominent neighbors to the northwest. A list of Chocho names from Coixtlahuaca in 1628 reveals that everyone had a Spanish first (baptismal) name and all but eleven had indigenous surnames, apparently based on the calendar (given the repetition of morphemes).[153] Seven of the nobles listed at the bottom of the document had Spanish surnames, and only 2 of the 102 had the title *don* (see table 5.4). A testament dated 1608 from Tamasulapa referred

TABLE 5.4
Some Chocho Names from Coixtlahuaca, 1628

Pedro Xishihi	Ysabel Rhantaa	Felipe Xindu
Cristóbal Zachziy	Francisco Xochziga	Juan Xicha
Bartolomé Zaquichzu	Jacinto Dachixo	Luis Ximi
Juan Rhanchu	Diego Dachisango	Melchor Xisango
Gerónimo Xunuña	Benito Xisango	Juan Ximi
Gregorio Rhataha	Francisco Zontaha	Bartolomé Xana
Gaspar Xathee	Gaspar Xuthee	Catalina Simi
Diego Xichziga	Juan Xiña	Diego Nina
Diego Xiña	Martín Xiña	Luis Xisango
Lucía Siñau	Luisa Rhaxi	

SOURCE: AJT-CR, 3:362.

to both Ñudzahui and Chocho men and women with calendrical names: the Ñudzahui were named Diego Siquaha and Catalina Ñucusi, and the Chochos were Agustín Xindayu, Melchor Tesacu, Gonzalo Tnatzee, and Cristóbal Dzihiña.[154] A testament of the year 1600 from Santiago Tiñuhu, near Tamasulapa, mentioned several Chocho with names such as Tomás Xaqhindu, Amtonio Tnacha, Ndiego Rhaxi, Domigo Xisij, Magdalena Tethee, and Pedro Tuchsinga.[155] References to Chocho calendrical names in Ñudzahui texts are seen in and around Tamasulapa as late as 1665.[156] Testaments of 1669 and 1695 from Coixtlahuaca, written in Chocho, reveal that everyone present had a Spanish surname.[157]

In summary, Ñudzahui personal names reflected degrees of social differentiation. The timing of the acceptance of Spanish names varied considerably, occurring first among yya and toho in the cabeceras of the region. Although Spanish names were adopted everywhere in the Mixteca by the end of the colonial period, the majority of ñandahi had not taken a Spanish surname by the end of the sixteenth century, several generations after the conquest. Others kept their calendrical names and merely added Spanish surnames, coming closer to the Spanish pattern of double names. The fact that calendrical names were still quite common in many places by the beginning of the eighteenth century attests to the survival of the ancient calendar, ritual naming ceremonies, and associated practices at least two centuries after the conquest. As the 260-day divinatory calendar faded into the past, ancient names gave way to a wide variety of Spanish names or simply names based on saints, which could also in a way be calendrical, since practically every day of the Christian calendar recognized a saint. Having two first names, as in Juan Diego or Ana María, was a sure sign of one's social and ethnic position in colonial society. Thus, personal names also distinguished most indigenous people from Spaniards.

Typically, yya and yya dzehe converted to the new system rather quickly. They came into contact with Spaniards most frequently, and their names revealed the extent of their connections. Even in the early period, men and women who bore the titles *don* and *doña* did not appear with an indigenous, calendrical name. Toho appeared early with Spanish surnames, but they adopted more homogeneous, predictable names. Ñandahi did not adopt Spanish names until much later because they had little reason or opportunity to do so; many people had Spanish names but little occasion to use them.

The introduction of a new naming system made a lasting impression on the historical memory of at least one community. A false title from the Valley of Oaxaca (discussed in chapters 2 and 9) begins by describing how Hernando Cortés arrived and gave names to the Ñudzahui people of Yuchayta. First Cortés (and presumably a priest) baptized and named the cacique don Diego Cortés, who was also called by the personal name Dzahui Yuchi, or "rain-flint." Then they baptized all the other yya, toho, and ñandahi in the order of their rank. Writing in the 1690s, the author(s) of the title described the legendary act of baptismal naming in the 1520s in terms of the social order.[158]

The following two chapters continue the discussion of social relations.

CHAPTER 6

❧

Yuhuitayu

THE *YUHUITAYU* UNITED two *ñuu* (local states) through the marriage of hereditary male and female rulers, *yya* and *yya dzehe*. Each ruler represented a separate, autonomous ñuu and its lordly establishment (the building, lands, relatives, dependents associated with a yya lineage). Preconquest and postconquest pictorial writings referred to the yuhuitayu with a familiar glyph: a married couple (*tayu*) seated on a reed mat (*yuhui*). Colonial native-language documents used the term consistently in reference to communities involved in these royal alliances. Thus, the yuhuitayu was both a place and a political arrangement created by dynastic alliances. Spaniards called the place a *cabecera* or *sujeto* and referred to the rights and properties of the yuhuitayu in terms of a kingdom, a *cacicazgo* or a *señorío*. Male and female hereditary rulers survived the conquest and continued to represent and govern multilevel sociopolitical structures despite significant colonial changes. The evolution of the yuhuitayu under Spanish rule exemplifies the complex nature of change and continuity in Ñudzahui society and culture.

The first part of this chapter describes the indigenous system of government at the time of the conquest, focusing on the representation of ñuu by yya and yya dzehe. In particular, I examine four important native concepts: hereditary authority, or *toniñe;* the royal palace or lordly establishment, known as the *aniñe;* one's duty or responsibility to community, called *tniño;* and the yuhuitayu, a system of joint male and female political rule. Despite local variation in the precise arrangements of hereditary government, all areas of the Mixteca shared these four fundamental concepts and institutions. The second half of this chapter focuses on the effects of colonial changes, particularly the implementation of Spanish-style municipal government, on native institutions and concepts.

Royal Titles

Native hereditary leaders were called *caciques* (male) and *cacicas* (female) in Spanish, based on an Arawak word adopted by Spaniards in the Caribbean and applied to all native rulers in the Spanish Indies. In the Ñudzahui language, leaders were called *yya toniñe*, "lord ruler," and *yya dzehe toniñe*, "lady ruler." As descendants of *yya tnuhu*, "royal lineage," they represented the yuhuitayu. Caciques and cacicas were also called *yya* in general and were customarily addressed or referred to with honorific titles, pronouns, and vocabulary. Hereditary rule was defined in terms of *sa toniñe*, or "the rulership." The *Vocabulario en lengua mixteca*, published in 1593, defines a *señorío* (lordship) as *sa si toniñe*, "that which belongs to the rulership," or *sa si yya*, "that which belongs to the lord(s)."[1] *Toniñe* also appears in association with "city" (*tayu toniñe*) and "pueblo" (*tayu toniñe* and *ñuu toniñe*).[2] The Ñudzahui *toniñe* is analagous to the Nahua *tlatocayotl*.[3] Another general term for a high lord was *stoho*. The *Vocabulario* lists "señor" as *stoho* and *yya*.[4] Three terms are given for "señor grande": *yya canu; yya toniñe;* and *yya canu toniñe*. The first of the three terms contains the word *canu* for "great" or "big" and simply means "great lord"; in this context, the term could also apply to important people such as Spanish officials or a bishop. It does not bear the significance of *toniñe*.[5] Sometimes *yya toniñe canu* is seen in reference to a very important lord. The addition of *canu* to *yya toniñe* is comparable to the Nahuatl *huey tlatoani*.[6]

In contrast to the frequent use of *toniñe* in reference to lords, the term *cacique* was not used by Ñudzahui-language writers. References to toniñe appear in the earliest colonial records. In 1573, don Felipe de Saavedra and his wife, doña María, were known as yya toniñe of Tlaxiaco and Achiutla.[7] In 1621, the cacique of Yanhuitlan, don Francisco de Guzmán, was called "our lord ruler" [costohonju yya toniñe].[8] In 1622, don Felipe de Velasco appeared with a group of lords and nobles in Teposcolula seeking a dispensation for the marriage of his son, don Diego de Velasco y Arellano, to a cousin named doña Micaela de la Cueva.[9] Eight "yhya toniñe" from eight separate yuhuitayu attended the ceremony. The provincial friar was called "yhya cano" in recognition of his high rank within the church. Don Felipe de Velasco was called "yhya toniñe cano" [great lord ruler] in general and, more specifically, "lord ruler of the yuhuitayu of Santiago Miltepec" [yhya toniñe nuu yuhuintayu sanctiago ndanduhua]. Doña María was referred to as the "yhya ñaha toniñe" [lady ruler]. In 1704, when "the lord ruler don Agustín and his brother-in-law, don Francisco, came to see the people working his lands" [yia toniñe don augustin sihi cadzaya don francisco nindicotoya ñayehui yositu nino ñuhudeyuya] in the community of Santiago Yolomecatl, the "yia toniñe" was greeted with gifts of chocolate, tortillas, and sugar.[10] The same terminology was used in the Mixteca Baja, where *toniñe* was pronounced and written as "toniy." For example, in 1643, don Rafael de San Miguel y Salazar was referred to as "ruler of the tayu of Tonalá and Etla" [yia toniy tayu ñoniy ñoduchi].[11] In a bilingual Nahuatl-Ñudzahui document from Atoyac and Tonalá (1584), the Nahuatl term *totecuiyo* is equated with the Ñudzahui "stohoyu" for "our lord," and the Nahuatl *tlatoani* is paired with the Ñudzahui "yia toniy."[12] This term *yya toniñe* continued to be used in the eighteenth century, although it was often reduced to *yya*.

Royal Residences

In the Mixteca, yya toniñe, or rulers of the yuhuitayu, lived in royal residences, the aniñe. *Toniñe* and *aniñe* are probably related words, much as the Nahuatl *tecpan,* "palace," is presumably derived from *teuctli,* "lord."[13] *Aniñe* was translated in Spanish-language documents as *tecpan,* and, in fact, palaces in the Mixteca were not unlike those in central Mexico.[14] Essentially, single-story stone structures, each with its separate entrance, were arranged around sunken patios and enclosed by an outer wall. The representation of a palace in the map of Teozacualco, painted in 1580, illustrates the general layout of the structure (see fig. 2.4). In this illustration, four separate units surround a patio, with one entrance to the entire structure. The aniñe of Yanhuitlan was described in sixteenth-century documents as a multicomponent complex of one-room houses and nine separate patios.[15] In the 1540s, lords assembled in the palace, called "the houses of the cacique" in Spanish, for many important matters, including sacred ceremonies and feasts.[16] This aniñe is depicted in the *Codex Yanhuitlan* (see fig. 6.1).

In Teposcolula, the royal residence was a structure that is known today as the "Casa de la Cacica." The structure in Teposcolula is a rare example of a surviving Meso-american palace in Mexico (see fig. 6.2).[17] The decorative disk motif on the upper part of the outer walls conforms with motifs on palace structures in the *Codex Nuttall,* the *Codex Yanhuitlan,* and other writings from the Mixteca (see fig. 6.3).[18] Central Mexican palaces represented in the *Florentine Codex* and the *Codex Mendoza* bear the same motif. In its association with palace structures, the disk motif symbolized the site of political and religious authority.[19] It is possible that the palace was named after the cacica doña Catalina de Peralta. In 1569, she and her husband, don Diego de Mendoza, formally took possession of the aniñe of Teposcolula, which stood "behind and opposite" the monastery, on or adjacent to land named "ytonocoyoo." This is precisely where the Casa de la Cacica stands today.[20] Doña Catalina was the chosen heir of Teposcolula (called Yucundaa in Ñudzahui), and her husband was lord of Tamasulapa (Tiquehui); she laid claim to her position with ancient paintings and the last will and testament of her uncle, don Pedro Osorio, which was written before sixty native witnesses in 1566. Cacique status was conferred legally by Spanish officials, after hearing testimony and reviewing all titles and documentation pertaining to the case. The caciques were confirmed and blessed by a priest in the church.

The aniñe was the household of the lordly establishment and the symbolic site of the yuhuitayu. The ceremony of 1569 associated the royal couple with images of the community's past. When doña Catalina took formal possession of her aniñe, as a ruler of the yuhuitayu of Teposcolula, she and her husband walked through the entire palace complex, accompanied by several male and female nobles. They entered the main patio and, before all the witnesses, sat together on a woven mat as a sign of true possession. The ceremony reenacted a scene from the codices: male and female lords seated on reed mats, usually inside or in front of a palace. This ritual act was repeated five separate times, as the couple proceeded through each separate *aposento,* or "room," of the complex.[21] In each room, the couple sat on *petates y asientos de indios* (reed mats and Indian seats), or "petates e yquipales" (from the Nahuatl *icpalli,* "seat"; the *petlatl icpalli* was associated with a royal throne in central Mexico). The only aposento in which

FIGURE 6.1. Stylistic representation of a royal palace in the *Codex Yanhuitlan* (upper left). Seated rulers on the right address community members. The Ñudzahui word *aniñee* is written on the palace structure. *Codex Yanhuitlan*, plate II.

FIGURE 6.2. The "Casa de la Cacica" in Teposcolula (Yucundaa). Photo taken by author in 1996.

they did not take a seat was the small *aposento de cocina* (cooking room), although both doña Catalina and don Diego entered and took possession of it together. Their royal residence resembles those described in central Mexico: separate dwelling places or "rooms," called *huahi* in Ñudzahui, were divided by patios and separate entrances.

Doña Catalina and don Diego passed through the individual units and patios of the palace complex, accompanied by the noble witnesses; the choreographed repetition of gestures must have made a lasting impression on the social memory of the community. They opened and closed doors, they threw stones from one side of a patio to another, and they received a written title from the Spanish official. Finally, the couple escorted everyone out of the house and locked them out. As part of a legal proceeding presided over by the Spanish *alcalde mayor* or an Audiencia judge, the ceremony clearly incorporated Spanish rituals, just as the palace had adopted European hinged doors and other architectural influences by this date. Despite the inclusion of Spanish ceremonial acts, indigenous rituals and symbols remained at the core of the ceremony in the account from Teposcolula. The act of tecpan possession is recorded for several other communities in the sixteenth and seventeenth centuries.[22] Only this earliest description of the ceremony from Teposcolula records the seating of male and female lords on reed mats. Later descriptions focus on formal Spanish acts, crowned by the transfer of palace keys from the alcalde mayor to the male cacique. The latest known example, when don Baltasar de Velasco y Guzmán inherited the palace of Yanhuitlan in 1629, focuses on the male *cabildo* members who participated in the ceremony.[23]

The aniñe was the site of a reed mat throne, the seat of power in Ñudzahui society. The palace possession ceremony exemplifies how the native nobility and Spanish authorities utilized ritual as a "performative language" to create and sustain community

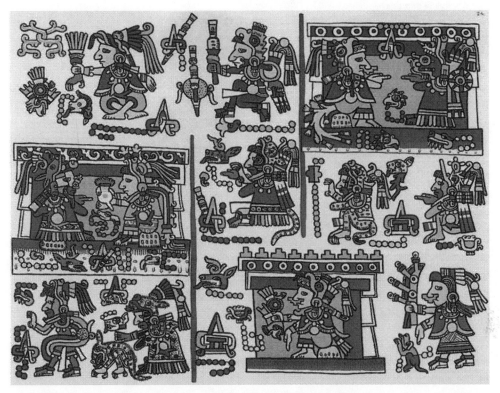

FIGURE 6.3. Images of the yuhuitayu and aniñe in the *Codex Nuttall*, p. 24. Codex-Zouche Nuttall, British Museum, London. Facsimile edition by Akademische Druck-u. Verlagsanstalt, Graz/Austria 1987.

memory.[24] The lords performed a series of repetitive postures and gestures before a noble audience, commemorating sacred events and ceremonies that are inscribed in the codices. Invoking images from the codices, the ceremony transmitted social memory in both textual (codices) and nontextual (performance) ways.[25] The ceremony invited a select group of nobles to participate in the symbolic construction of community. At the same time, the lords validated their status as hereditary rulers.[26]

Spanish influences on the ceremony also featured rituals of repetition and gesture, including the throwing of stones and slamming of doors. These acts emphasize the sanctity of private property, as if to say that rightful owners could do as they pleased in their own houses. If they wanted to throw stones across the patio and slam doors, then that was their prerogative. Similarly, kicking the sod, tearing up grass, and throwing sticks and stones were typical ceremonial acts associated with taking possession of land in New Spain, based on medieval traditions in Castile. As a final act of "true possession," the owners threw the guests out of the palace and locked the door behind them. Later in the colonial period, the transfer of keys from one male authority to another represented a Spanish choreography of authority and possession that excluded women. Public displays of power in Spanish ceremony tended to privilege male actors. Spanish ceremonies of possession were invented traditions that did not re-create the image of the yuhuitayu from the indigenous past. The formal recognition of native structures and institutions, verified by the ceremonial transfer of a written title, made the palace's legitimacy and maintenance dependent on Spanish law. Spanish influences on native ceremonies confirmed and reinforced colonial authority and control. Early colonial ceremonies of palace possession reflect the attempt or need of local elites to speak two symbolic languages: one that made sense to Spaniards and another that validated their authority before members of their own communities. Ultimately, Mixtecs directed their performance to the male authorities of New Spain.

The aniñe continued to maintain a distinct identity in the colonial period. The structure was assigned a specific name and attached to named lands within a named entity. For example, don Gerónimo García y Guzmán, yya from the *siqui* Yaaçahi of the yuhuitayu of Yucundaa (Teposcolula), stated in 1672 that his wife, doña Lázara de Guzmán, was to inherit "the walled houses of my palace" [huahi nama ñu aniñendi].[27] Several years later, the widow doña Lázara described the same aniñe more explicitly in her own testament: "the lordly tayu palace named Ñuuñañu belongs to this tayu cabecera" [yia tayu aniñe ñuuñañu maa tayu dzini ñuu yaha]. She bequeathed the aniñe to her three sons, saying: "I leave in the hands of my sons the tayu palace Ñuuñañu and all the cultivated lands of the palace and all the palace lands of Ñuuñañu" [aniñe tayu ñuuñañu sihi nee cutu solar ñuhu aniñe sihi ndehe taca ca ñuhu aniñe ñuuñañu yaha ndehe yonachihindi ndaha dzayandi].[28] Thus, don Gerónimo and doña Lázara kept their aniñe in a particular siqui of the yuhuitayu, which was attached to specific lands. Appropriately, the structure's name means "part of the ñuu."[29]

The record contains several references to named structures associated with the yuhuitayu and its subdivisions. In 1571, doña María López, yya dzehe toniñe of Tlazultepec, identified her royal dwelling with the yuhuitayu when she referred to "my yuhuitayu, my patio-house of Yucucuihi" [yuhuiteyudi cahihuehidi yucucuihi].[30] In 1572, doña María de Paredes, yya dzehe toniñe of Teposcolula, referred to her aniñe in the siqui called Tanduaa.[31] Don Benito de Zúñiga, yya toniñe of Coixtlahuaca in 1656, referred to his "tecpan" in a "barrio" of Tecomatlan called "Utziniyucu," including its lands and laborers.[32] In 1708, a group of nobles in Yolomecatl referred to the "palace of the lord don Agustín Carlos Pimentel y Guzmán called Dzahuico" [aniñe yia don Agustin Carlos Pimentel y Gusman yonani dzahuico].[33] The location of an aniñe within a particular subentity of a ñuu was also common in the Mixteca Baja. For example, don Jorge de la Cruz Alvarado's palace was located within a specific *dzini* of Tequistepec in 1678, which he called "my house palace in the dzini of Ñuchiyo" [huehiyu aniy dzini ñuchiyo].[34] Like most royal palaces, don Jorge's aniñe contained an archive of legal records and paintings supporting the patrimonial claims of his lordly establishment. In his testament, don Jorge explained that among the contents of the palace were a "satno tutu" [chest of papers] and a "satno ñuhu tutu" [chest of land documents], which contained "the land documents and testaments of my grandparents" [ñuhu tutu testamendo si siy sitnayu] and "all the papers concerning the lands and lienzos of the borders" [dihi cutu tutu saha ñuhu dayu dzoo dzaño].[35]

In many respects, the Ñudzahui aniñe resembles the tecpan of central Mexico, where it was closely associated with the *altepetl* as the palace or residence of the *tlatoani* (ruler) and the repository of the kingdom's records, histories, and titles. Each tlatoani of an altepetl was based in a particular *calpolli* of that altepetl, where his tecpan was located.[36] The aniñe is especially comparable to the eastern Nahua variant of the tec-pan—the *teccalli*.[37] The Nahua teccalli was a noble lineage with a titular lord who possessed lands and dependents. The teccalli referred as much to a lordly establishment (building, lands, relatives, dependents) as a physical structure, a sociopolitical entity as much as an actual residence.[38] The teccalli might be as large as the calpolli, and the leaders were often the same people. In Nahuatl, the literal meaning of the term *calpolli* as "big house" conveys a metaphorical association between the sociopolitical entity and the palace. The teccalli and tecpan were integrated into the calpolli-altepetl framework. Similarly, the aniñe was integrated into the siqui-ñuu-yuhuitayu configuration. As a big house, the aniñe was to some extent the basis and origin of these sociopolitical structures.

The Yuhuitayu as a Symbol of Power and Sexuality

The image of the yuhuitayu evoked by the ceremonial possession of the aniñe in Teposcolula symbolizes the convergence of social and political relations within the community. Let us review the discussion of the yuhuitayu as a sociopolitical entity, introduced in chapter 4. The term *yuhuitayu* is a metaphorical doublet: *yuhui* is "reed mat" and *tayu* is "seat" or "pair," depending on tone; as a convention in the codices, "tayu" is a tone pun for both the seat of authority and the married, ruling couple. *Tayu* is given for "par" in the *Vocabulario,* and the term for "marido y muger casados" is *tay nicuvui tayu,* or "those who were paired" or "seated [together]."[39] *Tayu* was also used occasionally for the royal palace or its establishment, although *aniñe* is a much more common word for the structure.[40] As a seat of power, the yuhui seated two rulers, uniting two ñuu until both were deceased. The emphasis on selecting heirs who descended directly from royal parents assigned equal importance to both members of the yuhuitayu and their respective lordly establishments.[41] In this arrangement, the couple embodied and exercised the rulership. The convention of the seated couple in the codices, represented by an actual ceremony, had a direct corollary in the terminology of sociopolitical relations.[42]

The image of the ruling couple stands out in pictorial writings from the preconquest and postconquest periods. The couple is customarily seated on a mat or on small stools or jaguar skins positioned on top of the mat (see figs. 6.3 and 6.4). Sometimes, the mat is missing, and the seated couple is perched on a *tablero* platform or frieze motif.[43] Often, the couple is seated before the temple or palace, or within the structure itself, facing each other. Occasionally, the couple faced the same direction.[44] Even when the mat's interwoven design is not detailed, as is often the case in the *Codex Nuttall*, it still appears as a yellow strip on which rulers are seated (the mat is usually colored yellow or brown).[45]

The petate or seat motif was a Mesoamerican symbol of authority.[46] In Nahua society, the petlatl icpalli (literally "mat seat") was a seat of power and government. In European terms, the mat was a royal throne. The Nahua historian Chimalpahin used the term as if it meant the "rulership" and suggested that it was synonymous with *tlatocayotl*.[47] However, consider the differences between Ñudzahui and Nahua images:

FIGURE 6.4. The Ñudzahui yuhuitayu. *Codex Becker II*, p. 4. Codex Becker II, Museum für Völkerkunde, Wien. Facsimile edition by Akademische Druck- u. Verlagsanstalt, Graz/Austria 1961.

whereas the Nahua tlatoani (male Nahua ruler) is depicted in codices from central Mexico seated alone on a reed mat with a raised back and his spouse may or may not have been depicted off to the side or behind him, the Ñudzahui man and woman shared the mat, faced each other, and actively gestured toward each other (see fig. 6.5).[48] Rarely is a Ñudzahui ruler seated alone. Alfonso Caso and other scholars have recognized this essential difference, but few have elaborated on its significance for the political authority of women.[49] In fact, Caso concluded that women were ineligible for the rulership, their prominent position in the codices notwithstanding.[50] The complex gestures and postures of seated men and women constitute a "gestural vocabulary" that is still largely unintelligible.[51]

Many Nudzahui writings produced before and after the conquest feature the rectangular, woven reed mat on which ruling couples are seated. Smith has noted a few appearances of the central Mexican petlatl icpalli (the reed mat throne with an extended back) in Ñudzahui manuscripts, including postconquest products such as the *Codex Yanhuitlan, Codex Tulane,* and some of the lienzos from the Coixtlahuaca Valley. In general, these are later works that bear a distinct Nahua influence. None of the preconquest-style manuscripts from the Mixteca contains the central Mexican–style petlatl icpalli. The rectangular mat motif is most prevalent in the codices *Bodley, Selden,* and *Becker II.*[52] Despite considerable variation in style, the flat, rectangular reed mat is the most common motif associated with the depiction of seated rulers in the Mixteca.[53]

The mutual influence of Nahua and Ñudzahui cultural forms is especially notice-able in the Mixteca Baja. For example, Yucuyuchi (called Acatlan in Nahuatl) was a Ñudzahui ñuu with a minority Nahuatl-speaking population in the sixteenth century. One document, written in 1601 on behalf of the cacique and cacica of Acatlan, is accompanied by a painting with Nahuatl-language glosses.[54] The *Codex Tulane,* which illustrates the ruling dynasty of Acatlan, reflects several central Mexican (and Euro-pean) stylistic influences in its composition.[55] The codex consists of strips of animal hide in the form of a roll or cylindrical scroll, which is read from the bottom upward. The codex contains several alphabetic glosses in the Ñudzahui language. Significantly, the painting depicts pairs of seated male and female figures who face each other. How-ever, the male cacique is seated alone on a central Mexican–style petlatl icpalli, wearing a central Mexican headdress and *tilmatli,* or cloak; the female cacica is seated in the central Mexican manner and wears typical central Mexican dress (see fig. 6.6).[56] The women are not seated on the mat, but they are paired with male rulers as if they were ruling couples.[57] This manner of depiction appears to represent a combination of ele-ments from two traditions, a compromised pose between the Ñudzahui ruling couple

FIGURE 6.5. The Nahua tlatoani on his petlatl icpalli. *Codex Mendoza,* f. 68. The Bodleian Library, University of Oxford.

FIGURE 6.6. Seated rulers in the *Codex Tulane,* plate II. Middle American Research Institute, Tulane University.

and the Nahua tlatoani.[58] Perhaps this hybrid rendering of sociopolitical relations is the pictorial equivalent of the *yucunduta*, discussed in chapter 4.

The image of the couple on the mat has been interpreted as the event of a royal marriage or a conference, but the glyph also represented a place and its seat of authority. The frequent use of the term *yuhuitayu* in colonial documentation in reference to specific places and political arrangements indicates that it was an authentic political structure. As a place, the combining form of *yuhui* and *tayu* resembles the metaphorical doublet *altepetl* (combining *atl*, "water," and *tepetl*, "hill"), the term applied to central Mexican local, ethnic states.[59] As an institution, the yuhuitayu encompassed the duties, privileges, goods, properties, dependent laborers, and influence derived from the rulership. Spaniards interpreted the rights and properties of the yuhuitayu in terms of a "kingdom-cacicazgo."[60]

The woven mat also symbolized fertility and sexuality. As a royal throne, the Ñudzahui yuhui or reed mat was a conjugal bed on which ruling heirs were conceived and born and the royal line perpetuated. Lineage was often depicted in lienzos and maps from the Mixteca as a vertical list of yuhuitayu, each couple bearing the progeny for future ruling pairs. A sixteenth-century painting on cloth from the Coixtlahuaca area, the Lienzo of Nativitas, employs this convention (see fig. 6.7).[61] Appropriately, a metaphor for sexual intercourse in the *Vocabulario* is *yoyuhuindiña*, literally "to mat someone."[62] This association of the mat with sex and marriage is exemplified by a description of a Nudzahui royal wedding. Recorded in 1579, the narrative informs us that the woman and man were literally joined together by their clothes; his cloak (*dzoo*) and her overblouse or *huipil* (*dzico*) were tied together before an assembly of family and nobles.[63] Seated on a mat, the couple divided a tortilla and a piece of meat and fed each other, placing bits of food in the other's mouth. Later, they consummated their marriage on the mat.[64] This wedding scene explains a metaphor for "the marriage of lords" recorded by fray Antonio de los Reyes in the sixteenth century—*yocuvui huico yuvuiya*—literally, "to celebrate a feast of the royal mat."[65] Sometimes the feasting and dancing went on for days.[66] Images of food offerings enhanced the sexual, reciprocal symbolism of the union. Another metaphor for marriage refers to the drinking of pulque, an alcoholic drink extracted from the maguey cactus. The representation of a pulque vessel on the mat was a potent symbol, considering the drink's metaphorical associations with sexuality (see fig. 6.8).[67] Finally, the mat was associated with fertility; codices depict women giving birth on stylized reed mats (see fig. 6.9).

As a prominent symbol in pictorial writings, the yuhuitayu venerated the importance of yya and yya dzehe. Women ruled alongside men as entitled members of the tayu. It is no coincidence that women stand out in Mixtec pictorial writings from the preconquest and early colonial periods. In the documentary record, cacicas are most conspicuous in postconquest sources as widows, when they alone managed the toniñe. But women continued to represent ñuu in the yuhuitayu throughout the colonial period. In comparison, various Nahuatl and Spanish sources indicate that Nahua women held the rulership only on rare occasions. Nahua women could sometimes influence the selection of a male ruler.[68] Although succession by males was clearly standard, the Nahua historian Chimalpahin did allow the possibility of *cihuatlatoque*, "women rulers." Nonetheless, female succession among the Nahuas was exceptional.[69]

FIGURE 6.7. Section of the Lienzo of Nativitas. Photo courtesy of Carlos Rincón-Mautner.

FIGURE 6.8. Depiction of the yuhuitayu and a vessel of pulque. *Codex Bodley,* p. 30. The Bodleian Library, University of Oxford.

Royal Marriage and Succession

Several historians have noted the prominence of hereditary cacicas in the Mixteca. Alfonso Caso concluded that women were ineligible to rule, although he did cite examples when the lordship was "transmitted" through the female line. In the case of Yanhuitlan, he observed that the first child inherited the patrimony of the father, and the second that of the mother.[70] Bárbro Dahlgren regarded primogeniture as the rule of succession, despite noting many exceptions to the rule in the *Relaciones geográficas,* codices, and archival record. Even when women did inherit a title, they were entrusted with passing it to a male relative and could not bequeath the patrimony directly, Dahlgren concluded.[71] Using archival records from the early colonial period and the findings of Caso, Ronald Spores was the first to posit that "females inherited, possessed in their own names, and passed on titles."[72] He noted that the "matter of sibling gender in determining succession" was unclear, and he was careful not to exaggerate the significance of female succession. A year later, in the introduction to their study of the population of the Mixteca Alta, Sherburne Cook and Woodrow Borah made the following observation regarding cacicas: "Inheritance could proceed through the female line in default of male issue, and a woman could inherit and hold the office of ruler. A peculiar and interesting custom that seems to have been uniquely Mixtec obtained when the female ruler of one state married the male ruler of another."[73]

Like Caso, Borah and Cook recognized a preference for male heirs, but they acknowledged the potential of women to rule. The second part of their observation, however, suggests that women ruled only by default, that all "cacicas" had no eligible male siblings. The nature of royal marriage alliances among a restricted group of high nobles would have made this scenario very unlikely. Mary Elizabeth Smith noted that

FIGURE 6.9. Depiction of birth on a reed mat. *Codex Nuttall,* p. 27. Codex-Zouche Nuttall, British Museum, London. Facsimile edition by Akademisch Druck- u. Verlagsanstalt, Graz/Austria 1987.

the "equal importance of men and women of the noble class is expressed pictorially in both pre- and post-hispanic Mixtec manuscripts."[74] As Spores observed, sixteenth-century lawsuits from the Mixteca Alta indicate that the choice of heirs and favored dynastic lines depended on the advantages to be gained from alliances rather than a particular gender bias.[75] At times, women were chosen over male siblings to inherit the rulership. Likewise, in the Valley of Oaxaca, William Taylor observed that cacicazgos favored male succession but that female descendants were not uncommon. Significantly, many examples of female succession in the valley involved Ñudzahui communities, including the prominent yuhuitayu of Cuilapan.[76]

    Despite a general recognition that the Ñudzahui system of hereditary rule was "peculiar and interesting" in the roles its alliances ascribed to cacicas, these "uniquely Mixtec" customs have not been fully examined from a gendered perspective. This section builds on earlier observations of the principles of hereditary rule and considers the role of women in the yuhuitayu. Early colonial sources from the Mixteca, including pictorial writings, native-language testaments, and civil cases involving caciques and their patrimonial estates or cacicazgos, reveal certain general patterns that I have organized into five parts. In discussing these patterns, I emphasize the shared features of hereditary rule in the Mixteca without ignoring extensive local variation and change.

First, the yuhuitayu was a marriage alliance. Ronald Spores summed up the situation neatly when he observed that "in every instance, a possessor of a title was married."[77] No lord or lady ruled alone, unless his or her spouse had died. Marriage united the patrimonies of a yya and a yya dzehe, who each represented at least one separate community or ñuu.[78] Through this interdynastic alliance, each of the ñuu could claim yuhuitayu status as an equal partner. The two ñuu might be located in the same area of the Mixteca, or they might be separated by considerable distance. Marriage among yya and yya dzehe was community exogamous, and residence patterns of the nobility were mainly ambilocal; in some places, especially the Mixteca Baja, there was an observable preference for patrilocal residence patterns.[79] Colonial introductions favoring male heirs, discussed below, promoted patrilocality as a strategy of political consolidation. However, the relative resources and prestige of lordly establishments continued to influence residence patterns more than any other factor. In reality, members of a ruling couple were likely to retain royal residences in both home communities.

Second, both sets of parents participated equally in the marriage arrangement, and both lordly establishments exchanged equal gifts at marriage, usually cloth, food, and prestige items. There was no dowry, as in the European tradition. Many informants of the *Relaciones geográficas*, recorded in 1579 and 1580, reported that parents consulted priests on the advisability of the marriage.[80] Many of these testimonies indicated that the groom's family initiated the marriage proposal. Groups of nobles and dependent laborers might move with their yya or yya dzehe to serve in the aniñe, as part of the lordly establishment. Such arrangements would account for multiple ethnic "barrios" and shifting populations. Marriage alliances were also arranged with lesser-ranking subunits, integrating smaller structures into larger networks by kinship.[81] The gifting and alliance-building strategies of the yuhuitayu were based on the principles of reciprocity and mutual benefit. Strategic marriages held more promise of long-term gain than the prospect of warfare.[82]

Third, on the death of one ruler, the other could continue the rulership alone and need not remarry, exercising control over the deceased spouse's estate until his or her own death. Remarriage did not affect the original yuhuitayu; new spouses and children could not inherit estates or titles from previous marriages. If a married heir apparent died without inheriting, the spouse held no right to succession.[83] When heirs failed to marry, they were usually not acknowledged.[84] Endogamous marriages within the ñuu were especially common among *toho*, or lesser nobles.

Fourth, each ruling member of the yuhuitayu kept his or her estate separate and chose a different heir distinctly for his or her half of the inheritance.[85] The yuhuitayu joined the resources of the two lordly establishments for one generation and yet bequeathed them separately to the offspring of interdynastic marriages. Even when the two estates were vested in the same heir, their distinct origins were acknowledged, and

validates proof of female legitimacy

each might be distributed separately among future heirs unless the two forged a more permanent alliance. Ideally, one heir or heiress would inherit the rule of a distinct patrimony and marry another yya or yya dzehe to continue or create a new yuhuitayu alliance. Two heirs were usually designated for the two separate patrimonies of an alliance, though properties or parts of each patrimony might be further divided among additional eligible children, in accordance with native principles of partible inheritance. The bequest of separate and comparable estates resulted in the far-flung distribution of rulerships and dispersed, cross-community landholdings. The scenario underscores the importance of recording named places, named lands, and named palaces in codices and similar writings.

Fifth, titles and properties were distributed to males and females rather evenly. Again, patterns of inheritance were flexible and varied according to local custom. The ruling couple determined the details of succession at marriage and usually confirmed their decision at the time of the widow's or widower's death. In the colonial period, each ruler declared or confirmed the order of succession in a separate last will and testament, as a speech recorded before an assembly of noble witnesses. Emphasis was placed on direct succession from parents of yya status, respecting the legitimacy of both dynastic lines; thus succession was not patrilineal. Women could be chosen among male siblings to inherit the principal part of a yuhuitayu. The *Relaciones geográficas* report from Juxtlahuaca—the source of the wedding feast narrative described above— stated in 1579: "The children of the royal couple were held to be legitimate and inherited the cacicazgo. And it made no difference whether a son or daughter was to inherit, because they did not distinguish between the lines. Because cacique married cacica."[86] This statement indicates that since none of the two *linajes* (dynastic lines) was favored, even if there were a preference for male rulers, it would not have any impact on the yuhuitayu. On the other hand, the *Relaciones geográficas* report of Mixtepec stated that male heirs were preferred and that daughters inherited the cacicazgo only in the absence of brothers.[87] Overall, there was an observable preference for male heirs in the colonial period, but there were also many exceptions to this pattern. In any case, parents did not single out one child to inherit their two separate patrimonies; thus, primogeniture was not the dominant practice. As Spores noted, the rights of secondary heirs were protected.[88] It was possible to consolidate two patrimonies in one heir, but it was a rare occurrence in the sixteenth century. Another form of consolidation was to arrange marriages between siblings.[89] Although this practice has been recorded (infrequently) in the codices, it has not been observed in the colonial period. In this system, bilateral cross-cousin marriage was common.[90] The colonial record contains an example of cousins who obtained an ecclesiastical dispensation for marriage.[91] The existence of polygyny in the preconquest period allowed the formation of multiple political alliances simultaneously, including alliances between dynasties of unequal rank and endogamous marriages. Nevertheless, the yuhuitayu consisted of a primary inter-dynastic, isogamous marriage and, in any case, there was a distinction between the offspring of royal parents and the children of extramarital sexual relations. Children born outside a royal marriage were theoretically ineligible to inherit royal title. The report from Juxtlahuaca states that other women served in the palace but that children produced outside the principal marriage were not eligible to inherit the cacicazgo.

The preconquest codices illustrate how some dynastic lines expanded their base of influence through multiple marriages.[92]

A case study from the Mixteca Alta illustrates the general principles of royal marriage and succession. One of the best-documented yuhuitayu in the colonial period is Yodzocahi, better known as Yanhuitlan.[93] At the time of conquest, lord Namahu and lady Cauaco (or Cahuaco) are shown in the preconquest *Codex Bodley* as rulers of the yuhuitayu of Yanhuitlan.[94] Namahu came from Tilantongo, and Cauaco represented Yanhuitlan; both were never baptized. Cauaco survived her husband and ruled until she died, around the year 1530. Her daughter doña María Cocuahu succeeded as ruler of Yanhuitlan and married (in the church) don Diego Nuqh, the yya toniñe of Tamazola, thereby uniting the two places (as well as Chachuapa, which was conjoined with Tamazola).[95] She was chosen as cacica of Yanhuitlan before her brother, don Domingo de Guzmán.[96] The ruling couple resided primarily in Tamazola. On their deaths, in accordance with an agreement reached at the time of their marriage, doña María and don Diego's older son, don Matías de Velasco, became ruler of Tamazola and Chachuapa and was raised there. Don Gabriel, their younger son, was appointed ruler of Yanhuitlan, where he was raised. Witnesses from Yanhuitlan testified in 1580 that it was customary in the Mixteca for the oldest child to inherit one place and the second child to inherit the other; in this case, Tamazola and Chachuapa went to the first and Yanhuitlan went to the second, even though Yanhuitlan was the more prestigious place. The informants affirmed that this decision was made when a cacique and a cacica married, but they did not suggest that male heirs were preferred, and they did not state that the first child was to inherit from his or her mother or father.[97] Don Matías and don Gabriel were to marry rulers who represented other ñuu, forging new yuhuitayu alliances with each generation.

However, don Gabriel de Guzmán, as the yya toniñe of Yanhuitlan was named, was too young to marry or to rule when his parents died. Thus, the brother of doña María and uncle of don Gabriel, don Domingo de Guzmán, served as interim ruler. If male heirs were preferred, don Domingo would have inherited the patrimony of Yanhuitlan in the first place. He was called a "regent" in Spanish documentation, although his identity as "cacique" was not qualified in any way during the Inquisition trials of the 1540s, when he was accused of idolatry, discussed in chapter 8. In his testament, written in the Ñudzahui language in 1558 and later translated to Spanish, he acted as if he were the legitimate cacique and governor of Yanhuitlan and made no reference to a regency. He affirmed that his older sister, doña María, was the "*señora* and cacica who had ruled in the past," that she had entrusted the rulership to him, and that it had belonged to him.[98] At the hour of his death, he gave the title to don Gabriel. The young don Gabriel took his seat on the reed mat when his uncle died in 1558 and ruled for thirty-three years until his own death in 1591. Through his marriage to doña Isabel de Rojas, he united his ñuu of Yanhuitlan with her ñuu of Achiutla. Don Gabriel outlived his wife and continued to control her patrimony until his death. After her death, he married María de Chávez, with no consequences for royal succession. Apparently, don Gabriel and doña Isabel had planned a complex inheritance scheme. Their daughter, doña María de Guzmán, would inherit her mother's patrimony, residing and ruling in Achiutla with her husband, don Miguel de Guzmán, the cacique of Teposcolula.[99]

Meanwhile, don Gabriel's son, don Francisco de Guzmán, became the ruler of Yanhuitlan and married the cacica of Tlaxiaco, doña María de Saavedra.[100] Don Gabriel de Guzmán enumerated the provisions for succession in his testament of 1591. If his son, don Francisco, died without children, then his patrimony would pass to don Gabriel's daughter, doña María (the cacica of Achiutla), and then to her children. If that line of succession failed, he stipulated that the patrimony should go to his youngest daughter, doña Inés (married to don Francisco de Mendoza), and then to her children. The epidemics of the late sixteenth century must have heightened anxieties about succession and forced lords to make additional alternative plans.

Don Francisco ruled as cacique until 1629, when he died without heirs. Don Gabriel's elaborate provisions were not made in vain. In his Ñudzahui-language testament, don Francisco passed the toniñe to his nephew, don Baltasar de Velasco y Guzmán, the son of doña María and don Miguel. Don Baltasar took possession of the aniñe before the native municipal council of Yanhuitlan and was acknowledged as cacique by the Spanish alcalde mayor, who handed him the keys to the palace.[101] When don Francisco de Guzmán died without legitimate heirs, a cousin of his named don Juan Manuel de Guzmán challenged don Baltasar's claim on the grounds that he was don Francisco's son from a subsequent marriage.[102] This type of succession dispute after a break in the line of descent was the bane of all hereditary forms of government. Apparently, a compromise was reached through the arranged marriage of don Baltasar's son, don Francisco Pimentel y Guzmán, to don Juan's daughter, doña María de Guzmán. These two rulers, in turn, bequeathed Yanhuitlan to their daughter, doña María Pimentel y Guzmán, who married don Diego de Villagómez, cacique of Acatlan, Petlacingo, and Silacoyoapan in the Mixteca Baja. They had a daughter, their oldest child, named doña Josefa Villagómez Pimentel y Guzmán, called the "cacica and señora" of Yanhuitlan and Xaltepetongo, who married don Luis Montezuma y Guzmán of Tepexe de la Seda in southern Puebla. When they had no children, the cacicazgo of Yanhuitlan went to her niece, doña Teresa de la Cruz Villagómez, who married don Martín Josef de Villagómez y Mendoza y Guzmán, cacique of Suchitepec. By this time, in the year 1717, doña Theresa was known as cacica of Acatlan, Petlaltesingo, Yanhuitlan and many of its sujetos, Silacoyoapan, Anañe, and Xaltepetongo.[103] From 1718 onward, the cacicazgo was attacked by factions within the "community" (*comunidad*) of Yanhuitlan. In 1720, the Royal Audiencia ruled in favor of the community, reducing the caciques' privileges in Yanhuitlan. Finally, after decades of petitions and appeals, the Audiencia ruled against the cacicazgo of Yanhuitlan in 1759—a process discussed in detail below. Figure 6.10 traces the succession of rulers in the yuhuitayu of Yanhuitlan from the early sixteenth century to the mid-eighteenth century.

The yuhuitayu of Yanhuitlan survived the conquest and more than two centuries of colonial rule, adhering to the basic principles of royal marriage and succession into the eighteenth century. These principles were based on an ideal of direct succession, whereby the legitimate child of a yya and yya dzehe inherited the patrimony and rulership, what the Spaniards called succession by *linea recta*. Twice lords were forced to appoint siblings, nephews, or nieces as heirs in the absence of children, a practice known as succession by *linea transversal*. In effect, the "regency" of don Domingo was simply a temporary application of transverse succession because don Gabriel was too

Yanhuitlan[a]	=	Other ñuu
1-Flower Cauaco	=	8-Death Namahu (Tilantongo)
2-House doña María Coquahu	=	6-Movement don Diego Nuqh (Tamazola-Chachoapa)
7-Monkey don Domingo de Guzmán[b]	=	?
don Gabriel de Guzmán	=	doña Isabel de Rojas (Achiutla)
don Francisco de Guzmán[c]	=	doña María de Saavedra (Tlaxiaco)
doña María de Guzmán	=	don Francisco Pimentel y Guzmán (Teposcolula)
doña María Pimentel y Guzmán	=	don Diego de Villagómez (Acatlan)
doña Josefa Villagómez Pimentel y Guzmán[d]	=	don Luis Montezuma y Guzmán (Tepexe de la Seda)
doña Teresa de la Cruz Villagómez	=	don Martín Josef de Villagómez y Mendoza y Guzmán (Suchitepec)

[a]Each yya or yya dzehe from Yanhuitlan, unless otherwise specified, descended from the previous royal couple.

[b]Don Domingo ruled on behalf of his nephew and heir apparent, don Gabriel, who was too young when his parents died. According to allegations made by witnesses in the inquisitorial trial in Yanhuitlan (1544–46), don Domingo was married three times. He married and then separated from a woman from Etlatongo named Yayuxi. He also married a native slave in the church to mock the friars. Finally, he married a niece from Tiltepec, named doña Ana, in a traditional ceremony. None of these allegations was confirmed. AGN-I, 37: 7–11.

[c]This couple produced no heirs. The inheritance was disputed between the nephew of don Francisco, don Baltasar de Velasco y Guzmán, and the cousin of don Francisco, don Manuel de Guzmán, resulting in an arranged marriage between the son and daughter of two claimants.

[d]This couple produced no heirs. Doña Josefa's niece, doña Teresa, inherited.

FIGURE 6.10. Hereditary succession in the yuhuitayu of Yanhuitlan, 1520s–1749.

young to marry and to forge a yuhuitayu alliance when his parents died. The record in Yanhuitlan makes no mention of don Domingo's wife, as if it did not matter. Although the interdynastic system was flexible enough to endure severe population loss, problems arose when nephews or nieces took over the toniñe, when breaks in the *linea recta* occurred. The first time prompted the challenge of two yya who reached a compromise, and the second occasion invited the opposition of the native cabildo. The case of Yanhuitlan demonstrates that the yuhuitayu was a complex arrangement of shifting alliances that integrated the resources of different Ñudzahui aniñe and ñuu from one generation to the next. Alliances could be made with rulers from either a nearby or a distant ñuu. This system promoted the diffusion of a shared social and political ideology that stretched from the Valley of Oaxaca to the Mixteca Baja and southern Puebla.

The basic principles of royal marriage and hereditary succession observed in the Mixteca Alta were also typical of the Mixteca Baja. To provide a brief example, in the early seventeenth century, doña María de Velasco, cacica of Ñucucu (also called Coculco), married don Gerónimo de Guzmán, cacique of Tisacu (Chinanco). Doña María died in 1633 and bequeathed Ñucucu to her son, don Raimundo de Santiago, who would receive it on his father's death. Doña María's testament instructed her husband to carry out this bequest. Before his death in 1642, don Gerónimo de Guzmán fulfilled his deceased wife's request and then bequeathed his patrimony of Tisacu to their other son, don Domingo Sacarías.[104] Each of the sons forged yuhuitayu alliances with other ñuu.

The *Codex Becker II*, a manuscript from the Mixteca Baja, illustrates how successive generations of ruling couples were depicted seated on reed mats (see fig. 6.11). The codex was written in a community whose identity remains uncertain, perhaps because it was unnecessary to inform a local audience of its origin.[105] Recognizable place glyphs in the codex include Tecomastlahuaca and Juxtlahuaca. The manuscript depicts nine generations of seated rulers. The last couple probably lived during the mid-sixteenth century, suggesting the possibility that this manuscript was produced for early colonial purposes. If so, it is probably a simplified version of genealogical claims, representing one community's point of view and executed in a linear, horizontal format. Each of the males (seated on left) and females (seated on right) possesses a name glyph, and each of the women proceeds from a place glyph representing her home community and that half of the yuhuitayu. The footprints proceeding from place glyphs might refer to patrilocal residence patterns, or they might simply record the origins of the exogamous marriage partner, namely, "this person is from this place." There is a marked preference for patrilineal inheritance (and possibly patrilocal residence) in this community, a pattern that was especially pronounced in the Mixteca Baja.[106] Presumably, the male successors were sons of the previous couple; visible portions of the codex reveal four

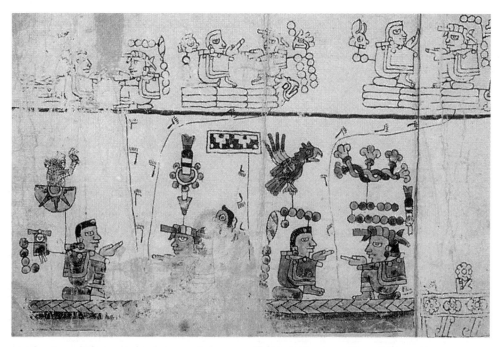

FIGURE 6.11. Royal succession depicted in the *Codex Becker II*, p. 3. Codex Becker II, Museum für Völkerkunde, Wien. Facsimile edition by Akademische Druck- u. Verlagsanstalt, Graz/Austria 1961.

daughters who forged yuhuitayu alliances in other communities, their footprints leading from the local yuhuitayu in the bottom register to new alliances in the upper part of the screenfold. Each time an outgoing alliance was made with a daughter of the ruling couple; the footprints emerge from a place glyph, encircle the female ruler on the mat, and issue forth to an heiress in the register above. Each marriage represented a new alliance, the formation of a new yuhuitayu.

The shifting nature of the yuhuitayu meant that little was written in stone. Portable codices recorded each generation of alliances before the conquest, and testaments served a similar function after the introduction of alphabetic writing. In addition, the oral tradition continued to play a crucial role in the collective memory of local history. As late as 1749, the yya toniñe of San Pedro Azumba, don Juan de Mendoza, testified to the importance of the oral tradition in legitimating rulers, when he said, "It is the custom among us to speak with our children and with others about our ancestors and the genealogies of the lords." Don Juan had "heard grandfathers speaking with other elders about the past . . . especially when they celebrated feasts." Thus don Juan was able to speak about his ancestors who had ruled nearly two centuries earlier.[107]

Yya toniñe had the right to choose any primary heir to succeed and, if necessary, to name substitute heirs in advance or when the need arose. For example, Doña Gracia de Guzmán, cacica of Chicahuastla (and nearby Chicahuastepec), named her daughter doña Ana de la Cueva as heir. When doña Ana died without children, her husband, don Gregorio de Mendoza, cacique of Coixtlahuaca, attempted to claim her future patrimony in the absence of other named heirs. But in 1640, doña Gracia blocked his attempt by choosing her son, don Jacinto de Guzmán, to inherit the patrimony. On her deathbed, she pronounced her last will and testament before the governor in her native tongue.[108]

In this system, every person of royal rank was a potential ruler by birth and marriage. For the ruling couple, the ideal was to bequeath a separate rulership to two heirs and to arrange good marriages for other children, in order to establish alliances with as many dynastic lines as possible. In the Mixteca, many aniñe looked to establish dynastic ties with prestigious places, such as Tilantongo; writers-artists in Teozacualco went out of their way in 1580 to detail such an alliance in their map for the *Relaciones geográficas*, discussed in chapter 2.[109] Alliances were made at different levels of sociopolitical organization. Rulerships could rise with advantageous marriages and fall with the failure to produce heirs. Investing the entire patrimony in one heir or heiress was risky but not impossible.[110] It is likely that surviving lordly establishments made claims to more places and lands in the colonial period, when the population of lords and commoners alike declined to a mere fraction of its original size. Women would not have been more eligible to rule as a result of the epidemics, as was the case in times of necessity in central Mexico, because a yuhuitayu always required a male and female ruler. On the other hand, male rulers had specific advantages over female rulers under colonial rule.

Colonial "Joint Person" Rule

The alliance of the ruling couple was defined in terms of a *conjunta persona*, or "joint person," in the legal terminology of New Spain.[111] The Spanish concept of joint person rule recognized a legal union that joined the couple's resources while distinguishing the origin of the two patrimonies. In sixteenth-century Spanish law, a woman possessed certain legal rights in marriage that represented the interests of her family, including the right to keep and bequeath property separately. Of course, Spaniards understood the basic concept of a queen or noblewoman with extensive privileges as heiress. Thus, colonial authorities respected the property and inheritance rights of native women and recognized the legitimacy of noblewomen who represented royal families. This fact is confirmed by the extensive use of the term *cacica* in the Mixteca to designate the *señora natural* (native female lord) of a cacicazgo. The use and evolution of this terminology reveal how Spanish authorities did and did not recognize the female half of the rulership, and how they understood and influenced native patterns of political authority.

From the earliest period, Spanish documents recognized female lords and specified when a male cacique's authority derived from a female cacica's patrimony. For example, in 1566, doña Catalina de Peralta and don Diego de Mendoza were called "caciques" of Teposcolula. However, it was doña Catalina who was born and raised in Teposcolula and who inherited the rulership; her husband, don Diego, came from Tamasulapa. Their relationship was clarified when they were called "caciques of Teposcolula, doña Catalina and the said don Diego as her joint person" [caciques de Teposcolula doña Catalina y el dicho don Diego como su conjunta persona].[112] Spanish law recognized his rights in Teposcolula vis-à-vis her position as cacica. In many ways, the same principle was applied to the properties and rights of married nobles and commoners. However, Spanish judges often interpreted native concepts in terms of their own cultural categories. For example, in the proceedings involving doña Catalina de Peralta and don Diego de Mendoza, one lawyer reasoned that don Diego had the right to be cacique of Teposcolula "as husband and lord of the dowry" [como marido señor de los bienes dotales], invoking the concept of a European dowry and the man as master in marriage. Judges and lawyers in legal cases over cacicazgos applied Spanish principles and ideas regarding inheritance and succession. As Woodrow Borah observed, citing this same case from Teposcolula as an example, Castilian rules of inheritance could be imposed at the expense of local custom.[113] Claimants appealed to Spanish principles of succession and tailored their descriptions of "ancient customs" to serve their own particular ends. In the case from Teposcolula, lawyers assailed the cacique of Tilantongo's argument as "bestial and against all reason" and dismissed his pictographic writings as lies.[114]

Male and female caciques continued to be recognized in the late colonial period. When doña Josefa Villagómez Pimentel y Guzmán married don Luis de Guzmán y Montezuma in 1698, the two were called "legitimate caciques of Yanhuitlan."[115] Similarly, in 1718, don Martín Josef de Villagómez y Mendoza y Guzmán was called cacique of the cacicazgo of Acatlan, Petlaltesingo, Silacoyoapan, Anañe, Xaltepetongo, and Yanhuitlan (and several of it subject settlements) as "husband and joint person of doña Teresa de la Cruz, cacique and cacica" [como marido y conjunta persona de doña Teresa de la Cruz, cacique y cacica]. In fact, don Martín was cacique of all but one of these places only by virtue of his marriage to doña Teresa. Later in the proceedings, his title was reduced to "cacique of Suchitepec." Despite his secondary status within the marriage, don Martín played a visible role in the proceedings as the male representative of the cacicazgo in a Spanish legal sphere dominated by men. Doña Teresa conferred additional legal status on him by granting him special license, as her "legitimate husband," to issue and collect bills of payment and rents in Yanhuitlan in her name.[116] The concern with tracing one's principal claim while acknowledging joint person rule was present even at the most basic level of the "barrio." For example, don Severiano Esquivel was cacique of Tepexillo and doña Teresa Andrade de San Miguel y Mendoza was cacica of the barrio of Guatepec in 1752.[117] Consequently, don Severiano was called cacique of the barrio of Guatepec "as husband and joint person of doña Teresa de Andrade."

Spanish legal protocol recognized women's hereditary right but gave preference to the public behavior and authority of men, nonetheless. One case from the coastal region confirms this preference. In 1729, don Juan Muñoz de Santa María was called the "cacique of Xicayan de Tobar, as husband and joint person of doña Manuela de Los Ángeles, the legitimate owner of the said cacicazgo."[118] Although doña Manuela was the "cacica and legitimate owner" [dueña legítima] of Xicayan and he was the cacique of Zapotitlan, he appeared in court as the cacique of Xicayan, by virtue of his marriage to her. Don Juan took formal possession of the lands belonging to her patrimony, even though she was presumably present at the ceremony (but not even mentioned in the record). In contrast to this formal ceremony presided over by men, the same legal case featured an incident involving a group of married couples who represented a community faction in a more informal, unofficial capacity. A delegation from the community of Cochoapa was headed by three married couples: Pedro Nicolás and María Lucía; Francisco Andrés and Antonia Isabel; and Luis Santiago and Nicolasa Isabel. These couples from Cochoapa gave flowers to the *teniente* (Spanish official) as a sign of peace and said to him, through interpreters, that they had come in the name of sixty married couples from their community to speak on behalf of justice for the caciques of Xicayan. Married couples represented groups at many levels of social organization. In this informal meeting between a Spanish official and community representatives, both married men and women took part in the ceremonial gesture of peace.

The Spanish custom of singling out men as the representatives of joint persons in legal proceedings had certain disadvantages, especially during times of crisis. In a dispute between San Miguel Tisaha and a ruling couple in 1798, doña Clara Sebastiana de Esquivel y Andrade, cacica of three communities in the jurisdiction of Acatlan, and don Francisco de Jesús Velasco, cacique of Tepexillo, were called "both caciques of the jurisdiction of Acatlan."[119] Clearly, she was recognized by commoners as the "cacique who inherited the cacicazgo" in 1774. In the midst of a long legal battle over the status of the three communities in Acatlan, don Francisco was jailed in Puebla and his goods were sequestered. Although the disputed patrimony belonged to her, he was recognized as the defendant. He bore the brunt of the legal proceedings in the case "as the cacica's husband." Meanwhile, doña Clara solicited funds (*derramas*) from the commoners attached to her cacicazgo in order to help finance the legal proceedings. This case illustrates how some Spanish-language documents used the plural term *caciques* in reference to a married royal couple, recognizing the female as hereditary ruler in her own right. In the late colonial period, some documents ignored the gendered distinction between *cacica* and *cacique*, even when referring to a single ruler. In 1820, for example, doña Juana Galiano was repeatedly called the "cacique de Yucuyache" in the course of a lengthy civil case.[120]

The Spanish principle of conjunta persona, when applied to members of the yuhuitayu, acknowledged the rights of women as more than mere consorts of the cacique. However, the category entitled men to represent the yuhuitayu in legal action, even when their separate patrimonies were not at issue. The joint person principle was invoked only when a cacique represented a cacica's patrimony; the reverse was not necessary. Since the yuhuitayu joined the resources of two yya, the partner's participation in important matters was to be expected. But even when women's rights were acknowledged by law, the accepted norms of Spanish public discourse preferred male actors in the legal and political realm. Because all Spanish officials were men, it is possible that native custom held men responsible for dealing with other male authorities, especially outsiders. The Spanish legal system accorded native noblewomen properties and titles by virtue of their birth and marriage, but they seldom spoke in the record, hardly ever wrote, and were barred from the formal political arena within their communities.[121] As with Spanish women, cacicas were especially prominent as widows in Spanish-language sources, when they exercised the dynastic rulership alone.[122] When a cacique and a cacica appeared together before Spanish officials, the woman's presence was often acknowledged, but the male generally represented them in the proceedings. This tendency became more pronounced in the later period. We may recall how the earliest palace and land possession ceremonies included the cacica and cacique of Teposcolula, compared with later ceremonies that tended to ignore the presence of women. Nowhere is the absence of native women more conspicuous than on the Spanish-style municipal council.

Spanish-Style Government

The introduction of Spanish-style government represented significant changes and continuities in local government. As in central Mexico and Yucatan, many elements of traditional native government endured in the Mixteca after the conquest.[123] In the mid-sixteenth century, Spaniards introduced the cabildo, a form of the Spanish municipal council. Many yya toniñe and noble functionaries maintained their traditional prerogatives and continued to play active roles on the cabildos until the late colonial period and beyond. Native cabildos mediated between their communities and Spanish authorities while continuing to fulfill many traditional functions of local government and administration. Often, the male yya toniñe occupied the council's highest office, while other elected positions rotated among the highest lords and nobles from the various constituents of the yuhuitayu. The cabildo's ability to provide corporate representation ensured its vitality. In form and function, the cabildo represented a tradition of autonomous self-government that included nobles and elders and surely drew on preconquest precedents. Many preconquest functions of local rule were transferred to the cabildo, including the supervision of tribute and labor and the dispensing of local justice. However, the cabildo excluded women entirely; none of the positions was open to yya dzehe. Let us begin with the most important position on the native cabildo—the *governador*, or governor.

Cacique and Governor

An appropriate native response in the *Vocabulario* of 1593 to the Spanish term "gobernador" was "one who guarded the tayu" (*tay yondadzi tayu*).[124] Similarly, the Spanish entry "to govern as a king" elicited a number of metaphors involving the Ñudzahui verbs "to provide cover" (*dzadzahui* and *dzaquete*), "to protect," and "to watch over."[125] The first of these was the most frequently used verb associated with governance in the *Vocabulario*, resembling the "shade and covering" metaphor of the Nahuatl difrasis *in pochotl in ahuehuetl* (cyprus and silk cotton tree). This phrase was used repeatedly in Nahua election documents from Cuernavaca in reference to the governor's protection of his constituency.[126] Mixtec terminology associated the governor with the yya toniñe.

The introduction of the cabildo began with the installation of governors before or around the mid-sixteenth century, in the most prominent yuhuitayu of the region.[127] By the early 1540s, Yanhuitlan, Teposcolula, and Tlaxiaco had governors who appeared with only baptismal names and the title of *don* and who spoke through Nahuatl and Mixtec interpreters. No other officers were present. The process of appointing governors in this early period undoubtedly favored some yya toniñe over others. Spaniards must have singled out the most visible leader and dealt with him alone as cacique, to the exclusion of other yya toniñe and women rulers. This process overlapped with the designation of cabeceras and sujetos in the 1530s and 1540s, discussed in chapter 4. When necessary, Spaniards manipulated rulers and encouraged rival candidates to compete against one another. In addition, the presence of Nahuas as guides, allies, and translators may have reinforced patterns established during the Mexica conquest. Again, the situation compares to central Mexico, where only one constituent of a complex altepetl might be designated for the governorship, while others were left unrepresented, creating a single head and consolidated rule that did not exist in the preconquest period.[128] Confusion abounded in the first decades of contact. Yanhuitlan had two governors and a cacique in the 1540s, confirming the complexity of that cabecera. The record refers repeatedly to don Domingo as cacique and don Francisco and don Juan as governors of Yanhuitlan.[129] Similarly, a dispute between Tlaxiaco and Teposcolula over boundaries in 1541 refers to don Josef, don Martín, and don Francisco as "caciques y gobernadores de Tlaxiaco" and don Pedro, don Domingo, and don Martín as "caciques y gobernadores de Teposcolula."[130] In each case, three men represented one place. As full cabildos were established within the next two decades, these anomalies were adjusted to conform with the cabecera-sujeto scheme of sociopolitical reorganization.

Governors were typically yya toniñe or caciques. Although all cabildo positions were subject to annual election, many caciques retained the governorship year after year in the Mixteca.[131] Extended terms of office through constant reelection conformed to a preconquest tradition of lifelong hereditary rule. For example, the cacique of Tamasulapa, don Fernando de Andrada, served as governor through much of the last quarter of the sixteenth century while other cabildo positions rotated on an annual basis. Fluent in Spanish, he enhanced his high status by cooperating with the Dominicans.[132] In fact, he and his wife, the cacica doña Gracia, gave land on two occasions to the Dominican establishment and helped arrange the payment of two thousand pesos for the painting of the church altarpiece.[133] Successive caciques of Tamasulapa retained control of the governorship throughout most of the sixteenth and seventeenth centuries.[134] In many cabeceras, caciques remained active as governors until the eighteenth century by ignoring electoral laws or by collaborating with native and Spanish officials to stay in office.[135] The equation of the hereditary lord, the yya toniñe, with the governor is reflected in native-language terminology. In 1709, a writer equated the two positions when he referred to "the ruler don Agustín Carlos Pimentel y Guzmán, governor of the tayu of Teposcolula" [yia toniñe don nagusti Carlo Pimentel y Guzmán tniño governador teyu yucundaa].[136] Likewise, the nobles of the *siña* of Ayusi referred to the governor of Yanhuitlan in 1681 as "yya toniñe governador."[137]

However, a separation of the governorship from the position of cacique did occur in some yuhuitayu as a result of annual elections and because of the unique nature of the yuhuitayu.[138] Namely, a male hereditary ruler could serve as governor in only the cabecera in which he resided.[139] A female hereditary ruler could not be elected to the municipal council of her ñuu; even when a widowed cacica ruled alone in the absence of her husband, she was ineligible for the governorship. Her son or a male relative might be eligible, but there was no guarantee that he would be recognized as governor. Some ruling couples responded to this predicament by arranging for male caciques to serve as governors in their wives' communities. For example, the cacica of Yanhuitlan, doña Josefa Villagómez Pimentel y Guzmán, married don Luis de Guzmán y Montezuma in 1698, who became "cacique and governor of Yanhuitlan."[140] In Tlataltepec, don Juan de Guzmán became governor in the late sixteenth century by virtue of his marriage to the cacica of that ñuu, doña Juana de Rojas.[141] Don Francisco de Paredes was governor of Quautla in 1583 because of his marriage to the cacica, doña Luisa de Mendoza.[142] This pattern also applied to other offices of the cabildo. In 1573, a noble of Texupa named don Juan de Zúñiga became a resident and alcalde of Coixtlahuaca through marriage.[143] And in 1606, don Francisco de Mendoza, cacique of Tocaçahuala, served as alcalde of Yanhuitlan and maintained a household there.[144] Obviously, Yanhuitlan's prestigious status and complex sociopolitical relations attracted some highly qualified candidates. This adaptation conformed to the ambilocal residence patterns of yya, who based their decisions on existing and potential resources and status.

A second strategy adopted by male yya toniñe in response to the prohibition against consecutive terms of office was to rotate between the two ñuu of a yuhuitayu alliance, alternating as governor in both places. Don Francisco Pimentel y Guzmán y Alvarado, cacique of Teposcolula and spouse of the cacica of Yanhuitlan, mastered this trick in his day. As early as 1649, he appeared as "cacique and former governor" of Yanhuitlan. And as late as 1675 and 1676, the electors of Teposcolula declared that they unanimously supported their cacique, don Francisco, as governor.[145] All positions except the governorship were elected that year; the electors simply signed a letter supporting a renewed term of office for their governor and cacique. The document that renewed don Francisco's term was signed by a former governor of Teposcolula, who was now serving as alcalde. Thus, don Francisco had served as governor of both places, residing in one or the other aniñe; it is clear, however, that he stayed more often in his own ñuu of Teposcolula. Serving as governor in two places was probably more of a possibility than a consistent practice.

A third response to electoral requirements was to recruit noble relatives or caciques from within the cabecera-sujeto configuration to serve as gubernatorial candidates. Many lordly establishments relied on male relatives or caciques from constituent parts of the cabecera to serve as governor in the event of an absentee cacique. At times, cabeceras called on yya in nearby sujetos. For example, a "sujeto" and "estancia" of Yanhuitlan named Mascaltepec, a ñuu that had attempted to assert its autonomy from the cabecera as early as the 1540s, had a cacique named don Domingo de San Pablo y Alvarado who was governor of Yanhuitlan in 1681 because there was no resident cacique of Yanhuitlan at the time.[146] Indeed, there were many caciques to choose as governors in this complex yuhuitayu; in 1587, Yanhuitlan counted seventeen caciques from fifteen sujetos among its cabildo members.[147] In the mid-seventeenth century, don Gerónimo de Guzmán, a yya in the ñuu of San Juan Teposcolula, served as alcalde and governor in the cabecera of San Pedro y San Pablo Teposcolula, and his son also occupied several cabildo positions.[148] Throughout the region, there were many places where the governorship was occupied by a yya who was not the hereditary ruler of that community. For example, don Baltasar de Chávez rotated in and out of office as governor of Tlaxiaco between 1581 and 1589 in the absence of the cacique, don Francisco de Guzmán, who resided in his home of Yanhuitlan.[149] Despite the ability of many yya to respond and adapt to the Spanish system of local government, it is clear that the separation of the governorship from the toniñe, so that many prerogatives would be exercised by the governor instead of the hereditary ruler, meant that hereditary rulers lost some of their authority.[150]

In at least one case, a toho, or lesser noble, aspired to the elected office of governor. In 1691, doña Lázara de Guzmán referred to "the elder toho, Lorenzo González, governor of the yuhuitayu of San Juan" [toho nisano loreso gosales governador yuhuitayu san juan].[151] San Juan was a former sujeto of San Pedro y San Pablo Teposcolula before it achieved autonomy in the late seventeenth century and adopted the same Nahua name as its parent community. Many sujetos developed full cabildos in the last quarter of the seventeenth century, when they attained autonomous pueblo status. In 1675, before it had broken away from the cabecera, San Juan Teposcolula was one of thirteen sujetos attached to San Pedro y San Pablo Teposcolula.[152] Perhaps toho aspired to the governorship only in smaller ñuu such as San Juan.[153]

Competition for the governorship was enhanced by the prospect of a sizable annual salary. In 1575, don Diego de Mendoza of Tamasulapa received 50 pesos per year for the "cargo de governador" [office of governor]; he was also entitled to two male and female servants each week. In return, he was obligated to pay each servant a daily fare of 25 cacao beans and to feed them.[154] In comparison, each of the alcaldes and *regidores* received an annual salary of 15 and 6 pesos, respectively. Salaries varied from one community to another. In 1574, the cacique of Coixtlahuaca, don Pedro, collected 150 pesos.[155] His brother don Juan received 70 pesos, and his two uncles, don Tomás and don Francisco, each collected 50 pesos. The governor (who was unnamed) received an annual salary of 80 pesos, while the two alcaldes each received 12 pesos, and the ten regidores received only 4 pesos apiece. In Texupa, don Gregorio de Lara received 310 pesos in 1587; don Gregorio had become governor by virtue of his marriage to the cacica of Texupa.[156] In the relatively humble ñuu of Chicahuastla, in 1575, the governor received twice as much money (30 pesos) as the cacique, don Juan de Fonseca.[157] In comparison, the cacique of Yanhuitlan, don Francisco de Guzmán, collected 400 pesos per year in 1591, in addition to many other privileges.[158] The fact that the governor of Mexico Tenochtitlan also received 400 pesos in this period confirms the relative importance of Yanhuitlan.[159] The separation of the governorship from the position of hereditary ruler could deprive caciques of a valuable source of wealth and political authority; naturally, hereditary rulers sought to maintain control of this position.

Female Rulers or Cacicas

Although the cabildo ascribed no roles whatsoever to women, most female cacicas received some form of monetary compensation from the *caja de comunidad* (community treasury chest) in the late sixteenth century, just as male caciques and cabildo members received annual salaries. In 1578, the cacica of Tlaxiaco, doña María Saavedra, received an annual salary or pension of 100 pesos; her income equaled the governor's and exceeded that of an alcalde and a regidor by five and ten times, respectively.[160] In fact, don Felipe, cacique and governor of the great yuhuitayu of Tilantongo, received no more in salary than doña María did that year.[161] Most salaries for cacicas were more modest, however. In 1575, doña Juana de Santa María and another woman named doña Juana, cacicas of Texupa and Tonaltepec, respectively, received 20 pesos per year.[162] In Quautla, doña Luisa de Mendoza was entitled to receive 30 pesos a year in 1583 but petitioned Spanish authorities to receive the tribute in goods and labor because the commoners in her community could not raise the money to pay her.[163] In 1573, doña Isabel Bautista, cacica of the "estancia" of Nepala, a sujeto of Coixtlahuaca, requested the service of two men and two women in her palace in exchange for a daily quantity of cacao beans.[164] It is unclear exactly how such non-cabildo salaries were determined or why officials in some communities were paid so much more than others. The amount must have varied with the availability of funds from the *sobras de tributos,* money remaining in the caja de comunidad after the payment of tribute and other necessities. By designating the monetary compensation and services of caciques and cacicas, to be paid from community treasuries, traditional privileges were subsumed under Spanish law and subject to the discretion of Spanish judges. The fact that Spanish officials acknowledged and compensated cacicas with salaries attests to their recognized authority in native society. It is likely that the practice of compensating cacicas with salaries resulted from negotiations between Mixtec and Spanish officials and that Mixtecs were the primary advocates of such a policy. Most cacicas received less money than the average governor, however. Cacicas may have benefited from money paid to spouses who served as governors, but the consequences of denying cacicas the governorship reached far beyond salaries and income.

Despite being recognized as hereditary rulers with certain property rights and privileges and receiving some form of monetary compensation, women were excluded

[handwritten marginalia: "generalized 'colonial period' status quo" / "is it fair to argue this" / "as a long-term movement of this period?"]

from official, political decision-making functions in colonial society. Women continued to exercise a considerable degree of authority as cacicas, but outside and apart from the daily responsibilities of the cabildo. The separation of political decision making and hereditary right altered yuhuitayu arrangements. The conquest introduced new constructions of political power, predicated on Spanish cultural attitudes, which marginalized women from formal sectors of colonial community rule.

The early political and religious reorganization is difficult to document. There is as little on the specific decision-making responsibilities of male rulers as there is on female rulers. Mixtec-language alphabetic writings do not speak directly to these issues. The near absence of women from cabildo-generated records reflects their exclusion from this group. But women continued to appear in the pictorial written record. Early colonial pictorial writings illustrate women's changing status in the new system of local government.

The *Codex Sierra,* an early colonial book of accounts from the Mixteca Alta, beginning in 1550 and ending in 1564, introduced in chapter 2, chronicles the movement to exclusive male political rule. This text is unique in that it combines parallel portions of pictorial and native-language alphabetic text (written in Nahuatl by Ñudzahui authors). In the earliest years of the work, the cacica doña Catalina is portrayed as a prestigious yya dzehe. She is named after the patron saint of Santa Catalina Texupa. Santa Catalina's feast day is symbolized in the manuscript by the instrument of her martyrdom, the saw wheel. Doña Catalina can be seen as early as 1551, when she is seated in the aniñe, in front of the unnamed governor (see fig. 6.12). The stylized post-and-lintel palace structure is attached to the place glyph of Texupa, as it was in the *Relaciones geográficas* map painted nearly thirty years later (discussed in chapter 2). It is likely that this anonymous governor was her spouse, who derived his position from her authority in the community. She wears her hair in the traditional braided manner, and the governor sports a plume-covered hat. She is called a "cihuapilli" (noblewoman) in the Nahuatl-language text. Doña Catalina appears several times with the governor and other *pipiltin* (nobles) as representatives of the community.[165] Each year, she is seated prominently in front of all the nobles, receiving quantities of food and

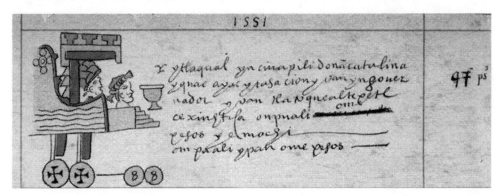

FIGURE 6.12. The cacica of Texupa (Ñundaa), doña Catalina, seated in the palace with the governor, receiving tribute in 1551. *Codex Sierra,* p. 4.

drink on their behalf. Doña Catalina is last seen in the year 1554. In 1559, a full cabildo appears for the first time, and now the governor is seated in front of a body of nobles who represent the various offices of the cabildo, listed in the Nahuatl portion (see fig. 6.13). Two years later, they appear in profile, facing the caja de comunidad and identified by name scrolls; thereafter, men perform an active role throughout the text (see fig. 6.14). As Woodrow Borah and Sherburne Cook remarked, the evolution of the full cabildo seems to have eclipsed the cacica's prominent position.[166] It is unknown whether doña Catalina died or was removed from the picture, but the manuscript depicts no woman in any official capacity after her disappearance, even though archival sources indicate that a daughter succeeded her as hereditary ruler, who in turn bequeathed the toniñe to her daughter.

Let us consider the situation in Texupa. In 1574, don Gregorio de Lara was entangled in a legal dispute with don Juan de Zúñiga over the cacicazgo of Texupa; as "joint person," don Gregorio represented the patrimony of his wife, doña Inés, the daughter of doña Juana de Santa María and the granddaughter of doña Catalina of Texupa. Specifically, don Gregorio possessed papers from his mother-in-law, doña Juana, "cacica and señora" of Texupa, who inherited the cacicazgo from her mother, doña Catalina.[167] In turn, doña Juana passed the cacicazgo on to her legitimate daughter doña Inés. An independent document confirms that, in 1575, doña Juana de Santa María received an annual salary of twenty pesos as cacica of Texupa.[168] The proceedings over the cacicazgo of Texupa revealed that in the 1550s the ruler of Texupa was a cacica named "Ychique Yatonatlesuchi," who was later called doña Catalina de Zárate. This "señora and cacica" married "Yacaotuta" (also called "Yacahuaco") in Texupa, a son of "Yaxiqui," who came from a "barrio" of Teposcolula named Texcaltitpat.[169] Doña Catalina de

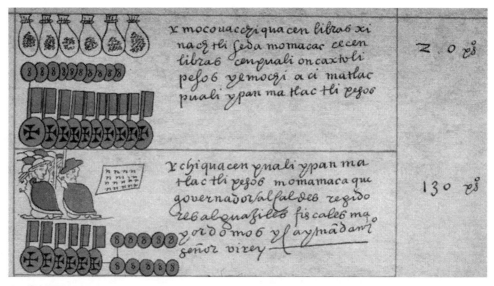

FIGURE 6.13. The first appearance of the all-male cabildo of Texupa in 1559 (bottom frame). *Codex Sierra*, p. 26.

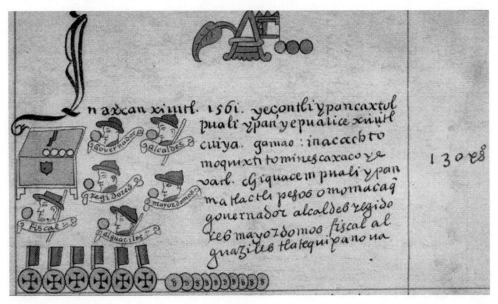

FIGURE 6.14. Members of the cabildo of Texupa receive salaries from the caja de comunidad in 1561. *Codex Sierra,* p. 35.

Zárate was called an "yndia principal" of Çaqualtongo, an "estancia sujeto" of Texupa. Spanish categories and Nahuatl names obscure the relationship between doña Catalina and Santa Catalina Texupa. In any case, it is clear that the cacica of Texupa depicted in the *Codex Sierra,* doña Catalina, bequeathed her patrimony to her daughter, who then passed it on to her daughter. The doña of the *Codex Sierra* came from a named entity within Santa Catalina Texupa. It is likely that this Santa Catalina was Çaqualtongo, a distinct ñuu or siqui subsumed by the colonial cabecera, Santiago Texupa. The relationship between the two places is uncertain, but it is possible that Santa Catalina possessed the most prestigious aniñe in that area.[170]

The case of doña Inés and don Gregorio was complicated by don Juan de Zúñiga's lawyer's claim that don Gregorio and his witnesses had lied about inheritance practices in order to support their case. The Spanish lawyer asserted: "An ancient custom in the Mixteca is that daughters cannot inherit cacicazgos when there are eligible sons, that they only inherit until the boys reach an age when they can rule."[171] While one side claimed descent from the maternal line, based on the principals of the yuhuitayu, the other side claimed that the absence of male heirs entitled the closest male relatives, based on patriarchal principles. This case suggests how Spanish lawyers could manipulate interpretations of traditional practices to advance the interests of their clients, even when their clients were indigenous.[172] The lawyer also claimed that don Gregorio and his witnesses were prone to habitual drunkenness, an irrelevant accusation that invoked the Spanish stereotype of the drunken Indian. The attorney even suggested that don Gregorio was a mere "principal" from a sujeto of the cabecera, questioning his noble status.

Spanish political and religious models viewed men as more suitable administrators and representatives of society. The Spanish distinction between hereditary rule and community government barred women from the cabildo, which subsumed, at least in part, decision-making powers previously shared by women and men. It may be that native men were normally responsible for dealing with outsiders, especially male outsiders.[173] But serving as intermediaries was only one function of the new cabildo. Before the conquest, the threat of intercommunity conflict may have encouraged the choice of male heirs who could personally direct a community's defense or lead other nobles into battle. Again, this was only one of many qualities associated with rulers. And the presence of several women warriors in the Mixtec codices suggests that warfare was not an activity reserved exclusively for men.

The fact that cacicas were ineligible for the important position of governor affected the yuhuitayu. Lords recognized the benefit of combining the toniñe and governorship in one person and place. The new system favored single, male heirs who were eligible to act as governor, unifying political authority in one head and sustaining the power of the dynastic line. After the "regency" of don Domingo de Guzmán in Yanhuitlan, who served as governor and cacique, the toniñe was bequeathed to a male heir who remained in Yanhuitlan. This strategy avoided the need to elect outsiders to the governorship. In the early eighteenth century, conflict occurred when the cabildo of Yanhuitlan rejected a cacique who sought the governorship by virtue of his marriage to the local cacica. When there was no resident cacique, the governor could be a yya or toho from a faction or subunit of the ñuu. Long-distance claims by nonresident lords were sometimes contested by local, competing factions, people usually associated with the cabildo, who forced caciques either to defend or to cede claims to distant lands, houses, and dependents.

Giving preference to the male heir brought succession practices closer to the practice of unigeniture. In the second half of the colonial period, many lordly establishments adopted this strategy to consolidate titles and properties by favoring one heir, especially a son.[174] The treatment of the cacicazgo as an entailed estate, or *mayorazgo*, encouraged the concentration of patrimonies in a single person who obtained clear titles to properties and was recognized by Spanish authorities. The tendency to consolidate patrimonies explains in part why so many postconquest lords are called caciques of multiple places and why they claimed so many lands in different places. The sixteenth-century sociopolitical reorganization complicated matters in that some lords were called caciques of a cabecera *and* all its sujetos. The lack of eligible yya and the extinction of dynastic lines caused by epidemic diseases also contributed to the consolidation of multiple holdings among surviving dynasties. Although consolidation may have empowered individual ruling couples, it reduced the number of yuhuitayu while extending the patrimonial claims of some caciques in the late colonial period.

This discussion of colonial government moves beyond the yya toniñe and yya dzehe toniñe to examine the cabildo as a group of male yya and toho. To consider how cabildo offices were understood in native terms, we return to a fundamental concept that organized Ñudzahui social and political relations, introduced in the previous chapter, tniño.

The Tniño of the Cabildo

Early colonial native-language terminology ascribed to cabildo positions reveals how Mixtec nobles interpreted cabildo offices in terms of traditional practices.[175] The perceived continuity and adaptation of Spanish models to indigenous practices facilitated a rapid transition to local municipal government.[176] Thus, it is significant that the term *tniño* was used to describe the cabildo's functions. As discussed in the previous chapter, tniño encompassed an entire range of activities governing the assessment and collection of tribute, labor and services, and other social responsibilities. *Tniño* is very similar to the Nahuatl *tequitl*. It may be translated as "work" or "task," including public responsibility and the charge of office. I translate it here as "duty" because the term involves service in an assigned position. The *Vocabulario* defines *oficio,* in the broadest sense of one's primary occupation, as tniño; appropriately, "public duty" was defined as *tniño yuvuitayu,* or "yuhuitayu duty."[177] The cabildo assembled in the *huahi tniño,* "duty house," and its members were called *tay natnay tniño,* "those who order/arrange the tniño."[178] The governor was called "one who commands the tniño" [tay yotasi tniño].[179] In Teposcolula, election records refer to cabildo officials as "yya, toho who arrange the tniño" [yya toho coo tniño].[180] A typical election record, written in Topiltepec, summarizes the duties of the nobility in the first line: "[Here is] a list of all the yya and toho who will perform the tniño of San Pedro Topiltepec in the year 1674" [memoria taca yya toho cadza tniño cuiya de 1674 san pedro yuqhtatne].[181] One native writer who adopted the loanword for "governor" still used *tniño* as a qualifying term when he referred to the cacique and governor of Teposcolula as "the ruler don Agustín Carlos Pimentel y Guzmán, tniño governor of Teposcolula" [yia toniñe don nagusti Carlo Pimentel y Guzmán tniño governador teyu yucundaa].[182] Clearly, the duties of office were perceived as tniño.

The Spanish term *Audiencia,* used in reference to the body of cabildo electors as well as the building in which they met, was called the *huahi sini tniño,* or "hearing duty house."[183] The Audiencia and the aniñe were the same building in most ñuu.[184] Before the conquest, yya and yya dzehe gathered in the aniñe to arrange the tniño and matters related to the toniñe. With the introduction of the cabildo, male lords assembled in the huahi tniño for the business of Spanish-style government. When the male hereditary ruler served as governor of the cabildo, the nobles met in his aniñe to organize the tniño, as in times past. Native-language records show that Ñudzahui writers adopted loanwords such as *audiencia* and *casa de la comunidad* for the structure. The association of the new Audiencia with the old aniñe persisted into the eighteenth century. A document written in 1708 reveals that the yya toniñe of Teposcolula, don Francisco Pimentel y Guzmán, met with nobles of the cabildo in the "aniñe comonidad," rendered in a subsequent translation as the "community tecpan."[185] One document from Achiutla reveals that the officials sometimes assembled on the roof of the "casa de la comunidad," as if it were a palace platform.[186]

Tniño was associated with tribute in kind, or *daha*. In the early colonial period, tniño and daha were the primary mechanisms for providing goods and services to Spanish officials, the *encomienda,* and the church. Labor and tribute benefited the aniñe and the corporate interests of the ñuu. The cabildo's tniño was to organize and direct the labor and tribute of all community members. The service-oriented nature of cabildo offices, staffed by yya and toho who represented the community's welfare, qualifies the impression of the native nobility as a dominant group of elites who lorded it over a subject class and enriched themselves through government.

By the mid-sixteenth century, basic cabildos were established in those places that had been designated cabeceras.[187] The *Codex Sierra* demonstrates that the cabildo of Texupa had already begun to take shape by 1550, though it did not reach full form until 1559. The book of accounts probably began as soon as there was a trained notary on hand to record the entries in Nahuatl. A central activity recorded in the *Codex Sierra,* which functioned as a record of community accounts, was the collection and expenditure of money. A prominent object in the *Codex Sierra* is the caja de comunidad, called the "caxaco" and the "caxaco comunidad."[188] The authors attached a Nahuatl locative suffix, *-co,* to a Spanish loanword to denote "inside the chest," in reference to the contents of an actual chest with lock and key and, by extension, the institution of the local treasury. The "caxaco" represents a monetarization of goods and services associated with tniño and daha. Salaries of cabildo officials were paid out of the chest. Sometimes, the manuscript depicted a hand protruding from the chest to represent the payment of tribute, relying on a Ñudzahui tone pun for "hand" and "tribute" based on *daha,* as discussed in chapter 2. An artist from the *Codex Yanhuitlan* filled an entire page with sketches of these chests. The creation of a cabildo and its treasury marked the existence of a colonial corporate community. The basic framework of indigenous municipal government that was established by 1580 in the Mixteca was maintained until the time of independence.

In the colonial period, offices rotated among various noble members of the cabecera and its sujetos according to annual election requirements. Rotation of the governorship was limited and inconsistent and only partially enforced in some cabeceras. Other offices rotated consistently among a fairly restricted group of nobles, analogous to the pattern observed among the Nahuas of central Mexico.[189] The order of rotation in any given community cannot be defined at present, because election records from the Mixteca are too dispersed in provenance and date to allow a focus on one cabildo over an extended period of time. Moreover, cabildos in cabeceras usually included elected representatives from sujetos, so that municipal offices were actually filled by representatives of multiple communities. In any case, it is clear that a limited group of people served multiple terms of office during their lifetimes.

After the governor, the next highest cabildo officers were the alcaldes and the regidores. Neither of these offices seems to have had a close native parallel. The former was rather vaguely associated with the staff of office, *tatnu,* and the entry in the *Vocabulario* for the latter term merely says "see governor."[190] Indigenous alcaldes were important lords and nobles who were closely connected to a lordly establishment. In the early period, alcaldes were the most likely candidates to bear the title *don* after the governor. Some alcaldes aspired to the governorship, while some caciques and former governors served as alcaldes. Alcaldes served as community judges and high officials who performed a number of important duties, from investigating criminal matters to keeping community accounts and verifying land transactions. In the late seventeenth century, the native-language record indicates that the cabildo of Yanhuitlan settled land disputes between siña and yya of the yuhuitayu, in the absence of Spanish officials.[191]

The indigenous cabildo was more fluid than its Spanish model. A high number of minor officials was designed to include the many nobles who customarily participated in the administration of corporate affairs and to serve as multiple witnesses for ceremonies and speeches. Judging by surnames and places of origin, most of the lower-level offices were staffed by lesser nobles. But even constables and underlings were nobles. The indigenous association of tniño or office with nobility corresponded with the Spanish system. In Spain, regidores were more prominent members of society, and alcaldes rotated annually; serving as alcalde could enhance one's chances of becoming a regidor. The position of alcalde involved the arduous task of civil and criminal adjudication. However, in peripheral or dependent settlements of Spain, where a full municipality was lacking, one alcalde would be the primary official, and a couple of subordinates would be called regidores. This latter system may have been a model for New Spain.[192]

The size of the cabildo in the Mixteca adhered to a general format throughout New Spain, confirmed by a royal *cedula* (decree) of 1618.[193] Cabeceras elected a governor, two alcaldes, four regidores, and numerous lower officers. Sujetos in the Mixteca sent one or two representatives to the cabildo, usually a regidor.[194] At times, yya from these sujetos managed to attain the governorship; more likely, however, they served as regidores or alcaldes. Election records show that in Teposcolula the assembly of yya and toho who served as electors numbered from about fifty to eighty men. The group numbered sixty-eight in Teposcolula in 1675, of which fifteen were from the cabecera and fifty-three represented thirteen sujetos. In 1707, the electors of Teposcolula comprised fifty-one nobles, sixteen who held office in the cabecera and thirty-five nobles and elders who represented eleven sujetos. The election record begins: "The account concerning the yya toho who will perform the tniño this year of 1707 to 1708. Eleven tribute ñuu [sujetos] and their head ñuu [cabecera] have assembled in this community palace [on] the first of December of 1707, [in the] yuhuitayu of San Pedro San Pablo Yucundaa (Teposcolula)" [memoria dzahua tnaha yya toho coo tniño cuiya huitna de mil siettesiento y siette años cuiya qhcueñe de mil siettesiento y ocho años ninataca ndihi usi ee ndaha ñuu sihi maa dzini ñuu yaha aniñe comonidad 1 de dzisiembre de 1707 años yuhuitayu santo san pedro san pablo yucundaa].[195] The document lists all the officials who were elected "to perform the tniño." Although the electors and the elected were normally yya and toho, some election records also referred to *ñandahi*, or commoners, whether as part of a formulaic statement or because they were present at the ceremony.[196] Another group of people who were sometimes present at elections, introduced in the previous chapter, were the *tay nisano*, or "elders."[197] Despite their attendance as witnesses to community ceremonies, age or prior service was not nearly as important as hereditary status in the choice of officials. Thus, it was not unusual for young men to occupy high positions of authority, especially if they had good family connections.

The office of the *escribano* (notary) was a key cabildo position. Escribanos were official clerks and notaries who wrote many different types of records, including legal proceedings of the cabildo, property transactions, and last wills and testaments. A cabildo was not really possible without a notary who was familiar with Spanish procedures and documentary genres. The Ñudzahui *tay taa tutu* (person who writes [on] paper), as the position of notary came to be called, inherited an ancient function associated with the noble group.[198] Preconquest writers-painters kept many different types of written records, as discussed in chapter 2. The colonial notary was not a voting member of the cabildo, but he was still a high-ranking, educated official drawn from the noble group. With the exception of a few incidental references, little is known about how the notary learned to write or how he practiced his craft. In Teposcolula, the notaries Juan Blas and Domingo de Velasco remarked that they customarily worked together on writing documents, indicating the collaborative nature of their work in that community.[199] There is some evidence that Ñudzahui notaries trained young relatives.[200] In Teposcolula, the Carrillo family passed on the offices of notary and translator through several generations; Juan Carrillo, an heir to this tradition, was a well-to-do noble in the early eighteenth century.[201]

Another important cabildo function was performed by the *alguacil* (constable), defined as *tay yonay tatnu,* or "one who holds the staff."[202] The term *tay tatnu* is found throughout Ñudzahui-language documentation and in many places never gave way to a Spanish loan in the colonial period, suggesting that the position fulfilled or at least resembled a preconquest function. Since the staff was a Spanish symbol of office, however, it is unknown if this was an indigenous concept or simply a fitting association.[203] The tay tatnu is the equivalent of the Nahua *topile.* An office associated with the alguacil was the *alcaide de la carcel,* or jailer, who was called the *tay yondaa huahicaa* (person who guards the iron house), sometimes abbreviated to *tay yondaa* (guard).[204] The municipal tribute officers and overseers, who in Mixtec were called *tay saquiñahi* (person who collects) and *tai yonahatniño* (person who collects the tniño), undoubtedly fulfilled a preconquest function.[205] Native terms were used throughout the period for these positions, suggesting a close preconquest analog.

The Spanish ordering of units enabled the transfer of many preconquest modes of organization to the function of the local cabildo; at the same time, Spanish-style government was reinterpreted to suit native organizational patterns. By the seventeenth century, cabildo members were known collectively as *oficiales de república,* "officers of the commonwealth," sometimes used in reference to all officials beneath alcaldes and regidores.[206] Although terminology of office increasingly reflected Spanish influences, the phrase *oficiales de república* acknowledged that the native body of officers differed considerably from the cabildo in Spanish American cities and in Spain.

Disputes over a candidate's eligibility for office were not unknown in the Mixteca, but they were few and far between in comparison with the incidence of election disputes in central Mexico or Yucatan.[207] Most disputes occurred in the late colonial period, from the last quarter of the seventeenth century onward. As a typical example, two sujetos of the cabecera of Teposcolula contested the election results of 1708 on the grounds that two high-ranking officials had been reelected.[208] Usually, factional disputes reflected existing sociopolitical tensions. Disputes suggest that factions could appeal to the enforcement of electoral procedures, even when those rules were not customarily followed.[209] Another type of political conflict in the eighteenth century involved cabildos or cabildo factions that rejected the patrimonial and political claims of caciques. This conflict was often closely tied to the issue of political office, particularly the governorship. Some of the conflicts involved disputes over the fulfillment of tniño and the changing role of the aniñe within the community. One example from Yanhuitlan illustrates how the potential disjunction between hereditary and municipal government, between the lifelong cacique and the annually elected governor, could lead to political and social conflict.

Caciques versus Communities

A legal dispute between the "caciques" and the "community" of Yanhuitlan in the eighteenth century posed questions about the rights and obligations of caciques that signified changing attitudes toward the aniñe and tniño. First, let us review the background of this landmark case. In 1669, Yanhuitlan forged an alliance with communities in the Mixteca Baja through the marriage of its cacica, doña María de Pimentel y Guzmán, to don Diego de Villagómez, cacique of Acatlan and other places. The couple had a daughter, doña Josefa Villagómez Pimentel y Guzmán, who inherited the combined cacicazgo of Yanhuitlan, Acatlan, and other ñuu, apparently as the sole heiress. In 1698, she married don Luis de Guzmán y Montezuma, cacique of Tepexe de la Seda in southern Puebla. As conjunta persona of doña Josefa, don Luis became governor of Yanhuitlan. Meanwhile, doña Josefa secured her position as cacica of Yanhuitlan and reserved the same privileges and rights accorded 140 years earlier to her great-great-great-grandfather, don Gabriel de Guzmán. She possessed his titles, his last will and testament, and many documents from his descendants as proof of her claim to the cacicazgo of Yanhuitlan. By the time doña Josefa wrote her will in 1717, she had amassed thousands of pesos by renting tracts of land in the Mixteca Baja and nearby southern Puebla to Spaniards and mestizos. Doña Josefa and don Luis produced no heirs, so Tepexe de la Seda reverted to relatives of don Luis, while doña Josefa bequeathed Yanhuitlan and her Mixteca Baja patrimonies to a niece, doña Teresa de la Cruz. Doña Teresa married don Martín Josef de Villagómez y Mendoza y Guzmán of Suchitepec, a former sujeto of Yanhuitlan. Through his marriage to doña Teresa, don Martín became the cacique of Suchitepec, Yanhuitlan, Acatlan, Petlacingo, Silacoyoapan, Tonalá, Anañe, Xaltepetongo, and their sujetos; most of these places were part of the cacica's far-flung patrimony.[210] She obtained power of attorney for him to transact legal business on behalf of the extended yuhuitayu, Yanhuitlan included.[211]

Don Martín and doña Teresa chose to reside in Yanhuitlan, the most prominent and centrally located community of their combined patrimonies. Her status as a niece of doña Josefa, who was not well known in Yanhuitlan, and his position as cacique of a relatively small community—a former sujeto of the cabecera—did not command much respect in their new home. He was not elected governor in Yanhuitlan, and, in fact, its cabildo challenged the couple's right to live in the tecpan and questioned their claim to lands within the community.[212] The governor, Domingo Hernández, and a group of nobles with surnames suggesting their middling or lesser-noble status (Gutiérrez, Cruz, García) complained that they had been reduced to poverty and slave labor for a cacique with dubious claims. At the same time, don Martín was described as "sumamente ladino" [extremely Hispanized], a perception that may have further undermined his credibility. The cabildo members especially objected to his possession of the aniñe or tecpan; they considered the building as the community Audiencia, or municipal palace, which housed the governor and all the high officers of the cabildo. The faction argued that the "casas de tecpa," where the governor lives, was never considered private property, not even when don Gabriel de Guzmán had lived there (don Gabriel served as cacique from 1558 to 1591). Rather, they were always considered "casas de la comunidad, casas publicas," where the community celebrated its feasts and elections. The cabildo members claimed that the last cacique, don Luis, lived there only because he served the community as governor; since don Martín was not governor, they reasoned, he had no right to live there. Thus, the question was posed: Was the colonial tecpan primarily the patrimonial property of the lord, or did it belong to the community as the meeting place of the cabildo? This question, posed within the Spanish legal system in terms of private and community property, involved a number of overlapping issues. A crucial issue involved the distinction between cacicazgo lands and community lands or, in Ñudzahui terms, the distinction between *ñuhu aniñe* and *ñuhu ñuu,* discussed in the following chapter. The rights and privileges of the lordly establishment within the ñuu were subjected to Spanish concepts of public and private.

The controversy escalated into a bitter assault on the cacica's hereditary claims and highlighted some long-term effects of Spanish policy and law on local political rule. Don Martín, as joint person of doña Teresa, struggled to protect their claim, which he called "clearer than the light of mid-day." How could it have been don Luis's property and not his? "A cacicazgo without lands and properties or without rights and privileges," he argued, "is only a title and I am only a cacique in name."[213] Nevertheless, in 1720, the Audiencia ruled in favor of the "community of Yanhuitlan" against the caciques. The costs of the case exceeded a thousand pesos. When don Martín died, doña Teresa de la Cruz took the lead in fighting for her cacicazgo. Finally, in 1758, the Royal Audiencia responded to yet another petition from doña Teresa and again ruled against the cacica. The Audiencia recognized a connection between the tecpan and cabildo office and distinguished between cabildo salaries and wealth associated with hereditary titles. The Audiencia dismissed extensive testimony on behalf of the cacica as evidence of "the ignorance and simplicity so common among the Indians, people who were as a rule dim-witted due to lack of education and culture."[214] The ruling stated that most of the lands claimed by the cacica belonged to individual communities, but she was allowed a certain amount of "private property." The ruling even questioned whether wills were valid legal instruments of possession, despite the fact that wills had fulfilled this widely accepted legal function since the sixteenth century. In the end, the Audiencia divested the cacicazgo of its palace and its lands, dismissed its titles as inconsequential, and denigrated its supporters as misguided fools. The *macehuales* deserve "liberty," the officials declared. By 1758, about two hundred years after don Gabriel de Guzmán took his seat on the reed mat, the yuhuitayu of Yanhuitlan was no longer recognized by law.

The Audiencia's ruling represented a formal redefinition of the community's social relations and obligations, but it also confirmed a changed situation. The decision undercut the cacicazgo only after its caciques had lost their base of local support. Sixteenth-century introductions had culminated in the demise of the hereditary rulership. By 1758, social relations had changed considerably in the two centuries since don Gabriel de Guzmán inherited the toniñe of Yanhuitlan. Most eighteenth-century legal disputes over the provision of labor and tribute to cacicazgos involved the issue of reciprocity. Spanish administrative and legal introductions that distinguished office from hereditary rulership opened the door to challenges from cabildo factions and other discontented groups who derived few benefits from the hereditary nobility. When lands and labor were disputed, both sides were forced to appeal to Spanish authorities. Spanish officials were receptive to hearing cases against local caciques that would break up their estates. If the colonial system benefited from patronizing these local power brokers in the early period, it had little need for them by the eighteenth century. In the case of Yanhuitlan, the "community" counted on several Spanish witnesses, including four friars, for support against the caciques. The ruling in Yanhuitlan represented a general policy to separate hereditary rule from municipal government in cabeceras and to establish salaries for elected officials while reducing the privileges of caciques. In the end, Spanish law reserved the right to confer or divest offices and titles, forcing native lords to abide by the rules that ultimately eroded their hereditary authority.

The timing of this extended process of change was subject to significant local variation. As a center of native-Spanish interaction and competition in the Mixteca Alta, Yanhuitlan was a place where native institutions were more prone to Spanish influences and colonial changes in the eighteenth century than many other communities in the region. Yanhuitlan was a cabecera in the largest valley of the Mixteca Alta, situated along the highway that links the Valleys of Mexico and Puebla with the Valley of Oaxaca. Although Yanhuitlan was not the first community to experience cacicazgo-related conflicts, it was a center of cultural interaction and social change. Yet, in comparison with central Mexico, Oaxaca was a remote region of New Spain with few resident Spaniards and mestizos by the end of the colonial period. The demise of hereditary rule in most central Mexican altepetl occurred much earlier than the mid-eighteenth century. If some caciques suffered setbacks in the eighteenth century, others adapted to colonial changes and avoided costly legal disputes with factions or won the favor of Audiencia judges.[215] This surviving group included many prominent female cacicas, despite legal and political incentives to favor males as heirs.[216] Certainly, the yuhuitayu survived the conquest and continued to function in many places throughout the colonial period.

Nonetheless, by the end of the eighteenth century, it is clear that most caciques were simply well-to-do investors in Spanish-style enterprises who could make little claim to hereditary authority.[217] Thus, many caciques survived into the nineteenth century and beyond, but many others were, to borrow don Martín's expression, little more than caciques in name.

CHAPTER 7

Land and Livelihood

IN THE MIXTECA the Spaniards encountered densely populated settlements that utilized terraces, irrigation, and reclamation techniques to achieve high levels of agricultural productivity. Agricultural goods and textiles were the primary sources of sustenance, wealth, and taxation. Regional and interregional trade networks and organized local market systems circulated a wide variety of prestige and mundane products and foodstuffs. In the first half of the colonial period, recurring epidemics reduced agricultural and nonagricultural production and commerce in the region to a fraction of preconquest levels. Meanwhile, Spaniards competed with Mixtecs for resources from the moment of their arrival. The introduction of money and credit, new enterprises, and new markets expanded material opportunities for some people but increased demands for resources and labor. Despite colonial introductions and demographic decline, traditional forms of agriculture, household production, and local markets remained the basis of subsistence and surplus throughout the colonial period.

The first section of this chapter uses native-language records and other sources to describe the organization and possession of houses and land in the colonial period. In particular, I examine the physical layout and organization of houses, land tenure categories, names and types of land, the distribution and uses of land, inheritance patterns, and conflicts over land and agricultural labor. Each of these topics sheds light on significant continuities and changes in native lifeways and social relations. The second part of the chapter examines patterns of native trade and tribute in the colonial period, including the work of men and women in nonagricultural enterprises such as weaving, local and long-distance commerce, and certain indigenous and introduced

198

occupations and enterprises. This section also considers the impact of money and competition with Spaniards for resources, markets, and labor.

Native-language documents reveal the structure and organization of native houses and lands soon after the conquest. But as Lockhart observed for the use of Nahuatl-language records, it is difficult to trace with great precision continuities and changes in native land tenure and distribution across the colonial period, mainly because the sources (primarily documents generated by native *cabildos*) record only certain types of economic data.[1] Whereas testaments and inventories typically noted the number of lands held by a household, they rarely specified the size, value, and productivity of those landholdings. Moreover, the nature of the native-language sources enables a broad study of patterns in multiple communities within a given jurisdiction over an extended period of time, rather than a more defined study of one community. Nonetheless, testaments and inventories from a cross section of Mixtec society reveal distinct patterns of wealth and economic activity. Finally, a sampling of similar records for Spaniards who lived in the Mixteca illustrates the extent of socioeconomic difference between these two groups.

The Household Complex

The Ñudzahui system of land tenure and use was based primarily on the household. People in the same household complex relied on one another to work certain lands and to produce textiles and other goods. The house was also a mainstay of most people's possessions, a type of wealth as well as a site of production. This section describes the physical layout of the Ñudzahui house and its central role in the structure of landholding.

The *Vocabulario* equates "house" with the word *huahi*.[2] Early colonial sources indicate that the Ñudzahui huahi shared many common features with the Nahua *calli*.[3] In both central Mexico and the Mixteca, several separate living quarters or "house structures," each with its own entrance, were arranged around a central patio, the Nudzahui *cahi* or the Nahua *ithualli*. Since there is no marked distinction between singular and plural nouns in the language, the term *huahi* could refer to the entire complex or individual units within the larger structure.[4] But judging by the numerous contiguous huahi some people claimed in their testaments, the term usually referred to the individual units. The complex was often walled off to create an enclosure, with one shared entry that united the household. Each huahi within the complex had only one entry, called *yuhu*, normally just an opening facing onto the patio. A typical structure consisted of one or more main huahi or separate rooms, a small cooking area, a sweat bath, and a storage space. No clear term stands out for the cooking area, or what Spaniards called the *cocina* (kitchen); the *Vocabulario* simply described it as a house where food is cooked (*huahi yocuvuihuaha sacasi*).[5] Whereas every huahi complex had a small, ventilated cooking huahi, not every household owned a *huahi ñehe*, or "sweat bath house" (*temazcalli* in Nahuatl); incidental references to people who went to bathe at their neighbors' or relatives' huahi ñehe suggest that they did not have one of their own. Storage spaces are rarely mentioned, yet some sources refer to agricultural products and equipment stored in the household complex. Finally, a few Spanish-language sources refer to huahi where saints were kept, comparable to the Nahua *santocalli,* or saints' houses, and Spanish *oratorios.*

The royal palace, or *aniñe,* was the most elaborate huahi within a *siqui* or *ñuu.* As discussed in chapter 6, the typical aniñe was a single-story, multicomponent complex with several rooms or single-room houses arranged around or adjacent to sunken patios, not unlike the *tecpan* in central Mexico. The aniñe of Teozacualco, depicted in the map of 1580 for the *Relaciones geográficas,* illustrates the general layout of a palace (see fig. 2.4). By this date, the rebuilt palace had incorporated arched doorways, but the walled-in structure retained its central patio and separate units. The aniñe complex of Yanhuitlan contained several one-room houses and nine separate patios in the sixteenth century.[6] In the 1540s, people referred to the complex as "casas del cacique," indicating the large size and multiple components of the building.[7] When don Juan Manuel de Guzmán stayed with his wife in the aniñe of Yanhuitlan, his quarters were described in terms of an *aposento,* "room" or "lodging," with its own patio, separate from and yet connected to the rest of the palace.[8] In 1630, the Jesuit Bernabé Cobo noted that the main patio of the palace complex was large enough for the running of bulls.[9] Likewise, the aniñe of Teposcolula was described in 1566 as multiple rooms (including an "aposento de cocina") arranged around several patios, including one large patio in front of the enclosed complex that exited to the street.[10] The main patio was said to be large enough to accommodate a hundred people.[11] Despite its grandeur, many *yya* spoke of the aniñe in terms of a large huahi. Don Miguel de Guzmán called his palace "my large palace house" [huehi aniy canuyu], and don Jorge de la Cruz Alvarado referred to his residence as "my house palace" [huehiyu aniy].[12] In 1571, doña María López, cacica of Tlazultepec, affirmed the fundamental association of a house with its patio when she called the palace "my patio-house" [cahi huehidi].[13]

The ordinary huahi did not differ in its basic structure from the aniñe; it was built with different materials on a smaller scale.[14] Scattered references to the huahi of *ñandahi,* or commoners, speak of small structures and patios.[15] For example, Diego Cotuta and his wife, Inés Xigua, lived in a huahi containing at least two units with separate entrances, arranged around a patio.[16] The continued use of native surnames in 1632 indicates that Diego, a *petate* maker in Tamasulapa, and his wife were humble people. Several other references to the huahi of common folk, including María Cahuitzo and Cecilia Nachi of Teposcolula, confirm the basic structure of single-room units organized around patios.[17] People assembled in their patios for a number of household activities; men and women cultivated maguey plants in their patios. Whereas the aniñe and houses of nobles were constructed with stone (*yuu*) or adobe (*ndoho*), ordinary houses were built from straw (*ita* and *tiyahua*). Usually, adobe walls were covered with roofs of wooden beams or poles and straw or palm.[18]

The number of huahi within a compound varied from one to several, depending on the size and resources of the household and the number of members living there. María Méndez, a noblewoman of the *siña* named Ticoho in Yanhuitlan, owned a house complex consisting of eight separate but contiguous sections or rooms organized around a patio; she referred to each of the units as huahi, whereas the translator called them aposentos.[19] Spanish translations often referred to these separate, single-room huahi as either aposentos or *salas* (large rooms). In turn, the *Vocabulario* defined *sala* as *huahi cani,* or "long house."[20] Some huahi in a compound were larger than others; often the main huahi was called a *huahi cano* (large house). The description of a house complex owned by María de la Cruz Çayucu, located on the plaza of Yanhuitlan, illustrates the huahi's organization into constituent units.[21] When a Ñudzahui-language transaction involving one of her houses was translated into Spanish, *huahi* was rendered as a "pedazo de casa," or "piece of house."[22] In 1713, Micaela Nicolasa of Teposcolula bequeathed "half" of her house to one heir and the other half to an image of a saint, specifying which huahi in the complex went to whom.[23] The *relación* of Tilantongo referred to houses as multiple small cells (*celdas pequeñas*).[24]

Typically, each nuclear family or adult independent member maintained an individual huahi within the household complex. The entire complex might be owned by a single person, or each unit might be held separately by its residents. Independent structures were likely to be inherited by members of the extended household. For example, Bernabé López of Tamasulapa bequeathed specific huahi and lands to his older grandson and his granddaughter, and he gave his younger grandson a sweat bath and a plot of land.[25] Bequests of land usually went to children or grandchildren within the household, rather than eligible heirs who lived in other households. Women owned land and houses as part of their entitlement to a separate patrimony in marriage. Although lands and properties were bequeathed to individuals, members of the household worked the land jointly; when a woman inherited land, men in the household helped in its cultivation. The dispersive consequences of partible inheritance patterns, that is, distributing property equally among multiple heirs, were offset by concentrating bequests to members of the household. Since tribute was based on the household, consisting ideally of at least a married couple, rather than the individual, every member contributed to the productive capacity of the huahi. Multiple houses organized around a shared patio constituted one household and tribute-paying unit. Dependents living inside the household complex were eligible to inherit property, especially in the absence of other heirs.[26]

The huahi is also described in terms of a general enclosure of walls (*nama*) around a house complex.[27] Some structures inside the compound were built against the enclosure, supported by the wall itself. A document from 1587 informs us that Mateo Higuera's house and patio in Achiutla were enclosed by such a wall.[28] And in 1672, don Gerónimo García y Guzmán referred to his "walled house palace" [huahi nama aniñe] in Teposcolula.[29] Many people spoke of the orientation of their huahi in terms of which cardinal direction its entrance faced, especially west or east. For example, Juana de la Cruz referred to her house as a structure facing east ("yondito nicana ndicandij"), or literally "looking where the sun emerged," whereas the huahi of Miguel Jiménez faced west ("yondito nicai ndicandij"), or "looking where the sun entered."[30]

Not all huahi were enclosed by walls, organized into compounds, or arranged around patios. Some descriptions indicate modest one-room structures that do not seem to be organized in any particular manner. The *report* of Ytnuhuaya for the *Relaciones geográficas* states that the common house was a simple straw structure with one "aposento" and a roof of poles and straw. Caciques and nobles lived in adobe structures with straw roofs consisting of two or three "aposentos."[31] Another type of dwelling was the temporary structure located on or near distant plots of land, the simple straw *huahi tiyahua*, where people might tend to a field without walking great distances every day.[32] This huahi tiyahua was often translated as *jacal* in Spanish, a word borrowed from the Nahuatl *xacalli*, suggesting its association with the Nahua structure. Regional variation, climate considerations, the availability of building materials, and the dwelling's function must have affected household structures and designs. Nonetheless, the huahi-cahi complex is mentioned repeatedly in the written record.

Observable changes in the household complex in the colonial period were mainly external, related to the introduction of new building techniques and materials. European-style swinging doors of wood with metal hinges became common features of nobles' houses, but windows were less common. The aniñe of Teposcolula had adopted both doors and windows by 1566, although it is clear that this structure was rebuilt after the conquest.[33] Those who had doors often acquired latches and locks. But the basic layout and organization of the huahi seems to have been maintained throughout the colonial period.[34] By the seventeenth century, loanwords were used to qualify the general term when referring to specific huahi within a complex, such as *huahi sala* (main house) and *huahi cocina* (kitchen). Some loanwords described a new function, such as *huahi tienda* (store) and *huahi fragua* (forge); it is unclear whether the latter structures were included in the household complex. The occasional reference to a *huahi casa* (house) suggests some variation on a common theme or simply a greater familiarity with Spanish. But most people continued to refer to huahi in the general sense of the word throughout the colonial period. Miguel Jiménez, the owner of a huahi tienda in Yanhuitlan, also possessed a *huahi nino* (a type of high, flat-roofed house), surrounded by forty maguey plants.[35] Rooftops of sturdily built houses may have been utilized for various purposes, including terraces and gardens. There is also some evidence for two-story houses in the Mixteca; for example, in 1610, Gonzalo López described his house complex in Topiltepec as "four large houses and three houses on top of them," apparently lined up "in the manner of a corridor."[36]

Throughout the colonial period, the contents and movable goods of the house included standard indigenous items such as *yodzo* (*metates*, or grinding stones), *yuhui* (petates, or reed/palm mats, used as beds and seats), *coho* (*tecomates*, or gourd containers), *tayu* (wooden stools), and *satnu* (native wooden or reed chests). Houses also contained quantities of perishable goods such as maize (*nuni*), which was kept in separate storage houses or granaries. Cloth and clothing were often the most conspicuous items in household inventories, especially among women's possessions. Women typically owned weaving instruments, thread (*yuhua*), cotton (*cachi*), and other indigenous materials such as maguey fiber and animal furs (especially rabbit); some nobles possessed considerable quantities of local and imported cloth, including new materials such as silk, wool, and taffeta. Men often owned digging sticks (*yata*) and iron-tipped digging sticks (*yata caa*). But the distribution of goods in testaments could be quite flexible; property associated with gender-specific labor, such as weaving gear, cloth, metates, oxen, and digging sticks, was often divided among men and women alike. Judging by testaments, women wore the same type of clothes as they wove, including the sleeveless, unfitted *huipil* (called *dzico* in Mixtec), a garment that extended from the neck to below the waist, and the *nagua,* or skirt (*dziyo*). In contrast, men rapidly adopted the Spanish *camisa* (shirt), *sombrero* (hat), *jubón* (doublet), and *calzones* or *zaragüelles* (trousers) in place of the Ñudzahui *satu,* or loincloth; most continued to wear their woven *dzoo* (*mantas,* or cloaks), however. Leather goods such as shoes, boots, and belts rounded out the new attire. In general, the contents of Ñudzahui and Nahua houses were identical.

Early colonial testaments and inventories reveal that yya and *toho* practically monopolized indigenous luxury goods, including feathers, headdresses, articles of finely woven clothing, masks, and animal skins. In the early colonial period, inventories of lords included gold, jade, turquoise, silver, jewels, and precious stones. Several nobles, especially men, referred to "dancing feathers" and dancing *cascabeles,* or small rattle bells. Nobles also possessed many introduced items, including European-style chests with locks and an array of iron goods such as knives, scissors, hammers, and other tools. The possession of tables, chairs, silverware, plates, glasses, jars, cups (including china), candles, and tablecloths suggest changes in dining customs among members of the upper social group. Some caciques owned swords and daggers and even obtained muskets by special license.[37] Introduced items included an assortment of religious images and art and items such as lockets, mirrors, ivory, and gold objects. In 1591, the cacique don Gabriel de Guzmán owned dozens of small ornaments of silver and gold, many bearing classical and religious motifs of European origin. He also owned several items associated with the valuable property of horses, such as bridles, saddles, and stirrups.[38] But don Gabriel also possessed an array of indigenous goods, including jaguar skins, five metates, and three blowguns. Like don Gabriel, male and female lords customarily owned paper, ink, Castilian feathers (quills for pens), writing boxes, printed books, chairs and desks, and legal titles to lands kept in wooden *cajas,* or chests. One yya from Tlaxiaco even owned a pair of eyeglasses in 1571.[39]

In general, most native yya owned furniture and a variety of European and native goods in the colonial period, whereas ordinary ñandahi possessed very few European items and kept mainly native goods in their huahi.

Categories of Land Tenure

In preconquest as in colonial times, Ñudzahui land tenure and use was based on the huahi. The separate units of a household worked lands individually, dividing responsibility for cultivating plots among its members. Although individuals worked specific plots, they did so as members of a household; in this sense, households held land, and its members exercised certain rights to individual plots. Each huahi was a potential landholder in the colonial period, and each male adult who was not a noble was a potential *tay situ,* or cultivator (*labrador* in Spanish). Men cleared, planted, cultivated, and harvested crops on plots maintained by the entire household, sometimes with the help of women. All yya and some toho counted on other people to work their lands. Variable tribute assessments were based in part on the yield of a household's lands and other resources. Thus, the native concept of "possession" was closely tied to use, responsibility, and inheritance.

Land was called *ñuhu* in the general sense and *ytu* in reference to the cultivable plot.[40] The site of the main land held by a household was called *ñuhu huahi,* or "house land," where the huahi and cahi complex was located. It was the site of a house as well as a sizable plot of cultivable land. Nuhu huahi resembles the Nahua category of land called *callalli,* which usually referred to the most fertile, valuable land of the house- hold.[41] As the best and oldest plot passed down from one generation to the next, house land was usually associated with *ñuhu chiyo,* or "patrimonial land." *Chiyo* referred to an "altar" or a sacred site associated with ancestors; the term was also used with *yata* for an "ancient site."[42] This type of inherited land was analogous to the Nahua *huehue- tlalli,* or "old land," in reference to patrimonial land. Likewise, the Ñudzahui *ytuchiyo,* "patrimonal field," was the same as the Nahua *huehuemilli.*[43] When Juana de la Cruz made her testament in 1681, she combined references to house and patrimonial land with the phrase "ytu chiyo huehendi" [my patrimonial house plot].[44] Lucía Hernández's description of her "ñuhu chiyo sata uahy" [patrimonial land in back of the house] illustrates the association of patrimonial lands with the house.[45]

Lords used the term *chiyo* in reference to their aniñe, or palace, lands. In 1672, don Gerónimo García y Guzmán, yya of Teposcolula, referred to his patrimonial and house land in terms of "my house field, the patrimonial field, and the house walls of my palace, the alluvial lands" [ytu huahindi ytu chiyo sihi huahi nama ñu aniñendi ñuhu ndayu].[46] His wife, doña Lázara, called land belonging to the aniñe "the patrimonial field of the ancient patrimonial palace named Palace [of] Duhuadoo" [ee ytu chiyo aniñe chiyo yata nani aniñe duhuadoo]. Thus, the aniñe of don Gerónimo and doña Lázara was attached to specific lands that, if not the actual site of the house, were con- sidered part of a contiguous, integrated unit. In 1676, don Raimundo de Santiago y Guzmán, a cacique in the Mixteca Baja, also referred to "cultivated alluvial fields" [ytu ñoho dayu] in relation to his "palace lands" [ñoho aniy].[47] These examples are royal versions of a standard arrangement of ñuhu, ñuhu huahi, and ñuhu chiyo in the Mix- teca Alta and Baja. References combining terminology for land (*ñuhu* or *ytu*) with *huahi,* qualified by *chiyo* (patrimonial), can also be found in the testaments of commoners throughout the colonial period. The concept of patrimonial land was shared by all households in Ñudzahui society, from stately aniñe to ordinary huahi.

Beyond the house land, other holdings, simply called ytu, were typically scattered within the community's borders and might be acquired and lost, bought and sold more frequently. If ñuhu chiyo was reserved for the highest-ranking huahi in the household complex, distant lands were probably marginal, less fertile plots in less desirable areas. But they were not necessarily poor lands; the system of multiple, separate plots must have distributed fertile lands more evenly among households within a community and facilitated native inheritance patterns of dividing goods and possessions among all heirs.[48] In addition, the cultivation of scattered supplemental plots encouraged a degree of agricultural diversity and subsistence, particularly in ecologically diverse zones of the Mixteca.[49] Surpluses were traded to other areas for supplementary goods. Lords kept numerous scattered plots of land, relying on nearby dependents to work them, and occasionally sent families to settle on or near distant fields. Commoners' lands were also based on the same model of ñuhu huahi and scattered ytu, though not every household possessed multiple lands, as demonstrated below.

Landholdings could be so fragmentary that some people referred to some tracts as *sichi ñuhu* or *sichi ytu*, as "parts" of cultivable land. Similarly, Inés and Josef de los Reyes used the term *sichi huahi* in reference to a "piece" of their house in Teposcolula.[50] This term may be influenced by the Spanish *pedazo*. Diego Gómez used the term *sichi* to refer to four parts of an ytu named "Ticahuiyo" that he divided among his heirs.[51] He also used another common term, *coo*, for a strip or row of land, usually planted with magueys (*yahui*). Spaniards often translated *coo* as *camellones*, or dividing ridges.[52] Another term synonymous with *coo* was *yuhua*, used especially in the Yanhuitlan area.[53] Plots of land were so scattered that men and women were sometimes forced to stay in temporary shelters near their fields to tend to their crops (*guardar milpa*).[54] The system of combined house lands and scattered plots accommodated combined clustered and dispersed settlement tendencies.

Some documents refer to corporate lands that did not belong to an aniñe or huahi and thus were not kept by a specific household. For example, in a land dispute with the yya of Mascaltepec, six toho from the siña of Ayusi argued that certain lands belonged specifically to their siña, calling the land in question "ñuhu siña Ayusi."[55] They also called these tracts of land "the fields of our fathers, our mothers" [simayndo ytu taa dzehendo], using a metaphorical couplet for their ancestors. They distinguished between "ytuniñe" [fields of the aniñe] and "ytusiña" [fields of the siña]. The term *ytuniñe* was interpreted as "lands of the cacicazgo" in a subsequent translation of the Ñudzahui-language document. The nobles defended the "lands of the people of the siña Ayusi" [ñuhu chay siña ayusi], but they did not refer to individual owners. Rather, the siña as a corporate unit claimed the land. This group of nobles from Ayusi also referred to lands belonging to another siña called Yuhuyucha. Similarly, in Santa Magdalena Yucucata (1693), an elder noble (*toho nisanu*) named María de la Cruz Avendaño referred to land belonging to a "barrio" of her ñuu and a plot of land belonging to the ñuu of Tecomatlan ("siytu bario may ñuu yaha sihi ytu Tiyaha").[56]

References to lands associated with subdivisions of the ñuu resemble the Nahua categories of *altepetlalli* and *calpollalli*, or land held under the jurisdiction of the *altepetl* and *calpolli*, presumably the same thing.[57] As corporate landholding units, the altepetl and calpolli assigned lands to individual households. A household could keep its land through inheritance if members were available to cultivate it. Any land left unworked was subject to reallocation by community authorities; custom dictated that a household should not own more arable land than it could cultivate.[58] Calpolli lands in the Nahua area were often contrasted with lands belonging to the lordly establishment. In the Mixtec case from Ayusi discussed above, nobles were careful to distinguish between lands of the aniñe, which belonged to the yya or cacique, and lands of the siña, suggesting that corporate lands were the opposite of lordly lands. This organization conforms to the pattern described for the Nahuas. Land claimed by the siña could also be reallocated according to local needs and demands. Usually, enterprising individuals cleared and worked unused lands as a precondition for claiming them. Individuals were obligated to notify community authorities of all land transactions, including leases and sales, and to obtain their collective approval. Households paid tribute to corporate authorities based, in part, on the extent of their landholdings. In the Nahua area, the term *tequitlalli* was used to designate land on which tribute was paid. I have found no equivalent term in the Mixteca.[59]

Another term that indicates a category of corporate land is *ñuhu comunidad,* "community land," employing a Spanish loanword. This term refers to the Spanish introduction of community fields, used to support a community's functions, feasts, and tribute payments.[60] Although this arrangement represented a type of land controlled by the corporate community, it was not an original native category of tenure. The concept is based on a Spanish loanword that was not adopted in place of the ñuu or its subentities (siqui, siña, or dzini). In fact, the term *comunidad* was often used in connection with proceeds of the community treasury, the *caja de comunidad,* and activities associated with colonial municipal government and finance. For example, in Topiltepec, the expression *ytu huahi tniño,* or "fields of the cabildo," was translated as "milpas de la comunidad" in 1711.[61] References to "ytu comunidad tniño" indicate that the lands were worked communally or were possessed by the ñuu.[62] It is unclear whether native officials of the ñuu could allocate these plots to individual households; in any case, they grew surplus crops on community lands and leased them to individuals for profit. By the second half of the colonial period, community lands had become a source of corporate revenue.

Despite the examples given above, sources from the Mixteca do not contain many references to lands belonging specifically to siqui or ñuu. In comparison, references abound to lands located in siqui or ñuu that belonged to the aniñe of lords, considered part of the colonial *cacicazgo.* The prominence of aniñe lands might be attributed to the frequent appearance of yya in the documentary record. At the same time, the relative scarcity of information on corporate lands suggests that noble houses subsumed many corporate landholding responsibilities in the Mixteca. The situation may be comparable to the eastern Nahua cultural area, where powerful noble houses around Puebla and Tlaxcala apparently subverted the structure and corporate powers of the altepetl and its subdivisions, the *tlaxilacalli* or calpolli.[63] This tendency seems most pronounced in the Mixteca Baja, where yya normally considered the lands and laborers of dzini as part of their patrimonies.

The continued use of terminology for ñuhu aniñe in the late seventeenth and eighteenth centuries reflects the enduring power of the lordly establishment in the Mixteca. In comparison, the use of Nahua terminology for nobles' lands in central Mexico was rare by the later period; the term *tecpantlalli* does not appear in extant Nahuatl-language documents after the early 1600s, and use of *pillalli* had faded by the second half of the seventeenth century.[64] Even if nobles' lands in central Mexico did not become entirely indistinguishable from corporate lands, the disappearance of these categories signifies changes in land tenure and use. These differences reflect the relative strength of Ñudzahui and Nahua lordly establishments within corporate communities. A decisive factor in the continued vitality of the Ñudzahui aniñe was the low rate of Spanish immigration to the Mixteca and the relatively slow development of Spanish estates in the region, which allowed yya to consolidate properties and to maintain access to labor, despite severe population loss. The Mixteca compares with the Valley of Oaxaca in this regard, where many cacicazgos remained intact by the late colonial period.[65]

In some cases, distinctions between the lands of ñuu, siqui, and aniñe are unclear. In fact, some siqui were founded by groups of people who lived and worked on a lord's distant lands. For example, in the 1590s, the yya of Tlaxiaco sent some dependents to establish a siqui called "Ñuyucu" in order to work his lands there.[66] The nearby ñuu of Malinaltepec complained about twenty years later that this group of ten married couples had encroached on lands belonging to the ñuu, since the fields were actually located within the boundaries of Malinaltepec. When the couples refused to pay tribute to Malinaltepec, they were accused of trying to break away from the ñuu. This dispute illustrates the unclear and contested distinction between cacicazgo lands belonging to the aniñe and corporate lands belonging to the ñuu. Another example of a yya who created a siqui by settling lands with dependents involves the cacica of Tlaxiaco, doña María Saavedra, who sent eleven married couples to settle ("poblar y guardar") a place called Acatlixco in 1581.[67] Soon this group came into conflict with the ñuu of Atoyaquillo, which demanded tribute from the new group because the lands they worked were located within the ñuu's territory. It is likely that tensions between corporate groups and lordly establishments over land and labor had always existed, but the demographic catastrophe, colonial changes regarding private property, and the involvement of Spanish officials must have complicated matters.

Native-language terminology for purchased land in the early colonial period suggests that a preconquest precedent existed for this type of land transfer, though buying and selling land surely increased after the conquest. Land acquired by purchase, even if the transaction had occurred many years earlier, was called *ñuhu nidzico* (sold land).[68] For example, in 1632, Diego Gómez of Santa Magdalena Yucucata possessed the standard arrangement of a huahi and its cahi, ñuhu chiyo, a few scattered ytu, and two *ytu nidzico*.[69] Similarly, in 1623, Lucía de la Anunciación referred to the ytu nidzico that she had purchased from Isabel Nahuiyo.[70] Often, testators simply stated that they had bought a plot of land from someone, instead of referring to the category of possession. In any case, the buyers nearly always specified the person who had sold them the land, even if the sellers were deceased.[71] Sometimes, they included the selling price and the date of purchase. However, testators did not refer to the inheritance of purchased land, suggesting that proof of possession was only necessary for one generation, nor did they speak of lands they had sold.[72] The Nahua equivalent of ñuhu nidzico was *tlalcohualli,* or "purchased land."[73] People who possessed purchased lands in the Mixteca were usually yya or toho. Although it was a normal aspect of the native land tenure system, sold land was not nearly as common as inherited land in the documentary record. The consistent use of terminology for purchased lands reflects the importance of proving origin and legitimacy of possession.

Finally, especially in the late colonial period, certain lands were designated for particular religious purposes, managed by *cofradías* (lay confraternities) or assigned to specific saints. This type of land tenure was based on the Spanish practice of contributing funds for the maintenance of an image or shrine and the celebration of a saint's feast day.[74] The arrangement resembled communal property in that proceeds from the land were allocated to finance community functions. Some testators bequeathed land to an image of the Virgin Mary. For example, Rosa Hernández and don Lorenzo Vásquez, a toho and a yya from Chilapilla, each gave a plot of land to the Virgin of Guadalupe

TABLE 7.1

Category	Translation and Description
Ñuhu ñuu	Land of the ñuu; claimed by the corporate entity and subject to use or allocation by it members; similar to Nahua altepetlalli
Ñuhu siña	Land of a subentity of the ñuu, called siña (or its regional variants, siqui and dzini); corporate lands are often contrasted with lands of the lordly establishment; similar to Nahua calpollalli
Ñuhu aniñe	Palace land; part of the hereditary patrimony of the lordly establishment, represented by a male or female yya, or both; contrasted with ñuhu ñuu and ñuhu siña; considered part of the colonial cacicazgo; similar to Nahua tecpantlalli or pillalli
Ñuhu huahi	House land; the plot or plots of land associated with a given household; refers to either the land on which the house stood or land adjacent to it; existed among commoners and lords; as the best and most inheritable land, it was often associated with ñuhu chiyo; in the colonial period, the Spanish term *solar* was adopted as a synonym; similar to Nahua callalli
Ñuhu chiyo	Patrimonial land, old land, or altar land; usually the site of the main household; the plot most likely to be bequeathed to members within the household and the least likely to be alienated by sale or reallocation; existed among both nobles and commoners; similar to Nahua huehuetlalli
Ñuhu nidzico	"Sold land"; most common among nobles during the colonial period; similar to Nahua tlalcohualli

in 1749; it is unclear who worked the fields, but it is certain that harvests from the land were designated for a cofradía dedicated to this venerable image.[75] In describing the borders of these lands, they referred to Mary as an owner not unlike their neighbors. Similarly, Juan Domingo, a toho of Topiltepec, gave some lands in 1711 to Jesus of Nazareth and to the Virgin of the Immaculate Conception.[76]

The complexity of Ñudzahui land tenure categories indicates that land tenure in the Mixteca contained few communal elements (see table 7.1). Corporate entities such as ñuu and siña had residual control over land within their territories, but most land was inherited and possessed by specific households, including lordly establishments. The number, size, and quality of holdings varied considerably, so that some households had much more land and access to labor than others. In fact, the Mixtec system of land tenure, in its tolerance of individual or household possession and inheritance, resembled European practices in many ways.

However, there were considerable differences between Ñudzahui and European land tenure systems. First of all, no native category of land corresponded entirely in meaning or function with any Spanish category. Second, the Ñudzahui system placed much more emphasis on a household's obligation to cultivate its lands, pay tribute based on the yields of those lands, and maintain a community consensus that periodically confirmed its right to possess and transfer those lands.[77] Acquisition, retention, and alienation of lands were subject to collective consent. Third, native landholding was not neatly divided into public and private domains. Land belonged to the ñuu, the siña, a specific household, and individual members who inherited and worked certain plots, but not exclusively to any one of these entities. Whereas in this system the individual's right to possess land was mediated by overlapping household and community rights, land was either private or public in Spanish society, and an individual's right was not contingent on use or consensus. I have found no words in the Ñudzahui language that signified "public" or "private." Even native lords who controlled lands beyond the jurisdiction of the ñuu and siqui needed to fulfill certain obligations with those who cultivated their lands, and to maintain social relations with members of that ñuu or siqui who acknowledged their authority. Claims to multiple lands without the ability to cultivate them, or claims in the absence of community consensus, were vulnerable to dispute and the lands subject to allocation.

Ñudzahui terminology for land tenure compares with Nahua terminology in its multiple distinctions and categories.[78] The use of land tenure categories in extant native-language records from the sixteenth to the eighteenth centuries demonstrates that land continued to be organized primarily within communities, despite the noticeable impact of Spanish concepts of land tenure by the late colonial period.

Names and Types of Land

Land was also classified by the quality of its soil. For example, in 1611, doña Juana Beatriz, cacica of San Juan Yolotepec and Cosoltepec referred to her "black lands" [ñoho dayu] and her "hill fields" [yucu ytu].[79] The term *ndayu* means "mud" or "black" and was often used in conjunction with *ñuhu* in reference to good, fertile valley soil.[80] The best lands in the region were the rich alluvial lands of valley floors, low slopes, and river systems. In the Mixteca Baja, yya typically associated ndayu with their dependent laborers. Black, alluvial lands may refer to the "lama-bordo" terracing technique, a technological and adaptive mechanism employed in the postclassic period to increase agricultural production and to cultivate slope lands not previously tilled.[81] This system involved the creation of channels that washed soil from hills to create an alluvium in terraces descending to the valley floor. The rich land of narrow valley floors lies in stark contrast to surrounding eroded hills and steep slopes.[82] Rain-watered fields and irrigated fields were called *ñuhu dzahui* and *ñuhu doyo*, respectively. When don Juan Agustín used these two terms in his testament (translated as "milpas de temporal y de la riega"), in addition to ñuhu ndayu, he distinguished between three different types of cultivable land.[83] Other types of land refer to their location. Don Andrés de Zárate referred in 1607 to ravine and slope lands ("ytu aniñe nduhua" and "ytu aniñe ytnu") associated with his aniñe in Santiago Tiñuhu.[84]

A few Spanish loanwords for plots and fields entered the Ñudzahui lexicon as early as the sixteenth century. For example, in 1573, don Felipe de Saavedra used a version of the loanword *huerta* (orchard) in combination with *ytu* and *ñuhu*.[85] The infrequently attested term seems to refer specifically to a field of introduced fruit trees. A more common loanword, employed by the early seventeenth century, was *solar,* or "house lot." Whereas Spaniards used the term to denote the land on which the house stood, many documents refer to it as cultivable land behind the house, using the term as a synonym for *ñuhu huahi*.[86] In 1682, a married couple from Teposcolula referred to their "house and solar land behind the house" [huahi sihi ñuhu solar sata huahi].[87] A cacica conflated the two terms when she referred to her "solar ñuhu aniñe" [palace land lot] in 1691.[88]

Unlike in central Mexico, there is little evidence of a native system of land measurement in the Mixteca.[89] In the early period, lands are merely named and not described or measured at all. When measurements were discussed, people spoke in terms of Spanish *varas, brazas,* or *yuntas.* The first two units are Spanish measurements of length; the third unit is an estimated measure based on the number of oxen required to plow a given amount of land.[90] No indigenous equivalents for these measurements appear in the record. The act of measuring lands usually accompanied title verification actions presided over by Spanish officials; such ceremonies became more common by the late seventeenth and eighteenth centuries, as the need for land titles became more urgent in the face of legal and commercial demands.

Perhaps the strong tradition of assigning names to lands in the Mixteca compensated for the lack of standardized land measurements. People used a complex naming system to identify the type and location of a given tract of land throughout the colonial period. This tradition also existed in the Nahua area, but it was practiced, or at least recorded, more consistently in the Mixteca.[91] References to an unnamed plot of land are quite rare in documentation from this period, especially before the eighteenth century. Sometimes, it is difficult to distinguish whether the name referred to a cultivated field or the general place where the land was located. Since every prominent feature of the landscape was named, field names could draw on local topographic names. Names usually consisted of two or three elements and do not appear to differ from place-names for sociopolitical entities. Typical elements mark the vicinity of the plot vis-à-vis prominent features of the landscape, such as a river (*yuta*), a ravine (*nduhua*), a road (*yaya*), a valley (*yodzo*), a hill (*yucu*), a slope (*ytnu*), or a forest (*yutnu*). Modifying elements further qualify the type of land and its appearance, color, size, shape, or unique physical or sacred features. Names sometimes incorporated descriptions of soil type. Words referring to animals, invoking some metaphor or association, were not uncommon. Lands were not named after people, however. Often, locative terms (based on body parts, as elsewhere in Mesoamerica) define the position of the field in relation to a feature of the topography.

The custom of naming lands enabled people to map their surroundings. In codices and other pictorial manuscripts, writers recorded lands in the form of place-name glyphs, which simply inscribed the collective memory of the local oral tradition. In the colonial period, alphabetic writing served a corresponding function, spelling out the place-name and its relative location. The attention to detail in this system was remarkable. In 1566, the cacica of Teposcolula, doña Catalina de Peralta, claimed at least fifty named lands as part of her patrimony; the lands were enumerated in the will of her uncle, don Pedro Osorio, which was witnessed by sixty native men and women.[92] Some lands were named after siqui, ñuu, and *yuhuitayu*, reinforcing the relationship between lands and sociopolitical entities. It is possible that the lands were simply located in those entities. Few disputes seem to have arisen from an ignorance of named lands;

rather, contending parties tended to acknowledge the land in question but disagreed on its precise boundaries. Again, land names could have referred to a general area rather than a specific tract. Occasionally, some lands were known by more than one name. For example, in 1693, doña Luisa de Orozco, cacica of Yanhuitlan, referred to a piece of land named "Sahayucunda," which was also called ("por otro nombre") "Yuqutiahuaa."[93] In multilingual areas, lands were often known by names in different languages.[94] When Juana de la Cruz of Tamusalapa listed her lands in her testament of 1720, she referred to five lands by their Ñudzahui names, and she pointed out that a sixth tract of land had a Chocho name.[95]

Domingo de Celís testified to the time-honored tradition of naming and describing lands.[96] Domingo was a noble from San Pedro Mártir Yucunama who traveled to Teposcolula in 1717 in order to make his last will and testament. He described the location of twenty-one named pieces of land and five houses in relation to eighteen place-names. He distributed his lands among three sons and a daughter as if he were going for a long walk along the borders of his landholdings. In his imaginary stroll, he named each piece of land, specified the adjacent lands and borders of other men and women in relation to the cardinal directions, and occasionally noted the borders of other communities and landmarks.[97]

Even Spanish-language documents noted the names of Ñudzahui lands. When don Domingo de Guzmán listed all 102 of his lands in his Spanish-language testament of 1591, every ytu was named and located within a named ñuu.[98] If names associated particular plots of land with features of the local and sacred landscape, it is possible that the range of terminology was unlimited or perhaps limited only to choices that avoided replication in a given locality. The system was also capable of incorporating new names; for example, in his testament of 1680, Gaspar de Silva of Yanhuitlan bequeathed an "ytu yuchasalucas" [San Lucas river land] to his granddaughter.[99] Naturally, communities must have drawn on a repertoire of common naming elements based on a familiar mountainous landscape; but in each ñuu, every ytu or cultivable plot of land had a separate identity. Only the smallest strips of land, the so-called coo, were usually unnamed. By the eighteenth century, some people referred to a sichi, ytu, or solar with no corresponding name, or they referred to multiple contiguous plots with one general name. Nonetheless, the Ñudzahui practice of designating separate ñuhu and ytu with recognizable names lasted throughout the colonial period and continues today.

Land Distribution and Use

The most profound change affecting land distribution and use was the drastic decline of the native population in the sixteenth century. In the first half of the colonial period, the native population declined about 90 percent. In theory, population loss increased a household's access to arable and semiarable lands in the sixteenth and early seventeenth centuries, but there were far fewer hands to work them. In the Mixteca, the epidemics forced the abandonment of many labor-intensive projects. Extensive terracing along hills, a prominent feature of the preconquest landscape, suffered irreversible losses, contributing to erosion and soil depletion.[100] Despite these significant changes, tay situ continued to cultivate the staple crops of maize, maguey, beans, and squash in the traditional manner. By the seventeenth century, tilling the soil with yuntas (yokes) of *ydzundiqui* (oxen, literally "horned deer") and plows was not uncommon on valley lands, although the yata (digging stick), now fitted with an iron tip, was still the most common cultivating tool.[101] Communities in temperate valleys were encouraged to grow wheat by *encomenderos* and Spanish officials on their community lands, but wheat production remained a marginal enterprise in the Mixteca.[102] Introduced fruits included apples, peaches, lemons, limes, oranges, figs, pears, quinces, apricots, grapes, melons, and olives. The silk industry spurred the planting of mulberry trees.[103]

Although the ñuu continued to organize land among its members, Spanish influences and procedures were perceptible by the mid-sixteenth century. By the 1550s Spanish law appropriated the power to entitle yya to their houses and lands, requiring them to possess titles to their properties by obtaining the approval of local lords and Spanish officials and by paying the obligatory royal fees. New possessors of titles performed ceremonial acts symbolizing their right to do as they pleased with their own private property. For example, when doña Catalina de Peralta and her husband, don Diego de Mendoza, took possession of lands belonging to her aniñe in 1569, the two rulers tore up grass, threw stones, and broke stalks of planted maize.[104] Acts of taking possession clearly followed a Spanish model, but some aspects of recorded ceremonies reveal native concerns and traditions, such as addressing the four directions and commemorating the occasion with a feast.

Just as the nobility had used pictorial writings to support and promote their claims before the conquest, their descendants understood the value of written documents in the early colonial period. Native rulers continued to rely on codices and *lienzos* in the sixteenth century to prove possession, but they also sought to establish and validate their claims with the new form of writing in the Spanish legal system. By the 1560s, the last will and testament had begun to serve an important function of documenting lands and properties among natives; lords and nobles were encouraged to write testaments before an assembly of local nobles to clarify possession in the event of property disputes. In 1591, for example, the cabildo of Yanhuitlan ordered nobles, merchants, and traders to make their testaments with native *escribanos* and witnesses in order to facilitate property transactions and to mitigate the number of property disputes.[105] Later in the colonial period, the title verification program, carried out by Spanish officials from 1696 to 1718, was designed to establish the limits of community holdings and to raise revenue by the granting of *títulos de composición*. The program forced communities to furnish or purchase proof of possession. By the end of the seventeenth century, increasing Spanish competition for access to land led many lords to establish their rights and to confirm all land transactions in the presence of Spanish officials. Native ownership was based on evidence of ownership at the time of the conquest, bequests, purchase, *mercedes* (royal land grants), and titles.[106]

The distribution of lands among households in the Mixteca varied considerably.[107] No Mixtec household possessed more land and wealth than the aniñe or the lordly establishment. The total sum of lands, palaces and houses, titles, properties, goods, and labor belonging to a lord's patrimony was known in colonial legal terms as the *cacicazgo,* a term that was not used in Ñudzahui-language documentation. Rather, native writers referred to the yuhuitayu, a system of hereditary rule discussed in the previous chapter, and the aniñe. In accordance with Spanish law, male yya and female yya dzehe controlled extensive cacicazgo landholdings as private property. For example, in 1571, the cacica of Tlazultepec, doña María López, possessed 38 pieces of land and several houses.[108] Of the 102 plots of land that *yya toniñe* don Gabriel de Guzmán owned in 1580, 56 were located in communities outside his home ñuu of Yanhuitlan, indicating the extensive cross-regional nature of landholdings associated with the aniñe.[109] This aspect of geographical separation inherent in the sociopolitical nature of the yuhuitayu is apparently unrivaled in postconquest Mesoamerica.[110] In the Mixteca Baja, the cacica doña Juana Beatriz of Acaquisapa bequeathed 26 pieces of land in 1611, carefully distinguishing them from her late husband's patrimony.[111] In the Valley of Oaxaca, doña Juana de Lara of Cuilapan possessed 43 cultivable plots of land, 7 solares, several orchards and small lots, and 2 *ranchos* for domestic animals.[112] It is unclear what percentage of any ñuu's land was controlled by its aniñe. In the Mixteca Baja, some yya and yya dzehe spoke of their dzini and ñuu as if they owned all the lands associated with those entities. The fact that many yya claimed lands in several different communities complicates an assessment of their holdings. Demographic decline may have concentrated patrimonial landholdings in the hands of fewer lords, contributing to multiple and even more scattered holdings.[113] It is also unclear, in the absence of relevant census data or specific counts, how many dependent laborers worked on these lands.[114]

Differences in landholdings among yya reflect degrees of socioeconomic differentiation within this group. For example, the late-seventeenth-century testaments of don Gerónimo García y Guzmán and his wife, doña Lázara de Guzmán, show that they possessed several tracts of good land in the ñuu of San Juan Teposcolula. But their holdings did not compare with the extensive properties of don Francisco Pimentel y Guzmán, yya toniñe of the yuhuitayu and *cabecera* of San Pedro y San Pablo Teposcolula. In Tlaxiaco, don Diego de Velasco was clearly a prominent yya with many resources at his disposal; he owned an iron forge, two African slaves, and numerous furnishings and books. However, don Diego claimed only four pieces of land in his testament of 1627.[115]

Although tracts of land were almost always listed and named separately, it is very difficult to ascertain an exact measure of land-based wealth because details on the length, width, and soil type were inconsistently recorded. However, a sample of 20 testaments and inventories of yya from the Mixteca Alta and Baja, concentrated in the period from 1570 to 1750, gives an impression of this group's wealth by the number of lands they claimed in their testaments (see table 7.2).[116] Yya in the sample claimed an average of 32.6 lands and numerous other possessions. The range of holdings in the sample was from 4 tracts of land to 102. Yya dzehe in the sample (eight of the twenty) possessed an average of 35 lands, indicating that gender was not a determining factor in the size of lordly estates. Landholdings represented the possessions of the aniñe more than the individual. Rather than enumerating separate huahi, lords tended to refer to the aniñe as a complex of dwellings. In the Mixteca Baja, in particular, many lords referred in general terms to lands belonging to a specific aniñe, or lands associated with a dzini ("barrio"), without enumerating those lands.

TABLE 7.2
Sample of Twenty Testaments of Yya

Name	Place/Date	Source
doña María López	Tlazultepec, 1571	AGN-T, 59:2
don Felipe de Saavedra	Tlaxiaco, 1573	AJT-C, 7:654
don Gabriel de Guzmán	Yanhuitlan, 1591	AGN-C, 516:3
doña Juana Beatriz	Acaquisapa, 1611	AGN-T, 245:2
don Diego de Velasco	Tlaxiaco, 1627	AJT-C, 2:263
don Gerónimo de Lara y Guzmán	Texupa, 1633	AGN-T, 3567:5
doña María de Velasco	Huaxuapa, 1633	AGN-T, 571:1
don Diego de Velasco	Chalcatongo, 1636	AGN-T, 637:1
don Juan Agustín	Huaxuapa, 1642	AGN-T, 245:2
don Rafael de San Miguel y Salazar	Tonalá, 1643	AGN-T, 657:2
doña Francisca Petronilla	Tequistepec, 1652	AGN-T, 245:2
don Gerónimo García	San Juan Teposcolula, 1672	AJT-C, 4:417
doña Lázara de Guzmán	San Juan Teposcolula, 1691	AJT-C, 4:417
don Raimundo de Santiago y Guzmán	Huaxuapa, 1676	AGN-T, 571:1
doña Beatriz Maldonado	Huaxuapa, 1677	AGN-T, 571:1
don Jorge de la Cruz Alvarado	Huaxuapa, 1678	AGN-T, 245:2
doña Juana de Lara	Cuilapa, 1717	AGN-HJ, 118
don Lorenzo Cortés y Salazar	Chilapa, 1744	AJT-C, 10:873
don Lorenzo Vásquez	Chilapilla 1749	AJT-C, 20:1684
doña Josefa de Salazar	Chilapa, 1750	AJT-C, 10:873

In comparison with the far-flung, extensive landholdings of yya, most lesser nobles, or toho, owned land only within the borders of their home ñuu. However, some toho possessed as many lands as yya in the colonial period, and, in general, there were considerable differences among the toho. Toho are often identified as such in their testaments and are also recognizable by their Spanish surnames, as discussed in the section on naming patterns in chapter 5. Their lack of the titles *don* or *doña* set them apart from yya and yya dzehe, whereas their wealth distinguished them from the vast majority of ñandahi. One toho from Topiltepec, Gonzalo López, owned 56 plots of land in 1610.[117] More typical of toho, however, was the estate of a woman from Yanhuitlan named María Méndez, who owned a large household complex of 8 huahi, a tract of patrimonial land, and 8 scattered pieces of land in 1646.[118] Some toho owned as few as 3 tracts of land, but they possessed other types of wealth. Many nobles acquired land in the colonial period through purchase. Again, there is no indication of the quality or size of these holdings. The choice of *sichi* (piece) or *coo* (ridge) over *ytu* (cultivable field) may indicate the relative size of tracts, but this possible distinction is obscured by the use of *sichi ytu* and *coo ytu* in reference to some plots. In any case, the extensive landholdings of nobles tend to reflect their general wealth; in addition to 56 lands, Gonzalo López had several houses, about 1,600 pesos, 27 mules, and 4 oxen. His possession of many mules indicates that he was involved in long-distance trade, an occupation associated with nobles. Whereas yya relied on dependent laborers to work on their multiple fields, as discussed in chapter 5, toho could not count on a large contingent of dependents to sow their lands. Still, some toho did have access to a limited number of dependents. For example, Juan López de Quiñones, a noble of Achiutla, bequeathed 4 houses and 6 lands, complete with their dependent laborers, in his testament of 1593.[119] Most nobles had one or more live-in dependents, sometimes married couples, who contributed to the productive capacity of the household by spinning, weaving, or working plots of land.[120]

A sample of 33 testaments and inventories of toho from the Mixteca Alta, concentrated in the period from 1590 to 1690, gives an impression of this group's landholdings and material wealth (see table 7.3). Counting various types of land together—including ñuhu huahi, solar, ytu, coo, and huertas—toho in this sample owned an average of 14.7 separate plots of land.[121] Toho possessed an average of 3 huahi, but some owned as many as 8 separate house units. Most owned a horse, at

TABLE 7.3
Sample of Thirty-three Testaments of Toho

Name	Place/Date	Source
Martín Cortés	Istepec, 1594	AJT-C, 1:161 bis.
Francisco López	Sayultepec, 1595	AJT-C, 1:161
Gonzalo López	Topiltepec, 1610	AJT-C, 8:705
Juan López Qhmañe	Yanhuitlan, 1616	AJT-C, 2:231
Catalina García	Yanhuitlan, 1621	AJT-C, 2:188
Diego de la Cruz	Tamasulapa, 1621	AGN-T, 1226:3
Miguel Jiménez	Yanhuitlan, 1621	AJT-C, 2:243
Lucía de la Anunciación	Teposcolula, 1623	AJT-C, 4:400
Lucía Hernández Ñuquihui	Teposcolula, 1633	AJT-C, 3:287
Melchor Mejía	Yucucata, 1641	AJT-C, 5:506
María Méndez	Yanhuitlan, 1646	AJT-C, 13:1109
Inés Juárez	Tamasulapa, 1665	AJT-C, 10:838
Juan Domingo	Topiltepec, 1668	AJT-C, 8:705
Domingo Pérez	Yanhuitlan, 1670	AJT-C, 7:686
Felipe de la Cruz	Topiltepec, 1678	AJT-C, 6:578
Gaspar de Silva	Yanhuitlan, 1680	AJT-C, 13:1109
Diego García	Suchitepec, 1681	AJT-C, Anexo 1:18
Bernabé López	Tamasulapa, 1687	AJT-C, 10:838
Domingo Hernández	Yanhuitlan, 1689	AJT-C, 5:535
Domingo Ramos de la Cruz	Suchitepec, 1710	AJT-C, Anexo 1:18
Domingo de Celís	Yucunama, 1717	AJT-C, 7:689
Salvador de Celís	Yucunama and Teposcolula, 1718	AJT-C, 7:689
Juana de la Cruz	Tamasulapa, 1720	AGN-T, 1226:3
Francisco de Avendaños	Yanhuitlan, 1726	AJT-C, 11:921
Miguel Aranda	Yanhuitlan, 1726	AJT-C, 7:686
Lázaro Aranda	Yanhuitlan, 1728	AJT-C, 7:686
Miguel Sánchez	Achiutla, 1742	AJT-C, 14:1199
Rosa Hernández	Chilapilla, 1749	AJT-C, 20:1682
Juan de Velasco	Texupa, 1752	AJT-C, 17:1464
Sebastián Sánchez Hernández	Yanhuitlan, 1754	AJT-C, 15:1232
Felipe Mariscal	Teposcolula, 1769	AJT-C, 13:1052
Pasquala Salazar	Amatlan, 1777	AJT-C, 14:1180
Manuel de Velasco	Atlatlahuca, 1787	AJT-C, 16:1303

least one mule, and a yoke of oxen. Eight toho in the sample possessed movable goods or cash valued at more than 400 pesos, with 1600 pesos being the highest sum. Women in this group (8 of the 33) claimed an average of 7.3 parcels of land, which is still a substantial amount, but it is half of the overall average for toho.[122] However, many noblewomen also possessed sizable inventories of cloth. There is little observable change over time in the number of toho landholdings. Of the 33 men and women in this sample, the earliest 15 cases (those before 1646) averaged 14 tracts of land per person. In terms of landholdings and general wealth, testaments and inventories indicate subtle, rather than sharp, degrees of difference between lesser yya and higher toho. Some toho resembled the high nobility in terms of their wealth, despite a lack of titles (don, yya, cacique) and prestigious surnames.

Most ñandahi households had access to only a few plots of land. In general, this group does not appear as often as nobles in my collection of testaments until the second half of the colonial period. The typical ñandahi can be identified by an indigenous surname as late as the end of the seventeenth century, or by a surname based on a saint's name. A sample of 75 testaments and inventories of ñandahi from the Mixteca Alta, concentrated in the period from 1650 to 1800, gives an impression of this group's landholdings and material wealth (see table 7.4). On average, ñandahi possessed 3.8 parcels of land and one main huahi or house.[123] The landholdings of a typical ñandahi consisted of one house lot, a field for maize cultivation, and one or two supplementary plots of secondary or marginal land for the cultivation of magueyes. Women in the group (29 of the 75) possessed 4.2 parcels of land, or slightly more land than the average commoner. In fact, the total sample of 128 testaments (45 women, 83 men) indicates that men and women owned comparable amounts of land; among yya, toho, and ñandahi, the average man claimed only one more plot of land than the average woman. There is no indication that men and women in the Mixteca owned different types of land or that women owned increasingly less land during the colonial period. However, the fact that extant testaments from the civil record represent nearly twice as many men as women suggests that men were more likely to write testaments. The implications of this fact are discussed in the following section on inheritance patterns. At this point, suffice it to say that among testators in my sample there was little observable gender preference for landholdings.

As with the yya-toho elite, the amount of land held by members of the ñandahi group varied greatly. In the sample, several men and women owned no land, whereas some people owned more than a dozen plots of land. To reiterate, the number of lands specified in a testament is only an estimate of land-based wealth. In 1716, Inés María of Xoxocotlan owned only two tracts of land in the Valley of Oaxaca, but one of those plots measured eighty yuntas—a substantial amount of land.[124] In the absence of descriptive terminology, the well-off ñandahi are difficult to distinguish from the lesser toho. A number of people in the ñandahi sample who possessed approximately five to fifteen plots of land might be placed in either group. Appropriately, many men and women in this intermediate category have surnames such as Cruz, López, and Pérez. I have placed them among the ñandahi when they are not called "toho" (or "principal" in supporting Spanish documentation) and when the surnames of their relatives and heirs suggest a non-noble social status. The fact that many people can not be distinguished as toho or ñandahi based on their landed wealth, despite the fact that significant differences in landholding continued to exist between the two groups, indicates that socioeconomic differences between the nobility and commoners in the colonial period represented a continuum rather than a rigidly stratified hierarchy. The ability to differentiate toho from ñandahi is increasingly difficult after 1700, when terminology of social differentiation became less pronounced. Landholding patterns observed in native-language testaments reveal gradations of difference rather than a process of social leveling in this period.

Despite the fact that many people in the record fall between the categories of well-off commoners and lesser nobles, most ñandahi can be recognized at a glance. Take, for example, a man from Yucunama named Pedro de San Pablo. In 1690, he bequeathed to his wife nothing more than a house and "everything inside and in back of the house."[125] Pedro specified that when his wife died, their two sons were to divide the house and movable property among them. In comparison, Petronilla de la Cruz was a relatively secure ñandahi woman. In 1627, Petronilla sold two small plots of land (one planted with magueys) and a chest filled with clothes to pay for her burial and masses.[126] Her remaining property consisted of a house, one ytu, three coo (camellones), and three metates. The testaments of Pascuala María and Nicolás Miguel, commoners from San Francisco Chinduhua, represent the extreme within this group.[127] Neither Pascuala nor Nicolás had any land or property, and, in fact, their testaments were little more than pious statements. They went through the motions of giving money to various saints, but the notary was forced to record zeros next to their mock offerings. Nothing more is known about these two humble ñandahi, who were so poor that they could have passed as landless dependents. Indeed, most live-in dependents resembled poor Pascuala and Nicolás.

Some testators made some provision for dependents in their wills by virtue of a general tendency to bequeath something to everybody. In the absence of heirs, especially children, dependents might receive a house and lands. More likely, dependents inherited a small amount of land, a few magueys, or movable property such as clothing. Sometimes, they received the generous bequest of a mule. For example, in 1728, Lázaro de Aranda of Yanhuitlan divided his estate of multiple lands and houses among his wife and two daughters. Before closing his testament, he addressed a man named Nicolás de Santiago, called "my son, a person whom I have raised" [codayanju chay nidacuanunju]. Like most nobles, he referred to his dependents as children.[128] Nicolás received a small patch of land (measuring 4 by 6 brazas, or approximately 6.7 by 10 meters), twenty magueys, and a "torito" (young bull). Similarly, a dependent named Andrés Pérez Sicuañe, who lived with a toho from Topiltepec, received a yoke of oxen in 1610.[129] In most cases, testators recognized dependents in their wills without giving them enough to become independent of the household. The testaments of yya and toho reveal the continued importance of dependent live-in laborers throughout the colonial period.

In contrast to lands distributed among households (aniñe included), another broad category of native land distribution and use was called "ñuhu comunidad," introduced earlier in the discussion on categories of land tenure. William Taylor identified various forms of corporate lands among communities in the Valley of Oaxaca, including fields

TABLE 7.4
Sample of Seventy-Five Testaments of Ñandahi

Name	Place/Date	Source
Catalina	Achiutla, 1581	AJT-CR, 1:25
Diego Siquaha	Tamasulapa, 1608	AJT-C, 6:635
María López Siñuu	Yucucata, 1625	AJT-C, 5:506
Diego Gómez	Yucucata, 1632	AJT-C, 5:506
Juan López	Yanhuitlan, 1642	AJT-C, 4:467
Alonzo Gómez	Tlacosahuaya, 1653	AJT-C, 4:482
María Gutiérrez	Yanhuitlan, 1658	AJT-C, 5:515
Juan de la Cruz	Tamasulapa, 1672	AJT-C, 4:412
Luis de Mora	Tamasulapa, 1679	AJT-C, 6:635
Petronilla García	Tamasulapa, 1680	AJT-C, 11:938
Juana de la Cruz	Teposcolula, 1681	AJT-C, 6:575
Diego de Vario	Yucucata, 1684	AJT-C, 5:506
Juan de la Mesquita	Yanhuitlan, 1686	AJT-C, 5:515
Pedro de San Pablo	Yucunama, 1690	AJT-C, 7:689
Miguel de Osorio	Teposcolula, 1700	AJT-C, 5:544
Petronilla de San Pablo	Yucunama, 1701	AJT-C, 5:548
Juan Miguel	Yucunama, 1704	AJT-C, 5:544
Juan Pasqual	Teposcolula, 1709	AJT-C, Anexo 1:19
Nicolás de Santiago	Teposcolula, 1712	AJT-C, 7:682
Micaela Nicolasa	Teposcolula, 1713	AJT-C, 9:758
Inés María	Xoxocotlan, 1716	AGN-T, 742:3
Pedro Nolasco	Chilapa, 1721	AJT-C, 18:1564
Matias Bautista	Tamasulapa, 1721	AJT-C, 10:838
Micaela Aguilar	Yolomecatl, 1721	AJT-C, 7:681
Josef Antonio Solano	Teposcolula, 1724	AJT-C, 9:758
Petronilla Calderón	Teposcolula, 1726	AJT-C, 8:726
Blas de la Cruz	Yanhuitlan, 1726	AJT-C, 9:781 bis
Juana María	Teposcolula, 1727	AJT-C, 8: 726
Juan Pasqual	Teposcolula, 1727	AJT-C, Anexo 1:19
Manuel de Santiago	Teposcolula, 1728	AJT-C, Anexo 1:19
Pasquala María	Chinduhua, 1730	AJT-C, 14:1124
Josef Rodríguez	Teposcolula, 1731	AJT-C, 8:726
Pedro de la Cruz	Teposcolula, 1734	AJT-C, 9:772
Micaela de Santiago	Teposcolula, 1737	AJT-C, Anexo 1:19
Nicolás Miguel	Chinduhua, 1737	AJT-C, 14:1124
Juan Nicolás	Chinduhua, 1737	AJT-C, 14: 1124
Manuel Hernández	Yolomecatl, 1738	AJT-C, 15:1268
Domingo de Tapia	Yolomecatl, 1738	AJT-C, 10:837
Mateo de San Pablo	Yolomecatl, 1738	AJT-C, 10:866
Nicolás Juan de la Cruz	Tonaltepec, 1738	AJT-C, 9:792
Petrona de Osorio	Yolomecatl, 1738	AJT-C, 10:866
Micaela de Santiago	Teposcolula, 1740	AJT-C, Anexo 1:19
Gaspar de los Reyes	Chilapa, 1740	AJT-C, 18:1564
Gertrudis María	Yolomecatl, 1743	AJT-C, 19:1655
Felipe Alvarado	Teposcolula, 1748	AJT-C, 17:1499
Blas Pérez	Teposcolula, 1750	AJT-C, 5:544

Table 7.4. *(continued)*

Name	Place/Date	Source
Florentino de los Reyes	Nduayaco, 1753	AJT-C, 17:1467
Manuel Pérez	Tataltepec, 1761	AJT-C, Anexo 1:51
Patricio Miguel	Xaltepetongo, 1762	AJT-C, 13:1042
Petrona María	Texupa, 1762	AJT-C, 17:1464
Nicolasa María	Chilapa, 1764	AJT-C, 18:1564
Pasquala de Paz	Tataltepec, 1764	AJT-C, Anexo 1:51
Domingo de la Peña	Tlaxiaco, 1765	AJT-C, 12:1009
María Cervantes	Yolomecatl, 1770	AJT-C, 17:1415
Nicolás de Santiago	Yolomecatl, 1772	AJT-C, 14:1195
Josefa María	Tisaa, 1773	AJT-C, 13:1100
María de la Cruz	Amatlan, 1775	AJT-C, 14:1180
Inés López	Adequez, 1776	AJT-C, 18:1516
Pasquala López	Tidaa, 1782	AJT-C, 18:1562
María López	Adequez, 1784	AJT-C, 18:1516
Pedro Antonio	Tlaxiaco, 1784	AJT-C, 15:1244
Juana María	Yucunama, 1785	AJT-C, 15:1251
Miguel Sandoval	Atlatlahuca, 1786	AJT-C, 16:1303
Domingo Barrios	Atlatlahuca, 1786	AJT-C, 16:1303
Santiago Bautista	Atlatlahuca, 1786	AJT-C, 16:1303
Agustín López	Atlatlahuca, 1786	AJT-C, 16:1303
Esteban Bautista	Atlatlahuca, 1787	AJT-C, 16:1303
Juliana Clemente	Tidaa, 1787	AJT-C, 19:1617
Mateo Barrios	Atlatlahuca, 1788	AJT-C, 16:1303
Manuel de la Cruz	Atlatlahuca, 1789	AJT-C, 16:1303
Ignacio Hernández	Adequez, 1789	AJT-C, 18:1516
Ignacio Ramírez	Tonaltepec, 1790	AJT-C, 21:1863
Felipa López	Adequez, 1798	AJT-C, 18:1516
Francisca López	Adequez, 1800	AJT-C, 18:1516
Casimero de los Santos	Tonaltepec, 1807	AJT-C, 18:1578

to pay the annual royal tribute (usually for growing wheat or maize), fields for community funds or surplus (usually maize), plots dedicated to religious feasts and saints (usually for herding, often managed by cofradías), and communal woods and pastures.[130] The same types of arrangements were made in the Mixteca. Communal lands were cultivated by laborers on a temporary, rotational basis according to the traditional *tniño*. Normally, communal lands consisted of a large tract of fertile land and a few marginal plots. The ratio of communal lands to household and cacicazgo holdings was flexible and subject to a number of variables, including the strength of the corporate unit, the profitability of certain enterprises, available labor resources, Spanish pressures to expand the size of community landholdings in order to ensure full tribute payments, and regional differences. In the sixteenth century, when depopulation exceeded the ñuu's capacity to reallocate lands, assigning unused lands to the category of "ñuhu comunidad" was an alternative to abandonment or alienation, Spanish usurpation and confiscation.[131] Many ñuu used these community lands for herding and leasing.

Inheritance Patterns

The principles of Ñudzahui inheritance, introduced in the previous sections on household structure and land tenure, require further examination in the context of land transfer and distribution. Although corporate lands were subject to reallocation by authorities, inheritance and interhousehold division were the principal means of transferring and distributing land in Ñudzahui society, as they were for the Nahuas and Maya.[132] Men and women inherited, possessed, and bequeathed property separately, even in marriage.[133] Many basic principles of possession described for the yya and yya dzehe of the yuhuitayu can be applied to toho and ñandahi, as well. As in central Mexico and Yucatan, property and wealth were divided rather evenly among principal heirs. Testators preferred consanguineal over affinal kin and children and grandchildren over siblings, uncles, and aunts.[134] Typically, all potential heirs received something in the end, but lands and houses were reserved for lineal descendants.[135] Although both men and women bequeathed property to their spouses, husbands and wives usually left each other very little; both men and women served as custodians of their spouses' wills, retaining property in their lifetime before confirming and fulfilling their spouses' wishes in their own last testaments.[136] Preferences for same-sex bequests are not apparent, though it was not unusual for women without children to favor female dependents.[137]

The tendency toward dispersal inherent in the native system of partible inheritance raises the question of how yya and toho managed to retain possession of multiple tracts of land. It is likely that population loss forced the concentration of more properties among fewer households and heirs, and it is certain that many yya and toho bought lands from ñandahi in this period. Caciques were also aided by Spanish law, which regarded the cacicazgo as a *mayorazgo* (entailed estate).[138] Ideally, each yya and yya dzehe of the yuhuitayu chose one heir to inherit the aniñe, the ñuhu chiyo, and ñuhu aniñe and then divided remaining properties among other children and heirs. By the late seventeenth century, inheritance patterns tended to favor male caciques, for reasons described in chapter 6, but female cacicas continued to inherit substantial properties. The retention of multiple landholdings by yya and toho was reinforced by inheritance strategies based on the centrality of the household complex. Testaments indicate how yya and toho consolidated bequests among heirs who resided within the extended household complex, a strategy corresponding to a preference for lineal kin.

A series of testaments from Topiltepec illustrates the extent to which land was consolidated among household members.[139] When the toho Gonzalo López divided his 56 lands in 1610, he gave 12 to his oldest son and 15 to his married daughter, and he divided the remaining 29 plots among three younger children (13 to a son and 8 each to two daughters). All lived in the same large household complex, which consisted of at least four huahi. Despite the dispersal of lands in his bequest, Gonzalo's grandson Juan Domingo possessed 51 plots of land in 1668, which he called the patrimony of his grandfather; only 4 of the 51 plots had been purchased in his lifetime. He bequeathed

46 of the 51 lands to his only child, setting aside 4 plots for his wife and horses for his sisters and nephews. Juan Domingo also gave one small piece of land to a live-in dependent named Ursula. When his son, also called Juan Domingo, wrote his testament in 1711, he possessed 44 lands and the testament of his great grandfather, Gonzalo López. In turn, Juan gave most of the land to his only son, Luis Domingo. Thus, after four generations, the López household had managed to retain about 80 percent of Gonzalo's original holdings. A loss of lands in the century between 1610 to 1711 may have been caused by household members splitting off to form their own complex as the family expanded, by alienation through sale, or simply by changing naming patterns that recognized fewer distinctions among plots. In any case, this series of testaments indicates that much of the extended household's property reverted to members of the main household throughout the century.

Some testators chose household members as heirs over more likely candidates who lived outside the household. A fine example of this tendency involves a toho named Lucía de la Anunciación (also called Lucía Siqhu), who made her testament in Teposcolula in 1623. Lucía left most of her property to two orphaned dependents, called *criados* (servants) or *huérfanos* (orphans) in Spanish, who were named Juana and Ana. In her native tongue, she called Juana "a child whom I raised myself" [dzaya nidzaquanomayndi]. To this statement she added: "I took care of the little one named Juana de la Cruz because there are no children of my own, I have nurtured the child as if I gave birth to her myself" [ninihidi sa dzuchi nani juana de la cruz saha yoo dzayamayndi dzahua tnaha dzaya nidzacacumayndi yotadziynindi].[140] Lucía gave Juana four adjoining houses (of which two were in need of repair), a parcel of land next to the plaza that she had bought from Isabel Nahuiyo, a cotton huipil, a central Mexican–style metate ("yodzo ñucoyo"), a wooden bed, religious images (including one of her namesake, Santa Lucía), an iron-tipped digging stick ("yata caa ticoo"), a chest with a lock, and some weaving equipment ("dzitu tnuquaa"). Lucía also bequeathed a great part of her estate to a dependent orphan woman from Chila (called a *criada* in Spanish) named Ana de la Anunciación (also called Ana Siqhu or "10-Lizard," based on the ritual calendar); it appears that Ana adopted Lucía's Spanish and native surnames (Anunciación and Siqhu). Ana had lived and worked in the household for so long that Lucía treated her "as if she were my own daughter" [dzahua tnaha dzayamayndi]. Lucía bequeathed to Ana the following property: two huahi; two fields of land; another field that Lucía cultivated jointly with a woman named Magdalena Hernández in order to pay the royal tribute ("daha Rey"); cloth, clothing, and weaving gear; and all the things inside the huahi, including petates, metates, plates, and cups.

Lucía de la Anunciación Siqhu left all her lands and houses to two dependents even though she had two brothers, named Melchor Hernández Qhcui and Mateo García Qhmaa, to whom she gave a generous assortment of magueys, weaving gear, religious images, metates, and metal-tipped digging sticks. The bequest of items associated with both men's and women's labor to the same heir was not uncommon.[141] Lucía left another two purchased tracts of land, some magueys, and two metates to a dependent or godchild named Juan de la Cruz (he was simply called *dzaya,* "child," but the translation referred to him as a godchild). Toward the end of the testament, she gave something to everyone, including a huipil to a woman named Mariana de la Cruz, fifteen magueys to Magdalena Sánchez, and eight magueys to a young godchild named Marcos, whom she called "a child whom I baptized in the church" [dzaya nisadocandi huahy ñuhu]. Her last bequest designated fifteen magueys to a Spanish woman ("señora") named María Velásquez. This case reveals that even live-in dependents were preferred as heirs to blood relatives who lived outside the household, particularly in the absence of children or grandchildren.

A third case demonstrates the flexible nature of inheritance patterns, even when lineal descendants were preferred. We have already been introduced to Lázaro de Aranda, the toho from Yanhuitlan who left his dependent a tiny patch of land and a torito.[142] In 1728, he divided an adobe house (huahi ndoho), three small structures (huahi tiyahua), a sweat bath (huahi ñehe), five plots of land (two purchased), a horse and oxen, and 600 magueys between two daughters and his wife. In particular, he gave the main house and two good tracts of land to his wife. To round out his bequests, he gave the following: 20 magueys to his mother; 10 magueys to his grandmother; a small lot of land, 20 magueys, and a young bull to his dependent; and a plot of land in the siña of Tindee to his godchild (*ahijado*), Juan Castañeda, whom he called "codayan-duchanju" (literally "my water child" in reference to his relationship through baptism). Finally, he set aside 150 magueys to pay for his burial.[143] Lázaro's even dispersal of property to his wife and daughters conforms to the general pattern of partible inheritance, but it departed from the strictly lineal manner in which he had inherited the property. Just two years earlier, his father, Miguel Aranda, had bequeathed all his property to Lázaro, with the exception of one tract of land that he gave directly to Lazaro's daughters.[144] Apparently, Lázaro had no brothers or sisters.

A case from Teposcolula reveals how difficult inheritance could become in the absence of household heirs. Petronilla Calderón, a widow of Teposcolula, had no children when she wrote her will in 1726.[145] She chose as heirs two orphan woman ("dzayandahui," or literally "poor children") named Juana María and Michaela Petrona, who had been like daughters to her. Petronilla described her household complex as two adjoining units, with two large walls (nama). She bequeathed the large house (huahi cano, also referred to as the huahi sala) to Juana, in addition to another adjoining house (huahi tiyahua, or "jacal") with its "house plot" [huahi ytu] of magueys. In addition, she gave Juana three ytu, or cultivable plots, and two yokes of oxen. Petronilla gave Micaela, the other orphan, a house named "mahñuñuu" and an adjoining solar planted with magueys. Petronilla also had three brothers; she gave a house to one brother and a plot of magueys that she had purchased from Inés Santiago to the other two. In 1727, when the orphan Juana María wrote her testament, she also had no children, since her sole child had died a few years earlier.[146] So she left the house and ytu huahi to her husband, Josef Miguel; she also gave a plot of land and some clothing to her younger sister and another plot of land to an uncle. Four years later, Juana's husband (now called Josef Rodríguez) was forced to make his testament.[147] Josef recalled the generosity of his "mother-in-law," Petronilla, and sold much of the property, including the houses, to pay for masses for the souls of his deceased wife and mother-in-law. He also set aside two plots of land, some magueys, and many clothes and lienzos for Micaela Petrona, the orphan companion of his wife. This case indicates how humble dependents could inherit substantial properties as members of a household and how an estate was partially dissolved because of a lack of household heirs.

If the disposal of inherited property was clearly at the discretion of the heir or heiress, the distribution of property attained in marriage was subject to negotiation. An inheritance dispute from Teposcolula reveals cultural attitudes toward sharing the fruits of household labor. When Tomás Hernández died in 1634, he left thirty mules, three hundred sheep, and an undisclosed amount of land and magueys to his son. His wife, Juana Hernández, challenged his testament in a petition to local authorities, claiming that when they had married, Tomás was so poor that he was obligated to serve in her father's household. Everything that he bequeathed in his will they had acquired during their marriage, she argued. Juana concluded that half of it belonged to her and that she should be able to dispose of it according to her wishes. She took the liberty of paying for his masses and extravagant offerings, including twelve cloaks and many *tomines* (a coin worth one-eighth of a peso) for the poor, with money from his share of the property. Moreover, Juana claimed that the lands and magueys that he had mentioned in his will were not his to give but rather belonged to her father. The only land to which he had any claim, Juana said, was the plot that they had bought together during their marriage. She intended to honor his half of that plot. Juana's defiant stand corroborates evidence suggesting that Tomás's son was not her child. Otherwise, she might not have objected to naming him as her heir in the absence of other children. In any case, Juana did retain possession of a part of the property, but we have no record of her will. Most important, the case illustrates cultural attitudes toward rights to non-inherited property that respected the access of each marriage partner.

Finally, some testators bequeathed property in general terms, dividing houses and lands equally among children in the household. For example, in 1672, don Gerónimo García y Guzmán of Teposcolula divided his estate among his children who "live together in the house" [sihiya cooya huahi].[148] He appointed his wife, doña Lázara de Guzmán, as custodian of the property. Don Gerónimo declared: "I leave her my house fields and all the patrimonial house land and my walled house palace; she will guard it for my children who live together in the house" [yonachihindi ytu huahindi ndehe taca ñuhu ytu chiyo sihi huahi nama (ñu) aniñendi ta cotneeya saha ysi siyo dzayandi sihiya cooya huahi]. The palace and patrimonial house lands (ytu chiyo huahi) were to be divided so that "each little one, each child will have an equal share" [dzuchi dzuchi cananihi ee ee dzayandi dzahuani]. Toward the end of his statement, he affirmed, "When my wife dies, it will be divided" [niquitnaha nino sasihi maa ñaha dzehendi quehui dzahua ca nachihitnuni yni niyasihi]. Nineteen years later, doña Lazara fulfilled her husband's last wishes on her deathbed.[149] In the name of don Gerónimo, doña Lázara divided among her three sons the aniñe, the "solar ñuhu aniñe," and all the "ñuhu aniñe" associated with the palace of Ñuuñaña. She also left them a plot of cultivated magueys that she had purchased and another tract of patrimonial land located in back of an aniñe called Duhuadoo, which she called the land of their ancestors, their "grandfathers and grandmothers" [syy sitnaya]. Finally, she possessed the testament of her husband's brother, who left his house and several adjacent lands to the three children because he had no children of his own. Doña Lázara left all these properties in the hands of don Pedro, don Josef, and don Domingo, without specifying how the property was to be divided among the three heirs. Again, this case illustrates the simultaneous distribution and consolidation of property among members of the household, among those who "live together in the house."

The notable tendency to transfer property to residents of a household brings to mind Lockhart's observation that the concept of "family" emphasized household members more than lineage relations in Nahua society.[150] This is true for the Mixteca, too. Ñudzahui inheritance patterns were as flexible as the structure of the household itself.[151] Most testaments conformed with Spanish principles of private property and legal right by making separate bequests to specific individuals, but testaments confirmed existing arrangements within the extended complex as much as they designated new individual rights.[152] Bequests to married sons or daughters invariably mentioned the heir's spouse as a co-recipient. A widow or widower often represented the property of an entire household complex by executing the wishes of his or her deceased spouse.

It is unclear what happened to the landholdings of individuals who moved away from the household complex, whether to start another complex or to relocate to a spouse's household. Outgoing members of a household were likely to possess few lands, perhaps some scattered ytu whose transference to another household, if acceptable, did not present any difficulties. In contrast, those who possessed ñuhu huahi and ñuhu chiyo were unlikely to move away from the house and adjacent lands. These issues of residency may shed light on the tendency for sons to inherit land more often than daughters, and consequently for men to write wills more often than women, despite the general adherence to an even distribution of property among men and women.[153] Namely, the pattern may be related to a preference for patrivirilocal residence arrangements. Although choice of residence after marriage was subject to considerable variation in this period, in part because such arrangements were based on existing or potential household resources, the sources confirm that couples were more likely to move into a husband's household after marriage.[154] Thus it was more pragmatic to bequeath land to sons, who were less likely to move away from the original household.[155] On the other hand, a woman's inheritance of lands and houses might have encouraged couples to relocate to her original household. One case from Chilapilla is very explicit about the relation between residency and inheritance. In 1749, don Lorenzo Vásquez bequeathed no land to his daughter, doña Luisa Vásquez, and her husband, don Antonio de Arellano, because "they chose not to reside in this ñuu."[156] Instead, he gave them cloth and clothing. Usually, men and women relied on an extended network of support from multiple households and stood to inherit some property regardless of their place of residence.[157] These flexible patterns of residency and inheritance deserve further systematic examination in future studies.

Land Sales and Leases

The shortage of labor in the wake of successive epidemics made large landholdings less valuable and encouraged a shift to less labor-intensive activities. Leasing lands to Spaniards, mestizos, and other natives became a source of considerable income for communities and caciques who could parcel off unused or unproductive lands, while reserving their best lands for agriculture.[158] As early as the 1560s, caciques such as don

Felipe de Santiago leased excess tracts of land to Spaniards, who used them for raising livestock.[159] But leasing to Spaniards was not especially common until the mid-seventeenth century. In the early period, Spaniards in the region preferred to invest more in interregional commerce than livestock or agricultural enterprises. After the 1620s, they became more involved in the buying and selling of *ganado* (cattle). Caciques in cabeceras populated by Spaniards were the largest lessors. María de los Ángeles Romero Frizzi found that of 140 lease agreements in the seventeenth and early eighteenth centuries, 82 properties were leased by caciques and 58 by communities.[160]

The transactions of don Francisco Pimentel y Guzmán, cacique and governor of Teposcolula and cacique of Yanhuitlan, illustrate the extent to which some caciques profited from this activity. He leased parts of his cacicazgo lands for periods of four to nine years, collecting twelve to thirty pesos annually for each plot of land. The duration of leases tended to increase with the growing demand for land after 1690. Don Francisco rented out lands at least ten times from the 1650s to the 1680s; when he died, his wife continued the business. His son, don Agustín Carlos Pimentel y Guzmán y Alvarado, cacique of Teposcolula, Tilantongo, Tututepec, and Jaltepec, turned the operation into a lucrative enterprise. Between 1703 and 1728, he leased lands to Spaniards at least fifteen times, charging annual fees of six to thirty pesos (most of the money paid in advance), and earned more than two thousand pesos over the period.[161] Each transaction was ratified by the native cabildo in order to demonstrate community consent and to avoid future disputes over the possession of leased lands, which were all too common in the later period. Sometimes caciques split the profits of leases with their communities.[162] Profits from leasing lands amounted to as much as one hundred pesos per year.[163]

The enterprise of leasing lands to Spaniards brought substantial profits by the end of the seventeenth century, when increasing demand for land corresponded with population growth and a revival in regional commercial activity. The vast majority of leases were made to Spaniards and Dominican or Jesuit establishments. The number of leases in the Mixteca Alta increased from about five in the fifty-year period between 1575 and 1624, to about twenty-five from 1625 to 1675, to more than eighty between 1675 and 1725.[164] In 1676, the Jesuits were leasing at least eighteen lands from native communities in the Mixteca. Dominican *conventos* not only leased lands from native caciques and communities but also rented herds out to non-Mixtecs who could not afford to purchase their own, dispensing with the need for labor.[165] After the 1670s, Spaniards also began to engage in agricultural enterprises on leased or owned *tierras de labor*, mainly growing wheat. Until this period, wheat was grown in modest quantities by Mixtecs or was transported from the Valley of Atlixco in Puebla. In the semitropical area around Tlaxiaco, lands were also leased for the growing of sugarcane after 1700; many of the *trapiches*, or sugar mills, employed African slaves.[166]

If leasing native lands to Spaniards was a typical practice in the Mixteca by the end of the seventeenth century, selling land was not. The sale of native lands was much more common among native nobles and lords.[167] Native analogues to the Spanish practice of buying and selling land, discussed above, must have facilitated this practice in the colonial period. References to ñuhu nidzico (sold land) appear in the written record, mainly as indirect statements in testaments. In 1633, for example, Lucía de la Anunciación

Siqhu of Teposcolula referred to land that she had bought from another Ñudzahui woman.[168] In 1684, don Francisco Pimentel y Guzmán sold twenty yuntas of land in Tamasulapa to don Pedro de la Cruz, a toho of the ñuu of Santa María (*sujeto* of Teposcolula) for 151 pesos.[169] Most ytu nidzico were small plots purchased for minimal amounts ranging from 4 to 20 pesos; land was especially cheap and plentiful before the last quarter of the seventeenth century. Testaments reveal that some nobles had purchased as many as a third of their landholdings.[170] For example, of the 56 tracts of land owned by Gonzalo López, he had bought 18 from ñandahi such as Miguel Cahuidzu, Luisa Cahuaco, and Luis Siñuu.[171] Of the 21 lands owned by Domingo de Celís, a toho of Yucunama in 1717, he had bought 6.[172] By 1633, Lucía Hernández Ñuquihui had purchased 6 of her 13 lands, paying an average of 10 pesos per plot.[173] Testators' careful distinction between inherited and purchased lands indicates the continued importance of specifying land tenure categories. Scattered ytu were more likely to be bought and sold than house lands or patrimonial lands.

Ñudzahui officials discouraged and even prohibited the sale of lands to Spaniards. Legally, all sales of native-owned property required a *pregón*, or public announcement of the intent to sell, at least thirty days in advance of the transaction.[174] Occasionally, testators advised their heirs not to sell patrimonial lands. For example, when don Diego de Velasco bequeathed extensive landholdings in and around Chalcatongo to his son in 1636, he admonished him not to sell the lands to anyone. If lands were sold, he stipulated, the yya and toho of Chalcatongo should collect the money.[175] Occasionally, tensions over land transactions spilled over into community politics. When an *alcalde* of Malinaltepec accused the governor in 1652 of having sold land to a Spaniard, the accusation agitated the assembly of people in the church patio, and the governor vehemently denied the charge.[176] The ability of the local ruling group to prevent sales to Spaniards contributed to the maintenance of corporate lands.

Land was also sold to non-natives infrequently because Spaniards were not especially concerned with acquiring large quantities of land throughout much of the colonial period. First of all, investments in trade and livestock were much more profitable than agricultural activities. Unlike the Valleys of Mexico and Puebla, the Mixteca was too distant from Spanish markets to supply agricultural goods. Trade in textiles and raw materials such as cochineal, cotton, and silk was a more lucrative investment. Second, it was more economical to lease land for pasture than to purchase marginal plots. Until the eighteenth century, few Spaniards and mestizos in the Mixteca owned more than a solar or a rancho and a few supplemental tracts of land. Leasing land was more common than selling it to Spaniards even in the late colonial period. Leasing could provoke litigation over possession and title, but it did not necessarily lead to permanent alienation of land from the community. This activity may have foreshadowed land sales and the growth of Spanish haciendas in the nineteenth century, a possibility that remains to be examined.[177]

Thus native communities and individuals retained substantial amounts of cultivable land throughout the colonial period. In contrast, Rebecca Horn has documented the relatively swift accretion of Spanish estates at the expense of native lands, primarily through piecemeal purchase, in Coyoacan, near Mexico City.[178] The situation in the Mixteca is more comparable to that in the Valley of Oaxaca.[179] However, despite the tendency toward native retention, Spaniards did acquire lands in the Mixteca by purchase and other means during the colonial period. Religious establishments led all takers in this category.[180] The Dominicans and Jesuits managed to acquire a number of sizable estates and scattered properties throughout the area through native donation, sale, and bequest. Friars solicited caciques to donate sizable plots of lands, on a temporary or permanent basis, to convents for the support of *capellanías* (chaplaincies). For example, in 1572, doña María de Paredes gave a plot of land to the friars when she made her testament.[181] And in 1581, don Gregorio de Lara allowed friars to sow wheat on one of his valley fields, located near the church of Texupa.[182] The religious orders engaged in every possible form of revenue-producing enterprise in the Mixteca, from growing wheat and sugarcane to raising livestock and running iron forges. They leased lands to other Spaniards, and they bought and sold African slaves. As a result of their constant acquisitions, the largest Spanish haciendas in the region were owned by the Dominican and Jesuit orders.

Caciques and communities did not speculate in the sale of lands; rather, native land sales to Spaniards usually occurred during times of crisis, such as bad harvests, drought, or debt.[183] For example, in 1674, Pedro de Meneses sold a plot of his land to a Spanish resident of Teposcolula because he owed him money.[184] People also leased lands for these purposes; when Inés Juárez owed Bernabé López thirty-six pesos, she leased a tract of land to him to repay the debt.[185] Some people sold houses and house lots, especially in cabeceras where properties were in relatively high demand. In 1671, for example, María de la Cruz Çayucu sold one of her houses in the plaza of Yanhuitlan to a Spaniard for two hundred pesos because she needed the money to pay debts and tribute.[186]

Sales to Spaniards in the second half of the colonial period represent the inability or unwillingness of some communities to enforce prohibitions against alienating lands. Increasing privatization and demand made selling more expedient or, in terms of paying debts, more compelling. As a group, Mixtecs had plenty of land but little cash or access to credit. The convergence of several developments in the last quarter of the seventeenth century, including population growth, increasing demands for land, and easy profits from leasing lands, led to increased competition, litigation, and conflict.

Competition and Conflict over Land

Competition and legal conflicts over the use and distribution of land in the last quarter of the seventeenth century reflect economic, political, and social changes in the Mixteca. By this period, the fragmentation of ñuu into constituent parts, the decay or loss of an internal record-keeping system, and the weakening of traditional authorities led many groups and individuals to seek recourse in the Spanish legal system, especially when local consensus could not be reached.[187] Conflicts over land in the Mixteca might be classified in general terms, from the perspective of the local community, as disputes of an external and internal nature. External conflicts involved neighboring communities or non-natives; internal disputes involved cabildos or political factions and native individuals, especially caciques.

The most common form of external conflict involved boundary disputes between two communities. Intercommunity conflict was an ancient phenomenon that was complicated by colonial introductions and changes, including the sociopolitical reorganization of the sixteenth century, the introduction of livestock, the leasing and selling of land, corporate fragmentation, and increasing demands for land and labor in the late period.[188] In lieu of border skirmishes, communities were forced to air their grievances before Spanish officials. Spanish legal institutions accommodated and adjudicated conflicts without always resolving them. In defense of their perceived corporate rights, competing communities often spent great sums of money for numerous hearings and appeals, some of which dragged on for generations.

Direct and indirect disputes with Spaniards were another form of external conflict. Several cases between competing communities involved Spanish estate owners who competed for access to land, water, and labor.[189] Disputed leases were fertile grounds for conflict and litigation, particularly when individuals leased untitled lands. When agreements were made informally, in the absence of written records and official titles, the existing arrangement could be called into question when the lease expired. For example, don Juan de Mendoza, cacique of San Juan de Achiutla, claimed that his father had leased a plot of land named Dayuxisi; when the lease expired, the land was never returned to the cacicazgo. But don Juan's claim to the land was tenuous without a title and vulnerable to a *denuncia* (accusation or statement of land claim). At the time of the suit, in 1629, the land was being cultivated and claimed by a woman named Catalina Bautista, who denied that the land had been leased.[190] Few Mixtecs possessed titles to their scattered landholdings, perhaps because they were so expensive. In the mid-eighteenth century, when land was in high demand, an individual title cost about twenty pesos; those who claimed multiple holdings were required to pay a substantial amount of money in purchasing titles.[191]

The introduction of numerous *rebaños* (flocks or herds) and *estancias* of livestock had a profound impact on intercommunity relations and the environment. First, the tremendous growth of this new animal population contributed to the introduction and spread of disease. Second, overgrazing of marginal lands contributed to soil erosion in many areas of the Mixteca Alta. Third, communities and individuals protested damages to their fields from the 1540s onward. Damages caused by ganado led to conflicts among some communities.[192] The *Codex Sierra* shows that Texupa had acquired ganado by the 1550s; by 1561, residents of Texupa complained that the beasts were trampling their crops.[193] In 1567, Spanish authorities attempted to confine damages caused by ganado by establishing limits of five hundred varas between estancias and the outer edge of nearby communities, modified in 1695 to six hundred varas measured from the church. This latter measurement served as the basis for the *fundo legal*, the minimal extension of an indigenous community's property.[194]

Internal conflicts between community factions and caciques were not uncommon by the eighteenth century. A typical example involved the community members of Chazumba, who attacked the cacicazgo in 1744 because they believed that their labor was simply enriching the private estate of the cacique.[195] The group accused don Felipe de Guzmán y Aguilar of using cofradía funds to pay for lawsuits to protect his cacicazgo, which he never repaid. The dissenters went on to question his right to dependent laborers and denounced him for renting so many lands to Spaniards. The lawyer of don Felipe and his wife, doña Teresa García de Mendoza, countered that the commoners derived many benefits from the cacicazgo: "They collect wood, palm, beehives, chiles, and clay to make pottery which they sell; they sow their milpas and pasture their livestock. They derive great benefits, all with the permission and benevolence of the caciques, who are Indians of noble lineage. In return, they work the caciques' fields at certain times of the year and they provide some people on a weekly basis for domestic service in their house."[196] The lawyers argued that dependents who worked their lands and served in their houses were considered part of the traditional cacicazgo in the Mixteca. After don Felipe died, his wife took up the suit, and the Audiencia eventually ruled in favor of the cacicazgo.

In the eighteenth century, Audiencia officials heard many cases against caciques and ruled either to uphold their position or to restrict their claims and privileges. The patrimonial rights of caciques were vulnerable when dependents and local officials contradicted their claims to authority. A typical compromise of this period was to award the land in question to caciques, but without laborers. This type of ruling confirmed the sanctity of private property but freed up labor from traditional arrangements, encouraging a general movement toward individually contracted wage labor. For example, in 1714, ñandahi worked land in Astatla for the cacica of Coixtlahuaca, doña María de Mendoza.[197] Her possession was disputed by the nobleman don Tomás de San Juan García, who presented documents written in Nahuatl, Ñudzahui, and Chocho that allegedly traced his possession back to 1551. Don Tomás was awarded the land without its laborers. Similarly, in 1743, doña Manuela de los Ángeles, cacica of Igualapa, won rights to some disputed lands, but without the laborers who worked them. In fact, they were ordered to move back to the cabecera from which they came, more than ten leagues away, and their houses on the cacica's lands were destroyed.[198]

Tensions between caciques and communities resulted in part from contending interpretations of land tenure. The controversial distinction between cacicazgo (aniñe) lands and corporate (ñuu) lands, a contested issue before the conquest, was complicated in the colonial period by the Spanish division of property into private and public categories.[199] Conflicts over cacicazgo rights and access to dependent labor often revolved around this issue. Under Spanish law, lands of the aniñe were considered the private property of individual lords; according to native tradition, these claims were contingent on the fulfillment of social relations and obligations. In general, the Ñudzahui system of land tenure placed much more emphasis on a household's obligation to cultivate its lands, pay tribute based on the yields of those lands, and maintain a community consensus that periodically confirmed its right to possess and transfer those lands. Caciques may have possessed Spanish titles to specific lands, but their access to labor depended on social relations. They could rely on dependent laborers as long as members of the ñuu continued to recognize their patrimonial rights and as long as dependents continued to derive some benefit from the arrangement. After decades of depopulation, when land was abundant but labor was scarce and when Spanish law had restricted caciques' access to labor, many yya resorted to leasing lands or using them to raise livestock. In some cases, they even sold lands to individual Spaniards or to the church. These responses to a dwindling labor supply tended to exacerbate local tensions. Caciques who managed their estates too aggressively were vulnerable to opposition in the later period, when the value of lands increased with population growth.[200] In cabeceras, where the Spanish presence was concentrated, the leasing of land was most common, and the demand for resources was most intense, caciques were especially prone to litigation.

Increasing litigation against caciques after 1700 corresponded with a surge in the number of lands leased to Spaniards.[201] Numerous caciques from the Mixteca Alta who rented lands in the early eighteenth century were faced with legal action. In response, caciques called on Spanish judges to enforce their "traditional" rights and privileges. When caciques fought these costly battles, they resorted to raising revenue by leasing or selling more lands to pay debts or by imposing *derramas* (additional or unauthorized tribute). All these responses invited further conflict and litigation. Often, caciques were forced to lease properties at low annual fees because they needed the money in advance.[202] At the same time, municipal governments were caciques' primary competitors in the land lease market. Some disputes between communities and caciques specifically involved proceeds from the renting of lands.[203]

One final case, discussed previously in relation to changes in the yuhuitayu, illustrates how challenges to cacicazgos involved the issues of land, labor, and reciprocity. The cabildo of Yanhuitlan, led by a governor named Domingo Hernández, disputed the cacicazgo rights of don Martín Josef de Villagómez and doña Teresa de la Cruz.[204] The cabildo argued that the community had been reduced to poverty by a cacique with dubious claims and that the dependent laborers were treated like slaves who received nothing in return for their work. The caciques' wrongful treatment of their dependents became one of the cabildo's central accusations. In 1759, the Audiencia ruled against the cacica and cacique, assigning the lands in question to the "cabecera of Yanhuitlan." The Audiencia dismantled the cacicazgo but saved some "private property" for the cacica.

In general terms, conflicts over land and labor between caciques and communities may be attributed to what William Taylor called a "growing lack of respect for the nobility." Taylor correlated the high number of land disputes after the period from 1650 to 1670 with caciques' declining political power. In the Valley of Oaxaca, dependent laborers increasingly asserted claims, especially after 1700, to the land they occupied.[205] The increased demand for labor encouraged private initiative and individually contracted wage arrangements at the expense of traditional corporate or cacicazgo obligations. Income derived from labor service and tribute was progressively reduced by population decline, legal restrictions, competition with Spaniards, and internal conflict.

At the same time, many caciques adapted to colonial changes and competition, avoided costly legal disputes with factions, continued to profit from extensive landholdings, and maintained traditional labor arrangements.[206] For example, the cacica doña Martina Morales García de Rojas continued to claim dependents on her cacicazgo lands of Cuquila in 1801.[207] In 1805, doña Clara Sebastiana Esquivel y Andrade and don Francisco de Jesús Velasco, caciques in the Acatlan area of the Mixteca Baja, confirmed their rights to specific lands, palaces, and laborers.[208] The case of don Bonifacio Pimentel y Velasco, a great-grandson of the yya toniñe of Teposcolula and Yanhuitlan, provides an excellent example of the enduring influence that caciques or descendants of caciques had on land tenure in the region. Don Bonifacio did some archival work in 1847 in order to establish title to old cacicazgo lands from the sixteenth century. He succeeded in his quest, and his son, don Francisco, leased some of those lands to mestizos in 1856 for a substantial profit.[209]

Trade and Tribute

In the Mixteca and other areas of Mesoamerica, men and women exchanged agricultural products, textiles, and prestige items in markets that were supplied by local and interregional traders. Professional merchants in the Mixteca traveled as far south as Guatemala and as far north as Cholula and Tenochtitlan to buy and sell goods. In the final decades before the Spanish arrival, the Mexica and their allies had expanded their sphere of influence into the Mixteca and commanded tribute items from several major yuhuitayu. According to tribute lists preserved in the *Codex Mendoza*, they demanded specific quantities of woven cloth, finely worked costumes, cochineal dye, quetzal feathers, and jade (see fig. 7.1).

In the first decades after the Spanish conquest, tribute was the principal mechanism of economic interaction between indigenous communities and Spanish officials. Pre-existing relations with the Mexica were used to determine the types of tribute goods available in a region and the location of *encomiendas*. The encomienda, a royal grant of labor and tribute given to a Spaniard, was introduced during the 1520s; the Mixteca was divided among about thirty *encomenderos* (holders of encomienda grants). Encomenderos demanded the provision of goods and services from local yya, who relied on the traditional system of rotational labor or tniño to supply the conquerors. Above all other commodities, encomenderos sought gold from temples, palaces, tombs, mines, and streams. Faded images from the *Codex Yanhuitlan,* produced around the mid-sixteenth century by native artists, depict men and women panning for gold in streams, directed by armed Spaniards (see fig. 7.2).[210] Some encomenderos reaped substantial profits from gold tribute in the early period; for example, the encomendero of Yanhuitlan received 783 pesos in 1550, in addition to many other goods. Ten years later, Yanhuitlan gave 1,500 pesos of gold (*oro común*) to the encomendero.[211] But placer deposits in mountain streams, as elsewhere in Spanish America, were quickly exhausted. Typically, the ephemeral gold-rush phase lasted only a couple of decades.[212]

In the first three decades after the conquest, Spaniards investigated all possible forms of wealth, relying on native labor, markets, and goods. As early as the 1520s, the encomendero of Teposcolula sent teams of native carriers to Veracruz, who transported wine and other Spanish goods to Guatemala in exchange for cacao and indigenous products.[213] Spaniards used ancient trade routes to exchange new products for indigenous commodities, which were resold to indigenous-Spanish markets in central Mexico. Encomenderos and the crown preferred payments in gold, but they took whatever they could get in the early period. Until the mid-sixteenth century, most tribute goods received by encomenderos were the same types of indigenous items given to native lords, including finished cloth, cotton, cacao, dyes, maize, turkeys, and other foods. Cochineal (a red dye derived from insects on the nopal cactus, called *duq* in Ñudzahui) was a highly valued indigenous product, second only to silver in the colonial export trade from New Spain in the colonial period. The first shipment to reach

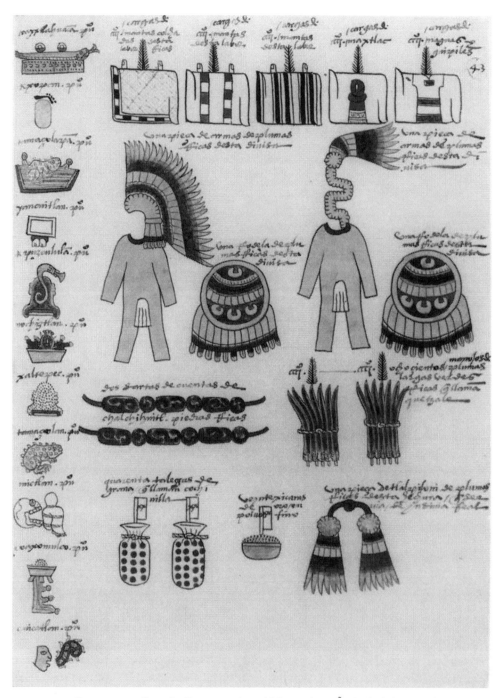

FIGURE 7.1. Preconquest list of tribute goods paid by various Ñudzahui ñuu to the Mexica. *Codex Mendoza*, f. 43. The Bodleian Library, University of Oxford.

FIGURE 7.2. Depictions of men and women forced by armed Spaniards to mine gold in streams. *Codex Yanhuitlan*, plate XIX.

Spain was in 1526, and by 1600 the annual cargo of cochineal from New Spain to Seville was valued at around six hundred thousand pesos.[214] The Mixteca was part of an extended territory of cochineal production in highland central and southern Mexico.

In the 1530s, Spaniards and the Dominican order introduced new tribute items, such as wheat and silk. Wheat served a limited, local market of Spaniards in the sixteenth century, and few native communities chose to cultivate the new grain.[215] In contrast, sericulture drew native communities into the Spanish economy and generated considerable profits in the sixteenth century. This industry continued to grow even as the indigenous population was devastated by a wave of epidemics from 1545 to 1548. Silk production relied on traditional native mechanisms of labor and needed only a small outlay of money; it required a great deal of seasonal intensive labor lasting only a few months.[216] Silk and cochineal were sold to Spanish merchants in Mexico City and Puebla. Encomenderos added silk to their lists of tribute items by the 1540s. Even communities that were no longer under the jurisdiction of encomenderos—that had escheated to the crown—paid the royal tribute with money raised from selling silk and cochineal. Teposcolula, the first community to come under direct control of the crown as a *corregimiento,* relied on silk to pay nearly seven thousand gold pesos in royal tribute in 1564.[217] The use of tniño labor to produce silk and cochineal enabled many communities to make tribute payments collectively and to generate *sobras de tributos* (surplus income after tribute payments) for the cajas de comunidades, community treasuries used to finance various expenses and to pay cabildo officials' salaries.

The *Codex Sierra* shows that Santa Catalina Texupa spent an average of 1,171 pesos annually from 1550 to 1564, while earning an annual average of 1,738 pesos in the last four years of that period.[218] Nearly three-quarters of the income resulted from the production of silk, but twice as much money was spent on costly Spanish-style goods (such as wine, cloth, candles, ironwork, and religious paraphernalia) as on indigenous products. The community spent about 15 percent of the money on tribute and nearly 60 percent on religious feasts and the church; 15 percent was reinvested in productive activities.[219] Aside from fulfilling ceremonial functions, fiestas distributed goods and foods among households through traditional mechanisms and according to existing social relations.[220]

Ganado, or livestock, was another new source of income for communities. Livestock raising required little labor. Caciques and communities actively sought estancias of *ganado menor* (sheep and goats) in the 1560s and 1570s. Running sheep and goats on marginal lands was a fairly lucrative enterprise. Ganado allowed communities and caciques to generate capital through the use of vacated lands, called *tierras baldías.* Individual grants to own *estancias de ganado menor* (sheep and goat ranches), with few exceptions, were restricted to the native nobility and communities, Spaniards, and religious establishments.[221] As early as the 1550s, the *Codex Sierra* depicts the purchase of sheep and goats by the community of Texupa, whose members derived more than 10 percent of their money income from ganado between 1561 and 1564.[222] By 1580, cabeceras such as Teposcolula acquired grants to purchase up to a thousand head of ganado menor as *bienes de la comunidad,* or community goods.[223] In 1590, don Felipe de Santiago, cacique and governor of Teposcolula, established an estancia on the border of the community; in the same year, don Gabriel de Guzmán of Yanhuitlan possessed

nearly fifteen hundred sheep and goats.[224] Between 1560 and 1620, Spanish authorities
issued about seventy *mercedes,* or grants, to native individuals or communities for estancias
in the Mixteca Alta and another thirty licenses to own rebaños not exceeding three
hundred head.[225] The sale and consumption of meat, cheese, animal fat, leather, and
wool made livestock a good investment and a supplementary source of income and
support for communities. The small amount of labor invested in livestock did not
affect agricultural yields in the early period; however, in the second half of the colonial period, when competition for land increased, some evidence suggests that the
profitability of livestock shifted community resources away from maintaining agricultural surpluses in favor of running herds.[226] By the eighteenth century, communities
came to rely heavily on herding and leasing lands for revenue.[227] Of course, Spaniards
also invested heavily in ganado, especially after the 1620s. Between 1625 and 1700, at
least twenty-seven Spanish *haciendas de ganado menor* were founded in the Mixteca Alta,
corresponding to a dramatic increase in the number of lands leased to Spaniards for
herding.[228]

The relative productivity of native communities in the Mixteca during this period
can be estimated from tithes. In 1598, the Mixteca contributed 5,468 pesos, or 74 percent of the total collected for the bishopric of Antequera; by 1624, this sum had dropped
to only 16 percent of the total, falling even further in 1634 to 8 percent of the total.
Population loss is one major reason for the decline. During the same period, the estimated Spanish contribution to the tithe rose from 14 percent in 1580 to 67 percent
in 1620. Another reason for declining tithes was the collapse of the silk industry in New
Spain, due in part to the import of low-priced silks from Manila after 1565, through
the nearby port of Acapulco. Although people continued to produce silk in the Mixteca throughout the colonial period, the industry went into serious decline after 1580.[229]
By the end of the seventeenth century, tithes rose to 10,000 pesos, or about a third of
Antequera's total, representing the recovery of the indigenous population and economic activity in the Mixteca.[230]

Thus, three major economic enterprises that were introduced in the sixteenth
century—silk, livestock, and wheat—did not require intensive Spanish participation.
Spaniards worked as advisors, or *mayordomos,* in the production of these Spanish
goods, but they constituted a very small percentage of the total labor involved in the
enterprises. For nearly everything they received, Spaniards relied on existing forms
of organization, production, labor, and tribute. Each ñuu applied a form of corporate labor to the production of silk and the growing of wheat. Livestock enterprises
were an adaptation to the availability of lands in the wake of severe population loss.
Silk production and livestock raising drew communities and individuals into the money
economy.

Despite population decline, corporate adjustments to Spanish economic introductions yielded considerable wealth in the third quarter of the sixteenth century. Woodrow
Borah's study of the silk industry documents the timing of this process in the Mixteca Alta.[231] Much of this new wealth went into building, decorating, and supplying
churches. The magnificent churches of the Mixteca, including the open-air chapels
of Teposcolula, Coixtlahuaca, and Cuilapan, were constructed with native labor in the
second half of the sixteenth century. Encouraged by local priests, some communities

contracted Spanish artists for thousands of pesos to paint *retablos* in their new churches; in 1581, Teposcolula paid Andrés de Concha five hundred pesos to paint a retablo in the church. Tamasulapa paid two thousand pesos in 1586 for his services, and Achiutla paid seven hundred pesos one year later. In fact, several communities hired the services of Concha and other Spanish painters in this period.[232] The splendid retablos represent the height of ecclesiastical extravagance in the Mixteca, before the onset of more epidemics and economic depression.

By the last quarter of the sixteenth century, Spaniards had also introduced a number of technical enterprises, including the indispensable business of ironworking. The preconquest professions of copper working and goldsmithing were suitable analogues for the working of iron in the colonial period. Native nobles played an active role in this new technology by running forges. For example, a toho named Lorenzo managed a "huahi fragua" (forge house) in the plaza of Teposcolula, which he had bought for 150 pesos (house and accoutrements) in 1618. By 1658, Juana de Zárate managed this same forge, which her deceased husband, Pedro de Zárate, had purchased from Lorenzo.[233] In the early seventeenth century, another noble, Tomás Hernández, owned a "huahi tihuicaa" (metal-working house) in the ñuu of Santo Tomás, near Teposcolula.[234] The yya toniñe of Tlaxiaco, don Diego de Velasco, owned a forge that was run by dependents and two African slaves.[235] Local ironworking, supplemented by iron products sold by Spanish merchants, represented a significant introduction and technical innovation of the early colonial period.

Native participation in silk production and ironworking indicates an active response to Spanish introductions. Likewise, communities and caciques who ran ganado on unused lands generated income for new tribute requirements and for other activities. However, the fact remains that all communities were forced to channel labor and tribute to many groups and individuals after the conquest, including encomenderos, the hereditary nobility, the local cabildo and caja de comunidad, the alcalde mayor and his staff, the crown, and the church. Encomienda obligations demanded periodic payments to a distant Spaniard. For example, in 1585, Tlaxiaco was required to pay six hundred pesos three times a year to an encomendero, Matías Vásquez, who lived in Mexico City. The encomendero sent a resident of Antequera on the first of April to collect the money on his behalf.[236] As many encomiendas in the Mixteca escheated to the crown by the end of the sixteenth century, encomienda tribute was replaced by royal taxation and, by the 1580s, *repartimiento*.[237] Repartimiento duties involved temporary labor assignments such as construction projects (churches and Spanish residences), silk and cloth production, cochineal gathering, working in mines, building and maintaining highways, and working on estancias and haciendas.[238] Consider the example of a repartimiento demand issued in 1616, which summoned two hundred laborers from each *alcaldía mayor* (the jurisdiction of an alcalde mayor) in the Mixteca to build a fort in distant Acapulco.[239] The demand for "tniño puerto," as it was called in the native-language decree, threatened to divert precious labor resources to the disease-ridden coast. The yya toniñe and governor of Yanhuitlan resisted the demand, complaining that the assignment was hazardous.[240] Despite the protests, the alcalde mayor rounded up two hundred men in May of that year. Surely, many of these obligations were burdensome projects offering minimal compensation to the people or communities involved.[241]

Money and Exchange

By the mid-sixteenth century, Spaniards had introduced money and credit arrangements throughout much of the Mixteca. The *Codex Sierra* demonstrates how ñuu such as Texupa were familiar with denominations of money by 1550 and how native writers applied the vigesimal system to tallying amounts while continuing to use Mesoamerican symbols for quantities, such as a feather for the number 400. The rapid adoption of coin in native society suggests a familiarity with the concept of exchange value, rather than confusion caused by a totally foreign introduction.[242] After all, both Mesoamerican and European societies had well-developed market systems and trading traditions. Although preconquest Mesoamerica did not rely on precious metals as an exclusive means of exchange, native artisans knew how to mine and work metals and fashioned exquisite artifacts from gold for ornamental and sacred purposes. More important, currencies had supplemented the bartering of goods before the arrival of the Europeans.

The main indigenous currency used in the early sixteenth century was cacao (called *dzehui* in Mixtec), cultivated in the Pacific coastal area of Oaxaca and the regions of Soconusco and Guatemala. Despite the impact of Spanish forms of currency, cacao continued to possess an exchange value in the early period. Throughout the sixteenth century, yya reciprocated the services of ñandahi in their aniñe mainly in the form of food and a given number of cacao beans. Native men and women continued to exchange cacao for products of modest value. For example, in 1575, Ana López of Teposcolula was caught selling a quantity of pulque to native men in exchange for forty cacao beans and was fined two pesos by the Spanish alcalde mayor.[243] The continued use of cacao as a beverage and delicacy ensured its high demand in the colonial period. In the seventeenth century, Central and South American cacao was shipped to the ports of Huatulco and Acapulco to supply the indigenous and Spanish thirst for chocolate beverages.[244]

By the last quarter of the sixteenth century, however, money was a familiar currency that coexisted with traditional forms of exchange.[245] References in native-language sources to money in the general sense as *dinero* or *monedas* (coins) are rare; rather, people referred to specific denominations, such as reals or tomines and pesos, sometimes qualified by Mixtec references to gold (*dziñuhu quaa,* "yellow precious metal") or silver (*dziñuhu cuisi,* "white precious metal"). Perhaps because most native people possessed little money, they often spoke of the lowest-valued denomination, the tomín, in reference to money in general. Like many Spanish merchants, some native lords compensated for a shortage of circulating money by obtaining lines of credit from Spanish officials, merchants, and priests. For example, don Gabriel de Guzmán had accumulated 671 pesos of debts and 464 pesos of credit by the time he made his last will and testament in 1591.[246] Some noblemen and -women lent small sums of money to a variety of people, as part of their overall trade and investments.[247] Among native individuals only lords and nobles had access to sums of money in excess of a few pesos, but even most members of this elite group possessed more lands and movable goods than liquid wealth. In 1573, a commoner named Mateo Nucua owed a total of thirty-eight reals and a variety of goods to seven native women and six native men. His state of affairs indicates that even commoners participated in the money economy by this early period but that he also continued to rely on the direct exchange of goods.[248] Normally, testators spent all their money on future provisions for their bodies and souls, on burials, masses, and alms; others who lacked the money sold a plot of land or cloth for these purposes. Many people preferred to sell maguey plants, or instructed heirs to sell maguey plants, in order to raise cash. Miguel Jiménez, a noble from Yanhuitlan who owned a store and two African slaves, sold forty maguey plants to pay for his burial in 1621.[249] Juan Ramírez, a small trader from Yanhuitlan, routinely accepted maguey plants as a form of payment in the 1740s and 1750s.[250] In the margin of his bilingual book of accounts, he frequently noted that clients had paid their accounts with magueys ("pagó con magueyes"). Maguey plants were valuable sources of pulque (a fermented alcoholic drink), among other products.

Cloth was *the* indigenous product that maintained its high value as an exchange commodity in the sixteenth century and beyond. Ñudzahui traders who traveled to Guatemala and other distant regions relied on cloth to obtain cacao, feathers, and dyes. The following two sections examine the indigenous cloth trade and long-distance commerce in the Mixteca.

The Cloth Trade

Before the conquest, woven goods were a major tribute and trade item in the Mixteca.[251] Images of cloth top the tribute lists of goods owed to the Mexica empire (see fig. 7.1).[252] The *Codex Mendoza* illustrates that every major yuhuitayu of the Mixteca gave five bundles of cloth, woven in specific patterns, to the Mexica of Tenochtitlan. No Mesoamerican group could claim to have a more "extensive repertory" of clothing.[253] In the preconquest-style codices, women and men are dressed in finely woven clothes and feathered costumes. Spinning thread and weaving cloth were activities associated with women's work to the extent that women are depicted in codices holding weaving gear and spinning cotton. In the colonial period, women in the Mixteca continued to weave garments for daily wear, gifting and tribute payment, and trade in local and distant markets. Cotton was acquired along the coastal plains of Oaxaca, and wool and silk were introduced in the early sixteenth century. In their testaments, many women revealed an inventory of finished and unfinished raw materials and cloth, and many possessed what Inés Juárez of Tamasulapa called "my woolen yarn and my wads of wool and my yarn stick" [yuhua ydzandi sihi tinduú ydzi sihi tnu ydzandi].[254]

Cloth was a valuable gift and tribute item in native society. At royal weddings, married couples received gifts of cloth from toho and ñandahi. This practice continued after the conquest. In 1591, don Felipe de Santiago, yya of Teposcolula, requested that the commoners spin eight *fardos* (bundles) of cotton for the marriage of his son, don Juan de Mendoza.[255] When the yya dzehe of Tlaxiaco, doña María de Saavedra, married in 1587, nobles presented her with forty fardos of cotton for mantas (capes or mantles, *dzoo* in Ñudzahui) and huipiles (overblouses, *dzico* in Ñudzahui), as well as cacao, fruits, pulque, and other gifts. The nobles affirmed that the bride and groom customarily exchanged finished and unfinished cloth on such occasions, a tradition practiced "since ancient times and even after conversion to Christianity."[256] The description of how nobles handed over gifts to the aniñe suggests that they organized the spinning and weaving of cotton among ñandahi. Aside from these ceremonial occasions, the aniñe received regular tribute payments in cloth produced by dependent laborers and commoners; yya redistributed part of this tribute as gifts to other yya and toho. A case from Chicahuastla suggests that nobles shared in the profits as intermediaries between yya and ñandahi in the organization of cloth tribute. Don Martín de Fonseca explained that it was ancient custom in that part of the Mixteca to give four bundles of cotton as gifts in a royal wedding, testifying in 1591 how "the nobles and commoners help with the wedding of the cacique, according to custom, by spinning four *arrobas* of cotton [a Spanish measure of about twenty-five pounds] in order to make mantas and huipiles to distribute among lords and nobles attending the wedding, and to dress the royal couple."[257]

Woven goods remained in high demand as tribute items after the conquest, partly because cloth was a highly valued item among the Spaniards, too. The earliest royal tribute exaction in the Mixteca Alta, from the corregimiento of Teposcolula in 1530, demanded a quantity of gold and one hundred black and white cotton shirts.[258] Meanwhile, native lords continued to receive cloth as a tribute item. For example, in 1548, the yya toniñe of Yanhuitlan received seven cargas of spun cotton that were to be woven into mantas.[259] In 1578, the tribute given by dependent laborers of Tecomaxtlahuaca included woven goods such as naguas (skirts, *dziyo* in Ñudzahui), huipiles, mantas, and *maxtles* (loincloths, *satu* in Ñudzahui).[260] The sophistication and importance of weaving are documented in the *Vocabulario* of 1593, which lists twenty-nine entries for manta (cloth), ten for *telar* and *texer* (loom and weaving), and fourteen for *hilar* (spinning).[261]

In the second half of the sixteenth century, alcaldes mayores attempted to standardize tribute payments and, in general, replace tribute in goods by tribute in money.[262] Whereas cloth tribute in kind declined in the Nahua region by the end of the sixteenth century, cloth remained an important source of tribute payment in the Mixteca until the early eighteenth century, more comparable to the situation in Yucatan.[263] Even when tribute was paid in coin, the money was often raised by selling cloth in the marketplace. In 1580, the report of Juxtlahuaca for the *Relaciones geográficas* stated that "women weave and spin and sell their goods in the markets, and trade among themselves, and buy other things that they need."[264] The relaciones of Tilantongo and Nochixtlan refer to Ñudzahui women selling clothing to Spaniards and natives.[265] Women often relied on their weaving skills and active participation in the marketplace to raise money for tribute. In 1596, several women appeared as prominent tribute payers in the ñuu of San Gerónimo, near Coixtlahuaca.[266] The community complained that the tribute collector had forced women to weave mantas worth four reals in addition to making normal tribute payments from the sale of cloth. Although most of the tributaries were men, only one man (Domingo Nachi) contributed as many pesos (seven) as the widow named Ana Sayu. Domingo Cacuaa was next with six, followed by Catalina Cacuii and María Qhquehui, who each paid five pesos; the majority gave only two or three pesos.

The case from Coixtlahuaca indicates that widows and other women on the list (who did not bear the title of widows) were considered heads of household and were subject to pay according to the resources of their households. The obligation of a widow or unmarried person to pay one-half of the normal royal tribute assessment based on a married couple recognized a woman's equal status as producer.[267] Because of their skilled and unskilled labor, resident kin or female dependents who could help pay community tribute assessments based on the household by spinning and weaving were desirable additions to the household. In the colonial period, marginalized women paid their share of the tribute by serving in the households of yya and toho, Spanish officials, and priests. These were the "female household servants" mentioned in the relación of Juxtlahuaca.[268]

Another means of tribute payment was by remitting spun cotton or finished cloth to Spanish or native officials. In their dual occupations as official tribute collectors and private investors in the local economy, Spanish officials blurred the distinction between collecting cloth for tribute payment and acting as intermediaries in the inter-regional cloth trade, an activity known as *repartos de efectos* or repartimientos. Typically, Spanish officials and merchants advanced cotton or money to community officials in exchange for finished or semifinished goods or cochineal, which would pay part of the tribute or fulfill an independent contractual obligation.[269] The terms of these arrangements invariably favored the Spaniard, who would resell the goods to other Spanish merchants or sell them directly in local or distant markets. Alcaldes mayores practiced this trade in the sixteenth century, but repartimientos are associated more with the late colonial period. Such "informal" agreements were seldom written down because they were illegal; according to Spanish law, alcaldes mayores were prohibited from engaging in trade within their jurisdictions. But the law was easily circumvented and rarely enforced. Therefore, these activities are observable only through incidental references and outright complaints. In 1601, men and women from Achiutla accused native nobles of collaborating with the Spanish alcalde mayor, who forced them to spin cotton, work silk, and weave cloth for his own profit.[270] In Yolomecatl, female yya and toho ("yia toho dzehe") were obligated in 1704 to provide cloth to the alcalde mayor, suggesting their roles as managers of cloth production and tribute.[271] These women also provided dzico (huipiles) and dzoo (cloaks) to local officials, such as the governor, the *maestro* (choirmaster), and the *fiscal*. The document demonstrates that women of Yolomecatl managed the weaving of cloth, as well as the production of wax and pulque.

In Santo Domingo Yanhuitlan, women from the ten "barrios" wove garments of cotton, feathers, and silk for various feasts, including the titular saint's feast day and Holy Week.[272] In 1677, tribute collectors distributed fifteen pounds of cotton and gathered a total of fourteen mantas, eighteen *ayates* (cloaks, usually of maguey fiber), and nine silk garments from the "women of each barrio" to be given as gifts to the provincial priest, the friars, the alcalde mayor and his staff, and the highest-ranking native nobles on the feast day of Santo Domingo. Even Juan Ortiz received a "manta de pájaros" (feathered manta) for fighting bulls that day. It is unclear whether the women received any compensation for their labor.

An outstanding example of the value attached to cloth in Yanhuitlan involves its use in a diplomatic mission. In response to a dispute with the neighboring community of Suchitepec, Yanhuitlan sent two cabildo officials in 1677 to appeal to the Royal Audiencia in Mexico City, bearing gifts of silk huipiles and silk mantas for the Spanish judges.[273] The presentation of huipiles and mantas to male judges of the Audiencia suggests that the Ñudzahui gifts were designated for couples, presumably the judges and their wives, as if the items were intended for yuhuitayu couples. Indeed, cloth was a supreme gift item and a readily accepted form of compensation for services in Yanhuitlan.

Tribute burdens forced some women to weave more than ever to pay the tribute with woven goods or money earned from the sale of textiles.[274] Sometimes, men and women objected to increases in tribute demands for weaving and spinning or perceived abuses of authority. Several disputes and local rebellions of the eighteenth century were directly related to the problem of increased tribute demands or a particularly rapacious alcalde mayor, and women accordingly played leading roles in many of the *tumultos* (riots), in defense of their labor and community.[275] Returning to the example from Achiutla introduced above, it is important to note how the *macehuales* targeted both Spanish and native officials in their petition. In addition to spinning silk and cotton and weaving, their uncompensated work included cultivating lands, providing food for feasts, tending to sheep and cattle, and providing domestic service.[276] At the same time, native officials who did not cooperate with Spanish authorities or who failed to produce the required tribute payments were subject to harassment and prolonged periods in jail.

Alcaldes mayores were notorious for appropriating women's textile production, silk, and dyes by negotiating with or bullying local cabildo officials and, if necessary, using their considerable authority to determine prices, enforce agreements, jail people, confiscate goods, and collect debts.[277] The record contains ample evidence of these abuses in the form of complaints. To choose one of many examples, in 1647, several communities in the Mixteca Alta accused the Spanish alcalde mayor of ignoring labor laws regarding *indios de servicio* that he was supposed to protect. They accused him of using native men and women for personal services, including the spinning and weaving of cotton, the collection of cochineal and silk, and the provision of food and drink.[278] All these duties were required in addition to normal repartimiento services and tribute payments, the petitioners stated, and all the activities involved women's labor. All together, in addition to community tniño obligations and periodic derramas, these demands amounted to considerable burdens and debts for impoverished people.

In times of crisis, leaders relied on cloth production to generate revenue in defense of the community. For example, the cacique of Tecomastlahuaca, don Francisco de Arellano, appealed to a gathering of community members for help with a land dispute against the nearby pueblo of Igualtepec.[279] Two tribute collectors, Domingo Cumau and Domingo Xaquihu, testified in 1563 that the cacique had presented the commoners with a choice: he could borrow the money from a Spaniard to pay for the lawsuit, or they could spin cotton for the Spaniard in exchange for the money. The commoners decided to spin enough cotton to earn the money rather than go into debt; when the Spaniard stalled in compensating the community for its work, a group of people from Tecomastlahuaca forced him to fulfill his obligation. When he offered to extend the arrangement at the same wage, the men and women declined. Nobles and commoners who testified in this case confirmed that the collective community usually had a voice in matters regarding the use of their labor. Nonetheless, periodic derramas, or levies for specific purposes, usually to pay for extended lawsuits on behalf of communities or caciques, amounted to additional burdens for commoners with limited access to money.

In addition to fulfilling tribute obligations, gifting, and raising funds for various corporate projects, the cloth trade offered native households the opportunity to earn money. Especially in the first half of the colonial period, some Ñudzahui noblewomen profited from a demand for traditional and introduced types of cloth. One of the best examples involves a noblewoman named Lucía Hernández Ñuquihui (6-Crocodile), from the siqui of Dzumañuu in Teposcolula. An inventory of her estate in 1633 reveals that she possessed thirteen plots of land (six purchased) and a large quantity of yarn and weavings.[280] Her inventory contained sixteen pounds of white cotton thread (*yuhua cuisi*), eleven pounds of woolen yarn (*yuhua ticachi*), and many types of cloth and clothing, including *dzama* (cloth), *cuitu* (fine cloth), *yadzi* (maguey fiber cloth), "tapita" (taffeta), *paño* "uaha" (good cloth [generally woolen]), and *ñoo* and *tnoo* (dyes). With these she made dziyo (skirts or naguas), dzico (huipiles), dzoo (cloaks or mantas), *dzono* and "camissa" (*camisas,* shirts), "jompon" (*jubones,* doublets), and "calçone" (*calzones,* cotton trousers for men). Lucía's list resembles the inventory of a store, though she apparently ran the business out of her house or in the marketplace. Not counting the value of her textiles, her lands, or her houses, her cash assets from sales and credits amounted to 446 pesos; in addition, six native men and women owed her a total of 50 pesos for loans apparently unrelated to her cloth business. It is no coincidence that Lucía's late husband was a long-distance trader who owned several mules; he probably conveyed her products to distant markets. Typical of married Mixtec couples, she kept and bequeathed her own property and money separately from her husband's lands and mules. It is unclear whether Lucía produced the woven goods herself, received cloth in tribute, managed the cloth production of dependents, or bought finished and unfinished cloth from other women. Noblewomen may have received some finished or unfinished goods from the community. By comparison, in the Nahua area, native informants in the sixteenth century confirmed that *cihuapilli* (noble women) received cloth as tribute.[281] But noblewomen were not exempt from weaving. In both Teposcolula and Yolomecatl, for example, sources indicate that *yya toho dzehe* wove in the colonial period, and it is likely that some type of hierarchy existed based on the types of materials woven and the quality of the finished products.[282] In any case, Lucía Hernández Ñuquihui's assets represent a substantial amount of money in the 1630s, especially for an indigenous person.[283] Not even the value of her husband's assets was comparable to her own. She earned some of the profit by trading with women from Tilantongo and Puebla, and she bequeathed part of the estate to her granddaughter, Isabel Ramírez, a noblewoman from Teposcolula who resided in Puebla. Her connections with Puebla suggest that she played the role of a small producer in the interregional cloth trade.

Many people in the Mixteca Alta possessed notable quantities of woven goods and money, especially in the first half of the colonial period. The testament of a woman named Catalina, who lived in Achiutla until her death in 1581, reveals that she owned a chest of huipiles, several mantas and other weavings, ten rolls of cotton, and fifty-three pesos of gold in a cloth bag, in addition to several tracts of land.[284] María Sihueyo, of the siña of Yuchaychi in Yanhuitlan, possessed four hundred pesos in 1588, including seventy pesos in cloth, large quantities of yarn and cloth, weaving gear, six mules, and three pieces of land.[285] Again, the possession of mules suggests that María's household was involved in long-distance trade. In 1604, Esteban Mendoza of Yanhuitlan and Tomás Pérez of Chapultepec, a ñuu in the Valley of Oaxaca, appeared in Achiutla with two hundred pesos and a sizable quantity of locally produced cloth.[286] The two men had worked together for four years transporting cotton and cloth from the coast to the Mixteca Alta.

In response to a demand for cloth and the potential for profit, Spaniards instituted mills or shops, called *obrajes*, that produced Spanish-style textiles with European technology, operated by men and women. Although obrajes were not introduced in the Mixteca during the colonial period, Spanish merchants shipped cloth produced in Puebla to the Mixteca and other southern destinations, including the Valley of Oaxaca, Tehuantepec, Socunusco, and Guatemala.[287] By the seventeenth century, goods produced by mechanical looms in obrajes and imported cloth competed with local household production for profit and even use. Inventories of traders in the early 1600s contained significant quantities of *paño* (Spanish-style cloth, usually woolen), taffeta, and even *sinabafa* (a type of cloth from Holland). This pattern was especially pronounced by the eighteenth century, when traders such as the toho named Sebastián Sánchez Hernández of Yanhuitlan possessed so many types of foreign cloth that he consistently used the term *ñudzahui* to distinguish local products from goods associated with Brittany or Britain (Bretaña), Germany, China (most likely the Philippines), Castile, Venice, Guadalajara, Puebla, and Cholula.[288] Likewise, a book of accounts kept by the toho Juan Ramírez, a small trader from Yanhuitlan, lists a wide variety of woven goods.[289] But their records also reveal that cloth produced in the Mixteca, the "dzama Ñudzahui" of Sebastián's inventory, continued to serve a multiethnic demand in the eighteenth century.[290] Let us now consider the interregional dimensions of the indigenous cloth trade.

Long-Distance Traders

In the preconquest period, long-distance traders, or *tay cuica*, provided precious imports such as salt and cotton from the coastal region and cacao and feathers from Guatemala.[291] The importance of traders in the Mixteca is confirmed by many references to ancient cults associated with merchants, described in the following chapter. In the first half of the colonial period, native merchants from the Mixteca continued to carry indigenous goods along traditional trade routes, traveling from central Mexico and Puebla to Soconusco and Guatemala. Native traders left a trail of documentation in the colonial archival record because they often kept written inventories of their goods, unlike local market sellers. In addition, most traders attempted to settle their accounts in testaments. In fact, they were encouraged to do so by local authorities. The cabildo of Yanhuitlan decreed in 1591 that all nobles, traders, and merchants—speaking of the three in unison—should make their testaments with native notaries and witnesses.[292] Civil suits over property and debts relied on testaments and inventories to settle claims; these documents were filed with records of the legal proceedings in judicial archives.

Ñudzahui tay cuica were particularly active in and around Yanhuitlan, along the ancient road that connects the Valley of Oaxaca with Puebla and the Valley of Mexico, the *ychi yaya cano*, or "great road."[293] In 1563, the alcalde mayor of Yanhuitlan complained that men from Texupa went to the province of Guatemala and other places for lengthy periods in order to trade goods, leaving their wives behind to take care of things.[294] His observation was intended to explain why Texupa had failed to fulfill its tribute obligations. His recommendation that indigenous men concern themselves more with local agriculture than commerce reflects a dual desire to eliminate the competition of native traders and to channel their labor into the fulfillment of tribute demands.[295] Spanish officials frequently complained how the activities of native merchants diminished agricultural productivity, mainly owing to their own economic interests in the trade. However exaggerated, the alcalde mayor's remark confirms repeated references to traders in documentation from this area of the Mixteca Alta.

Guatemala was a popular destination of goods from the Mixteca. The sale of Ñudzahui cloth in and around Santiago de Guatemala by native and Spanish traders was a thriving trade in the sixteenth century.[296] Martín Cortés was one of the many men who transported woven goods to Guatemala in return for cacao and other items.[297] A toho from Santiago Istepec (called Tiyyu in Mixtec), he used seven mules to carry cloth and clothing on behalf of the cacique of Istepec, don Diego de Rojas, as well as products belonging to him and his wife, Inés de Velasco. In 1594, he fell ill while en route to Guatemala, was forced to make his testament in haste, and arranged for his goods to be sent back to his home in the Mixteca Alta, near Yanhuitlan. The inventory of goods he was taking to Guatemala included dozens of huipiles, *tochomite* (rabbit fur), doublets, varas of blue cloth, and sinabafa. Martín's Nahuatl-language testament indicates that he and his wife kept their finances separate; in fact, he owed her 40 pesos at the time of his death. He divided his movable goods between his wife and his daughter from a previous marriage, Petronilla. Witnesses in Tiyyu, in the siña of Titnee, affirmed that Inés took possession of cloth and clothing valued at 697 pesos. Martín also possessed four houses and some forty plots of land in 1594.

Another tay cuica who traded clothing for dyes, feathers, and cacao in Guatemala was Gregorio García, who came from Santa María Ysquisuchitlan, a community near Yanhuitlan. In his testament of 1621, which he was forced to make in Guatemala because of illness, he bequeathed thirty-eight mules, a large quantity of clothing, quetzal feathers and feathered headdresses, and eighteen arrobas of *ñuma* (wax) to his wife, Catalina Pérez.[298] Shortly after her husband's death, Catalina made her Ñudzahui-language testament in Yanhuitlan; she owned forty-two arrobas of wax, four plots of land, and a wide assortment of material goods and sacred images.[299] Her testament includes a separate inventory of wax goods and accoutrements worth more than a thousand pesos.[300] Since the source of the wax was never mentioned and she did not bequeath any bee hives, Catalina may have been an intermediary in the local wax business, while her husband transported wax and other goods on mules to distant markets. Since the alcalde mayor owed Catalina more than three hundred pesos in 1621, we can assume that he was involved in their trading activities.

A third example of a long-distance trader is Francisco López of Sayultepec, another ñuu near Yanhuitlan, who took eight mules and two horses to "Yutnucucha" (the Ñudzahui name for Guatemala) to sell cloth. His wife, María Ñuquaa, helped to produce or supply part of his cargo.[301] Francisco also carried goods for other people, most likely for a percentage of sales; in fact, several people owed him a total of 720 pesos at the time of his death in 1595, including the Spanish alcalde mayor, the encomendero, and a few native nobles. Juan López, a regidor from Nochixtlan who was in Guatemala at the time of Francisco's death, owed him 400 pesos. He instructed his wife and executors to collect the debts. Francisco also owned seven tracts of land and a yoke of oxen in his home of Sayultepec.

These examples of interregional traders, selected from many similar cases, indicate a clear pattern for the Mixteca Alta: all were nobles from the Yanhuitlan area who prospered in the late sixteenth and early seventeenth centuries by selling cloth in markets to the south.[302] Some of these traders may have descended from merchant families or households, or perhaps they simply resembled nobles by virtue of their profits.[303] All possessed typical noble (or lesser noble) native surnames—López, Hernández, Cortés, García, and Pérez. As intermediaries between ñandahi and yya, toho played an important role in the accumulation and trade of indigenous goods in the first half of the colonial period. Many of the traders also carried goods on behalf of other native nobles or Spanish investors. In their possible associations with the nobility, they resemble the Nahua *pochteca* or *tlanecuiloque* of central Mexico.[304] But it is impossible to tell whether they inherited their roles as long distance traders or whether they were simply nobles who owned a pack of mules. By the end of the sixteenth century, native traders relied more on pack trains than on the traditional *tay sidzo* or *tlamemes* (human carriers).[305] Natives who possessed numerous mules and a horse or two in their wills were surely involved in long-distance trade.[306] The demands of interregional trade did not deter traders from possessing land, however.[307] In fact, profits derived from their activities, sometimes amounting to huge sums by indigenous standards in this period, enabled them to buy parcels of land during the great depopulation.

Whereas men owned the means of transport (mules and horses), women often managed the production and provisioning of cloth. Ñudzahui tay cuica counted on their wives to produce or supply them with goods for their journeys.[308] The complementary arrangement of female producers and male long-distance marketeers suggests a continuation of preconquest crafts and trades among the nobility in the colonial period and conforms to the normal pattern of married couples contributing equally to the livelihood of their households. The married couple was the productive basis of a household. In the absence of a marriage partner, single women or widows hired men to sell their goods in distant markets. For example, in 1605, Catalina de Rojas and her mother, María, two noblewomen from the siña of Ticoho in Yanhuitlan, hired Melchor de Espinar to sell chiles in Mexico City, Puebla, and Tepeaca.[309] Melchor's humble status suggests that commoners were also employed to transport agricultural goods to distant markets. The difference between toho and ñandahi traders is reflected in their carrying capacity and the types of goods transported.

Eventually, all tay cuica competed with Spaniards. Commerce along the "southern trunkline" extending from Guatemala to Mexico City was profitable enough to attract the attention of Spaniards, who became involved as early as the 1530s, when encomenderos used tlamemes to transport goods from Veracruz to Guatemala. Alcaldes mayores participated in the trade, ignoring laws prohibiting their investment in the regional economy. Some officials circumvented laws against their involvement in local trade by involving other family members in the business. For example, in 1603, doña Francisca de la Vega, the Spanish wife of the alcalde mayor of Teposcolula, invested five hundred pesos for the purchase and transport of woven goods to Guatemala in return for cacao to be sold in Mexico City.[310] He was not allowed to involve himself in such a legally binding contract, so his wife invested the money on their behalf. In this case a Spanish couple operated as a commercial team.

The involvement of Spanish *tratantes*, or petty traders and merchants, in interregional trade, often involving indigenous goods, confirms the maxim that Spaniards eventually took over any enterprise in the colonial period that showed a strong profit potential.[311] Late-sixteenth-century legislation enhanced their advantage; native individuals were prohibited in 1597 from owning more than six mules without special license. Although the law was undoubtedly difficult to enforce, numerous complaints from native nobles in the first decade of the seventeenth century indicate that alcaldes mayores reserved the right to confiscate mules from traders who violated the law.[312] The intent of such legislation was to restrict indigenous traders to local activities, leaving interregional trade to Spaniards. Mixtec traders responded by petitioning Spanish authorities for license to own as many as fifteen mules in the early seventeenth century.[313]

In the sixteenth century, a hierarchy of Spanish traders existed, from the itinerant tratantes who exchanged small amounts of cash or credit for finished goods or raw materials in native communities, to more established *mercaderes* who remained in centers such as Yanhuitlan and Teposcolula, to mercaderes in Puebla and Veracruz who accepted *cartas de obligación* in exchange for goods on credit. Spanish merchants exploited traditional indigenous markets by selling cloth produced in the Mixteca, Puebla, and Europe to southern markets in exchange for cacao and dyes, which were then resold in central Mexican markets.[314] From the Mixteca, Spanish traders brought silk and cotton goods to Puebla and Guatemala; by the end of the sixteenth century, they controlled much of the production and shipment of cotton from the coastal regions of Oaxaca. Despite the Spaniards' competitive advantage, a thriving trade in indigenous goods allowed native traders a share of the commerce. Some served as intermediaries for Spanish merchants, who expanded their operations by extending credit to small tratantes. For example, one Spanish mercader in Tlaxiaco employed eight natives and twenty non-natives as intermediaries in the first decade of the seventeenth century.[315]

By the last quarter of the sixteenth century, the collapse of the silk industry, the constant decline of the native population, and the onset of depression contributed to a shortage of money and credit in New Spain.[316] This trend was particularly pronounced from 1620 to the 1650s. Romero Frizzi has argued that the contraction of credit made interregional commerce less viable and halved the number of Spanish traders in the Mixteca Alta during the period from 1600 to 1650.[317] In this half century, many Spanish *vecinos*, or residents, of the Mixteca invested in livestock to compensate for sluggish trade and a shortage of labor. Alcaldes mayores relied on repartos de efectos, advancing unfinished goods rather than reals, to exploit labor resources in this period. Many native individuals and communities paid tribute in goods such as cochineal, cotton, cloth, wheat, and ganado instead of money.

The first half of the colonial period offered opportunities for native nobles such as Martín Córtes, Francisco López, and Gregorio García to drive pack trains loaded with indigenous goods down to the Valley of Oaxaca, across the Isthmus of Tehuantepec, and over to Chiapas, Socunusco, and Guatemala. After the mid-seventeenth century, evidence of native nobles' involvement in interregional commerce is scarce. By the 1660s, a resurgent economy and renewed prospects of credit attracted Spanish traders to the region again; their numbers in the Mixteca Alta doubled from about sixteen in 1650 to thirty-six in 1675.[318] Meanwhile, merchant houses in Puebla consolidated commercial ties with Spanish mercaderes in Teposcolula, who used lines of credit to dominate trade by the last quarter of the seventeenth century. In this period, Oaxaca City became an important market for goods from the Mixteca. Spanish merchants who drew on thousands of pesos of credit left little room for tay cuica. The lengthy inventories of Ñudzahui traders and producers in the earlier period are rare in the later period. As Romero Frizzi observed, they came to rely increasingly on credit from Spanish merchants in Teposcolula and were restricted to driving small pack trains, reselling goods of little value to local native markets.[319] Moreover, Spaniards were likely to hire mestizos or *mulatos* for this secondary, transport role. For example, in 1641, Antón Sánchez de la Torre and his wife, doña Ana de Chávez, contracted a mulatto living in Yanhuitlan to drive a team of mules to San Antonio Suchitepec in Guatemala.[320] They gave him 456 pesos to conduct a pack train of twenty-five mules with woven goods from the Mixteca, Puebla, and Europe. This was precisely the type of work that had been performed by tay cuica in the earlier period.

The marginalization of Ñudzahui traders corresponded with the overall uneven distribution of wealth between Spaniards and natives in the region. For example, a petty Spanish trader named Juan de Iriarte possessed more than 2,000 pesos of goods and money (after debts) when he made his will in 1597.[321] This was a vast sum of money by native standards, yet it was still comparable to the total assets of some native traders during this early period. By the later period, Spaniards who specialized in trading Spanish goods for cotton in Teposcolula and Yanhuitlan, such as Luis de Haro and Gabriel de Bolaños, repectively, owned estates worth 7,367 pesos in 1673 and 6,960 pesos in 1718.[322] Of course, there were considerable differences in wealth among the Spanish group, and their assets were probably only a fraction of those of the Spaniards who operated in the commercial center of New Spain, in Mexico City and Puebla.[323] But even a mestiza such as Antonia de la Peña, vecina of Tlaxiaco, possessed 2,695 pesos in 1683 by dealing in the cotton trade.[324] The average Spanish or mestizo merchant reaped sizeable profits from doing business in the Mixteca; a sample of eighteen testaments of non-native merchants and muleteers from 1650 to 1724 indicates that the average net value of a trader's estate (debts included) was just over 6,300 pesos.[325] One Spanish vecino of Teposcolula accumulated a fortune of nearly 54,000 pesos in 1701, whereas only one Spaniard died in debt.[326] Muleteers included in the sample possessed as many as seventy-six mules, each capable of carrying at least two hundred pounds of goods. Clearly, Spanish traders could draw on greater economic and social resources than their Mixtec counterparts.

By the end of the seventeenth century, Spanish and mestizo merchants consolidated control over regional and interregional markets and accumulated small fortunes. The competition of Spanish tratantes and mercaderes, the system of tribute and repartos, and colonial legislation placed indigenous traders and producers at a decided disadvantage. Whereas Mixtecs traded quantities of indigenous goods and raw materials in exchange for European products or remitted goods to pay tribute, Spanish traders converted large quantities of indigenous goods into profits. For the most part, native trade was confined to petty commerce and local marketplaces in the second half of the colonial period.

Local Markets

Despite many references to long-distance travel in the written record, most people traded and worked locally, and much of this daily and weekly exchange among ordinary men and women went undocumented. In fact, market activity is an extremely underrepresented area of activity in Ñudzahui-language sources. Testaments, inventories, and other records give us a sense of what some people sold in the marketplace, but we catch only fleeting glimpses of their transactions. For example, Juana López, who sold straw or hay (*zacate*) in the market of Teposcolula in 1630, appears to us only because she fought with a Spaniard who was buying fodder for his horse. She bought the zacate from Pedro Naxa (8-Eagle), who came from an outlying ñuu, and sold it for a small profit.[327] These are the types of mundane transactions that were hardly worth writing down. Yet local markets were vital redistribution points that invited open exchange among men and women within and among communities, including non-natives. Indeed, Spaniards came to rely on native markets in the Mixteca for many of their own provisions.

Public markets represented another convergence of indigenous and Spanish custom, and thus markets were not dramatically transformed by the arrival of Europeans.[328] In the colonial period, the aniñe (also the cabildo meeting place), the church, and the market constituted the nucleus of a ñuu. This center was the obvious location for the Spanish church and plaza. The term for "market" (*yahui*) was applied to the Spanish word *plaza*, identifying the new space with a familiar function. Perhaps many markets had been located in these ceremonial-administrative centers. Some areas organized strategically located market communities, such as Suchitepec in the Yanhuitlan area, which attracted people from adjacent ñuu. In the 1540s, people from Yanhuitlan and vicinity attested to the dominant role played by the Suchitepec market, where one could purchase anything from slaves to prestige items. Exchange also occurred along the borders of communities.[329] Markets were held every five days in the preconquest period but were restructured to fit a seven-day week after the conquest. In 1575, Coixtlahuaca petitioned to return to a five-day market schedule, based on the native calendar, on the grounds that its new fixed day of Saturday competed with other nearby markets. Its protest suggests an indigenous precedent for the rotational, interregional organization of local market activities.[330]

Spaniards attempted to monitor and profit from the flow of goods in local markets by imposing taxes and requiring licenses.[331] By 1576, several toho from Teposcolula had been forced to obtain licenses to sell European and local ("de la tierra") goods.[332] In 1580, five noblewomen from Yanhuitlan and Yucuita—Ana López, Lucía López, Ana Gutiérrez, María Hernández, and Catalina de Cabrera—protested that Spanish officials had obstructed their sale of meat, chickens, and other goods with excessive taxation.[333] Taxation and interference in local markets were sources of tension and resentment. In 1587, in the market town of Suchitepec, 104 people from eleven separate communities in the Yanhuitlan area protested the collection of tribute and taxes in the market.[334] The alcalde mayor had infuriated the group of commoners and nobles by aggressively collecting a total of 1,787 pesos from local sellers. In 1591, the Audiencia ruled that all native merchants of Yanhuitlan were entitled to sell goods of any kind as long as they paid a sales tax (*alcabala*).[335] In that same year, six women and six men from Yanhuitlan petitioned to sell native goods in public markets of the region without being assessed the tax because, they argued, the alcabala applied only to the sale of Spanish-style goods. The petitioners, all nobles, identified themselves as dyers and vendors of rabbit fur.[336] It seems as if resentment of taxation reached its limits when it came to the household production and sale of pulque. The record contains countless cases of common folk who were fined for selling small amounts of pulque, as well as many complaints against native and Spanish officials who sought to enforce laws against the sale of pulque in order to raise revenue. A group of people from Yanhuitlan lodged a typical complaint in 1591 that officials frequently entered houses at night in search of informal taverns or *pulquerías*.[337]

Whereas disputes over lands usually involved cabildo officials and caciques, men and women did not rely on cabildo representation to air their grievances in the marketplace. Market activities among the Nahuas seemed to have gone without corporate regulation in the colonial period, possibly because of the small money value of these activities or because this sphere of activity fell under the jurisdiction of Spanish authorities from an early period.[338] The examples from Yanhuitlan seem to confirm the transcorporate nature of market activities and participants despite the considerable amounts of money involved in their transactions. Perhaps the cabildo played a limited role in representing markets because local trade involved so many corporate groups and communities that it was impossible or impractical to control them. In the Yanhuitlan area, the ñuu of Suchitepec hosted the largest market, but the majority of participants came from Yanhuitlan and other nearby communities. Among the 104 people who confronted the alcalde mayor in the market of Suchitepec in 1587, there were 56 people from Yanhuitlan and only 3 from Suchitepec. Spanish attempts to regulate markets may have contradicted a general tolerance of open intercommunity trade. Early colonial sources suggest that long-distance trade was not necessarily controlled by the aniñe or the cabildo, either. Caciques and nobles supplied traders with wares, furnished by their tribute and surplus production, but they did so more as individual investors than as corporate sponsors. In the sixteenth century, long-distance traders were generally free agents who carried goods to distant markets for a number of individuals, including their wives, nobles from other communities, and even Spanish investors. Thus, local and long-distance markets were integrated by a network of household relations among local producers and sellers and long-distance traders.

Outside the marketplace, some toho ran small stores or traveled locally to sell their wares. For example, Miguel Jiménez ran a "huahi tienda," or "store house," near the center of Yanhuitlan.[339] In 1621, when he made his testament, he was forced to sell two African slaves and rent his store to pay off debts; his testament suggests that the shelves of his huahi tienda contained little more than an arroba of wax and some odds and ends. His main assets consisted of a house and forty magueys. In general, stores were owned by Spaniards who could draw on their contacts with Spanish merchants and access to credit. Rodolfo Pastor cites a number of examples of Spanish store owners in the cabeceras who exchanged imported goods for cochineal, cloth, wheat, wax, and wool from Mixtecs, an arrangement known as *repartimientos de mercancía*.[340]

In the second half of the colonial period, bilingual Ñudzahui merchants managed to resell an assortment of Spanish and indigenous goods to local native and non-native clients, traveling to communities or attending periodic local markets. These men were the successors of long-distance merchants from the early period. A book of accounts kept by a toho trader in the mid-eighteenth century provides some insight into this local trade. Juan Ramírez's accounts, dated from 1740 to 1758, document transactions with men and women who bought, bartered, and sold a variety of goods, including *fanegas* of wheat and maize, soap, books, clothing, wool, shoes, and even religious items such as crucifixes, lienzos, and reliquaries.[341] The value and volume of his trade were relatively modest. Some of his native clients lacked cash to the extent that he occasionally accepted payment in magueys, noting the form of payment in the margin and drawing a line through the entry to indicate a completed transaction. The bilingual entries in his sixty-eight-page book represent how Juan relied on a multiethnic clientele, supplying Mixtecs from "Yucundaa" as well as Spanish speakers from "Theposcolula" (the Spanish-Nahuatl name for Yucundaa), writing place-names in entries of his book according to the language of his client. His sales were confined to the Yanhuitlan-Teposcolula area. One of Juan's clients was his *compadre*, Sebastián Sánchez Hernández, another toho from Yanhuitlan (from the siña called Tindee). Sebastián's thirty-eight-page Ñudzahui-language testament and inventory, covering the years from 1754 to 1758, overlaps with Juan's book of accounts.[342] Apparently, Sebastián and his son carried on a local resale trade in cloth and other goods. His estate, valued at nearly three thousand pesos, included a wide variety of imported items and Ñudzahui goods. He was careful to distinguish between the two types of goods throughout his inventory. His testament does not indicate the nature of his business, and the only sign that he sold cloth is the fact that he possessed so much of it and that many people owed him small amounts of money, although he could have also lent money to people. It is likely that Sebastián resold goods that he purchased from other traders or acquired by other means. Nevertheless, much of his wealth was derived from the forty-three tracts of land he possessed (eight purchased), four houses, two jacales (huahi tiyahua), two horses, and six yokes of oxen. Sebastián resembles wealthy toho traders from the earlier period, but he did not own a single mule.

By the eighteenth century, commerce was dominated by Spaniards in all but the most local venues of exchange, involving the sale of agricultural commodities and indigenous crafts or the resale of imported goods. Mixtec traders in the late period, though still identifiable as relatively well-to-do toho, did not carry large quantities of cloth or supply valuable raw materials to distant markets in Guatemala, Puebla, and Mexico City, as their predecessors had done in the sixteenth century. Rather, they sold an assortment of Spanish and native goods to local buyers, working for Spanish merchants or stores on commission, or they resold items for a modest profit. In comparison, many Spanish and mestizo mercaderes earned small fortunes by native standards, by exporting cotton, dyes, and other indigenous products from the Mixteca and importing goods produced in Puebla, central Mexico, Spain, and the Philippines.

CHAPTER 8

⧼⧽

Sacred Relations

SOCIAL AND SACRED RELATIONS are intertwined. Ñudzahui *yya* and *yya dzehe* maintained reciprocal relations with male and female sacred ancestors. Mixtec codices traced the origin and descent of the *yuhuitayu* from a primordial creator couple to the ruling couple who commissioned the painted writings. People imagined the sacred past in terms of the lived present. Christian priests sought to transform these relations by smashing and burning all hallowed objects and writings, desecrating or taking over ancient ritual spaces, and persecuting native priests. They aimed to replace the entire system with new buildings, images, books, ceremonies, personnel and a new calendar. They introduced new ideas about sin and salvation, life and death. The collision and convergence of Mixtec and Christian ideologies in the sixteenth century, the creation of new Ñudzahui sacred relations, and the many "great persistences within great changes" are among the topics addressed in this chapter.[1]

It is important to acknowledge from the beginning that the historical record fails to represent the complexity and diversity of local religious practices in the Mixteca. Preconquest codices depict numerous sacred personages, places, objects, and events, but the writings were not intended to describe the meaning of these images to outsiders. Colonial sources offer only glimpses of native practices and beliefs, mainly at the corporate level of *cabeceras*. Most direct commentaries on native religion were written by Spanish priests and administrators, who interpreted what they saw, heard, or imagined in terms of their own cultural perspectives. Most of the sources were written decades after the conquest, following a period of considerable transformation and crisis. Ñudzahui-language writings on religion are limited to church-sponsored texts, Christian statements of faith in last wills and testaments, and a few archival documents. There is nothing from the Mixteca comparable to the *Florentine Codex,* the *Primeros memoriales,* or other Nahuatl-language commentaries on native religion.

On the other hand, a remarkable collection of preconquest codices, early colonial pictorial writings, and sixteenth-century Inquisition records sheds light on some religious practices in the early sixteenth century, especially at the corporate level. Whereas the first two types of sources have been discussed in chapter 2, the third requires some introduction. In 1544, the Inquisition investigated alleged idolatries in Yanhuitlan.[2] The trial elicited testimony on local religious practices and responses to Christianity. Three Ñudzahui lords from Yanhuitlan, in the heart of the Mixteca Alta, were accused of reverting to ancient practices and subverting the faith. Dozens of Spanish and indigenous witnesses testified to alleged practices, including unbaptized native priests who described their ritual ceremonies and sacrifices. The situation in Yanhuitlan was so threatening to the Dominicans that the friars abandoned their *convento* (church and living quarters) twice before 1544, even though Yanhuitlan was one of the richest and most populous settlements in the Mixteca. The Inquisition proceedings generated some of the earliest Spanish records in the region. A second inquisitorial investigation in Oaxaca complements the case from Yanhuitlan. In the same year, 1544, three lords from Coatlan were accused of rejecting Christianity and committing numerous crimes against the church, including human sacrifice and the desecration of Christian images.[3] The two cases are related in that the lords of Coatlan referred to meetings with nobles from Yanhuitlan and other prominent communities in the Mixteca Alta.

Although Inquisition records refer to sacred beliefs and practices, it is important to keep in mind the limitations of these sources. First of all, the questions asked of witnesses in the proceedings were based on European categories of thought about pagan religion. The inquisitors' questions and preoccupations, prepared in response to accusations made by Spaniards, dictated the flow of information in the trial. In general, native witnesses responded to questions about "idols," sacrifices, and any inkling of opposition to Christianity. Reconstructions of native beliefs and practices based solely on these trials are likely to be superficial and slanted. Second, not all the testimonies are entirely credible, considering how both Spaniards and natives used the inquisitorial process to defame their adversaries. Numerous factors motivated witnesses to testify against the accused. Third, observable practices in the 1530s and 1540s represent responses to a state of crisis and change provoked by conquest, repression, and disease. The trials in Yanhuitlan and Coatlan coincided with an epidemic of disease and drought that lasted until 1548. Fourth, in these Spanish-language documents, native witnesses spoke through two translators, one who spoke Mixtec and Nahuatl and another who spoke Nahuatl and Spanish. Obviously, the transmission of concepts was subject to distortion and reinterpretation.

And yet, despite these biases and distortions, Inquisition records can be very useful.[4] Let us reconsider some of the limitations. First, it is true that the questions were usually limited to a narrow focus on certain notorious practices, but many of the practices in question were, by the 1540s, known to Christians as fundamental elements of Mesoamerican religious systems. Witnesses who responded to the questions did not necessarily conceal the truth. Sometimes, they raised additional issues in their testimonies, which the inquisitor pursued in subsequent questioning. Questions and answers are important for other reasons. Discrepancies between the inquisitor's questions and the respondent's answers, representing how each side viewed the same matter, can be most revealing. Notable discrepancies between native and Spanish testimonies suggest ideological and cultural gaps. Second, if witnesses fabricated tales to implicate their enemies in idolatries, they nonetheless articulated specific rituals and acts that were embedded in their own cultural imagination and experience. Multiple native descriptions of ceremonies, taken as a whole, represent a collective commentary on ritual practices. Some of these descriptions correspond with representations of ritual acts in preconquest codices or are corroborated by contemporary Nahuatl-language sources or records of the oral tradition. Native priests and lords who described their own participation in sacrificial rituals had little to gain by such confessions.[5] Although many accused native nobles simply denied everything, others spoke freely, and a few recanted their statements when they realized the full implications of their confessions. Finally, it is true that one should not place too much emphasis on specific terminology elicited in the course of the trial, unless the original native language was retained; in general, the names of people, places, and deities are the only native-language items preserved in the documentation. But in terms of bridging language gaps, most Mixtec nobles knew Nahuatl as a second language, and the translation process that relied on Nahuatl as a lingua franca was well developed in the Mixteca by the 1540s. Thus, despite their limitations, inquisitorial records are valuable sources of information for the early period. Like all sources, they should be used with discretion.

The first part of this chapter uses codices, colonial pictorial writings and legends, and Inquisition trials to examine certain aspects of Ñudzahui religious practices and beliefs in the early sixteenth century, when Christianity was introduced. I use the same types of sources (except the codices) to consider native responses to Christianity in the early period. The first part also benefits from several other Spanish-language sources, including the *Relaciones geográficas* of 1579–81, discussed in chapter 2. In particular, question number fourteen of the *Relaciones* inquired about the "adorations, rituals, and customs, good or bad" that each community had in the ancient past.[6] Some communities said very little in response to this provocative question, but others replied at length. The second part of this chapter considers how Ñudzahui people came to understand Christianity in their own terms, in ways that made sense to their own cultural imagination and experience. I use church-sponsored native-language texts and a variety of archival records in consideration of this topic.

Let us begin, appropriately, with a Ñudzahui origin legend about the birth of ancient deities and the coming of Christianity.

Origins

In the early seventeenth century, fray Gregorio García wrote down a story in Cuilapan, a yuhuitayu in the western Valley of Oaxaca. The story was based on a book in the possession of the Dominican vicar of Cuilapan. According to García, the priest had a "hand made book composed of images, like those written by Indians of the Mixtec kingdom in their books or rolled parchments, with descriptions of what the images meant, relating their origin, the creation of the world, and the flood."[7] García wrote down the origin legend as it was recounted in the book. The text, translated from Spanish, begins:

> In the year and the day of obscurity and darkness, before there were days or years, the world being in great darkness, when all was chaos and confusion, the earth was covered with water. There was only slime and mud on the surface of the earth. At that time, the Indians imagine, a God who had the name of 1-Deer and the surname of Lion Serpent, and a very attractive and beautiful goddess named 1-Deer, whose surname was Tiger Serpent, made themselves visible.[8] These two gods are said to have been the origin of all the other gods that the Indians possessed. The histories of this people relate that when these two gods became visible in the world, when they appeared in human form, with their omnipotence and wisdom they established and founded a large rock, upon which they built some very magnificent palaces, constructed with the finest workmanship, where they made their seat and residence on earth.

The legend from Cuilapan attributes the beginning of life to the time when a female deity and a male deity, both bearing the same calendrical name of 1-Deer, built a palace in which they seated themselves as rulers. In other words, they constructed the first yuhuitayu. This primordial yuhuitayu appears on the second page of the *Codex Vindobonensis*, a preconquest screenfold manuscript from the Mixteca Alta.[9] Of all the preconquest manuscripts discussed in chapter 2, the *Vindobonensis* is the only extensive account of the creation of the world. The first page of this finely painted text (obverse 52) introduces an enigmatic scene (see fig. 8.1).[10] Reading from right to left at the bottom of the page, ten nameless figures hold ceremonial objects and perform rituals; the barefoot male figures wear white loincloths and their bodies are painted black. They are followed by ten place signs, located above them. The entire scene on this page is bounded at the bottom by a sky band, a blue ribbon with eight celestial bodies, suggesting the location of these events, when the earth was still covered with water.[11] The narrative moves from right to left, up and over the vertical line and down to the left-hand corner of the page. After the emergence of twenty days and nights (a month in the 260-day ritual calendar) and other phenomena depicted on the right side of the vertical line, two stylized *aniñe*, or palaces, appear at the top (left side) of the page. I interpret the parallel structures as sacred palaces or temples. Below the temples, an unnamed couple is seated facing and gesturing toward each other. The aged, toothless personages are covered with headdresses of long green and blue feathers, indicating their sacred and powerful status and associating them with the star band on which they are seated, as creatures of the sky. A female personage is seated on the left, and her male counterpart is seated on the right. Below them is another (possibly the same) unnamed, aged couple seated on red and white platforms or altars. The very next scene on the following page depicts a third seated couple (or the third image of the same couple), a male named 1-Deer (left) and a female named 1-Deer (right), who hold sacred offerings of tobacco and a smoking incense ladle (see fig. 8.2). Both appear with skeletal jaws, and both wear the mask of a prominent deity in the codex, 9-Wind.[12] The Cuilapan legend referred to this 1-Deer couple as the "father and mother of all the gods."

After the primordial couple had seated themselves on a paradisal mountain site near Apoala, a *ñuu* in the Mixteca Alta, they produced two sons. The legend continues:

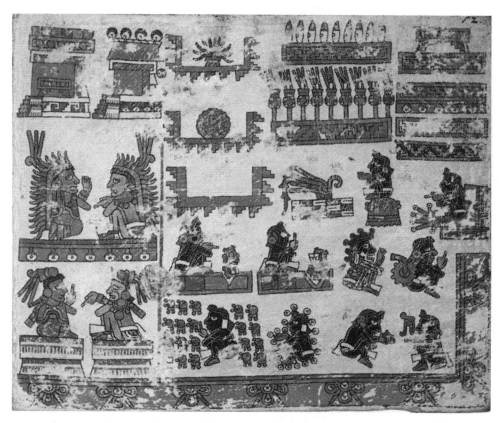

FIGURE 8.1. The origin of life, from the *Codex Vindobonensis,* obverse 52. Codex Vindobonensis Mexicanus I, Österr. Nationalbibliothek, Wien. Facsimile edition by Akademische Druck- u. Verlagsanstalt, Graz/Austria 1974.

"Thus these gods, father and mother of all the gods, in their palaces and royal courts, had two very handsome male sons who were clever and wise in all the arts. The first was called Wind of 9-Snake, a name taken from the day he was born. The second was called Wind of 9-Caves, which also was the name of his birth date."[13] The two children possessed magical powers, including the ability to transform themselves into animals, fly through the air, and pass through objects. They made the "first offerings" in the world to their parents, burning incense or ground tobacco in their honor. They were the first priests to forge a reciprocal arrangement with the primordial deities, their parents. They created a garden of luxuriant fruits and herbs and a field to grow the sacrificial items they needed. So that their parents might clear the earth of its waters, they sacrificed drops of blood from their ears and tongues, splattering the blood over the branches of trees and plants. Many of these acts are depicted in the *Codex Vindobonensis.*

The preconquest codex is far more elaborate and complex than the colonial legend. The compact writing of the codex conveys much of García's narrative in only a few pages. The codex includes numerous important scenes that are not addressed by the legend, including the appearance of 9-Wind, the Mixtec variant or prototype of the central Mexican deity "Quetzalcoatl."[14] The venerable 9-Wind lifted the sky and waters upon his shoulders and revealed a familiar landscape of hills, rivers, and cultivable val-

FIGURE 8.2. The "father and mother of all the gods," from the *Codex Vindobonensis,* obverse 51. Codex Vindobonensis Mexicanus I, Österr. Nationalbibliothek, Wien. Facsimile edition by Akademische Druck- u. Verlagsanstalt, Graz/Austria 1974.

leys.[15] Several pages later, a symbolic tree in Apoala gives birth (see fig. 8.3). A nude male figure emerges from the crotch of the tree; he is paired with a newborn female figure who stands above him.[16] These two twins represent the first of more than fifty descendants from the tree.[17] The base of the tree features the head and face of a grimacing woman who is planted face first in a carpet of feathers. The tree's outspread limbs, V-shaped cleft, swollen trunk, and human head represent a woman's body. But the tree itself contains both male and female symbols.[18] Two male personages apply writing instruments to the trunk of the tree, painting the progenitor's body.[19]

In the *Codex Vindobonensis,* two descendants of the tree birth procreated a third line of descendants associated with Apoala (after the primordial couple and the tree). The yya 5-Wind and the yya dzehe 9-Crocodile are seated together on a reed mat, facing each other (see fig. 8.4). Between the couple is a frothing vessel of chocolate. With their round eyes and fanged teeth, each bears the visage of Dzahui, the rain deity. The woman on the left, 9-Crocodile, is distinguished from the man only by her posture, dress, and hair. The place sign below the mat depicts a blue river (*yuta*) and a bunch of feathers (*tnoho*), representing Yutatnoho, the name for Apoala in the Ñudzahui

FIGURE 8.3. The tree birth at Apoala (Yutatnuhu), from the *Codex Vindobonensis*, obverse 37.
Codex Vindobonensis Mexicanus I, Österr. Nationalbibliothek, Wien. Facsimile edition by Akademische Druck- u. Verlagsanstalt, Graz/Austria 1974.

FIGURE 8.4. A sacred couple who descended from the tree and founded the first yuhuitayu in Yutatnoho (Apoala). From the *Codex Vindobonensis,* obverse 35. Codex Vindobonensis Mexicanus I, Österr. Nationalbibliothek, Wien. Facsimile edition by Akademische Druck- u. Verlagsanstalt, Graz/Austria 1974.

language. Cognate scenes in the codices *Bodley, Nuttall,* and *Selden* confirm the importance of this couple in the land of Dzahui.[20] The Dzahui pair founded a yuhuitayu at Yutatnoho, the legendary and sacred origin of all other royal dynasties in the Mixteca.

Fray Antonio de los Reyes addressed the famous tree birth legend in the prologue to his *Arte en lengua mixteca,* published in 1593. The story recalled a time when gods and lords emerged from named trees that grew in a river near Apoala, called Yutatnoho. After promptly dismissing the legend as false and ridiculous, he explained that the lords who emerged from Yutatnoho divided the Mixteca into four parts and introduced laws to the land.[21] Before their birth from the trees, the land was inhabited by people who had emerged from the center of the earth called "tay nuhu" or "ña nuhu."[22] The lords from Apoala who conquered the land were the "true Mixtecs and lords of the language that is now spoken in the Mixteca."[23] Nearly a century later, fray Francisco de Burgoa recorded the same Apoala tree birth. In his version, written in the 1670s, two trees "produced the first caciques, male and female," whose descendants populated the land.[24]

The obverse side of the *Codex Vindobonensis* speaks of the origin of life and natural forces, the birth of sacred ancestor deities, the ceremonies and rituals they established, the creation of yuhuitayu alliances, and the foundation of ñuu, or settled places, in the Mixteca.[25] The overwhelming attention to sacred ñuu and *ñayehui* (people) in the second half of the codex presents a coherent view of the *ñuu ñayehui*, the Ñudzahui term for the "world." Whereas the codices convey extended narratives and worldviews, the Spanish storytellers ventured only so far. Fray Gregorio García cut short the Cuilapan legend with the following words: "So as not to disgust the reader with these fables and nonsense that the Indians tell, I omit and overlook a great many things. In conclusion, after referring to the sons and daughters that those gods had as husband and wife, and the things that they did, where they had their seats and residences, and the labors and effects attributed to them, the Indians say that there was a great flood where many gods drowned. After the flood passed, heaven and the earth were created by the God whom they called in their language 'Creator of All Things.' The human race was restored and, in this manner, the Mixtec Kingdom was founded." When fray Gregorio decided to spare the reader from all the "nonsense," he brought the entire sacred realm of male and female deities to an abrupt end. After a great flood had drowned the gods, heaven and earth were created by the one God who founded the new "Mixtec Kingdom" and restored the human race. Perhaps fray Gregorio appended this biblical end and new beginning to the story at the point when he interrupted the narrative. Although floods were a familiar theme in Mesoamerican lore, there is no sign of a great flood in the *Codex Vindobonensis*.[26] Or perhaps it is possible that native storytellers of the late sixteenth century incorporated the arrival of the Christian God into their ancient legend. In any case, García's version of the legend says that "many" gods drowned in the flood. Others survived the tidal wave of the conquest and surfaced in the historical record. Who were these gods, and how were they imagined?

Images and Deities

Spaniards typically used the words *demonios* (demons), *diablos* (devils), and *dioses* (gods) in reference to native numina, often qualifying the last term with the word *false*. Until now, I have used the more neutral and general term *deity*, although this concept is rooted in the Western tradition, too. The Ñudzahui term for a sacred being was *ñuhu*. Sixteenth-century sources speak of specific, named ñuhu rather than ñuhu in the general sense. Usually, people referred to ñuhu in terms of images made from stone, jade, or turquoise.[27] Some of the images were inlaid with gold and precious jewels; most measured between a foot to two feet in length. Spaniards referred to these images as *ídolos*, "idols."

Writings and oral traditions represented the sacred past in terms of the secular order; male and female ñuhu were created in the image of the yuhuitayu. Local beliefs reproduced the coupling of gendered deities in the codices. In Yanhuitlan, a native priest testified in 1545 that the community possessed two male and two female jade deities.[28] Another witness stated that Yanhuitlan had two principal jade images, one in the figure of a man and the other in the figure of a woman.[29] The *relación* of Coatlan states that, in ancient times, after their cacique had learned how to offer sacrifices from other caciques in the Mixteca, the people of Coatlan made offerings to a pair of gendered deities. The male image was described as an "ídolo casado," a "married image." According to the relación, women made offerings to the female image, while men made offerings to the male image. Male captives taken in warfare were sacrificed to the male deity, whereas female slaves were sacrificed to the female deity.[30] Thus, when the priests of Coatlan sacrificed one male slave and one female slave to their deities in 1538, they paid tribute to the primordial couple.[31]

The relación of Ixcatlan, an Ixcatec community located in the northeastern corner of the Mixteca Alta, presents a superb description of gendered deities that resonates with descriptions from the region. In ancient times, the Ixcatecs worshiped two deities: a deity of the men and a deity of the women.[32] The male deity was named Acatl (reed) and the female deity Ocelotl (ocelot). On a nearby hill, the community maintained a temple for these deities, built with stone and covered with a cedar roof. The walls were whitewashed and adorned with finely woven and painted cloth hangings, feathers, and animal skins (especially *tochomite,* or rabbit fur). The sacred images were made of jade and decorated with gold ornaments; they stood just over a foot in height. The deities were bundled in straw, reed mats, or baskets and covered with worked cloth. They were not to be removed from their bundles during the year. For the feast of fire or light, the two images were placed on altars of flowers, upon their respective seats ("icpales"), in plain sight of community members.[33] People danced and sang around the seated figures while burning offerings of copal. On the feast day of the ocelot, dedicated to the female deity, different types of birds were sacrificed to her. On the feast day of the reed, dedicated to the male deity, quetzal feathers were offered to him. The local male ruler who led the ceremony gave gifts of food and cloth to the community. The fourth feast was the principal feast of Ixcatlan, when men and women, dogs, birds, quails, and paper were offered to the deities. Heart sacrifice was performed on a circular stone on top of the temple platform. According to the elders of Ixcatlan, the hearts were given to the images and burned, and the bodies were given to the priests for burial.[34] Thus, the relación of Ixcatlan speaks of a male and a female deity who represented the community and whose names, Acatl and Ocelot, were probably based on the ancient calendar. The community's stepped temple was the deities' palace, their sacred seat of rule. Ceremonies involved the entire community in both general and specialized feasts to the male and female deities.

Nobles from Molcaxtepec, a ñuu in the Mixteca Alta, admitted that their community had at least two images in the 1540s: "quacu sachi" and "quacu ija conhu."[35] These names can be translated as "cuacu 7-Wind" and "cuacu 3-Monkey," based on the days and months of the 260-day ritual calendar. The term *cuacu* (also spelled "quacu") referred to an image in general. It is defined in the *Vocabulario* as "idol of the forests and hills."[36] *Cuacu* precedes the names of many images in the *Relaciones geográficas* of 1579–81, when it was interpreted by Spanish officials as part of the deity's name. For example, in Juxtlahuaca, people adored a stone image named "Cuaqusiqhi," or the cuacu of *siqhi*, the calendrical name 10-Movement.[37] In Acatlan, informants spoke of a figure named "Cuacu sacuaha" (the cuacu of 7-Deer), an image of "emerald" no more than a foot in height.[38]

Each cuacu was bundled in woven cloth or a reed mat. Priests unwrapped the bundles (called *petacas* or *bultos* in Spanish) for sacrifices and feasts. A native priest from Yanhuitlan stated that when he removed Dzahui, the rain deity, from its bundle, he could not put it back until he had made the appropriate offerings.[39] The wrapping and unwrapping of bundles was an extremely important ritual.[40] Bundles in Ixcatlan were opened only on special occasions. Before the conquest, in Ixcatlan and in Tilantongo, the images were kept on a human-made hill (temple), with a palm-covered house at the top.[41] Tecomahuaca had a stone image of "Cihuatecutli," or "woman lord" (in Nahuatl), who resided in a temple on a hilltop.[42] With the destruction of temples and images, the conquest drove many cuacu and bundles into hiding. Priests carried portable images, wrapped in bundles, to hilltops, caves, palaces, and bordering communities. In the early colonial period, the lords of Yanhuitlan were forced to keep images in their houses and in the mountains.[43] In Coatlan, one lord admitted to keeping two "petacas" of images on a nearby hill.[44] The codices abound with images of bundles. Usually, the sacred *bulto* is depicted as a white, spherical bundle, tied at the top with a large knot.[45] Often, the bundle sits inside a temple, at the top of the stairs. It is likely that these bundles contained cuacu or ñuhu. Sometimes, a head or face protrudes from the top of the bundle.[46]

The Inquisition proceedings of the 1540s uncovered four principal ñuhu in Yanhuitlan: "çaagui," defined in the Spanish record as "demonio del agua" [water demon]; "tiçono," defined as "demonio de corazon" [heart demon]; "toyna," defined as "dios de ellos" [their god]; and "xitondoço," defined as "dios de los mercaderes" [god of the merchants].[47] The first ñuhu, Dzahui or Dzavui (literally "rain"), was known throughout the region and is discussed separately below. The second ñuhu, Tidzono, resembles the jade image called "Corazon del Pueblo" [heart of the pueblo] that fray Benito Hernández found in a cave at the summit of a mountain near Achiutla.[48] The image had a snake coiled around it and a carved bird on top. The third ñuhu, Toyna, shares a name with deities in two Mixteca Baja communities that border on the Alta region. Puctla and Mixtepec had merchant deities called "toyna yoco" and "yoco toyna," respectively.[49] In Chila, people spoke of an "emerald god," about the size of a six-year-old child, named "toyna xiñuho," to whom they sacrificed war captives.[50] The fourth ñuhu of Yanhuitlan, Xitondodzo, was associated with trade. In 1545, a native of Molcaxtepec named Xaco, a priest who had served the cacique of Yanhuitlan for eight years, said that Yanhuitlan had four jade deities; two of the images were in the shape of men, and two were in the shape of women.[51] Perhaps these four images were the same as those listed above. Xaco noted that there were figures of other deities, too. Indeed, the four primary images were merely the tip of the iceberg. Domingo, another native of

Molcaxtepec, said that the governor of Yanhuitlan had a subterranean cave in a certain part of his palace complex where he kept many images, including one called "que-
quiyo" (9-Reed), which belonged to the community.[52] A noble of Etlatongo named
Diego testified that Yanhuitlan had two principal images that were made of jade. The
first was the figure of a man, named "syquyui" (10- or 13-Crocodile), and the other was
the figure of a woman named "xiu" (probably 10- or 13-Serpent).[53] Diego said that the
people of Yanhuitlan also kept many images on a hill by the road to Coixtlahuaca, near
Soyaltepec. Don Juan, the cacique of Nochixtlan, claimed that the cacique of Yanhuitlan, don Domingo, had an unbaptized priest in his house who guarded twenty bundles
(*envoltorios*) of images. Each of the twenty images had its own name, such as "Qua-
quxio" and "Quaquxique," or the cuacu Xio and the cuacu Xique.[54] People referred
to and treated the cuacu as a ñuhu. Priests sheltered the many cuacu, carried them on
their back, conversed with them, placed offerings at their feet, and dressed and anointed
them. People gave food and other tribute items to the images as if they were living yya
and yya dzehe. Priests instructed people to provide sacrificial items on a regular basis,
including quails, doves, cloth, precious stones, feathers, and copal incense.[55] These
were the same types of prestige goods that lords received in tribute.

The inquisitorial investigation in Coatlan provides intimate glimpses of how the
lords communicated with their deities. In 1546, the lords stated that a priest had come
to Coatlan about eight years ago. He demanded that they hand over their "idols."
In response, three lords and four *tequitlatos* (tribute collectors) secretly assembled the
images and separated the most esteemed and noble ones ("los mayores y principales")
from the lesser ones ("los menores"). They gave the least favored images to the Christian priest while keeping the most precious ones for themselves. Then they made a
speech before the remaining images, the "principales," or important ones. One of the
lords of Coatlan, don Alonso, recalled what they had said to the images on that sad day
in 1538: "We reasoned with them, telling them how the priest had come for them and
that in order to meet his demands, we gave him the lesser ones, which were separated
from the rest. The remaining ones will be hidden and guarded where nobody can find
them. And we promised that we would keep them as gods, like before, and that they
should not be angry, and that they should remain calm."[56] The cacique, don Hernando,
remembered the speech in similar terms. He said to the images: "You already know
how the Christians have come asking around for you and looking to burn you, and
that we would be mistreated and killed if we did not give them anything. So it is better that we gave the priest those lesser ones."[57] He pleaded with them not to be angry.
Once the priest had gone from Coatlan, they honored the remaining images by sacrificing a male and a female slave before them, offering the victims' hearts to them as a
propitiatory gesture. In don Hernando's words, a priest performed the sacrifices "so
that they [the images] would not be angry." The third brother, don Juan, recalled how
they had confessed to the images their fear of the Christians and how they had reaffirmed their resolve to worship and take care of them as before. The three lords of
Coatlan conversed with their deities in very respectful terms. Some of the deities were
ranked higher than others, reflecting the society in which they were adored. The least
noble of the images were sacrificed to the Christian priest for the greater good of the

most esteemed. The images possessed human emotions of anger and passion, but they were capable of listening to reason, too. They expected their guardians, the three lords and four tribute collectors, to look after their interests.

Funerary practices suggest how yya and yya dzehe were considered sacred or how they attained sacred status upon death.[58] Deceased lords were bound in bundles of cloth or reed mats, in a seated position; a jade or turquoise mask, fashioned after the deceased person's face, was secured to the outside of the bundle. Upon the death of doña Ana, the wife of don Francisco (the *cacica* and cacique of Yanhuitlan), native priests cut some of her hair and tied it to a mask of turquoise.[59] They put a precious stone in her mouth, bundled her, attached the turquoise mask to the bundle, feasted in her presence, and made the same types of sacrifices before her as they made before the sacred images.[60] Eventually, they buried or stored the bundle. Some people claimed that don Francisco kept bundles and images of his wife, mother, and father in a subterranean cave inside his large household complex.[61]

Fray Benito Hernández, the author of the *Doctrina en lengua misteca*, encountered a cache of masked funerary bundles in the mid-sixteenth century.[62] According to Burgoa, fray Benito detected a large cave at the summit of a mountain called "Cumbre de Cervatillos" (Young Deer Summit), near Achiutla. Inside the cave he found many richly dressed, bundled corpses propped up in a row on stone benches along the walls. The bundles were adorned with gold, jewels, and stringed beads. As he came closer to the bundles, Hernández claimed that he recognized some of the corpses as local caciques who had recently died, including some whom he had considered "good Christians." Farther inside the cave he found niches in the walls, images and figures of precious metal, carved wooden objects, and cloth *lienzos* with pictorial writing.

People worshiped yya ancestors as ñuhu. The codices illustrate the descent of all yya and yya dzehe from sacred ancestors.[63] Some figures in the codices "impersonate" certain ñuhu by adopting their attire or appearance. Those who arrayed themselves in the likeness of a particular ñuhu may have wielded powers associated with that sacred force.[64] Throughout Mesoamerica, certain ancient ñuhu represented specific forces of nature, such as rain, wind, and the sun. But these forces were also imagined in terms of men and women with distinctive features, dress, calendrical names, origins, and personal histories. In the codices, local variants or prototypes of Quetzalcoatl, Xipe Totec, and Cihuacoatl were known as 9-Wind, 7-Rain, and 9-Grass, respectively.[65] Most deities possessed the same type of calendrical name as any Ñudzahui noble or commoner before the complete adoption of Christian names (see chapter 5, section on naming patterns).

Multiple ñuhu reflected the local nature of Mesoamerican religion and the inherent autonomy of sociopolitical organization.[66] Each corporate entity, and each household for that matter, had its own sacred ancestors. Corporate, ethnic deities are the most prominent cuacu or ñuhu in the record. Some local images commanded devotion across the Mixteca. Burgoa reported that people traveled from afar to honor a deity in Achiutla, which he called an "oracle."[67] In the *Relaciones geográficas*, people also associated certain deities with social or occupational groups; for example, warriors were dedicated to the sun, while tillers of the soil devoted themselves to the rain deity. In Juxtlahuaca, ancient images were dedicated to "hunters, merchants, farmers, and other occupations."[68] Certain primordial pan-Mesoamerican deities were known throughout the region. The Mexica deity Huitzilopochtli does not appear in the Mixteca, however. Central Mexican deities were reinterpreted or had a minimal impact on local ideologies.

One of the most powerful forces in the Mixteca, the deity of rain and water, commanded respect throughout Mesoamerica. This ñuhu was known as Dzahui in the Mixteca. Naturally, the *tay ñudzahui*—the "people from the rain place" or "the people from the land of Dzahui"—had much to say about Dzahui.

The Rain Deity

The lone entry for the Spanish term *ídolo* in the *Vocabulario* of 1593 is "dzavui."[69] But this was not the word for an "idol." Rather, Dzavui or Dzahui was the first image that came to mind in response to the Spanish category. Whereas *cuacu* was the general term for a physical image or embodiment of the deity, Dzahui was the name of a particular cuacu, a powerful sacred force associated with thunder and lightning and a central figure in the codices. In the 1540s, the first and foremost of four deities in Yanhuitlan was "çaagui," defined by the inquisitors as "demonio del agua" [water demon]. In reference to the rain god's provision of sustenance, some Spaniards in Yanhuitlan referred to Dzahui as "diablo del agua y del pan" [devil of water and bread]. Dzahui was comparable in many respects to the Nahua Tlaloc, the Zapotec Cosijo, and the Maya Chac. The pan-Mesoamerican rain deity was so important in central Mexico that the Mexica elevated Tlaloc to an esteemed position alongside their ethnic deity, Huitzilopochtli.[70]

People continued to make offerings to Dzahui after the conquest. Men and women from the Mixteca Alta stated that when it had not rained for a long time, they invoked Dzahui, performed sacrifices, and drank pulque. Don Juan, the governor of Etlatongo, said that they made offerings when there was no water, when there was illness, and when they harvested the fields.[71] Many witnesses who testified in the inquisitorial trials of the 1540s reiterated this statement. Even friars recognized the relationship between sacrifice and drought.[72] In Topiltepec, when it had not rained for many weeks, the lords assembled people from the surrounding communities for a sacrificial feast in honor of Dzahui. Sacrifices were performed in a cave on a hill near Etlatongo because it had not rained in a long time. In times of drought or sickness, priests sacrificed slaves, feathers, jade, and cloth on a hill near Jaltepec. When it had not rained for a long time, the priests of Yanhuitlan brought charcoal from a nearby mountain, which they used to make a black dye or ink. A lord of Yanhuitlan, don Francisco, stripped and painted himself with the charcoal ink, let blood from his ears, burned copal, and sacrificed quail to Dzahui.[73] By painting his body with black ink, he impersonated Dzahui and his blackened priests. People gathered in and around the palace to invoke Dzahui. Don Domingo, the governor of Chachuapa, testified that the lords of Yanhuitlan used to assemble in the palace, while the commoners gathered outside, to summon and make sacrifices to Dzahui.[74] Ritual drinking was an important means of summoning the rain deity.

The Inquisition trial from Yanhuitlan abounds with references to Dzahui, including the rare testimony of a native priest who had dedicated his life to serving the rain deity. One of the four priests of Yanhuitlan who appeared in the trial, named Caxaa (1-Eagle), admitted to having guarded the image of "zaguii."[75] An unbaptized native noble from Molcaxtepec, Caxaa testified in 1545 that he had performed feasts, sacrifices, and ceremonies throughout the year, according to the customs of his ancestors. After serving as an apprentice, he took charge of the rain deity as a young adult, when another priest who had held that position died. In response to the question of how he had made sacrifices to the rain deity, he stated that in times of drought he would take out his stone image and place it before him with much reverence. He would squat before the image, sitting on his heels, and offer it copal incense and feathers. He talked to Dzahui for a while, informing the image that the commoners were suffering from hunger and drought. He promised Dzahui that he would sacrifice doves, quail, dogs, parrots, and a person, conforming to his wishes. He filled a small bowl (*jícara*) with water and sprinkled it on the offerings. Then he took a rubber ball and bounced it on the ground. He burned the ball and smeared the image with the resin. He relied on the lords of Yanhuitlan to provide the offerings that he made to Dzahui, including a child who was to be sacrificed. Asked by the inquisitor how he sacrificed the child, he replied that he went to the highest hill with the image and the child. He set the image down in a suitable place, burned offerings of copal smoke before it, and spoke to Dzahui. Then he placed the child before it and performed the sacrifice, tearing out his heart and placing it at the base of the image. He remained on the hill for two days or more, before burning the heart and placing the ashes with the other offerings. He made a bundle of all the offerings for the deity. The priest would not wrap the stone image in its bundle until it had received all the offerings.

The priest named Caxaa confirmed that priests sacrificed only children or young people to the rain deity. This was the reason why there were always children reserved ("en deposito") for sacrifices, he confessed. Caxaa stated that he had killed four children in the service of Dzahui. A native of Molcaxtepec named Xaco (7-Rain), a priest who had served don Domingo for eight years, also admitted to sacrificing children to the rain deity.[76] He testified that about six years earlier, when it had not rained for a long time, don Domingo ordered him to sacrifice a child. Juan, a former slave of don Francisco, testified that five boys were sacrificed to Dzahui on a hill called Yucumaño, four years prior to the trial.[77] The slave claimed that he had witnessed the ceremony. Of the four slave boys who were sacrificed, Juan testified, two were very young and two more were slightly older, because he remembered that they could walk well. The fifth alleged victim was a young man who had served in the church. Juan also stated that about six years earlier, when it had not rained for a long time, don Domingo ordered a priest named Xixa (10-Eagle) to sacrifice a child.

It is possible that the witnesses exaggerated or even fabricated these sacrifices. On the other hand, the priests Caxaa and Xaco had little to gain from detailing their own roles in these activities. Their testimony did not exonerate them from punishment. Later, they were arrested and placed in chains. Moreover, the testimonies reveal patterns of ritual behavior observable in other parts of Mesoamerica, particularly in central Mexico. The *Primeros memoriales*, a sixteenth-century Nahuatl manuscript from central Mexico, also states that children were sacrificed to Tlaloc and that Tlaloc or Tlaloque (plural) were supplicated in times of drought by means of blood sacrifice. Tlaloc was associated with mountaintops and caves, and he was smeared with burned rubber by Nahua priests.[78] Likewise, the *Codex Magliabechiano* associates child sacrifice with Tlaloc and other feasts connected with the rain deity.[79] Nahua informants of the *Florentine Codex* described Tlaloc as a venerable deity whose face was covered with the soot of incense and painted with liquid rubber.[80]

A witness in the Yanhuitlan trial associated the so-called *voladores* ("fliers") with the rain deity. The ceremony of the voladores featured men who "flew" through the air by swinging themselves around tall, upright poles planted in the ground.[81] The vicar of Apoala, Juanés de Angulo, found evidence of this practice on a hill near Chachuapa called Quiavi, where poles ("palos voladeros") were planted in the ground. The vicar was informed that a priest would hang and swing from the poles while appealing to the rain deity for water. The *Vocabulario* refers to this act with the verb *yosicoyahandi*, "to fly as an eagle."[82] Beneath the poles, the vicar found evidence of sacrificial offerings.[83]

Nahua participants in the *Florentine Codex* project called Tlaloc "the provider." He caused things to grow, including maize, but he also made thunderbolts and caused people to drown. The relación of Puctla called "zahuy" a deity of the farmers.[84] According-ing to Burgoa, a friar named Gerónimo de Abrego realized that people continued to appeal to Dzahui for sufficient rains and harvests. Abrego had heard about a large cave in the Yanhuitlan area that was dedicated to the rain deity.[85] One day the friar surrep-titiously followed a native priest to this cave, which was situated high in the mountains. Inside the cave was a large area where incense had been burned and animals had been sacrificed. In one corner, the priest saw a pyramidal column of ice that glistened like crystal, sculpted in the form of a statue, and many other smaller ice statues. The angry priest broke up the large ice statue and began to drink the melting image before the native priest and his accomplices in order to "show them how foolish they were."

In the mid-sixteenth century, a Mixtec artist sketched the rain deity on a paper associated with the *Codex Yanhuitlan* (see fig. 8.5). The sketch was furnished in 1707 by the cacique of Yanhuitlan, don Agustín Pimentel y Guzmán. The artist drew another standing figure who faces Dzahui, but the page is torn, and only the feet and garment of the personage remain. Judging by the hem of a *huipil*, the missing figure is that of a woman. Perhaps this missing personage was a female version of Dzahui, or a local version of Chalchiuhtlicue, a deity who was often paired with Tlaloc and associated with the Tlaloque in Nahua lore.[86] Naturally, Dzahui was paired with another ñuhu. Today, Dzahui continues to reign over the Mixteca.[87]

Priests and Diviners

Native priests were nobles whose *tniño*, or responsibility, was to shelter, honor, and feed the deities. Priests organized feasts, collected tribute in sacrificial items and prestige goods, and performed certain rites for the images. Ñudzahui terminology for priests, called *papas* in Spanish, is unclear because native-language archival records do not refer to these people, and there are no sources for the Mixteca comparable to the *Florentine Codex* or works of a similar nature. The term in the *Vocabulario* of 1593 given for an "ancient high priest" [sacerdote mayor de los indios en su gentilidad] was *nahaniñe*, which I interpret as "person of the palace."[88] A minor priest ("sacerdote menor") was

FIGURE 8.5. A sketch of the rain deity Dzahui and the remnants of a female personage (left), drawn in Yanhuitlan around the mid-sixteenth century. AGN-V, 272:3, f. 505.

known as a *tay saque,* which may be related to the term for tribute collector, *tay saque ñehe,* although the meaning of *saque* is unclear.[89] The fact that these two positions shared a common name suggests that priests were responsible for collecting tribute on behalf of the images they guarded, including sacrificial items. The association is especially clear in Coatlan, where four tequitlatos, or tribute collectors, guarded the deities and participated in sacrifices in the late 1530s. The relación of Tilantongo refers to priests called "tay saqui" who guarded the images and made sacrifices to them.[90] Burgoa described how native priests at the temple of Achiutla learned to practice devotion through fasting, abstinence, cleaning the temple and its possessions, and sweeping the floors. He also noted that apprentices learned how to use the calendrical portions of codices to plan ritual ceremonies and were schooled in the histories of their ancestors.[91] Witnesses in the Coatlan Inquisition trial made a direct association between priests, codices, and ceremonies. A noble from Tututepec named Diego de Albino said that people from Coatlan were notorious for continuing traditional practices. According to Albino, eight months earlier, in 1544, the cacique of Coatlan received emissaries from Yanhuitlan, Xaltepec, Tilantongo, Elotepec, Teosapotlan, Tiltepec, and many other places. The gathering was intended to determine how they should respond to Christianity. The cacique, don Hernando, sponsored a grand feast in which they became drunk, painted codices, and performed autosacrifice, among other practices.[92] By these accounts, painting was a sacred activity performed by nobles and priests.

   The Inquisition trial from Yanhuitlan provides the most information on Mixtec priests.[93] The unbaptized priest from Yanhuitlan named Caxaa testified in 1545 that he had guarded the images of the community for several years.[94] Caxaa performed this noble task with three other priests, named Cagua (1-Dog), Cahuizo (1-Ocelot), and Caguiyo (1-Reed). Each of the four priests, who were named after the first day of a calendrical cycle, was in charge of serving a particular deity. Caxaa specialized in the care of the rain deity, performing feasts, sacrifices, and ceremonies throughout the year. He recalled that when he was a child, he was ordered by the lords of Yanhuitlan to live with priests who were in charge of the images of the community. Until 1545, he lived with other priests in a large house in Tamaxcaltepec; he had neither seen Christians nor stepped inside a church. When he began to take care of the rain deity, he was forced to leave his pregnant wife, he said.

   Lords relied on priests to ensure that the images were kept and honored properly. In a community near Yanhuitlan called Cuzcatepec, there was an unbaptized elder priest named Caco (1-Rain) who performed sacrifices and conversed with deities. There was another elder priest in Xicotlan named Xiquibe (10- or 13-Crocodile) who was in charge of guarding images. Many priests worked and lived in a lord's palace. In the 1540s, two priests (Coquaa, or "3-Deer," and Cocuyui, or "3-Crocodile") guarded images in the palace of the governor, don Francisco. Xaco, a priest who had served don Domingo for eight years, said that he had met several other priests while living in the aniñe, including Xixa, Nahuaco, Xintla, and Quihuizo.[95] According to Xaco, don Francisco ordered the priests to ask the deities for advice on certain matters, such as when they should dance and whether they should dance in the church or in the palace.[96] A priest's duty was a serious, sacred charge; one priest of Yanhuitlan who had improperly attended to an image was allegedly put to death by the lords.[97] According to many of the relaciones, priests in the Mixteca fasted for days before a feast, smoking tobacco in pipes called *sane* and chewing tobacco. During the fast, priests abstained from sexual pleasures and pulque. The violation of this code of conduct was supposedly punishable by death in Mixtepec.[98] On the night before a feast, the priests let blood from their ears and tongues with slivers of obsidian and performed various sacrifices.[99] For this reason, all the native priests from Yanhuitlan had scarred ears and tongues.[100] Priests in Tilantongo guarded images in the temple and made offerings of copal, birds, dogs, turkeys, deer, and human hearts.[101] There were four principal priests who determined the day of sacrificial offerings, the amount of feathers and cloth, and other important matters.

   Women may not have performed the same roles as male priests, but they did engage in similar activities. Don Francisco, a noble from Etlatongo, testified in 1545 that don Francisco's wife, named Cocuañe (2-Grass), had performed many sacrifices. A sister of don Juan, the governor of Yanhuitlan, Cocuañe was never baptized and had never set foot inside a church. After don Francisco was imprisoned for his alleged crimes against the church, Cocuañe performed sacrifices each night for her spouse. This accusation was made by Quxi of Molcaxtepec, who had served as a slave in the household of don Francisco and Cocuañe for many years. Quxi said that don Francisco's wife made many sacrifices of doves, quail, dogs, and copal and invoked the deities when her husband was imprisoned. Like many lords, Cocuañe offered sacrifices directly to the deities. When Cocuañe died, don Francisco took it upon himself to perform the proper ceremonies and sacrifices at her funeral.[102]

The trial from Yanhuitlan introduced a woman diviner named Xigua (10-Dog). Catalina, a slave of don Francisco, testified that Xigua had lived in don Francisco's house, where she performed divination by hand casting to predict the future and to foretell death.[103] When the bishop and other ecclesiastical officials entered the community, she cast beans to determine whether the images would be safe. Xigua also cast beans to warn the lords when Spaniards were approaching the community and to predict when the Christians would leave Yanhuitlan forever. In one of her visions, when she saw a friar coming to the community, she advised the lords to set an image along the road where she knew he would stop to sleep, so that he might never awake. The proceedings in Coatlan also refer to a woman prognosticator. One witness said that a woman advised the lords when and what to sacrifice to the deities.[104] References to women's participation in sacred ceremonies and magic in the early colonial record resonate with depictions of women in the preconquest codices. The codices show women in various types of ceremonial activities, holding vessels of ceremonial drinks (pulque and cacao), staffs (perhaps of religious or political office), sacred bundles, sacrificial birds, finely carved bones, torches, precious feathers, weaving instruments, stone figures, incense burners, pipes, and tobacco. These postures and gestures suggest an active role for Mixtec women in sacred ceremonies.

Priests who served local deities in temples and palaces of the community tend to dominate the discourse on local religion in the Mixteca. I suspect that the lone example of Xigua in the Inquisition trial does not represent the full range of specialists or diviners who possessed sacred knowledge and power. The *Vocabulario* contains many terms for these men and women, whom the Spaniards called *hechizeros* (wizards) and *bruxos* (witches). Most of the native-language terminology is unattested in the native-language record. But references to the Mesoamerican belief in *nahualism*, the ability of a person to transform into an animal, among other things, appear in the *Vocabulario*.[105] Under the entry "witch who deceives, who is said to turn into a lion," the responses included "tai ñaha quete" [one who is a person-animal], "tay sanduvui" [one who goes along at night], and "tai sandacu" [one who imitates or descends].[106] These terms correspond with another entry, "sorcerer, deceiver who is said to turn into a tiger."[107] An interesting term for the latter entry is "tay yondaa tnoo," or "one who applies the black." Priests often appear in the codices with blackened faces and bodies. Another "sorcerer" of sorts, "a deceiver who flies through the air," is the "yahui" or "yaha yahui."[108] As John Pohl has observed, *yahui* figures play a prominent role in the Mixtec codices.[109] The two sons of the legendary 1-Deer couple who became the first priests possessed the powers of yahui. They flew like eagles (*yaha*) and could fly through objects. Under the term *hechizero* (sorcerer), the *Vocabulario* contains two descriptive references to these beings with supernatural abilities: "tay yoquidza siyo yuu," or literally "one who passes through stone"; and "tay yodzacuico siyo yuu," or "one who flies through stone."[110] The fact that yahui are usually depicted holding flint knives and human hearts indicates their ability to cut through objects and their association with sacrifice.

The terminology for these "diviners" and "sorcerers" who possessed special powers, and the prominent roles assigned to many of them in the codices, indicate that conventional European distinctions between priests and sorcerers, religion and magic, did not apply in the Mixteca.

Feasts and Offerings

The *Vocabulario* refers to the act of committing idolatries as *yoquidzahuico*, "to make feasts," and *yoquidza ñuhu yuu quacu*, "to make stone images."[111] The term for feast was *huico*, and an "idolater" in the *Vocabulario* was simply a *tay yoquidzahuico*, or a "person who makes feasts." The verb "to make feasts" (*quidzahuico*) was also used for the Spanish *sacrificar*, "to sacrifice."[112] Those who contributed to the *Vocabulario* associated feasts with sacrifices because ritual celebrations always involved offerings of food and drink to the ñuhu. Priests also offered cloth, feathers, paper, birds, incense, precious stones, jade, and slaves.

Ritual feeding and drinking reproduced social relations at the sacred level. Priests were obligated to feed and shelter the images, relying on everyone to contribute to this tniño, or obligation. One priest from Yanhuitlan said that certain households were designated to pay tribute for sacrifices to certain deities. The governor of Chachuapa testified that the lords of Yanhuitlan often requested sacrificial birds from his community. Sacrificial goods of all kinds, including slaves, were also acquired in the marketplace.[113] According to the governor's testimony, the market of Suchitepec sold copal incense, feathers, and other sacrificial items "just as before, when there were no Spaniards in the land."[114] Witnesses testified that the lords of Yanhuitlan also used tobacco and hallucinogenic mushrooms to hear the images speak. At the age of fourteen, the lord of Yanhuitlan, don Francisco, ate mushrooms for the first time.[115] The ritual ingestion of pulque and mushrooms is illustrated in the *Codex Vindobonensis*.[116]

According to a noble from Molcaxtepec, there were four annual feasts celebrated in and around Yanhuitlan in the 1540s: Xicuiyo (10-Reed); Xiyo (10- or 11-Serpent); Cachi (7-Wind); and Xacuv (7-Movement).[117] These four named deities play key roles in foundation rituals in the *Codex Vindobonensis* and *Zouche-Nuttall*, attesting to the relationship between named deities and feast dates.[118] The sacrificial feast commemorated an ancestor's birthday, recalled by his or her name.[119] The image of the yya or yya dzehe was revealed and "reborn" on that day.[120] Both ancient ñuhu and recently deceased lords were honored with feasts. In the 1540s, don Domingo paid tribute to his deceased uncle, the former *yya toniñe* of Yanhuitlan, with annual feasts and sacrifices.[121] There were also feasts that were apparently unrelated to named deities. For example, a slave of don Juan, the governor of Yanhuitlan, said that each year during the maize harvest there was a feast called "huico tuta," when the priests unwrapped their bundles, took out the images, and made offerings to them.[122] The witness added that this festival coincided with the Christian feast of All Souls' Day.

Priests made their sacrifices on hills and temple platforms and inside caves and palaces. Temples may have mimicked hills, but the sacred hill, or *yucu*, still dominated the landscape. As openings into hills and the source of springs, caves (*cahua*) were important sites of sacred activity. In the 1530s friars found a cave near the market of Suchitepec that was filled with sacrificial offerings. In another cave on a hill near Etlatongo, slaves were allegedly sacrificed in the midst of a drought. Consequently, many caves in the Yanhuitlan area, near Tlataloltepec, Chachuapa, and Acamulco, contained evidence of sacrifices in the 1540s.[123] In the mid-sixteenth century, fray Benito Hernández found several caves on hilltops where priests continued to make offerings, including two near Chicahuastla and Achiutla.[124] The palace was yet another sacrificial site. Don Francisco, his wife, Cocuañe, and two priests allegedly sacrificed doves, quail, and dogs in the aniñe.[125]

A human heart was the most precious gift a priest could offer to a deity. The act of heart sacrifice was mentioned by too many native witnesses in the Inquisition trials of the 1540s, including priests and lords who jeopardized themselves by admitting to their own roles in the act, to have been fabricated. Sacrifices were usually performed, at least in the early colonial period, by a solitary priest or group of priests on a hilltop, in a cave, or in the middle of a cultivated field.[126] According to witnesses' descriptions, the act of human sacrifice was normally performed by four or five priests who held the arms, legs, and head of the victim. One of them used an obsidian blade to slice open the chest from the left side, reached into the open wound, and quickly tore out the heart. After removing the heart, the priests usually burned it before the image and buried the body. Slaves taken as captives in warfare or purchased in the marketplace were the most likely donors of the precious gift. One native witness said that don Domingo, the lord of Yanhuitlan, had a native woman named Xiyo who bought slaves for sacrifice in the market. In Coatlan, the cacique don Hernando admitted that he had bought a male and a female slave from Tetiquipac in 1538 for seven gold pesos apiece. Their hearts were sacrificed to the ñuhu of the community, he confessed.[127] In 1545, a slave woman named Catalina, who had served for ten years in the house of don Francisco of Yanhuitlan, testified that priests sacrificed her seven-year-old sister, named Xaxa (7-Eagle), on a mountain called "Yucumayu." She was sacrificed when don Francisco had fallen ill two years earlier. Catalina claimed that they killed another slave who was purchased in the market.[128]

Sacred rituals reflected certain inequalities in the social order. Yya and *toho* made offerings on behalf of everyone except slaves. As outsiders who were usually captured in warfare, slaves were a vulnerable group. The testimony of slaves reveals a subordinate group's perspective on practices that undermines the notion of a "collective mentality."[129] The slave woman from Etlatongo named Catalina, who served in the household of a male lord from Yanhuitlan and whose seven-year-old sister was sacrificed for the health of her lord, fled from don Francisco's house because she thought that she was next in line. Spaniards sought out this subordinate group to testify against their former lords. Judging by their statements, many slaves failed to see the sacred qualities of human sacrifice. A slave named Juan suggested that sacrifices were at times little more than vengeful acts. Juan testified that don Francisco ordered the immediate sacrifice of a slave who was having sex with a woman of his household.[130] When the slave found out his fate and tried to escape, he was caught on the road and sacrificed by a priest. In a similar fit of vengeance, don Juan allegedly sacrificed a girl who had killed his female African slave in a dispute.[131] The latter example hints at the complexity of subaltern relations in colonial society, even by the early 1540s.

In contrast to the slaves' point of view, lords looked upon human sacrifice as a remedy for disease and hunger. Don Hernando of Coatlan stated that when he was sick, the entire community made offerings for him. Later, when there was sickness in Coatlan, when the "commoners' children were dying," he made a "very solemn sacrifice" for everyone's health.[132] To don Hernando, sacrifices were reciprocal gestures. Similarly, don Alonso testified that in late 1544, when an epidemic disease raged through the community, he instructed a priest named Canautli to make offerings on behalf of the commoners.[133] Sickness caused constant concern and fear in native communities from the 1530s onward. The propitiatory act of sacrifice must have peaked by the time of the trials in Yanhuitlan and Coatlan, when another major epidemic struck in the 1540s.

People from Coatlan stated in 1580 that they had not known the custom of sacrifice in ancient times until one of their caciques met with other caciques in the Mixteca, who taught him sacrificial rituals. Perhaps the oral tradition simplified a complex history of cultural influence in this border area.[134] In any case, people in Coatlan allegedly performed sacrifices in times of sickness and drought, when they planted and harvested maize, and to sanctify important events such as weddings and funerals. In February 1543, don Juan of Coatlan married his daughter to the cacique of Suchitepec, who brought a slave to Coatlan to be sacrificed.[135] Witnesses also alleged that when don Hernando's daughter died, the priests of Coatlan killed two female slaves by burying them alive with her in a cave.[136] The priests of Coatlan also performed propitiatory sacrifices. When they were forced to give some of their images to a priest, the lords of Coatlan appeased the remaining deities by speaking to them and sacrificing a male and a female slave before them.[137] They laid the hearts of the victims before the images and buried the slaves' bodies on a hill near Coatlan. In one case, an image was literally fed a human heart. Two Spanish priests and two native nobles encountered a cave near the road to Tututepec, in which they found an image with a human heart lodged in its mouth. The witnesses testified that the image itself was covered in blood and that they found more than a dozen human skulls, about fifty small containers, and numerous other offerings in the cave.[138] The lords of Coatlan also made offerings to appease Spaniards or the Spanish deity. One time, when news spread that a vicar was approaching the community, priests and commoners performed autosacrifice at different points along the road, so that he would not be angry and vindictive when he reached Coatlan.[139]

In the Yanhuitlan trial, one native priest and three native witnesses claimed that the priests and lords of Yanhuitlan ate the body parts of sacrificial victims.[140] These witnesses did not describe the act in any detail. Surprisingly, the inquisitors did not ask them to elaborate on their claims. In contrast to the terse remarks of these few witnesses, some Spaniards imagined the most diabolical scenes. Luis Delgado testified that he saw one feast in an *estancia* of Yanhuitlan in which people were boiling about thirteen or fourteen pots of blood that contained the body parts of victims.[141] One of the pots, he claimed, contained fresh blood, which was only three or four days old, and the head of a recently murdered Spaniard. Delgado swore that they were cooking human flesh for their feast. No other witness corroborated this wild tale. Clearly, he could not have known that the blood was "fresh" and that the head belonged to a Spaniard. The vision of a Spanish head bobbing in a boiling pot of blood appears to be a paranoid fantasy. In this case, Spaniards were the only witnesses who claimed that victims had been eaten. Bartolomé Sánchez, a vicar of Coatlan who admitted to his fear of being murdered, claimed that the people of Coatlan once killed a Spaniard, cooked his flesh, and ate it with hot chilis.[142]

It is impossible to estimate the frequency of human sacrifice; native priests spoke about it as an event that occurred on special occasions or in times of crisis, perhaps a few times a year.[143] In the codices, the act of human sacrifice appears only rarely, although some scenes depict human hearts without illustrating the act itself.[144] A priest from Coscatepec named Caco, who was about sixty years old, confessed that he had sacrificed twelve children and two adults in his lifetime.[145] Preconquest-style codices and postconquest testimonies illustrate that birds, incense, and animals were more typical offerings.[146] Another form of offering was autosacrifice; lords, commoners, and especially priests let blood from their ears and tongues with sharp bones or spines. A noble from Tututepec testified that he had seen the nobles of Coatlan make sacrifices from their ears, tongues, and private parts ("miembros y partes vergonçosos").[147] Ear perforation was the most common form of autosacrifice.[148] Often, people spattered blood onto native paper, straw, or reeds. Sometimes, they performed these acts on sacred ground. Fray Bernardo de Santa María said that he had seen people letting blood from their ears in the patio of the church on the site of the old temple in Yanhuitlan. He reprimanded them in sermons and punished them with lashes.[149]

As indigenous practices continued in the early colonial period, vigilant Christians sought to extirpate "idolatries." Many Spanish witnesses related how they had forced their way into houses and confronted men and women in the act of idolatry. Luis Delgado, a Spanish resident of Mexico City and Tilantongo, the lieutenant of the *corregidor,* was especially zealous. Delgado recalled the time when he broke up a feast by riding into town, firing his musket, and scaring everyone off. He found several empty cooking pots; convinced that they used the large pots to cook human flesh, he concluded that they had eaten all the flesh before he arrived.[150] Another time, Delgado and a friar entered don Domingo's house when he was not home, despite his wife's loud protest. They stormed into the house and found "a *cu* [stepped structure] that was about a foot high, made of the seeds that they eat in this land."[151] On top of this miniature temple was a sacrificed bird and a serpent made of feathers. The friar confiscated the tiny temple and used it in a sermon to demonstrate the "childishness" of native beliefs. It was a fitting trophy for the "spiritual conquest" of Yanhuitlan.

The Spiritual Conquest

In 1529, the Dominicans officially founded a convento in Yanhuitlan, the first community in the Mixteca Alta to receive the faith. They left the establishment temporarily, refounded it in 1535, and then abandoned it again just before the beginning of the inquisitorial proceedings in 1544.[152] By the time of the trial, most Spanish witnesses agreed that the faith had failed to take root in the region. Despite repeated attempts to preach and to punish idolatries, they lamented, people persisted in their ancient ways.

In 1544, Licenciado don Francisco Tello de Sandoval, a member of the Council of the Indies, who had served as inquisitor for the archbishop of Toledo, assumed the position of apostolic inquisitor of New Spain. He relieved fray Juan de Zumárraga, the first bishop of Mexico City, who had been criticized in Spain for his handling of native idolatries, from his inquisitorial duties in Mexico.[153] It was Zumárraga who had condemned don Carlos Mendoza Ometochtzin, cacique of Texcoco, to a sentence of death in 1539. Even though the accusations against don Carlos did not involve allegations of human sacrifice, don Carlos was hanged and burned at the stake for his open defiance of church and crown. In December 1544, Tello de Sandoval ordered the arrest of don Francisco and don Domingo of Yanhuitlan, while Bachiller Pedro Gómez de Maraver, dean of the cathedral of Oaxaca and visitor of the bishopric of Oaxaca, continued gathering evidence against the lords.[154] The resulting investigation involved many Spaniards and Mixtec nobles from the area, including indigenous slaves and priests who had served in the houses of the lords of Yanhuitlan.

A Spaniard named Martín de la Mesquitta, the corregidor of Texupa and a resident of Antequera (Oaxaca City), provided the first testimony against don Francisco, the native governor of Yanhuitlan. Mesquitta went to Yanhuitlan to arrest the son of don Francisco for his alleged participation in a violent confrontation with officials from Etlatongo. When Mesquitta arrived at don Francisco's house, a man ran out carrying a cloak filled with bloody feathers, straws, and reeds. He peered into the interior of the house and noticed some small images in a dark chamber, several bundles, and stacks of *cajetillas,* or small bowls for food and offerings.[155] This was the first of many accusations against don Francisco and the nobles of Yanhuitlan.

The first round of testimony seemed to confirm the fears of the Dominicans that preconquest beliefs thrived in the most populous and prosperous area of the Mixteca, at the very center of their regional operations. The arrival of Christianity seventeen years earlier, in 1527, had made little impression on these people. Fray Martín de Santo Domingo, a resident of Coixtlahuaca, confessed that the faith was unknown in communities around Yanhuitlan. In Molcaxtepec, the church was a straw shed that could accommodate no more than ten people. When saying mass in the shed, fray Martín complained that he could barely elevate the host during the Eucharistic celebration without scraping it on the ceiling.[156] Ironically, the richest community in the Mixteca had the worst church building, images, and adornments and the worst reputation for continued idolatries and drunken feasts. The friars' exaggerated claims that other communities in the Mixteca had embraced the Christian faith heightened the tragedy of Yanhuitlan. In reality, the church suffered from an utter lack of resources in this densely populated, mountainous region. The Spanish presence consisted of a small group of friars and a handful of administrators who were scattered in fewer than a dozen cabeceras. In the many dispersed ñuu around Yanhuitlan, there were no churches or resident priests by the 1540s. Language barriers had forced the friars to rely on a few bilingual boys to translate their sermons into the native language. Many native priests confessed that they had never seen a friar before the trial. Despite acknowledging these limitations, the friars laid the blame squarely on the shoulders of the native lords and the Spanish *encomendero* of Yanhuitlan. The Inquisition trial provided a suitable stage for this Dominican drama.

The Ñudzahui governor of Yanhuitlan, an aged man in his seventies, was the first defendant to testify before the grand inquisitor of the Holy Office in Mexico City. With the assistance of two translators, don Francisco sidestepped or denied every accusation made against him. He had nothing to do with drunken feasts, he said, and his use of tobacco and other herbs before or during mass was intended to give him strength in his old age. If he appeared inattentive during mass, it was because he was a sick, old man. He did his best to encourage people to accept the new faith, but since Yanhuitlan was spread out over an area of about five or six leagues (about twenty-five to thirty-five kilometers), it was difficult to assemble everyone at the same time. The only offerings that he had made to his deceased wife were the same types of offerings that Christians made to the dead (wine, bread, and candles). If boys had been sacrificed, he replied, let their parents come forth and complain, and let their relatives make paintings of them in order to identify them. Don Francisco had an answer for every accusation. Finally, when asked if he knew anybody who was opposed to Christianity, he answered wisely, "I don't know anything about anybody." He admitted that the friars were very disappointed because things had not gone according to plan, but he thought that they had abandoned Yanhuitlan because of their conflict with the Spanish encomendero, Francisco de las Casas, and not because he or any other native noble had challenged Christianity.[157]

In his defense, don Francisco exposed a bitter feud between the local encomendero and the Dominican order. In the proceedings, many friars openly criticized the encomendero for obstructing their mission. Fray Francisco de Mayoraga blamed continuing idolatries on the encomendero's unwillingness to cooperate with the friars. One friar said that the encomendero continually impeded evangelization efforts because he wanted "the natives to go through him first" and, for that matter, "he wanted everything to go through his hands."[158] Fray Bernardo de Santa María claimed that the encomendero's lack of support had forced the Dominicans to abandon the convent. The encomendero intervened when friars punished Indians for their sins, he interfered with plans for the building of a grand church, and he even encouraged Mixtec nobles to ignore the friars. The Dominicans clearly resented the encomendero's influence and used the trial as a means to humiliate and attack him.[159]

The feud represented a classic confrontation between friars and encomenderos over the control of indigenous resources. The *encomienda* in Yanhuitlan was disputed from the start, when Hernando Cortés assigned the grant to his cousin, Francisco de las Casas.[160] To the encomendero, the establishment of a large convent in Yanhuitlan posed a formidable challenge for access to native labor and tribute. The friars would want to build a huge church, and they would expect many things to go through their hands. Even the business of confiscating images was subject to competition. Native witnesses testified that Francisco de las Casas had instructed them to bring their images to his house, and not to the friars. One cacique reported that they brought some very good stones to him, and he took them in secrecy.[161] Since some of the images were inlaid with gold and precious stones, it is easy to imagine the encomendero's motivation for making this secret pact. In Coatlan, the lords accused secular priests of confiscating idols for this same purpose.[162] Friars were not above this practice, either. When fray Benito Hernández discovered a cave full of images and offerings, he used the jewels and gold from the images to purchase silver and vestments for the sacristy of the church in Achiutla.[163] Tombs and images provided start-up capital for the Christian enterprise; likewise, temples provided building materials for new churches.

Indigenous nobles found themselves caught in the middle of this worldly conflict between Spaniards, but they were not passive victims. Just as groups in central Mexico used ecclesiastical conflicts to support their own interests, including rivalries among the orders and competition between the secular and regular clergy, the lords of Yanhuitlan exploited a conflict between the encomendero and the friars.[164] Don Francisco defended himself with terse replies to the charges, focusing attention on the conquerors' power struggle. Apparently, the lords of Yanhuitlan and the encomendero had reached a working agreement that excluded the friars. The agreement was simple: the encomendero would not meddle too much in local affairs if he received his tribute. Since the encomendero did not live in Yanhuitlan, he did not pose an immediate threat. A distant lord who demanded tribute was nothing new; resident priests who sought to smash and burn temples and images and persecute their rivals were without precedent. Perhaps it was true that don Francisco had told the encomendero that he did not want friars living in the community.[165]

At the same time, deep-seated conflicts of interest and rivalries divided the native participants of the trial.[166] Don Francisco understood this fact. He acknowledged that Yanhuitlan was involved in separate legal disputes with Etlatongo, Nochixtlan, Jaltepec, and Suchitepec, which had reached the Royal Audiencia in Mexico City. The Spanish political reorganization that made Yanhuitlan a cabecera over many other ñuu had made matters only worse. Nobles and caciques from these communities seized the opportunity to denounce Yanhuitlan and its rulers. Etlatongo led the attack. Apparently, don Francisco's son had provoked a skirmish with officials from Etlatongo over some native slaves. This incident resulted in the initial confrontation between the Spanish corregidor and don Francisco, when officials sought to arrest don Francisco's son. The fact that lords from Yanhuitlan possessed slaves from Etlatongo suggests that the two communities had engaged in warfare at some point in the recent past. In 1544, Etlatongo filed a legal suit against Yanhuitlan and its encomendero. The nobles of Nochixtlan, whose yya dzehe toniñe (female ruler) was married to the yya toniñe (male ruler) of Etlatongo, supported their yuhuitayu partner by filing a suit against Yanhuitlan. Don Francisco and don Domingo singled out the rulers of Suchitepec, an ally of Etlatongo, as embittered rivals who resented their status as a *sujeto* of the cabecera of Yanhuitlan. Rather than serving the cabecera, they sought to establish their own autonomy.[167] Political conflict had produced many hostile witnesses against Yanhuitlan. Local allegiances were so strong that the only witnesses from Yanhuitlan who denounced the lords were boys in the service of the friars. The slaves who condemned the lords for their idolatrous words and actions were from elsewhere; even the native priests who testified in the trial came from outlying ñuu. Rival lords offered the most enthusiastic denunciations. Colonial changes complicated preexisting conflicts among autonomous ñuu.

Spaniards offered damaging testimony against the lords of Yanhuitlan for their own reasons. Some of the witnesses had quarreled in the past with people from Yanhuitlan. Don Francisco dismissed the testimony of the Spaniards who had accused him; in particular, he singled out Martín de la Mesquitta as an arrogant troublemaker. One of the most vocal accusers, Bachiller Gómez de Maraver, had insulted the lords of Yanhuitlan more than once, calling them "no more Christian than a horse."[168] Luis Delgado, a lieutenant of the Spanish alcalde mayor who prided himself as a Christian vigilante, could scarcely conceal his contempt for the nobles of Yanhuitlan.

Witnesses in favor of don Francisco included four Spaniards who confirmed the bitterness of intercommunity rivalries and acknowledged the conflict between Francisco de las Casas and the friars. Whereas no Dominican defended the lords of Yanhuitlan, a secular priest named Juan de Ruanes could not resist the opportunity to contradict the friars.[169] He called don Francisco a good Christian who had done his best to attend church regularly, and he dismissed many of the accusations as petty gossip. He said that he had witnessed don Francisco preaching to groups of native people in the church patio. The Spanish witnesses defended don Francisco and the other lords of Yanhuitlan on several counts. Don Francisco ingested tobacco, they admitted, but many indigenous people, Africans, and even some Spaniards used tobacco to stave off hunger, alleviate the pain of headaches and toothaches, and revive themselves. One witness thought that the Mixec officials of Yanhuitlan, rather than encouraging drunkenness, tended to punish it too harshly. Another witness stated that the lords positioned men at the back of the church so that people could not sneak away from the mass. In fact, four Spanish witnesses testified that Yanhuitlan was being victimized by native and Spanish factionalism. Their testimony belies the impression of the trial as an attack on the colonized by the colonizers. Although the relationship between these witnesses and the encomendero is unclear, I suspect that they favored the encomendero's position for their own personal motivations. The spiritual conquest spawned struggles for power and influence in Yanhuitlan.

Chaos reigned in Coatlan, too. Coatlan was a complex cabecera with multiple estancias in a border area settled by Nahuas, Mixtecs, and Zapotecs.[170] Hundreds of indigenous people died in a violent two-year rebellion against the Spanish invasion, beginning in 1525. Repression and disease followed in the 1530s. A dispute over the encomienda was settled in favor of Andrés de Monjarraz, whose son Gregorio inherited half after it was divided by the crown. Meanwhile, the Dominicans relinquished Coatlan to the secular clergy in 1538, probably because of a lack of resources.[171] In December 1544, a secular priest of Oaxaca, Pedro de Olmos, submitted a report concerning idolatries and sacrifices in Coatlan. Tello de Sandoval ordered an investigation based on Olmos's report. Whereas the encomendero Francisco de las Casas did not appear in the record of the trial in Yanhuitlan, Gregorio Monjarraz testified against the lords of Coatlan. He accused them of multiple crimes and sins, from organizing sacrificial slaughters and burning a Christian cross in the marketplace to having sex with his female Indian slave.[172] He recommended harsh punishment for the lords. Although less is known about the specific circumstances of this case, it is clear that political intrigue and local enmities fueled the fires of the Inquisition in Coatlan.[173]

Ambivalence and Resistance

When the native governor of Chachuapa testified in 1545 that the people of Yanhuitlan sacrificed things to their ancestors' images and to the "one God from Castile," he said that the "people of Yanhuitlan were of two hearts."[174] This ambivalent, two-hearted allegiance was an understandable response to Christianity in the early period.[175] To the people of Yanhuitlan, the introduction of an ethnic deity after the conquest came as no surprise.[176] Apparently, many people had accepted the "God from Castile." But the acceptance of a new deity did not warrant the exclusion of all others, nor did the continuation of ancient practices and beliefs signify a rejection of Christianity. Don Francisco had acknowledged the God from Castile by attending mass and observing many Christian customs, but he had not embraced Christianity wholeheartedly. When asked if he knew any Christian prayers in Latin, Castilian, or Mixtec, he replied that he knew a few words; when asked to recite those words, he responded that he could not remember them.[177] In truth, he did not know a single word of any Christian prayer. Several witnesses claimed that the people of Yanhuitlan were "lukewarm" in matters of the faith.[178] They accused the lords of "going through the motions" without truly knowing or caring about God. When the lords attended mass, they went reluctantly and did not pay attention. After mass, they joked that they had not understood a single word of the sermon. Don Francisco was accused of chewing tobacco, refusing to kneel, looking inattentively away from the altar, putting his head down, and falling asleep during mass. After mass, they sat around and drank pulque. They ate meat on Fridays and made their servants work on the Sabbath. The friars saw these transgressions as signs of blatant indifference or latent resistance.

The lords of Yanhuitlan tried to appease or bargain with zealous Spaniards, hoping to convince them that they had accepted Christianity. Luis Delgado recalled the time when nobles from Yanhuitlan gave him gifts of clothing and gold so that he might leave them alone.[179] The nobles had tried to reason with him: since they were baptized and had no more images, there was no need to look for images. In this case, the strategy did not work. Armed with a musket and sword, Delgado confiscated several images from a cacica in Tacosaguala who confessed that she was guarding them on behalf of the lords of Yanhuitlan. In response, nobles of Yanhuitlan attempted to rescue the images from Delgado's house by bribing him. In the end, Delgado smashed and burned the images before the nobles. The Spaniard reminisced how a noble named Domingo Estumeca broke down and cried at the sight of the destroyed cuacu.[180]

Amid the chaos and confusion, the lords of Yanhuitlan began to wonder whether their half-hearted acceptance of the Castilian God had angered their own deities and had brought sickness and drought upon them. Disease was widespread in the 1530s and 1540s, especially in 1538 and from 1545 to 1548.[181] According to one witness, when the lords of Yanhuitlan assembled in the palace of don Francisco to discuss how to cope with drought, disease, and hunger, they concluded that the recent baptisms and masses had angered Dzahui, the rain deity. Don Francisco reasoned: "If Jesus Christ were a god, he would not give the commoners such hunger." They decided to assemble the necessary items for sacrifice, drink pulque, and invoke Dzahui .[182] Don Francisco said that "the god of the Christians is a lie and because some of us follow him our gods are angry."[183] When don Francisco painted himself with charcoal and made sacrifices to Dzahui, he allegedly cried out, "Now I'm no Christian, I'm what I used to be."[184]

The trial in Yanhuitlan introduced considerable evidence of resistance to Christianity.[185] The nobles of Yanhuitlan had acquired a reputation for mocking the faith and denouncing the friars and their new converts. According to several witnesses, don Francisco bragged about not being Christian and reminded his people that their ancestors had not come from Castile and that they did not understand the ways of the Christian god.[186] People from Yanhuitlan mocked native Christians from other communities with gestural and verbal insults. The cacique of Nochixtlan testified that the nobles and commoners of Yanhuitlan insulted them when they passed along the borders or on the road, shouting, "There go the Christians of Castile, the chickens."[187] The governor of Chachuapa recalled the time when, in the market of Suchitepec, they were accosted by officials from Yanhuitlan and accused of abandoning their ancestors' ways. The officials scorned them with derisive gestures, exposing their genitals to them and saying, "Well, since you are Christians . . ."[188] The governor claimed that they wanted to bar Christians from going to the Suchitepec marketplace because it was the principal source of their sacrificial items.

Mockery verged on mimicry when don Domingo allegedly married a native slave in the church. After mocking the Christian sacrament of matrimony, he married a niece from Tiltepec in a traditional ceremony that lasted several days. One time, after a six-day feast in his palace, don Domingo allegedly invited a friar to say mass in his house on the seventh day, mimicking the Christian observance of the Sabbath.[189] Sometimes, people consciously intermingled native and Christian practices. According to a slave of Molcaxtepec who served in the palace of Yanhuitlan, don Francisco instructed people to worship the deities of their ancestors in the church patio, where the temple used to stand. Another native witness was more explicit about the church's location on sacred ground: don Francisco told people to invoke the ancient spirits, to burn copal, and "to worship in the place where the houses and temples of the deities used to be, which is the southern side of the church patio."[190] This was the place where many people, including don Francisco, had been accused of letting blood from their ears on the ground. As he admitted in his own confession, don Francisco had been "disciplined" with lashes by fray Bernardo de Santa María for his performance of this ritual act.[191]

Christianity forced nobles to participate in the destruction of the old system or to stand aside and witness its demise. One Spaniard recalled don Francisco's reaction on the day when the remains of the old temple were demolished. When fray Dionisio de la Anunciación ordered commoners to tear down the temple remains that were left standing next to the church, don Francisco tried to impede their efforts. According to Luis Delgado, when they began to raze the structure, don Francisco warned them that the gods would get their revenge.[192] According to several witnesses, don Francisco prohibited people from surrendering their images to the friars. When the cacique of Molcaxtepec tried to hand over his images to a friar, don Francisco confronted him with the question, "Why are you bringing your gods to the friars? These are your ancestors whom you should guard and adore."[193]

Clandestine activity was a predictable response to sporadic and limited repression in the first decades of the colonial period. Certain ritual acts were confined to concealed spaces and remote places, involving fewer people. Small, bundled images were worshiped in houses or carried to remote mountains and caves. Fray Diego de Santa María, who claimed that he had burned piles of images, was the first to admit that people hid many things from the friars.[194] Even native priests hid or changed their appearance by dressing differently and washing when the friars came around.[195] In fact, one priest named Cuizo (2-Ocelot) was *alguacil* (native constable) of Yanhuitlan until the *señor juez* (Spanish official) removed him from office in 1544.[196]

Christians had time on their side. Secret rites divided communities into factions, pitting converted natives against their unconverted neighbors. Diego Hernández, a native church attendant of Yanhuitlan who translated sermons into the Ñudzahui language, said that the lords had tried to kill him because he preached Christianity and defiled the ancient "demons."[197] He complained that most people in Yanhuitlan would not speak with him because they thought of him as a spy. Friars trained boys for these specialized church skills, encouraging them to identify elders who had not converted. The introduction of generational policing in a society that held age in high regard must have horrified the elders. Outsiders with prying eyes were most threatening because they were not subject to local authorities, peer pressure, or intimidation. When many people from Yanhuitlan and surrounding communities gathered in Topiltepec for a sacrificial feast to Dzahui, nobles warned the commoners in speeches not to say a word about the ceremony to anyone else, especially to native Christians from Teposcolula, Nochixtlan, and Etlatongo.[198] When this type of large-scale, corporate activity was no longer possible or expedient, when the collective nature of ritual practices was reduced to a few people who performed secret rites in remote places, clandestine cults posed little threat to Christianity.

The case from Coatlan smacked of resistance to Christianity. Agustín de San Francisco, a native church official in Tututepec, was informed by merchants of his community that people in Coatlan continued to perform many ancient practices, including human sacrifice.[199] According to Diego de Albino, a noble from Tututepec, emissaries from the communities of Yanhuitlan, Xaltepec, Tilantongo, Elotepec, Teozapotlan, Tiltepec, and many other Mixtec, Zapotec, and Nahua communities gathered in Coatlan in 1543 to discuss how to deal with the Christian threat. They celebrated a feast in which they ate and drank, painted, sacrificed themselves, and performed many other rites and ceremonies. When the feast was over, Albino recalled the following speech that don Hernando made to the assembled group: "Brothers, I beg you to tell your caciques and nobles what you have seen here, and I beg them that they should do the same there. They should sacrifice and call upon their gods as they have done before, and they should not listen to the doctrine of the [Christian] priests. Here are the gods of our ancestors; they should resuscitate their gods. . . . I am the valiant and great lord don Hernando, I have many bows and arrows and many people, and if I were to kill the priests or the Christians, then the tatuan [*tlatoani*] of Mexico will pardon me."[200] He warned against giving images to Christian priests, who sought them for their gold and precious stones. When don Alonso, the cacique of Mistepec, suggested that it might be better to give up the images in order to retain power in the region, don Hernando insulted him before the other nobles who had assembled in the patio of his palace.[201] He challenged don Alonso to explain why he had not buried his father in the traditional manner, and he berated the other nobles who had accepted Christian practices and who had spoken with priests. He was proud to have guarded the ways of his ancestors and to remain "lord in his own land." The quote attributed to don Hernando suggests that after more than two decades of Spanish rule, he still thought of the tlatoani of Tenochtitlan as the ultimate political authority in the land.

Apparently, don Hernando of Coatlan despised Christian priests, whom he called *gallinas* (hens).[202] Pedro de Olmos attributed the following speech to don Hernando: "If the Christians have their god, then we have our own gods, and if they have their laws and commandments, then we have ours, too. We should not associate ourselves with the Christians, nor should we accept the sticks [staffs of office] that the viceroy sends because they are not our friends. We have listened to the priests and dealt with Christians for more than twelve years, but we have not accepted their words, nor do we want to accept what they say, because it is all lies."[203] One day, when Bartolomé Sánchez, the vicar of Coatlan, was preaching to nobles and commoners, don Hernando stood up and shouted at him that the gospels were nothing but lies written down on paper. Another time, when Sánchez began to reprehend the nobles in his sermon for not attending mass regularly, they walked out of the church and into the market, leaving him to say mass alone. When the priest later confronted them for ignoring him, they threatened to beat him.[204] Sánchez also recounted how he had entered don Hernando's house one day, when he suspected that they were committing idolatries. He found don Hernando and other nobles with their war clubs, bows, and arrows, getting drunk. When the priest tried to enter, don Hernando grabbed him by the beard and sexually insulted him.[205]

The lords of Yanhuitlan and Coatlan struggled to abide by certain Christian practices while resisting the destruction of their sacred relations. Ultimately, they were persecuted for their ambivalence and resistance. The lords of Yanhuitlan were imprisoned for two years, and more than forty witnesses came forth to denounce or support them.[206] Meanwhile, the community was forced to pay for the proceedings. In 1546, the cabecera paid five hundred pesos for the legal expenses of the Holy Office.[207] In 1547, Coatlan was ordered to pay one thousand pesos for the cost of the trial.[208]

In 1546, the inquisitors began to exhume corpses in and around Yanhuitlan in search of evidence of human sacrifice. In the house of don Juan's neighbor, where don Juan allegedly had buried a sacrificed girl, they exhumed the body of a boy or girl whose skull was broken into fragments; there were several "blue stones" (turquoise) next to the body. Nearby, the corpse of an adult was bundled in a reed mat, surrounded by jade stones, pieces of silver, and eight jars.[209] The owner of the house testified that the bones belonged to a mother and her child. The investigation proved inconclusive. The accounts of witnesses who claimed to have seen sacrifices and burials led the inquisitors on a wild search for bodies. In Molcaxtepec, officials dug around in a canyon called Yuchaco, where the sacrificed corpses of several boys were said to be buried, only to find the bones of one adult. In Tiltepec, officials dug several holes at the foot of a hill named Yucumano, where boys were allegedly sacrificed and buried. They found nothing.[210]

While Spanish officials searched for bodies, seven Mixtec priests were arrested and placed in chains. Two of the priests were too sick to walk, and another was an elderly, feeble man, so only four of the priests were interrogated. Two of them had testified previously. One of the most talkative priests, Caco of Coscatepec, admitted earlier in the trial that he had performed numerous sacrifices. For example, he said that he had sacrificed boys when the cacique of Coscatepec died. When the cacique of Yanhuitlan died in 1539, don Francisco and don Juan ordered him to make sacrifices. This time, when Caco was called on to clarify his testimony, he retracted part of his statement. Specifically, he denied that the lords of Yanhuitlan had ordered him to make any sacrifices. Meanwhile, the other three priests gave evasive replies to the inquisitors' questions. Cuizo denied sacrificing humans and concluded that "he did not know anything" about the lords of Yanhuitlan. When the judge admonished him to tell the truth, he replied that he did not know anything more. Cocoane and Xixa, both about twenty years old, denied that they had ever been priests. They also denied letting blood from their ears or tongues. When asked about the severe scars on his tongue, Cocoane said that it was from eating maize stalks. In response to questions about the scars on his ears, Xixa said that his mother had pierced them when he was a boy. [211] By this time, the defendants had realized that it was best to deny everything. As testimony against the lords of Yanhuitlan continued and the lords and priests continued to deny the charges made against them, the documentation comes to an end. The case is incomplete. The last page ends in the middle of don Domingo's denials. We can only guess how long the trial continued beyond the last page of the document and whether the inquisitors applied torture to the accused, as they had done elsewhere in New Spain. It is possible that the trial was suspended indefinitely when the inquisitor Tello de Sandoval returned to Spain in 1547. [212] It is likely that the entire case was dropped.

The record of the trial in Coatlan also ended without a verdict in 1547. Whereas the lords of Yanhuitlan denied every serious charge, despite explicit confessions by native priests with whom they were closely associated, the three lords of Coatlan confessed to guarding images and performing sacrifices, even after baptism. Don Hernando defended himself with the disclaimer that he had been deceived by the devil and that he was not opposed to Christianity. By his own admission, he did not know a thing about the faith. He remembered that he had been baptized by a tall priest from Castile, whose name he did not know. He admitted that the baptism had meant nothing to him. At the end of his confession, he begged the court for mercy and promised to live as a Christian. When the documentation ends in 1547, the three lords languished in a Mexico City prison.

In Yanhuitlan, the trial had strengthened church and crown in the Mixteca Alta. Indigenous lords were forced to declare their allegiance to Christianity, and the Dominicans reasserted control over the indoctrination of Yanhuitlan by 1548. In that year, the encomienda of Yanhuitlan was limited to half of its original grant; the other half fell under crown control as an *alcaldía mayor*. Francisco de las Casas bequeathed this half to his son, Gonzalo de las Casas, who assisted in financing construction of the church of Yanhuitlan. [213] Don Domingo survived as cacique until 1558, when his nephew, don Gabriel de Guzmán became the officially recognized yya toniñe of Yanhuitlan. In sketches of the *Codex Yanhuitlan,* drawn a few years after the trial, don Domingo appears before a seated ecclesiastical official, as discussed in chapter two (see fig. 2.9). After the inquisitorial investigations of the 1540s, it is fitting that priests appear as prominent, overbearing figures in the sketches.

Ñudzahui Christianity

When don Domingo's nephew, don Gabriel de Guzmán, was confirmed as cacique of Yanhuitlan in 1558, he addressed the nobles and commoners of Yanhuitlan and its sujetos and lords from many other ñuu in the Mixteca Alta.[214] He admonished them to respect their authorities, learn the Christian doctrine and attend mass, prohibit drunkenness and other vices, stop drunken feasts and sacrifices of any kind, purge all idolatries, despise adultery, and avoid all sins. As yya toniñe of Yodzocahi, don Gabriel fulfilled an obligation to speak to his people. His ceremonial speech addressed many of the same issues as the "long discourse with which the ruler admonished the inhabitants of the altepetl when he spoke for the first time," recorded in Nahuatl by fray Bernardino de Sahagún in the *Florentine Codex*.[215] As lord of Yanhuitlan, don Gabriel played a pivotal role in the local colonial order. Like the many Nahuatl-language speeches collected by Sahagún, don Gabriel's address was a moralistic lecture on proper behavior. But don Gabriel's speech was also infused with the spirit of Christian values. These were the Christian morals that, only a decade earlier, don Gabriel's uncle had been accused of violating. The friars must have been pleased. In don Gabriel they had found a spokesman who could deliver the Christian message to the people of Yanhuitlan.

Don Gabriel cooperated with the friars and supported the church in Yanhuitlan.[216] He and his wife, doña Isabel de Rojas, donated a large plot of land to the church for the establishment of a *capellanía* (chaplaincy or chantry) in 1576.[217] In turn, don Gabriel benefited from being a good Christian. As he helped organize labor drafts for church construction, he redirected part of the labor pool to build a palace in the 1560s.[218] His repeated terms as governor earned him an annual salary of four hundred pesos and many other privileges. He claimed more than one hundred plots of land and lived in a palace complex with nine separate patios. He used the legal system to his advantage and participated actively in the local economy. He was recognized as the cacique of Yanhuitlan for thirty-three years until his death in 1591.

Don Gabriel de Guzmán was obviously tutored by the friars as a boy. He could read, write, and speak Castilian and Ñudzahui by the time he became an adult. As the ultimate native authority in Yanhuitlan, he signed his name to many legal documents from the period. An inventory of his goods reveals that he possessed a desk with drawers, a writing box, and books. Since don Gabriel could read Spanish, it is likely that he read the books in his personal collection. One of his books, *Contemptus Mundi*, is a passionate discourse on the evil vanities and vices of the world.[219] The book urges the reader to despise the pleasures and honors of life on earth, for "the world turns like a wheel, and in the fury of its turning it flays them who love it most." Accordingly, titles, privileges and royal descent have no value because "only mortality is inherited." The book contains 120 chapters of self-flagellating material designed to help "shut up one's senses to the vain blasts of this miserable world."

When don Gabriel prepared to leave this "miserable world" in 1591, when he made his last will and testament in Spanish, he paid considerable attention to Christian detail.[220] He acknowledged that Jesus Christ had died for him and had redeemed his many sins and that Christ's precious blood would redeem his soul. He desired an elaborate burial in a sepulcher inside the church. He asked several friars and all the *cantores* (church singers) to accompany the procession of his corpse from his palace to the church. The many *cofradías* (lay confraternies) to which he belonged would provide candles for the procession. He arranged to have fifty masses sung on behalf of his soul, and he gave money to each of the cofradías of Yanhuitlan. He possessed numerous Christian relics and icons, including a silver-plated reliquary of the Agnus Dei, four images of the Virgin Mary, three gold rosaries, and gold figures of Santiago, the Baby Jesus, cherubs, and Jesus the Savior.[221]

By all appearances, don Gabriel was a devout Christian who personified the post-Inquisition achievements of the church in Yanhuitlan. The Dominicans used the investigation to establish their presence in the Mixteca, where they dominated the instruction and administration of the Christian faith. Between 1538 and 1548, they founded establishments in the major cabeceras of Teposcolula, Coixtlahuaca, and Tlaxiaco. They founded a dozen more convents within the next three decades, from Cuilapan in the Valley of Oaxaca to Chila in the Mixteca Baja.[222] Parishes were based on the colonial sociopolitical order and the main outline of encomiendas. By 1590 the Dominicans maintained sixteen convents in the Mixteca.[223] They sought to finance their operations by investing in all possible economic enterprises. At the same time, they encouraged native lords to donate lands and money to support the church, and they relied on native tribute and labor mechanisms to support their various activities. The last will and testament provided a steady supply of pious bequests. By the end of the colonial period, the accumulation of native bequests and aggressive land purchases made the church and its various institutions, especially the Dominicans and Jesuits, the largest corporate landowners in the Mixteca.[224]

The success of the local church depended on the participation of the native nobility. As intermediaries between Spaniards and the indigenous majority, nobles were targeted for cultural and spiritual conversion. Some male nobles, including don Gabriel, were trained and tutored by priests at a young age. The church created a formal hierarchy of male nobles who represented the community and served as intermediaries between priests and the congregation. By the 1550s, most cabeceras sponsored a group of native church officials, whose duties complemented the activities of the native *cabildo,* or municipal council. This group was called the *tay huahi ñuhu,* or the "church people," the equivalent of the Nahua *teopantlaca* or *teopannenque.*[225] The *Codex Sierra* depicts the church people of Texupa in 1550, when they were being trained by Nahuas. Nahua aides had received the faith earlier and could communicate effectively with Ñudzahui speakers. Like the cabildo, the native church hierarchy was an all-male body.[226] Spanish custom and Christian doctrine excluded women from positions of authority.[227]

In the preconquest period, political and priestly offices overlapped and were held by the same ruling group of yya and toho. The highest native church office, that of *fiscal,* was usually occupied by a literate noble who sat on the cabildo when not serving the church. The fiscal was described in the *Vocabulario* as *tay ñoho tniño huahi ñuhu,* or "person who organizes the church duties," a descriptive term that was rapidly replaced by the Spanish loanword, if it was used at all.[228] The fiscal was the steward and manager of the local church and its activities. The use of *tniño* (duty, office) in reference to the responsibilities of the governor and the fiscal suggests how the two positions were related. The governor was called *tay yotasi tniño*, "one who commands the tniño."[229] In many respects, the fiscal was the equivalent of the governor in religious concerns. The remaining offices consisted of a *tay tatnu huahi ñuhu* ("church staffholder," for *alguacil de la iglesia*) and a *tay taa tutu huahi ñuhu* ("church writer," for *escribano de la iglesia*). The former was a constable who often performed the symbolic duty of cleaning and sweeping the church, and the latter was the church notary. The *sacristan* was described simply as "one who takes care of the sacristy" [tay yondaa sacristia], relying on the loanword, or "one who takes care of the sacred things" [tay yondaa sasi ñuhu].[230] Finally, there could be as many as twenty *cantores*, or singers (*tay daa huahi ñuhu*), including musicians such as the *tay sadzi organo*, or "one who strikes the organ."[231] Church people enjoyed a modest salary and received small bequests from testators for their participation in funeral rites.

The local *cajas de comunidades* (community treasuries) paid for the construction, adornment, and maintenance of church buildings; the vestments, wine, and precious objects of the sacristy; the sponsorship of Christian feasts; and the daily bread of local priests. Communities purchased everything from organs and bells to silver chalices and ornate altarpieces.[232] In the sixteenth century, the silk industry generated revenue to pay for basic and lavish expenditures alike. Christian grandeur in the Mixteca peaked in the 1580s, when the Spanish artist Andrés de Concha was commissioned to paint works in the new churches of Tamasulapa, Achiutla, Teposcolula, Yanhuitlan, and other communities for large sums of money. For example, in 1586, he was paid two thousand pesos to paint the altarpiece of Tamasulapa.[233] Cofradías, or lay brotherhoods, contributed to the finance of church-related activities and objects. They were organized in some places by the 1570s and 1580s, but they were especially common by the second half of the colonial period.[234] Cofradías were dedicated to generalized concepts or personages, such as the Holy Cross or Saint Mary of the Rosary. Members, or *cofrades*, paid dues and participated in feasts and processions dedicated to the advocation. Leadership often overlapped with that of the cabildo and the church hierarchy. However, whereas the native church hierarchy was exclusively male, these organizations allowed women an active, participatory role. Cofradías engaged in commercial enterprises, such as the cacao trade, the herding of sheep and cattle, and agriculture.[235] Their financial activities were often indistinguishable from the corporate affairs of the ñuu.[236]

The second half of the sixteenth century was a period of major church construction in the Mixteca. Church building in Yanhuitlan began around 1550; by 1579, workers were chopping wood for the grand altarpiece.[237] Magnificent churches in Teposcolula, Coixtlahuaca, and Cuilapan, with their vaulted open-air chapels and large patios, were designed to accommodate thousands of people at mass. The open-air chapels were a distinctly Mexican feature of church architecture. When the Jesuit Bernabé Cobo passed through Yanhuitlan in 1630, the church inspired him to write that the "buildings of Peru were huts in comparison to the ones here."[238] Ironically, by the time these imposing structures were completed in the final decades of the sixteenth century, the congregation had been reduced to a mere fraction of its former size. Continuing disease and depopulation cast a somber shadow over the lofty, visible achievements of the church.

Sacred Houses

No sign of the new faith stood out more than the church edifice. The use of the term *huahi ñuhu,* "sacred house," in reference to the church building, rather than the borrowing of the Spanish word *iglesia,* suggests how people identified the new structure with a preconquest analogue.[239] Native-language writings never incorporated the Spanish loanword for the church during the colonial period. The new structure was normally built on the same site as the preconquest temple, often using stones from the razed temple. After the conquest, people in Yanhuitlan recognized the fact that the "houses and temples" of their ancestors and deities were buried under the southern side of the church patio. Nobles and commoners performed autosacrifice in this patio.[240] Ñudzahui neophytes continued to use new sacred spaces in familiar ways. In Yanhuitlan, don Francisco addressed large audiences from the top of the stepped platform of the cross, which stood in the middle of the church patio.[241] In effect, the lord spoke from a raised platform in the church patio, standing on or near the site of the old temple platform. Juan de Ruanes, a secular priest, was impressed with don Francisco's ability to command an audience, even though he could not understand the speeches. We can only imagine what don Francisco said from this platform in the church patio.

In the *Codex Yanhuitlan,* the churches of Teposcolula and Yanhuitlan are marked by identifying glosses: "huey ñuhu yucundaa" [the sacred house of Teposcolula] and "huey ñuhu yodzoquehe" [the sacred house of Yanhuitlan]. The latter is spelled out below as "la yglesia de Yanhuitlan."[242] The rendering of the churches combines preconquest-style two-dimensional depiction and three-dimensional European drawing. That of the church of Teposcolula, viewed from the left side, depicts two towers in the foreground and a cupola in the back; the structure is elevated by steps (see fig. 8.6). Beside the church, the remnants of a reed mat are visible from a damaged part of the page, as if a native ruler were seated beside the church. The church of Yanhuitlan is viewed from the right side, on top of the place glyph for Yanhuitlan and a flight of steep stairs (see fig. 8.7).[243] Both structures have conical, thatched roofs. The platforms, stairs, and roofs of the two churches resemble characteristic features of temple structures in the preconquest-style codices.[244]

Churches, temples, and palaces figure prominently in early colonial pictorial manuscripts in the Mixteca.[245] The church came to represent the ñuu. In sixteenth-century maps and lienzos, ruling couples were seated near or in front of the church, in the same manner as they appeared before temples in the codices. In the Lienzo of Zacatepec, rulers are seated between the church and the palace/temple; both structures stand on the same *tablero* ñuu frieze (see fig. 8.8).[246] Every map from the Mixteca that was drawn for the *Relaciones geográficas* depicts the preconquest temple or palace next to the church. As discussed in chapter 2, the artist(s) from Teozacualco placed the church alongside the native palace (see fig. 2.4). The writer from Amoltepec

FIGURE 8.6. Depiction of the church of Teposcolula, "huey ñuhu yucundaa," from the *Codex Yanhuitlan*, plate XVIII.

FIGURE 8.7. Depiction of the church of Yanhuitlan, from the *Codex Yanhuitlan,* plate XX.

FIGURE 8.8. A church, a yuhuitayu, and a palace in the Lienzo of Zacatepec. CNCA-INAH-MEX, Biblioteca Nacional de Antropología e Historia.

placed the church next to the ruling couple's temple (see fig. 2.5). The artist from Texupa drew the new *monasterio* and the old temple, even though the latter had been destroyed by the time of the painting (see fig. 2.6). The artist from Nochixtlan drew the palace and the church in the town center (see fig. 2.7). Question number ten of the *Relaciones* questionnaire requested artists to sketch the community church on their maps, but it did not ask them to depict temples or palaces. And it certainly did not expect artists to draw temples that no longer existed.

A map from Cuquila illustrates how artists continued to associate the church structure with the preconquest temple and the ñuu in the late sixteenth century (see fig. 8.9).[247] The church and temple of Cuquila share the same tablero motif as the ocelot-hill place glyph. The disk motif on the band below the church bell, symbolizing political and religious authority, was a standard feature of temples and palaces (see figs. 6.2 and 6.3). Another map from Cuquila depicts churches in a similar manner (see fig. 8.10).[248] The drawing was presented in a legal dispute between the community of Cuquila and doña Pascuala Feliciana de Rojas, the cacica of Ocotepec and Ñundaco, over a tract of land. Drawn on paper around 1595, the map relies on preconquest-style motifs for the depiction of hills, roads, and rivers. But the artist used stylized depictions of churches to represent the ñuu of Cuquila, Mistepec, and Chicahuastla. Appropriately,

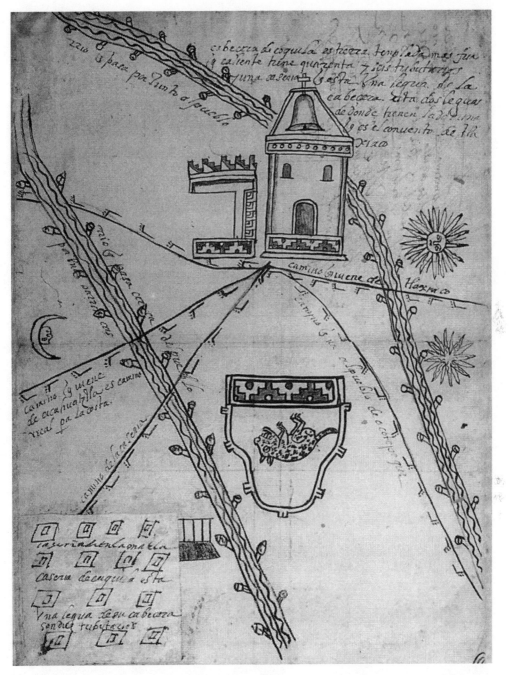

FIGURE 8.9. The temple, church, and place glyph of Cuquila (Nuucuiñe). AGN-T, 3556:6, f. 175.

FIGURE 8.10. A map of Cuquila and two nearby ñuu. AGN-T, 876:1, f. 122.

each church bears the preconquest symbol of the ñuu, the tablero motif, on its facade. Ñudzahui artists relied on familiar conventions to portray churches as symbolic centers of colonial ñuu.

Churches signified local autonomy. Conflict and competition between sociopolitical units were often expressed in terms of church construction, attendance, and patronage. For example, in a dispute between Yanhuitlan and Tecomatlan in 1582, officials from the sujeto of Tecomatlan complained that the colonial designation of cabeceras and sujetos had forced them to supply labor for the construction of Yanhuitlan's church, attend mass there, and pay tribute for its maintenance.[249] They had not performed these acts or provided these services before the conquest, they argued. This example indicates that not all communities willingly engaged in church construction, especially when the church was not theirs. In response, representatives of Yanhuitlan simply cited the fact that people from Tecomatlan had always attended mass in their church as proof of its own superior, cabecera status. The same markers of religious allegiance and political deference applied to relations between communities and their constituent units. In the last decade of the sixteenth century, a group of ten married couples established a settlement called Ñuyucu, which was near Malinaltepec.[250] The group attended mass, brought flowers to decorate the church of Malinaltepec, and participated in community labor projects. In return, Malinaltepec treated them as if they were a "barrio." About fifteen years later, people from Ñuyucu no longer attended mass in the church and refused to give labor or tribute to the cabecera. Officials from Malinaltepec accused them of attempting to break away from the cabecera and worshiping the devil. Representatives from Ñuyucu insisted that they were living on lands belonging to the cacique of Tlaxiaco and that they had only attended mass and given tribute as a gesture of friendship. It is easy to imagine how Ñuyucu's eventual desire for autonomy would be accompanied by plans to build its own church. In 1612, the cabildo of Malinaltepec attempted to preclude this possibility by bringing legal action against Ñuyucu. When many ñuu gained independence from cabeceras in the late seventeenth and eighteenth centuries, a second wave of church construction swept the Mixteca.[251]

The Spiritual Dialogue

The period of great church construction in the sixteenth century coincided with the beginning of native-language writing and the appearance of ecclesiastical publications. Friars engaged native nobles in a religious dialogue designed to define Ñudzahui terminology and metaphors to approximate basic concepts of the Christian faith. In describing new ideas and objects, friars preferred to find native equivalents rather than relying on meaningless loanwords. But if the two cultures offered an expansive arena for dialogue, based on what was identifiable and familiar to the other, they also possessed different cultural constructions that shaped their imagination of sacred relations.[252] The study of language is one point of entry into the cultural and ideological gap. This section considers native-language terminology for Christian concepts and evaluates the usage of those terms in a variety of texts and contexts.

One of the most important sources for the study of Ñudzahui-language Christian terminology is the *Doctrina en lengua misteca*. Published in 1567 and again in 1568, this four hundred-page doctrinal manual, written entirely in the native language, was designed to assist friars in delivering sermons and to educate literate native nobles. We have already discussed in chapters 2 and 3 how native nobles participated in writing the texts, even if they did not design the basic content and format of church publications. The *Doctrina* introduces and discusses many elements of the Catholic faith, including the four major prayers (Credo, Pater Noster, Ave Maria, and Salve Regina), the articles of faith, the Ten Commandments, the sacraments, the five commandments of the church, the seven mortal sins, the five senses, the seven virtues, the fourteen acts of mercy, a discourse on sin and morality, and the feast days of the church. Many of the sections are organized in the format of a question-and-answer dialogue; a priest (*dzutu*, or "father") poses the questions, and the *dzaya*, or "children," respond in proper form. The *Doctrina* represents a systematic effort to address every fundamental aspect of the faith, from the origins of life on earth to the Kingdom of Heaven above.

The friars sought to supplant native codices and sacred writings with the *Doctrina*. It is no coincidence that the author of record, fray Benito Hernández, had a reputation for destroying codices and painted lienzos in the area where it was first published.[253] According to Burgoa, fray Benito had annoyed the people of Achiutla to the point that they barricaded him inside his quarters and refused to give him food or drink.[254] The dialogue between Mixtecs and friars that produced the *Doctrina* was a colonial discourse between the dominant few who attempted to impose their version of the truth and the subordinate many who were expected to listen and learn.[255] The new truth was revealed in a new form of writing. The power of the written word is suggested by an illustration in the *Doctrina* (see fig. 8.11).[256] The woodcut depicts a friar who reads a printed book as he ascends the "stairway to heaven." He symbolizes the Dominican order, one of the knowledgeable few. God the Father is seated above. The caption reads "yyacaa taniño ychi andehui" [look here, an illustration of the path to heaven].[257] The Latin "scala celi" [stairway to heaven] is written below. The image and caption indicate that the Bible is a road map to paradise. The *Doctrina* used several woodcuts to illustrate Christian themes.

The *Doctrina* also featured song with native-language verse (see fig. 8.12). Following an exposition on the meaning of certain prayers and the Ten Commandments, the priest poses a question to the neophyte in the form of a dialogue:

QUESTION: Precious child, do you know how to sing the words of the Doctrina written here?
RESPONSE: I know, precious father.
FATHER: Sing, child.
           We always say: guard the commandments;
           for if we do not guard them well, we will never behold the lord.

P. Dzaya manisinindo sa catando dudzu Doctrina yondaa yaha?
R. Sini ñadzaña dzutu mani.
P. Cata dzaya.
    Dehe tna qhehui nacahando: saconaahuaha huidzo dzaha;
    da dzahuata ña yonaauaando, va cuhui cotondo nanaya.[258]

FIGURE 8.11. Woodcut of the "stairway to heaven," in the *Doctrina en lengua misteca*, by fray Benito Hernández (1567, f. 62v). The Huntington Library.

The term *huidzo dzaha*, literally "words, speech," appears in Reyes's vocabulary of reverential terms for "the law of the lord."[259] It was a common metaphor for authority, applied to the Commandments and the Christian doctrine in general.[260] This passage illustrates the power of the "dudzu Doctrina yondaa," the written *Doctrina* words that could be sung aloud. Those who refused to know and obey the Lord's Commandments would never look upon his face. In its use of images, song, and metaphor, the *Doctrina* incorporated key elements of the codices.

¶ Dzayamanıfınındo facarando oudzu Doctrina pondaayabar ꝶ. Sini fıadzaña ozutumani. P. Cata ozaya.

De betna quebui na-

cabado:facona abuaba

buıdzodzaba:oadzabua-

ta ñagonaauaado: va cub

buıcotodo nanaya.
¶ Yubayodaa articulos.

Dzaeeni dios vni pfonas qbiındifa nee ynindo dzutu Dios iu dzagaya dpe Spiritu fancto Dios nıfaandigaya andebui ñuuñagebui guliyondo fadzebui ycan dios nitab uiñaba.

faba gꝰa adeuinyttauido yotaliya fandoo fanina. fabuaba yonyitabuindo: yofini nanıyadoo ñayeui, q̃buiñatubui quachido, dpe qbnidifandoo ñayeui faba andebuinnbudo.

dzayan Dios nicubuiya ñayebui, faba gracia Spiritu fctõ, fancta Maria nidzacacu ñuuñayebui ozayaya.

¶ Jefu chrifto ozayã dios tayꝛee nicubuiya, faba gracia fpiritu fancto, nicubuibuabacoñoya, fancta Maria yyaneeñuẽ nidzatubui nanaya fabandoo taꝛvdzatebui, dica cruz nindoboya, oanicavozicava Limbo, nifaa vni queui nidotoya.
dꝯ

Many of the metaphorical expressions of the *Doctrina* appear in the religious pre-amble of the earliest native-language testaments. Friars worked closely with a select group of native nobles who played a leading role in the dissemination of writing in the region. The first extant Ñudzahui-language last will and testament, written on behalf of doña María López, indicates that she possessed a copy of the *Doctrina*, which had been published only four years earlier.[261] The native-language testament is a valuable source of information on local interpretations of Christianity in the Mixteca. In particular, the religious preamble contains direct statements by native testators on Christianity. This part of the Spanish/Christian model testament consisted of a supplication, a meditation on death and the final judgment, and a profession of faith. The profession of faith usually included a statement of belief in the church and affirmed basic tenets of the Christian faith, followed immediately by the encommendation of the soul and body. Then the testament moved onto matters of burial, masses, pious bequests, the division of one's estate, and the naming of one's executors and witnesses to the will.[262] Much of the preamble in native wills conforms to the formulaic invocations of Spanish testaments; however, some Ñudzahui-language testaments went beyond the usual oblig-atory words and dedicated many lines of reverential expressions to this part of the doc-ument. Solemn invocations and declarations of belief articulate native statements about the Christian faith.[263] The declaration usually affirms the testator's belief in basic Chris-tian principles, especially the Ten Commandments and articles of faith; often, requests are made for the intercession of the Virgin Mary and other saints on behalf of the soul and one's entry into heaven.[264] Although the words in this part of the document were based on the ideals and models of native-language ecclesiastical writings and teachings, native testators and notaries elaborated on the language of native-Christian discourse in meaningful ways.[265] Of course, these statements reflect only an impression of one's faith, but they do reveal how men and women actually referred to fundamental Chris-tian concepts. Most Spanish translations of testaments ignored or simplified most of these terms and moved on to the business of bequests.

The following sections use Mixtec ecclesiastical texts, last wills and testaments, and other nontestamentary genres of mundane writing for evidence of how native writers conceptualized Christian phenomena. The use of multiple types of sources is impor-tant. Native-language records of community accounts, for example, refer to religious activities in a matter-of-fact manner, in the absence of friars and without recourse to the formula of testaments. Normally, the notary had no direct connection to the native church hierarchy. In describing images, feasts, processions, and saints, the writings re-veal ordinary usage intended for a native audience. First, let us consider how Ñudzahui Christians imagined and envisioned God, the Kingdom of Heaven, Jesus and Mary, and the angels and saints.

The Kingdom of Heaven

The word for God was *stoho Dios*, meaning "lord God," using the loanword *Dios*. It often appears as "stohondo Dios," as in "our Lord God." The term *stoho* denoted an esteemed noble person, comparable to the term *yya*. The two honorific titles approx-imated the Spanish *señor*. God was also called a *ñuhu* and a *yya toniñe*, the ancient term for a deity and the title of a male ruler, respectively.[266] Jesus Christ was usually introduced by the same titles and names. A straightforward loanword was adopted for the Holy Spirit (*Espíritu Santo*), presumably because this concept was too difficult to convey in the native language. As we have seen in the "stairway to heaven" woodcut, the word *andehui* (sky) was employed for "heaven," much like *cielo* in Spanish. Similarly, in Nahuatl, the term *ilhuicac*, "in the sky," was adopted for "heaven." However, the "Kingdom of Heaven" was called "yuhuitayu andehui gloria," employing Ñudzahui vocabulary for the largest political entity (yuhuitayu) and the sky, modified by a Spanish loanword (*gloria*) in reference to its everlasting quality. Often the term *toniñe* (rulership) was added to the phrase. This phrase *yuhuitayu toniñe andehui*, "yuhuitayu rulership in the sky," appears in the earliest Ñudzahui-language records from the Mixteca and in the *Doctrina*.[267] Actually, the *Doctrina* used many versions of this phrase for the Kingdom of Heaven, including "tayu toniñe andehui" and "tayu andehui."[268] This metaphor lasted throughout the colonial period; the full phrase "yuhuitayu toniñe andehui" appears in a testament written in 1807.[269]

People envisioned the sacred realm in the image of the secular order.[270] Christian ideology portrayed God as the King of Heaven, superior to earthly monarchs. All others in his celestial court were subordinate figures and potential intercessors between God the Father and his children on earth. Popular and official conceptions of God cast the Creator in patriarchal terms, as an almighty father figure seated in the Kingdom of Heaven. The "stairway to heaven" image features a lone, bearded male seated in the sky. Sometimes, the *Doctrina* used the loanword *rey* to reinforce the notion of kingship, calling Jesus "iya Rey andehui ñuu ñayehui" [yya King of Heaven and Earth].[271] The Christian Kingdom of Heaven also featured a "Queen of Heaven," the Mother of God. The Ñudzahui "kingdom" placed as much emphasis on the female as the male ruler of the married couple. As discussed in chapter 6, the term *yuhuitayu* was used in reference to a place and, in particular, to a sociopolitical alliance of male and female rulers who represented lordly establishments. Origin legends and codices depicted sacred male and female creator couples who descended from the primordial couple. Colonial sources confirm the fundamental belief in gendered ñuhu and cuacu pairs. Just as popular conceptions of the Kingdom of Heaven in early modern Spain were based on a projection of the earthly sociopolitical order, modeled on the European court, the Ñudzahui *yuhuitayu andehui* represented a celestial version of male and female rulers on earth.[272] Thus, Mary figured prominently in popular conceptions of the yuhuitayu andehui.

A woodcut in the *Doctrina en lengua misteca* depicts Mary with Jesus in the yuhuitayu andehui (see fig. 8.13).[273] Mary gestures toward her male counterpart as a yya dzehe toniñe would gesture in the codices, with one finger pointing downward and one open palm extended upward. This familiar pose can be seen in many preconquest writings, including the *Codex Nuttall* (see fig. 8.14).[274] The gesture refers to agreement and acceptance. On the other side, Jesus gestures in the traditional Christian manner. This image is introduced by a text describing the "rulership, sacred house, seat in the sky" [tayu toniñe huay ñuû tayu andehui], where "the lords Jesus Christ and his precious mother Saint Mary live" [yosica hitohoyo Jesu Christo hyy ceê maniya Sancta María]. They are accompanied by "all the angels and saints" [deê taca Ángeles deê taca sanctos],

FIGURE 8.13. Woodcut of Mary and Jesus in the yuhuitayu andehui, from the *Doctrina en lengua misteca,* by fray Benito Hernández (1567, f. 52v). The Huntington Library.

FIGURE 8.14. Female ruler (left) and male ruler (right) gesturing in the preconquest *Codex Nuttall*, p. 30. Codex-Zouche Nuttall, British Museum, London. Facsimile edition by Akademische Druck- u. Verlagsanstalt, Graz/Austria 1987.

who are assembled to the right of the seated couple. Below is a multitude of believers, called "all we children" [deê taca çayando], who pray to the sacred couple above.[275] "A villainous, evil person called the Antichrist" [taa çana taa ñahuaâ nanita Antechristo] lurks in the space below.

The image of the yuhuitayu andehui suggests that indigenous aides took part in the production of images for church-sponsored texts. If indigenous men participated in the gathering of data and the writing and typesetting of publications, it follows that native artists also produced images for the texts.[276] This image, more than any other illustration in the Docrina, resembles the type of hybrid art production discussed in chapter 2. The composition is based on a European model, but the depiction of Mary is unique. She is presented in a combined frontal-profile pose, a trademark of the sixteenth-century hybrid style. The awkward positioning of her arms is reminiscent of scenes in the *Codex Yanhuitlan* (and the *Florentine Codex*). Her position in the corner suggests that she was added to the composition after Jesus had been drawn. The visual representation of Mary as yya dzehe toniñe in the yuhuitayu andehui illustrates how native artists conceived of new sacred figures in familiar ways. Mary was interpreted as a female ruler who is seated with a male ruler and who actively gestures to her counterpart. In this role, she resembles the female creator figures 1-Deer or 9-Crocodile in the *Codex Vindobonensis*. Christian concepts and personages were adapted to the local context of Ñudzahui culture.

References to Mary in statements of faith confirm the general impression of the *Doctrina* image. In a testament from Chalcatongo, for example, don Diego de Velasco offered his soul to the lords ("hitoho") God and Mary and to all the saints and angels that accompanied them in the Kingdom of Heaven.[277] The passage reads: "I offer my soul to our lord God and our lady Saint Mary, and to all the saints and angels who are with them in the yuhuitayu rulership in the sky of glory" [yonaçocondi animandi noo nana hitohoyo ndios hiy noo nana hitooziyyo sata maria hiy noo nana ndiy taca sato hiy ageles hihi yohi taca daa yuhuitayu toniñe adihui gloria]. The writer referred to Mary and God in the same breath, using parallel honorific titles for the two lords. Literally, he offered his soul "in the presence of our lord God" [noo nana hitohoyo ndios] and "in the presence of our lady Saint Mary" [noo nana hitooziyyo sata maria]. In this case, the reference to heaven was translated into Spanish as *corte del cielo*, "celestial court," instead of *reino*, or "kingdom." Many Ñudzahui Christians emphasized Mary's noble, ruling qualities, as yya dzehe toniñe of the yuhuitayu andehui. Salvador de Celís of Teposcolula referred to Mary as "yya dzehe toniñe Santa Maria del Rosario," employing the titles for lady or noblewoman (yya dzehe) and ruler (toniñe), just as Jesus and God were called "yya toniñe" (male ruler) in the course of the same document.[278] Likewise, doña Lázara de Guzmán referred to Mary as "yia dzehe toniñe santa maria" [lady ruler holy Mary] and "stoho dzehendo toniñe santa maria" [our lady ruler Saint Mary]; in the course of her testament, she referred to God with the same superlative titles, "stoho" and "yia toniñe."[279] This aspect of Mary as ruler conforms to a woman's status in the yuhuitayu and resembles the Christian title "Queen of Heaven."[280] The *Doctrina* referred to Mary as a queen ("iya çeê toniñe") in the prayer Salve Regina and elsewhere.[281] Some people thought of Mary as a goddess. Domingo de Celís referred to Mary as "ñuhu Santa María," using the word for "sacred" or "deity" (*ñuhu*) usually applied to God. Petronilla Calderón called Mary "ñuhu yya dzehe toniñe Santa Maria," combining the words for "deity" or "sacred" and "female ruler."[282]

Most people recognized Mary as a sacred mother. Petronilla Calderón referred to God as "dzutu maniya" [precious father] and Mary as "dzehe maniya" [precious mother], in the manner of a creator couple.[283] Domingo de Celís called her the "noble mother of the precious child of the true God" [yya dzehe santa maria mani dzaya ndisa ñuhunDios] and "the mother of all of us" [yya dzehe sindehe tacando].[284] In the case of Mary as "our mother," the *Doctrina* makes a clear distinction that testaments do not always make: God is called "the father of all of us" [dzutu ndehe taca ñadzaña], whereas Mary is called "the precious mother of the lord God" [zehe mani yya Dios].[285] In the exposition of the Ave María prayer, Mary is described as the "mother of the son of the lord God" [dzehe dzaya yya nDios].[286] The invocation of the Virgin in testaments as "our precious mother" is comparable to the Nahuatl phrase *tonantzin* or *totlaçonantzin*.[287] As Lockhart has noted for the Nahuas, the interpretation of Mary as "our mother" seems to represent a native innovation.[288] Mary "our mother" complemented God "our father."

The *Doctrina* tended to emphasize Mary's pureness, as "the lady Saint Mary, the entirely divine, entirely sacred precious lady mother of the lord God" [stoho dzeê sancta María iya nee iy nee ñuhu dzehe mani yya Dios].[289] Her consummate qualities as Virgin are conveyed by the parallel construction "nee iy nee ñuhu," in which *nee* means "whole," "entire," or "everywhere."[290] This term is similar to the Nahuatl *cenquizca*, "entire," "perfect," or "consummate." In Nahuatl, the Virgin Mary was described as *cenquizcaichpochtli;* the word *ichpochtli* refers to an unmarried female who has reached puberty, or a maiden.[291] In the Ñudzahui language, no clear term stands out for "maiden." The *Vocabulario* lists several terms under "donzella virgen," combining ñaha (female) with *nee* (entire), *yy* (divine), and *ñuhu* (sacred). One description refers to a woman's body.[292] The last of nine terms, *ñaha quachi*, stands out in mundane writings;

typically, girls and maidens were called *ñaha dzuchi* or ñaha quachi, using the diminutive with "woman." Unlike the *Doctrina*, few testaments emphasized Mary's virginity, and few testators used the name *Virgen*.

The Nahuas of central Mexico found a similar attraction in the Virgin of Guadalupe and other images of Mary, considering her as much a goddess as the mortal mother of Jesus, even if they did not associate her specifically with Tonantzin, a preconquest female deity.[293] In the Mixteca, Tonantzin and Guadalupe had no impact on Ñudzahui interpretations of Mary in the sixteenth and seventeenth centuries. In general, references to the Virgin of Guadalupe do not appear in Ñudzahui testaments until the eighteenth century, and most references were made in the second half of the century. The most prominent image of Mary in the Mixteca was the Virgin of the Rosary, the Dominican patroness.

Nobody adored Mary more than the Spaniards, and no group promoted Marian devotion in New Spain more than the religious orders. If Mary was an ideal successor to pre-Christian female deities in Europe, she won over the hearts of Ñudzahui Christians, too.[294] Medieval Christianity viewed the Virgin Mary as a prominent queen or empress in the Kingdom of Heaven, a mortal who became a saint because of her motherly virtue. In sixteenth-century wills from Madrid, Carlos Eire points out that Mary was the most popular intercessor between God and testator and that she was often implored to act in her role as mother of Jesus.[295] Spaniards in the sixteenth and seventeenth centuries emphasized her virgin qualities, her role as the suffering bearer of the sacred child, and her ability to act as mediatrix.

In the yuhuitayu andehui, Jesus and Mary were joined by many saints. People referred to "all the saints who live in the Kingdom of Heaven" [taca santos ysi siyo yuqua yuhuitayu toniñe andehui gloria].[296] The *Vocabulario* describes them as yya who suffered on earth and joined God in heaven.[297] In general, saints did not bear high titles such as *stoho* or *yya toniñe* and were not usually called *ñuhu*. Often, they were called *yya*, but most people simply referred to them with the Spanish *santo* or *santa*. However, the general rule did not always apply. In Yolomecatl, Nicolás de Cervantes referred to saints in the same terms as he referred to God, using "stoho" [lord] and "stoho dzehe" [lady]. On three separate occasions in 1704, when the community gave gifts to a friar on his patron saint's day, Cervantes referred to the saint as a "stoho" and a "ñuhu" [deity].[298] Whereas saints were generally understood as sacred yya who had lived in the past and had ascended to the yuhuitayu andehui, angels defied the imagination. The *Vocabulario* calls angels *yya ñayeque ñacoño*, literally "lords without bones or flesh."[299] This is a confusing image, considering the usual depiction of angels in art from the period as fleshy, little creatures. The *Doctrina* simply used the loanword *ángeles*.

Certain fundamental Christian acts were described in terms that signified minimal understanding of the act's sacred meaning. For example, "to baptize" was translated as "to sprinkle water on someone" [sadzonduta ñaha]. A baptized person was simply "one who received water" [tai ninihinduta].[300] The phrase "to receive water" was used for the sacrament of baptism in a document from Yolomecatl.[301] Holy water was "sacred water" [ndutañuhu] or "precious water" [dutamani]. The Eucharist was the "precious flesh of the lord" [coñomaniya].[302] People who went to mass said that they "saw mass," using the loanword *missa* with the verb "to see" (*sito*), instead of the customary Spanish expression "to hear mass."[303] These equivalents focus on the visible acts of the ceremony.[304] This terminology was especially common in the *Doctrina*, qualified by the early use of loanwords such as *baptismo, penitencia,* and *sacramento.*[305] Despite the friars' desire to avoid meaningless loanwords, the *Doctrina* of 1567 relied on quite a few mysterious terms associated with heaven that had no equivalent in the native language. Presumably, the friars and their aides chose to use the original word instead of introducing some obfuscating construction, such as the boneless, fleshless angel. The *Doctrina* introduced the following words (in Spanish or Latin): soul, saint, the Holy Spirit, apostle, prophet, cross, limbo, commandment, martyr, eternal paradise, earthly paradise, purgatory, glory, justice, angels, archangel, cherubim, seraphim, grace, virtue, evangelist, and power (*potestad*).

On the way to the yuhuitayu andehui, all baptized and faithful Christians hoped to make an expeditious passage through purgatory, which was called by many testators the *huahi caa purgatorio,* or the "jail of purgatory" (jail is literally "iron house"). This metaphor seems to portray purgatory as an undesirable holding place before one's final judgment. The *Doctrina* relied on the loanword *purgatorio* and described judgment day with the loanword *juicio.* The association of a jail with judgment probably comes from a familiarity with the Spanish legal system; people were usually imprisoned until found innocent. The iron house of purgatory threatened to delay one's ascent to the yuhuitayu in the sky. Even worse, a guilty verdict on judgment day would condemn one to a fate of fire, brimstone, and the dreaded owl-person.

The Devil, Hell, and Sin

When a gathering of nobles from Chalcatongo and Miltepec came to Teposcolula in 1622 to arrange a dispensation for marriage between don Diego de Velasco y Arellano and his cousin, doña Micaela de la Cueva, the fiscal swore the noble witnesses to the following oath:

> Then I, the fiscal, said to them: Listen you three, kiss this cross, so that you respond truly and correctly to every word that I ask you. Let there be no dishonesty on your chest or in your heart from the words you speak. If you lie, the owl-person devil will take your souls to hell, and in hell your souls will burn, suffer, and be tormented. If you speak truthfully, God will save your soul and will protect your soul in heaven, and there you will be content and joyous forever, I said. The three nobles responded, they said amen, they said it will be done. Then they placed their right hands on the holy cross, which was on top of the staff of justice; the three nobles extended their hands and kissed the cross.

> Yca nisiyñaha nduhu fiscal: Conahandi unindo, ntaayuhundo cruz, yaha saha dzahuidzo ndaa dzahuidzo cuitindo nuundi niy cutu ndudzu cacatnuhu ndisindo. Huacuhui canehendo dzacuiy caynindo ndudzu cachindo. Ntanacahanehendo tiñomi ñaha diablo qhundacañaha animando andaya, andaya cocayu condoho coneni animando. Nicaa niqhuhon tandaa cuiti dzatna dzahuindzo cachindo ndios qhunindahui ñahaya nuhu animando andihui gloria nocoocando si cocuhui dziy cocuhui huatu yni animando andihui gloria niycaa, niqhuhuni nidzahuidzondi. Hunito nicachito amen nicachito nacuhui dzahua. Taquiyeni queyndaha cuaha ndiunito nisaqhi santa cruz, yodzo nuu dzini bara de justiçian, nisinondahandi nintaatuhuiyuhu ndihuni toho.[306]

The fiscal used the phrase *tiñomi ñaha diablo* for the devil, combining *tiñumi* (owl) and *ñaha* (person) with the Spanish loanword *diablo.* The *Vocabulario* also defined the *demonio* as "teñumi ñaha."[307] This owl-person is the equivalent of the Nahua *tlacatecolotl*, from *tlacatl* (person) and *tecolotl* (owl).[308] In Nahua lore, the owl-person was a malevolent creature of the night who possessed the ability to change shape and to bring sickness and death. It is possible that Christian concepts first developed in central Mexico were brought to the Mixteca by Nahua aides or by the friars themselves. On the other hand, the owl-person may have been a widespread Mesoamerican belief; the term would not have been used if it did not make sense to native speakers. In any case, friars relied on the term *tiñumi ñaha*, one of many preconquest spirits, to represent the devil in the early colonial period. It is used throughout the *Doctrina* of 1567, often coupled with *demonios* in the same manner that the fiscal used *tiñomi ñaha diablo* in his speech to the nobles. The *Doctrina* even defined a "ñuhu named the Antichrist" [ñuû nani Antechristo] as the son of the owl-person ("çaya tiñomiñaâ").[309]

The *Doctrina* portrayed the devil as one who "deceives men and women" [jha cay taa yee ñaâ çeê].[310] In criminal records, many people claimed that they had been tricked into committing sins or crimes by the devil.[311] Accordingly, a second term for *demonio* in the *Vocabulario* is "ñuhu cuina" [deity who robs or tricks].[312] The notion of calling the devil a ñuhu, the same word reserved for God, was problematic. Use of the term *ñuhu* is comparable to the Nahuatl *teotl*, which some friars feared might encourage the equation of preconquest deities with the Christian God. Despite the use of native-language terms for the devil, many people had adopted the loanword *diablo* by the end of the sixteenth century. In 1581, María García invoked the name of the diablo when she conspired with Andrés Trujillo to kill her husband, Agustín García. The attempted homicide in San Andrés Chalcatongo elicited three native-language testimonies, recorded immediately after the crime.[313] In the middle of the night, when Agustín was fast asleep, Andrés crept into his house with a knife. Agustín awoke, grabbed the knife, and began to stab Andrés, who cried out for María to "smash this devil's head" [çatahui sini diablo yaha]. Later, when Andrés and María were apprehended, María confessed that "the devil(s) deceived me" [diablos nicay nuu yninza].[314] María used the term *diablos* to refer to one or more demons who had tricked her into killing her husband, whereas Andrés used the term in reference to Agustín.

Hell was called *andaya*, the term for the "underworld," sometimes modified by the loanword *infierno*. The *Vocabulario* describes hell as a dark and wretched place within the earth, but it is more of an abstract, circumlocutory entry than a useful equivalent.[315] This term does not translate as "place of the dead," like the Nahua equivalent for "hell" (*mictlan*). The association between the underworld and the owl-person is unclear. Hell was also envisioned as a "house of demons" [huahi demonios].[316] In the end, the native term for hell did not convey the sense of divine punishment and damnation associated with the Christian concept.

Finally, the term for "soul" in the passage written by the fiscal of Teposcolula relies on the Spanish loanword *anima*. Again, the *Vocabulario* employs a long and confusing circumlocution for the soul that refers to the heart; it is unlikely that the phrase was used by native speakers.[317] Employing the heart as a metaphor for the soul was bound to cause confusion, especially since the term *ini*, "heart," was used in numerous expressions to signify emotion and volition. If the friars found rough equivalents for hell and the devil based on preexisting concepts, there was little in the native vocabulary to approximate the Christian meaning of the soul. Thus, to the neophyte, hell was a place inside the earth (where everyone was buried), the devil was a malevolent native spirit or a deceitful deity (one of many spirits who had always existed), and the soul was a foreign, abstract concept. We know that conceptions of the soul and sin were crucial components of Christian ideology. If the idea of a soul was vague, how was it possible to define the concepts of sin and personal salvation in concrete terms?

The Mixtec *Vocabulario* defines "sin" and "crime" as *cuachi. Cuachi,* or "quachi," resembles the Nahuatl *tlatlacolli* and is associated with both serious crimes such as homicide and minor offenses such as theft as well as common mistakes and defects. The verb "to sin," *dzatevui,* literally means "to cause damage," resembling the Nahuatl verb *tlatlacoa.* The complex surrounding *cuachi* is extensive; the word is often modified by other terms to impart a different meaning, depending on the context.[318] For the Nahuas, the term *tlatlacolli,* adopted for the concept of sin, fell short of reaching the full meaning with which the Christian concept was imbued.[319] This is true for the concept of cuachi, both today and in the sixteenth century.[320] The word appears in Ñudzahui-language criminal records from the colonial period. In a murder note written in 1684, Pedro de Caravantes of Yanhuitlan employed the term *cuachi* to refer to his crime of murder. But he also used *cuachi* a second time in reference to his *anima* and God. Thus, the author of the murder note conveyed a Christian concept by extending the semantic range of a native-language word in conjunction with a basic loanword (anima). Unfortunately, his ability to talk about sin did not restrain him from committing, in the words of the *Doctrina,* a "cuachi mortal."

The authors of the *Doctrina* wrote a great deal about cuachi. Mortal and venial sins were modified by the respective loanwords. Pride, conveyed by the loanword *soberbia,* was called the "mother and father of all sins" [dzehe dzutu si ndehe ndu quachi].[321] In talking about hell and sin, the *Doctrina* frequently evoked the metaphor of the road or path.[322] The devil tricked people into following the *ychi andaya,* the path to hell. It was a "dangerous path, a harmful path, a dangerous and harmful path" [ychi nicuhui cana nicuhui neni ychi neni ychi cana].[323] Discussions of sin emphasize the dangers of nature and the need to avoid the temptations of the "flower fields [garden] of earthly paradise" [ytuyta parayso terrenal]. In life, one was forced to choose between the *ychi andehui* (road to heaven) and the *ychi andaya* (road to hell). One could not follow both roads at the same time. In the same vein, one could not have "two hearts." In a section on the meaning of confession, the *Doctrina* states that "we sinned before our lord God" [nidzatehuindo nuu nana yyanDios] because "we were of two hearts" [nicuhui uhui ynindo].[324] In the Inquisition trial of Yanhuitlan, a native witness used the expression of having two hearts when he accused the nobles of Yanhuitlan of worshiping their old deities and the Christian deity at the same time. The *Doctrina* discouraged this ambivalence by drawing a sharp line between the good (*sa huaha*) and the bad (*sa ñahuaha*), warning people about the "evil in the world" [sa ñahuaha caa ñuu ñayehui].[325] The act of confessing (*nanama*) was crucial to steadying one's course, one's heart on the ychi andehui. The *Doctrina* provided a model of how to confess oneself, written in a most reverential language, which emphasized the straightening of the heart. The model began: "I am a sinner. I set straight, I make clear my heart. I reveal my sins before our lord God and before the noblewoman, the entirely divine, entirely sacred

Saint Mary and the apostles Saints Peter and Paul and all the saints who have gone on to heaven, who have become sacred, who have ascended to the Kingdom of Heaven" [ñadzaña tay sadzatehui yoquidzandaa yoquidzacuite yni ñadzaña yonacuaayuhu ñadzaña quachi ñadzaña nana stohondo nDios sii nuu nana yya dzehe Santa María yya nee ñuû nee yy nee caa sii apostoles san Pedro y San Pablo dehe taca santos sii santas ysisiyo andehui ysindehe ñuhu ysita candaa yuhuitayu andehui]. The metaphor for straightening one's heart, based on *yni* and the verbal couplet *quidzandaa quidzacuite,* corresponds with a Nahuatl term for the rite of confession.[326]

The discussion of sin naturally leads to a consideration of guilt and shame. Like crime and sin, guilt is also defined as *cuachi,* distinct from shame. Guilt is so closely associated with criminal and sinful acts that the same word is applied to all three concepts. The term focuses more on the act of doing something wrong than on an internal feeling of regret about the act. In this sense, it is more like "guilty." To approximate shame (*vergüenza*), the author of the murder note from Yanhuitlan used *caha,* verbalized as "yocuhuicahanuu ñadzaña" (literally, "I am shame-faced" or "there is shame on me/my face"). He was ashamed because, in his own words, his wife's alleged lover was "a thief and his wife had been stolen," not because he had killed her. The verb associated with "casting shame" is also listed in the *Vocabulario* as an entry for adultery.[327] Thus, his wife's adulterous behavior had cast shame on him. The context of shame in this case connotes more the idea of public humiliation than internalized regret.[328]

The early colonial dialogue between friars and native nobles produced reasonably equivalent terminologies for Christian concepts. And yet, despite fertile grounds for shared understanding, native-language vocabulary and loanwords had certain inherent limitations. Some native-language terms and metaphors possessed ambiguities or associations unrelated to the original concept. Other terms did not transmit the moral and ethical essence of Christian concepts, such as sin, guilt, penitence, and personal salvation. In most cases, Ñudzahui speakers continued to rely on native terminology, conventions, and ideological constructs to describe and understand Christian phenomena throughout much of the colonial period. In other words, they understood Christianity in their own terms.

This survey of Christian moral terminology in the native-language record represents another aspect of the complex and dynamic interaction of cultures in colonial Mexico. A comparison of the Nahuatl- and Ñudzahui-language Christian dialogue, with all its similarities and differences, sheds light on the local and regional dimensions of native Christianity.[329] The creation of a Ñudzahui-Christian religious ideology, articulated by native-language writings and art, was no simple syncretic process. The dialogue reveals as many points of disjunction as convergence. The terminology of native-language testaments indicates that models worked out in the *Doctrina* and other church-sponsored texts were subject in practice to many local interpretations. The dynamic, parochial nature of religious practices and beliefs suggests that the process of cultural exchange and influence was never complete or homogeneous.[330]

Let us now go beyond the analysis of words and woodcuts to consider some of the many local religious practices associated with Ñudzahui Christianity in the colonial period.

Christian Images

Ñudzahui Christians paid special attention to the care and maintenance of their Christian images—the saints. An important part of every last will and testament involved the offering of money to holy images inside the local church. Since the typical huahi ñuhu housed many images, one's offerings could amount to a substantial donation. Nobles and commoners offered coins to these images, even if they had to sell things to acquire the money. Even the poorest people managed to give a few *tomines* to images of Jesus Christ and the saints.[331] People sustained the images in their churches and their tayu (altars) by feeding their *satnu* (offertory boxes) with coins. The standard phrase for the act of offering was *yodzocondi nana* (I offer before) or *yodzocondi satnu* (I offer to the box) of a certain image. On a saint's feast day, part of the money in the satnu was used to sponsor a celebration that fed members of the community, or at least those who belonged to the cofradía that maintained the image. Sometimes, the word *satnu* was even defined as "cofradía" in subsequent translations of testaments, referring to the coffers of the religious sodality.[332] Offerings to the saints provided food and drink to fellow community members.[333]

The offerings of don Gerónimo García y Guzmán are especially notable. In 1672, he bequeathed money to a "Santo Christo tay ñudzahui" [holy Christ of the Ñudzahui people] and a "Santo Christo español" [holy Christ of the Spaniard(s)].[334] He did not elaborate on the ethnic distinction. It is likely that the images of Christ belonged to specific cofradías in Teposcolula.[335] There were at least five different images of Christ in the church of Teposcolula at this time. Don Gerónimo also left money to three different images of the Virgin in his church of Teposcolula: "yya dzehe solidad" [the Lady of Soledad]; "yya dzehe Rosario Español" [the Lady of Rosario of the Spaniard(s)]; and the unnamed "yya dzehe chisi coru" [the Lady beneath the choir]. A few years later, don Gerónimo's wife gave money to multiple images of Christ but only referred specifically to one as a "santo christo español."[336] In 1731, Josef Rodríguez referred to a "yia dzihi rosario yia castilla" in the church of Teposcolula, which was translated as "Nuestra Señora del Rosario de los Españoles."[337] Ethnic saints and their sponsoring cofradías represented defined constituencies of the local church and community. However, it was not uncommon for Ñudzahui testators to make offerings to Castilian images in the spirit of giving something to all the cofradías. In 1726, when Petrona Calderón of Teposcolula gave money to various cofradías, she reserved an offering for the "satnu animas yya castilla," translated as the "box for the Spanish souls in purgatory."[338]

Multiple images of Christ, Mary, and the saints lent themselves to the complexity and micropatriotism of sociopolitical organization in the Mixteca.[339] Each corporate entity desired its own image of a saint or Jesus Christ. The Christian conception of the patron saint accommodated an ancient yearning for local autonomy. Even in distant Mexico City, a group of people from the Mixteca had established a cofradía by the early seventeenth century and proudly paraded their own image of the Virgin of the Rosary.[340] In the Mixteca Alta, the *ñuu siña* of Ayusi kept an image of the crucified Christ, which they brought out each year for the Holy Week procession "in the same manner as the other barrios that made up the pueblo of Yanhuitlan." The organization of processions and feasts respected the ordering of barrios; Ayusi claimed to be the first barrio in the processional rotation. Officials from Ayusi recounted how they elected a *mayordomo* from the nobles of their siña who would guard the offerings and goods for the dressing and procession of the sacred image. In 1711, the mayordomo of Ayusi guarded the following items belonging to the image of Christ: twenty pounds of wax, forty sheep and goats, about fourteen *fanegas* of maize, eight pesos, two candle holders, and some wool. Ayusi's saint represented its separate status within the greater entity of Yanhuitlan. All the community lacked was a separate church to solidify its autonomy. Significantly, nobody referred to a cofradía or even mentioned the word in the proceedings. According to nobles from Ayusi, the mayordomo protected goods and money belonging to their "Santo Christo," and to the siña of Ayusi in general, also referred to as the "comonidad" in the native-language record. The "mayordomo of the community" was elected along with other cabildo and church officials, including two tequitlatos ("ña saque"), two regidores, and the fiscal.[341]

Some ñuu managed to achieve a limited degree of autonomy with their saints. As a sujeto, Santiago Yolomecatl struggled to achieve independence from the cabecera of Teposcolula.[342] In 1704, the residents of Yolomecatl had their own small church, feasts, and processions. They proudly maintained a pair of images, a "stoho" Santiago and a "stoho dzehe" María. But they also continued to pay allegiance to Teposcolula by sending periodic offerings of money to the church of Teposcolula.[343] They participated in the cabecera's Holy Week procession and sent their dancers to Teposcolula on Corpus Christi day, instead of sponsoring these events in their own community. Yolomecatl also provided labor for church-related activities in the cabecera, including what it called "tniño ytu dzutu yucudaa," farming the lands of the friars of Teposcolula.

Communities sought intercession from the saints, as Christians did in sixteenth-century Spain. Spaniards prayed to Mary for rain and fertile harvests in the sixteenth century; entire communities called upon Mary to rescue them in times of drought or severe weather.[344] Ñudzahui Christians drew on a rich tradition of Christian lore and hagiography. In October 1704, officials from Santiago Yolomecatl paid for a mass to "stoho dzehendo del pilar de zaragosa" [Our Lady of Pilar of Zaragosa] in the hope that she would petition God to protect their crops from frost.[345] The legend of Pilar's apparition to Santiago was widespread in Spain by the sixteenth century.[346] Thus, the people of Santiago Yolomecatl appealed to a specific image of Mary who had appeared before their own patron saint in the sacred past. In her capacity as intercessor in times of drought, Mary fulfilled the specialized function of the rain deity, Dzahui. Some people continue to think of Mary and Dzahui as a complementary pair. Mixtec prayers and chants, recorded by Maarten Jansen and Aurora Pérez in Chalcatongo in the 1970s, associated the two ñuhu and addressed them simultaneously.[347] In Santiago Nuyoo, John Monaghan observed that people respected the "ñu'un Savi" ("ñuhu Dzavui" in the colonial orthography), whom they define in Spanish as "the saints of rain."[348]

Communities sponsored masses on behalf of many special projects and concerns. For example, in Yanhuitlan, a mass was said in 1677 for the men who went to chop wood.[349] In Yolomecatl, a mass was said so that "stohondo Dios" might ensure a good yield from the lime kiln. When they fired the oven, officials and men involved in the work drank pulque, as if to seal their appeal with a traditional oblation.[350] In fact, they drank pulque every time the kiln was fired. They also drank pulque when they began work on a community field. Sometimes, the community also provided the workers with food, but the amount of money spent on pulque always exceeded money spent on food. The sacred implication of making lime and chopping trees brings to mind some of the "superstitions" documented by Hernando Ruíz de Alarcón in the Nahuatl-speaking area of Guerrero. In the first quarter of the seventeenth century, the priest observed elaborate rituals connected with preparing lime kilns and chopping wood, complete with incantations and pulque drinking.[351] In the case from Yolomecatl, leaders appealed to God with a mass in the church on Sunday and then drank pulque and performed other rituals when they stoked the flames of the kiln on Monday. They made parallel propitiatory offerings to ensure a good yield.

If saints lent themselves to corporate concerns, they also appealed to the more intimate, personal needs of the household. Most people possessed Christian images and objects in their home. Don Gabriel de Guzmán's inventory, discussed above, was extraordinary in this regard, but many yya and toho accumulated comparable stores of sacred items. Don Diego de Velasco, a yya of Tlaxiaco, had accumulated twenty-five lienzos and images (both called *naa* in testaments) by the time he made his will in 1627.[352] Similarly, Sebastián Sánchez Hernández possessed fifteen lienzos and images.[353] Catalina García, a noblewoman from Yanhuitlan, owned two crucifixes, some banners from the church altar, and multiple images of the Virgin Mary. She also possessed "a house and all its images" [huahi sihi nee cutu naa], a one-room structure set aside for devotion, resembling the Nahua *santocalli*, or "saint-house."[354] These separate houses were called *oratorios* in Spanish. According to Herrera, most people in the sixteenth century had "oratorios in their houses where they make offerings and perform sacrifices on behalf of their needs."[355] The colonial record contains fleeting references to household saints. In 1681, for example, a sick man from Teposcolula named Nicolás Vásquez entered his "oratorio" from the patio of his house after drinking a remedy made from an herb called "Santa María."[356] The aged widower addressed himself to each of the saints in the one-room structure and prayed to each of them twice.

Some testators bequeathed tracts of land dedicated to saints, or lands that were attached to specific images of saints, to household members.[357] The produce of that land was used to maintain the image and to sponsor feasts on the saint's day. For example, doña Josefa de Salazar maintained multiple images of saints in her house and possessed several lands dedicated to them.[358] In her testament of 1750, she divided her deceased husband's estate by bequeathing one saint and at least one piece of land to each of five heirs. She disposed of her own, separate estate in the same manner, thereby consolidating saints, houses, and lands among the same heirs. Finally, she bequeathed the saints and houses of her grandmother to one of the five heirs. The extended Vásquez y Salazar family owned as many saints as plots of land, suggesting an ideal ratio of one saint for each field. Juan Domingo of Topiltepec was even more explicit about saints' lands when he gave a tract of land named "yodoñuñami" to the Virgin of the Immaculate Conception ("yya dzehe la lipia consepsion") and a plot of land named "ytnuanchihi" to Jesus of Nazareth. In 1711, these lands were located next to the community lands ("ñuhu comunidad").[359] Presumably, the lands of the household images were to be worked by household members. Similarly, Rosa Hernández gave some of her land in Chilapilla to the Virgin of Guadalupe in 1749; another testator from the same ñuu, don Lorenzo Vásquez, made the same bequest a few months later.[360] In 1713, Micaela Nicolasa gave half of her house, including the "huehe cucina" [kitchen house] and a plot of land behind the house, to San Pedro Mártir.[361] The practice of bequeathing lands to saints who were associated with a particular household accommodated a general concern for concentrating landholdings among members of the household, discussed in chapter 7.

Saints were also the symbolic or actual owners of community lands. The community of Santiago Yolomecatl dedicated plots of community land to one male and one female saint, called "the field of Our Lord Santiago and the field of Our Lady of Rosario" [ytu stohondo santiago sihi ytu stoho dzehendo del Rosario].[362] The fields were cultivated by rotational, collective tniño labor. In the Valley of Mexico, tracts of lands dedicated to saints were run by either the community, cofradías or their mayordomos, or specific households that were obligated to contribute specified amounts to masses and feasts.[363] Sometimes, it is difficult to distinguish between these categories. In Yucatan, the economic enterprises of the community (represented by the *caja de comunidad*) and cofradías were one and the same.[364] Even in the case of nonagricultural properties, this arrangement applies to Yolomecatl in 1704. When community officials held a small feast after shutting down the lime kiln, they killed a goat that belonged to "our lord Santiago" [stohondo Santiago]. Presumably, they meant the cofradía of Santiago.[365] The community did not reimburse the cofradía for the animal. In fact, the lengthy document does not make any direct references to a cofradía.

The saints represent a diverse, colorful collection of sacred Christian ancestors. People treated the images as they had treated the cuacu or ñuhu, making little distinction between the image as representation and the divine essence, as if the material substance were the sacred being they venerated.[366] They endowed them with human attributes, dressed them, housed them, feasted with them, cleaned them, spoke to them, and made offerings before them. In their multiple advocations and attributes, saints adapted well to the local, corporate nature of social and sacred relations. Saints represented corporate aspects of local religion in sixteenth-century Spain, as well. The saints were also treated as household members. Ñudzahui communities and households accepted and appropriated the santos and santas. The Christ of the Ñudzahui people of Teposcolula exemplifies this process of localization. The celebration of the cult of saints in the Mixteca resembles patterns observed for the Nahuas and Yucatec Maya in the colonial period. When Spanish culture offered a recognizable practice with some indigenous analogue, indigenous people usually adopted the Spanish tradition while maintaining the essence of their own practices and beliefs.[367] The collective, corporate nature of feasts was another aspect of sacred and social relations that made sense to both Spanish and Ñudzahui Christians.

Feasts and Religious Expenses

The authors of the *Doctrina* made a conscious choice not to use the term *huico* to describe a Christian feast. Perhaps the term was linked too closely to preconquest-style feasts and offerings, as discussed above. It used the term in reference to the seasons, such as summer ("huico dzahui") and winter ("huico yuhua").[368] Instead, the *Doctrina* used the more neutral term *quehui* (day), often qualified by *cano* (large or great). Native writers of mundane records continued to use *huico* for feasts, however. In many respects, the colonial huico represented a fundamental continuity in sacred practices.

The cult of the saints depended on the periodic huico. Like the ancient native calendar of ceremonies, the Christian calendar was marked by multiple feast days that were dedicated to sacred ancestors and commemorated sacred events. The local patron saint's day was the greatest and most elaborate celebration of them all. In Santa Catalina Texupa, the community spent nearly twice as much money on the feast day of Saint Catherine as it did on any other annual feast in the mid-sixteenth century.[369] Since Santa Catalina Texupa was represented by a woman named doña Catalina in the 1550s, the community simultaneously celebrated its patron saint and its female ruler.[370] In addition to the feast of its patron saint, the community of Texupa allocated money from its caja de comunidad for the celebration of at least eleven other feast days.[371]

A major general feast was the combined celebration of All Saints' Day and All Souls' Day in November, generally called "Todos Santos." According to fray Diego Durán, who wrote in the 1580s, Nahuas observed a "feast of the little dead" and a "feast of the adults," complete with offerings of food and candied fruits, that corresponded with the Christian celebrations. He suspected that Nahuas continued the preconquest tradition in a Christian guise.[372] This holiday is known today as "Día de los Muertos."[373] People in Yanhuitlan associated Todos Santos with a preconquest feast as early as the 1540s. A Mixtec witness in the Inquisition trial spoke of a feast called "huico tuta" that coincided with All Souls' Day. In this huico, celebrated after the rainy season and during the maize harvest, native priests unwrapped their images and made elaborate offerings to them.[374] In effect, people shared the fruits of the new harvest with their sacred ancestors. In the colonial period, many testators made special provisions in their wills for this Ñudzahui-Christian celebration. In 1625, María López Siñuu sold a house and an adjoining plot of land to pay for masses and to sponsor a feast on the day of Todos Santos, which she called "huico tucu santo santa."[375] Typical of many Ñudzahui testators, María emphasized the gendered aspect of saints by using the parallel construction of male "santo" and female "santa," choosing not to use the male gender as a generic form, and replacing *todos* with the native equivalent *tucu*.[376] In Tamasulapa, Juan de la Cruz referred to the feast of All Saints' Day with the parallel couplet "uico santo uico santa."[377] When Domingo Pérez of Yanhuitlan made his testament in 1670, he asked his son to place votive candles on his grave on All Saints' Day and to remember him on the feast days of other "santos" and "santas."[378] The honoring of household ancestors was an important feature of this feast, but it was celebrated at the corporate level, as well. Texupa allocated money to sponsor a huico for Todos Santos in the 1550s.

A feast was not a feast without dancing. Ceremonial dances, called *mitotes* in Spanish, derived from the Nahuatl *mitoti*, accompanied Christian celebrations in the Mixteca.[379] For example, in 1581, everyone in Tlaxiaco went to see the dances in the church patio on Easter Sunday.[380] On that holy day, Diego Hernández brought gifts of food and cacao to his *compadres* (ritual kinsmen). After eating and drinking pulque, they went to the church to watch the dances. Communities made careful plans to provide dancing during feasts. A recurring expense in a record of accounts from Yanhuitlan, written in 1677, concerned the payment of a native dance instructor who trained nobles to perform mitotes, especially for the feast days of Corpus Christi and Santo Domingo.[381] In preparation for the feast of Santo Domingo, the community's patron saint, the instructor met with a group of dancers at least four times between July 25 and August 4. Each time they met, the *maestro* and the dancers were remunerated with food and cacao. In 1707, the community of Topiltepec also paid an instructor to prepare dancers for the "huico corpus," the feast of Corpus Christi.[382] And in 1704, dancers from Santiago Yolomecatl went to Teposcolula in May to participate in the "huico corpus."[383] Maestros who trained nobles how to perform these elaborate rituals were knowledgeable specialists who fulfilled an ancient responsibility. The record makes numerous references to ritual dancing during Christian celebrations.[384] As Robert Ricard observed for Indians of New Spain in general, "in their feasts and dances, they mingled Christian elements with the practices and beliefs of their old religion."[385]

Ritual dances required precious feathers. The act of dancing with feathers in church-related feasts exemplifies how Christianity in the Mixteca incorporated local practices.[386] Feathers retained their sacred value in the colonial period, even though Spaniards did not value feathers. In 1561, Texupa spent the considerable sum of seventy-five pesos for quetzal feathers in order to "decorate" the community.[387] Many testators counted feathers among their most important bequests. In 1678, Felipe de la Cruz, a noble from Topiltepec, owned a "dancing vestment with four large, green feathers."[388] In 1710, Domingo Ramos de la Cruz of Yucuita possessed some 860 green feathers, 94 Castilian feathers, 4 dancing outfits, and a music book.[389] In 1621, a noblewoman from Yanhuitlan named Catalina García referred to her possession of numerous feathers by various names, such as "yodzo," "ndoço," "vichi," and "tiqueva."[390] The translator defined them as "plumas para bailar," or "dancing feathers." Her estate included *tecomatillos* (small gourds) adorned with feathers, an elaborate headdress of feathers, and several masks. Catalina's inventory, an eclectic mixture of Christian images and native prestige items, represents the material culture of Ñudzahui Christianity.

Most communities allocated a significant amount of their annual budgets to food, pulque, and chocolate for their feasts. In Santiago Yolomecatl, 62 percent of total expenses in 1704 were spent directly on food or drink, mainly for feasts.[391] There is little doubt that the importance of ritual drinking in native ceremonies and feasts persisted in the colonial period. The Inquisition trials of the 1540s indicate that indigenous and Spanish witnesses equated inebriation with traditional practices, especially rites associated with the invocation of Dzahui. Throughout the colonial period, drinking was a highlight of Christian celebrations, including the Sabbath. The ritual use of pulque during the colonial period may be interpreted as an example of syncretic behavior.[392] Despite the friars' attempts to curb excessive drinking during feasts, pulque continued to flow on special occasions.

Religious expenditures in general represented a significant portion of a community's annual budget. In the Valley of Mexico, Gibson estimated that communities spent three-quarters or more of their income on church supplies and activities in the seventeenth and eighteenth centuries.[393] The *Codex Sierra* indicates that the community of Texupa spent a substantial amount on church activities and religious objects from

1550 to 1564, including feasts for saints and food for priests. On behalf of the church, the community bought everything from trumpets and chalices to fancy vestments of taffeta and velvet. Woodrow Borah and Sherburne Cook calculated that religious expenses, including feasts, constituted more than half of Texupa's total expenditures for the period covered by the manuscript.[394] María de los Ángeles Romero Frizzi used the same source to calculate that 58 percent of Texupa's expenses from 1550 to 1564 were related to religious feasts, goods for the church, and food and wine for priests.[395]

In Santiago Yolomecatl, a detailed list of expenses and revenue from the early eighteenth century confirms the data from Texupa. The record of 1704 indicates that the community allotted 56 percent of its annual expenses to church-related activities, including feasts.[396] Yolomecatl in the early eighteenth century was a poor community in comparison with Texupa in the mid-sixteenth century. Several expenditures in the *Codex Sierra* ledger would have exceeded Yolomecatl's means.[397] Nonetheless, the percentage of funds spent on religious activities and materials is comparable. In Topiltepec, church-related expenditures represented an overwhelming part of the community's budget in the early eighteenth century. A list of accounts for the year of 1707 shows that only about 16 percent of total expenditures were not allocated to a feast, a mass, a church item, the tithe, or a priest.[398]

Some communities established special funds for feasts. In 1677, twenty-one tequitlatos, or tribute collectors, of Santo Domingo Yanhuitlan, including two women, collected money and goods from nine siña or "barrios" to pay for religious feasts.[399] The money was called "duayaqua" in the Ñudzahui language, defined as "*tequios* reserved for the church."[400] This fund was intended to help sponsor the four principal feasts of the community: Easter, Corpus Christi, Christmas, and Santo Domingo, the community's patron saint. Nobles also collected cloth "mantas de pájaros" [feathered mantas] and other woven materials from women in each siña for the tutelary saint's celebration. On the day of the feast, August 4, officials distributed cloth gifts to priests, Spanish officials, native nobles, and the bullfighter who entertained them.[401]

The organization of feasts in the colonial period resembles the redistributive mechanisms of the civil-religious hierarchy in contemporary native communities. The religious feast system was a structured mechanism that supported community members with periodic banquets and social-sacred events.[402] We have already seen in the case of Yolomecatl how more than 60 percent of annual expenditures went toward food and drink. The community spent another 15 percent on clothing given as gifts, paid to the women who produced the clothes. Some expenditures simply listed "food for the community," even when there was no feast. It is likely that much of this food went to nobles of the "casa de la comunidad." The feast system respected social differences rather than leveling them. But even if the food and gifts were not always distributed evenly, religious feasts continued to fulfill a basic function of feeding people in communities.

Money spent on feasts was money that priests or Spanish officials could not appropriate for their own needs or interests. Officials and priests required certain goods and services that were paid out of the cajas or came from special funds set aside for such purposes. Sometimes, these responsibilities were assigned to specific households on a rotational basis. For example, in Yolomecatl, the obligation to feed local priests was delegated to households. Apparently, many people did not fulfill their obligations. In

1704, the notary of Yolomecatl recorded fifty-nine separate entries when individuals or groups of people paid a fine to the caja for failing to feed the local friar or for not working on church lands. The fines amounted to approximately 15 percent of the community's total income for that year. Additional fines were levied against those who failed to work for the friars in Teposcolula. Apparently, many people preferred to pay the fine than to feed the priests.[403]

Even though references to processions in the Mixteca are few and fleeting, certain important observations can be made from existing references. Processions and feasts reinforced political and sacred ties among contiguous communities. For example, in 1592, the alguacil of the church of San Andrés, a sujeto of Teposcolula, went to the community of Santa María Magdalena to ensure that the officials there would bring ashes to San Andrés on Wednesday, the first day of Lent. In turn, a group of nobles from San Andrés were in charge of bringing the ashes to Teposcolula.[404] The procession brought together indigenous officials from three separate communities. Women participated in processions, as well. In Yolomecatl, a procession on February 26 featured "women who carried our sacred lady of the Soledad and her black cloth hood" [ñaha dzihi nisiyo dee ñuhu stohodo de la solidad saha cobija ndeyu].[405] Processions and feasts attracted people from other communities. In Yanhuitlan, the spectacular Holy Thursday procession of the "penitents of blood" drew a crowd of curious onlookers from other parts of the Mixteca.[406] The supracommunity tendency of feasts and processions suggests how local forms of Christianity were shaped by certain shared, regional influences. Finally, procession routes and shrines marked the sacred boundaries of a community.[407] For this reason, conflict between communities often involved their saints and procession routes.[408]

Concealed Continuities

In matters of faith, the written record leaves us wondering what was never written and hence what is concealed from view. Many historians have discussed continuities in native rituals and beliefs in terms of spaces and places. In public spaces, at the corporate level, mixed or syncretic native-Christian practices predominated in centers of cultural interaction. On the other hand, in peripheral places where few priests or Spaniards ventured, Christian practices and beliefs made less of an impression. In both places, households and fields were sites of traditional life cycle rituals and ceremonies. The colonial record informs us primarily about the first space, the public arena of the community. Most Spanish and Ñudzahui notaries wrote in the administrative and religious centers where the Christian presence was most perceptible. Outside the cabeceras, religious practices are concealed from our view. Some practices were deliberately hidden and thus are doubly concealed. For this reason, it is important not to project across the entire region ethnohistorical findings based on sources in church-dominated centers.

Nevertheless, the historical record reveals that the adoption and adaptation of Christian images, ideas, and activities and the acceptance of friars did not obliterate all traditional practices and beliefs in the colonial period. For the Nahua area, no source demonstrates this fact better than Ruíz de Alarcón's "Treatise on Heathen Supersitions," recorded in Guerrero in the early seventeenth century.[409] Ruíz de Alarcón encountered a world of daily rituals, performed by specialists and ordinary folk alike, that seemed unaffected by Christian teachings. He vacillated between dwelling on the practices as serious idolatries and dismissing them as silly superstitions. There is no work like that of Ruíz de Alarcón for the Mixteca. But the absence of such sources does not mean that similar activities did not occur in nearby Oaxaca.

The continued use of the 260-day ritual calendar is perhaps the best evidence for the practice of indigenous ceremonies in the colonial period. Until they adopted full Christian names, all Ñudzahui men and women were named after their calendrical birth dates, consisting of a number and a sign from the ritual calendar. The 260-day cycle of the calendar corresponded to the human gestation period. The continued use of native surnames in the eighteenth century, discussed in chapter 5, proves that namers and prognosticators continued to operate in many communities in the Mixteca. The birth and naming ceremony was performed by male or female namers who had mastered the calendar and who were familiar with the symbolic meaning of days. Burgoa spoke of diviners or "astronomers" in the Mixteca who possessed a knowledge of the stars and who memorized the day signs and numbers of the ritual calendar.[410] Midwives also played a crucial role in birth ceremonies. In their capacity as healers, midwives possessed specialized knowledge of herbal medicines and ritual incantations. Respondents of the *Vocabulario* associated midwives with curing.[411] Naturally, people continued to seek out traditional male and female healers throughout the colonial period.[412]

Many writers in the colonial period used the Christian and ancient calendars simultaneously. The authors of the *Codex Sierra* made constant references to the ancient calendar and its equivalent Christian dates. When don Felipe de Saavedra, the lord of Tlaxiaco, gave his last will and testament in 1573, he qualified the Christian year with the native calendrical equivalent "coo quaa" (2-Deer).[413] In 1647, one indigenous writer combined references to the ancient and Christian calendars in the margins of the *Doctrina*. In a copy owned by the Huntington Library, one line reads: "today, Saturday, the 14th of September, 1647, was born the child of María de la Cruz, on the Ñudzahui day 10-deer" [huitna sabado 14 de septembre de 1647 aᵋ nicacu sidzaya mᵃ de la crus quihui ñudzahui siquaa].[414] In another edition of the *Doctrina* owned by the Huntington, someone wrote the date "quehui ñudzavi qh chi," literally "the Ñudzahui day 5-Wind."[415] It is ironic and somewhat suggestive that native writers referred to the ancient ritual calendar in a Christian doctrinal manual. The latter example may actually refer to a feast day associated with the ancient calendar, since *quehui* was the term for "feast" used in the *Doctrina*. The continued use of the calendar in places such as Yolomecatl, where many people possessed native surnames in 1704, indicates the persistence of divinatory household rituals. These were the types of activities that are barely observable in the record because they were doubly concealed.

In the Mixteca, evidence of "idolatries" after the Inquisition proceedings of the 1540s is scarce. This fact may be attributed more to the limited abilities of the church to investigate such possibilities than to the actual disappearance of traditional practices. Very few friars lived in the Mixteca. Many ñuu had no resident priests. On the other hand, some areas of Oaxaca came under close scrutiny in the late colonial period, especially the Zapotec and Mixe regions of the Sierra. In any case, persecuted practices were driven into houses and out to caves, fields, and hills. Caves continued to serve as sites of non-Christian ritual activity. As openings into the earth and sources of springs, caves are considered sacred places in the Mixteca.[416] And as concealed spaces, caves were perfectly suited for clandestine sacrificial offerings. Two examples of cave ceremonies illustrate how preconquest-style practices, reminiscent of those found in Yanhuitlan during the 1540s, continued in some places.

The first example of clandestine ceremonial activity involved a native noble named Diego de Palomares, the alcalde of Malinaltepec, who was accused of making sacrifices in a remote cave.[417] Apparently, Diego had a reputation for challenging authority. One time, he disrupted the governor's speech on the need to abstain from drinking pulque by accusing him of selling some land to a Spaniard. His accusation broke up the gathering in the church patio. In 1652, he allegedly invited a group of men and women to participate in a ceremony; they took candles, copal incense, and torches to a cave where he kept a bundled stone image with a finely carved face. One witness claimed that he accidentally found the image, surrounded by flowers and feathers, when he went into the cave to look for beehives. Other witnesses said that Diego made offerings to the bundle in times of drought, imploring the image to bring rain. He invited other people to participate in the ritual drinking that accompanied his visitations. When the Spanish alcalde mayor and a group of men investigated the cave, they found a sculptured stone image with eyes, mouth, and other features. Beside the image were two candles and some copal incense. They also found another small stone image that was carved in the pattern of a checkerboard. They confiscated the two images. When they questioned Diego de Palomares about the cave, he denied any knowledge of the sculptures. He responded that he had accompanied a friar to the cave in search of idols but they found none. The case was complicated by the testimony of two witnesses who accused the governor of planting the images in the cave in order to frame the alcalde. The case ends after an exchange of denials. The descriptions of bundled figures in caves, copal incense, feathers and flowers, ritual drinking, and supplications for water conjure up rituals associated with Dzahui that were described more than a century earlier. Clearly, preconquest-style practices continued in some clandestine capacity. If it were not for factional conflicts in Malinaltepec, this concealed activity would not have entered the historical record.

Spanish officials made another shocking cave discovery in 1706. In a remote, inaccessible cave near Tutla, outside Tamasulapa, officials found fifty-five skulls surrounded by sacrificial offerings.[418] They described some of the skulls as very old, some as more recent, and some as bloody. A rock in the middle of the cave was covered with copal incense and feathers. There were also many blades of obsidian glass, of the type that priests used to bleed their tongues and ears.[419] Whereas local indigenous people professed total ignorance about the cave, Spanish residents reacted with a mixture of horror, fear, and wild speculation. Spaniards feared that the bodies belonging to the heads had been devoured during a recent sacrificial feast. Some believed that the skulls belonged to Spaniards, presumably because they had reddish hair. Spanish officials and priests burned the skulls and buried the ashes inside the church; the feathers and remains of other sacrifices from the cave were burned and thrown in the river.

As Christian rituals became the dominant public form of religious expression in the sixteenth century, centered around the huahi ñuhu, the santos and santas, and the huico, many ancient practices were driven out of sight or were combined with Christian forms and structures in new, dynamic ways. Local religious practices defy generalization and reflect a spectrum of responses to Christianity. The most extreme responses to Christianity, outright resistance and full acceptance, were perhaps the least common. Factions within the same community contributed to the unpredictable and multidimensional nature of the process. In reality, the evolution of local religions is an ongoing process.

Nearly four decades ago, Charles Gibson observed that "our fullest evidence for preconquest survivals derives from modern practices rather than from colonial records," owing to the unsystematic nature of the archival record.[420] In other words, the lived present reminds us that the historical record presents a restricted view of local practices. No doubt, Christianity exerted a profound influence throughout the region. Contemporary ethnographies have documented an array of Ñudzahui-Christian practices. But in many places, multicultural forms exist alongside indigenous traditions that appear to be unaffected by Christianity. Some practices are unmistakably rooted in sacred relations that predate the conquest.[421] As a final example, in the community of Santiago Nuyoo, according to Monaghan, people refer to many male and female ñuhu, including several rain deities. These ñuhu behave very much like humans.[422] They meet to discuss activities that affect the well-being of the community, including the amount of maize that they will produce for the next year. They might produce a bounteous crop, or they might cause hunger and famine. The decisions of the ñuhu regarding how much work they will invest in tending to the maize crop, how they intend to fulfill their tniño or obligation, are influenced by the quality and quantity of sacrificial offerings that they receive from people in Santiago Nuyoo. Today, as in the past, sacred and social relations are intertwined.

CHAPTER 9

~

Ethnicity

MANY CULTURAL MARKERS OR TRAITS distinguished Ñudzahui people from other
ethnic groups in colonial Mexico. One received a Ñudzahui name at birth based on a
particular version of the Mesoamerican 260-day ritual calendar and was affiliated with
a named social group, as a *yya, toho,* or *ñandahi.* One spoke a regional variant of a widespread language and belonged to a household within a named *ñuu* and one of its named
siqui. One wore certain clothes that associated him or her with a particular place and
station. Men and women shared local and regional sacred beliefs and practices. One
category of ascription and identification, which transcended an affiliation with the local
ñuu, embodied these shared practices and values, the "cultural content" of the group.[1]
The term *Ñudzahui* represented a conscious identity based on these cultural attributes,
a subjective feeling of belonging to an ethnically defined group. The frequent use of
the term in the native-language record reflects how Ñudzahui-language speakers maintained the boundaries of that group.

   The frequent expression of Ñudzahui identity in native-language sources from
the area, and the complex and changing contexts of those expressions, are the subject
of this chapter. First I examine articulated expressions of ethnic identity after the
conquest—namely, how the so-called Mixtec Indians referred to themselves, their language, their region, and things associated with their culture in their own terms. The
examples are intended to show how people used the term *Ñudzahui* and to suggest
how specific social and cultural circumstances influenced an individual's reference to
his or her ethnic self. The construction and articulation of Ñudzahui identity are then
compared with expressions of ethnicity among two other ethnic groups in Mesoamerica, the Nahuas of central Mexico and the Maya of Yucatan. The second part of this

318

chapter considers multiethnic interactions in *cabeceras* of the Mixteca Alta and in the Valley of Oaxaca where Mixtecs came into close contact with ethnic others.

The Mixteca is an ideal setting for the study of interethnic interactions in the colonial period. The western area of the Mixteca Baja, extending from modern Guerrero to the southern edges of Puebla, shared boundaries and even communities with Nahuatl-speaking peoples. The northern perimeter of the Mixteca Alta was inhabited by Chocho, Cuicatec, and Ixcatec groups, and the southern Baja and coastal area included Trique, Amuzgo, and Chatino populations. In the east, the Mixteca spilled into the Valley of Oaxaca and overlapped with a cultural area known as the Zapoteca. After the conquest, the arrival of Spaniards, more Nahuas, mestizos, Africans, and other Europeans contributed to the multicultural milieu. This scenario is far more complex and interesting than the traditional biracial discussion of Indians and Spaniards in colonial Mexico.

Ñudzahui Identity

The term *Mixtec Indians* represents a Nahuatl and a Spanish designation for a people who, in preconquest and colonial times, called themselves by neither name. Native writers from the area did not use either term.[2] In contrast, Spanish-language sources, including translations of indigenous documents, make repeated references to "Mixtecos" and "Indios."[3] We associate the region of the Mixteca with the people who bear its name, but that name was not their own. *Mixteca*, the plural form of the Nahuatl *mixtecatl*, means "people of the cloud place." People from the Mixteca Alta called themselves *tay ñudzahui*, "people from the rain place" or "people from the place of Dzahui." *Dzahui* means "rain" or "a divine or esteemed thing" and is the name of the rain deity or deities, as discussed in the previous chapter. The term *Mixteca* indicates that Nahuatl speakers recognized the people of this adjoining cultural area as a homogeneous group; the term refers to the people of a given region, rather than from a specific ñuu such as Yanhuitlan or Teposcolula. Since the Nahuatl term is relatively close in meaning to *Ñudzahui*, perhaps the Nahuas derived their version from the genuine self-appellation. But the two terms are not synonymous. The Ñudzahui term for "cloud" is *huico*. "Cloud" and "rain" are distinct words in Nahuatl, too. Although the two words *dzahui* and *huico* may share a morpheme (*hui*) and a natural association, it is unlikely that the Nahuatl term based on clouds was a semantic equivalent of the Ñudzahui concept. Many Nahuatl names for other people and places did not correspond in meaning with local terms. The "Popoloca" surely did not adopt the pejorative name assigned to them by Nahuas, which refers to incomprehensible babblers.

A famous legend suggests how the Nahuas came to name the Mixteca and people from the region after clouds. In the sixteenth century, fray Toribio de Motolinía wrote that the Mixtecs were named after Mixtecatl, the fifth son of a lord originating from Chicomoztoc, the famous "place of the seven caves" in Mexica mythology.[4] Other sources identify this lord as Mixcoatl or Camaxtli, a prominent deity in Tlaxcala and Puebla. The report of Acatlan for the *Relaciones geográficas*, recorded in 1579, states that Mixtecatl was a Mexica lord who came to settle there. This Mixtecatl was either the leader of a Nahua faction that moved into the area or a local ruler who adopted a

Tolteca-Chichimeca origin. The area from Tututepec in the south to Acatlan in the north was a corridor of Nahua-Mixtec interaction in the postclassic period. Thus Nahuas may have named the area after this legendary figure who expanded Nahua influence into the region. Mixtecatl was peripheral to Nahua cults and practically unknown in Ñudzahui lore. The legend was widespread enough, however, to come to the attention of chroniclers such as Motolinía, Durán, Torquemada, and Burgoa.[5]

Dzahui is a sacred and esteemed life-giving force in the Mixteca. The deity Dzahui resembled the Nahua Tlaloc, the Zapotec Cocijo, and the Mayan Chac. The Inquisition trial of Yanhuitlan, discussed in the previous chapter, demonstrates the powerful presence of Dzahui in the Mixteca Alta before and after the conquest. The written record contains more information on Dzahui than on any other *ñuhu*. Dzahui continues to command a presence in the Mixteca.[6] The sacred association of the Ñudzahui name with a prominent native deity confirms its ancient origins. I do not believe that the term was invented after the conquest or that its use was encouraged by friars in an attempt to promote a homogeneous and distinguishable *nación* among other "naciones de Indios." The term was used throughout the native-language *Doctrina*, published in 1567, but the work nonetheless was titled *Doctrina en lengua misteca*. Maarten Jansen has observed the use of this name as a glyph in two preconquest-style codices, the *Codex Selden* and the *Codex Bodley*, as well as the early colonial Lienzo of Zacatepec.[7] The glyph consists of the *tablero con grecas* ñuu motif, combined with the familiar face of Dzahui, and accompanies both personal names and place-names.[8] Although the precise function of the glyph in these cases is unclear, its presence in pictorial writings is further evidence of its preconquest origins.

In native-language documents, the term *Ñudzahui* has been attested more than a hundred times in texts from the 1560s to the 1760s. Writers used the term in reference to the region, language, individuals and groups of people, communities, material objects, flora and fauna, and the ritual calendar. The term appears in sixteenth-century church-sponsored religious and language texts, but the best indication that this self-appellation was genuine and widespread is its frequent attestation in native-language archival sources, produced for mainly internal audiences, often made in the absence of Spaniards. The term was especially common in the Mixteca Alta and the Valley of Oaxaca. In contrast, the term is unattested in the Mixteca Baja. Since extant documentation from the Baja represents only a small percentage of extant native-language archival documentation, however, it is difficult to draw any firm conclusions from its omission. As for the tropical coastal region, no Ñudzahui-language records have appeared to date.

Today, the self-ascribed term, written as "ñudzahui" or "ñudzavui" in the colonial period, is spelled and pronounced many different ways, but it is still the operative term for "Mixtec" among those who speak a Mixtecan language.[9] The term always modifies a noun, whether *tay* (person or people) or *dzaha* (language). *Mixteco* is generally used as a self-ascribed reference only when speaking Spanish. The term *Indio* tends to be avoided altogether because it is a contrived category used mainly by outsiders and because of its pejorative connotation in Mexican society. Unlike *Indio*, *Ñudzahui* does not imply a homogenized and marginalized identity.

The following four sections analyze a variety of references to the term *Ñudzahui* in postconquest native-language texts.

Ñudzahui Land

In the prologue to his *Arte en lengua misteca* (1593), fray Antonio de los Reyes defined the region of the Mixteca in terms of its legendary origins and territorial subdivisions:

> There was an ancient legend that the lords who left from Apoala had divided them-selves into four parts, in such a way that they took over all of the Mixteca; they called the Mixteca Alta *ñudzavui ñuhu,* which is a divine and esteemed thing, from the verb *yeheñuhu,* to be held in esteem. They called the Chocho part *tocuijñuhu* for the same reason and *tocuij ñudzavui,* which is the Chocho Mixteca, due to the interaction, com-munication, and close kinship that they have with the Mixtecs. They called the part toward Oaxaca *tocuisi ñuhu* because it is also esteemed land; they gave the name *ñuñine* to the Mixteca Baja because it is hot country, and the whole mountain range as far as Puctla, the beginning of the coast, is called *ñuñuma* because of all the fog that one ordi-narily sees there, which in its thickness appears like smoke, called *ñuma* in Mixtec. The coast of the South Sea [Pacific Ocean], which continues beyond Puctla, they called *ñundaa* because it is flat lowland, and *ñunama,* which is the maize stalk [cane, reed], and *ñundeui,* because the horizon, called *sahaandevui,* meaning the foot of the sky, can be seen better in that land.[10]

Thus, the Mixteca was divided into four parts: the Alta, Baja, Costa, and Valley of Oaxaca. However, Reyes later translated "all pueblos of the Mixteca" as "neecutundu ñuu ñudzavui" [all Ñudzahui ñuu], applying the term for the Mixteca Alta to the entire cultural region.[11] His reference to the Mixteca Alta as a "divine and esteemed" place refers to the fact that the written word *ñuhu* can be interpreted as a deity, land in gen-eral, or a "divine and esteemed thing," depending on tone. As we have seen in the pre-vious chapter, the ñuhu called Dzahui (or Dzavui) was both divine and highly esteemed.

The four-part division of the Mixteca is a pattern of organization based on the cardinal directions; each of the four areas corresponds roughly to a direction.[12] In addition, many of Reyes's terms for regions correspond to specific ñuu located in each area. For example: Ñuniñe is the name of Tonalá; Ñuñuma is the name of Puctla (derived from the Nahuatl Poctlan); Ñuñama is the name of San Pedro Amusgos; and Ñundehui is the name of Pinotepa Nacional.[13] The pattern of naming a region after a prominent place is evident in the use of *Ñucoyo* as a reference to Tenochtitlan ("place of reeds," same as Tula), as well as the Nahua cultural area in general (discussed below). In contrast, the regions of the Mixteca Alta and Ñuutocuij (the Chochona) do not appear to be named after one prominent sociopolitical center. However, there are at least two places that are named after rain in the Mixteca: Ñudzavui (called Xicayan de Tovar) on the coast and Yucuñudahui, "Ñudzahui hill," in the Alta. It is conceivable that Yucuñudahui lent its name to the entire region, for it was a dominant political/ cultural center in the late classic period.[14]

Native informants of the *Vocabulario en lengua mixteca,* published in 1593, defined *misteca* unequivocally as "ñuu ñudzavui," "place of the Ñudzahui."[15] Two qualifying entries are included for the Alta and the Baja. The "misteca alta" is called "ñudzavui

ñuhu" and "dzini ñudzavui"; the first has been frequently attested, and the second is a
literal equivalent of "alta," as in the "high Mixteca."[16] The "misteca baxa" is called,
among other terms, "ñuu cani" in reference to the humid climate.[17]

Ñudzahui Language

The earliest dated and extant example of alphabetic writing in the Ñudzahui language
is the *Doctrina,* published in the Achiutla variant of Mixtec in 1567 and printed again
in the Teposcolula variant a year later. This book contains dozens of references to the
term *Ñudzahui;* moreover, the marginalia and notes of two copies owned by the Huntington Library (dated 1567 and 1568) confirm that native writers from the Mixteca
Alta used the term. The name appears in a variety of contexts, especially in relation to
language. The 1567 version makes repeated references to "duçu ñudzahui" [Ñudza-
hui speech] and "duçu Castilla" [Castile speech].[18] Likewise, the 1568 version speaks
of "dudzu castilla" [Castile speech] and "dzaha castilla" [Castile language], as opposed
to "dudzu ñudzahui" and "dzaha ñudzahui." Christ's message was directed to "those
who speak Castile speech, the Castile language, as well as those who speak the Ñudzahui
language" [tay yocaha dudzu Castilla dzaha Castilla da tucu tay yocaha dzaha
Ñudzahui].[19] The following phrase, in reference to the subtle meaning of prayer, conveys the distinction between two tongues and the difficulty of conveying Christian concepts in the native language: "perhaps you will not understand the speech which was
translated to your own Ñudzahui language" [adzi ñasinindo dudzu nindico cahua
ñudzahui dzaha maando].[20] Five handwritten, unnumbered folios in the back of the
Huntington's copy of the 1567 edition were written in the Yanhuitlan variant, even
though the text's language represented that of Achiutla. These ten neatly written
pages are prayers and responses to be said in mass, with alternating Ñudzahui and Latin
refrains. The instructions contain several references to "ndudzu ñudzahui" [Ñudzahui
speech], also spelled as "ñudzavi" in the text, translated from the "ndudzu latin" [Latin
speech].[21]

The term of self-ascription was also used by native-language speakers and writers
to distinguish the local language from Castilian. For example, a noble named Pedro
de Caravantes wrote a murder note in 1684, drawing a distinction between the language of his letter (*dzaha ñudzahui*) and the language to which it would be translated
(*dzaha castilla*): "Let this letter in the Ñudzahui language be read by don Tomás, he
will read this letter and then translate it to Castilian for the lord *alcalde mayor* to hear"
[yodzanacahui tutu yaha dzaha ñudzahui d. tomas yca yya cahui tutu yaha yca yya dza
njico cahua dzaha castilla saha nachacu siyya allde maro].[22] The writer was so conscious of a language difference that he directed a specific person to translate his letter
into the official legal language. Thinking about the "other" reinforced his own ethnic
and linguistic identification. At the same time, he was concerned with the constraints
that his ethnicity placed on his ability to communicate with colonial authorities. He
was so concerned, in fact, that he attempted to close his letter with three lines of garbled Spanish. The services of the translator, don Tomás, were required for this part of
the murder note, too.

Ñudzahui People

The *Doctrina* employs ethnic terminology for native peoples, as in the phrase "tai ñuu Indios, tay ñudzahui" [people from Indian communities, Ñudzahui people].[23] This use of *Indio* in native-language texts is without parallel in the archival record. The couplet appears to draw an implicit distinction between "deê taca yndios" [all the Indians] and "deê taca taa ñuçahui" [all the Ñudzahui people].[24] The first is a contrived term describing all other indigenous groups without designating them separately; the second is a more genuine and specific term referring to the people of the region in which the texts would be read. It is also possible that this couplet is a parallel construction, hence the equivalent of "Ñudzahui Indians." But considering the usage of the phrase in the texts, *Ñudzahui* appears to be a specific qualifier of the more general term *indios*. For example, in discussing Cortés's arrival to New Spain and his introduction of the faith, the *Doctrina* recalls: "when the Marqués entered the land of the Indians, he captured a place called Cozumel" [quehui niquehuiyya marques ñuu yndios, niniyya ee ñuu, nani acuçamil].[25] The context and usage of the term in this example suggest a more general meaning of "ñuu yndios." In contrast, a discussion of the Fourth Commandment of the church simply refers to "ndoô taa ñuçahui" [we Ñudzahui people].[26] The *Doctrina* also makes several references to Ñudzahui rulers, as in the "yya ñuu ñuçahui" [lord(s) of Ñudzahui ñuu].[27]

A legal document from Yanhuitlan, written in the year 1699, evoked a clear expression of ethnic identity that was linked to a broader ensemble of identities.[28] The plaintiff introduced himself to the native Audiencia as "Juan Domingo, a Ñudzahui person from this ñuu chayu of Yanhuitlan, a tributary of our lord king from the barrio siña of Ticoho" [Ju° domingo chay ñudzahui ñuu chayu Yodzocahi yaha tributario costohondo Rey barrio siña ticoho]. This introduction constitutes a summary of Juan Domingo's multiple self-ascribed identities, including references to his ethnicity ("Ñudzahui"), his community ("ñuu chayu"), his colonial social status ("tributario"), and the local subentity of his ñuu ("barrio siña"). In the documentation, he is referred to as "chay ñuu," that is, "a person from a ñuu" and thus simply a person, since everyone came from some ñuu or another. However, this term also conveys the sense of an ordinary commoner, a status confirmed by his double first name. He was also called by the more neutral term of "chay nani Juan Domingo" [a person named Juan Domingo]. The wording of Juan's introduction resembles the Spanish formula of petitions. In this case, "Indio" was substituted by "Ñudzahui," and "cabecera" was given as "dzini ñuu" (head pueblo), an expression invented for the new concept, as discussed in chapter 4. Some loanwords were combined with native terminology to denote equivalences or to recognize colonial versions of native entities, such as "barrio siña."

The ethnic term was assigned to groups of tributaries in the same manner. In Yolomecatl, a petition by Manuel de la Cruz in 1708 refers to "taca tributarios tay ñudzahui" [all the Ñudzahui tributaries]. It is translated in the proceedings merely as "indios," avoiding the redundant term *Indian tributary*, since only native people were subject to pay tribute in the colonial period.[29] In response, native officials proclaimed that "the royal laws and ordinances of our lord king order that all the Ñudzahui tributaries be assembled" [yotasitnuni Reales leyes y ordenansas stohondo Rey saha cuhui tahui ndehe taca tributarios tay ñodzahui]. As in the preceding example of Juan Domingo, the association of Ñudzahui people with the responsibility of paying tribute indicates that ethnicity was linked to issues of status and class in the colonial order.[30] But the term was used in reference to the nobility, as well.

The Ñudzahui label was applied to community officials. In 1700 the officers of the Yanhuitlan *cabildo* were called "all we Ñudzahui officials" [taca njuhu Justiss[a] ñudzahui] by the notary Agustín de la Cruz in reference to the local officials (himself included, the governor, alcaldes, and *regidores*).[31] The opening of the proceedings went as follows: "Today, Thursday, the 21st day of the month of March, in the year of 1700, the lord lieutenant ordered that all the Ñudzahui officials, the governor, alcaldes and all the regidores, the officials of the Republic, be informed of the statement that our lord king has made to all the officials of this great cabecera yuhuitayu of Santo Domingo [Yanhuitlan]" [Uitna Jueves 21 quehui yoo de Março cuiya de 1700 años nitasitnuni yya theniente saha cuvañaha taca njuhu Justiss[a] ñudzahui gov[or], alldes, sihi taca Regidor officiales de Repu[ca], saha huidzo dzaha costohondo Rey Yocuhui tacanju Juss[a], dzini ñuu chayu cánu sancto domingo yaha]. Similarly, in 1684, Pedro de Caravantes referred to the local "gustisia ñuudzahui" [Ñudzahui officials] of Yanhuitlan, using the term to distinguish native alcaldes from Spanish administrative and judicial authorities.[32] Caravantes wrote in his note: "I am responding before all of you lords who are officials [justices], the señor lieutenant or the señor alcalde mayor, or the Ñudzahui officials, concerning what I have done" [yyodzahuidzoñadzaña si nuu dehe taca njisi yya yocuhui yustisia señor tiniñende adzi sr[nor] tallde maro adzi yustisia ñudzahui saha niquidzañadzaña]. This distinction between native and Spanish officials was not represented in a subsequent translation of the document. Caravantes was well aware that two sets of officials had jurisdiction over criminal matters, especially serious crimes such as homicide. He knew when he wrote his murder note, after killing his wife, that Spanish officials would investigate the murder.

Ñudzahui people had their own religious confraternities. When Salvador de Celís wrote his testament in 1718, he referred to his people in general terms when he gave offerings to the various *cofradías* of Teposcolula.[33] Salvador said: "I offer half of a peso to the coffers of all the confraternities belonging to us Ñudzahui people" [yonadzocondi me[o], me[o], satno ndehe taca cofradía maa ndoo ñayehui ñuudzahui]. When this part of the testament was translated several years later, the writer omitted the Ñudzahui reference and wrote: "I offer half of a peso to each of the various cofradía boxes."[34] The original wording indicates that the ethnic term distinguished one group from others. Spaniards who resided in this cabecera had their own confraternities.

Ñudzahui people also had their own images of Christ. In 1672, don Gerónimo García gave money to a "Santo Christo tay ñodzahui," a "Holy Christ of the Ñudzahui people," in Teposcolula. It was translated as merely "santo christo." Translators often omitted Ñudzahui references, as if the distinction needed no emphasis from their perspective or for the legal proceedings that required the document's translation. Don Gerónimo also mentioned a "Santo Christo Español," translated as "santa cruz de los Españoles," in reference to an image of Christ on the cross.[35] He also referred to a "yya dzehe Rosario Español" [Spanish lady of the Rosary], translated as "señora de los

Españoles." The distinction between a Spanish and a Ñudzahui Christ probably refers to a specific cofradía image kept in the church, resembling the reference to ethnic confraternities in the preceding example from Teposcolula. In 1691, the widow of the late don Gerónimo García, doña Lázara de Guzmán, mentioned the same images in her testament but simply called them "stohondo santo christo español" and "stohondo santo christo" (*stohondo* means "our Lord").[36] She specified only the other, Spanish Christ.

Ñudzahui Things

Native writers used the term *Ñudzahui* to refer to many things, including the ancient calendar. For example, the *Doctrina* texts in the Huntington Library contain marginalia referring to calendrical dates. On one page of the 1567 edition, someone wrote "quehui ñudzavi qh chi," literally "the Ñudzahui day 5-Wind." Similarly, on a page in the 1568 edition, some writer referred to the birth of a certain María de la Cruz as an event that took place on "quihui ñudzahui siquaa" [the Ñudzahui day 10-Deer] in the year of 1647.[37] Personal names based on the ancient calendar were still quite common in the Mixteca at this time, a topic discussed in chapter 5. The two books bear the names and dates of many native writers who left their marks in the books, which were probably circulated among owners and borrowers. The application of an ethnic term to days of the ancient calendar, recorded in a Christian sacred book, reflects a recognition of two ways of marking time and naming people.

The record contains numerous references to the style or origin of Ñudzahui material objects. In the *Vocabulario* of 1593, native informants defined several material objects with the term *Ñudzahui*. For example, "papel de estraça o de la tierra" [coarse paper or local paper] is defined as "tutu ñudzavui," "tutu ñuu dzúma," and "tutu ñuhu."[38] This entry refers to the coarse, native fig bark paper produced in Mesoamerica; the first native-language equivalent obviously refers to a type of paper associated with or produced in the Mixteca. The second refers to paper from central Mexico (this and other terminology for Nahuas are discussed below). The third term is a literal equivalent of the Spanish phrase *de la tierra*, in reference to a locally grown or produced thing.

Ethnic references to local objects and artifacts abound in mundane writings. Cloth and clothing are the most common items associated with ethnic identity. Clothing served as a distinctive social and ethnic marker throughout Mesoamerica. Specific references to Ñudzahui clothing could refer to the material itself or to its place of manufacture, similar to the Spanish concept of *ropa de la tierra*. This label could also refer to a specific regional style of dress. For example, references to a "Coixtlahuacan cape" in one criminal record implied that it bore some unique pattern, color, or design.[39] When Diego Miguel of Teposcolula wrote an account of his possessions in 1674, he was careful to include his "calzone dzama ñudzahui" [Ñudzahui trousers] and his "camissa dzama ñodzahui yotnahandaha dzunu" [Ñudzahui shirt with sleeves].[40] In both cases, a Spanish loanword accompanied the indigenous equivalent. At the same time, Diego also referred to a "tay castilla" [Castilian person] who owed him money. His contact with persons from other ethnic groups and their material culture reinforced a sense of cultural difference.

Ñudzahui textiles are prominent items in the testaments and inventories of Sebastián Sánchez Hernández, his spouse María de la Cruz, and their daughter María. Three documents, dated 1754 to 1758, detailed the possessions of the family, which included hundreds of pesos' worth of cloth and woven goods. Alongside imported cloths from Britanny (or Britain), Germany, China, Spain, and Venice and Mexican goods from Guadalajara and Cholula, the family from Yanhuitlan owned many Ñudzahui articles of clothing. The three documents employ the label *Ñudzahui* fifteen times.[41] All the local goods were woven products, such as white cloth Ñudzahui mantas ("dama cuisi doo ñudahui"), large Ñudzahui cloths ("manteles doo ñudahui"), cloth mantas of Ñudzahui thread ("paño ditu yuhua ñudahui"), small Ñudzahui cloths ("mantelito doo ñudahui"), and a Ñudzahui napkin cloth ("servilleta ñudahui"). Some items are accompanied by Spanish loanwords such as *paño* and *manteles*. Most of the local products were made from cotton, since "dama ticachi," or "woolen cloth," (from the name given to sheep, which is in turn derived from *cachi*, "cotton") is often mentioned separately. Thus, the term *Ñudzahui* was employed to distinguish imports from places as nearby as Cholula and as far away as China from local or regional products.

Products originating from outside the region, whether introduced items previously unknown to the area or simply imported products, were usually qualified by their place of origin, whereas indigenous equivalents, however close the approximation in function or appearance, were referred to by their usual names. A full range of European items that resembled indigenous equivalents were described as Castilian in the sixteenth century, naturally associated with the people who brought them and used them. Thus, wheat was called "nuni castilla" [Castile maize], and bread made from wheat was "dzita castilla" [Castile tortillas]. Likewise, the domesticated chicken was called "tiñoo castilla" [Castile turkey] after its association with the indigenous bird. Although a complex arose by the end of the sixteenth century to describe these new objects without using an ethnic term and without resorting to adapting a Spanish loanword, the use of *castilla* prevailed until the eighteenth century and beyond in many places. At times, choosing to employ this terminology was a matter of perspective. In Ocotepec, don Pedro Sotomayor wrote in Nahuatl of a "mexico tutuli" and a "castilla tutuli" (from the Nahua *totollin*), a Nahua turkey and a Castilian turkey, most likely referring to the indigenous turkey and the still foreign chicken or hen.[42] Similarly, among the many food items listed for the feast of Santiago in Yolomecatl, a distinction was made between the "tiñoo ñudzahui" [Ñudzahui turkey] and other fowl.[43] The turkey was used to make tamales and was distinguished from a number of Spanish items such as saffron, bread, rice, and olive oil, which were purchased mainly for the friars and Spanish officials of Teposcolula. Finally, a merchant in Yanhuitlan named Juan Ramírez sold a wide variety of indigenous and Spanish goods. Juan kept a book of his accounts during the 1740s and 1750s; most of the time he wrote in his own language, except when dealing with Spanish-speaking clients. He sold a type of local herb for cleansing called "nama ñudzahui," which he distinguished from European tallow-based soap.[44] This was the equivalent of *jabón de la tierra* (local soap), a term seen in Spanish-language documents.

Sometimes the actual term *Ñudzahui* was implied but not employed. For example, in 1623, Lucía de la Anunciación bequeathed several grinding stones, or *metates*, called *yodzo* in Ñudzahui, including a "yodzo ñuundo" [metate from our ñuu/region]. This part was translated into Spanish as "metate misteco." The document also mentions a "yodzo ñucoyo" [Mexican metate].[45] Cultural distinctions between local household products probably referred to their place of manufacture or their distinctive shape or design.

The eventual borrowing of Spanish loanwords for many introduced items may have signified a more complete integration of the object or concept into the native language and material culture, a reduction of cultural difference over time. That some of these castilla-based constructions were still used by the late colonial period indicates the complexity of this process and suggests that people continued to perceive a limited set of cultural features as different.[46]

The Construction of Ethnicity

The use of the term *Ñudzahui* as an ethnic and cultural qualifier appears in native-language documentation from both the early and later colonial periods (see table 9.1). The term was especially prominent in writings from the 1670s to the 1720s, particularly in and around the cabeceras of Teposcolula and Yanhuitlan. This pattern can be attributed, in part, to the provenance and date of extant native-language sources. Scribes from these two yuhuitayu produced about half of all native-language sources used in this study, and the amount of documentation generated by civil and criminal disputes in the Mixteca, native-language sources included, increased dramatically after the 1670s. So it is not surprising that expressions of Ñudzahui ethnicity were especially common in this area of the Mixteca Alta during this period. However, the frequent articulation

TABLE 9.1
Some Attested References to "Ñudzahui" in Native-Language Sources

Date	Place	In Reference to:
1567	Achiutla	People, region, language, calendar, places
1568	Teposcolula	People, region, language, calendar, places
1593	Teposcolula	People, region, language, places, objects
1593	Teposcolula	People, region, objects
1625	Yucucata	Fauna
1672	Teposcolula	Christian image or people
1674	Teposcolula	Clothing
1684	Yanhuitlan	Language, writing, people
1696	Chapultepec	People, community
1699	Yanhuitlan	Person
1700	Yanhuitlan	People
1705	Yolomecatl	Fauna
1708	Yolomecatl	People
1718	Teposcolula	People
1740	Yanhuitlan	Flora
1754	Yanhuitlan	Objects
1756	Yanhuitlan	Objects

of "Ñudzahui" identity was not simply a factor of increased notarial production. The need or occasion to articulate one's belonging to an ethnic group was prompted by particular social and cultural circumstances. First, it should be noted that colonial administrative and commercial centers such as Yanhuitlan and Teposcolula contained the largest population of non-native peoples in the Mixteca. By the second half of the colonial period, Ñudzahui people in cabeceras came into increasing contact with Spanish-speaking groups. Changes in the last quarter of the seventeenth century, discussed in each of the seven previous chapters, tested the boundaries of Ñudzahui ethnicity in this period. Second, the increase in judicial records for this period was related to socioeconomic and demographic changes associated with increased contact. Increased competition for local resources provoked a more assertive expression of ethnic and corporate identities in response to new challenges. Ethnic boundaries were reaffirmed by the dichotomy between "us" and "others" inherent in the ascriptive, exclusive term.[47] In some cases, the expression of ethnic identity represented a recognition and validation of colonial social relations. Some people used the term to promote their particular interests within the Spanish legal system, as members of "repúblicas de indios." As we have seen, native-language speakers preferred the ascription *Ñudzahui* to *indio* when identifying their ethnic status within the colonial system.

References to Ñudzahui identity in the record indicate that individuals chose to invoke their ethnic affiliation when they perceived a need to identify themselves with a familiar, unambiguous term that did not compromise their belonging to other local groups and places, such as the ñuu and siqui. In most cases, contact with other ethnic or racial groups provided the context of expression. Most Ñudzahui men and women did not need to articulate a specific ethnic identity when writing or speaking within their own immediate circles. Similarly, in Spanish-language documentation, Spaniards often appeared without special designation, whereas "indios" and individuals associated with other racial categories, including "mestizos" and "negros," were consistently labeled accordingly. When in doubt, however, Spaniards used the term *español* to affirm their social and ethnic status.

The geographical boundaries of Ñudzahui ethnic identity in the colonial period are unclear. The term appears consistently in writings from the Mixteca Alta, and it has been attested in documents from the Valley of Oaxaca. Although I have not located any native-language writings from the coastal region, several documents from the Alta specifically refer to the coast and its inhabitants. In 1593, Reyes listed *Ñundeui*, "place of the sky or horizon," as one of the terms for the Mixteca coast. A document from Teposcolula, dated 1633, called a person from the coastal area "tay ñundevui" [person from the land of the horizon or sky], which was later translated as *costeño*, or "coastal person."[48] A record from San Bartolomé Tiyacu (Almoloyas), written in the year 1701, alluded to the coastal region twice as "ñuu dehui."[49] In Yolomecatl, in the year 1705, the coastal area was called "ñudihui."[50] In the testament of don Diego de Velasco, written in Tlaxiaco in the year 1627, "tee ñudihuiy" was translated as "yndio de la costa."[51] These five references provide evidence of a specific term for the coastal region and its inhabitants. In any case, *ñundehui* was the most frequently used term for the coastal region by people from the Mixteca Alta.[52]

The Mixteca Baja is a distinct subregion of the Mixteca that merits further study in the colonial period. The classic-period "Nuiñe" style seems to represent a unique cultural and iconographic tradition.[53] Linguistic data suggest that the Baja was an area of significant lexical innovation, distinct in many ways from other regions in the sixteenth century.[54] Although there are relatively few extant native-language documents from the area, the sources reveal some interesting patterns. First of all, there is no reference in this documentation to either a Ñudzahui or a Ñuniñe identity.[55] In addition, writings from the Baja conspicuously lack the reverential language so typical of documentation from the Alta. Neither the typical *ñadzaña* pronoun nor the *-ya* reverential suffix appear in a sample of twenty-five documents, even though most of the sources are legal records pertaining to high nobles in the seventeenth century, when one would expect to encounter such usage. Another notable feature of native-language sources from the Baja was the influence of Nahua culture and language, a topic discussed below. Thus, it is unknown whether people from the Baja region used the term *Ñudzahui* in reference to ethnic identity.

Comparisons with Nahuas and Maya

A consideration of how other Mesoamerican groups referred to themselves in the colonial record lends a useful comparative perspective to the findings presented above. Comparisons are possible for two other groups: the Nahuas of central Mexico and the Maya of Yucatan. The terms *Nahua* and *nahuatlatolli* and related terminology appear regularly in church imprints, beginning with the work of fray Bernardino de Sahagún and fray Alonso de Molina. In his *Vocabulario en lengua castellana y mexicana*, Molina began and concluded his work with an unequivocal reference to "nauatlatolli" [Nahua speech], which he translated as "nahual o mexicana" [Nahuatl or Mexican].[56] However, he did not attribute the term *Nahua* in the text to a group of people, or a region, or even a language. The term for the language, *Nahuatl*, is defined as a clear and intelligible sound, as "something that sounds good, like a bell."[57]

Although *Nahua* does appear in many of the earliest church texts as a limited term for the language of a people, it was not employed consistently by Nahuas themselves. The term *Nahuatl* was rarely used alone and appears mainly in reference to speech.[58] In fact, it was most frequently employed in reference to the language of books, particularly ecclesiastical publications (*doctrinas,* chronicles, dictionaries, and the like).[59] The people of central Mexico who spoke Nahuatl sometimes called themselves *Nahuatlaca* (Nahua people), but the term appears very infrequently in the colonial documentary record. As Lockhart observed, the Nahuas tended to "emphasize the narrow ethnicity of the local altepetl and calpolli-tlaxilacalli rather than broader ethnic categories . . . even when the contrast between indigenous and Spanish was specifically at issue."[60] *Nahua* is the best name for the larger culture group, certainly better than *Mexica* or *Aztec*, but the term is not prominent in the archival record.

The phrase *nican titlaca*, "we people here," was the initial operative reference to the larger ethnic self among Nahuas in the sixteenth century, almost replicating the meaning of the word *native*.[61] The relative scarcity of any ethnic term in Nahuatl-language notarial sources was compensated by a widely used designation connoting a similar sense of the common person, though it lacked a specific ethnic or regional reference. By around 1600, *macehualli* was the primary word applied to the bulk of the population, used very much in the sense of "human being" or "person" and the general Nahuatl approximation of "Indian" in the seventeenth and eighteenth centuries.[62] As in Ñudzahui documentation, *indio* rarely became a loanword in Nahuatl during the colonial period.[63] Similarly, Alvarado translated "maçegual" in the Mixtec *Vocabulario* of 1593 as "ñanday" and "tay ñuu," whereby the former refers to social status and the latter means simply "a person from a ñuu," resembling the general sense that the Nahuatl word came to signify.[64] But *ñandahi*, the Ñudzahui equivalent of the Nahua *macehualli*, was not adopted in place of *Ñudzahui*. In contrast, Spanish documents and translations identified people as "indios," often qualifying the general term as "indios mixtecos" or "indios mexicanos." Translators of Ñudzahui-language documents usually labeled the local person as an Indian; for example, in Teposcolula, the phrase "tai nani nJuá García" [person called Juan García] was translated as "el Indio Juan García."[65]

On the fringes of the Nahuatl-speaking area in Oaxaca, Tenochtitlan was the point of reference when speaking of the Nahuatl language or the cultural group called the Nahuas. In Nahuatl documentation from the fringes of the Mixteca, references to Nahuas and Nahuatl always employed the term *Mexico*. One such document is from Ocotepec, a Ñudzahui yuhuitayu that possessed a Nahuatl-speaking minority population in the sixteenth century, as well as Amuzgo and Trique populations. A writer drew up a list of goods in 1612, distinguishing between what he called "mexico tutuli" [Mexican turkey] and "castilla tutuli" [Spanish turkey], whereby the first designation was practically synonymous with "indigenous."[66] Similarly, in his Nahuatl testament of 1594, Martín Cortés, who was identified as an "indio misteco de Santiago Ystepec," a *sujeto* of Yanhuitlan, referred to a book or a document in Nahuatl as "amal meçico tlatoli" [paper-Mexico-speech].[67] Finally, in Tonalá, a bilingual Ñudzahui/Nahuatl document was written in 1584; the Nahuatl version bears the caption "yn cuepca mexico tlatoli" [turned into Mexico speech].[68]

In summary, Nahuatl documents written in the Mixteca contain references to the Nahuatl language as "mexica tlatolli"; the terms *Nahua* or *Nahuatl* were not used. This practice may have been a pattern on the Nahua fringe. Nahuatl writings from Guadalajara in the north and Socunusco in the south repeatedly refer to "Mexico." Perhaps the term was reinforced by Spaniards, who used it from the earliest period onward.[69] Although *Nahua* has not been attested outside central Mexico, Nahuas living in the Valley of Oaxaca possessed a keen sense of ethnic identity in the colonial period; this issue is addressed below in the discussion of Nahuatl and Ñudzahui primordial titles from the Valley of Oaxaca.

Comparisons with the Yucatec Maya shed additional light on the nature of Ñudzahui identity. Studies have indicated that the Maya of Yucatan seldom used a term of ethnic self-description and apparently lacked an overarching identification with any entity beyond the local *cah*. The rare appearance of the term *Maya* in the notarial record is limited to references to language and to documents named after Chilam Balam.[70] Indeed, people did not use the term in reference to themselves and, in fact, the origins and meaning of the term are obscure.[71] When one would expect to find the word in reference to indigenous objects or people, the term was not used. Whereas Ñudzahui and Nahuatl speakers distinguished the indigenous turkey from foreign fowl with terms such as "tiñoo ñudzahui" and "mexico totollin," Matthew Restall found one reference to a "hunpok maseual" [macehual turkey].[72] This use of a Nahuatl loanword for "commoner," borrowed before the Spanish conquest, in reference to something "Mayan" indicates how writers from Yucatan used anything but *Maya* in reference to themselves and things from the region. It also indicates a parallel process in Yucatan and central Mexico in which the term *macehualli* came to signify "indigenous" or to approximate *indio*. In addition, the Yucatec Maya tended to refer to foreigners as outsiders, or *dzulob* (plural of *dzul*), rather than associating them with a specific place or ethnic group. I know of no such term in the Ñudzahui language. The multiethnic and multilingual nature of the Mixteca, where several ethnic groups came into frequent contact with one another and even lived together in some communities, precluded a dichotomy between insiders and outsiders inherent in the concept of dzulob.

Thus, the self-ascribed term *Ñudzahui* was much more prominent in the written record than corresponding expressions of ethnic identity (that transcended the local state) among the Nahuas and Yucatec Maya. As Frederik Barth observed, ethnic distinctions do not depend on the absence of cultural contact and mobility; in fact, the opposite holds true.[73] Whereas the Yucatec Maya represent a somewhat predictable extreme, given their relative isolation in the colonial period, the Nahuas do not conform to expectations. In general, the Nahuas of central Mexico came into intensive contact with other native groups and Spanish speakers, but they did not articulate a broader ethnic term beyond an affiliation with the local *altepetl* (local ethnic states). Even in the seventeenth century, when expressions of an older Ñudzahui identity were renewed in response to colonial changes in the Mixteca, there was no close equivalent in central Mexico. Comparisons with the Nahuas and Maya of Yucatan illustrate the unique nature of Ñudzahui ethnic identity in colonial Mesoamerica.

Ñudzahui Names for Others

Before the conquest, interethnic contact on the Nahuatl-speaking frontier or perimeter to the west and northwest of the Mixteca exerted a profound impact on the construction of Ñudzahui identity. Mutual interaction created ethnic enclaves or barrios in communities from Mexico City and southern Puebla to the Valley of Oaxaca. Ñudzahui people had their own names for Nahuas and various Nahua altepetl. They consistently called Tenochtitlan *ñuu coyo,* "place of the reeds," and the people from Mexico were known as *tay ñucoyo,* or "people from the place of reeds."[74] This term, extended to apply to anyone from the general region of central Mexico, associated a cultural area and its people with a most prominent place. Likewise, the Spaniards derived *Mexico* and *Mexicano* from the Mexica of Mexico.

In 1593, the *Arte en lengua mixteca* referred to Tenochtitlan several times as "ñucoyo."[75] Native contributors to the *Vocabulario* listed several responses for the term *mexicano:* "tay saminnu" (*sic,* saminuu), "tay ñuudzuma," "tai yecoo," and "tay ñuu coyo."[76] The first, "tay saminuu," means "person with burnt face or eyes." This name does not appear often in Ñudzahui-language sources, but it does appear as an ethnic marker in pictorial writings, in which personages are represented with blackened eyes and faces.[77] The second and third entries for *mexicano* have not been attested in the archival record, though "ñuudzuma" also appears in the *Vocabulario* under "papel de la tierra," as discussed above. The last term for *mexicano* listed by Alvarado's informants, "ñuu-coyo," or "place of reeds," is by far the most common name in the native-language record.

The *Codex Sierra* makes several references to Ñucoyo, as a familiar ñuu place glyph from which bunches of reeds (*coyo*) protrude (see fig. 9.1).[78] One scene in the manuscript identifies an individual Nahua by elaborating on this convention. A Nahua noble who was recruited to instruct the local church people is shown carrying a reed on his shoulder in reference to his Ñucoyo origins (see fig. 9.2).[79] The reference to "place of reeds" invokes the image of Tollan or Tula; the depiction of Ñucoyo in the *Codex Sierra* resembles representations of the place sign for Tula in the Historia Tolteca-Chichimeca, only the latter sign lacks the *tablero* ñuu motif. Perhaps the glyph was based on an association of the Mexica with their Toltec predecessors, or maybe it referred to the natural landscape of Tenochtitlan.

The *Codex Sierra* illustrates that people in Texupa, a ñuu in the Mixteca Alta, came into closer contact with Mexico City than with Oaxaca City in this period. The text contains thirty references to Mexico, whereas Oaxaca is mentioned only once. Spanish settlement patterns and trade patterns undoubtedly reinforced existing contacts between the Mixteca and Mexico City. Nahuas appear in the manuscript performing various tasks, instructing the *teopannenque* (church people) in 1554 and bringing medicinal

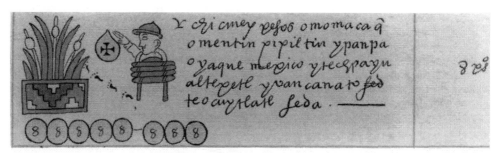

FIGURE 9.1. Depictions of Mexico Tenochtitlan or Ñucoyo, "place of reeds," in the *Codex Sierra*, p. 38.

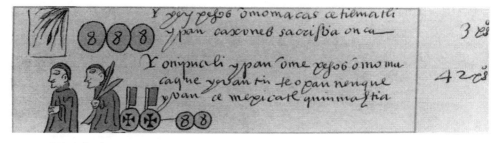

FIGURE 9.2. Depiction of a Nahua in the *Codex Sierra*, identified by the reed he carries over his shoulder, p. 12.

drugs from Mexico in 1559. There was also a "tlacuylo mexicatl" [Mexica painter] in 1560.[80] References to migration and travel to Mexico appear regularly in the colonial record. In 1613, Mixtec migrants proudly paraded their image of the Virgin of the Rosary around Mexico City.[81] This procession came from a parish in Mexico City called "Mixtecos."[82] Charles Gibson observed that migration of Mixtecs from Oaxaca to Mexico City resulted in a permanent settlement with its own officials. Likewise, Nahuas settled as individuals and as groups in the Mixteca Baja and Alta and the Valley of Oaxaca.

The Chochos were another major language and cultural group in the northwestern Mixteca Alta. In the postclassic period, this group interacted with Nahuas to the extent that they shared a common migration legend; Chocho alphabetic writing appears on the first page of the *Historia Tolteca Chichimeca*.[83] The Chocho also possessed a well-established pictorial writing tradition associated with the so-called Mixteca-Puebla style.[84] Chocho influence stretched north from the populous sites of Texupa and Tamasulapa into the Coixtlahuaca basin and as far north as the steep continental divide. Reyes confirmed the historical relationship between tay ñudzahui and "tay Tocuij." *Tocuij* may be a reference to the color green (*cuii*) and nobility (*to* from *toho*), but its specific or metaphorical meaning is unclear. The Chocho region was also known as "tocuij ñudzavui," according to Reyes's *Arte*, in reference to its esteemed qualities and close association with the Mixteca Alta ("ñudzavui ñuhu").[85] In any case, the key term has been attested in a Ñudzahui-language criminal record of 1596, which refers to "los chochones" as "ñuu tocuiy."[86] Its usage referred to people from a specific place in the region of the "Chochona" as "chai ñuu tiquehui ñuu tocuiy yaha" [a person from the ñuu of Tamasulapa, here in the Chochona]. Several communities in the northwestern Mixteca Alta were inhabited by both Ñudzahui and Chocho speakers in the colonial period, including Texupa, Tamasulapa, and Coixtlahuaca. Barrios were organized along ethnic lines in these multiethnic communities.[87] Place-names conformed to the language of the speaker: Coixtlahuaca (called Yodzocoo in Ñudzahui) was referred to as the "xade" of "Nguichee" in Chocho.[88]

The Mixteca's eastern border extended into the Valley of Oaxaca. Several Ñudzahui communities were centered around Yuchaticaha (Cuilapan) in the Valley of Oaxaca. Some lordly establishments in the Mixteca Alta established marriage alliances with communities in the valley during the late postclassic period. The Zapotec community of Zaachila, known as Teozapotlan to Nahuas and Ñuhu Tocuisi to Ñudzahui speakers, was probably the most prominent site in the Valley of Oaxaca. It was so prominent, in fact, that Mixtecs named the entire valley after the site, calling the Zapoteca *Tocuisi ñuhu*. Similar to the name for Chochos, this term combines a color (*cuisi*, white) with a reference to nobility (*to*). Zapotec people were called "tay ñucuisi" by Ñudzahui speakers. The association of a cultural group with a prominent place-name resembles the way *ñucoyo*, named after Tenochtitlan, became the general term for Nahuas.

Spaniards were named after a region of the Iberian Peninsula, the kingdom from which most of them came. Spaniards were called *tay castilla*, or "Castile person(s)." They were also known as *tay español* or simply *español*, but *tay castilla* was a more common term. Similarly, Nahuas applied the term *caxtiltecatl*, or "inhabitant of Castile." Nahua writers used *español* as early as 1550, but *caxtiltecatl* was used earlier and more frequently. The two false titles from the 1690s, discussed below, refer to the Spaniards as "españoles." By the end of the sixteenth century, the general term for Spaniard was often supplemented by a more precise reference to a person's local origins; for example, in 1585, Manuel Rodríguez was called "ee español ñuunduhua nanita Manuel" [a Spaniard from Oaxaca named Manuel].[89] But the late colonial terms *criollo* and *peninsular* have not been attested. Sometimes, the Spanish loanword *vecino*, or "resident," was used in reference to a non-native person who resided in a particular community, a rough equivalent of the term *natural* that was applied to indigenous people. One document from Yanhuitlan, written in 1700, referred to a Spaniard as a "besino ñuu" or a resident of the ñuu.[90] The writer chose not to use the more common term *tay ñuu*, (person from a ñuu), which would have suggested that he was a native person. The term *señora* has also been attested more than once as a reference to a Spanish woman.

In Nahuatl and Mixtec, all the ethnic terms used by Spaniards except *Indian* became loanwords.[91] The native word for "black" was used for persons of African descent; Nahuas used *tliltic*, "something black," rather than the Spanish loan *negro* throughout the colonial period.[92] In the same manner, *tnoo* was used in the Ñudzahui language. For example, in 1621, Miguel Jiménez of Yanhuitlan referred to a "ñaha tnoo" [black woman] and her seven year-old son, whom he had bought for three hundred pesos.[93] The term conveys a racial designation; however, the category "white" was not used for Spaniards or other Europeans in the colonial period. The native-language record contains only a few references to mixed racial categories. For example, in the year 1632, a certain "ndomigo mestiçu" was accused of murder in Tamasulapa.[94] In the Spanish summary of the document, the suspect was introduced as "Domingo de la Cruz mestiço y natural de Tamasulapa." Similarly, in 1703, one native writer referred to a "mulato" from Tlaxiaco.[95]

Ethnicity in the Valley of Oaxaca

The confluence of cultures and languages in the Valley of Oaxaca indicates how multiple indigenous groups and individuals interacted during the colonial period and how they referred to themselves in relation to others. At the time of the conquest, the Valley of Oaxaca's population consisted of a Zapotec-speaking majority, a significant Mixtec minority, and a small group of Nahuas from central Mexico. The yuhuitayu of Yuchaticaha (Cuilapan) was one of the largest communities in the valley throughout the colonial period. In the mid-sixteenth century, after the congregation of several small communities in the 1530s, Cuilapan had seventeen subject settlements.[96] Nonetheless, many ñuu continued to maintain separate identities throughout the colonial period. Ñudzahui ñuu in the Valley of Oaxaca included Chapultepec (Yuchayta), Xoxocotlan (Ñuhuyoho), Ixtlahuaca, Azompa, Amilpas, and Tlanichico. Several mixed communities, such as Tlapacoya, Zegache, and Zaachila, contained a Ñudzahui barrio; Ñudzahui settlements also existed in the eastern Etla branch of the valley at Huitzo, Suchilquitongo, and Tenexpan.[97] Many of these multiethnic communities continued to function as such into the eighteenth century. For example, in 1715, Santa Anna Zegache, a ñuu in the jurisdiction of Cuatro Villas (part of the Marquesado del

Valle), elected to the cabildo twelve officers from its "Mixtec barrio" and twenty officers from its "Zapotec barrio."[98]

The Spanish conquest complicated this multiethnic setting. A contingent of central Mexican Nahuas accompanied the Spaniards to the Valley of Oaxaca and settled in and around Antequera: in Villa de Oaxaca to the northwest (the cabecera of Cortés's Marquesado del Valle); Jalatlaco to the northeast; Mexicapan to the southwest; and Xochimilco to the north.[99] Their numbers were estimated at four thousand. The Spanish city of Antequera (named after a town in Andalusia) was founded just east of the Nahua tribute collection garrison at Huaxyacac (later called Oaxaca); Antequera eventually subsumed the settlement called Jalatlaco, which became a barrio of the city. Jalatlaco's residents included Nahuas from various central Mexican altepetl, Ñudzahui people from the Cuilapa area and the Mixteca Alta, Zapotecs from the valley and Sierra, and even a contingent of Guatemalans. Jalatlaco had its own cabildo by 1565 and was subdivided into ten named barrios or *tlaxilacalli* that reflected the diverse origins of the Nahua population and the loyalty of each satellite to its home altepetl in central Mexico.[100] Nearly half of Jalatlaco's population consisted of Nahuatl speakers; less than a tenth of the people were Guatemalan, and about 45 percent were either Ñudzahui or Zapotec, mostly from the valley but also a small percentage from the Zapoteca Sierra and the Mixteca Alta. According to John Chance, marriage records indicate that the number of barrios in Jalatlaco named after valley Zapotec communities had increased by the early seventeenth century.[101] Meanwhile, Ñudzahui members were grouped into barrios called in Nahuatl *Mixtlan,* or "place of the clouds," and by extension place of the "Mixteca" or Mixtec people. As the number of barrios increased, the term *Mixtlan* always accompanied the new title: Mixtlan, Mixtlan en los Solares, Mixtlan Toctlan, Mixtlan en las Huertas, Mixtlan de Alonzo Martín, and Mixtlan de Diego García. Since the sources are recorded in Spanish, it is unknown how Mixtecs actually referred to these barrios. Nonetheless, it is significant that the Ñudzahui barrios were named after a collective ethnic identity rather than specific communities in the Mixteca from whence they originated. In comparison, neither the Zapotec nor the Nahua barrios were named after the larger ethnic groups.

The fact that multiple ethnic barrios continued to reflect original corporate entities or were based on language affiliation confirms the maintenance of specific ethnic and local identities among indigenous groups in an urban setting. These specific ethnic identities impeded the formation of a homogenized "Indian" identity. On the other hand, Chance found that cabildo members from Jalatlaco countered accusations of being mestizo by affirming themselves as "Indio puro," or "pure Indian," in order to justify their right to office.[102] In this case, however, I suspect that the term *indio* was an imposed legal category, articulated by translators (in Spanish) before colonial officials. The use of such a concept to defend against accusations of mestizo interference shows how an externally imposed racial identity was constructed within a specific colonial context. The question remains: How did native groups in the Valley of Oaxaca refer to themselves in their own languages, and to what extent did they articulate a shared ethnic identity?

A land dispute in the Valley of Oaxaca elicited two native-language documents, written in Nahuatl and Mixtec, that enunciate clear expressions of self-ascribed identity.

Southwest of the city of Antequera, across the Atoyac River, two neighboring communities furnished competing "titles" to disputed lands in the 1690s that were falsely dated from the 1520s. Representatives of the communities claimed to have recently found the documents. The titles present interpretations of events surrounding the Spanish arrival into the Valley of Oaxaca, relating how the residents' ancestors negotiated deals with the Spaniards and how they came to possess the lands that they claimed at the end of the seventeenth century. The Nahua document, produced by San Martín Mexicapan, is dated 1525 and consists of twenty-four pages of Nahuatl-language text; the eleven-page Ñudzahui-language document, written in San Juan Chapultepec (Yuchayta), bears the date of 1523 and is accompanied by a map.[103]

As mentioned in chapter 2, the titles genre constitutes one of the most discursive, unpredictable forms of indigenous writing in the colonial period.[104] Judging by language, handwriting, and dates of presentation, no known example from highland Mexico predates the mid-seventeenth century; however, most titles purport to be early-sixteenth-century accounts of the arrival of Cortés and the subsequent settlement and possession of lands. Many are accompanied by pictorial portions. They are known as *títulos primordiales,* or "primordial titles," in reference to their use as antiquated claims to land. The títulos are also called "false titles" because they were forged legal documents, written and painted by native authors who intended to impart an ancient appearance to the manuscripts. They were in some shape or form based on Spanish land titles, though they rarely fooled Spanish officials. Native authors produced many of the falsified documents in response to Spanish demands for the verification of legal land titles, or *títulos de composición,* beginning in the late seventeenth century, as discussed in chapter 7. Untitled lands were subject to confiscation and resale. Local authorities who failed to submit legal titles were forced to produce some record of their claims for the surveyors, whether maps and paintings or other written materials. In the absence of official documentation from the early colonial period, some people produced their own titles, not fully aware of the legitimate format, content, or language. Drawing on authentic oral and written traditions, titles express a local, popular remembrance of the past that is rarely seen in other sources.

Boundary disputes with neighboring indigenous communities also occasioned the production of titles. In this case, the conflict between Mexicapan and Chapultepec in the 1690s stemmed from the Spanish conquest. The Nahuatl title from Mexicapan (literally "for the Mexica") evokes events and dialogue that explain and justify the presence of the Mexicatlaca (Mexica people) in the area.[105] The title opens with a character identified as the "noblewoman of the Zapotecs," who narrates how she requested help from Hernando Cortés and the Nahuas of central Mexico because the Mixtecs were beheading and cannibalizing her children.[106] Four Mexica warriors responded to her plea for help and approached Cortés, who is called the "Ruler of the Children of the Sun," with the idea of rescuing the Zapotec noblewoman. They convinced Cortés of their martial prowess by staging a mock battle; Cortés was so impressed that he immediately sent them off to war. The warrior-heroes battled their way through the Mixteca and into the Valley of Oaxaca, where they defeated the Mixtecs amid a windstorm and an earthquake. By helping the Zapotecs, they won a place to settle in the valley. But then Cortés entered the Valley of Oaxaca and began to wage war on the Mexica warriors who had saved Lady Zapoteca. In defense, the Mexica unleashed a flood from underground, confounding the Spaniards and forcing them to retreat from the torrent. At first, Cortés appeared surprised, but then he grew angry when the Mexica continued to raise the water to perilous heights. After a furious last stand, the Spaniards were forced to submit to the "truly famous Mexicans." The Mexica proudly proclaimed that they had defeated everyone and had even captured a few black slaves in the battle. They called their victory the "original conquest," employing Spanish loanwords in the Nahuatl text.

The Ñudzahui community of Chapultepec told a very different story in its title. Its people claimed to have received Cortés in the manner of a high lord when he first came to Oaxaca. The Spaniards needed a place to settle, so the Ñudzahui ruler, don Diego Cortés Dzahui Yuchi, the narrator of the title, gave his Spanish counterpart some land as a gift. The Nahuas were conspicuously absent from these proceedings. All was well until Cortés came a second time, accompanied by a group of Mexica, with whom the Ñudzahui people began to fight. The Spaniards intervened, but not before the Nahuas were forced to surrender. Out of respect for Cortés, and to avoid further conflict, the Ñudzahui ruler graciously granted the Nahuas some land to settle. Thereafter, Mixtecs, Nahuas, Zapotecs, and Spaniards coexisted peacefully in the Valley of Oaxaca.

The titles addressed specific concerns that were relevant to each community. The Nahuatl-language title consists of five sections or "scenes" in which the Zapotec-Ñudzahui conflict affords the Nahuas a pretext to establish a foothold in the region, sanctioned by Cortés himself. Each successive episode legitimates the Nahuas' historical presence in the area and, specifically, Mexicapa's possession of the contested land. They defeated the Mixtecs, defended their newly won land from the Spaniards, and established a lasting peace that recognized their permanent settlement in the Valley of Oaxaca. The Nahuas claimed to have conquered Oaxaca before Cortés had even arrived. As conquerors rather than secondary allies, the Mexica needed no assistance from the Spaniards. After the conquest, the title informs us that the new community's borders were marked and the nobility adopted local Spanish-style government. The Ñudzahui version is more condensed than the Nahuatl account because there was no need to establish or justify a presence in the valley. Chapultepec presented itself as a faithful Spanish ally rather than a defeated enemy. The narrator, don Diego Cortés Dzahui Yuchi, said that "we the Ñudzahui people of the pueblo of San Juan Chapultepec gave land to the Mexicans" [nduyu chee ñodzahui ñoo sa ju° yuchayta nisahañahandi ñoho chee ñocoo].[107] Land was given to the Nahuas only out of loyalty to Cortés, not because of defeat. According to this version, instead of rescuing the Zapotecs, the Nahuas were uninvited meddlers who disturbed a peaceful situation. Mesoamerican assumptions about conquest and alliance frame the document's narrative; namely, a community could claim full possession of lands only if it had never been conquered.

The titles present a selective remembrance of things past. The opening scene of the Nahua title is clearly based on the historical rivalry between Zapotec and Mixtec groups in the Valley of Oaxaca. The recounting seems to blend preconquest and postconquest events, since the Nahuas had arrived in the valley several decades before the Spaniards and had temporarily allied with the Zapotecs against the Mixtecs. Sixteenth-century sources suggest that the Zapotecs had allied with Nahuas from central Mexico against a cluster of Mixtec communities around Cuilapa.[108] Thus, the noblewoman of the Zapotec represented a Zapotec community or group. The Nahuas exploited existing rivalries to establish a foothold in the area; implicit in Nahua aid to the Zapotecs was the promise of new lands and tribute. Similarly, Nahuas who went with Spaniards as "allies" on expeditions were awarded lands to settle in the conquered region. A group of Nahuas who accompanied Spaniards to the Valley of Oaxaca settled in the satellite community of San Martín Mexicapan; the new settlement was divided into barrios that represented different altepetl from central Mexico. The telescoping or accretion of preconquest and postconquest events in the first few pages of the title was typical of the oral tradition.

The two titles from Oaxaca define groups by the corporate communities to which they belonged. Like most Nahuatl-language documentation, Nahuatl titles tend to identify strongly with the local altepetl and its subdivisions rather than broader ethnic categories.[109] The titles attempted to preserve or extend privileges in the name of the Ñudzahui ñuu and Nahua altepetl, on behalf of the community or vested interests therein. The Nahuatl title describes how groups from specific central Mexican altepetl came to settle in separate barrios and retained their corporate identities in distant Oaxaca, while the Ñudzahui map and title serve the defined interests of specific ñuu and yuhuitayu.

However, the titles also enunciate broader, overarching ethnic identities. The Nahuatl narrative employs a range of ethnic terminology: "mexica"; "mexicatlaca"; "mexicanos"; "mixteca"; "mixtecatlaca"; "tlacame mixteco"; and "zapotecatl." Although the Nahuas hailed from various central Mexican altepetl, they were collectively called Mexica or some derivative in the title and were thus associated with the one most prominent Nahua altepetl of Tenochtitlan. Expressions of ethnic solidarity are prominent in both the Ñudzahui and Nahuatl titles: the three Nahuatl-speaking communities of Mexicapan, Xochimilco, and the Marquesado forged an alliance based on common ethnicity.[110] Likewise, San Juan Chapultepec received help in fighting the "chee ñucoyo" [Nahuas] from the other two Ñudzahui yuhuitayu of the valley—Cuilapa and Xoxocotlan. The authors of this title clearly distinguished themselves as "chee ñodzahui," distinct from the "chee ñucoyo" or "saminuu" and the "chee españole." The local corporate identity of Yuchayta was not compromised by a broader Ñudzahui identity. The titles provide little evidence for the colonial construction of a homogenized Indian identity in the Valley of Oaxaca, at least not in the late seventeenth century. The native-language writings make no reference to "Indians."

The title from Chapultepec utilized ethnicity as a strategy for corporate action in the competition for land.[111] The title's authors and backers claimed the disputed land on the grounds of historical events told from an ethnic perspective. They descended from a Ñudzahui yya who had fought off the Nahuas and graciously received the Spaniards, and who had set aside certain lands for the Ñudzahui people. By maintaining the boundaries of their ethnic identity, they sought to maintain the boundaries of their lands.

Interracial Interactions

As we have seen, people articulated a specific Ñudzahui identity most often when they came into contact with ethnic others, especially in the cabeceras of the Mixteca, where interracial interaction was most common. Even in cabeceras, however, nonindigenous people constituted a small ethnic minority in the Mixteca throughout the colonial period. According to the census of 1746, non-native households or families constituted only 3.6 percent of the total population of the Mixteca Alta (373 of 10,343 households). Teposcolula, the seat of the alcaldía mayor, had the highest non-native population (160 out of 717 households). In Yanhuitlan, only 35 of 900 households were non-native. Of the 65 communities that participated in the census, 56 reported that only indigenous people resided within their borders.[112] In the sixteenth century, the number of non-native residents in the Mixteca was even smaller. In 1612, for example, the alcalde mayor could not find a single Spanish resident to witness legal proceedings in the cabecera of Teposcolula.[113]

In general, few Spaniards went to Oaxaca in the colonial period because the region offered relatively little prospect for profit. Unlike central Mexico, the Mixteca had no great mines, few haciendas, and no *obrajes* (Spanish-run textile enterprises). Traditional production methods continued to meet colonial demands for goods such as cotton cloth and cochineal dyes. Nonetheless, Spaniards were concentrated in a handful of administrative and commercial centers and exerted considerable political and economic influence in the region.[114] In the first half of the colonial period, the Spanish presence was largely confined to priests, administrators, and traders. A few dozen priests lived in residences attached to the largest churches. The alcalde mayor and his staff of *tenientes* (deputies), *escribanos* (notaries), and translators were the main Spanish officials located in the cabecera of a given jurisdiction. This group of friars and officials constituted the core of the local Spanish presence throughout the colonial period. A limited number of petty traders, or *tratantes,* resided in the cabeceras. Some *mercaderes* owned small stores. These itinerant or established traders, discussed in chapter 7, did not exceed more than a few dozen at any time before the eighteenth century.[115] There were also *mayordomos* who worked on Spanish estates as foremen or supervisors of native labor, and herders who ran sheep in the area. By the seventeenth century, many mestizos and mulattoes filled these types of positions. A few Spanish-speaking women lived in some of the major cabeceras; usually they were mestizas who married native nobles or mestizos. Alternatively, they lived out of wedlock with Spanish or mestizo men, typically working in both native- and Spanish-type enterprises.

Religious establishments and Spanish officials engaged in the traffic of African slaves.[116] Some Mixtec nobles owned African slaves as early as the 1540s, but it was mainly Spaniards and mestizos who purchased and sold slaves. Of forty-one Spaniards and mestizos living in the Mixteca from 1590 to 1724, ten owned a total of twenty-three African slaves.[117] One mestizo in Tlaxiaco owned a married slave couple in 1626.[118] Spaniards relied on the labor of African men and women for many types of work, from raising livestock on haciendas to driving pack trains. Aside from isolated references in the record, little to nothing is known about Africans who lived as servants in Ñudzahui households.[119] References to African slaves in the Mixteca before the introduction of sugar mills indicate that they tended to work in Spanish-style enterprises, such as iron forges and stores, whether in the service of Spanish or Ñudzahui owners.

In theory, Spanish law prohibited nonindigenous people from residing in "repúblicas de Indios." The laws were designed to prescribe situations of contact between native peoples and Spaniards and to regulate the extent of their relations. Constraints were placed on both groups for different reasons. Special license was granted to officials, traders, and those who married native men or women. Interracial marriage was not prohibited, but it was rare. In the first half of the colonial period, Ñudzahui officials lodged numerous complaints against Spaniards and others who did not belong in their communities. Take the year 1591, for example. In that year, officials from Atlatlahuca filed a formal complaint against Spaniards living in the area and petitioned the alcalde mayor to expel them.[120] In Yolotepec, the cabildo expelled a mestizo named Cristóbal de Acuña, who had married a native woman; he was accused of instigating trouble and litigating excessively for his own selfish ambitions.[121] The community of Mixtepec tried to expel a resident mestizo for the same reason.[122] Officials from Teposcolula refused to provide free food and lodging to Spanish travelers in the community inn (*mesón del pueblo*) and complained that many Spaniards were recruiting native labor illegally.[123] In the same year, 1591, nobles from Achiutla protested that resident Dominican friars imprisoned, whipped, and fined fifteen people who had challenged their claim to several pieces of land in the community.[124]

By the mid-seventeenth century, complaints against the presence of Spaniards and others living in "pueblos de indios" reached a pinnacle in the Mixteca. Many petitions called for the enforcement of the royal decrees of 1578 and 1591, which prohibited "Spaniards, mestizos, blacks, mulattoes, vagabonds and drifters" from entering and living in native communities. By law these outsiders were restricted to a maximum three-day stay. In 1612, the cabildo of Yanhuitlan attempted to expel a resident Spaniard named Felipe de Aguilar because he owned several houses, pastured many sheep and cattle, and "contributed nothing but insults and debts to the community."[125] One complaint from Yanhuitlan in 1647 lamented that outsiders "serve no good, instead they cause great trouble . . . they solicit Indian women and steal things . . . they possess bad customs and odious vices."[126] The petition singled out *mulatos*, blacks, and mestizos as the worst of the troublemakers, but it also blamed Spaniards for manipulating land and house sales, entering houses unlawfully, and compelling people to serve them for little or no compensation. Moreover, their cattle, goats, and sheep destroyed maize fields, the plaintiffs alleged. They demanded that houses not be built for Spaniards in communities, under the penalty of confiscation. Protests against the presence of Spaniards in native communities suggest that laws prohibiting intrusion were ineffective. No colonial law could prevent cultural contact, especially in the region's cabeceras. The frequency of petitions and decrees from around 1590 to 1660 indicates that the law was violated on a regular basis and had become impractical by the second half of the seventeenth century.[127] After the 1660s, protests fade from the record as such laws became increasingly unrealistic and ineffectual.

A few non-Spanish Europeans lived and worked in the Mixteca. For example, in 1620, a Portuguese man named Duarte Pereira served as the mayordomo of a sheep hacienda owned by the Dominican friars of Tlaxiaco. We know about Pereira because, in that year, he became involved in an altercation with a noble who was related to the royal family of Tenochtitlan, don Fernando de Andrada y Montezuma, and who lived in Tlaxiaco.[128] While don Fernando was visiting his aunt, doña Mariana de Andrada, Pereira entered and accused him of taking one of his small money chests. The two exchanged some heated words before don Fernando called the mayordomo a "portugues puto judio borracho" [drunken Portuguese Jewish homosexual]. Pereira drew his sword, don Fernando countered, and they began to fight in the street. Pereira's cousin, Domingo López, suddenly jumped in to the fray and stabbed don Fernando in the face. Doña Mariana ran from her doorway and screamed at Duarte: "ladron borracho portugues" [drunken Portuguese thief]. Let us consider the circumstances of this unfortunate cultural encounter. Don Fernando was a highly respected noble who carried a sword and spoke Castilian well enough to hurl Spanish racial, sexual, and cultural insults at Duarte Pereira.[129] His slur associating Jews with evil and Portuguese with crypto-Jews proceeded from Spanish cultural attitudes. The irony of native people insulting Europeans with their own stereotypes suggests the extent to which dominant cultural attitudes and prejudices were perpetuated within colonial society. It is especially interesting to note that two Nahua women from central Mexico, who were servants in doña Mariana's household, testified in this case. One woman who served doña Mariana, Ana de Peña, was actually a *comadre* of Pereira the Portuguese man. Thus, the native nobles don Fernando and doña Mariana were of a higher social status than Pereira.

An Italian petty trader named Luis Bocarón fits the social profile of a marginal European in the Mixteca. Bocarón was called a Spaniard until the criminal proceedings against him revealed his true origins as a native of Genoa. In 1589, Bocarón attacked Juan Gregorio, a Nahua who lived in Tecamachalco, knocking him to the ground and slashing his face with a butcher's knife.[130] Gregorio nearly bled to death before natives from Tamasulapa hurried him to a Spanish surgeon. The injured Nahua dropped the charges and settled for a cash payment from the Italian, citing his faith in God, local pressures, and the money as reasons for his decision. As for Bocarón, he denied any wrongdoing but agreed to pay fifteen pesos to Gregorio and thirty pesos to the surgeon. He was exiled from the Mixteca Alta for four years and fined an additional forty pesos for the costs of the case. As in the previous example, this incident shows how European outsiders did not hesitate to brandish knives and swords in violent conflicts with native men. Colonial law and custom gave European men a decided advantage in this capacity because native men were not allowed to carry a sword, dagger, or musket without a special license. Whereas don Fernando possessed such a license, Juan Gregorio did not. These cases suggest why some native officials wanted to keep Europeans out of their communities.

Of course, not all interethnic contact amounted to conflict. Criminal records tend to emphasize violent conflict over peaceful coexistence. Actually, the record contains ample evidence of the latter. For example, baptismal registers reveal a network of *compadrazgo* ties (ritual co-parenthood) among Spaniards and Mixtec nobles. Even in criminal records, Mixtec defendants sometimes called upon Spaniards as friendly character witnesses. On the other hand, evidence of interethnic conflict in criminal records should not be dismissed as unrepresentative, aberrant behavior. Patterns of conflict reveal underlying tensions in colonial society. Most important, the ordinary criminal record offers extensive testimony on the mundane circumstances of social interaction. Each case contains incidental information, not necessarily related to the crime in question, that sheds light on patterns of everyday behavior and normal contact. Often, this information is more insightful than the specific details of the crime itself.

Marital and extramarital unions represented the most intimate form of cultural contact in the Mixteca. Sources suggest that most interethnic sexual relations in this period involved a native woman and a mestizo or Spanish man, or a native nobleman and a mestiza woman. The following four cases present examples of mestizo men who lived with native women in the Mixteca Alta; the first three cases aroused the disapproval of local native authorities, especially because the couples were not married. The final case presents two mestizas who were married to native noblemen and illustrates the emergence of a complex multiethnic society in Yanhuitlan.

At the end of the sixteenth century, Juan Bautista Grimaldos, a mestizo translator of Teposcolula, carried on an illicit affair with a younger native woman named Lucía López.[131] Lucía was a widow whose husband, a native translator, had died a few years earlier. She presumably met Juan through her husband's line of work; the two men had collaborated in the past, translating Spanish, Nahuatl, and Mixtec for the alcalde mayor and his staff. As his partner, Lucía cooked for Juan, cleaned his house, and washed and wove his clothes; she went back and forth from his place to the house of her mother, whom she continued to support. In exchange, Juan paid their tribute. When the local priest came around, she simply stayed at her mother's house in order to conceal their cohabitation. Fearful of being punished, she claimed that she had tried to leave more than once but that Juan had always convinced her to stay and once even forced her to return. Local native officials denounced them to the alcalde mayor when they were certain that she was living with him. This accusation might have been a pretext for harassing the mestizo. Just two years earlier, in 1595, the cabildo of Teposcolula had lodged a formal complaint against Juan Bautista. The native officials called the mestizo translator a rebel, a thief, a liar, and a fraud, and they accused him of sleeping with a native woman (Lucía).[132] The petition concluded in no uncertain terms: "we all hate him." Finally, Juan confessed to his affair with Lucía but claimed that he had intended to marry her. He was fined ten pesos and the costs of the case, and Lucía was exiled for six months to Yanhuitlan, where she served in a Spanish woman's house. The couple was ordered never to meet again, or she would be exiled for six years. This case suggests that native women could achieve a measure of financial security through their relations with Spaniards and mestizos. But women who were not married were vulnerable to community vigilance, even when they were widows. Obviously, the fact that native officials had declared their hatred for Juan, and that the petition made explicit his affair with a native woman, did not bode well for his relationship with Lucía. Witnesses in this case represented a cross section of society in the cabecera of Teposcolula, including Mixtecs who spoke Spanish fluently, Mixtecs who spoke only their native language, Spaniards, an African woman, and a mestizo.

Mixed-race marriages were not common in this period, but they were not necessarily opposed, either.[133] Informal sexual unions between mestizos and native women were subject to local disapproval, while adulterous affairs were subject to censure and punishment, especially in the case of interracial couples. In Yanhuitlan, one couple inspired the moral condemnation of their peers for their behavior; they simply could not be kept apart, despite their spouses. Pedro López Hordónez was a mestizo married to a native woman of Yanhuitlan; María Jiménez was a Mixtec woman married to a Mixtec man who was often away on business in Mexico City.[134] Pedro was a bell maker, and María supported herself by weaving garments; they lived in different siña (barrios) of Yanhuitlan. Local officials admonished them not to meet again after they were caught sleeping together in 1604. Pedro was fined sixteen pesos and two *tomines,* and María was "deposited" in the house of doña Beatriz de Azevedo, the wife of don Francisco de las Casas, the *encomendero.* But Pedro visited María at doña Beatriz's house, and they continued to have secret sex. A year later, when María was free, officials caught the couple at the house of Pedro's comadre, a native woman named Juana López. Cornered and frustrated, Pedro threatened officials with a loaded musket and shouted to María in her native language to flee. But they were captured and brought to jail. The alcalde mayor stripped Pedro's privilege of carrying a sword or a musket, fined him thirty pesos, and exiled him from the community for two years. If he were to meet or even speak with María under any circumstances, he would suffer the penalty of two hundred lashes and a fifty-peso fine. As far as we know, Pedro and María went their separate ways. In the end, the lovers' long-term consensual union jeopardized their status within the community. It is interesting to note that Pedro, a bilingual mestizo, had a native wife, a native mistress, and a native comadre. Another mestizo witness in the hearing, Domingo López, required the services of a translator because he did not know Spanish. This case illustrates how mestizos who lived in Ñudzahui communities were immersed in the local culture and language, despite colonial pressures to identify with the dominant group.

Some mestizos in the Mixteca Alta were drifters whose behavior aroused the suspicions of local officials. Pedro Juan was one such character. A mestizo tailor from Guadalajara, he had moved from one place to another before coming to Teposcolula in the early seventeenth century.[135] He lived with Francisca, a Nahua woman from Tepeaca who spoke Spanish. In Teposcolula, they sold pulque out of their home to Mixtec men and women. Pedro was not new to the Mixteca; several years earlier, he had fathered a child with a widow named Catalina, who lived in Mistepec. Pedro and Catalina had been punished by Mistepec officials for that illicit union. In 1618, Pedro and Francisca were accosted by the native officials of Teposcolula, but they defended themselves by claiming to have been married in Puebla ten years earlier. As an uprooted mestizo tailor, Pedro Juan had a foot in both worlds. He knew a European trade, spoke Spanish well, and could even sign his name. Yet he married a bilingual Nahua woman, and together they practiced the typical native trade of selling pulque.

A final example of interracial contact reveals the complexity of local society in Yanhuitlan by the end of the seventeenth century. In 1684, Pedro Caravantes murdered his wife, María Montiel, and left a murder note on her body before fleeing the community.[136] The three-page letter, written in the Ñudzahui language and addressed to native and Spanish officials, attempted to explain that he killed his wife because he had caught her committing adultery. As discussed earlier in this chapter, Pedro Caravantes was conscious that his note, written in the Ñudzahui language, needed to be translated into Spanish for the colonial officials who would investigate the case. Like many *toho* of his day, Pedro lived in a world of fluid ethnic boundaries. Pedro was a native noble who knew some Spanish, but not enough to communicate his thoughts in writing, although he tried to write a few lines of Spanish at the end of his note. María Montiel, Pedro's wife, was a bilingual mestiza.

The witnesses from Yanhuitlan who knew the accused and his victim constituted a cross section of a complex colonial society: Antonio de la Cruz, a middle-aged Ñudzahui man who knew Spanish; María Machete, a Ñudzahui woman with an odd surname (probably a nickname); Juan Tomás, a Ñudzahui boy who knew some Spanish; Ursula de Torres, an elderly mestiza; María Antonia, a young free mulatta; María de la Confesión, a Ñudzahui woman who claimed she knew Spanish but, nonetheless, relied on the services of a translator; María de la Cruz, an "india ladina"; Domingo de la Cruz, a Ñudzahui man who knew Spanish; Juana Montiel, a young mestiza who was related to the victim; doña María Rodríguez, a "Spanish" woman; María de la Concepción, an "india ladina"; and Sebastián García, a Ñudzahui man who did not know Spanish. This case introduced nearly as many mestizos who spoke Mixtec as Mixtecs who spoke Spanish. An individual's ethnic status was often blurred in the cultural milieu; no witness called María Montiel a mestiza, and her husband did not feel obligated to mention the fact in his letter. The victim's mestiza status was confirmed only during the second round of the proceedings, when the victim's alleged lover was apprehended by local authorities. In this case, women played a crucial role in forging intercultural ties in Yanhuitlan. María Montiel and her sister, Juana Montiel, had married native nobles and befriended women of other ethnicities; the people who testified on María's behalf included a mulatta, two mestizas, and a Ñudzahui woman. When Juana the mestiza approached the authorities concerning María's disappearance, she counted on the help of a native doña.

These examples illustrate the mundane circumstances of interethnic and multicultural relations in the most prominent cabeceras of the region. In the second half of the colonial period, even people who lived in relatively isolated sujetos came into contact with Spanish-speaking people who resided in cabeceras, haciendas, or Spanish cities such as Oaxaca or Puebla. Interracial interactions prompted and reinforced conscious expressions of ethnic identity within a colonial context of difference. Even though few non-native people lived in the Mixteca, it is impossible to speak of separate Spanish and Ñudzahui worlds in the colonial period.

CHAPTER 10

Conclusions

THIS WORK USES pictorial writings, native-language records, and Spanish-language sources for a history of the Ñudzahui, or Mixtec, people in the colonial period. I am especially concerned with how indigenous individuals, groups, and institutions responded to colonial changes. Each chapter considers the impact of colonial changes and the presence of Spanish-speaking people on some aspect of Ñudzahui culture and society. Each chapter could serve as the basis of a separate study, and it is hoped that future studies will test and extend the findings presented here.

Much of this study draws on evidence from the Mixteca Alta, particularly the western half of the Alta, in and around the valleys of Nochixtlan, Teposcolula, Tamasulapa, and Tlaxiaco, where Spanish-Ñudzahui interaction was concentrated in the colonial period. The repetition of familiar cultural patterns and conceptual vocabulary in each subregion has allowed me to make certain general conclusions that apply to the Mixteca as a whole. Native-language terminology for an entire range of cultural categories, from sociopolitical organization to land tenure, is consistent in the Alta, Baja, and valley. Despite the existence of local and regional variation, general patterns prevail.

Common cultural attributes were the basis of a distinct self-ascribed ethnic identity. People referred to themselves as *tay ñudzahui,* translated as "people of the rain place" or "people from the land of Dzahui," the rain deity. Writers identified their language, the region, *ñuu* and *yuhuitayu,* individuals and groups of people, the ancient calendar, sacred images, flora and fauna, and material culture with the term *Ñudzahui.* References to the term appear in the earliest and latest native-language writings, especially those from the Mixteca Alta. Many people in the region shared a distinct culture, conveyed in the vocabulary of a common language and the conventions of an elaborate

345

writing system. The frequent use of the term *Ñudzahui* represents the need and ability to distinguish one's affiliation within a multiethnic and multilingual milieu. Ñudzahui people were surrounded by other native groups and communities for whom they had specific names, especially Nahuas (*tay Ñucoyo*), Zapotecs (*tay Ñucuisi*), and Chochos (*tay Ñucuij*). Ñudzahui vocabulary consistently identified groups and individuals with an ethnic qualifier, usually based on their place of origin, and did not have an equivalent term for "foreigner" or "outsider" (such as the Yucatecan Maya *dzul*). The term *Ñudzahui* did not compromise a more specific local identity with a ñuu and *siqui*. Nor did it entail political unification. The population became more complex after the Spanish arrival, when *tay Castilla*, "people of Castile," and other ethnicities settled in several *cabeceras*. In the course of the next two centuries, population decline, the growth of the Spanish sector, and the proliferation of Spanish concepts, language, and material culture prompted a conscious distinction between the indigenous and the intrusive. The written expression of Ñudzahui ethnicity was especially prominent in the late seventeenth century, a period of increased contact with Spanish-speaking peoples. Today, the term *Ñudzahui*, spelled and pronounced many different ways, is used as a term of self-ascription by many Mixtecan language speakers in Oaxaca.

A common culture did not preclude subregional differences. I found no references to the term *Ñudzahui* in about thirty native-language records from the Mixteca Baja.[1] Texts from the Baja exhibit significant phonetic and lexical differences in comparison with writings from the Alta. Sources from the sixteenth and seventeenth centuries contain no trace of the honorific register associated with lordly speech in the Mixteca Alta. The subunits of the ñuu had a distinct name in the Baja (*dzini*), which were often attached to the patrimonies of lords. Even though *yuhuitayu*, *ñuu*, and *dzini* were the operative terms for sociopolitical entities in this region, writers also used the term *yucunduta*, "hill and water," the semantic equivalent of the Nahua *altepetl*. The Baja's proximity to the eastern Nahua area suggests a complex history of interaction and influence that merits further study.[2]

Shared concepts and local variations on familiar themes reflect centuries of interethnic interaction. The following section compares some key Ñudzahui cultural attributes, in the light of new findings, with those of neighboring Mesoamerican groups.

Mesoamerican Comparisons

Native-language alphabetic sources are known to exist in only a few areas of Mesoamerica, in central Mexico, Oaxaca, and Yucatan. No language group in the Americas has left a legacy of native-language writings comparable to that of the Nahuas. The entire collection of known Ñudzahui-language writings is modest in comparison with the existing Nahuatl-language corpus. There are no extensive writings of an epic quality, such as the annals of the Nahua historian Chimalpahin or the encyclopedia of Nahua culture and language compiled by fray Bernardino de Sahagún in Tlatelolco. Whereas Nahuatl notarial records number in the thousands, Ñudzahui-language sources amount to a few hundred. Nonetheless, the Ñudzahui record is rich enough to make possible multiple detailed comparisons between the Mixteca, central Mexico, and Yucatan. I will focus on the following comparative topics: writing; language; sociopolitical organization;

lordly establishments and systems of government; the organization of households and lands; social differentiation; gender relations; religious practices; and expressions of ethnicity.

The Ñudzahui system of writing in the postclassic period compares with pictographic writing traditions in central Mexico to the extent that the famous *Codex Borgia* group was clearly influenced by Mixtecan style, even though the screenfold manuscripts were probably produced in the Puebla-Tlaxcala area. In anthropology and art history, the mutual influence in style and various shared conventions have been recognized by the term *Mixteca-Puebla*. Most of the extant preconquest-style codices from highland Mesoamerica come from the Mixteca, where pictographic writing flourished at the time of the Spanish arrival. In the Maya region, the highly stylized hieroglyphic writing of the classic period was still practiced to some degree in the early sixteenth century. In the colonial period, the Maya did not produce maps or *lienzos* in Yucatan comparable to those of highland Mexico, probably because the Maya writing system relied less on pictorial conventions. The continued practice of Ñudzahui pictorial writing after the conquest registers significant continuities and changes; by the mid-sixteenth century, many native artists had begun to adopt European style as a complement to their own conventions. The creation of a hybrid or mixed pictorial tradition and the rapid adoption of alphabetic writing were parallel processes in central Mexico and Oaxaca. The main differences result from the timing and extent of interaction with Spaniards. Alphabetic writing began later in the Mixteca, and the pictorial tradition lasted longer. Pictorial manuscripts from Oaxaca illustrate the persistence of indigenous style in the colonial period.

In terms of language, the lordly "*yya* speech" of the sixteenth century compares in many ways to Nahuatl high speech, or *huehuetlatolli*. In both Nahuatl and Ñudzahui, the honorific register was a manner of speaking properly and respectfully more than a separate vocabulary. Ñudzahui conventions consisted of honorific pronouns (such as *ñadzaña* and *ya*), nouns, and verbs. The terminology typically referred to the actions of the elite, their body parts (including relational terms based on body parts), and elite material culture. Nahuatl reverential conventions included the use of applicative and causative affixes inserted within the verb phrase and the addition of the diminutive *-tzin* to nouns and pronouns. The two languages featured similar metaphorical expressions and the use of semantic couplets, so that two separate nouns or verbs imparted a particular meaning when combined. Shared linguistic conventions and a common calendar promoted the diffusion of comparable writing systems throughout central Mexico and the Mixteca. And yet, despite constant interaction across the fluid boundaries of these two cultural areas, there is little evidence for the lexical influence of one language on the other. In comparison, Yucatec Maya and Mexican Spanish borrowed numerous loanwords from Nahuatl.

This book examines the Ñudzahui corporate community, the interrelation of its structures, and the basic principles and patterns of sociopolitical organization. The ñuu and its constituent parts represent a complex scenario comparable to Nahua sociopolitical organization in many important ways. These named entities existed throughout the Mixteca. The ñuu was a potentially autonomous state or community with a defined territory, a governing nobility, constituent units, temple and palace structures, and an organized labor and tribute-producing system. The yuhuitayu consisted of an alliance between two ñuu, each ruled by a male or female lord according to the principles of direct descent. The term *yuhuitayu* referred to both the ñuu and the ruling couple involved in such an alliance, signifying both a place and a political relationship.

The native-language record reveals three comparable subdivisions of the ñuu in three different regions of the Mixteca: the siqui in the Teposcolula and Tamasulapa areas, the siña in the Yanhuitlan area and the Valley of Oaxaca, and the dzini in the Mixteca Baja. Documentation from a siña of Yanhuitlan named Ayusi indicates that siña were microcosms of ñuu with their separate nobility, palaces, temples, lands, and patron deities or saints. Each siqui was a potential ñuu and each ñuu a potential yuhuitayu, a possibility that accounts for the ambiguity of terms such as *ñuu siña* and *ñuu tayu* and the inherent tension between these dynamic entities. In many ways, the organization of the Ñudzahui ñuu is comparable to the Nahua altepetl. In central Mexico, the altepetl consisted of a number of separate, self-contained units called *calpolli, tlaxilacalli*, or *chinamitl*. As in the Mixteca, differences among the three Nahua names for the subunit may be related to regional variation or structure. Ñudzahui and Nahua constituent units had distinctive names that resembled other place-names. Unlike the names of ñuu and altepetl, however, siqui and calpolli names rarely included the word *hill*. In both cases, a subunit could conceivably break off and become a larger unit without changing its name or internal political arrangements. Some Nahua calpolli were contiguous and either formed two parts of a former whole or participated in some type of dual organization. Terminological evidence for this phenomenon exists in siqui names designating upper and lower versions. In addition, several ñuu contained a subentity of the same name, suggesting that the smaller entity lent its name to the larger. At the level of macrounits, the ñuu of a yuhuitayu resembles the *tlayacatl*, the constituent altepetl of a composite state in central Mexico. In both forms of organization, each constituent had a separate ruler. But the ñuu of yuhuitayu were not united permanently or joined as contiguous units within a bounded territory, as were the Nahua complex altepetl, such as the four altepetl of Tlaxcala. In fact, the constituent ñuu of a yuhuitayu might be separated by considerable distance. The shifting, cross-regional nature of the yuhuitayu brought people from different ñuu into contact with one another.

Ñudzahui siqui and Nahua calpolli contributed goods and services separately to the ñuu and altepetl through organized, rotational systems known as *tniño* and *tequitl*, respectively. In general, the altepetl consisted of a fairly symmetrical ordering of constituent parts. In contrast, symmetry was not a consistent pattern in the Mixteca. However, colonial attempts at congregation and other changes associated with the creation of cabeceras and *sujetos* obscure the preconquest arrangement in most places. For the Mixteca, there are no historical accounts that address the topic of preconquest sociopolitical organization comparable to those of the Nahua historian Chimalpahin. Yanhuitlan's inclusion of multiple siña (about forty in the sixteenth century) compares with the multiple tlaxilacalli of Nahua Coyoacan and Cuernavaca, where complex and constituent units were all reduced to one cabecera, thereby distorting the original configuration. The appearance of Ñudzahui settlement patterns in the sixteenth-century Spanish-language record—the center with hamlets or subordinate satellite settlements and the center without hamlets—reflects postconquest conceptual changes that were articulated in the language of the earliest Spanish documents. Population loss and the consolidation of larger units reinforced these conceptual changes. Despite the reorganization, indigenous writers continued to use their own terminology for all these structures throughout most of the colonial period. In both the Nahuatl and Mixtec languages, terms were invented for Spanish introductions.

This work examines the *aniñe* as a palace structure, the center of a lordly establishment, and a corporate landholding entity. In its function, floor plan, and exterior decor, the aniñe resembled the Nahua *tecpan*. The aniñe was a sacred site, a place of assembly for the nobility, a focal point of feasts, and the center of a ñuu or siqui. Each aniñe had a specific name and was located in a particular siqui (siña or dzini) of the ñuu. The relationship between the Ñudzahui aniñe, the ñuu, and its constituent siqui is comparable to that of the Nahua *teccalli* or tecpan, the altepetl, and its constituent calpolli. In the Mixteca Alta, the Ñudzahui siqui, like the Nahua calpolli, claimed a portion of its ñuu's territory for the use of its members. However, there are many more cases of aniñe that exercised control over extensive landholdings. Some siqui were actually created by lords who relocated people to serve as dependents on their land. The distinction between lands of the siqui and aniñe was ambiguous and, at times, contested. The strength of the aniñe in the Mixteca, particularly in the Mixteca Baja, where some lords referred to entire dzini and their inhabitants as part of their patrimonies, may have subsumed many landholding rights at the expense of the dzini or ñuu. This pattern resembles the eastern Nahua teccalli, especially in Tlaxcala and Cuauhtinchan.[3] Lordly establishments were so strong in the Mixteca that many continued to function throughout the colonial period.

The configuration of yuhuitayu, ñuu, and siqui allowed considerable autonomy. In this mountainous region of multiple small valleys, dispersed settlement patterns and small population clusters were more appropriate than highly nucleated settlements. The region was not unified politically, but many ñuu and yuhuitayu were integrated into a network of rotating dynastic alliances and overlapping trade and tribute networks. In reality, sociopolitical organization in central Mexico and the Mixteca had much in common. Essentially, multiple autonomous ethnic states were unified by a shared culture and language more than by political rule. The Mexica "empire" was an "ephemeral imperial agglomeration" of altepetl more than it was a unified state.[4] This is one reason why the Spaniards were able to undermine the empire so rapidly, with the assistance of many other altepetl. In the Mixteca and in central Mexico, comparable structures underwent similar processes of change in the colonial period, even though the rate and extent of change varied considerably in the Mixteca. In both cultural areas, resistance to the cabecera-sujeto hierarchy began in the early colonial period and culminated in the late colonial fragmentation of larger structures into smaller units. In both regions, the resulting configuration of pueblos was based on the outline of original sociopolitical structures.

In the light of comparisons between the Ñudzahui ñuu and the Nahua altepetl, the Maya *cah* seems very different. Maya-language documentation indicates that the Maya cah had no discernible sociopolitical subentities such as the Nahua calpolli and tlaxi-lacalli or the Ñudzahui siqui, dzini, and siña, and no macrounits such as the Nahua complex altepetl and its constituent tlayacatl or the Ñudzahui yuhuitayu and its constituent ñuu.[5] Despite the persistence of elite families, the cah had no defined palace or lordly establishment comparable to the Nahua teccalli or Ñudzahui aniñe, and a vague counterpart to the systems of corporate, organized labor, the Nahua tequitl and Ñudzahui tniño.[6] The integral relationship between lordly establishments and sociopolitical structures in central Mexico and the Mixteca does not compare with the situation in Yucatan. Sociopolitical organization in Yucatan was shaped by agricultural practices and settlement patterns that relied on periodic population movement. The implications of these cultural and organizational differences for the comparative study of native peoples under colonial rule are considerable. Patterns of change in Yucatan were not different simply because it was a more remote region in the colonial period.

At the level of the household, the organization and structure of the Ñudzahui *huahi* and *cahi* (house and patio) complex correspond in nearly all respects to the Nahua *calli* and *ithualli*. In both central Mexico and the Mixteca Alta, several separate living quarters or "house structures," each with its own entrance, were arranged around a central patio. The terms *calli* and *huahi* could refer to the single structures of a household or the entire compound. People often walled off the compound to create an enclosure, with one shared entry, that united the household. The royal palace, or aniñe, was the most elaborate huahi of the siqui or ñuu. The typical aniñe was a single-story, multicomponent complex with several rooms or single-room houses arranged around or adjacent to sunken patios, not unlike the tecpan in central Mexico.

The organization and tenure of land in the Mixteca resembled the general pattern described for the Nahuas. The average possession consisted of a main holding on which the house was located and a number of scattered plots; primary responsibility for separate fields was divided among household members. Land tenure categories included *ñuhu huahi* (house land), *ñuhu chiyo* (patrimonial land), *ñuhu aniñe* (palace land), *ñuhu ñuu* (land belonging to the ñuu), *ñuhu siña* (land belonging to the siña), and *ñuhu nidzico* (purchased lands). These categories correspond with the Nahua *callalli, huehuetlalli, tecpantlalli, altepetlalli, calpollalli,* and *tlalcohualli,* respectively. The basic distinction between *ñuhu aniñe* and *ñuhu ñuu* in the Mixteca resembles the distinction between *tecpantlalli* and *altepetlalli* in central Mexico. One possible difference between palace lands in the two areas is the extensive cross-regional nature of aniñe landholdings; many lords claimed substantial amounts of land located outside the boundaries of their home ñuu. Although ñuu authorities could reallocate corporate lands, inheritance and interhousehold division were the principal means of transferring and distributing land in the Mixteca, as in central Mexico and Yucatan. Inheritance patterns, the sale and purchase of lands, and many other features of land tenure, organization, distribution, and use are comparable to patterns described for the Nahuas. Trade and tribute mechanisms, long-distance traders, and a highly organized local market system were common features in both central Mexico and Oaxaca.

A fundamental Nahua organizational principle is based on the tendency to create larger entities by the agglomeration of separate, self-contained parts arranged in a numerical or symmetrical order. This tendency is what James Lockhart has called cellular or modular organization.[7] The Nahua altepetl exemplifies the principle of cellular organization. Similarly, the yuhuitayu can be seen as a larger entity created from two separate and essentially equal ñuu. In turn, each ñuu consisted of multiple constituent siqui. Each siqui was a potential ñuu, and each ñuu a potential yuhuitayu. A feature of cellular organization was the tendency to repeat the same basic patterns at different levels. Another pervasive Mesoamerican concept is the frequency of four as a principal number of organization, based on the cardinal directions.[8] The origin legend of Apoala, as told in Reyes's *Arte,* speaks of four rulers who set out from separate "barrios" to rule the four parts of the Mixteca. Some ñuu were divided into four parts, although many ñuu contained multiple subunits. In central Mexico, constituent Nahua calpolli usually numbered between four and eight parts.

Ñudzahui and Nahua social relations were very similar. Both societies consisted of two hereditary categories of nobles and commoners. Ñudzahui yya and *toho* were considered members of the same nobility, distinguishable from the much larger body of *ñandahi,* or commoners, similar to the Nahua division of *pipiltin* (nobles) and *macehualtin* (commoners). In both societies, nobles were distinguished from commoners by their titles, privileges, material wealth, housing, clothing, speech, and ceremonial roles. Every Ñudzahui yya or *yya dzehe* (female lord) presumably held title to a specific lordship involving subordinate nobles, commoners, dependents, and lands. Like the Nahua *teuctli* (lord), he or she represented an aniñe within a specific ñuu. In Yucatan, *batab* and *almehen* were the approximate Mayan equivalents of yya and toho, although they did not possess palaces, dependent laborers, or patrimonial lands in the colonial period.

Ñudzahui commoners were identified as *ñandahi* or *dzaya dzana.* The Nahuatl term *macehualli* came very close in usage and meaning to *ñandahi.* Apart from tribute-paying commoners, the marginal group of dependent laborers did not work land belonging to the ñuu and were not obligated to perform public duties but instead lived on the land or in the household of a lord and performed duties and services for that establishment. It was thought that the term *tay situndayu* was applied to this group, called *terrazgueros* in Spanish. However, native-language sources from the Mixteca Baja and Alta indicate that the conventional terms for commoner, *ñandahi* or *dzaya dzana,* were used consistently for dependents, suggesting that dependent status was not rigidly defined or permanent. The ambiguous distinction between lordly dependents and commoners may be related to the contested relation of the aniñe to the ñuu and siqui structure. Similarly, in Nahua studies *mayeque* were thought to have constituted a distinct social category with a separate name and to have been lower in status than ordinary commoners (macehualtin). However, Nahuatl-language sources show that the terminology for dependents varied, and they were actually called *macehualtin* more than anything else. Thus, in central Mexico and the Mixteca, dependent laborers were a type of commoners, not a distinct category. Finally, in both areas, slaves were bought and sold and captured in warfare until Spanish law prohibited these practices among indigenous peoples. In Yucatan, one of the great Maya mysteries is why the term *macehual,* derived from the Nahuatl macehualli, became the term used by Maya speakers for a commoner.[9] Normally, loanwords were adopted for introduced concepts or objects when there was no equivalent in the native language.

The present work has identified the yuhuitayu and described many aspects of political organization in the Mixteca, building on the pioneering studies of Alfonso Caso,

Ronald Spores, and Maarten Jansen. The yuhuitayu was a metaphorical couplet, represented in the preconquest-style codices and early postconquest pictorial manuscripts by a married couple seated together on a woven reed mat, facing and gesturing toward each other. An early colonial description of the ceremonial possession of a royal palace in Teposcolula, described in chapter 6, illustrates how the image of the yuhuitayu in the codices was performed and reenacted before members of the community. In each room of the palace, the royal couple sat together on a reed mat before an assembly of noble witnesses. The male *yya toniñe* represented one ñuu, and the female *yya dzehe toniñe* represented another. In this particular case, the female ruler represented Teposcolula, and her husband represented the ñuu of Tamasulapa. The ruling couple unified two ñuu and any additional entities belonging to the patrimony of each member. Women ruled jointly as equal members of the yuhuitayu, or alone as widows. The hereditary system of direct, bilateral descent valued both male and female lines equally. In the absence of legitimate heirs, provisions were made for siblings or their children as a last resort.

As a symbol of authority or government, the Mixtec yuhui resembles the Nahua *petlatl icpalli*. The Nahua historian Chimalpahin and the authors of the *Primeros memoriales* referred to the reed mat as a metaphor for the rulership. However, the Nahua mat refers more to the seat as the throne of the male *tlatoani*. In pictorial writings from central Mexico, the tlatoani is seated alone on a reed mat. The Nahua tlatoani inherited his position as a member of a royal genealogy or dynastic line associated with that particular rulership. Descent was traced primarily through the male line in each rulership, yet the female line was relied on in times of necessity.[10] Many candidates inherited the rulership of an altepetl when their mothers were from that place or when their mothers came from an important outside altepetl. Although succession by males was clearly the norm, Chimalpahin did allow the possibility of *cihuatlatoque,* "women rulers." Nonetheless, female succession was exceptional among the Nahuas.[11]

The yuhuitayu assigned high status to noblewomen. Thus, women stand out in pictorial and alphabetic writings from the Mixteca. The codices depict women almost as often as men. The sacred realm was imagined in terms of the political order; the *Codex Vindobonensis* traces the origins of life to a male and female creator couple, the mother and father of all the deities. Marital alliances of the yuhuitayu guaranteed that women were as likely to succeed to the reed mat throne as men. But inheritance patterns were subject to considerable local variation. In the Mixteca Baja, one codex indicates a preference for patrivirilocal residence patterns and the choice of male heirs. Nonetheless, each man married a woman who represented another ñuu. In the Mixteca Alta, early colonial evidence indicates that several factors, including the birth order of children, influenced inheritance patterns among the high nobility. In any case, each ruling member of the yuhuitayu bequeathed his or her patrimony separately to male and female successors.

In the colonial period the yuhuitayu was simplified and reinterpreted as the "kingdom-*cacicazgo*." Spanish officials recognized and validated the hereditary authority and rights of the local nobility, but the rulership of yya toniñe and noble functionaries was reorganized by Spanish-style municipal government. In form and function, the *cabildo* represented a tradition of autonomous self-government that included nobles and elders and surely drew on some preconquest precedent. As in central Mexico and Yucatan, many elements of traditional native government endured and even thrived in the Mixteca after the conquest. The electors and members were all yya and toho, and officeholding was interpreted in terms of preconquest structures and functions. The cabildo effectively represented the ñuu from the mid-sixteenth century onward. Many preconquest functions of local government were transferred to the cabildo, including some aspects of dynastic rulership, the supervision of tribute and labor, the organization of feasts, the dispensing of local justice, and writing. In many cases, the aniñe became the meeting place of the cabildo.

The cabildo excluded women from official, political functions. Noblewomen continued to exercise informal power and controlled a considerable degree of wealth as *cacicas,* as Ronald Spores has shown.[12] They received annual salaries in the early period in recognition of their high rank, and they controlled as much land and labor and possessed as many prestige goods as men. But they could not serve on the local Spanish-style municipal council and thus could not participate in the daily government of the ñuu. If noblewomen had exercised political responsibilities as ruling members of the yuhuitayu and were involved in ceremonial and ritual acts of a sacred nature, as they appear to have done in the codices, they were limited or excluded in the new order from many public aspects of these functions.[13] The fact that cacicas were ineligible for the important and lucrative position of governor encouraged the appointment of male heirs. Nonetheless, cacicas continued to represent communities as long as the institution of the yuhuitayu survived.

The fact that women ruled, not as the result of an untimely break in the male line of rulership but as entitled members of the yuhuitayu, is an exception to known Mesoamerican patterns. For the sake of comparison, recent studies of Nahua women in Mesoamerica have qualified earlier interpretations of gender hierarchy and have shown that, despite marginalization within the colonial political order, some Nahua noblewomen continued to exercise considerable local authority.[14] Nonetheless, Nahua men were more visible than women at the corporate level. In terms of political authority, the Ñudzahui case clearly differs from the Yucatecan Maya system, where women were ineligible for the position of batab and where patriarchal representation, even at the household level, was the norm. Farther afield, the prominence of male and female rulers in the Andean area (called *curacas* and *coyas,* respectively) and the significant roles attributed to women before the Inca conquest seem to present an arrangement comparable to the Ñudzahui case.[15] But the lack of native-language records in Quechua or Aymara places considerable emphasis on evidence drawn from seventeenth-century Spanish-language histories of the preconquest period, especially the work of Guaman Poma de Ayala. In comparison, I have drawn on information from the preconquest codices, sixteenth-century pictorial records, native-language writings, and early colonial Spanish documentation on cacicas. The yuhuitayu seems to offer an example of a political system in a "complex" society that is based on "egalitarian concepts of gender."[16]

Evidence of gender equality within the yuhuitayu raises the question: Did the same principles apply to gender relations beyond the high nobility? Scholars have linked the cultural practice of female succession to political office with the inheritance and possession of land and other forms of wealth.[17] An examination of 128 testaments from the Mixteca Alta indicates that female testators owned about as much land and property as male testators. Repeated examples of married couples who collaborated in the long-distance trade of cloth and other indigenous products suggest how members of a household allocated other forms of wealth. Some noblewomen made substantial profits from the cloth trade in the first half of the colonial period. In each case, women kept their money separate from their husband's accounts. The same basic patterns and principles regarding work and property are observable among commoners, as well. The general adherence to an even distribution of property and wealth between men and women, based on cultural expectations of reciprocal responsibilities and rights within the household and community, implies a considerable degree of gender equality in Ñudzahui society. On the other hand, patterns of male violence in disputes over accusations or incidences of adultery, and the justifications used by men to defend themselves before male authorities, undermine the ideal of gender equality within the huahi and ñuu. The judicial record contains numerous examples of how unfulfilled expectations or perceived transgressions of gender norms resulted in public shaming and violent confrontation. In cases of domestic violence, the vast majority of aggressors were men. Yet women were not passive or helpless victims in these contested situations, and it is misleading to focus exclusively on cases of assault or homicide to assess gender relations in native societies.[18]

In the realm of religion, preconquest Nahua and Ñudzahui practices and beliefs represent a complex synthesis of shared Mesoamerican features and local autonomy. The two cultural areas possessed palace and temple complexes, priests and specialists, sacred books, stone and jade images of male and female deities, an elaborate feast system based on a shared calendar, similar ritual offerings, and so forth. One of the most prominent deities or sacred forces associated with rain and water, Dzahui, is the Mixtec counterpart of the Nahua Tlaloc, the Maya Chac, and the Zapotec Coçijo. Whereas Dzahui was the most prominent deity in the Mixteca Alta, Tlaloc shared the great temple of Tenochtitlan with the Mexica patron deity, Huitzilopochtli. Even though the Mexica had conquered much of the Mixteca region before the arrival of Christianity, there is no sign of Huitzilopochtli in the early colonial Mixtec record. Mixtec codices depict central Mexican deities, but they ascribed unique local characteristics and names to them. This process of localization foreshadowed Mixtec responses to Christian introductions.

After the conquest, native-language terminology for new concepts provided the basis of a shared conceptual vocabulary. The church or *huahi ñuhu*, "sacred house," came to represent the native community, much as the *teocalli* did in central Mexico. The malevolent owl-person represented the Christian devil in both cultural areas, and the concept of sin was subsumed under a general category of error. The interpretation of Mary as a mother deity who complemented God the Father, and the importance of *santos* and *santas* in both areas, suggest a generalized interpretation of Christian personages in terms of sacred male and female figures. In the Mixteca, Nahuas contributed to the dialogue between friars and Ñudzahui nobles in the early period. It is unclear whether parallel responses to introduced phenomena represent Nahua influence or simply confirm the fact that Mesoamerican cultures responded in comparable ways to Spanish contact. It is likely that both interpretations are valid. The religious systems of both areas shared so many features that it is possible to treat the general evolution of native-Christian forms as a single process. This general evolution was subject to significant local variation, however.

The prominence of Dzahui in early colonial Inquisition records from the Mixteca Alta confirms the sacred content of the ethnic term *Ñudzahui,* "place of Dzahui," articulated by people from the Mixteca Alta and Valley of Oaxaca. This term appears dozens of times in many different types of native-language writings from the colonial period. In comparison, although *Nahua* does appear in many of the earliest church texts in reference to language, the term was not employed consistently by Nahuas themselves. In fact, *Nahuatl* was most frequently employed in reference to the language of books, particularly ecclesiastical publications. The people of central Mexico who spoke Nahuatl sometimes called themselves *Nahuatlaca,* "Nahua people," but the term appears only infrequently in the colonial record. Nahuas tended to emphasize their belonging to the local altepetl and calpolli rather than broader ethnic categories, even when the context invited a contrast between indigenous and Spanish. As a second point of comparison, in Yucatan, the term *Maya* rarely appeared in the written record, and, in fact, the origins and meaning of the term are obscure. When one would expect to find the word in reference to indigenous people or objects, the term was not used. Ironically, people used the term *macehual,* a Nahuatl loanword for "commoner" or "person" that was borrowed before the Spanish conquest, to distinguish local from introduced objects. In Yucatan and central Mexico, then, a version of the word *macehualli* came to approximate the meaning of indigenous or "Indian." Mixtec speakers did not use "ñandahi" in the same way.

This work places recent studies of the Nahuas and Maya in a broader Mesoamerican context. Detailed comparisons between Ñudzahui and Nahua culture challenge the dominant impression that the Nahuas and a prominent group at the time of the Spanish arrival, the Mexica or "Aztecs" of Tenochtitlan, had surpassed the peoples of adjacent cultural areas in their political and cultural development. Contrary to earlier assessments, the Mixteca was not a province of petty chiefdoms on the periphery of an empire with a more sophisticated center. In reality, the Nahua and Ñudzahui cultural areas had much in common, owing to centuries of interaction and mutual influence. In the densely populated, multiethnic highland areas of Mexico, local and regional variations on shared cultural themes were the rule rather than the exception. It remains to be seen whether similar native-language sources may be applied to the study of other groups. In Oaxaca, documents written in Zapotec and Chocho offer promising possibilities for comparative research.[19] Outside Oaxaca, the Otomí of central Mexico and the Purhépecha of Michoacan, among other groups, wrote in their own languages during the colonial period.

The existence of similar structures and modes of organization among the Nahuas and Mixtecs raises the possibility of shared responses to colonial rule and comparable patterns of cultural change. The following section considers the second main objective of this work—to assess the impact of colonial changes and interactions with Spaniards and other ethnic groups on Ñudzahui culture.

Interaction and Change

Europeans had a profound impact on society and culture in the Mixteca. Nothing remained the same after the Spanish invasion of the 1520s. The conquest affected everyone within a few generations, unless they were isolated from contact with Europeans, and even then they were affected by their isolation.[20] The profit motive of capitalism determined where Spaniards went during the colonial period and the intensity of contact between indigenous populations and Spaniards.

Recent studies based on Nahuatl-language sources have characterized cultural change in terms of a long, gradual process. James Lockhart has proposed three stages of postconquest change for the Nahuas of central Mexico, based primarily on increasing contact between indigenous and Spanish-speaking populations.[21] The beginning of the stages is defined more by the extent and nature of contact than the actual date of conquest. The model is most applicable to the gradual nature of language change throughout the Nahuatl-speaking area of central Mexico, caused by the increasing frequency and intensity of contact between native and Spanish speakers. The first stage in central Mexico proceeds from the arrival of the Spaniards to around 1550. In this period of about thirty years, there was virtually no change in the language itself, and new concepts and objects were expressed fully within Nahua conventions. Stage two extends from the mid-sixteenth century until around the mid-seventeenth century and is characterized mainly by the borrowing of Spanish nouns. By this time, a generation of Nahuas had become more familiar with Spanish introductions and were incorporating a full range of words into their daily vocabulary. But aside from this lexical augmentation, the language remained little altered in other respects. The onset of stage three in central Mexico is characterized by a relative gradualness, stretching across much of the mid-seventeenth century. After the 1650s, Nahuas went beyond borrowing nouns to using loan verbs, prepositions, adverbs, and conjunctions. Some Nahuatl speakers translated idiomatic expressions from Spanish and adopted Spanish principles of pluralization. These types of changes reflected a broad movement in the direction of bilingualism and eventual native language loss.

In the Mixteca, the cumulative nature of the *Vocabulario en lengua mixteca*, printed in the 1590s, represents both the first and second stages of contact. The text relies on numerous identifications, extensions, circumlocutory descriptions, and a few Spanish loan nouns (including loanwords derived from Nahuatl) to refer to Spanish introductions. The first extant Ñudzahui-language archival records, written in the 1570s, exhibit signs of stage two in their use of loan nouns. Nonetheless, loanwords in these writings are few and confined to nouns. When a loan was appropriated into the language, or when it was still new to a particular speaker, it was paired with a semantic equivalent in the indigenous language. In stage two, both Nahuatl and Mixtec speakers described new actions by incorporating certain Spanish nouns into a native verb phrase or by borrowing the infinitive form of Spanish verbs in the same manner. For example, to describe the introduced act of signing one's name, Ñudzahui writers combined the native verb *quidza*, "to do," with the loan noun *firma*, "signature," or the infinitive of the verb *firmar*, "to sign." Writers never abandoned the native verb, *quidza*, to describe

the new act. The imperfect equivalent of stage-three Nahuatl was not evident in cabeceras in the Mixteca until the 1670s and 1680s, and it was much less pronounced.
Mixtec speakers borrowed a full range of loan nouns from Spanish and adopted uninflected Spanish verbs. In this period, writers were more likely to borrow the Spanish
verb, *firmar,* than the loan noun but nonetheless continued to rely on verbs in their
own language. By the end of the eighteenth century, language contact in the Mixteca
was minimal in comparison with central Mexico. Similarly, Yucatecan Maya exhibits
only certain characteristics of stage-three Nahuatl by the mid-eighteenth century. The
extent of linguistic change in the administrative and commercial centers of the Mixteca Alta lagged behind Nahuatl by at least a quarter century and much longer in more
remote areas. Moreover, the cultural unity and contemporaneity of linguistic change
in central Mexico do not apply to the Mixteca. Language change in the Mixteca occurred neither as rapidly nor as evenly as in central Mexico.[22]

We may apply the stages model to change in many other cultural categories. In the
first stage, when interactions between Mixtecs and a small group of Spaniards were
minimal, contact is observable through pictorial records and a few Spanish-language
sources. Changes in writing mark a shift to stage two. In the first decades after the conquest, the tradition of writing on deerskin declined, but native nobles continued to
produce preconquest-style writings on cloth with few intrusive elements. By around
1550, the hybrid style of the *Codex Yanhuitlan* shows the extent to which friars in Yanhuitlan had worked with native artists in the wake of the Inquisition trials. Nonetheless,
the sketches portray the Spaniards as ominous, unnamed newcomers. In the 1550s
and early 1560s, writers in Texupa combined pictographic text with Nahuatl writing
in the *Codex Sierra,* illustrating how Nahuas served as cultural intermediaries and
nahuatlatos (interpreters) between Spaniards and Mixtec nobles during this period. In
the late 1560s, when the first Ñudzahui-language church publication was printed,
native-language writing and Spanish-style municipal government were practiced in the
ecclesiastical and administrative centers of the region. Whereas Nahuatl-language writing began in the 1540s, native-language writing did not begin in the Mixteca until the
1560s and 1570s. In comparison with central Mexico, the onset of a second stage in
the cabeceras of the Mixteca was delayed approximately two to three decades, but it
was subject to considerable local variation in the Mixteca. For example, maps drawn
for the *Relaciones geográficas* of 1579–81 exhibit a range of traditional and innovative
styles and conventions. The pattern discussed for writing can be applied to the timing
of other colonial introductions. The evolution of temporary labor mechanisms from
encomienda to *repartimiento,* for example, suggests the number of Spaniards in a given
area and the demand for labor. Repartimiento labor did not begin in the Mixteca
until around the 1570s and 1580s, whereas it began around 1550 in central Mexico.[23]

The third stage involves a deeper and broader Spanish influence. After a long
period of epidemics, the indigenous population reached a nadir around the 1640s and
began to grow gradually in the 1670s. Ñudzahui writing reflects this trend; the number of native-language sources in my collection falls to a low point in the early seventeenth century and begins to increase after 1670 until it reaches a peak in the first
quarter of the eighteenth century. Population growth spurred a growing demand for

land. In the second half of the seventeenth century, the *composiciones de tierras* (the legalization of land titles) and the restriction of corporate landholdings to the *fundo legal* (town site) caused an increase in litigation over land. Civil disputes elicited native-language documentation, especially last wills and testaments and other land records, as evidence of possession. Some nobles responded to increasing demands for land by leasing marginal plots to Spaniards. In the Mixteca Alta, the caciques don Francisco Pimentel y Guzmán and his son, don Agustín Carlos Pimentel y Guzmán y Alvarado, profited by leasing lands to Spaniards from the 1650s to the 1720s. In the Valley of Oaxaca, Ñudzahui groups produced *títulos primordiales* in the 1690s to claim disputed land in the absence of proper titles.

The growth of bilingual, mestizo populations in the cabeceras of the Mixteca became increasingly apparent by the last quarter of the seventeenth century. Toward the end of the sixteenth century, Ñudzahui authorities filed numerous petitions against the presence of Spaniards and other non-native individuals in the Mixteca; around the mid-seventeenth century, the complaints against perceived outsiders reached a peak, as laws prohibiting the residence of nonindigenous people in *pueblos de indios* were no longer realistic. Native-language sources refer to the presence of others in both direct and subtle ways. In 1672, don Gerónimo García y Guzmán distinguished between a Christ of the Spanish people and a Christ of the Ñudzahui people in the church of Teposcolula.[24] In 1684, when Pedro de Caravantes wrote a letter to Ñudzahui and Spanish officials, he revealed a familiarity with Spanish law, the local judicial system, the business of translating documents from Mixtec to Spanish, and the Spanish language.[25] The subsequent proceedings convened a cross section of the cabecera's complex population, including friends and relatives of Pedro's deceased spouse, a mestiza named María Montiel. The presence of ethnic others in these places occasioned clear references to a specific Ñudzahui identity.

Cultural influence ran both ways in colonial Mexico. Mexican Spanish contains hundreds of Nahuatl loanwords, most ending in the vowel *e*. Although I know of no Mixtec loanwords that have entered Mexican Spanish, it is clear that bilingual mestizos were as common as *ladino* Mixtecs in the colonial period. Records from Yanhuitlan reveal many mestizas who were married to native nobles. One bilingual mestizo had a Mixtec wife, a Mixtec mistress, and a Mixtec *comadre*.[26] One of his mestizo acquaintances required a translator to testify before the *alcalde mayor* because he could not speak Spanish. In Teposcolula, we have seen a mestizo translator who lived with a Mixtec woman and paid her tribute.[27] Another mestizo knew a European trade and spoke Spanish, but he married a bilingual Nahua woman, and together they sold pulque to a native clientele.[28] Mixed racial marriages and extramarital sexual relations brought most mestizos into direct and intimate contact with indigenous people. The same may be said for people of African descent who lived in the Mixteca. In the Mixteca, mestizos did not always choose to identify with the dominant Spanish culture. In many ways, the dominant culture was Mixtec. Many people were related to Mixtecs through marriage, parenthood, or ritual kinship (*compadrazgo*). Their participation in religious feasts and other church activities drew them into local Christian practices. Ñudzahui culture and language had a profound influence on all non-native people who lived in the area.

In comparison with central Mexico, changes resulting from contact with Spaniards were more gradual and uneven in the Mixteca. Simply stated, the timing of certain changes was delayed by at least two or three decades because there were fewer Spaniards in Oaxaca. By 1800, only about 5 percent of the population of the Mixteca Alta was non-native, and this group lived in a limited number of cabeceras.[29] These centers of contact were surrounded by multiple ñuu in which very few people, if any, spoke Spanish. Other sites of interaction, such as Spanish estates, were relatively few and far between in the Mixteca. Even in the Valley of Oaxaca, where the Spanish population was larger and more concentrated, William Taylor found that indigenous communities and individuals maintained ample amounts of land by the end of the colonial period. The regional, local variants of contact have great implications for the continued vitality of native cultures and languages. Today, in terms of population and languages, Oaxaca is one of the most indigenous states of Mexico.

The location of speech communities reflects the uneven impact of the Spanish presence in the Mixteca. Today, people who live in the former cabeceras of the Mixteca Alta and the Valley of Oaxaca, or in ñuu located near the Pan-American Highway, no longer speak Mixtecan languages. In comparison, native languages are spoken in many ñuu where Spaniards did not live in the colonial period. Ironically, the places where native-language writing originated and flourished, and where literacy was most prevalent, were the first in which Mixtecs began to write and speak Spanish.

The maintenance of native terminology for many institutions and social categories in the eighteenth century demonstrates the vitality of Mixtec forms of organization. Among the nobility, the continued importance of male yya and female yya dzehe, the aniñe (palace) and ñuhu aniñe (palace lands), the yuhuitayu, and the tniño of dependent laborers is confirmed by the survival of the cacicazgo in many places. Unlike hereditary rulers in central Mexico, many Mixtec nobles managed to retain their titles, lands, and many of their privileges throughout the colonial period. Don Gabriel de Guzmán of Yanhuitlan exemplifies the ability of lords to adapt to changes in the sixteenth century. Tutored by the friars as a boy, he could read, write, and speak Castilian and Mixtec by the time he came of age. When don Gabriel was confirmed as cacique of Yanhuitlan in 1558, he admonished nobles and commoners alike to respect and obey authority, embrace Christianity, prohibit drunken feasts and sacrifices, and avoid a host of sins. His speech resembles the long discourse with which the tlatoani admonished the people of the altepetl, recorded in Nahuatl in the *Florentine Codex*.[30] Unlike the previous generation of lords, who had not accepted Christianity wholeheartedly and who suffered imprisonment and interrogation at the hands of the Inquisition from 1544 to 1546, don Gabriel cooperated with the friars. He donated land to the Dominicans and helped organize labor drafts for construction of the colossal church in Yanhuitlan, while enriching his own lordly establishment. He lived in a new palace complex with nine patios, maintained more than a hundred landholdings, collected an annual salary as governor, owned numerous horses and livestock, invested in the local economy, and enjoyed many other privileges as cacique of Yanhuitlan for thirty three years. His frequent appearance in the written record reveals a shrewd understanding of the Spanish legal system. In his last will and testament, written in 1591, don Gabriel showed off his knowledge of the faith and spelled out his detailed plans for a proper burial in the local church. Don Gabriel was the consummate Christian cacique who responded actively to colonial changes in order to maintain his high status in the new order. The colonial system relied on the cooperation of caciques and nobles such as don Gabriel.[31]

One of the most subtle but convincing signs of cultural maintenance in the late colonial period is the continued use of the ritual 260-day Ñudzahui calendar. In 1705, for example, many people from Santiago Yolomecatl had native surnames based on the ancient calendar. In comparison, calendrical surnames had disappeared in central Mexico by the second quarter of the seventeenth century. In 1647, a native writer calibrated the Mixtec and Christian calendars when he or she referred to the birth of a child in the margins of a 1568 edition of the *Doctrina en lengua misteca*.[32] A knowledge of the ancient calendar suggests the continuation of associated ritual practices and beliefs, especially divinatory household rituals.

Throughout Mesoamerica, Spaniards relied on indigenous mechanisms and concepts that were familiar to them as Europeans. In many ways, native concepts and forms of organization defined the extent and nature of interactions between the two groups and the types of adaptations on each side. The impact of externally imposed changes was moderated by what the two cultures had in common. Most successful introductions were based on existing native mechanisms or some preconquest precedent, so that Mesoamericans came to view many introductions as their own, or they recognized that an introduction corresponded to some familiar practice or concept. At times, Mixtecs used the terms *Ñudzahui* (or *Ñudzavui*) and *Castilla* to distinguish local people from Spaniards and indigenous things from introduced equivalents.[33] But people were not always concerned whether the origin of something was native or foreign. They adopted new and useful objects, ideas, or words that complemented existing practices or mechanisms and adapted foreign concepts to local ways. Each side perceived the other according to its own cultural vision and sought to serve its own interests. Lockhart's concept of "Double Mistaken Identity" describes how each culture interpreted familiar traditions and concepts in the light of its own beliefs and practices, hardly recognizing the other's different interpretation. This concept of mistaken identity was at work in the Mixteca, as well. The woodcarving of the *yuhuitayu andehui*, depicted in chapter 8, is an example. Mixtecs imagined Mary as a *yya dzehe toniñe*, a female ruler, in the Kingdom of Heaven. Ultimately, both Mixtecs and Spaniards venerated her image in their homes and churches.

The Ñudzahui convention for adopting Spanish verbs exemplifies a tendency to borrow selectively in order to complement, rather than to substitute, indigenous forms or concepts. To describe new actions, Mixtec speakers borrowed Spanish words and incorporated them into their morphology, creating a new form that was neither entirely Spanish nor indigenous. This process of "complementary adaptation" created new forms by incorporating introductions into an existing framework, adapting them to familiar ways. The new form did not supplant an older one, nor was it the simple sum of two parts. New forms were subject to further elaboration to the extent that, over the course of generations, they became indigenous creations. Complementary adaptation occurred in many cultural arenas. For example, native artists complemented the existing pictographic system of writing by adapting elements of European art style to their paintings. The new forms and functions of expression facilitated communication with a multicultural audience. Despite Spanish influences, the hybrid or mixed art style that emerged in highland Mexico during the sixteenth century was a unique form of native expression, produced only by native artists. Finally, Mixtec writers adopted the Roman alphabet to defend, maintain, and advance corporate and individual interests in the colonial legal system.

This study provides numerous examples of newly created forms and practices, which emerged from a convergence of cultural influences, rather than a substitution or a replacement of the indigenous by the European. The evolution of Ñudzahui Christianity relied on the process of complementary adaptation. The celebration of feasts and dances for the *santos* and *santas* in the *huahi ñuhu* (sacred house), including the patron saint of the ñuu, complemented local, corporate religious traditions. As "the mother of all of us," Mary resembles a female creator deity who complements God the Father in the Kingdom of Heaven. The native-Christian discourse, designed to achieve comprehensible descriptions and explanations of the faith in the native language, suggests the limitations of the conversion process even among those few people who were consistently exposed to the friars' teachings. Mixtecs understood Christianity in their own terms. In the colonial period, the evolution from native practices and beliefs to Christianity was never consistent or complete. Complementary adaptation did not create a complete or perfect whole. New religious systems continue to evolve from the convergence of Christianity and local native beliefs and practices. Today, Mary, Jesus, and the saints coexist with rain and earth deities in some places. In the communities of Santiago Nuyoo and San Andrés Chalcatongo, for example, people believe in Dzahui and other ñuhu, including Mary.

The Ñudzahui expression "to be of two hearts" about something (*cuhui uhui ini*) signifies the complexity of indigenous responses to colonial changes. In the Mixtec language, *ini* has a broad semantic range from heart, breath, and spirit to desire, volition, and emotion. Mixtec witnesses used this phrase in the 1540s to describe the ambivalent beliefs of nobles who worshiped the "one god from Castile" as well as their ancient deities. In the 1560s, the Mixtec *Doctrina* used the same phrase to admonish neophytes to renounce their polytheistic tendencies. Ambivalence is the existence of mutually conflicting emotions and thoughts, an uncertainty as to which course to follow. To be ambivalent is to be of two minds about something. As a response to colonial changes and introductions, ambivalence falls between the two extremes of adaptation and resistance. Both extremes tend to emphasize rational choice, the conscious decisions of individual actors or the normal responses of groups who acted on behalf of their own interests. This work presents ample evidence for both types of responses. But in their emphasis on agency, these interpretations downplay the confusion, indecision, and paralysis of indigenous actors. In comparison, the concept of ambivalence recognizes the fact that people, as groups or individuals, did not always adopt clear or consistent strategies in response to introductions and changes. This was especially true for the chaotic years of the early colonial period.

In the process of change outlined above, comparatively little is known about stage one, when many dramatic changes and losses were undocumented. Even though many introductions were based on existing indigenous mechanisms and modes of organization, certain areas of cultural experience underwent marked change in the earliest period of contact. Those aspects of native culture that were most subject to persecution were those that the Spaniards perceived as unfamiliar and threatening. In the Mixteca, the profound reorientation of the early postconquest period predates native-language writing by at least two or three decades. The burning and destruction of temples, mummy bundles, sacred images, and codices are thinly documented, but the damage was done, nonetheless. The Inquisition trials of the 1540s reveal a worldview in a state of confusion and crisis. The lords of Yanhuitlan and Coatlan clearly resisted the friars' attempts to transform their sacred relations, while struggling to placate the powerful, prying newcomers. Ñudzahui lords and priests made desperate offerings to Dzahui during a period of severe disease and drought. In Yanhuitlan, they performed bloodletting rituals on the southern side of the new church patio, where the deities once stood.

The epidemic diseases that decimated one generation after another brought about a most dramatic transformation in the Mixteca. One brief but poignant source from Chalcatongo, written in 1591, testifies to the havoc wreaked by disease. Native officials informed the Spanish alcalde mayor that they intended to move from the main cabecera to an estancia named Santa Cruz because "the majority of people here have already died and many of those who have survived are sick, and every day we are dying in great numbers."[34] Perhaps the officials exaggerated their plight in an attempt to resist congregation, but similar accounts confirm the basic truth of the matter. A document from 1545 states that thirty to forty people in Coixtlahuaca were dying each day and that so many people were dying that they could not be buried quickly enough.[35] The authors of the *relación* of Coatlan, written in 1580, associated recent diseases and death with Spaniards and the Christian God when they observed that "the day the Spaniards arrived was when Our Lord began to punish us."[36] In response to the last part of question number fifteen of the *Relaciones geográficas*, which inquires whether people "were healthier in ancient times than now, and the reason for the difference," everyone agreed that they had been better off in the past. People from Teozacualco declared that "the land was once filled with people, but now it is depopulated."[37] People from Tilantongo, home of the most prestigious royal dynasty in the Mixteca Alta, said in 1580 that they had suffered through three major illnesses since the arrival of the Spaniards, that three-quarters of the people had died, and that there were no remedies for the diseases.[38] Some ñuu, such as Yucunama, had been reduced to a few households by the time of the survey. Aside from the relación of Yucunama and its distinctive map, I know of no other historical records from this ñuu. Immediately after the survey, another virulent epidemic raged across the region in the early 1580s, only to be followed by another epidemic in the 1590s. The demographic catastrophe transformed native society and culture in untold and unimaginable ways.

Population loss, combined with the introduction of livestock, transformed the physical environment. The loss of a labor supply large enough to maintain the complex preconquest terracing system in the Valley of Nochixtlan, for example, contributed to unchecked soil erosion. Grazing and overgrazing made matters worse. One can see the long-term effects of this irreversible process today. Likewise, the competition for resources and the privatization of land affected everyone eventually. Spanish and mestizo traders and alcaldes mayores took over the long-distance trade in indigenous products from Mixtec *tay cuica*, who transported goods to and from Guatemala, the Pacific Coast, Mexico City, and Puebla. Impeded by legislation designed to privilege Spanish traders and unable to compete with Spaniards' access to capital, Mixtec traders were cut off from traditional long-distance trade routes by the mid-seventeenth century. As a result, Mixtec traders confined their activities to local, regional markets.

Some transformations affected men and women differently. In the first two generations after the conquest, the political status of women within the yuhuitayu was transformed by the institution of all-male Spanish-style municipal government. The decision-making responsibilities of women at the community level were not recognized in the new system, even though Spanish officials acknowledged male and female hereditary rulers in the Mixteca. By the time native notaries had been trained by friars to record the activities of the cabildo, the exclusion was complete. Consequently, men and male activities dominate the corporate written record. Few noblewomen were trained to write because Spanish law and the church privileged male authority.

Many historians have identified the late colonial period as a time of profound transformation. At the center of cultural contact, in the Valley of Mexico, Charles Gibson located dramatic change and decline in the seventeenth century, when the indigenous population continued to shrink in size and strength.[39] Even though Gibson focused on indigenous institutions and forms of organization, rather than Spanish actions and introductions, as the basis of understanding historical processes of change in colonial Mexico, he concluded with the specter of Spanish hegemony. In the more peripheral region of Yucatan, Nancy Farriss documented the Maya ability to survive and adapt after the initial shock of the conquest, but she observed the devastating effects of a late colonial "second conquest," which she attributed to the Bourbon reforms and the growth of the Atlantic economy.[40] I have not found evidence for a similar second conquest in the Mixteca, but this study focuses on the early colonial period rather than the later period. Looking ahead to the nineteenth century, it is safe to say that the Mixteca was not transformed by haciendas or engulfed by terrible "caste wars." Incidences of local violence in the Mixteca did not escalate to the level of regional uprisings, as they did in Chiapas and Yucatan. William Taylor counted nineteen recorded rebellions in the Mixteca Alta from 1680 to 1811; most of the civil disturbances targeted tribute demands or abusive colonial officials and involved members of the entire community.[41] In all cases, the *tumultos* were confined to a single community. Still, it remains to be seen how changes in the late colonial period and the nineteenth century, including the abolition of corporate landholding status, affected the ñuu. Historians of Oaxaca and of Mexico in general have only begun to understand the impact of nineteenth-century changes on native communities.[42]

A final example of transformation involves the imposition of dominant cultural attitudes after the conquest. This attitude was articulated by a plainspoken ruling of the Spanish Audiencia in 1758, which ignored the extensive collection of titles and testaments presented by the cacica of Yanhuitlan and dismissed the testimony of witnesses on her behalf. The Audiencia attributed the loyalty and apparent servitude of the witnesses to "the ignorance and simplicity which is so common among Indians, a dimwitted people who lack education and culture."[43] The ruling concluded that caciques had no hereditary privileges outside the cabildo and decreed that the ancient palace belonged to the "community," which was represented by the Spanish-style cabildo. The Audiencia's decision signified the culmination of long-term changes and circumstances associated with the interpretation of private property and other changes within the ñuu. The tenor of the ruling also reflects a cultural attitude that was present from the very beginning of Spanish rule and persisted throughout the colonial period—that Ñudzahui people were secondary, tribute-paying subjects of the crown who were less than equal to their Spanish superiors. This cultural attitude represents a major introduction of the sixteenth century and a long-lasting legacy of colonial rule.

We may also speak of Ñudzahui legacies. Today, Mixtecan-language speakers continue to refer to themselves with the term *ñudzahui*, pronounced and spelled many different ways. About a quarter of a million people live in hundreds of ñuu. The ñuu is a crucial continuity from the ancient past. The ñuu survived Spanish attempts to congregate dispersed settlements, redefine sociopolitical relations, and restrict indigenous landholdings. In response, people in many ñuu sought autonomous status. Autonomy was a distinct and desirable feature of Mixtec organization. People had more incentive to seek autonomy in the late seventeenth century, when Spanish law and increased demands for land reduced the corporate holdings of all ñuu to a minimum. However, when many ñuu broke away from cabeceras in the eighteenth century, and some ñuu split into multiple pueblos, the divisions did not drastically alter existing settlement patterns. The resulting configuration of communities was based solidly on ancient structures, the ñuu and their constituent siqui. One glance at a map of the state of Oaxaca will confirm the viability and adaptability of these smaller units. The Mixteca has one of the highest concentrations of pueblos per square kilometer of any region in Mexico.[44]

The duties or responsibilities that each adult owes to his or her community, called *tniño*, continue to regulate social relations inside the ñuu. Tniño is as central to the ñuu today as it was in the colonial period. One's belonging to a ñuu is based on the tniño one performs. John Monaghan observed that *tiñu* (same as tniño) concerns all Mixtecs who live in the six hamlets that make up the ñuu of Santiago Nuyoo.[45] Tiñu is synonymous with *cargo* or *tequio* (derived from the Nahuatl *tequitl*). Organized by households, tiñu or cargo service amounts to several weeks of work during the year. In 1985, for example, adults from Nuyoo served an average of sixty days a year. As in colonial times, tiñu refers to both office and labor, and the most important duties require the most resources and investment of time. Office is considered more of a service than a potential source of enrichment or empowerment. Tiñu is so formidable that it is often feared, especially by those who have the most to give. Some people migrate to escape tiñu service, but most return or remit money to buy their way out of a cargo.

Today, many Mixtecs leave their ñuu for destinations to the north, where they work on others' lands. About fifty thousand Mixtecs live and work in the Central Valley of California, for example. Mixtecs migrate as far north as Alaska in search of work. Some people who stay in Oaxaca, and even some who leave, work to promote cultural revitalization. One goal of this movement is to write local histories and stories in Mixtec, a task that is complicated by the existence of multiple Mixtecan languages. Most people do not realize that alphabetic writing flourished in the region during the colonial period. Ironically, these forgotten texts from the past may serve as useful models for writing in the present. I hope that this book and future studies of Mixtec-language writings contribute to that goal and to a greater appreciation of Ñudzahui history.

APPENDIX A

Some Ñudzahui Place-names and Associated Nahuatl-Spanish Names

Ñudzahui Name	*Nahuatl-Spanish Name*
Anduhua	Tlacosahuaya
Antutu	Amatlan
Atata	Sinaxtla
Atoco	Nochixtlan
Ayata	Tecomatlan
Ayuu	Xochitepetongo
Chiyocanu	Teozacualco
Daanduvua	Miltepec
Disinuu	Tlaxiaco
Ñoñaña	Coyotepec
Ñucucu	Coculco
Ñudzai	Huaxuapa
Ñundaa	Texupa
Ñundecu	Achiutla
Ñunduhua	Oaxaca
Ñuniñe	Tonalá
Nuucuiñe	Cuquila
Nuundaya	Chalcatongo
Nuuquaha	Atlatlahuca
Ocoñaña	Tilantongo
Ticondoo Tiyta	Atoyaquillo

Ñudzahui Name	*Nahuatl-Spanish Name*
Tiquehui	Tamasulapa
Tisacu	Chinanco
Tiyuqh	Sayultepec
Tiyyu	Istepec
Tnohuitu	Huapanapa
Yniyoho Yuchiquaa	Yolomecatl
Yodzocahi	Yanhuitlan
Yodzocoo	Coixtlahuaca
Ytnuñute	Xaltepetongo
Ytnutnono	Igualtepec
Yucuañi	Maninaltepec
Yucucuihi	Tlazultepec
Yucuita	Suchitepec
Yucuite	Ocotepec
Yucunama	Amoltepec
Yucundaa	Teposcolula
Yucundayy	Tequistepec
Yucundii	Tonaltepec
Yucunduchi	Etlantongo
Yucunicata	Zahuatlan
Yucusatuta	Zacatepec
Yucuytayno	Xochitepec
Yucuyuchi	Acatlan
Yuhuacuchi	Huaxolotitlan
Yutacanu	Atoyac
Yutañani	Chachuapa
Yutaticaha	Cuilapa
Yutatnuhu	Apoala
Yutayaca	Michiapa

Transcriptions and Translations

NOTES ON TRANSCRIPTIONS AND TRANSLATIONS

The transcription divides or groups letters into words by modern principles, whereas the original document frequently does not do so. I have avoided dividing words or complete phonological phrases at the end of a line. Brackets in the native language texts are used to indicate words or letters that are unclearly written or missing because of a damaged spot and that contain what I think may be included. Blank brackets indicate missing material with no clear indication of content. Brackets in the translation include implied, but not actually stated, words.

I.   Personal letter written by don Diego de Guzmán in Atoyaquillo and sent to nobles in Tlaxiaco, around the year 1572, concerning the status of some lands. AGN-T, 44:1, f. 195.

dzutu manindza

juan lopez dzahua ndiy tacani tucu yia yuhuiteyuni santo juan baptista ticondzo tiyta yaha yio chuhu ndzayani nindihi pentiçion dundzuni tacani ninaqhnindi jhee tniño yocachi juan yondzonume jhee yocachini jhee taca cuiti yu ytuto ytu caa yucu ndjeñu dzahua vitna yocachindi conahani ndihe ytu chuhu caa vitna dijhe cachi chuhu yiqh castila chuhu yio nuu ñuhu vitna conahani dihe nindihi ndundzuto ninaqhnidi ninaqhni taca ndziy dzutudi alldes regidores dzoco huata cuhui tnuni ca nayyondindze dzo[c]uhui nayiondindze tahitnonindi nayiondindze chiytnuniynindi jhe cuhui hito vata natacu cahicandi dundzu tucu dzuhua conahani dzahua vitna mayndi yonaha vitna taca toho hi cuhui dzii ndzutundi yonaha [ni] na yiotahitnunidi nayiondindze ndudzundi day naqhnito dzuhua conahani jhe yocachini jhe yni ndihi ca ndudzu taca ni ninaqhnidi yio huaha yocachi tacani nacuvi dzahua mayndi yonaha vitna nayiodidze cuhui dzahua conahani yocachindi conaha ndiy tacani ninu condee tutu vitna jheni tuhu sexta quehui sancta maria quehui lones yia yuhuiteyuni s. juan baptista tiyta yaha

    ñadzaña sidzayani
    Don diego de gusma

My precious fathers,

Juan López and all you lords, here I am in your yuhuitayu of San Juan Bautista Ticondzo Tiyta (Atoyaquillo). I am your son. I have heard the petition and all your words on the matter from Juan Yodzonume. It is true what you say about your fields, the cultivable fields in Yucundjeñu. Now I say, you should know that the fields are planted with Castile (Spanish) melons. Know that I have heard your words. All my mothers and fathers, the alcaldes and regidores, have heard your words. From now on we will know how it is held, how we are to arrange it, how we are to work it. Let the words that I have written be read so that now all of you know that all of the nobles, my mothers and fathers, and I agree with you. This is how I order it. You will know what I say, you will know what is written on the paper. Today, after the sixth feast day of Santa María, the day of Monday, here in your yuhuitayu of San Juan Bautista Tiyta.

I am your son,
don Diego de Guzmán.

II. Testimony of Agustín García, María García, and Andrés Trujillo after the attempted murder of Agustín by his wife, María, and her lover, Andrés. The testimony was recorded in Chalcatongo in 1581. AJT-CR, 1:35, ff. 1–2.

huitna viernes 22 quihui hica yoo sebtiebre cuiya 1581 años niquihaadi yaha san andres duhu don al° de castilla di° ortiz alldes yocahandi yfromaçion haá augustin garcia haá nicánitnahate hiy tee nani andres trujillo nihicátnuhundite ñanacuhui nicánitnaándo hiy andres

te niçahuiçote conaha nihi toho naa tee nani andres nihaate hueyza ytu yondee qnmiza de yucu haquaanaha yoquisiza caaza hiy ñaciyza nihaate nicoocuiñete yuhu yahi te yone[i]te yuchicaa nihaate ñaciyza te nicáyña yuchii te nicoócahua doço yuchi nuu ndicaza te nindotoza nicayza yuchi yñete yuhu yay te nicaa[c]uitaza te nicanitnahaza hiynte sina candaamaaza nihaa ycáça niquihidaha andres ycáça nituhuiza yuchi çuqnte nituhuitucuza yuchi çiqui çuhute ycáça nihini uhui andres nicachite nihini ñaciynza maria cay yuu cay yutnu çatahui sini diablo yaha te nicayña tnucaa nicaniña siniza çuhua nicuhui hitoho cuiti ndaa yu nitneyte hiy ñaciyza haa cániñahate da cuiti yonacachiza hitoho ñatuhui pleytos ñuhuza hiyte ça na aca yyoza ñahiniza ha caniñahate çuhuani yonacachiza hitoho

te nindacatnuhutacundi tee nani andres truxillo ñana [ni]quácoocáninda augusti daa nacachindo na ndisa nicuhui asi ñaha pleytos ñuhudu hiynte

te niçahuiçote dahui nicuhui hitoho yonacachindaaza nuu ndihi hitohoza alldes mey ñaçiyte m^a gr^a nicachiña nihiniza quihui lunes nihaáña yute nicachiña andres haaday ñu quihui jueves ytundi cáninda yeendi çuhua nicachiña nihiniza te nicachiza huiy nacooçaa çuhua nihiyzaña te nihaatnaá quivi jueves s. m.° te nihacáynooza yuchi ñaniza andres tahinoo yuchindo nanaçahandi ndahandi çuhua nihiyzate te niniyza yuchi he neeza quáhaza te nihaaza ytute tuhuica te nihi yondetuza niquaa ycáça nihaa ñaçiyte nihaacáaña nicachiña andres he yoquisite huitna ça noo nitahaada çuhua nicachiña te nihaáza nihaáza yuhu yay nihaaza ñaçiyte yuchi nicayña te ça nicoócahua[ña] doço ca yuchi nuu dicate yca nidotote te nicaacuitañahate nicánitnahaza-hiyte te nituhuite yuchi çuqnza te nituhuitucute yuchi çiqui çuhuza ycáça nihiniuhuiza te nicachiza nihini ñaciyte m^a cay yuu cay yutnu çatahui sini diablo yaha te nicáyña tnucaa nicániña sinite te yocánitnahaza nitahuiza nuute nicachiza nihinite augusti ñana nicuhui yocánido duhu zañandi nanuhundi dahuindi ñani te yocuhuiynindo canidondi ça ee quáha ninacuhuindi asi niniynquay doho asi niniyquay duhu ñatuhui tnuhu cachindi cáni sitondi ñanidi duhu nihita cachindi cánite te ña nihaádetu tee siñaçiy ycaça niducundeyza nihinoza quáhaza çuhua nicuhui hitoho te ninuuza huey qnmi ytu di° te nituhui nihaá tee çuchi di° ycá nihiyza te nidicáhate ñaniza simo ninahaacuiçoteza ñaquándihiza te ninaniyza tee nicanitnaha hiyza yondecañaha sitote m° satuval te nicoócooza ychi te nihehi sita taandiçoñaha yca nicachi agusti andres conahando ñani nanooquachiyo naquihuindoyo tnuhu niçahayo tatahindi çónondi hiy nee çoondi ca chihindo nanooquachiyo asi ndiy nduhuiyo niniyquaytucu cachite te nihiyzate huadecúni nicachidi henooquachiyo ñanihaándo çaa nihiyzate yonini simo

Today, Friday, the twenty-second day of the month of September of the year 1581, we the alcaldes, don Alonso de Castilla and Diego Ortiz, came here to San Andrés to verify a crime involving Agustín García, as to how he fought against a man named Andrés Trujillo.

We asked him: "Why did you fight with Andrés?" He replied: "You will know, lords, that the man named Andrés came to my house in the hills where I was tending to my fields. It was already very dark. I am asleep, lying with my wife. He came, entered and stood at the doorway; he held an iron-blade knife in his hand. He gave it to my wife. Then she took the knife and dropped it on my chest, on my breast. I awakened and I grabbed the knife. I attacked him and fought with him as he stood in the doorway. First, I cut him, I injured him so that Andrés began to flee. And then I stabbed him with the knife in the shoulder and I stabbed him again with the knife above his ear. So Andrés was in pain, and he cried out to my wife: 'María, grab a rock, grab a stick and smash this devil's head.' Then she took an ax and struck me on the head. Thus it happened nobles, truly and honestly. He arranged it with my wife to kill me. I tell you the truth, nobles. I did not have any quarrels with him that would cause him to hate me, I do not know why he would kill me. Thus I declare it, nobles."

Then we asked the man named Andrés Trujillo: "Why did you attempt to kill Agustín? Tell us clearly what is true; did you perhaps have a quarrel with him?"

Then he responded: "It was a pity, nobles. I tell you the truth, my lords, alcaldes. His same wife, María García, said to me on Monday, when she came to the river, she said 'Andrés, come on Thursday night to my field to kill my husband.' This is what she said to me. Then I said, 'all right, good.' That is what I told her. When the Thursday of Saint Matthew came, I went to get a knife from my brother Andrés. 'Lend me your knife, I am going to cut branches.' This is what I told him. Then I took the knife that was given to me and went away. I went to his field, and then I waited nearby until it was dark, when his wife came. She came to tell me, she said: 'Andrés, he is already sleeping now. Come in a little while.' That's what she said. Then I went to the doorway, I gave the knife to his wife. She took it and then she dropped the knife on his chest, on his breast. So he awoke and attacked me, I fought with him and then he stabbed my shoulder with the knife and then he also stabbed me above my ear, so I was in pain. Then I cried out to his wife: 'María grab a rock, grab a stick and smash this devil's head'. She then took an ax and struck his head and I fought with him and cut his face. And then I said to Agustín: 'Why are you fighting, I will back down, I will retreat, I am weak brother. If you want to kill me, then just be done with it. I will die. You are suffering and wounded as I am wounded and suffering. I will cover it up, I will say to my brother and my uncle "I fell down," that is what I will tell them.' But the woman's husband would not consent. So I broke away and fled. Thus it happened, nobles. Then I arrived at the house, next to Diego's field. Diego's boy came and found me and I told him to go call for my brother Simón, who came to carry me. I could no longer walk. Then I met the man who had fought with me, his uncle Mateo Sandoval was carrying him. We sat by the

lopez thomas perez m° satuval ça yaha nicuhui hitoho daa cuiti yonaqu[ ]çuhuiza
nuundihi justiçia

te nindacátnuhundi ñahani mᵃ grᵃ cachindaa cachicuitindo ñananicuhui hua
coocánindo yeendo agustin

te ninacachiña diha çaa hitoho diablos nicay nuu yninza diha quihui lunes
nihaáza yute yca ninaniyza tee nani andres ychi nicachiza nihinite andres haaday ñu
quihui jueves cánida yeedi te nicachite huiy nacooçaa te yonahate nihaate nuu ytuza
tuhuica te nihaáza nuu yondeete nicachiza nihinite andres he yoquisi yeedi huitna
ça noo nitehaada çuhua nihiyzate huiy cachite te ninucahuaza hiy yeeza te nihaate
nicoócuiñete yuhu yay te nitahite yuchi nicayza ça niçacoocahuacaza yuchi yca nidotote te tnahani nitniytnahate nicánitnahate nituhuite yuchi çucu andres te nituvitu-
cute yuchi siñe nuute ycaça nihini uhuite nicachite nihiniza mᵃ cay yuú cáy yutnu
çatahui sini diablos yaá nicachite te nicáyza tnucaa nicoóza sinite te nihinoza ninde-
hiza nihaáza huey mᵃ s.tuval ytuña te ña nihiniza [. . . na] nicuhui ndi se nizañatna-
hate te he nituhui ycá ça ninahayeeza nuu yondeeza huey mᵃ s.tuval ycá ça nihaa sitoza
m° s.tuhual ninahaaquacañahate quándihiza ça yaha nicuhui yonacachindaaza nuu
dihi justiçia te çaa nicachi andres te nihiynyeedo te nducundo tee huaá coóhiyndo
huacuhui coo duhu hiyndo he hoo nicuhui justiçia haayo çuhua nicachite nihiniza
huiy nacooçaa hiyza te çuhuani yonacachidaamaaza ça tnaha nicuhui conahani hitoho

diy çaa yaha duçu ninacachindaa diy nuni tee nicaacánitnaa agusti grᵃ hiyn andres
truxillo mᵃ grᵃ tucu cuiti ndaa yuhu duçu maate yuhu nduçu maay ña ninaá niduhui
nuu ades don a°l de castilla di° ortiz   [signatures]

duú niteetutu lucas maldonando escribano

road and the people who carried us ate tortillas. Then, Agustín said: 'Andrés, you know, brother, that we must forgive one another, we must cleanse ourselves of this. We are badly hurt. I will give you my shirts[s] and all my capes for you to wear. We must forgive one another and be reconciled. We are both suffering from wounds,' he said. Then I said to him: 'Last night I told you that we should forgive one another but you did not agree.' That is what I said to him in the presence of Simón López, Tomás Pérez, and Mateo Sandoval. So this is what happened nobles, truly and honestly have I related this before you justices."

And we asked María García: "Speak truthfully and honestly: why did you attempt to kill your husband Agustín?"

She said: "It is truly cruel, nobles, the devil deceived me. It is true that on Monday, I went to the river and I met the man named Andrés on the road. I said to him: 'Andrés, come on Thursday night to kill my husband.' And he said 'all right.' When he came, he came right up to my field and then I went to meet him, I said to him: 'Andrés, my husband is already asleep now. Come in a little while.' That is what I said. He said 'all right.' Then I lay with my husband. Then he came and stood in the doorway, he gave me the knife and I took it but I dropped the knife and then he awoke and they came together, grabbed and fought one another, he stabbed Andrés's shoulder with the knife and he also stabbed him on the side of his face. Then he was in pain and he cried out to me: 'María, grab a stone, grab a stick and smash this devil's head,' he said. So I took an ax and struck his head, and then I ran away and came to the house of María Sandoval's field. Then I didn't know what had happened, whether or not they had separated. Later, my husband came and found me at María Sandoval's house and then my uncle Mateo Sandoval came to get me and I went away. This is what happened, I have spoken the truth before you officials. And Andrés has said since then: 'when your husband has died, then find a good man that you desire, I will not be yours for someone has already informed the officials about us.' That is what he said, and I said: 'all right, that would be good,' I said. Thus, I have spoken the straight truth, so that you will know what happened, lords."

These were all the words spoken truly by all three persons who fought with one another: Agustín García, Andrés Trujillo, and María García. True and honest are the words from the mouth of each man and the woman who appeared before the alcaldes, don Alonso de Castilla and Diego Ortiz.

I wrote this document, Lucas Maldonado, notary.

*IIIa. Testament of don Gerónimo García y Guzmán, written in Teposcolula in 1672.
AJT-C, 4:417, f. 16–16v.*

saha sa nani ni dzutu ndios ndehe dzaya ndios ndehe dzaya ndios ndehe espiritu
santo ndios ndehe nuni persona dza ee ni ndisa ñuhu ndios ndehe huaha ndehe
cuhuiya yosinindisa nduhu Don gr^mo garcia siqui yaacahi yehe ndahuindi sihi yonahi-
huahandi nee cutu mandamiento articulos de la fen sa usi sahu simaa stohondo ndisa
ñuhu ndios ndehe huaha ndehe cuhui dzahua nacuhui saha sananiya Jesus

dzahua huitna naconaha ndehe taca yya toho yondu ndehe cotondaa tutu testamentondi yaha yoquidzahuahandi huitna hua dzehui saha cuhuindi ndahua dzehui
saha cacundi yondiyoynindi sa dza yochihindatucaynindi ta quadzuhua siqui codzo
cahui yuquiti quahi Justiçia si maa stohondo ndios yotnahanino yequicoñondi dzoco yyo
casiynindi yocachindaa yocachicuitindi ndehe ndudzu ñuhu ynindi condaa tutu yaha
ndudzundi yaha nacuhui cutu nacuhuindaa nee chihi taa qhhu huacuhui yoonacane
huacuhui yoodzatuhu huacuhui yoodzatihui

dzahua tnaha yotasitnunindi huitna sa cuhui sianimandi sihi yequicoñondi tucu
dzahua huitna dzinañuhu dzina huii yonadzocondi animandi nuu nana stohondo
ndios yonatniñondi nduhua ndayaya cuhui uhui sichi yonachihitnahandi yequicoñondi
ñuhu ndayu sa nisiyonahi nuu nisiyonahi yecandi neecutu nisiyo nisicandi ñuu ñayehui
yosicatahuindi huahi ñuhu cano condusi yequicoñondi yodzocondi usi pesos dzahua
quehui nasaa 9 quehui nisiyohuaha yiquicoñondi yosicatahuindi vigillia ee missa cano
ndatu tahui animandi yodzocondi 2 pesos dzahua quehui saa uhui dzico quehui nisiyohuaha yequicoñondi yosicatahuindi bigillia sihi uni dzutu cachi missa ndatu tahui
animandi yodzocondi 4 pesos

dzahua sa yonadzocondi nana stohondo ndios tucu nana sacramento yodzocondi
uhui rr.—nana san p^o, san pablo yodzocondi ee rr.—nana yya dzehe solidad yodzocondi
me.^o—nana S.^to Dgo soriano yodzocondi me.^o—nana S.^to Cristo Español yodzocondi
me.^o—nana yya dzehe Rosario Español yodzocondi me.^o—nana Jesus nasareno yodzocondi me.^o—nana sa Reymondo yodzocondi me.^o—nana sa xacindo yodzocondi me.^o—
nana s.n miguel yodzocondi me.^o—nana s.^to dgo yodzocondi me.^o—nana s.^to Christo
tay ñodzahui yodzocondi me.^o—nana santiego yodzocondi me.^o—nana yya dzehe
chi[s]i coru yodzocondi me.^o—sianima yodzocondi me.^o—ndehe dzahua sa yonadzocondi nana stohondo ndios ta nicuhuindiya sani naquacaya animandi

dzahua huitna saha sa siñuu ñayehui sa nisinindahui ñaha stohondo ndios nicuhuitahuindi sihi ñaha dzehendi Donña lasara de gusman saha maa ñaha dzehendi con-
ducundaha stohondo Rey sindi sihi ndaha maaya yonachihindi ytu huahindi ndehe
taca ñuhu ytu chiyo sihi huahi nama ^ñuña aniñendi ta cotnee ya saha ysi siyo dzayandi
sihiya cooya huahi dzahua tnaha yyo ya huitna yca saha yoqhtasindi toho nisano p^o de
andrada si alcaldes loreso gonsales nduhui to cuhui albaçeandi yuhu nuu animandi
qhhu saha to dzanumini no quiye to coo huaha yequicoñondi sihi cuhui sihi toñaha
dzehendi coto to tniño ñuu ñayehui sindi tucu nda

In the name of God the father, God the son, God the son [*sic*], and God the holy spirit, three distinct persons, but one true and good God in whom I believe, I, don Gerónimo García, from the siqui [named] Yaacahi. I am a poor man who keeps all the commandments and articles of the faith, the ten [commandments] of our true lord God, so that good will be done in the name of the lord Jesus.

Today it will be known to all the lords, nobles who are present and to all who will see this testament of mine that I now make. Whether I die or I am saved, I truly desire only that I obtain complete satisfaction in my heart, despite this sickness that is the justice of our lord God. My body is sick but I am clear hearted. I speak with certainty, I speak honestly, and with God's will I put down my words on this paper. This will be done, all will be recorded and written. Nobody is to obstruct it, nobody is to deny it, nobody is to change it.

Thus I now arrange things for my soul and my body. Now first and foremost, I offer my soul before our lord God, whom I have served as a slave. Second, I give my body to the earth, the mud. All that I have possessed, living in this world, I have borrowed. I ask that my body be buried in the great church. I offer ten pesos. Then, when nine days have passed, and my body has been cared for, I beg that a high vigil mass be said on behalf of my soul. I offer two pesos. Then when forty days have passed, and my body has been cared for, I ask for a vigil and that a mass of three priests be said for the benefit of my soul. I offer four pesos.

Then, I offer to our lord God and also to the sacraments two reals; before San Pedro [and] San Pablo I offer one real; before the lady of Soledad I offer half a real; before Santo Diego Soriano I offer a half a real; before the Spanish Santo Cristo I offer half a real; before the lady Rosario español (Spanish Rosario) I offer half a real; before Jesus of Nazareth I offer half a real; before San Raimundo I offer half a real; before San Jacinto I offer half a real; before San Miguel I offer half a real; before Santo Domingo I offer half a real; before Santo Cristo of the Ñudzahui people I offer half a real; before San Diego I offer half a real; before the lady below the choir I offer half a real; to the souls I offer half a real. This I offer before our lord God. If I am worthy, may you collect my soul.

Now as to the things of the world that our lord God bestowed upon me while I have lived with my wife, doña Lázara de Guzmán: my same wife will hand over the tribute to our lord king. And in her hands I place my house lots and all the patrimonial lands and the houses of my palace, where my children live together in the complex. Thus, now I appoint the elder noble Pedro de Andrada and the alcalde Lorenzo Gonzales to be my executors. So that my soul will be taken, take care of things quickly. Take care of my body. Keep my wife company and see also to my worldly obligations when I die.

dzahuata nicuhuindiya may stohondo ndios niquitnaha ninosasihi maa ñaha dzehendi quehui dzahua cana chihi tnuni yni niyasihi nduhui albaçeandi tanda ytu chiyo
huahi dzuchi dzuchi cana nihi ee ee dzayandi dzahua ni yotasitnunindi nuu taca Justiçia
yondito nuu ndehe taca yya toho yyo yaha testigo çebastian de palma andres de tapia
gr.ᵐᵒ Baup.ᵗᵃ

sa ndaa cuiti yuhu ndudzu may yya yocuhui nitaa nduhu Ess.ⁿᵒ nombrado huitna
biernes sa ñeni caa uni oras 6 de mayo 1672 a.ˢ yaha yuhuitayu san p.ᵒ san pablo
yucundaa.

Ess.ⁿᵒ Domingo de Belasco

May our lord God guard my wife until her final day, and may she consult with the executors who will divide the patrimonial house lots between each child. Each child will have some of it. Thus, I order it before all the officials who are now in attendance, and all the lord nobles who are witnesses to this: Sebastian de Palma, Andrés de Tapía, Gerónimo Bautista.

True and certain are the words and speech of the lord which I, the named notary, have written. Today, Friday, three hours in the afternoon on the sixth of May, in the year 1672, here in the yuhuitayu of San Pedro and San Pablo Yucundaa (Teposcolula).

Domingo de Velasco, Notary

IIIb. Testament of doña Lázara de Guzmán, written in Teposcolula in 1691.
    AJT-C, 4:417, ff. 18–19.

saha sananini dzutu dios ndehe dzaya ndios ndehe espiritu santo ndios ndehe uni persona dza ee ni ndisa ñuhu ndios ndehe huaha ndehe cuhui yosinindisa nduhu ñaha nani doña lasara de gusman nisiyo ñuqhihi ndahui tnahandi siqui bario yaacayhe sihi yonehehuahandi mee cutu mandamiento articulos de la fee sa usi sayu simaa stohondo dios dzahua tnaha yotasitnuni dzehemanindo santa ygleçia Romana sihi nee cutu misterio yia dzehe toniñe santa maria saha niyehetnahandi tutu cofradias simaa stoho dzehendo toniñe santa m^a

dzahua huitna naconaha ndehe taca yia toho cotondaa tutu testamentondi yaha huytna yio casiynindi sihi ndehe hoho sa sinimanidi yonacachindaandi yonacachi-cuitindi saha nicuhuitahuindi sa usa santto Çacramento sihi yia tondiye don geronimo g^a y gusman yia tayu aniñe ñuuñañu maa tayu dziniñuu yaha nani nicuhuytahuindisi-hiya nisiyotacundi ñuu ñayehui nicuhuytahuindisihiya uni dzico cuyya nisiyondisihiya nicuhuitahuindi nana stohondo dios sihiya usi huhui dzaya usa dzaya dzehe nda hoho yia yee ninacuacañaha stohondo ndios ndehe usa yia dzehe nda uhui yia yee yca yotacu uni ca yia yee—yia yehua yonaniya don domingo g^a y gusman yia cuhui uhui yonaniya don Joshe g^a y gusman yia cuhui uni yonaniya don p^o g^a y gusman—ndehe nuni yia yaha nicuhuitahuindi nuu nana stohondo ndios sihi tondiye don geronimo g^a y gusman—sa dzehuy ndehe nuní yia yaha dzayandi yonacuatuñahandi siya qhuni tnani nahaya cotoya sacuhui aiandi cocuhuiya Aluaçeandi nani yondito cotacuya yaha ñuu ñayehui sa dzihui nindihi nuniya yondadzandi erederondi quihi ndahaya ndehe taca ñuhu ndayu sihi sa sistohoya don g^rmo g^a y gusman tondiye yeendi

yosicatahuindi nana dzutu ñuhu prior cura saha qhu nimaniñahaya ñuhu yy con-dusindi yni huehe ñuhu conondaa yonduhuihuatundi yaya qhuni mani ñaha ya sin-duhu ñaha ndahui tani satnaha ni nacuaca ndios aiandi yonahandihi taca yia toho saha ñaha ndahui nicuhuindi sihi yio ndahui nisiyondi ñuu ñayehui—ycasaha yodzo-condi limosna yosicatahuindi vigilia misa saha cuhui ndodzo yequicoñondi tanisa tnaha sa sihindi yodzocondi uhui ps^o tomines—sihi yodzocondi limosma yahui ñuhu yahui santa cruz vigilia santta missa ndehe taca dzahua yodzocondi limosma hoho peso tomines sihi saha canda caa ndehe taca dzahua yodzocondi sihi yahui maestro can-dores saha quicuaca yequicoñondi ta nicuhuindiya ndios nisihindi—4 ts—dzahua qui-huy saa 9 quihuy yosicatahuindi vigilia missa sacuhui siaiadi yodzondi uhui ps^o tomines limosma—dzahua tucu yodzocondi limosma nana stohondo santissimo sacramentto—1 ts yodzocodi limosma nana yia dehe del Rosario—1 ts yodzocondi me^o stohondo santo christo—yodzoconnndi me^o si sa mig^l—yodzocondi me^o si san diego—yodzocondi me^o si aia—yodzocondi me^o sistohondo Jesus nasareno—yodzocondi me^o nana sto-hondo santo chris español ndehe dzahua nisayo nadzoconndi limosma nuu nana stohondo ndios—

dzahua tucu saha tniño ñuu ñayehui yocachindaa yocachicuitindi yodzatuhuindi ndehe taca sa nicuhuitahuindi nuu nana stohondo ndios sihi tondiye don geronimo g^a y gusman ndiye yeendi aniñe tayu ñuuñau sa dzihui ndu dzahua nee cutu solar

In the name of God the father, God the son, and God the holy spirit, three persons but only one true God in whom I believe. I, the person named doña Lázara de Guzmán, who comes from the siqui barrio of Yaacayhe, and who keeps all of the commandments and articles of faith, the ten laws of our lord God and that which is declared by our precious mother Holy Roman Church, and all the mysteries of the lady ruler Holy Mary, and the cofradía of our lady ruler Santa María to which I belong.

Now let it be known by all the yya and toho who see this, my testament, that today I am clear in my heart and my five senses. I speak truthfully, I speak honestly that I have received the seventh sacrament with my deceased husband, don Gerónimo García y Guzmán, lord of the palace named Ñuuñañu, which belongs to this yuhuitayu cabecera. I had the gift of life with him, I lived with him in the world for sixty years. I lived with him in the presence of our lord God, who gave us twelve children, seven daughters and five sons. Our lord God took all seven daughters and two sons, so that three male lords remain. The first lord is called don Domingo García y Guzmán, the second lord is called don Josef García y Guzmán, and the third lord is called don Pedro García y Guzmán. All three of these lords have received the favor of our lord God and the deceased don Gerónimo García y Guzmán. These three lords here, my children, are to take care of and look after my soul and they are to be my executors as long as they live in this world. Likewise, I appoint all three as my heirs. They will take in their hands all the fertile lands and everything that belongs to the lord don Gerónimo García y Guzmán, my deceased husband.

I ask the holy father priest to bury me in the sacred ground inside the church, to make sure that I am buried in this way, as a poor person who awaits the hour when God will take my soul. Let all the yya and toho know that I am a humble person who has lived humbly on this earth. Thus I give alms. I ask for a vigil mass for the burial of my body when I die, I offer two pesos. And I offer alms to pay for a vigil mass of the holy cross, and also I offer to pay the choirmaster for singing when God has taken my body, four tomines. And on the ninth day I ask for a vigil mass for my soul, I offer two pesos tomines in alms. Also I offer alms to our lord the holy sacrament, one tomín. I offer alms to the Lady of the Rosary, one tomín. I offer half a tomín to our lord holy Christ. I offer half a tomín to San Miguel. I offer half a tomín to San Diego. I offer half a tomín to the souls. I offer half a tomín to our lord Jesus of Nazareth. I offer half a tomín to our lord the holy Spanish Christ and I also offer alms to our lord God.

As for duties of the world, I say truthfully, I say honestly, I make clear that all that our lord God gave to me and the deceased don Gerónimo García y Guzmán, my deceased husband, the palace Ñuuñañu and all the palace lands and all the lands belong-

ñuhu aniñe sihi ndehe taca ca ñuhu aniñe ñuuñañu yaha ndehe yonachihindi ndaha
dzayandi ndehe nuniya don domingo don joshe g^a don p^o n coo cano coo cutu cua
tniño ndehe nuniya huacuhuy naaya dehe nuniya nuu caa qhuhu—sa dzihui ndu dzahua tucu huehe yahui nisaandi caa siqui dzumañuu sihi yotnaha solar ñuhu sata huehe
solar diquisi sihi solar chisi huehe ndehe nduhui—

dzahua tucu yocachindi sa caa ee chiyo aniñe chiyo yata nani aniñe duhuadoo caa
si yuhu nduhua ndicuana yotnaha tnaha huehe ndiye Petronilla sima sihi solar ndehe
taca yonachihindi ndaha dzayandi ndehe nuniya conee saha sasi siy sitnaya—

dzahua saha huehe caa nu siqui huehe dioniçio delgado dzito tindiye yeendi yonehehuahandi ee testamento yonachihindi ndaha ndehe nuni dzayadi don domigo g^a y
don joshe g^a y don p^o g^a sihi ndehe taca solar ñuhu dzahua tnaha yondaca tnaha huehe
ndehe taca yonachihindi daha dzayandi dzahua yocachinuu testamento yonehendi—

ndehe dzahua yaha yuhu ndudzu maa [ñaha] yocuhui doña lasara y gusman saha
ndaa cuytiya yonini g^{or} alldes r^{or} fiscal sihi yoqhutasindi qhumi testigos toho nisano
loreso gosales g^{or} yuhuitayu san Ju^o qhumi dzico cuiya ta nicuhuitahuito ñuu ñayehui
sihi maestro domingo de çelis uhui dzico hoho cuiya nicuhuitahuito yocuhuito testigo
toho Ju^o de santi^o y cortes yio oco usi cuiya to yocuhuito testigo sihi niculas Clementte
maestro yio oco yñu cuiya yocuhui testigo saha ndaa cuisi dzahua tnaha yocachi nuu
testemento yaha yca saha yotniño dzihui ndehe taca Justiçia nuu tutu yaha g^{or} alldes
r^{or} fiscal huitna martes a 9 quihui yoo de enero cuiya de mil 1691 a^{o}s yaha tayu s^n p^o,
pablo yucundaa

    g^{dor} D^n Gabriel Ortiz de Tapia
    allde Geronimo Miguel de Sarate
    Domingo de la Crus
    fiscal Ju^o Nicolas
    saha ndaa cuiti yoyuhu ndudzu may yia yocuhui nitaa nduhu Ju^o Domnigo

ing to the palace called Ñuuñañu, I declare that it all be placed in the hands of my three children, don Domingo, don Josef, and don Pedro, so that all may share it and work it as three forever. Let nobody contest it or fight over it. Also, there is a purchased house, which is located in the siqui called Dzumañuu, with a field of house land behind the house, a field above the house, and a field below the house, which are all together.

Also I say that there is a field of patrimonial land behind the palace named Du-huandoo, which is at the edge of a canyon named Ndicuana, next to the house of the deceased Petronilla, and a field; I place all of it in the hands of my children. The three of them will have that which belonged to their grandparents.

Also there is a house in the same siqui as the house of Dionisio Delgado, an uncle of my deceased husband. I possess a testament [for it]. I place it in the hands of my three children, don Domingo García, don Josef García, and don Pedro García. I place all the plots of land and all the adjoining houses in the hands of my children. Thus I say it in my testament.

These words of doña Lázara de Guzmán are heard clearly by the governor, alcaldes, regidores, fiscal, and the four elder noble witnesses whom I designate: Lorenzo Gonzales, governor of the yuhuitayu of San Juan, who has had the gift of life for eighty years in this world; and the maestro Domingo de Celís, who has had the gift of life for fifty years, is a witness; and the noble Juan de Santiago y Cortés, who has lived for thirty years, is a witness; and maestro Nicolás Clemente, who is twenty-six years, is a witness. What is said in this testament is true and certain. Thus all the officials make their names on this paper, the governor, alcaldes, regidores, and the fiscal. Today, Tuesday, the 9th day of the month of January, in the year of one thousand [sic] 1691, in this yuhuitayu of San Pedro San Pablo Yucundaa (Teposcolula).

governor don Gabriel Ortiz de Tapia
alcalde Gerónimo Miguel de Zárate
Domingo de la Cruz
fiscal Juan Nicolás
true and clear are the words of the lord that I have written, Juan Domingo

*IV. Proceedings of the cabildo of Yanhuitlan over a land dispute in 1681. A last will
     and testament, written in 1642, was presented as evidence by the plaintiffs. AJT-C,
     4:467, ff. 40–45v.*

presentasion

yaha chayu santo domingo yodzocahi uitna miercoles 30 de Jullo de 1681 años
nisitonjuhu Justicias governador do Domingo de san pablo y alvarado alcaldes ordinario do pedro de san miguel mexia y gusma alcaldes Juan miguel tutu petiçio yaha
yca saha yonjaayecanju saha dzaqhcuvi tacanju dzava tnaha ndehe sa yosicanino
tacacha nuu tutu petiçion yaha

    don Pedro de san Miguel mexia y guzman
    governador don Domingo de san pablo y alvarado

petision

agustin adradas Regidor geronimo peres domigo de tapia bartasar gome yona-
siñotuvi taca ñadzaña sinana njisi governador don don diego de san pablo y alvarado
alcaldes ordinario don pedro de san miguel mexia y guzman y juan miguel sihi taca
Regidor saha uidzo dzaha costohondo ndios dzina nuu ni sihi saha dzaha costohondo
Rey don carlo secundo yocuvi tacani yuhu nuu taadza dzehe ndehe taca ñadzaña ña
ñuu ñanjahi yaá audiensia yodzocahi yaha sa yio arma sistohondo Rey sihi nee caa
ndaha ñuu si huitna yosicanino ndehe taca ñadzaña Justicia si domingo ramo si gaspar ramo pablo de ramo chay nicacu siña yuhuyucha saha niyehuidzanacha yosinicha
ñuhu chay siña ayusi sanaha sa yotasi taa si dzehe maa ñadzaña chay yyo huitna tucu
ñuhunjayu ytu siña ayusi yca yocuvi sa si may taca chay yocuvi tributario siña ayusi sihi
yoquidzatniño ñuu chayu tucu dzava tnaha yonacachi testamento niquidza Juan Lopez
siña ayusi saha ndaa cuitayu yonatuhui sa yocuvicha chay dzayocahi queye nica yca
saha nadzatuhuicha tutu testamento adzi escritura yonayhuahacha cha ndaa cuiteyu
nicuvi sasi maycha ytu siña yuhuyucha yonaha taca maycha nicahiqueyeni cacha ytu
ayusi sanani yuhuicani sihi yodzo nuu ñuu sanani ytuniñe nicuvi uvi sichi huitna yoc-
ahitucucha ytu yucua yca nani yuchayeye sitnu caca yca satasitnunini sa yosicanini taca
ñadzaña ñanjahi ñu siña ayusi ndehe dzaani sa yonatniñoñadzaña sinjiya taca njisi Justicia yuvichayu yodzocahi nisacuva peticio taca ñadzaña yaha huitna miercoles oco usi
quevi sica yoo de julio cuiya yonjacañaha yyondo huitna qhmi tuvi yodzo qhmi dzico
he cuiya nitucusinana costohondo—nduhua njaya ni yochaayuhu taca ñadzaña stoho

Agustin de adrada   geronimo perez   Miguel de spinal   bartaçar gomes   Jhoa
de spinosa

auto

nisitonjuhu governador alcaldes petiçion yaha yca saha yotasitnuninju coautonju
yaha cha nichacusinjoho chay nani domingo ramos sihi pedro ramos de la cruz coautonju yaha cha queyeni cuaynjatundo dzaqhcuvindo dzava tnaha tniño yotasitnuninju
saha va sa cutundo yuvi yuchayeye sa yñe sitnu caca sa yosahanindo vitna saha yaha
niquesi taca chay ñuu siña ayusi niquidzatu[vi]cha e testamento sihi tutu petiçion yaha

Presentation

In the tayu of Santo Domingo Yodzocahi (Yanhuitlan), today, Wednesday, the 30th of July, 1681, we officials, the governor don Domingo de San Pablo y Alvarado, the alcalde ordinario don Pedro de San Miguel Mexía y Guzmán, and the alcalde Juan Miguel, saw this petition. Thus we all attend to the concerns of all those who request counsel in this petition.

[signatures] don Pedro de San Miguel Mexia y Guzmán

governor don Domingo de San Pablo y Alvarado

Petition

Agustín Andradas, regidor, Gerónimo Pérez, Domingo de Tapia, Baltasar Gómez, all of us appear before you, the governor don Diego de San Pablo y Alvarado, the alcalde ordinario don Pedro de San Miguel Mexía y Guzmán, and Juan Miguel and all the regidores, according to the royal law of our lord God, first of all, and for our lord King don Carlos the second who looks after our fathers and mothers and all of us commoners from the ñuu, in this audiencia of Yanhuitlan, where the [Royal] arms of our lord King and those of all the sujetos are located. Today, we officials ask about Domingo Ramos, Gaspar Ramos, and Pablo de Ramos, who come from the siña of Yuhuyucha, who have knowingly usurped lands of the people of the siña of Ayusi, which are given to us by our fathers and mothers (ancestors), those who are living on the alluvial, cultivable plots of the siña of Ayusi and all those who are tributaries of the siña of Ayusi and who work for the ñuu tayu. Let it be said that the testament made by Juan López, from the siña of Ayusi, is legitimate. Let it be shown if those who have seized it can produce a legitimate testament or writing that shows that the fields belong to the siña of Yuhuyucha, if what they seized really belongs to them. The fields of Ayusi are called Yuhuicani, and those on the plain of the ñuu are called Ytuniñe. There were two plots of land. Now they want to take away the fields there that are named Yuchayeye and the lime furnace. We commoners of the ñuu siña of Ayusi appeal to all you officials of the yuhuitayu of Yodzocahi (Yanhuitlan). We have made this petition today, Wednesday, the 30th day of the month of July in the year four [×] four hundred [+] four [×] twenty + one [= 1681] years since our lord was born. We all kiss your feet and hands, lord officials.

[signatures] Agustín de Andrada   Gerónimo Pérez   Miguel de Espinal

Baltasar Gómez   Juan de Espinosa

Writ

We the governor and alcaldes have seen this petition. Thus we order you with this writ, Domingo Ramos and Pedro Ramos de la Cruz, you are notified by this writ of mine to immediately obey and comply with the obligation that I order, that you not work the ravine named Yuchayeye, where there is a lime furnace. Now you know that the people of the ñuu siña of Ayusi have come to present a testament and this peti-

cha dzaa tucu yotasitnunitucunju saha nadzatuvindo tutu testamento adzi escritura
saha nicuvi saha simayndo ñuhu yositundo yuvicani sa yñe yutnudzichi sihi sa nisaqh-
ndo nduchicha va dzevi sasimayndo yocuiña sini ñuhu cutundo va cuvicahinjaa queye
nadza si nani tnahando sihi ñuhu dza caa hooni ca sa nani Realego nja liçeçia cota-
canjuhu Justicia governador alcaldes yca nacutundo nanjaa si mihi yocuvivatuynindo
cutundo yca saha yocootasinju pena nuundo vitna saha va e ca quevi qhndehuidzanando
nja ca caa ñuhu caa hooni ca canindo cutundo cadzando saha simayndo ytu taa dzehendo sihi ytu ñoho yahui sindo yca nicutundo chava cuaynjatundo va dzaqhcuvindo
dzava tnaha yotasiynuninju tniño yahuindo usi qhmi peso sihi oco usi quevi vahi caa
cha ña nacadzava yaha ni yotasitnuninju yaha audieçia sistohondo Rey vitna miercoles
30 de Jullo de 1681 años

> governador ndomingo de san pablo y alvarado
> don pedro de san miguel mexia y guzman
> ante mi nicolas de villafaña escribano de cabildo

yaha nichacusiñadzaña chay ndahui ñanjahi stohondo dios sihi ñanjahi stohondo
Rey dzaa ñanjahi taca stohondo justicias governador alcaldes Regidores yochidzodzeque
ñadzaña dzaha mani taca stohodza dzoco natuhuiñadzaña nana taca Justicia nadzavidzo
ñadzaña adzi chay ñuu tucu nicuvi ñadzaña yca cuvi cocachi taca chay yaha sahavasi
ndehuy dza ñadza ñuhu njayu yuhuichayu yodzocahi yaha yca saha nacototuhua tacacha
nanjidza dzavidzocha stoho ñadzaña
Domingo de ramos

notifi[on]
vitna miercoles 30 de Jullo dzava tnaha caa 3 oras nicahuinjuhu escribano tutu
auto sihi petiçio yaha ñu domingo de rramos yca nidzavuidzo saha yodzavidzo yosayn-
jatu dzaha stohondo Rey sihi dzaha yya justicias governador alcaldes yca saha yosayn-
juhu escribano fee sahandaa saha njisayu yca saha yotniñonju firmanju sihi Rexidor
sihi nidzavidzocha saha tutu petiçio yaha saha yyo candudzu dzavidzocha yia nisaha
nitniñocha firmacha nuu tutu yaha sihi testigos

> nicolas de villafaña escribano de cabildo
> testigo Josephe de Byllafaña   Juan bautista

testamento
de 1642 años
siña ayusi Jhoan lopes yyo ndaha
¶ saha tnuni cruz et[a] saha sanani dzutu ndios ndehe dzaya ndios ndehe spiritu
santo ndios dzavua nacuvui saha sananini jhesus njuhu Jhoan Lopes vuitna yyo cahui
yocuvuiconju ta yocuhuiconju vuitna yyondaa coyninju yossininjisanju sanctisimo trinidad uni persona dza ee ninjisa ñuhu ndios sihi yyondaa coyninju yossininjisanju sa usi
qhmi sichi sa sininji sa nani articulos de la fee sihi yyonda coyninju yossininjisanju saha
niquicavui chai yee costohondo Jesus xpto yaha ñuu ñayevui cosahanjoo chai dzatevui
sihi yyondaa coyninju yossininjisanju yya dzehe Santa Maria del Rossario sidzehe mani

tion. Also, I order that you present testaments or other writings for your lands that you sow [named] Yuhuicani, where there are pitahaya trees and where you have sown your beans. Do not sow land that is not yours, do not take away what really belongs to your neighboring brothers. Even if the land is known as realenga (land without a formal owner, untitled land), you may have it to sow only through the license of us officials, the governor, the alcaldes. Thus, today I impose on you a penalty so that you will not enter or encroach on the land. Sow the fields of your fathers and mothers (ancestors) and the fields that belong to you by purchase. If you do not obey what I have declared, you will pay fourteen pesos and you will spend thirty days in the jail. Thus we declare in this audiencia of our lord King, today, Wednesday, the 30th of July, 1681.

> governor don Domingo de San pablo y Alvarado
> don Pedro de San Miguel Mexía y Guzmán
> before me, Nicolas de Villafaña, notary of the cabildo

Here I have heard, as a poor commoner of our lord God and a commoner of our lord King and a commoner of all our lord officials, the governor, the alcaldes, and the regidores. I hold in my head the precious words of all my lords, but I will appear before all the officials and I will respond as to whether we people from the ñuu did this and all of us people here will speak about the alluvial lands of the yuhuitayu of this Yodzocahi (Yanhuitlan). Thus all will see how they respond to our lords.

> Domingo de Ramos

Notification

Today, Wednesday, the 30th of July at 3 hours, I the notary read this decree and petition before Domingo de Ramos, who responded in the following manner, he said that he obeys the words of our lord King and the words of the lord officials, the governor and the alcaldes. I, the notary, record it faithfully, certainly, and very truly. Thus I make my signature and the regidor [does the same]. They have responded to this petition, they respond to the lords. The witnesses gave, made their signatures on this paper.

> Nicolas de Villafaña, notary of the cabildo
> witness Josef de Villafaña   Juan Bautista

Testament
in the year 1642
Juan López, [from] the siña of Ayusi, a tributary
¶ By the sign of the cross etcetera. In the name of God the father, God the son, and God the Holy Spirit, it will be done in the name of Jesus. I, Juan Lopez, am now gravely ill. Even though now I am sick, my heart is certain. I truly believe in the holy trinity, three persons but one true God. I truly believe in the fourteen articles of faith. I truly believe that our lord Jesus Christ came into this world as a man to redeem sinners. I truly believe in the lady Holy Mary of the Rosary, the precious mother of God. I truly believe what the holy church believes and what all Christians who live in this

ndios sihi yyondaa coyninju yossininjisanju ndehe dzavua tnaha yossininjisa santa yglesia sihi dzavua tnaha yossininjisa taca christianos sihi yonee caa cutu ñuu ñayevui yaha
sihi yyonda coyninju yonadzoconju coanimanju siña nana ndios sihi coyequecoñonju
cha nisihinju yosicatahuinju yni huahi ñuhu condusi coyequecoñonju yodzoconju . . .
1 peso

¶ 2 reales yodzoconju sacanja caa cha nicuvuisinjiya ndios ninana coanimanju

¶ 2 reales yodzoconju siyahui dzoo njayu

¶ 2 reales yodzoconju saquidzica cruzmanga quiquaca coyequecoñonju

¶ 2 reales yossinindahuinju cantores saha quiquacato coyequecoñonju

¶ 2 reales yodzoconju si yya dzehe santa maria del Rossario sacana yte cofradias
cha nisihinju satnoo taca xptianos xptianas quiquaca coyequecoñonju

¶ ee missa yosicatahuinju sacuvui cosaha animanju quevui cuvui 9 quevui nisihinju
yodzoconju . . . 1 peso

¶ njuhu maria garcia yosica ee missa sacuvui saha anima coyeende quevui cuvui
29 quevui cha nicuvuinjiya ndios nisihi ña yodzoconde . . . 1 peso

¶ dzehui mainde yosicatahui ee ca missa sacuvui quevui cuvui 49 quevui tucu yodzoconde . . . 1 peso

¶ njuhu diego hernandez yosicatahui ee missa resada sacuvui saha anima cocom-
padrenju yodzoconju . . . 4 reales

¶ njuhu Jhoan gutieres yosicatahui ee missa resada sacuvui saha anima cocompa-
drenju yodzoconju . . . 4 reales

¶ njuhu sebastian hortis yosicatahui ee missa major sacuvui saha anima cotaanju
yodzoconju . . . 1 peso

¶ njuhu Ynes Lopes yosicatahui ee missa resada sacuvui saha anima cocompadrende
yodzoconde . . . 4 reales

¶ huitna yonacahuinju sa comainju sa nissinindahui ñaha mai stohondios conju
quevui nisiyonjainda tnanju yaha ñuu ñayevui yca yyo ni covuahinju sa nidzacaa con-
dahamainju sihi yavui siñoho nee chiyo nacahi tucu ndehe saa nisa comainju yca ni
yonacuhuanju codzayunju chai dzina chai nani andres saha mai cha conducu condahanju cha nicuhuisinjisa ndios nisihinju sa yoo cuvui conducu condahanju

¶ sihi he sichi ytu yuchayeye yoneenino sa yyo sitnee caca

¶ ndehe dzavua yaha nicoyuhundudzunju yoquidzanju testamento vuitna jueves a
11 de diçienbre de 1642 años sanjisa sandaayu ninachihitnuniyninju ndehe dzavua
tnaha yonjaatnuni tutu yaha saha cuvui cosaha animanju sihi sacuvui si coyequecoñonju
sanjisa sandaayu saha vua yoo ñaha cachisa quaha savica si sihi vua yoo na cani ninoco-
juhu ndudzunju tucu yca saha yonjito nuu miguel peres sihi Jhoan gutieres sihi Juan
Lopes testigos ndehe 3 testigos yaha yonjito niquidzanju testamento sanjisa sandaanju
vuitna yochaatniñonju miguel peres cuvui alguaçea chihi mai coanimanju cha nisihinju
ndehe dzavua yaha ni niquidzanju testamento ndehe dzavua yaha nisiyuhundudzu
Jhuan Lopes nichaatnuninjuhu thomas sanche escribano testamento sanjisa sandaanju
saha cabildo nombrados

conuunjuhu

Thomas Sanche escribano

world believe. And with all my heart I offer my soul to God and [as for] my body, I ask that my body be buried in the church when I die, I offer 1 peso.

¶ I offer 2 reals for the tolling of the bells when God has taken me, when my soul has departed.

¶ I offer 2 reals for the purchase of the black cloth.

¶ I offer 2 reals for those who bring the cruzmanga, who accompany my body.

¶ I give 2 reals for the noble singers (cantores), who accompany my body.

¶ I offer 2 reals to the lady Holy Mary of the Rosary and candles from the cofradía for all those male Chistians and female Christians who accompany my body when I die.

¶ I ask that a mass be said for my soul nine days after I die, I offer 1 peso.

¶ I, María García, request that a mass be said for this man's soul 29 days after God takes him and he has died, I offer 1 peso.

¶ For myself, I ask that another mass be done [in] 49 days, I offer 1 peso.

¶ I, Diego Hernández, request that a high mass be done for the soul of my compadre, I offer 4 reals.

¶ I, Juan Gutiérrez, request that a high mass be done for the soul of my compadre, I offer 4 reals.

¶ I, Sebastián Ortiz, request that a high mass be done for the soul of my father, I offer 1 peso.

¶ I, Inés López, request that a high mass be done for the soul of my compadre, I offer 4 reals.

¶ Now I declare what is mine, that which the lord God has given me when I lived in health on this earth. My three houses which I built with my own hands and the magueyes on the patrimonial land and all that is mine I give to my oldest child named Andrés so that he might pay my tribute, and when God takes me and I die he will no longer hand over my tribute.

¶ And a field [named] Yuchayeye that goes all the way to the lime furnace.

¶ And thus I have spoken. I make my testament today, Thursday, the 11th of December, the year of 1642. Truly and certainly, I have fulfilled my wish to write this document for the sake of my soul and my body. Truly and certainly, let nobody interfere with what I have ordered, and let nobody dispute my words. Thus it is seen by Miguel Pérez and Juan Gutiérrez and Juan López, witnesses, and these three witnesses here see that I make my testament truly and honestly. Now, I appoint Miguel Pérez to be the executor who cares for my soul when I die. Juan López has also spoken in this testament that I have made. I, the notary, Tomás Sánchez, have written this testament truly and certainly for the named cabildo.

before me,
Tomás Sánchez, notary

pen^{on}

yaha chayu santo domingo yodzocahi vitna martes 12 de agosto de 1681 años nisito
njuhu governador do domingo de san pablo y alvarado alcaldes ordinario do pedro
de san miguel mexia y gusma alcaldes Juan miguel tutu peticion yaha yca saha yecayu
dzaqhcuvi tacanju dzava tnaha Justicias yosicatahui nuu tutu petiçion yaha
    governador don domingo de san pablo
    don pedro de san miguel mexia y gusma

    peticion

domingo de rramos y pedro rramos de la cruz y gaspar de suniga y pablo de la cruz
chay ñuu chayu santo domingo yodzocahi ñadzaña chay nicacu siña yuhuyucha yona-
siñotuviñadzaña yaha audiensia si costohondo Rey sanjita arma Real saha yodzica taca
stoho ñadzaña justicias yya yocuvi dzini dzeque sindehe taca ñadzaña yya toniñe governador, alcaldes sihi ndehe taca rexidores yonadzavidza ñadzaña nana taca stoho
ñadzaña yy justicias saha yoquidzañadzaña contradiçion petiçion sihi testamento si
chay ñuu siña Ayusi saha yocuvi nulo sihi falso testamento saha yosayhinitacacha nichi-
hicha ee yuqh caniyu letra yca yocuvi letra yyohini testamento yaha siletra toho nisanu
domingo de san pablo ycasaha yosicatahui taca ñadzaña justicias nana taca stoho
ñadzaña saha naconjatu domingo de san pablo sihi Jeronimo peres huahi caa saha
cuhuañadzaña yformaçion testigo nana taca stohoñadzaña saha ndaayu yocuvicha
chay yodzatevi nino testamento sihi chay yocahinjaa queye yahuicata ñuhunjayu sistohondo ndios sistohondo Rey sihi ñuhunjayu si ñanitnahacha cha cuadzu yocachi petiçion taca maycha saha ñadzaña yocahinjaa ñuhunjayu yahuicata ñanitnaha ñadzaña
dzoco vata ee ca testamento cadzañadzaña falçear dzava tnaha yoquidzatacamaycha
testamento niquidzacha preçentar nana taca stohodza vitna saha yocuvihinicha dzu-
hucha cuayqueyecha ñuhunjayu yaha stoho yca saha yosicatacañadzaña justicia nacu-
visicha saha va ee caquevi cadzecha tniño yaha saha dzandahuicha costohondo ndios
sihi costohondo Rey dzaa taca stohodza justicia governador alcaldes N^a sihi yosicatahui tucu taca ñadzaña saha nadzatuvicha titulo merced ñana yya ñana toho yocuvicha
ñuu siña Ayusi cha yodzicocha yavi siñoho nee cutu ytnu Ayusi sihi yavi ñoho ñuhu
yuchañana dzava tnaha ndudzu ninachaa taca yya toho santa maria yuchanani
[co]tani nacoto nana yya governador don Pedro de San Miguel Mexia y Guzman cuiya
caa cay saha may Jeronimo Pérez yaha nidzicoyavi yaha sa dzevi Jeronimo yaha yodzi-
coyavi dzeque ayusi yosay chay añoo chay nani gregorio sihi ca sica ñayevi yosay yavi
stoho sihi yodzadzahacha ñuhu dzava tnaha niquidzacha si ndiego de mentoza yosan-
jacha yutnu saha cutucha cha nisacuicoñaha may Jeronimo peres sadzevi ndudzaa
niquidzacha si chay ndahui chai nani grabiel chay vasi tiquevi nisadzadzahacha yavi
yotahuicha ndehe dzava yaha yformaçion testigo cuhua ñadzaña nana taca stohodza
Justicia et^a

canuyu yosatutahui taca ñadzaña saha nacuvitahui taca ñadzaña Justicia dzava
tnaha yosicatahuiñadzaña saha naconjatu nducucha huahi caa sihi cachi ndahuinjiya
taca stoho ñadzaña saha cuhua ñadzaña yformaçion testigo cha ña yonducuvatunjiya
taca stohodza saha cuvitahuiñadzaña ndehe taca justicias yosicaninoñadzaña nanduvi-

Presentation

In this tayu of Santo Domingo Yodzocahi (Yanhuitlan), today, Tuesday, the 12th of August, 1681. I, the governor, don Domingo de San Pablo y Alvarado, the alcalde ordinario don Pedro de San Miguel Mexía y Guzmán, and the alcalde Juan Miguel saw this petition. Thus all of us officials attend to what is requested in this petition.

governor don Domingo de San Pablo

don Pedro de San Miguel Mexía y Guzmán

Petition

Domingo Ramos, Pedro Ramos de la Cruz, Gaspar de Zúñiga, and Pablo de la Cruz, people who are from the ñuu tayu of Santo Domingo Yodzocahi (Yanhuitlan), who were born in the siña of Yuhuyucha, we appear here in the audiencia of our lord King and the royal arms, where all of our lord officials, the lords who are the head of all of us, the lord ruler governor, the alcaldes, and all the regidores. We are responding to all of our lords and officials by contradicting the petition and testament of the people of the ñuu siña of Ayusi. The testament is null and false because it is obvious to everyone that a line of handwriting was added to the testament, one can see that the handwriting in this testament is the handwriting of the elder noble Domingo de San Pablo. Thus we all ask for justice before all of our lords, that Domingo de San Pablo and Gerónimo Pérez be placed in jail so that we can have an inquiry [and] witnesses before all of our lords. It is true that the people who damage the contents of the testament and the people who seize and enter the alluvial lands of our lord God and our lord King and the lands of their neighbors, they all jealously order a petition against us, [claiming] that we seize the lands of our neighbors. But we will not falsify a testament like the testament that they make, that they presented before all our lords. Now, they would rob and harm these lands, lords. Thus we all ask that justice be done to them so that they will not benefit from this business of tricking our lord God and our lord King and all our lord justices, the governor, our alcaldes. And we also ask that they present titles and grants, the lords and nobles who live in the ñuu siña of Ayusi, who sell the magueyes that are grown on all the slopes of Ayusi and the magueyes on the land called Yuchañana. Concerning the words that were written by all the lords and nobles of Santa María Yuchanani (Chachuapa) to the lord governor don Pedro de San Miguel Mexía y Guzmán last year, as to how this same Gerónimo Pérez sold magueyes here, and how the same Gerónimo sells magueyes that are [in the hills] above Ayusi to a person from Añoo named Gregorio, and to other people who buy magueyes, lords. And they defend the land, as they did with Diego de Mendoza, who chops down trees in order to cultivate it. The same Gerónimo Pérez ran him off the land. He did it with a poor person who comes from Tiquevui (Tamasulapa) named Gabriel, who had defended the magueyes. All of this should be presented in the investigation of witnesses before all our lords and our officials, etcetera.

Together we request, we ask for justice, we ask that the accusers be placed in jail and that our courteous lords grant us an inquiry with witnesses. If all our lords do not intend to do as we ask, we ask all the officials to permit us to present testimonies, petitions, writs, and testaments before the lord alcalde mayor (Spanish official) so that he

tahui ñadzaña testimonio ndehe taca petiçion sihi auto sihi testamento saha natu-
viñadzaña nana yya alcalde mayor saha nacotoya tniño ñadzaña dzava yaha ni justicia
yosicatahui taca ñadzaña va dzevi tnuhu ñena tnuhu dzuhu saha ndaa sahanjisayu yca
saha yoquidzañadzaña jurameto crus nuu tutu petiçion ñadzaña yaha stoho ñadzaña
nacotocha costa sihi ñaña ndehe ca tniño cuvi stoho

    diego de rramos   pedro rramos de la cruz   gaspar de suniga
    pablo de la crus   jasinto ortis

    nauto
nisitonjuhu justicia governador alcaldes tutu petiçion yaha yca saha yotasitnuninju
cha nichacusinjoho chay nani domingo de sa pablo sihi geronimo peres coautonju
yaha cha queyeni cuaynjatundo dzaqhcuvindo dzava tnaha tniño yotasitnuninju saha
conjatundo huay caa yaha saha justicia yosicandehe taca chay yocaha nuu petiçion yaha
saha cuhua cha yformaçion testingo dzava tnaha yosicaninocha nuu petiçion yaha yca
saha cadza tacanju Justicia dzava tnaha tniño yonjaayecanju saha cuaynnju juramento
sihi nacuaynju yuhu ndudzu ndehe taca testigos nadzaha testigos cadzapresentar parte
contrario yca nananihindo auto sihi yformaçio saha nadzavidzondo dzava yaha ni yotasitnuninju yaha audieçia

    don pedro de san miguel mexia y gusman
    governador don domingo de san pablo y alvarado
    ante mi nicolas de villafaña escribano de cavildo

    noti[on]
vitna dzava tnaha caa 2 oras nindevinjuhu escribano de cavildo yni huahi caa sa
yyo·domingo de san pablo sihi geronimo peres nisacahuinju auto dzeque si yaha nuucha
ndehe nduvicha yca nidzavidzocha saha yosaynjatucha yodzaqhcuvicha sividzo dzaha
costohondo Rey sihi si yya Justicias dzava yaha nidzavidzocha yca saha yonini testigos
sihi nitniñocha firmacha sihi njuhu escribano de cabildo sihi firma testingo tucu

    ante me nicolas de villafaña escribano de cabildo
    domingo de san pablo   geronimo peres

    pre[on]
yaha chayu santo domingo yodzocahi vitna miercoles 17 de setienbre de 1681 años
nicuhui presentar petision yaha conuunjuhu alcalde ordinario don Pedro de san miguel
mexia y guzman saha yonadzavidzo taca chay ñuu siña ayusi yca saha dza yocuhuinju
dzava tnaha justicias yosicatacacha conuunju yaha audiensia

    domingo de san miguel mexia y gusman
    escribano miguel abendaños

    peti[on]
angustin de adrada regidor geronimo peres domingo de tapia bartasar gomes yon-
adzahuidzo tucu ñadzaña sinana njisi yya toniñe governador don diego de san pablo
alvarado alcaldes don pedro de san miguel mexia y guzman Juan miguel sihi taca Regidor natniño nana tacani huitna saha yosicaninoñadzaña dzava tnaha peticion sihi
yformaçio nitasi domingo de ramos saha yocachi saha yosaycaynitacañadzaña saha tes-

may see our concern here. We do not ask for justice falsely or maliciously; truly and honestly we make an oath of the cross on our petition here, our lords.

They will pay the costs for all the work done by the lords.

| Diego de Ramo | Pedro Ramos de la Cruz | Gaspar de Zúñiga |
| Pablo de la Cruz | Jasinto Ortiz | |

Writ

We officials, the governor, the alcaldes, have seen this petition and I hereby order Domingo de San Pablo and Gerónimo Pérez to hear this writ and to immediately obey and comply. I order that you stay in the jail here. For the sake of justice, I ask that all those who have spoken in this petition give testimony as witnesses so that what is requested in this petition will be done by all of us officials, as it is the duty that we are obligated to perform and to which we are sworn. And we will hear the words of all the witnesses, the speech of witnesses who will present the other side so that you will have a ruling and an inquiry in order to respond. Thus I declare in this audiencia.

don Pedro de San Miguel Mexía y Guzmán
governor don Domingo de San Pablo y Alvarado
before me, Nicolás de Villafaña, notary of the cabildo

Notification

Today, at around 2 hours, I, the escribano of the cabildo, entered inside the jail where Domingo de San Pablo and Gerónimo Pérez are. I read the writ before the two of them and they responded that they obey and comply with the laws of our lord King and of the lord officials. This was how they responded. The witnesses heard this and they made their signatures and I, the notary of the cabildo, signed as a witness, also.

before me, Nicolás de Villafaña, notary of the cabildo
Domingo de San Pablo   Gerónimo Pérez

Presentation

In this tayu of Santo Domingo Yodzocahi (Yanhuitlan), today, Wednesday, the 17th of September, 1681, this petition was presented to me, the alcalde ordinario, don Pedro de San Miguel Mexía y Guzmán. All the people from the ñuu siña of Ayusi respond. Thus we provide justice to those who ask it of us in this audiencia.

Don Pedro de San Miguel Mexía y Guzmán
notary Miguel Abendaños

Petition

Agustín de Andrada, regidor, Gerónimo Pérez, Domingo de Tapia, Baltasar Gómez, all of us respond before you, lord ruler governor, don Diego de San Pablo Alvarado, alcaldes don Pedro de San Miguel Mexía y Guzmán, Juan Miguel, and all the regidores who work in your presence. Today we ask about the petition and inquiry given by Domingo de Ramos, which says that we insert things in the testament of Juan López,

tamento Juan Lopes siña ayusi cha cuaniñaha yocuviynitacacha vahy tniño taca testamento yucua dzo he ca tutu testamento saha ninanihi huitna si may stohodza governador don domingo de san pablo alvarado saha nda ayusi ñuhunjayu si yya toniñe
yocuvi sihi taca dzayadzanasiya siña ayusi ndaa cuiteyu tniño yaha vacuviyu saha dza-
cuaycayni taca ñadzaña si nana tacani ndehe tniño yaha dzaani yonatniñoñadzaña
njiya tacaninisacuva peticion ñadzaña huitna viernes 12 de sentiebre cuiya 1681 años
etcetera

    sinjaya mani tacani yochaayuhudza
    geronimo peres   domigo de tapia   bartasar gomes

    auto
    nisitonjuhu justicia alcalde ordinario tutu petision yaha yca saha yotasitnuninju
cha nichacusinjoho Donmigo de ramos pedro ramos de la cruz pablo de la crus gaspar de suniga coautonju yaha cha queyni cuaynjatundo dzaqhcuhuindo tniño yotasitnuninju yaha saha ñaha sini ñuhu cadzasaando ñuhu yuchayeye sihi dzeque ayusi saha
yocachi petision yaha saha yonahi yya governador Don domigo de san pablo y alvarado
e ca tutu testamento saha yochachi saha ñuhunjayu simay yya governador yocuhui
ñuhu yuchayeye sanino sitnu caca sihi nee cutu dzeque ayusi yca saha yocootasinju
pena nuundo saha va sadzasaacando ñuhu yucua saha yyo ca stohosicha vacuayn-
jatundo vadzaqhcuvindo dzava tnaha tniño yotasitnuninju nuu coautonju yaha tniño
yahuindo yñu peso sihi tasiñahanju vahi caa sau quevi dzava yaha ni yotasitnuninju yaha
audiencia sicostohodo Rey chayu san domingo yodzocahi yaha

    don Pedro de san miguel mexia y gusman
    ante mi miguel de avendaño escribano de cabilndo

of the siña of Ayusi, in order to deceive people. Of all the testaments that they keep inside the duty house (audiencia), there is one testament that has been found today that belongs to our lord governor, don Domingo de San Pablo Alvarado, which shows that the alluvial lands of Ayusi belong to the yya toniñe and all his dependents of the siña of Ayusi. This matter is true and very certain. We have not attempted to insert things. Before all of you, we take care of this matter together, we have made a petition before all of you. Today, Friday, the 12th of September in the year 1681, etcetera.

We kiss your precious hands,

Gerónimo Pérez   Domingo de Tapia   Baltasar Gómez

Writ

I, the alcalde ordinario, have seen this petition and hereby declare that you, Domingo de Ramos, Pedro Ramos de la Cruz, Pablo de la Cruz, and Gaspar de Zuniga, have heard this writ of mine. You are to immediately obey and comply with the obligation that I order here, that nobody should touch the land or enter on the land [called] Yuchayeye and those that are above Ayusi, because this petition states that it belongs to the lord governor don Domingo de San Pablo y Alvarado, one testament says that the alluvial lands belonging to the lord governor are the lands [called] Yuchayeye, where the lime furnace is, including all the [land] above Ayusi. Thus, I will impose a penalty on you who do not leave the land there, the place that belongs to the lord; those who do not obey and comply with what I have ordered here in my decree will pay six pesos, and I will place them in the jail for fifteen days. This is what I order here in the audiencia of our lord King, in this tayu of Santo Domingo Yodzocahi (Yanhuitlan)

don Pedro de San Miguel Mexía y Guzmán

before me, Miguel de Avendaño, notary of the cabildo

GLOSSARY

alcalde [S] Member of a Spanish-style municipal council (cabildo) who acts as judge.

alcalde mayor [S] Spanish judicial and administrative official in charge of a given jurisdiction; often synonymous with corregidor.

altepetl [N] Local, sovereign, ethnic Nahua state; called pueblos by Spaniards.

aniñe [M] "Place of royalty"; palace or multicomponent dwelling structure; establishment of a ruler or lord.

barrio [S] Subdistrict of municipality, often equated with divisions of the ñuu—siqui, siña, and dzini.

cabecera [S] Head town; municipal status assigned to larger towns.

cabildo [S] Spanish-style municipal council; body of political officers.

cacica [S] Female indigenous ruler, an heiress to a cacicazgo; wife of a cacique.

cacicazgo [S] The sum of all privileges and rights pertaining to the title of cacique; associated with Spanish establishment of "mayorazgo."

cacique [S] Indigenous ruler, equivalent of yya toniñe in Mixtec or tlatoani in Nahuatl; derived from Arawak word for ruler and applied by Spaniards to any ruler; in later period, the term was used by any prominent indigenous person.

cah [Y] Local ethnic Maya state, roughly equivalent to altepetl or ñuu.

caja de comunidad [S] Municipal treasury.

calpolli [N] Constituent part, subunit of an altepetl.

chinamitl [N] "Enclosure"; constituent part, subunit of an altepetl.

cihuapilli [N] Noblewoman, lady.

codices [S] Indigenous pictorial writings, usually painted on deerhide.

cofradía [S] Sodality, lay religious brotherhood.

compadrazgo [S] Ritual kinship ties between godparents and natural parents.

congregación [S] Resettlement of indigenous people to effect a greater concentration of inhabitants.

corregidor [S] Often used interchangeably with alcalde mayor.

corregimiento [S] The jurisdiction or office of a corregidor.

cuiya [M] "Year".

daha [M] Tribute in kind.

daha ñuu [M] "Tribute ñuu"; neologism adopted for Spanish "sujeto."

don [S] High title attached to the first name of a male; like English "Sir."

doña [S] High title attached to the first name of a female; like English "Lady."

Dzahui [M] Rain deity in the Mixteca.

dzaya dzana [M] Commoner, similar to ñandahi, used also in reference to dependents of lords.

dzini [M] Subentity of yuhuitayu in Mixteca Baja; local units that Spaniards were to call "barrios."

dzini ñuu [M] "Head ñuu"; neologism adopted for Spanish "cabecera."

encomendero [S] One who holds an encomienda grant.

encomienda [S] Grant to a Spaniard of the right to receive tribute and labor from the indigenous people of a given community or communities through already existing tribute mechanisms.

escribano [S] Notary, clerk.

fiscal [S] Church steward, used here as the highest indigenous ecclesiastical office in a given church district.

gobernador [S] Governor; used here as an indigenous person exercising the highest office in the municipal government, usually the cacique in the Mixteca.

hacienda [S] Landed estate for agriculture and ranching.

huahi ñuhu [M] "God house"; term adopted for a church, presumably based on the term for a preconquest temple.

huehuetque [N] "Old men," elders, usually referring to municipal authorities or ancestors.

indio [S] "Indian"; term used by Spaniards for all indigenous people.

ladino [S] Spanish-speaking or acculturated indigenous person.

lienzo [S] Early postconquest indigenous pictorial writing on cloth.

macehualli [N] Nahua commoner.

maguey [S] Agave, term taken from Arawak; source of alcoholic drink pulque and of threadlike fibers for multiple uses.

mayorazgo [S] Entail.

mestizo [S] Person of mixed Spanish and indigenous ancestry.

Mixteca [S] Area mainly of western Oaxaca inhabited by the Mixtec or Ñudzahui people and several other cultural groups.

Mixtecs English term adopted from Spanish "Mixtecos," from the original Nahuatl designation for people who called themselves "Ñudzahui."

mulato [S] Person of African-European ancestry.

naboría [S] From Arawak, used by Spaniards to denote a permanent dependent of an indigenous noble or ruler.

nahuatlato [N] "Clear speaker"; term adopted in sixteenth century for "interpreter" or translator of any indigenous language.

ñandahi [M] Commoner; called "macehuale" in Spanish (derived from the Nahuatl term *macehualli*).

Ñucoyo [M] "Place of reeds"; Ñudzahui name for Mexico and Nahuas in general, perhaps associated with ancient Tula.

Ñudzahui [M] "Place of rain," or "precious place"; term of self-ascription applied to the people, region, language, and culture of the distinct indigenous group known also as the "Mixtecs"; also spelled "ñudzavui."

ñuhu aniñe [M] "Palace land"; part of the hereditary patrimony of the lordly establishment; similar to Nahua tecpantlalli or pillalli.

ñuhu chiyo [M] "Patrimonial land", "old land", or "altar land"; usually the site of the main household; the plot most likely to be bequeathed to members within the household and the least likely to be alienated; similar to Nahua huehuetlalli.

ñuhu huahi [M] "House land"; the lot or lots of land associated with a given household; refers to either the land on which the house stood or land adjacent to it; similar to Nahua callalli.

ñuhu ñuu [M] "Land of the ñuu"; claimed by the corporate entity and subject to use or allocation by it members; similar to Nahua altepetlalli.

ñuhu siña [M] Land of a subentity of the ñuu, called "siña" (or its regional variants, "siqui" and "dzini"); similar to Nahua calpollalli.

ñuu [M] Local ethnic Mixtec state, equivalent to Nahua altepetl and Mayan cah.

ñuu siqui [M] Hybrid term for sociopolitical unit's ambivalent, perhaps transitional, status between siqui and ñuu.

ñuu tayu [M] Hybrid term for sociopolitical unit's ambivalent, perhaps transitional, status between ñuu and yuhuitayu.

obraje [S] Factorylike establishment for producing textiles, run by Spaniards.

peso [S] Monetary unit, consisting of eight reals or tomines.

petlatl icpalli [N] "Reed mat and seat," and by extension royal throne; considered in central Mexico a symbol of high authority.

pilli [N] Nahua noble (plural: pipiltin).

pochtecatl [N] Professional Nahua long-distance or interregional merchant.

principal [S] Spanish term for a prominent indigenous person, often equivalent to Ñudzahui toho or Nahua pilli.

pueblo [S] Spanish term for an indigenous municipality (altepetl, ñuu, cah), applied to any autonomous or identifiable settlement.

pulque [S] Alcoholic beverage obtained from maguey.

real [S] A silver coin worth an eighth of a peso.

regidor [S] Councilman; member of a cabildo.

repartimiento [S] Most frequently, labor draft based on indigenous mechanism of rotary labor service.

siña [M] Subentity of yuhuitayu in Yanhuitlan and surrounding area; local units that Spaniards were to call "barrios."

siqui [M] Subentity of yuhuitayu in Teposcolula and Tamasulapa area; local units that Spaniards were to call "barrios."

stoho [M] Lord or ruler.

sujeto [S] Subject town, indigenous settlement subordinate to a cabecera.

tay cuica [M] "Trade person," or merchant, equivalent perhaps of Nahua pochteca.

tay nisanu [M] "Grown person," or body of elders, equivalent of huehuetque.

tay Ñudzahui [M] Ñudzahui person, often simply Ñudzahui.

tay saquiñahi [M] "One who gathers things"; term used for tribute collector.

tay situndayu [M] "One who works the land"; term thought to have been applied to dependent laborers of the lord.

tayu [M] Same as yuhuitayu; ñuu with a royal ruling couple.

teccalli [N] Lordly house or establishment, containing nobles, dependents, and lands.

tecpan [N] Palace, establishment of ruler or lord; literally, "where the lord is."

teocalli [N] "God house"; a preconquest temple and, by extension, a Christian church or chapel.

teopantlaca [N] "Church people"; the indigenous attendants of the church, including choir members.

tequitl [N] Duty, labor, obligation.

tequitlato [N] "Tribute speaker"; sub-cabildo officer, tax collector.

terrazguero [S] Serf or dependent laborer; term used by Spaniards for various indigenous dependents of lords or lordly establishments.

teuctli [N] Lord, titled ruler of a lordly house with lands and dependents.

títulos [S] Land titles.

tlatoani [N] Dynastic ruler of an altepetl.

tlatocayotl [N] The right of dynastic rulership.

tlaxilacalli [N] Altepetl subunit or constituent, apparently same as calpolli; what Spaniards would call "barrio."

tlayacatl [N] A constituent altepetl of a large, complex altepetl, the former with its own dynastic ruler.

tniño [M] Labor, duty, obligation, and service (including political office) on behalf of the ñuu or yuhuitayu.

tnuhu [M] Lineage or dynastic line of rulers, called "linaje" by Spaniards.

toho [M] Noble not entitled to rule a yuhuitayu.

tomin [S] A coin or value worth an eighth of a peso.

toniñe [M] Dynastic rulership based on direct descent from high lords.

topile [S] "One with a staff"; constable or low-level official in a supervisory position (derived from Nahuatl).

yahui [M] Market, plaza.

yucunduta [M] "Water and hill"; literal Ñudzahui equivalent of Nahuatl altepetl, attested only in writings from the Mixteca Baja.

yuhuitayu [M] "Reed mat and couple/throne"; the establishment of a ruling lord and lady who join two dynastic lines in marriage, and the place or places that are considered part of that united patrimony.

yya [M] High lord, applied to rulers and sometimes important Spanish officials.

yya dzehe [M] Noblewoman, lady.

yya toniñe [M] High ruling lord; called "cacique" by Spaniards and "tlatoani" by Nahuas.

ABBREVIATIONS

AGEO	Archivo General del Estado de Oaxaca, Oaxaca
-AM	Alcaldías Mayores
AGI	Archivo General de las Indias, Seville
-AMG	Audiencia de México, Gobierno
-C	Contaduría
-ESC	Escribanía de Cámara
AGN	Archivo General de la Nación, Mexico City
-C	Civil
-CR	Criminal
-G	General de Parte
-HJ	Hospital de Jesús
-I	Indios
-INQ	Inquisición
-M	Mercedes
-T	Tierras
-V	Vínculos
AJT	Archivo Judicial de Teposcolula, Oaxaca
-C	Civil
-CR	Criminal
Alvarado	*Vocabulario en lengua mixteca,* by fray Francisco de Alvarado (1593), 1962 ed.
BNAH	Biblioteca Nacional de Antropología e Historia
MFHL	Mormon Family History Library, Los Angeles
Reyes	*Arte en lengua mixteca,* by fray Antonio de los Reyes (1593), 1976 ed.

NOTES

CHAPTER 1 — INTRODUCTION

1. *Ñudzahui* is the most commonly attested form of the word in native-language writings from the colonial period, even though some friars who studied the language and who attempted to develop and promote a standardized orthography in the Mixteca Alta distinguished *vui* from *hui* and wrote *dzavui* instead of *dzahui*, for reasons explained in chapter 3. I am aware of this distinction, but I have observed that most native writers ignored it and wrote -*dzahui*. The phonetic value of *dz* ranged from [d] and [đ] to [z] and [s], depending on dialect area. This term is still used by many Mixtecan speakers in reference to themselves and is spelled and pronounced many different ways, as it was in the colonial period. Aware of this fact, I have decided to use the most common form of the term in the colonial period, as it appears most often in the record. Chapter 3 contains a relevant discussion of pronunciation, and chapter 9 focuses on the articulation of this self-ascribed ethnic term in the colonial period. Chapter 8 demonstrates the importance of the rain deity, Dzahui or Dzavui, in the Mixteca.

2. *Mesoamerica* refers to the indigenous (usually preconquest) cultural area that extends from central and southern Mexico to Guatemala.

3. See Paddock 1966 and Flannery and Marcus 1983 for essays on ancient Oaxaca.

4. *Codex Mendoza*, ff. 42v–43r.

5. Spores 1984, 97. The first extant records of tribute paid to the crown appear in that year, when the *corregimiento* (colonial administrative and legal jurisdiction, same as *alcaldía mayor*) of Teposcolula paid a quantity of gold and cotton cloth. AGI-C, v. 657, f. 767.

6. All population figures for the Mixteca Alta are taken from Cook and Borah 1968. William Autry is completing a demographic study of the Mixteca that qualifies these numbers but does not dispute the extent of rapid population decline.

7. Today, there are about three hundred thousand Mixtecan speakers in Oaxaca, other Mexican states, the United States, and Canada.

8. See Lockhart and Schwartz 1983, 96–100, 133–34, on trunklines in Spanish America.

9. Gerhard 1986, 296, from the census of 1797. This jurisdiction consisted of no fewer than seventy-four Mixtec communities or pueblos.

10. See Spores 1984, 107–8.

11. See Gibson 1952, 1964.

12. Farriss 1984.

13. Cook 1939; Borah 1943; Borah and Cook 1960, 1979; Cook and Borah 1968.

14. Taylor 1972, 1979.

15. Chance 1978, 1989, 1996, 1998, 2000.

16. Romero Frizzi 1986, 1990, and Pastor 1987.

17. Caso 1949, 1960, 1965, 1966a, 1977–79, for example.

18. In a famous essay titled "El mapa de Teozacualco," published in 1949, Caso discovered the relation between an ancient dynasty depicted in the preconquest *Codex Zouche-Nuttall* and a genealogy from the Ñudzahui community of Teozacualco, drawn in 1580 for the *Relaciones geográficas*. He used the colonial map, discussed in chapter 2 of this work, as a "Rosetta stone" to link the origin of several codices to the Mixteca.

19. Dahlgren 1954.

20. Spores 1964, 1967, 1976, 1983a–e, 1984, 1997. For related archaeological studies, see Lind 1979; Flannery and Marcus 1983; Byland and Pohl 1994.

21. Smith 1973a,b, 1983a–d; Smith and Parmenter 1991.

22. Boone 2000.

23. Furst 1978.

24. Jansen 1982.

25. Anders, Jansen, and Pérez Jiménez 1992a,b; Jansen 1994; Jansen and Reyes García 1997.

26. Pohl 1984, 1994a,b; Byland and Pohl 1994.

27. To name a few works not mentioned above: King 1988, 1990, 1994; Marcus 1992; and Boone 2000. At the annual Mixtec Gateway, Nancy Troike organizes workshops on the codices.

28. Monaghan 1995; for the relevance of ethnographic work on the codices, see also Jansen 1982 and Monaghan 1990a,c.

29. Anderson and Dibble 1950–82. See also Garibay 1971.

30. For example, Karttunen and Lockhart 1976; Anderson, Berdan, and Lockhart 1976; Carrasco 1976b; Reyes García 1977; Karttunen 1983; Cline and León-Portilla 1984; Lockhart, Berdan, and Anderson 1986; Lockhart 1991.

31. Lockhart 1992.

32. Wood 1984; Cline 1986, 1993; Haskett 1991a; Schroeder 1991; Kellogg 1995; and Horn 1997. For representative works on the translation and use of Nahuatl-language church-sponsored texts, see Andrews and Hassig 1984; Burkhart 1989, 1996; Sell 1993; Sousa, Poole, and Lockhart 1998; Sullivan et al. 1997.

33. Roys 1933, 1939; Scholes and Roys [1948] 1968. Roys transcribed and translated several important collections of Maya documents during the 1930s and 1940s, before the beginning of historical and philological research based on the Nahuatl language.

34. Thompson 1978 and Restall 1997. See also Restall 1995 for a collection of eighteenth-century Maya wills from Ixil, and Restall 1998 on Maya primordial titles. See Karttunen 1985 for a comparison of Nahuatl and Maya language contact phenomena. In addition, Robert Hill (1987) has translated and analyzed a collection of Cakchiquel-language documents.

35. Maarten Jansen and Aurora Pérez have worked with Mixtec-language sources from the colonial period and present five translated documents in Jansen 1994, 113–42. Josserand, Jansen, and Romero Frizzi surveyed a sampling of archival documents from the colonial jurisdiction of Teposcolula for phonetic data (1984). For translations of colonial Mixtec documents, see Terraciano and Sousa 1992; Jansen 1994, 1998; and Terraciano 1998. I translated ten documents in the appendix of my dissertation (1994).

36. I have benefited from several modern studies of Mixtec, especially Pike 1944; Dyk 1951, 1959; Pike and Pike 1982; Josserand 1983; and Bradley and Hollenbach 1988–92. For references to linguistic studies of Mixtecan languages, see chapter 3.

37. The archive that contains the best collection of Ñudzahui-language sources is the Archivo Judicial de Teposcolula (AJT), located in Oaxaca City. When I began my research in 1988, the documents were piled in partially cataloged bundles and boxes. I spent several years looking through all of them. A preliminary review and commentary of Mixtec-language archival documentation, primarily from the AJT, appear in Josserand, Jansen, and Romero Frizzi 1984. In appendix 3, the authors include a partial catalog of documentation (pp. 186–220). Unfortunately, the archive has been reorganized, recataloged, and relocated three times since that publication. The Huntington Library owns two copies of a doctrinal text written in Mixtec, dated 1567 and 1568. The Byron McAfee Collection of the UCLA Library contains microfilm copies of native-language church-sponsored materials. In addition, the Mormon Family History Library contains microfilm copies of colonial native-language baptismal registers from the Mixteca Alta.

38. I have acquired a reading proficiency in Mixtec by way of several complementary and ongoing endeavors. First, I utilize the instructional materials of the period, compiled under the auspices of the Dominicans, who mastered the language and developed a fairly standard orthography with the indispensable assistance of their indigenous aides. The *Vocabulario* and *Arte*, compiled by fray Francisco de Alvarado and fray Antonio de los Reyes, respectively, have been essential. Second, I have used

the colonial records themselves. Some of the documents contain partial or full translations, which are useful for identifying vocabulary and checking attested forms against entries in the *Vocabulario* and elsewhere. These translations are not wholly reliable, since they often omit parts that are considered irrelevant to the particular legal case that elicited the native-language document. In general, contemporaneous translations are more reliable than those done long after the original document was written. Third, I have compiled a working dictionary of attested forms from these various types of sources. Fourth, I have used studies of contemporary Mixtecan languages, and I have consulted native speakers. Finally, I have used two brief studies of colonial Mixtec published in the 1960s (Alvarado, and Arana Osnaya and Swadesh 1965).

39. It is surprising that any records from the early colonial period have survived in local archives. Most communities do not have archives. Stacks of papers are simply bundled with twine and stored wherever possible. Usually, they are exposed to the elements. In most cases, there are precious few resources to store the materials and little knowledge of archival restoration. Cases that went before the Audiencia in Mexico City and are now stored in the Archivo General de la Nación in Mexico City are the best-preserved early colonial records. Likewise, the Archivo General de las Indias in Seville has some very early cases. In contrast, most communities do not possess many records that were written before the eighteenth century.

40. I have not located books of testaments, such as the collection from Culhuacan. See Cline and León-Portilla 1984.

41. Unfortunately, the remains of other alcaldías mayores do not contain comparable records. The Teposcolula collection is extraordinary in this regard.

42. Spivak's discussion of the role of language in the "construction of the subaltern" by colonial and postcolonial elites sheds light on how Spaniards imposed categories of thought and modes of organization on indigenous peoples. These categories stand out in Spanish-language sources when they are read against native-language writings. See Spivak 1988.

43. Likewise, nineteenth-century historians such as J. A. Gay seldom cited the sources of their information and tended to reiterate and synthesize earlier histories.

44. In comparison, the lengthy and unpublished commentary of the Peruvian author don Felipe Guaman Poma de Ayala is without parallel in his adaptation of a Spanish genre and his use of the Castilian language for the purpose of criticizing the colonial system. I refer to the "good government" section of *El primer nueva coronica y buen gobierno*, completed in 1615. See Guaman Poma [1615]1980.

CHAPTER 2 — WRITING

1. In simple terms, writing may be defined as "a system of human inter-communication by means of conventional marks" (Gelb 1963, 12). In the Ñudzahui case, the marks were made with ink or paint on paper, cloth, and deer hide surfaces. To be more precise, one could define writing as ideas that are graphically represented and organized within a structured format and that correspond to the spoken language of the writer. The Ñudzahui system included conventional forms and symbols that communicated specific information without relying on a corresponding language element. On writing, see Diringer 1962; Goody 1986 and 1987.

2. This precedent helps explain the proliferation of alphabetic writing in Mesoamerica, especially in central Mexico, Oaxaca, and Yucatan, in comparison with the dearth of alphabetic writing among native peoples in other regions of the Americas, including the Andes. In general, Spanish introductions worked best when they corresponded to a close preconquest equivalent. Autonomous Mesoamerican writing traditions developed in the Mixteca, the Maya region, the Zapoteca, Nahua central Mexico, and the Tlaxcala-Puebla area. See Marcus 1992 and Goody 1997, 18–23.

3. On the Mixtec codices, see the following representative works: Caso 1949, 1950, 1960, 1977–79; Smith 1973a,b; Furst 1978; Nicholson 1978; Troike 1978, 1982; Jansen 1982, 1992, 1994, 1997; Pohl 1984, 1994a,b, 1996; King 1988, 1990; Monaghan 1990a,c; Smith and Parmenter 1991; Anders, Jansen, and Pérez Jiménez 1992a,b; Byland and Pohl 1994; and Boone 2000. Kubler has pointed out that the term used for these painted manuscripts is a misnomer, that "codex" usually refers to an illuminated European manuscript consisting of bound pages (1962, 100, 336).

4. Another format divides the "page" into two registers, with one genealogy appearing in the lower and another in the upper, such as *Becker II* and *Sánchez Solís*. The *Codex Bodley* employs a third format by dividing the screen into four sections. See Smith 1973a, 217, on the various formats employed by extant Mixtec codices. Another format begins a vertical line of succession at the bottom and works its way upward toward the present, as demonstrated by the map of Teozacualco, the geneal-

ogy of Tecomastlahuaca, and the *Codex Tulane*. The *Selden* employs a winding pattern from the bottom to the top. See Caso 1949; Smith 1973a, 10; and Smith and Parmenter 1991.

5. The *Codex Nuttall* (*Zouche-Nuttall*), for example, is 11.23 meters in length, consisting of 47 pages with images on a total of 86 pages (obverse and reverse combined). The rectangular pages measure 25.5 centimeters in width and 18.8 centimeters in height. The *Codex Vindobonensis Mexicanus I* (also called *Vienna*) is 13.5 meters long and consists of 52 folds, each measuring between 25 and 27 centimeters in length and 21.5 and 22.5 centimeters in height (Furst 1978, 2). The *Codex Bodley* is about 6.6 meters long and 25 centimeters wide. A characteristic feature of Ñudzahui codices is the style of depiction, whereby all figures are drawn in color encased by a thin black outline; colors include varying shades of red, blue, yellow, green, purple, brown, black, gray, and the white of the stucco surface. See Smith 1973a, 9–19, for a summary and illustration of the viewing techniques.

6. For a discussion of these techniques in central Mexico and Oaxaca, see Robertson 1959; Caso 1965; Dibble 1971; Benson 1973; Nicholson 1973; Smith 1973a; Galarza 1979; Lockhart 1992; Marcus 1992; and Gruzinski 1993.

7. See Caso 1965, 948–61, and Caso 1977–79, 2:27–29, 34. See also Smith 1973a, 47–49, and Jansen 1982, 65–67, for geographical terminology and the use of conventional signs related to the language. Gelb defined "visual morphemes" as "forms which convey the same meaning only in writing" (1963, 15). The depiction of footprints to indicate movement and direction is an example of a "sublinguistic ideograph." Ñudzahui place signs are often called "logograms," pictorial representations of a place-name in which the pictorial units prompt or suggest one or more words. An example of a visual morpheme or tone pun is the place glyph for Coixtlahuaca, called "Yodzocoo" in Ñudzahui. Because *yodzo* means "plain" or "feather," depending on tone, and *coo* can be translated as "snake," the conventional depiction for Yodzocoo in many codices consists of feathers and a snake, or a feathered serpent. Toponymic hieroglyphs (place signs) follow the Ñudzahui practice of giving names to the diverse features of the landscape and generally consist of two elements: a natural or cultural feature and a specifying element, such as a color, animal, plant, structure, or other object (Smith 1973a, 36–54). Place-names bear calendrical dates related to their founding, much like the calendrical birth names of personages (Jansen 1992, 24).

8. Jansen 1982, 81–84; King 1994; Byland and Pohl 1994, 8–11.

9. See Mitchell 1986, 1994; Boone and Mignolo 1994.

10. In the early period of research Ñudzahui writing was considered "essentially pictorial" (Covarrubias 1957, 300). Smith called it a "limited system" that utilized logograms for names, places, and persons, and analogues for some simple verbs; she concluded that "many of the narrative conventions utilized in the Mixtec histories are pictorial, without reference to language" (1973a, 175). At the same time, Smith was well aware of the potential for interpreting the writing through an understanding of the language, as she demonstrated in her own work. It is true that Ñudzahui writing did not use columns of hieroglyphs or any form of syllabic writing that was not accompanied by pictorial elements. Recent contributions by Maarten Jansen, Mark King, John Monaghan, Aurora Pérez, and John Pohl have placed greater emphasis on the language component. See the bibliography for multiple works by these authors.

11. Seler 1904; Burgoa 1989b, 210. For this reason, there was a tendency to paint on only one side of the screenfolds; most, if not all, of the two-sided examples appear to have been added later (Jansen 1982, 38). The fresco remnants of the Church Group at Mitla, in the Valley of Oaxaca, served the same function.

12. On song and the relation between music and writing, see Jansen 1982, 46; King 1990, 141–51; Monaghan 1990a, 134–39; León-Portilla 1969. King compares the narrative structure of the codices to a musical score with guides that direct the singer/performer in ways suggestive of sheet music. Monaghan uses the example of medieval oversized hymn books to describe how codices were displayed to be viewed simultaneously by multiple performers.

13. Aurora Pérez Jiménez and Maarten Jansen have interpreted passages from the *Codex Vindobonensis* and the *Codex Nuttall* in terms of the oral tradition and language of Chalcatongo. See Anders, Jansen, and Pérez Jiménez 1992a,b. John Monaghan has demonstrated the relevance of myth and "verbal performance" from Santiago Nuyoo and Santiago Ixtayutla for the study of the *Codex Vienna*. See Monaghan 1990a, 133–39, and 1990c, 559–69.

14. See Vaillant 1944; Nicholson 1966, 1978; Pohl 1994b; and Byland and Pohl 1994, 10–11. The *Codex Borgia* group (including the *Borgia, Cospi, Fejérváry-Mayer, Laud, Magliabechiano*), which is attributed to the Tlaxcala-Puebla area, exemplifies the many shared conventions. The Mixteca-Puebla style

has also been applied to other media, such as ceramics and jewelry. Donald Robertson (1959) proposed the term "international style" in recognition of its widespread use in postclassic Mesoamerica.

15. On the influences of writing on religion, see Goody 1986, 172–73.

16. John Pohl attributes the development and widespread use of this style to the existence of "alliance corridors" that united Tlaxcala, Puebla, and Oaxaca in the postclassic period. See Pohl 1994a, 153–56. Unlike Maya and Zapotec hieroglyphic writing, which relied on a single linguistic base, Mixtec writing employed many visual elements to communicate with a multilingual audience.

17. Repetition and the presence of cognate scenes and events in different codices from the same region expand the possibilities of interpretation. For example, both the *Codex Nuttall* and the *Codex Colombino Becker* present extended narratives concerning the rise to power of a ruler of Tilantongo named 8-Deer.

18. Burgoa 1989a, 1:210.

19. Ibid. I interpret Burgoa's use of "una tercia" as one-third of a *vara*, which is about twenty-eight centimeters. Elsewhere, he described them as: "algunas historias pintadas, en papel de cortezas de árboles, y pieles curtidas, de que hacían unas tiras muy largas de una tercia de ancho, y en ellas pinturas de sus caracteres, con que los indios doctos en estas leyendas les explicaban sus linajes, y descendencias, con los trofeos de sus hazañas, y victorias." Burgoa 1989a, 1:288.

20. Burgoa 1989a, 1:396.

21. In the *Vocabulario* of 1593, there are five equivalents given for "contar historias": *yondaanuutnuhundi,* "to write about lineage"; *yonandasininondi yaa tnuhu,* "to recount the speech (song) of lineage"; *yonacanindi tnuhu,* "to order lineage"; *yonatnayndi tnuhu,* "to arrange lineage"; *yonacahuindi tnuhu,* "to read or speak of lineage" (Alvarado, 52v). A more general term for "history" is "relacion hazer de alguna pasada," listed as *yondacu nahindi* and *yondacu cachindi,* "to relate (repeat, imitate, recreate) the past" [I interpret *nahi* as *naha*] and "to relate what is said." Alvarado, f. 181.

22. Pohl 1994a.

23. Glass and Robertson 1975. Caso observed that the reverse side of the *Codex Selden* had vestiges of earlier painting in some of the cracks and that erasure seemed intentional; at least two painters seemed responsible for the *Codex Vienna* (Caso 1950; Smith 1973a; Furst 1978; Jansen 1982).

24. See Burgoa 1989a, 1:275–77, 289. He considered many of the authors to have been "astronomers who possessed a great knowledge of the stars and other astronomical phenomena, and calculated the ancient calendar."

25. On the function of sacred knowledge as a means of social control, see Goody 1987, 129–38, 161–66.

26. Smith 1973a. The first four codices listed predate the conquest. Seven of the eight manuscripts are currently owned by museums or libraries in Europe.

27. For example, the latest date of the *Codex Selden* is 1556, and at least the last two pages of the manuscript treat rulers who were alive at the time of the conquest or were born in the early colonial period. Incidentally, there is no indication of the Spanish conquest on these pages. See Smith 1983d, 266.

28. Smith's discussion of the Lienzos of Zacatepec is the best description of their stylistic characteristics. See Smith 1973a, 89–121; see also King 1988, 41–56.

29. Included in this group are lienzos from Coixtlahuaca, Aztatla, Tequixtepec, Ihuitlan, Tlapiltepec, Nativitas, Tepelmeme, Tulancingo, Tamasulapa, and Ixcatlan. I thank Carlos Rincón-Mautner for a list of Coixtlahuaca Basin lienzos and a summary of the languages glossed on those manuscripts. See Glass and Robertson 1975, 244, for a preliminary list of sixteenth-century lienzos from the Mixteca with Nahuatl and Ñudzahui glosses; see also Parmenter 1982; Rincón-Mautner 1994, 1999. John Pohl has shown how many of the lienzos in this group combine representations of migration sagas, typical of the Tolteca-Chichimeca tradition, with strings of genealogical descent lines associated with the Mixtec-Zapotec tradition (Pohl 1994a, 147–53).

30. On native maps of New Spain, see Cline 1972a,b; Gruzinski 1987, 1993, 40–46; Leibsohn 1994, 161–87, and 1996, 264–81; Mignolo 1996, 296–313; Mundy 1996; and Boone 2000.

31. The term comes from colonial discourse analysis, especially from Homi Bhabha (1984, 1992). For a dicussion of cultural hybridity, see Young 1995; on hybrid images, see the essays in Farago 1996. On representation, see Goody 1997.

32. Speaking in reference to the Historia Tolteca-Chichimeca and colonial maps in general, Leibsohn observed that glyphs do not visually distinguish, at least for the uninformed, between landscape features and communities (1996, 270). In the Mixteca, during the colonial period, all prominent

features of the landscape, cultivable fields, and sociopolitical entities were named and thus could be represented in writing by a place-name glyph.

33. Gruzinski has described native cartography as "a representation of space that distributed place names in a regular, geometric manner, a bit like our underground [subway] maps" (1993, 40).

34. Acuña 1984, 2:17, from the 1577 "Instrucción y memoria de las relaciones. . . ."

35. Mundy 1996.

36. As discussed in chapters 4 and 9, all Nahuatl-Spanish place-names had Ñudzahui counterparts. Native speakers in the colonial period rarely used the introduced Nahuatl names. *Chiyo* is "altar" or "patrimonial place," and *canu* is "large."

37. See the relación of Teozacualco in Acuña 1984, 2:131–47. See Caso 1949 for the first ground-breaking article on this map. For a discussion of places represented on the map, see Anders, Jansen, and Pérez Jiménez 1992a, 23–57. See also Pohl 1994a, 139–40, Mundy 1996, 113–17, and Boone 2000, 30–36. For information on population and settlements in the colonial jurisdiction of Teoza-cualco, see Gerhard 1972, 275–77. No book-size illustration can do justice to this multicolored mas-terpiece. The map contains seventeen glosses in Spanish. The original is owned by the Benson Library at the University of Texas, Austin.

38. The cross on the summit of the hill apparently marks a sacred space; it is the only cross on the map that is not mounted on a church.

39. In this sociopolitical scheme, several estancias, or outlying settlements, were made subject (*sujeto*) to one cabecera, or "head town," in a given region. As discussed in chapter 4, the hierarchy did not necessarily correspond to a preconquest arrangement. The extension of the arc at the top right represents the changed colonial status of a community called Elotepec, which initially fell under Teozacualco's jurisdiction but by 1580 was considered part of the Nochixtlan jurisdiction. See Ger-hard 1972, 199–203, 275–77; Anders, Jansen, and Pérez Jiménez 1992a, 51; Mundy 1996, 113–14.

40. Anders, Jansen, and Pérez Jiménez 1992a, 39–53; see also Mundy 1996, 116–17.

41. According to Caso, the lineage is traced as far back as the Christian year A.D. 972. However, Emily Rabin's recent unpublished work has revised Caso's earlier estimates for the chronology of events in the Mixtec codices. See Caso 1949; Smith 1973a, 10, 308; and Anders, Jansen, and Pérez Jiménez 1992a, 55–57.

42. In the codices, the rulers were identified by calendrical names, based on their dates of birth, as well as personal names, allowing Caso to construct a chronology of the dynasties.

43. I use Emily Rabin's chronology here, rather than Caso's, following Jansen's analysis (1992a).

44. This meeting of warriors seems to represent Teozacualco's recognition of Tilantongo's author-ity. A delegation of seven men make the same offerings to two powerful rulers in the distant past, including the legendary 8-Deer's son. In all three cases, the delegation of men are drawn but not painted, unlike all other figures on the map. Yet all the men in these delegations bear calendrical names, unlike the rulers. Each time, the ruler who receives the delegation is preceded by a torch, and the ceremony is followed by the establishment of a yuhuitayu alliance. Each time a woman from Tilan-tongo wears a serpent headdress (or any headdress, for that matter) in the map, she is involved in the creation of a new alliance with Teozacualco.

45. Spores 1967, 225–27; Caso 1977, 152–53.

46. See Anders, Jansen, and Pérez Jiménez 1992a, 60–61.

47. Acuña 1984, 2:228.

48. See Miller 1991 and Mignolo 1995, 226–313, for the way that space and time are concep-tualized in native maps.

49. See Mundy 1996, 116–17, for a discussion of how the circular motif conforms to native con-ceptions of bounded space. Smith suggested that the circular shape was based on the European *mappa mundi* (1973a, 166). It is possible that a European map served as a conceptual model for the map from Teozacualco. The map resembles the circular style of medieval world maps, such as the Ebstorf and Hereford maps, or the map of Tenochtitlan attributed to Cortés. The attention to landscape indi-cates a definite familiarity with European paintings. In this case, the church and palace of Teozacualco occupy the center of the map but not the center of the circle. The placement of the sun in the east, at the top of the map, may represent another convergence of European and Mesoamerican conceptions (Anders, Jansen, and Pérez Jiménez 1992a, 39–40), although it seems based more on the European tradition. The *Vocabulario* defined "mapa" with one entry, as "an image of the entire world" [taniño nee cutu ñuu ñayevui], suggesting the introduction of a new concept. Alvarado, f. 146.

50. See Acuña 1984, 2:147–51. The original size of the map is 86 by 92 centimeters, utilizing twelve sheets of paper.

51. This community is not to be confused with another one by the same name in the Teposcolula jurisdiction, called San Pedro Mártir Yucunama, which was also known to outsiders as Amoltepec in this period.

52. The relación states that Amoltepec was a sujeto of Teozacualco, about fourteen leagues southwest, with only about fifty *vecinos* (married male residents) in 1580. Gerhard suggests that it maintained separate status until it was nearly devastated by population loss in the 1550s (1972, 275–77). In reality, Yucunama had closer relations with coastal Tututepec than it did with Teozacualco. This fact was recognized by the artist-writers of Teozacualco, who did not represent Yucunama on their map. This is a good example of how cabecera-sujeto designations often departed from preconquest sociopolitical arrangements, a topic of discussion in chapter 4.

53. Acuña 1984, 2:215–22. The map is 56 by 41 centimeters in size. For studies of the map of Texupa, see Bailey 1972, 452–72; Leibsohn 1996, 275–76; and Mundy 1996, 79–80, 101.

54. See Bailey 1972, 465–68, and Borah and Cook 1979, 409–32, for a study of Texupa in the sixteenth century. Bailey cites Ross Parmenter's finding that an unfinished church was built on the remains of this old temple before the site was abandoned. Thus the older structure would not have existed when the map was painted in 1579; nonetheless, the artist chose to represent the sacred site with a conventional image. On the slope of the hill behind, near the river, is another small temple structure that probably represents another settlement associated with Ñundaa. Settlements were located in the foothills to allow the full cultivation of the fertile flood plain and for defensive purposes. On the Spanish policy of *congregación*, see chapter 4 of this work.

55. Preconquest-style codices depicted a conquered place as a glyph (usually a hill) pierced with arrows. The painting depicts a multitude of human heads inside an enclosure at the summit of the hill. This place was clearly conquered, but it is not the place glyph for Texupa. The Nahuatl name of the hill given in the relación was Miahualtepec, which is written with the logograph of a maize tassle sprouting from its top: from *miyahuatl* (maize tassle and flower), *tepetl* (hill), and the locative suffix *c*.

56. See Bailey 1972, 454–55, and Borah and Cook 1979, 422, for a comparison of the painting's traza with a plan of the town's modern layout.

57. Goody defines *ambivalence* in terms of "being in two minds" about something or "looking both ways," a result of the absence of certain cultural activities or forms of representation in a society. The tensions between east and west reflect an ambivalent view of colonial Texupa from the perspective of the new map mode of representation. See Goody 1997, 22–31. See Bhabha 1984 on the concept of ambivalence in colonial discourse theory.

58. Acuña 1984, 2:362–72 bis. The map measures 41 by 30 centimeters. As in the other maps, east is located at the top.

59. See Pohl and Stiver 1997, 215–18, for a discussion of glyphs associated with the market and plaza.

60. The map's market and gridwork motif bring to mind Frederic Jameson's discussion, in his article titled "Cognitive Mapping," of the "space of classic capitalism," which he describes as "a logic of the grid, a reorganization of some older sacred and heterogeneous space into geometrical and Cartesian homogoneity, a space of infinite equivalence and extension" (Jameson 1988, 349). On the dominating aspect of the grid and congregation in native maps of New Spain, see Leibsohn 1996, 276.

61. AGN-T, 59:2. See Spores 1964; Smith 1973a, 170. The two legal-sized pages were reversed when they were sewn into the volume. The drawing is accompanied by a Ñudzahui-language testament, written in 1571.

62. An observation first made by Smith 1973a, 168–71. See also Gruzinski 1987, 1993, 45–46.

63. For example, Kubler 1948 and Robertson 1975 interpreted the "mixed" style in terms of a spectrum, ranging from preconquest native to European. More recently, scholars such as Boone, Leibsohn, Mundy, and Dean have viewed hybrid forms as neither European nor native but a new creation.

64. The "Testerian" manuscript might be considered an example of a Spanish model based on native conventions, intended to communicate with a native audience. This is a rare exception to the rule, however. Moreover, these instructional devices were short-lived experiments.

65. Bhabha 1984, 125–33; Farago 1996, 12.

66. Jiménez Moreno and Mateos Higuera 1940, 55. See also *Códice de Yanhuitlan* 1994 for a facsimile of the codex, including a related fragment from the AGN first published in Berlin 1947. The pages are 31 centimeters in length and 22.5 centimeters in width.

67. For example, the depiction of culturally specific objects such as the *petlatl icpalli*, the central Mexican-style reed mat with a high back, which does not appear in preconquest codices from the Mix-

teca, seems to indicate the possibility that Nahuas were involved in training native artists in Yanhuitlan. Moreover, the clothes worn by some of the women in the codex (in particular, the *huipilli*, or long unfitted blouse, with a rectangle in front) resemble central Mexican dress. Finally, some place-name glyphs may be based on the Nahuatl language. In the *Codex Sierra*, a contemporaneous manuscript discussed below and in chapter 9, Nahuas played a role in training church aides and in painting.

68. *Codex Yanhuitlan*, plate XVI. The rosary is a symbol of the Dominican order and its devotion to the Virgin of the Rosary, a point made by Maarten Jansen (personal correspondence). Sepúlveda y Herrera suggested that it refers to a specific friar named Tomás del Rosario (*Códice de Yanhuitlan* 1994, 127–28).

69. On the symbolism of gesture, see Bremmer and Roodenburg 1991.

70. Their gestures are reminiscent of an illustration on f. 491 of Guaman Poma de Ayala's *El primer nueva coronica y buen gobierno,* in which two Spanish officials discuss money matters.

71. The chair is arranged in a contradictory profile and frontal position. See Berlin 1947, 64–66, on this image and Jiménez Moreno and Mateos Higuera 1940, 69–76, on Caso's chronology for the Mixtec calendar. The date is 5-Flint.

72. Berlin 1947, 65.

73. *Codex Yanhuitlan*, plate VIII; Berlin 1947, 64–66, plate E.

74. *Codex Yanhuitlan*, plate XIX. The artist made no attempt to replicate alphabetic script on the blank paper. The glyph in the bottom left corner is a place sign for Teposcolula; its function or meaning is unclear. Perhaps the event took place in Teposcolula, or the priest was from this nearby community. It is possible that the artist intended to place the two men behind the priest and thus rendered them smaller in order to lend dimension to the composition. But the left foot of the man who is closest to the friar overlaps the chair leg, as if he were in front of the chair. The implication of this latter possibility is that the artist seems to have represented the friar as an important man who commanded the attention of his native acquaintances, who literally look up to him as an authority figure.

75. Jiménez Moreno and Mateos Higuera 1940, 63, plate XIV.

76. *Codex Yanhuitlan*, plates I and IX. The torn battle scene page apparently depicts the siege of Tenochtitlan, as some of the indigenous warriors fight from canoes.

77. See Goody 1997, 239, on the distinction between surface meaning and deep structure; in brief, the former signifies the meaning of the act to the actor, and the latter refers to the underlying functional meanings of acts that may be hidden from the actor. This distinction could also be made in terms of "emic" and "etic," or "thin" versus "thick" description.

78. The fragment was furnished by don Agustín Pimentel y Guzmán y Alvarado in a case against the community of Sola in 1707 over disputed lands (AGN-V, 272:3, ff. 452–508). On the fragments and their relation to the *Codex Yanhuitlan*, see Berlin 1947, 53–58.

79. The Ñudzahui complex of terminology surrounding the act and instruments of writing corresponds to Nahuatl terminology, as delineated in Lockhart 1992, 326–27. I believe this is a pattern based on a common Mesoamerican experience, more than Nahuatl influence on the response of other indigenous groups to the introduction of Spanish elements. See also Jansen 1982; King 1988.

80. Alvarado, f. 168v: "pluma para escrevir" is the entry. Perhaps the finely carved bones in the Tomb 7 treasure from Monte Albán are representations of these writing instruments. See Caso 1965, 956–57. For the use of bones by Nahua artists, see the exaggerated bone instruments in the illustrations of book 9, chapter 21, of the *Florentine Codex*.

81. Alvarado, f. 46.

82. *Tutu* also means "book." Another term recorded for this ancient paper is *dzoo ñee ñuhu*, "manta of skin from the earth," similar to the term for *lienzo*, which is merely *dzoo cuisi*, "white manta."

83. Alvarado, f. 161.

84. In the verb *yotaandi, taa* is the verb stem, *yo* is the indicative marker, and *-ndi* is the first-person subject pronoun. Most verbs in the *Vocabulario* appear in this form.

85. Similarly, "pintada cosa" is defined as *sanicuvui tacu*, "that which was painted," and *sayondaa tacu*, "that to which paint was applied." Alvarado, f. 168. In his grammar of 1593, Antonio de los Reyes defines *tay huisi* as "maestro y para saber el oficio que tiene," a term that could be applied to all trades. Reyes, pp. 8, 10–11.

86. Alvarado, f. 102. Reyes, p. 27, refers to the passive form of *yotaandi* as *yondaandi*. The term *yositondaandi tutu* could also mean "to see paper clearly," if *ndaa* is interpreted as an adverb referring

to truthfulness and intelligibility (like the Nahuatl *melahuac*). The use of the verb "to count" may be linked to the year count, as in histories or annals.

87. On continuity in the basic function of writing among Nahuas, see Lockhart 1992, 331, 364–68.

88. Smith 1973a, 163.

89. These are the codices *Colombino, Sánchez-Solís, Becker I,* and the Hamburg section of *Becker II.* See Smith 1973a, 9–19; Smith 1973b, 47–49; Smith and Parmenter 1991, 92.

90. Smith 1963, 276–88; Smith 1966; Smith 1973a, 170.

91. See Smith 1973b, 50–58. The *Codex Muro* has several different layers of pictorial and alphabetic text and exhibits stylistic changes with each successive generation depicted, much like the tribute record of Tecomastlahuaca.

92. Lockhart 1992, 582 n. 48.

93. León 1933. See also Gruzinski 1993, 26–28, 46.

94. *Codex Sierra,* pp. 2, 5, 8, 11, 15, 19, 24, 29, 35, 47, 48, 49, 54, 55, 56, 60, 61. In the last year of the codex the author uses *año* as well as *xihuitl* and *cuiya* when referring to the date. The last two references to the year exclude *cuiya* from the formula and substitute *año*. The use of *cuiya* with Ñudzahui calendrical signs and numbers was never recognized or translated in León's edition of the codex, which he ultimately attributed to the Popoloca culture group. In fact, León himself did not translate the Nahuatl text, so it is possible that he was not aware of these omissions from the translation. Bárbro Dahlgren noted the references to the Mixtec calendar, however. See Dahlgren 1954, 284–87.

95. See Smith 1973a, 23, for a list of studies concerning this vocabulary. See also the correlation of the vocabulary with the thirteen numerals taken from the Lienzo of Nativitas on pp. 24–26 and n. 24 about the origins of the Ñudzahui calendrical system. For a discussion of the honorific register, see chapter 3 in this work on language; for a summary of the calendrical lexicon, see the section on naming patterns in chapter 5.

96. *Codex Sierra,* pp. 19 and 25, 42, 49, 55, 61. Sometimes the hand is holding a tiny head: pp. 49, 55, 61. Actually, the arm and hand together, from the elbow down, are called daha.

97. Ibid., pp. 14, 35, 43 for church; tlacuylo on p. 13.

98. See ibid., festival of Saints Peter and Paul on pp. 26, 60; Saint Peter on p. 16; feasts on pp. 22, 38; spirit on pp. 25, 31, 38; Santiago on p. 39.

99. Ibid., pp. 18, 28, 48, 62.

100. Ibid., p. 41.

101. See ibid., goats on p. 8; painting p. 17; *varas* p. 29; *fanegas* pp. 40–41; absence of pictorial script pp. 45–46, 56.

102. Examples abound of interpreters who relied on Nahuatl in southern Mexico. In the 1560s, for example, Francisco Martín knew Nahuatl and Castilian, while Antonio Hernández "yndio ynterprete" spoke Nahuatl and Ñudzahui (AJT-C, 1:16 for Achiutla, 1564; 1:19 for Tlaxiaco, 1565). By 1585, people such as Pedro Sánchez knew Spanish, Nahuatl, and Ñudzahui in Tlaxiaco (AJT-C, 1:90, ff. 23, 24). In the Valley of Oaxaca (Cuilapa), the Spaniard Martín de Rojas knew Castilian and Nahuatl, and Alonso García, "yndio natural" from Teozapotlan, knew Nahuatl and Ñudzahui in 1558 (AGN-T, 243:4, f. 15). Likewise, in the Chocho-speaking region, in 1595, Tomás Gerónimo knew Chocho and Nahuatl, and Gabriel García spoke Nahuatl and Castilian in multilingual Coixtlahuaca (AJT-CR, 1:132). In 1596, Agustín Francisco de Arista and Domingo Esteban were responsible for Chocho, Ñudzahui, Nahuatl, and Spanish (AJT-CR, 1:52).

103. AJT-C, 1:12. One document from Yolomecatl referred to the translator as a *yya caha dzaha,* "lord who speaks languages" (AJT-C, 6:568).

104. Fray Bernardino de Santa María of Teposcolula, fray Alonso del Espíritu Santo of Teposcolula, and Fray Francisco Marín of Coixtlahuaca served as interpreters. AGN-INQ, 37:10.

105. AJT-C, 1:91, f. 15. The community of Tamasulapa contained both Ñudzahui and Chocho populations in the sixteenth century.

106. Ibid., 7:654. The document was copied verbatim in 1649.

107. *Codex Sierra,* pp. 15, 28, 48, 50, 57. Sometimes the translator is identified by a preconquest speech scroll issuing forth from his mouth. In Texupa, officials had to deal with four languages: Nahuatl, Ñudzahui, Chocho, and Castilian.

108. AGI-ESC, 162c, f. 516.

109. AJT-CR, 3:352.

110. AGN-V, 272:3.

111. AJT-C, 6:638. Another Chocho document is contained in the folder, but it is damaged and practically illegible. It may have been written as early as the 1580s, to judge by the smudged date. Another example involving Chocho comes from Tecçistepec, a sujeto of Coixtlahuaca, where Chocho-speaking officials apprehended a horse thief in 1601 and sent a Nahuatl-language letter to officials in Coixtlahuaca. The news was then relayed to officials in Teposcolula by a letter written in the Ñudzahui language. Either Chocho was not written on a regular basis in this area, or the authors thought that Nahuatl would be better understood in Coixtlahuaca and Teposcolula. AJT-CR, 1:151. A Ñudzahui barrio of Coixtlahuaca continued to use Ñudzahui-to-Nahuatl and Nahuatl-to-Spanish interpreters in 1596, indicating a continued reliance on Nahuatl as a lingua franca in this multilingual region. AJT-CR, 1:52.

112. AGN-T, 232:1. The originals are not contained in the expediente, but they are translated.

113. The Biblioteca Nacional de Antropología y Historia owns at least one hundred testaments written in Chocho, contained in a leather book titled "Libro de testamentos de Teposcolula" (CA. 777). They are cataloged as Mixtec testaments, but only the third one is written in Ñudzahui, from a place called Santiago Tiñuhu. They are not from Teposcolula. The collection runs from the beginning to the end of the seventeenth century. Additional Chocho sources exist in the Archivo Judicial de Teposcolula, as well as in community archives in the Coixtlahuaca Basin. Bas van Doesburg is currently working with a large corpus of Chocho-language documents.

114. AGN-C, 2303:3, ff. 5–11v. Bartolomé de Santiago was the appointed interpreter who knew Nahuatl, Ñudzahui, and Spanish. It is possible that Tonalá had a Nahuatl-speaking minority.

115. AJT-CR, 1:40.

116. AJT-C, 2:213; AGN-T, 3328:2, ff. 44–56. A very interesting Nahuatl-language document is the testament of Martín Cortés, a long-distance trader from Santiago Istepec, which is near Yanhuitlan. While traveling to Guatemala in 1594, Martín fell ill in a place called Huey Xiquipilan and was forced to record his last will and testament in Nahuatl. I have not been able to locate this community. AJT-C, 1:161.

117. For example, Antonio Nieto, a prominent translator in the Mixteca during this period, was fluent in Ñudzahui and Spanish.

118. AGN-T, 400:1, f. 56. A good example of a Spanish-language document written by a Ñudzahui escribano in the sixteenth century comes from Yanhuitlan. In 1584, cabildo officials wrote a petition in simple Spanish, misspelling Yanhuitlan as "yaguitlana," omitting a nasal consonant and attaching a vowel to the end of the unfamiliar word, as there are no consonant-final names in Ñudzahui. *Yanhuitlan* is derived from the Nahuatl place-name; it was called Yodzocahi in the Ñudzahui language. Typical errors include "ynterrocatoro" for *interrogatorio;* "gon" for *con;* "nustro" for *nuestro;* "pesentados" for *presentados;* and the phrase "quere azer povança" for *quiere hazer probanza.* Of course, Spanish escribanos were prone to take liberties, especially in this period, but these versions are particularly notable because they conform to Mixtec pronunciation, as discussed in chapter 3. AGI-ESC, 162c, ff. 82, 188.

119. Samples of writing in several Mesoamerican indigenous languages have survived the test of time. The existence of church-sponsored imprints in an indigenous language is usually a general indication that writings were produced by native speakers in the colonial period. In Oaxaca, in addition to Mixtec and Nahuatl, I have come across samples of Zapotec, Chocho, Mixe, and Cuicatec, though the last two are very rare. An example of Cuicatec writing is displayed in a map from Tutepetongo, a nearby Cuicatec-speaking area in the northeastern corner of the Teposcolula colonial jurisdiction. The map, enclosed in a land dispute of 1756, is drawn in partially preconquest style and consists of Cuicatec place-names and borders with Spanish glosses. AGEO-AM, 32. For an analysis of the Cuicatec map, see van Doesburg 1996.

120. The Huntington Library in San Marino, California, owns copies of both the 1567 and 1568 works. The 1567 copy contains an additional 5 folios of handwritten addenda in the back. The 1568 copy is slightly larger at 201 folios. The Biblioteca Francisco de Burgoa in Oaxaca City also owns a copy of the 1568 *Doctrina.* The production of church-sponsored texts written in the Ñudzahui language continued through the colonial period, albeit on a modest scale compared with similar Nahuatl-language materials (see Sell 1993). Later extant church-sponsored works include a manuscript dated 1584 titled "Catecismo de la doctrina Christiana en la lengua Mixteca," which appears to be a version of the Dominican theologian fray Gerónimo Taix's work of 1576. Another catechism was translated into Ñudzahui by fray Antonio González, curate of Nochixtlan; it was published in Puebla in 1719

and again in 1755 and appears to be a Ñudzahui version or summary of the catechism of fray Gerónimo de Ripalda (a Nahuatl version was printed in 1758). The Byron McAfee Collection of the UCLA Research Library owns microfilm copies of both the 1584 and 1719 works. I thank Barry Sell for bringing these to my attention. Other works of the eighteenth century include an *Arte, Vocabulario y Manual* of Guerrero Mixtec by fray Miguel de Villavicencio in 1755 and unpublished works by fray Antonio de Morales and fray Francisco Ortiz (Jiménez Moreno 1962, 99–103; Smith 1973a, 23; Josserand 1983, 154). A catechism was published in Puebla in 1837 under the title *Manual en lengua mixteca de ambos dialectos bajo y montañez*. In addition, according to Burgoa, a certain fray Martín compuesto "in the manner of comedies, representations of the mysteries or miracles of the Holy Rosary" that were performed in the churches, both in Spanish and in Mixtec, much to the delight of the locals. But Burgoa was not so amused, claiming that this theater was so full of doctrinal errors and corruptions, and some of the *cantores* had taken such liberties, that he was forced to find and burn the papers (Burgoa 1989b, 417–18).

121. AGN-T, 59:2.

122. In many ways the alcalde mayor, with his legal advisers and staff, personally administered justice at this level. But native individuals could appeal provincial decisions or move the entire proceedings to either the Juzgado de Indios (General Indian Court) or the Audiencia (viceregal council and judicial body of New Spain) in Mexico City. Both courts exercised overlapping and supersessory jurisdiction over provincial cases involving indigenous people, who could appeal a case in one court and then, if necessary, approach the other. Even when the case was tried at the provincial level, the alcalde mayor consulted a lawyer from the Audiencia or Juzgado, who reviewed the complete dossier on the crime and ratified, overturned, or issued a sentence. In fact, provincial courts in criminal proceedings could not impose sentences of death, mutilation, or slavery on assailants without consulting Audiencia officials. Sentences passed by trained agents of the court might be influenced by several factors: early Spanish American precedent and law; the concerns of the colony or province; and the Castilian code of law promulgated in 1567, which applied to the Indies as well as Spain (drawing on a medieval Castilian compilation called the Siete Partidas). In theory, local native custom also merited consideration as long as it did not conflict directly with natural law or Christian precepts. In reality, although it allowed a range of checks and appeals, the legal system was vulnerable to corruption and prejudice. See Borah 1983, 43, 223.

123. This summary is drawn from Taylor 1979; Borah 1983; Spores 1984; and my own work with civil and criminal records.

124. Testament writing benefited the church considerably. Some Ñudzahui-language testaments are accompanied by indulgences. In Teposcolula, for example, Pedro de la Cruz and his wife purchased two indulgences for two silver reals apiece. AJT-C, 9:772.

125. An observation that Lockhart has made for the Nahuas (Lockhart 1992, 367–72). That the earliest testaments are not accompanied by any pictorial element, however, seems to contradict the theory that the testament fulfilled a preconquest writing function. If so, we might expect overlapping alphabetic and pictorial portions in this genre, as with annals, for example. But was there an indigenous precedent of recording individual landholdings in writing? Even land transactions did not usually attempt any pictorial representation. All maps and lienzos normally display place-name glyphs that mark the boundaries of the community, not individual holdings. But there are frequent references in both Ñudzahui- and Spanish-language documentation to the possession of land papers (especially testaments) as well as paintings (lienzos and mapas) by nobles, in reference to their estates, discussed below.

126. On the use of testaments as evidence in European courts, see Goody 1986, 149–54.

127. For example, the Lienzo of Nativitas, the genealogy of Tecomastlahuaca, and the *Codex Selden*.

128. AGN-I, 6.2:176, f. 41.

129. For a discussion of testament writing among the Nahuas, see Cline and León-Portilla 1984; Cline 1986; Lockhart 1992. Lockhart noted that the last indigenous will and testament "remained residually a speech to a surrounding circle" (1992, 368–69).

130. See Molina [1571] 1977, ff. 58v–60, and Lockhart 1992, 471.

131. AGN-T, 24:6, f. 4v.

132. Sahagún 1950–82, bk. 6, chap. 7, p. 34. The original text is as follows: Ca quil in iehoantin mixteca: yn oc ipan intlateutoquiliz, in iquac ie ceme miquiznequi: quinotza in tlapouhqui in nonotzqui, ixpan muchi quitoa, muchi ixpan quitlalia, in tlein oax, in tlein oquichiuh in itlapilchioal, in inequal, in inequavitec: in at ichtec, in at itla quitecuili, muchi quitoa: atle quitlatia, atle quinaia.

Auh in tlapouhqui, in manoço ticitl: quinaoatia in cocuxqui in tetlaxtlaviliz, in quitecuepiliz in teaxca in tetlatqui.

133. AJT-C, 7:654.

134. AJT-CR, 1:35.

135. AJT-C, 2:215. When some communities claimed that they could not understand the mandamiento, the alcalde mayor sent a bilingual Spaniard to explain it. Many did not want to acknowledge the burdensome demand, and at least one cacique openly opposed it.

136. Ibid., 3:366.

137. AGN-T, 637:1, ff. 66–73.

138. AJT-C, 4:482. Some of the documentation was subsequently translated by an interpreter whose command of Mixtec was much better than his ability to write Spanish. For example, he wrote "ndeclaramos legua misteca" for "declaramos en la lengua misteca," typically omitting and inserting the nasal consonant at will and leaving out prepositions and articles.

139. Ibid., 4:482.

140. The case from 1681 is discussed in relation to land tenure in chapter 7. These examples are analogous to the 1746 case from Amecameca analyzed by Karttunen and Lockhart (1978), where civil proceedings were carried out in the absence of Spaniards, completely in Nahuatl.

141. AJT-CR, 5:581. See Terraciano 1998 for a transcription, translation, and analysis of this document.

142. AGN-T, 57:2. Nahuatl-language examples of personal letters can be found in Anderson, Berdan, and Lockhart 1976, 198–209.

143. AGN-T, 637:1, f. 68.

144. AJT-C, 4:405.

145. Ibid., 6:568.

146. For Topiltepec (1707), see ibid., 6:578; for San Bartolomé Tiyacu (1701), see AJT-CR, 6:675; for Yanhuitlan (1677), see AJT-CR, 6:644.

147. For example, the Lienzo of Xicayan and the *Codex Colombino-Becker* contain glosses. To date, archival Ñudzahui-language documentation has not been found for this expansive coastal region. First of all, the climate is not conducive to the long-term preservation of paper; second, disease decimated the population of the area during the colonial period.

148. Burgoa 1989a, 1: 349–50, 379, and Josserand, Jansen, and Romero Frizzi 1984, 180. Unfortunately, none of these works is known to have survived.

149. A manuscript dated 1584 in the Biblioteca de la Sociedad Mexicana de Geografía y Estadística is titled "Catecismo de la doctrina Christiana en la lengua Mixteca" but appears to be a version of the Dominican theologian fray Gerónimo Taix's work of 1576 on various aspects of Dominican history, *cofradías,* and the Virgin of Rosario. The manuscript was clearly written by a Mixtec. The Byron McAfee Collection of the UCLA Research Library owns a microfilm copy of the 1584 work. For a translation of excerpts of the Taix manuscript, see Jansen 1998.

150. Cited in Pastor 1987, 329–30.

151. AJT-C, 2:263, ff. 3–4.

152. AGN-T, 400:1; Spores 1967, 242.

153. AJT-C, 12:1029. The word *nani* means "named." He distinguished between the Ñudzahui *tutu* ("paper," also used as "book") and the Spanish *libro.*

154. AJT-CR, 1:150. His possessions included little more than a pair of pants, a *manta* (cloak), a *sombrero* (hat), a collection of feathers, one metate (grinding stone), and a chest with a lock.

155. Ibid., 5:508. This is a very curious native-language document that, unfortunately, is water-damaged and barely legible. Some aspects of the case are clear, however. Read aloud by the *pregonero* (town crier) in the church patio, the decree threatened to punish all those who did not produce their testaments. The reason for demanding that all testaments be brought forward to the "casa de la comunidad" is never made explicit, but it probably involved taxation. The decree also singled out and named fifty-four unmarried adults who may have evaded community service (*tniño*) and taxation by not marrying, and it encouraged them to marry at once. The order to marry appears to be a drastic moral or fiscal measure. Apparently, the Spanish alcalde mayor was not involved in this action; after a public outcry in response to these demands, he intervened to halt the order and jailed several cabildo members who were involved in drafting the decree.

156. AGN-T, 637:1, ff. 74–79.

157. AJT-C, 6:578.

158. AJT-CR, 5:594.

159. AGN-T, 571:1, ff. 75–77.

160. Ibid., 245:2, ff. 77–79.

161. AJT-C, 1:80.

162. For a discussion of Nahua literacy in colonial Cuernavaca, see Haskett 1991a, 132–43. Haskett found that literacy was rather rare among members of the cabildo and that their signatures were easily forged.

163. I have found one case of a father who tutored his children: in 1626, don Agustín Maldonado, a noble of Tamasulapa, taught his two sons how to read and write. AJT-CR, 3:357.

164. AJT-C, 10:866 (in the year 1738); ibid., 10:873, f. 9 (in the year 1750).

165. Ibid., 4:512. For example, doña Lucía de Orozco y Cortés, cacica of Teposcolula and widow of don Francisco Pímentel y Guzmán, signed her name clearly to a document in the year 1693.

166. Ibid., 1:102. Of course, this fact does not prove that none of the women could write. The absence of women's signatures in the legal record may simply reflect Spanish attitudes toward the public role of women, a topic discussed in chapter 6.

167. There is little evidence of any Nahua or Maya women who wrote in colonial times. See Karttunen, 1982, 415. The only known depiction of a woman writing in the codices comes from the Nahua cultural area. The *Codex Telleriano-Remensis* depicts the scribe of the *tlatoani* Huitzilihuitl, who may have also been his wife. See Quiñones Keber 1995, 63, 213.

168. AGN-T, 24:6, f. 13v. Smith presents similar evidence of a bias against indigenous pictorial writing, quoting one Spanish official who argued that a native *mapa* was worth nothing because it had been painted to suit one's desire and because it was not written in letters. Ibid., 1182:3-bis, f. 13, quoted in Smith 1973b, 57–58.

169. This opinion was perhaps best expressed by Juan Ginés de Sepúlveda, who wrote in 1548 that indigenous peoples of the Americas did "not even know the letters, nor [did] they preserve any monument of their history, except for an obscure and vague reminiscence of some things which [were] consigned to certain paintings." (Ginés de Sepúlveda 1941, 105). On European attitudes toward nonalphabetic writing systems, see Mignolo 1995, xi, 29–67, 128.

170. AJT-C, 6:578. See Boone 2000, 245–49, for a discussion of how Mixtecs and Nahuas continued to use pictorial writings in the colonial period.

171. AGN-T, 308:1. Sinastla was a sujeto of Yanhuitlan. The scaled-down hill glyph is similar to the one in the map of Cuquila (Smith 1973a, 309, from AGN-T, 876:1, f. 122).

172. AJT-C, 4:467, Yanhuitlan 1642 [*sic*]. There is no date on this document, and it appears misplaced in an expediente that refers neither to the family tree nor to the individuals depicted in the sketch. The handwriting seems to belong to a period earlier than 1642.

173. For example, the map of Xoxocotlan is dated 1771. Smith 1973a, 170, 202–10.

174. For a more detailed discussion of the título primordial genre, see Lockhart 1982, 1992; Wood 1984, 1991; Borah 1991; Terraciano and Sousa 1992; Gruzinski 1993, 98–145; and Restall 1998.

175. AGN-T, 236:6. This Ñudzahui title is also accompanied by a lengthy Nahuatl-language title from San Martín Mexicapan, a Nahua satellite community in the Valley of Oaxaca. See Terraciano and Sousa 1992 for a translation of both titles.

176. AGN-T, 236:6, ff. 10–11.

177. Glass and Robertson declined to include this "crude" pictorial in their catalog of Native Middle American Manuscripts because they considered it to be "too removed from the native tradition for inclusion in the census" (1975, 75 n. 42). Smith reproduced the map in her work on Mixtec pictorial writing but agreed that there were few vestiges of preconquest native iconography. She analyzed the place glyphs along its boundaries and noted its relation to the 1771 map of Xoxocotlan. See Smith 1973a, 202–10, fig. 164 on p. 340; for map of Xoxocotlan, see figs. 162–63 on pp. 338–39.

178. See Haskett 1996 for a discussion of the symbolism of coats of arms in Nahua primordial titles.

179. See Haskett 1991a, 143–45, for a discussion of ladino natives in Cuernavaca.

180. AGN-T, 400:1; AJT-C, 1:90, ff. 9–10. In these cases, all lands and place-names were still listed in Mixtec.

181. Ñudzahui place-names are still prevalent in the testament. AJT-C, 10:847.

182. Ibid., 16:1303. The document is obviously written by a Ñudzahui speaker in rudimentary Spanish. Singular and plural are constantly confused, as in the phrase: "dios padre, dios hijos, dios espiritu son tres persona." There are also some notable grammatical mistakes.

183. Ibid., 10:838. The other related documentation is dated 1634, 1648, 1656, 1665, and 1687.

184. Five well-written testaments are included in this case from Santa Catarina Adequez (dated 1776, 1798, 1784, 1789, 1800). Four are written on behalf of women. The Spanish in the testament of María López (1784) reveals that it was written by a Ñudzahui speaker, as does the judgment in the proceedings of the case, considering the use of words such as "mungeres" for *mujer,* "totnasa" for Tomasa, "loniete" for *poniente,* "tiquiclato" for *tequitlato,* and "quanreta," "quarreta," and "quanrenta" for *quarenta.* Ibid., 18:1516, f. 51.

185. Ibid., 4:458. In the year 1673.

186. Ibid., 13:1109. Again, the Ñudzahui text is full of loan vocabulary.

187. Ibid., 12:1029.

188. Ibid., 6:586. In the year 1708.

189. AGN-T, 400:1, f. 382.

190. For example, the testament of Nicolasa María of Chilapa (written in 1764) is very brief, contains no religious formula, and is little more than a simple listing of lands and goods. Appropriately, the case includes two posterior testaments (1776, 1787) of relatives written in Spanish. AJT-C, 18:1564.

191. For example, San Miguel Ñuucani (Tisaa?) produced a neat and elaborate testament in 1769 with very few loanwords and an extensive vocabulary. Members of the cabildo were present and signed their names. Ibid., 13:1052.

192. Ibid., 18:1578.

CHAPTER 3 — LANGUAGE

1. Today, Mixtecan languages are spoken by about a quarter of a million people in the states of Oaxaca, Guerrero, and Puebla. Thousands more Mixtec speakers have migrated to the north, to places such as Mexico City, Sinaloa, the Borderlands, the United States, and Canada.

2. For studies of colonial Mixtec, see Jiménez Moreno 1962; Arana Osnaya and Swadesh 1965; Jansen 1982, 1985; and Josserand, Jansen, and Romero Frizzi 1984.

3. Since the 1940s, studies have in general focused on tone, regional and subregional variation, and proto-Mixtec reconstruction. One example of a grammatical sketch of a modern Mixtec language is Dyk and Stoudt 1965. Bradley 1970 includes phonological, morphological, and grammatical descriptions and texts, as well as lexical material from linguistic sketches from coastal Jicaltepec in Oaxaca. One example of a morphological and grammatical treatment is a study of Peñoles Mixtec in Daly 1973. Modern vocabularies include Dyk 1951 for San Miguel el Grande; Pensinger 1974 for Jamiltepec; and Alexander 1980 for Atlatlahuca. A compilation of modern texts from San Miguel el Grande is Dyk 1959. Relevant articles on Mixtec languages include Pike 1944, 1945a,b, 1946, 1947a,b,c, 1949, 1975; Merrifield and Stoudt 1967; Pensinger 1974; Kuiper and Merrifield 1975; and Pike and Pike 1982. Bradley and Hollenbach have organized and edited four volumes of syntactic sketches (1988–92). They report the syntactic structure from dialect areas defined by Josserand's study of proto-Mixtec (1983) and also record the grammatical similarities and differences among them. In this series, volume 1 includes studies of Jamiltepec (coastal Oaxaca) by Audrey F. Johnson; Ocotepec (southwestern Alta near Tlaxiaco) by Ruth Mary Alexander; and Silacayoapan (western Baja toward Guerrero) by Jäna K. Shields. Volume 2 includes work on Ayutla (extreme southern Baja) by Robert A. Hills and Coatzospan (northern Alta toward Cuicatlan) by Priscilla C. Small. Volume 3 covers Alacatlatzala (Guerrero) by Carol F. Zylstra; Diuxi-Tilantongo (eastern Alta) by Albertha Kuiper and Joy Oram; and a preliminary sketch of Concepción Pápalo Cuicatec by David P. Bradley. Volume 4 includes Yosondúa (southern Alta toward the coast) by Edwin R. Farris and Copala Trique by Barbara E. Hollenbach.

4. Nebrija 1926, 3–6.

5. Mullen 1975, 49.

6. Ibid., 37.

7. AGI-AMG, 880, unnumbered, first expediente in legajo. The friars suggested that their secular counterparts failed to match their multilingual talents. By 1770, they purported to know eighteen native languages among members of their order. AGI-AMG, 2586.

8. Ricard [1933] 1966, 47, from Dávila Padilla [1596] 1955, 79.

9. Reyes, p. 12, for example, in his discussion of the inalienable, abstract possessor and his general use of terms such as "mazehuales," "tequio," "tianguez," and other Nahuatl-based words. Many of these words had already trickled into the Spanish language as loanwords in central Mexico, such as "maçegual" (commoner) and "petate" (reed mat).

10. AGI-AMG, 880.

11. AJT-C, 11:923. He owned a "Vocabulario Misteco" and a "Vocabulario Manual Mexicano."

12. AGN-INQ, 37:7, ff. 184v–185; Jiménez Moreno 1962, 20.

13. Burgoa 1989b, 35.

14. Burgoa 1989a and Dávila Padilla [1596] 1955, summarized in Jiménez Moreno 1962, 20–24.

15. Jiménez Moreno 1962, 23; Burgoa 1989a, 1:305. The compliment was paid by fray Juan de Córdova, who had studied the Zapotec language.

16. Dávila Padilla extolled his unique and successful method of using paintings and pictures to preach (1955, 255–57). Actually, Lucero simply adopted a form of communication that resembled the native use of pictorial writing, a technique also employed in the "Testerian" manuscripts of central Mexico.

17. Fray Domingo de Santa María supposedly wrote a book titled *Doctrina Cristiana y epístolas y evangelio en lengua mixteca,* published around 1543 (Dávila Padilla 1955, 172, 653), and another titled *Arte en lengua mixteca* (Jiménez Moreno 1962, 25); apparently neither book has survived. See also García Icazbalceta 1954, 210–16, 482, and Burgoa 1989a, 1:283–84.

18. AGN-INQ, v. 37, exp. 9, f. 271.

19. Jiménez Moreno 1962, 26; Burgoa 1989a, 1:305–6.

20. Burgoa 1989a, 1:344–47; Jiménez Moreno 1962, 33.

21. By 1564, he served as vicar of Teposcolula; see AJT-C, 1:14, for example.

22. Reyes's *Arte* is divided into twenty-eight brief chapters, with a prologue on origin legends, geography, and dialectal variation. The *Arte* is modeled on a Latin grammar. The first chapter acknowledges that despite all its "imperfections," the language contains the eight parts of speech common to Latin and "other perfect languages." Four chapters follow on nouns, adjectives, pronouns, and conventions of speech based on age, gender, and kinship. Chapters 5–20 treat various aspects of verbal constructions, including transitive, intransitive, and passive verbs, simple and compound verbs, verb-incorporated prepositions and adverbs, verb conjugations, and irregular verbs. The following chapters cover the remaining parts of speech: relationals, adverbs and modifiers, interjections, and conjunctions. The final four chapters focus on specific topics: a brief vocabulary of reverential expressions used when addressing lords; a vocabulary of body parts; kinship terminology; and a list of Nahuatl place-names in the Mixteca and other parts of New Spain, with their Ñudzahui equivalents. There are two manuscript versions of the *Arte* that are said to contain information that was left out of the reprinted Charancey facsimile published in Paris in 1889. The Vanderbilt University Publications in Anthropology series reproduced the latter in 1976. See Jiménez Moreno 1962, 36, and García Icazbalceta 1954, 409.

23. AGN-T, v. 59, exp. 2. The Tlazultepec variant corresponded closely with that of Achiutla.

24. Reyes, pp. v, viii.

25. AJT-C, 1:117; ibid., 1:169. Reyes was vicar of Teposcolula again in 1591 (ibid., 1:118).

26. In the prologue, he paid tribute to the "very serious and energetic religious who in their most beneficial study of the Mixtec language had written about it in many notebooks." In praise of his own Dominican order, he extolled the "holy conquerors of souls" who were sent to the Mixteca and who represented the "only order in that province." He remarked that some of the elders who were still alive at the time of publication had helped him with the vocabulary (Alvarado, prologue, f. vii).

27. In Nahuatl, grammar books were produced as early as 1547 (by Olmos) and 1571 (by Molina, revised in 1576). The problem of translating entries from Mixtec into Spanish was not addressed until Jiménez Moreno compiled a vocabulary based on Reyes's *Arte* in 1962, included in the reprint of Alvarado's *Vocabulario.* Jiménez Moreno's reprint of the *Vocabulario* was the most significant recent contribution to the study of the colonial language. Three years later, Arana Osnaya and Swadesh compiled a brief but important dictionary of "Ancient Mixtec," featuring a Mixtec-to-Spanish section of about two thousand words, using Reyes, Alvarado, and word lists from modern language studies. See Jiménez Moreno 1962, 109–53; Arana Osnaya and Swadesh 1965.

28. Alvarado, prologue.

29. Ibid., f. 155.

30. Burgoa 1989a, 1:282.

31. Reyes, pp. iii–viii.

32. Josserand 1983, 469; Reyes, p. 8.

33. Reyes, pp. ii–iii.

34. Ibid., p. v. Reyes called the other "lenguas" of the region "hijas de la de Teposcolula."

35. Ibid., pp. v, viii.

36. Josserand, Jansen, and Romero Frizzi 1984, 149; Josserand 1983.

37. Burgoa 1989a, 1:277–78. It is unclear whether Burgoa was qualified to make such a statement, however.

38. Acuña 1984, 1:178. He wrote, "There are differences in speech, but it is all one language."

39. To some extent, the *Arte* and *Vocabulario* were designed to promote homogenization and standardization. See Mignolo 1995, 46, for an interpretation of the politics of language studies by friars in the colonial period.

40. For example, in a twelve-line letter written in 1699 to the alcalde mayor in Tlaxiaco, from the community of Santiago Ñuyoo, the writer spelled *house* four different ways: "huey," "huay," "huahi," and "huehi." AJT-CR, 6:666.

41. Dahlgren 1954, 40–42.

42. Jiménez Moreno 1962, 51–52.

43. Josserand, Jansen, and Romero Frizzi 1984, 127–28, 155.

44. Josserand 1983, 470.

45. Ibid., 459–61.

46. See Karttunen and Lockhart 1976, 6, for Nahuatl comparison.

47. Josserand 1983, 106–19.

48. Ibid., 462–63.

49. Ibid., 463. It is currently unknown how far the Baja/Huaxuapan variant extended in the colonial period, because of the paucity of extant records from this region outside the immediate Huaxuapan area.

50. See Moser 1977 on Nuiñe material culture.

51. Josserand 1983, 112, 463.

52. Ibid., 149–50. The boundaries between Mixtec languages drawn from linguistic data reflect differences between types of speech but not the precise nature of these boundaries to the speakers themselves. In other words, the testing of mutual intelligibility is subject to many variables.

53. According to Josserand, many of the modern phonological systems are superficially quite similar, with common phonemic inventories. But many significant differences are obscured by surface structural units that appear alike but have different patterns of morphophonemic alternation, reflecting their different historical developments (1983, 458).

54. Ibid., 180–81. Mixtec variants differ in their number of lexical tones. These tones are carried by the vowels of each syllable of a root, which is characteristically bisyllabic. In addition to the basic lexical tone of each word, there are rules for modifying tones when words are combined into phrases, called sandhi rules.

55. In comparison, there was a great deal of ambiguity in Nahuatl orthographies that did not distinguish between long and short vowels and did not record glottal stop. Carochi resolved some of these problems in the seventeenth century.

56. Alvarado, prologue.

57. Dávila Padilla 1955, 64.

58. Cited in Jiménez Moreno 1962, 28. He said: "Deprendió muy en breve la lengua de aquella nación, que es dificultosa de saberse por la gran equivocación de los vocablos, para cuya distinción es necesario usar de ordinario el sonido de la nariz y aspiración del aliento."

59. The use of *h* was also a Spanish convention for the rearticulation of vowels. Nahuatl also inconsistently used *h* for glottal stop, but the digraph *hu* indicated a labial glide, not a glottal stop. In Maya, the symbol represented phonetic [h].

60. For Nahuatl, Carochi did the opposite, placing a grave accent on vowels to indicate following glottal stops.

61. Reyes, p. 2.

62. Josserand 1983, 158. Ñudzahui speakers acknowledge this fact.

63. For example, one entry appears as: "abatirse el ave para hazer presa: yocóótneete; yocôô-cahite; yocôôcuidzote." Other entries reveal little regularity, such as "abaxar por descendir: yocôôndi; yonoondi." Alvarado, f. 2.

64. Reyes, p. 54.

65. Ibid., p. 2.

66. He said: en la pronunciación de la dz herimos blandamente en la d, y más rezio en la z. Ibid., p. 2.

67. Josserand 1983, 146. Recent evidence indicates that sixteenth-century [z] was not pronounced

as theta, however. For the changing phonetic value of [s] and [z] in Spain and Spanish America, see Parodi 1995, 73–82.

68. AJT-C, Anexo 1:50. The document is dated 1745.

69. AGN-INQ, 37:5, 7–11.

70. See Josserand 1983, 470, for the relative location of northeastern Alta, eastern Alta, and western Alta. Incidentally, the digraph *dz* was also introduced for Maya in the later colonial period for the glottal counterpart of *tz* (Karttunen 1985, vi).

71. Actually, this was simply [t] followed by a nasal vowel, but it is such a common syllable-initial occurrence that it seems as if it is an invented digraph.

72. Reyes, p. 3.

73. Josserand 1983, 121. In Nahuatl, *hu* indicated a labial glide, even though *h* was used for glottal stop.

74. AJT-C, 6:635; Ibid., 13:1060; AGN-T, v. 986, exp. 1. These examples, taken from Tamasulapa, Tlacosahuala, and Xaltepetongo, are discussed below in relation to the pronunciation of Spanish words.

75. Note that the phonetic value of Spanish *ll* changed in the course of the colonial period, approaching [y] by the eighteenth century. Originally, no Nudzahui equivalent corresponded to *ll*.

76. In Castilian, initial [i] was written as *y* in this period.

77. Previous studies have questioned whether the yya "lengua" of which Reyes spoke should be considered a separate language or merely a metaphorical vocabulary. Arana Osnaya called it a "language" that might be related to Popoloca, Zapotec, or Cuicatec. Maarten Jansen was among the first to observe that it should not be considered a separate language and that the reverential vocabulary consisted of "metaphors and elegant expressions rather than cognates of other languages." See Jansen 1982, 496 n. 34, and 1985, 8–11, and Arana Osnaya 1960, 217–30. See also King 1988, 106.

78. The first-person pronoun *ñadzaña*, sometimes shortened to *-ñadza* or *-dza* when attached to the verb stem, was substituted for *duhu* (*njuhu, yuhu,* depending on variant). The second-person *disi* or *ndisi* was substituted for *doho* and often preceded the verb stem; the suffix *-ni* was also used as a singular and plural second-person subject pronoun. The third-person *ya* or *to* was substituted for *ta* and *ña*. The particle *to* (from *toho*, "lord") was also used as a prefix to indicate nobility (Reyes, pp. 14–15; these conventions have also been attested in colonial documents). In some modern Mixtec languages, a form of *ñadzaña, ni,* and *ya* is still used. For example, for the use of *-dza* as a respectful way of speaking to another person, see the syntactic sketch of Diuxi Mixtec, near Tilantongo, by Kuiper and Oram 1991, 194, 278, 281.

79. Burgoa 1989a, 1:331.

80. Reyes, pp. 74–81. Earlier in the work, he wrote that the reverential speech was used "when commoners [*macehuales*] or lesser nobles [*principales comunes*] speak with the lord, or when commoners speak with nobles, and sometimes when those same lords speak with nobles, their inferiors, in order to honor them" (1976, 14).

81. AJT-C, 7:654.

82. Reyes, p. 77. The term is also employed for a knife, as well as a type of sharp reed; see the entry "iunco ancho y aspero" in Alvarado, f. 128. Just as the term *yuchi* (flint) was extended to mean "tooth," the *Florentine Codex* presents a Nahua riddle in which teeth are likened to flint knives: "What is it which grinds with flint knives, where a piece of leather lies, enclosed in flesh?" The answer is "our mouth." See Anderson and Dibble 1950–82, bk. 6, chap. 42, p. 238.

83. For example, "buscar por rastro" has seven corresponding entries followed by a reference to its metaphorical nature. Alvarado, f. 39.

84. See also Jansen 1982, 292–95.

85. Karttunen and Lockhart 1987; Anderson and Dibble 1950–82; for modern honorific Nahuatl speech, see Hill and Hill 1986. Of course, many other oral traditions practiced this type of epic style or "Homeric" language.

86. Molina [1571] 1977, f. 116 *cuitlapilli hatlapalli;* Karttunen and Lockhart 1987, 51–62.

87. See Karttunen 1985, 15, for some features shared by Nahuatl and Yucatec Maya.

88. For example, in Mixtec *ini,* "heart" or "insides," was often bound with a large class of verbs (such as *catni* and *ndiyo*) to express desire and emotional states in general.

89. Karttunen 1985, 16.

90. As in Nahuatl, Mixtec describes east as "the place where the sun comes out" (*sa yocanandicandij*) and west as "where the sun goes in" (*sa yocaindicandij*). See Alvarado, ff. 159, 171, for the

relevant terminology. In Ñudzahui, "west" could also be interpreted as "where the sun goes under," "exits," or "falls."

91. For a discussion of how dissimilar languages shared some characteristic areal features typical of Mesoamerica, see Karttunen 1985. Yucatec Maya did incorporate some Nahuatl vocabulary, but relatively little in comparison with Spanish loanwords.

92. I have detected only one example of a Nahuatl loanword in a Ñudzahui-language text that did not originate from a Spanish borrowing. In his testament of 1749, don Lorenzo Vásquez of Chilapilla referred to his child Venturina as "socoyota," derived from the Nahuatl *xocoyotl,* "youngest child." The translation simply repeated the word as if it were a first name. Whereas some loanwords entered into Mixtec speech through Spanish and are recognizable by the syllable-final vowel *e* (for example, *atole,* derived from the Nahuatl *atolli*), the loan noun "socoyota" seems to represent a Ñudzahui borrowing.

93. See Karttunen 1985, 4–14.

94. Ibid., 46. Formal texts, including speeches and doctrinas, tend to avoid the use of unnecessary loanwords.

95. Karttunen and Lockhart 1976; Lockhart 1992, 429–436.

96. Karttunen and Lockhart 1976, 49–51; Lockhart 1992, 262.

97. On peripheral Nahuatl, see Dakin 1981 and Lastra 1986a,b. For Nahuatl in colonial Oaxaca, see Terraciano and Sousa 1992, nn. 41, 42 on pp. 80–81.

98. Statistical frequency counts with a mass of documentation are not attempted in this work, nor is there sufficient space to present a list of loan vocabulary.

99. See Lockhart 1992, 429–36.

100. Ibid., 266 and n. 6.

101. Karttunen and Lockhart 1976, 16–26; 40–43.

102. Karttunen and Lockhart 1976, 42–43; Lockhart 1992, 265.

103. For example, in Nahuatl the early colonial "candle" was called *xicocuitlaocotl,* or "beeswax torch." Karttunen and Lockhart 1976, 41–42; Lockhart 1992, 265.

104. Dyk 1959, 227. The latest attestation of *ydzundiqui,* "horned deer," for oxen is 1752 (AJT-C, 17:1464).

105. Lockhart has shown how Nahuatl developed an extensive vocabulary referring to everything associated with iron and the horse, employed from its introduction and persisting in some cases to the end of the colonial period. See Lockhart 1992, 270–75; see also Karttunen and Lockhart 1976, 41.

106. See Lockhart 1992, 272–75.

107. The extended, surrounding complex gradually yielded to loans, but the basic term and certain derivations are still used today (Lockhart 1992, 275 and n. 27).

108. This usage has been attested in several archival documents. See Alexander 1980 for use of *caa* for "key" and "time"; see also Dyk 1959 for "bell," "metal," and "coins." For Nahuatl, "striking clock" involved the use of the word *tepoztli: tlapohualtepoztli,* "count iron" (Lockhart 1992, 274). In the Mixtec *Vocabulario,* "clock" ("relox") is also defined using the *caa* complex, as *caa cánda maa* and *caa cuhua.* The latter is literally "measuring iron," and the former is an interesting stage-one descriptive circumlocution: "iron which divides into many parts from the middle" (cross-listed in the entry "dividir algo en muchas partes"). See Alvarado, ff. 181, 182. In the *Vocabulario, tiempo* is simply *huico* (season), *quevui* (day), and *cuiya* (year), and there are no entries for "seconds" or "minutes." The equivalent of the "hour," listed as "ora" in the *Vocabulario,* refers to measuring the path of the sun: *cuhua ndicandij.*

109. Lockhart 1992, 274–75. *Tepoztli* means "firearm" in modern Nahuatl (Key and Key 1953, 221; Brewer and Brewer 1971, 225).

110. Mixtec also occasionally employed *quiti,* "animal," for horse, usually modified by *ydzu.*

111. Maya did apply "deer" to the cow but had borrowed *vaca* by the time of the Motul dictionary in the 1580s (Karttunen 1985, 52).

112. Lockhart 1992, 272 and nn. 15 and 16; "deer" was extended to "elephant" in Molina, similar to the way "deer" was extended to "oxen" in Ñudzahui.

113. Lockhart 1992, 270–71.

114. *Codex Sierra,* pp. 18–20, for example.

115. AJT-CR, 1:151.

116. Alvarado, f. 46v. See, for example, the use of the loanword in "suelta de caballo: yoho coho saha cavallo" (f. 192).

117. Lockhart 1992, 276–79. Likewise, "one from Castile" in Ñudzahui was *tay castilla,* so that the original loan noun was not altered; in Nahuatl, it was changed to *caxtiltecatl.* In their dictionary of

contemporary San Lucas Quiaviní Zapotec, Pamela Munro and Felipe Lopez have located more than two dozen words that include a form of *castilla*, pronounced as *x:tíílly*. See Munro and Lopez 1999, 364.

118. Karttunen 1985, 70–71.

119. AJT-C, 15:1232. Similarly, in English, "china" is used to describe the name of the ceramic ware most associated with its place of origin, naming the object after the place. In the case of cloth and other goods, a place-name does not guarantee that the product actually came from that place; rather, it indicates that the product was of a type associated with that place. British *cashmere* (via India) or *taffeta* could have been worked or finished in Seville or even Puebla. *Sinabafa* was a type of cloth primarily associated with Holland, but I have seen examples of "sinabafa china."

120. Alvarado, ff. 16, 45 *carnero*, 54 *cordero*, 135 *lana*.

121. See, for example, Alexander's study of Ocotepec (1988, 255). Pamela Munro informs me that Zapotec speakers from San Lucas Quiaviní use the same word for "wool," "cotton," and "sheep." See Munro and Lopez 1999, 378–79.

122. Karttunen and Lockhart 1976, 42; Lockhart 1992, 265–67.

123. Alvarado, f. 168v. This *caa* refers to the location of something, often equated with the Spanish verb *estar*, not *caa*, "metal."

124. Indeed, these examples are so much like the Nahuatl *itlacoa, tlatlacoani,* and *topile* that one wonders whether they were affected by Nahuatl conventions.

125. Fray Luís de Villalpando supposedly produced a Maya dictionary, grammar, and Christian *Doctrina* within a decade after the founding of Mérida in 1542, but none of these works has survived.

126. Karttunen and Lockhart 1976, 16–26; Lockhart 1992, 284–85.

127. Even in the postconquest period, the only attested Nahuatl loan (thus far) in Ñudzahui-language archival documentation is *atole*, yet this term appears to have been Hispanized already, considering the *e* suffix typical of Spanish borrowings from Nahuatl. The loan appeared in Santiago Yolomecatl, in 1705. AJT-C, 6:568. Josserand wrote that interdialectal loans occurred for numbers and several nouns (trade items such as salt and feathers). She also wrote that a few loans from Nahuatl are widespread but gave no specific examples (1983, 467). Nahuatl also shows little borrowing from other indigenous languages, but this does not come as a surprise given the dominant nature of Nahuatl in central Mexico.

128. The language of sixteenth-century church-sponsored imprints reveals many similarities between early colonial Ñudzahui and Nahuatl. The language of the texts is consistent with documentation generated by indigenous notaries, though there is generally less loan vocabulary in the formal texts. The typical loanword is a noun, and there is a small inventory of frequently used items related to predictable vocabulary domains. There was a conscious and deliberate effort to use whatever speech conventions already existed, such as polite rhetoric and reverential expressions. The religious orders generally adopted a conservative approach to new terms; they encouraged the extension or careful reinvesting of well-known terminology with new meaning. Loanwords and potentially confusing terms were avoided. All terminology had to be readily intelligible, universal, and clear. Some of the very same processes were at work in Nahuatl- and Ñudzahui-speaking areas. For an overview of language contained in church-sponsored native-language texts from New Spain, especially those in Nahuatl, see Sell 1993. See chapter 8 of this work for a discussion of Ñudzahui-language Christian terminology.

129. Lockhart 1992, 292.

130. AJT-CR, 4:439; ibid., 3:366. As late as 1769, "yuqh chiyo sancta yglesia" was used for the church (*yuq* is "temple" and *chiyo* is "altar" or "patrimonial"), combining two archaic words with the Spanish loanword *yglesia*. In Alvarado, "yuq" is listed as a response to "yglesia" (f. 129v). Pamela Munro and Felipe Lopez (1999) have documented many examples of semantic equivalents or combined native words and loanwords in modern San Lucas Quiaviní Zapotec. The examples are so old that the etymologies are not always apparent to native speakers.

131. Lockhart 1992, 292–93. One of the most important of these loanword complexes was, of course, the horse, *cavallo*, written as "cahuallo," "cavalu," and so on.

132. Ibid., 299–300, 304–6.

133. The earliest example of the use of a Spanish infinitive with *quidza* is dated 1622, when a *fiscal* (church steward) from Teposcolula wrote *niquidza presendar,* "he presented." This example may be considered somewhat unrepresentative of the general pattern, since it comes from an ecclesiastical dispensation written by a highly trained noble in the presence of friars, inside the church of Teposcolula. AGN-T, 637:1.

134. Most loanwords were actually written according to Spanish orthographic norms, even in the early period, a point made by Karttunen and Lockhart (1976, 7) and confirmed by my own work with Ñudzahui texts. But the appearance of substitutions and other phenomena reflects indigenous speech; this is especially apparent among those writers who seemed unfamiliar with the standard Spanish orthography of the time and thus seemed to write words based on what they heard more than what they had previously seen in writing.

135. For a more detailed study of postconquest Nahuatl, see Karttunen and Lockhart 1976, 1–15, and for Nahuatl and Maya, see Karttunen 1985, 79–107. See also Restall 1997, 293–303, on colonial Yucatec Maya.

136. AJT-C, 4:467; Yanhuitlan, 1681. The document includes the signatures of "Bartasar gome" (Baltasar Gómez) and "Bartaçar lope" (Baltasar López); AJT-C, 10:838.

137. It has been attested as early as 1740: AJT-C, 18: 1564.

138. AJT-C, 2:179; AJT-CR, 1:25; AJT-C, 2:231; AJT-C, 5:506; AJT-C, 8:705; AJT-C, 2:188.

139. AJT-C, 2:215; ibid., 4:400.

140. Ibid., 6:635; AGN-T, 986:1. These examples are discussed above in relation to Ñudzahui orthographic conventions involving *hu* and *vu*.

141. AJT-C, 2:231; ibid., 5:506; ibid., 13:1109.

142. In modern Diuxi-Tilantongo, Juan is pronounced "nshú'á," and Chico is "nchikú." See Kuiper and Oram 1991.

143. Karttunen and Lockhart 1976, 8–14. Karttunen has suggested that the phonological process shared by Nahuatl and Maya of syllable-final segment weakening may be a main contributing factor to the phenomena of nasal omission and intrusion. Syllable-final consonants in loanwords are invariably omitted in Ñudzahui. See Karttunen 1985, 23, 105–7.

144. Dyk 1959, 227–48; Karttunen 1985, 83.

145. The basic Ñudzahui phonological phrase is oriented: tense / verb / object pronoun / subject pronoun. Nahuatl is essentially oriented the opposite way: subject pronoun / object pronoun / verb / tense.

146. Lockhart 1992, 307–8. The use of *chihua* plus the infinitive convention was retained in the far south of the Nahua culture area (see Karttunen and Lockhart 1976, 32; Lockhart 1992, 568 n. 122).

147. The Nahuatl verb *tequipanoa*, "to do work (for someone)," is the equivalent of the Ñudzahui *quidzatniño*. The Nahuatl term consists of the noun *tequitl* (labor) with the relational *pan* (on) and the *-oa* verbalizing suffix. The Nahua inclusion of *pan* complicates the comparison; however, many Ñudzahui verbs also incorporate the relational word *nuu*, "on."

148. Pamela Munro has observed similar types of what she calls "complex verb constructions" in contemporary San Lucas Quiaviní Zapotec, especially with the verb *ruhny*, "to do." These constructions consist of a native verb plus a second uninflected element; the second element may be a Spanish loanword such as an infinitive. In most cases, the second element, especially when an infinitive, cannot be identified as an object. See Munro and Lopez 1999, 18, 30, 286–301.

149. See Alvarado, f. 164.

150. This is analagous to *tlaçocamati* in Nahuatl.

151. Reyes commented that "*huaha* does little more than help the verb that it modifies" (p. 10). I think *huaha* is comparable to the use of the Nahuatl *huel*, "well," which often serves as an intensifier without contributing any distinct lexical meaning of its own (Karttunen 1983, 86). *Huel* may come from *hueli*, "to be able to."

152. The question whether these borrowed infinitives are syntactically nouns or objects needs to be examined further. They follow verbs in the same position in which nouns as objects normally occur, but it is unclear at this point whether they are treated as accusatives. Hence, I tend to use the more neutral term, *complement*, in reference to these borrowed verbs. The incorporation of borrowed infinitives in this manner is related to the nature of Ñudzahui "complex verb" constructions described above.

153. AJT-C, 9:792, f. 7.

154. AGN-T, 657:2, f. 47. This document was from Tonalá, in the Mixteca Baja.

155. Nduayaco, 1753. AJT-C, 17:1467.

156. Yucatec Maya adopted a similar strategy of verb borrowing using the infinitive form, though few verbs were borrowed. See Karttunen 1985, 59. By the late eighteenth century, Maya used a verbalizing suffix *t* with an infinitive of the verb, which came closer to the Nahua strategy of applying the *-oa* suffix (James Lockhart, personal communication).

157. In Nahuatl, there are some 40 recorded loan verbs and 720 loan nouns over the colonial period; many were technical, with an emphasis on the legal discourse of notarial documents. See Lockhart 1992, 305.

158. Ibid., 309.

159. AJT-CR, 4:439 (1635); ibid., 5:549 (1681); ibid., 5:550 (1681); ibid., 5:552 (1681); ibid., 5:594 (1686).

160. Prepositions do not appear in Yucatec Maya texts until the middle of the nineteenth century (Karttunen 1985, 65, 76).

161. Karttunen and Lockhart 1976, 25–26; Karttunen 1985, 64; Lockhart 1992, 303–4 and n. 108. The possible exception to the rule of indigenous people as the originators of borrowing is ecclesiastical terminology, in which case introduction seems to have been sponsored by friars in the earlier period of contact. Religious loanwords were surprisingly small because a finite number of religious concepts were covered very early, and friars attempted to be as conservative as possible in the introduction of new and possibly obfuscating terms.

162. In Tlaxiaco, in 1573, "ytu a la huerta ñuhu" appears in the testament of don Felipe de Saavedra three times (AJT-C, 7:654). In Coixtlahuaca, in 1596, it was written as "ytu a la huerta" (AJT-CR, 1:85, f. 13). In Teposcolula, in 1682, it appears as "a la buerta" (AJT-C, 7:689, f. 32). In Texupa, in 1752, it was simply "huerta" (AJT-C, 17:1464). Another occurrence has been noted from Tonalá, in 1643, when the writer referred to a "sitio yuhuiyta nana la guerta," or a "piece of land named yuhuiyta that is in front of the orchard" (AGN-T, 657:2, f. 47v). This example uses the Spanish article *la*, without the preposition. The preceding native preposition, *nana*, just happens to end in *a*, however.

163. Some nouns caused confusion because they resembled Ñudzahui possessed forms in their original. For example, in Yanhuitlan, the first-person possessive pronoun consisted of a *co-* prefix (unlike in other dialect areas) and a suffix written as *-nju*. A Spanish loanword such as *compadre* (or *comadre*), beginning with *co*, was often reduced to "copadrenju " in testaments, leading some interpreters to gloss *compadre* as *padre* in the translation. This scenario resembles the confusion caused by the ubiquitous *in* article of Nahuatl, which was often presumed to be present in any Spanish word containing similar initial sound segments.

164. On the other hand, Ñudzahui *kw-* is usually followed by [a] and [i], and not [e].

165. Santa Catarina Adequez, 1798 (AJT-C, 18:1513, ff. 2–3); Adequez, 1800 (ibid., 18:1513, f. 4–4v.). The orthography of these two documents is very inconsistent, but the meaning is apparent after much repetition. The term has also been attested in Chilapa, 1721 (ibid., 18:1564); Yanhuitlan, 1750 (ibid., 12:1029); Chilapa, 1750 (ibid., 10:873); Amatlan, 1775 (ibid., 14:1180).

166. For Ocotepec, see Alexander 1988, 261. For Yodzondua, see Farriss 1992, 132. For Diuxi-Tilantongo, see Kuiper and Oram 1991, 221, 223, 282. For Chalcatongo, personal correspondence with Aurora Pérez Jiménez. For Silacayoapan, personal correspondence with Priscilla Small and Joanne North.

167. Karttunen 1985, 66.

168. Yanhuitlan, 1681 (AJT-C, 4: 467); Topiltepec, 1738 (ibid., 9:792).

169. Chilapilla, 1749 (ibid., 20:1682).

170. Ibid., 11:921; 7:686; 17:1464; 15:1232.

171. Ibid., 15:1232, in the year 1754.

172. Lockhart 1992, 311; Karttunen reports the appearance of such "replacement vocabulary" by the early eighteenth century (Karttunen 1985, 62).

173. Yanhuitlan, 1686 (AJT-C, 5:515).

174. Yanhuitlan, 1740–58 (ibid., 12:1029). The phrase *yocuviquentacha* can be analyzed as follows: *yo-*, indicative; *cuvi* or *cuhui*, "have"; *quenta*, "account"; *cha*, "he, she."

175. For calques in Nahuatl, see Karttunen and Lockhart 1976, 43–48; Lockhart 1992, 312–15.

176. See Ravicz 1965; Josserand 1983, 115, 463–67. The virtual absence of spoken Mixtec languages in most contemporary centers complicates studies aimed at defining dialectal patterns and areas and the identification of the influential centers around which they were formed.

177. The many late colonial native writings in Spanish deserve a separate study that would test and extend the analysis provided here.

178. Actually, Tlaxiaco is removed from the main highway, yet it was an important administrative center located along the road linking the Pacific coastal region and the Mixteca Alta. Yolomecatl, another intermediate area that lies along the road between Tlaxiaco and Teposcolula, won autonomy from Teposcolula by the end of the seventeenth century and thereafter began to generate written records from its newly created cabildo. Achiutla and Chalcatongo are two administrative centers

where native language was maintained, in part because of their relative isolation. The situation is somewhat comparable to patterns of language loss and maintenance in Yucatan, where communities located along railroad lines and Hispanic centers have lost Maya as a first language. There are fortunately enough mobile Maya speakers, however, to reinforce the number of native speakers in many communities where the language is in competition with Spanish. In central Mexico, most Nahuatl-speaking communities are relatively isolated. See Karttunen 1985, 128.

CHAPTER 4 — COMMUNITIES

1. For classifications of the Mesoamerican corporate community, see Redfield 1941, 1960; Wolf 1957, 1962; and Aguirre Beltrán 1979. For more recent studies, see Sandstrom 1991 on a Nahua community and Monaghan 1995 on a Mixtec community.

2. See, for example, Haskett 1991a; Schroeder 1991; Lockhart 1992; and Horn 1997 for the Nahuas, and Restall 1997 for the Yucatec Maya.

3. By "structures" I mean something made up of a number of parts combined, organized, and held together in a specific way and the interrelation of those arranged parts within the whole.

4. This interpretation considers the two words a metaphorical couplet. Alternatively, it may be considered "place of people."

5. Alvarado, ff. 174v, 195, 79, 139v, 27v. Again, it is important to note that the appearance of a term in the *Vocabulario* of 1593 merely indicates its potential use in the language.

6. Ibid., f. 69v.

7. Ibid., f. 27v. The Spanish entry reads: "asiento hazer en alguna parte."

8. Ibid., ff. 63v, 46.

9. Reyes, p. 74.

10. The word *tay* (Teposcolula-area spelling) is the personal agentive. "Gente" (people) and "maçegual" (Spanish word, derived from Nahuatl, for "commoner") are glossed as *tay ñuu*. A "nation of peoples" is listed as *tay ñuu tucu*, or "people from various ñuu." Alvarado, ff. 115, 142, 154.

11. The most populous and prominent Ñudzahui places were assigned a Nahuatl name that was subsequently adopted by the Spaniards. Smaller or more remote places were never assigned a Nahuatl name and have maintained their Ñudzahui place-name to the present day. Today, many Mixtecan-language speakers from places that did receive Nahuatl names continue to refer to their home communities by their Ñudzahui names, especially when speaking in their native language.

12. AJT-C, 7:654.

13. Ibid., 7:654, f. 3.

14. See Jansen 1982, 59–63; Smith 1983c, 243–44; Jansen 1985, 9 n. 13; Smith and Parmenter 1991, 18–20; and Jansen 1992, 25. I had seen the term repeatedly in documents before realizing that it is represented in codices and postconquest pictorials as a royal couple facing each other, seated on a reed mat. This correlation came into focus when Carlos Rincón-Mautner showed me a photo of the Lienzo of Nativitas in Oaxaca. Later, I realized that Maarten Jansen had made the connection between the pictorial symbol and the sociopolitical term that appears in colonial documentation.

15. Smith seems to suggest that the *petlatl icpalli* motif was a central Mexican influence expedited by the conquest, explaining why the motif was comparatively rare in some manuscripts (Smith 1983c, 244).

16. Alvarado, ff. 63v, 174v, 40, 28, 135, 174v. The phrase *sacaayuvuitayu* (where there is a yuhuitayu) is also a response to "corte de Papa" and "corte de rey" (f. 55v). Another entry for "ciudad" is *tayu nann*, which I think should be *tayu nanu* (very big tayu). The vocabulary contains quite a few misspellings, usually involving an inverted or transposed letter. In archival documentation, Mixtecs wrote "yuhuitayu" as often as "yuvuitayu," for reasons discussed in chapter 3.

17. AJT-C, 7:689.

18. AGN-T, 571:1.

19. AJT-C, 4:467.

20. Alvarado, f. 63v. *Yucunduta* is the fifth term listed for "pueblo" and the third term listed for "ciudad."

21. AGN-C, 2303:3, ff. 5–11v. Bartolomé de Santiago, the appointed interpreter, knew Nahuatl and Mixtec; he wrote in Nahuatl (as did Gonzalo Pérez) and signed his name to the Spanish parts of the proceedings, but he indicated that he could not write Mixtec. Don Pedro de San Miguel of Atoyac (Yutacano) wrote and signed the Nudzahui-language document. It is likely that Nahuatl was well known in both Tonalá and Atoyac and that a familiarity with the Nahuatl term *altepetl* engendered the use of *yucunduta* in Mixtec. Gerhard states that Ñudzahui and Nahuatl were spoken in this area (1972, 132).

22. AGN-T, 85:2. This testament was untranslated, so it is not possible to see how the word was interpreted.

23. His bequest refers to "the lands of the yucuduta, the commoners on the estancia, and all my tribute laborers of the yucuduta" [ñoho yucuduta nu ñadehi estacia niy cutu cuvui nisiyo daayu chiño yucuduta]. He also referred to "the commoners on the estancia of my yuhuitayu" [mey ñadehi estacia yuhuitayu siyu]. This is a rare mention of the Spanish term *estancia*. See Lockhart 1992, 53, on the rarity of such a term in Nahuatl texts.

24. AGN-T, 245:2. This phrase was translated rather liberally in 1709 as "pueblo de los oficios que tube en el cavildo de Tequistepeque." The term *chiño yucunduta* is the equivalent of the Nahuatl *altepetequitl*.

25. Ibid., 571:1. He also referred to Ñudzay (Huaxuapa) as a yuhuitayu.

26. For example, the description of borders in Tequistepec. Ibid., 571:1, f. 71.

27. In the Valley of Oaxaca, for example, Yucuyta (Chapultepec) produced a document in the 1690s that referred to "yuhuichayu" and "ñoo," representing the pronunciation of these two terms in that area (ibid., 236:1). Since documentation has not survived from the coast, the generalization does not include that area.

28. Schroeder 1991, 210.

29. Alvarado, f. 33.

30. Ibid., ff. 48, 6.

31. Ibid., f. 202. The implication of using *ñuu* as a response to "barrio" in this case is discussed below.

32. Ibid., f. 58.

33. Ibid., f. 167. See Molina [1571] 1977, ff. 61–63v; for a translation into English and analysis of the testament, see Lockhart 1992, app. B, pp. 468–74. Of course, native testators never adopted the term *perrochia* in place of the native terminology. Whether *sichi* was an actual term for a subunit used at the time is unknown. It can be translated as "section" or "piece" and is usually used in association with plots of land. The *Vocabulario* also lists "parishioner" as *tai yehetnaha siña huahi ñuhu* (one who is attached to a church siña).

34. Alvarado, f. 55v. Jansen translated this term as "sede de ñuhu, santa sede" (1982, 295). In addition, the Spanish term *assiento proprio*, "one's site," is listed as *siñandi* and *tayundi*, whereby the *-ndi* suffix is the first-person possessive pronoun. Alvarado, f. 28.

35. Alvarado, f. 57v.

36. Arana Osnaya and Swadesh 1965, 119–21.

37. Reyes called "los primitivos mixtecos que salieron del centro de la tierra" *ñañuhu*, or "people from the earth" (p. 11). There is also a version of siña that is associated with vacated or empty space, since *ña* is also a negative particle associated with *ñaha*, or "nothing."

38. Alvarado, f. 168v, "razimo" is given as *dzitni*.

39. I do not think that the siqui was a general term for maçehual kinship, as Pastor proposed (1987, 34).

40. The same could be said for the Nahua calpolli. See Lockhart 1992, 17. Pastor considered the barrio or siqui to be a strictly endogamous group (1987, 34). But the documentation contains many examples of exogamous marriages. For the Nahuas, see also Offner 1983, 163–226.

41. The same could be said for *-tepec* in Nahuatl.

42. Spores 1983d, 246.

43. AGI-ESC, 162C, ff. 307–307v.

44. AGN-C, 516:3, ff. 6–7. The barrios are also listed in Spores 1967, 159.

45. This list represents a synthesis of references to estancias in 1580 and 1584. The spellings are especially dubious because they were written by Spaniards. AGI-ESC, 162C, ff. 307–307v.

46. Yodzocahi (Yanhuitlan) might have been one constituent siña or ñuu of the whole yuhuitayu, whose dynastic rulership controlled the *toniñe*, or rulership. It is unclear whether in this case the whole ñuu or tayu might have been called Yodzocahi or if the original siña (or ñuu) lent its name to the whole.

47. AJT-C, 18:1512.

48. AJT-CR, 1:113. The original Ñudzahui-language documents are badly damaged. It was likely called Yuhuyucha with an *h* instead of a *y*, which is the semantic equivalent of the Nahuatl place-name Analco.

49. Spores questioned whether barrios were corporate landholding units (1967, 92).

50. AJT-C, 4:467, f. 40, lines 11–15.

51. AGN-INQ, 37:5, 7; Gerhard 1972, 298.

52. AJT-C, 6:605. The translation of this passage, written by a Mixtec, reads: el juramento de domingo juan, mayordomo del bario de siquitongo que llaman en la lengua misteca ayusi en nombre de rey nuestro señor como justicias que lo mas de esta cabesera de santo domingo yanguitlan.

53. Ibid., 5:535.

54. Ibid., 1:161.

55. *Chinamitl* is another term used for calpulli or tlaxilacalli, seen south of central Mexico (e.g., in the early Cuernavaca-region censuses). See Lockhart 1992, 16, and n. 12. It is listed in Simeón as: "separación, cerca de cañas; por ext. barrio, suburbio" (1988, 103). Molina gives *chinamitl* as "seto o cerca de cañas" (f. 21). The rendering of Santiago Istepec as "yetztepel" suggests that the writer was unfamiliar with these Nahuatl-derived names. See chapters 2 and 7 for additional commentary on this document.

56. The interpretation of *chinamitl* as a larger entity resembles the Highland Maya use of *chinamitl* in Guatemala, for example. See Hill and Monaghan 1987.

57. I have also seen a reference to Xihuitongo in 1600, but since it is a Nahuatl name, it is unclear whether it was a Nahuatl version of a Ñudzahui name or an actual Nahua subunit, so I have not included it here. Interestingly, the barrio of Ayusi in Yanhuitlan was called "Xiquitongo" in Nahuatl. Elsewhere, it was called "Siquitongo." Could this be the Nahuatl diminutive *-tonco* added to siqui?

58. Horn found an upper (*acohuic*) and lower (*tlalnahuac*) distinction between tlaxilacalli in Coyoacan that served as the basis of labor and tribute rotation within the altepetl (1997, 20–24; 38–43; 59–64). In that case, it appears as if such an ordering was based on the location of subunits. On upper and lower organization among the Nahuas of Culhuacan, see also Cline 1986, 56–57.

59. Reyes, p. vii. Reyes also reported that the dialects of the two places are very similar.

60. AJT-C, 4:400. A case could be made in these two examples for an appearance of the term *ñuu siqui*, which is elaborated below.

61. Ibid., 4:417.

62. MFHL, microfilm roll #0671267, unnumbered pages corresponding to the years 1646–87. Since the book covers the entire cabecera and its sujetos, it is not always clear if a given siqui was part of Yucundaa (Teposcolula). Some entries refer specifically to a siqui of the cabecera, some refer to siqui of ñuu that were sujetos, and some list siqui but do not indicate their affiliation. In most cases, it seems as if siqui in the last category belonged to the cabecera. In any case, it is clear that Yucundaa had multiple siqui in the second half of the seventeenth century.

63. The siqui from San Juan included Tinañu, Ynitutni, Ynisaa, Ndiquhuaa, Dzutundoco, Yuqhdzadza, Ndiqhhuadzo, and Yuqhsichi.

64. AJT-C, 9:758. In 1724, the "person named Joseph Antonio from the siqui Dzayata" [tey nani joseph antonio siqui dzayata] made his last will and testament before several members of the cabildo.

65. Another in a Spanish-language document is named Çagualtongo, but since it is a Nahuatl name, it may already be represented in the group. To reiterate, Ñudzahui-language writings did not use Nahuatl names. I have discounted another named Nduhuande because it may be an alternate spelling of Nduhua or Ñundee.

66. AJT-C, 6:635.

67. Ibid., 6:635.

68. Ibid., 10:838.

69. Ibid., 10:838.

70. AGN-T, 245:2, f. 75. The accompanying translation of this section, done in 1707, rendered the original as "tierras, varrios, y terrasgueros." The meaning of *tuta* is unclear here; the handwriting of this document is very difficult to read in places.

71. Ibid., 571:1. The eighteenth-century translation of this document on f. 81 is deficient. Even the date is mistranslated as 1676 instead of 1633. The quoted passage is translated: "mando por mi pueblo san bartholome Coculco y todas las tierras y terrasgueros, sitios y mojoneras y linderos y seppas y bienes de cassas segun y como mi entrego mis padres y madre y antepasados todo le entriego a mi hijo don raimundo con sus ocho barrios donde vibían los hijos terrasgueros del dicho pueblo de san bartolome coculco." Perhaps so much was skipped because it is difficult to read; the brackets in the Mixtec text indicate one or two letters cut off by the binding.

72. Ibid., 779:1.

73. Ibid., 2692 (2): 16.

74. "Grasshopper" in Mixtec would be *tica*, but the writing of *d* for *t* was not uncommon.

75. For Achiutla, Texupa, Nochixtlan and Sayultepec, see Gerhard 1972, 292–99, from *Suma de Visitas*. It is unclear in many of these early reports, however, what is meant by "barrio" and "sujeto."

The definition may not have been consistent. Most barrio names are given in Nahuatl, further obscuring matters. There is some evidence in the *Codex Sierra* that Texupa had six barrios. Some of the entries divide things into six parts; for example, quetzal feathers that were bought in 1561 for seventy-five pesos to decorate the community are divided neatly into six bundles (*Codex Sierra*, p. 44). For Tlaxiaco, AJT-C, 6:624. For Coixtlahuaca, personal correspondence with Carlos Rincón-Mautner.

76. The phrase "la vieja" may also indicate congregation from an earlier location, though in this case it refers to an inhabited site and not a former one. See Wood 1984, 105. Note that the name of a siqui in Teposcolula corresponded with the Ñudzahui name of the ñuu (Yucundaa).

77. AGN-C, 1429:3. Yucundayy (Tequistepec); Tnohuitu (Huapanapa); Ayuu (Xuchitepetongo); Daaduhua (Miltepec); Yucuytayno (Xochitepec); Ñoñaña (Coyotepec); Yuhuacuchi (Huaxolotitlan).

78. The term first appears in the record of a land transfer near Texupa. Don Gabriel Martín Corado hails from a place called "bario iniyada" (AJT-C, 6:638). The term has appeared in Ñudzahui-language records from Achiutla (1632), Ytnotnono (1681), Yucucata (1693), Tlaxiaco (1713), Xoxocotlan (1716), Texupa (1752, 1762), and Tonaltepec (1790).

79. In comparison, Haskett reports that "tlaxilacalli" faded in the beginning of the eighteenth century in Nahuatl-language records from Cuernavaca and was increasingly replaced by "barrio." This did not occur with altepetl, however (1985, 88).

80. Alvarado, f. 69v.

81. Ibid., f. 202.

82. AJT-C, 13:1109.

83. Ibid., 4:467.

84. Ibid., 6:605. The translation reads: "mayordomo del bario de siquitongo que llaman en la lengua misteca ayusi." I am convinced that a Ñudzahui person translated this document. Ayusi appears elsewhere as Xiquitongo, and Yuhuyucha is called Analco in Spanish writings. I suspect that Ayusi and Yuhuyucha were prominent enough settlements to acquire names derived from Nahuatl. The use of Xiquitongo represents a rare appearance of a Nahuatl name used in a Ñudzahui writing.

85. Ibid., 3:287.

86. AGN-T, 1226:3, f. 9.

87. AJT-C, 10:838.

88. Spores 1967, 78.

89. See Cook and Borah 1968.

90. Acuña 1984, 2:147.

91. Jiménez Moreno 1962, 16–19; Romero Frizzi 1990, 55–58.

92. Romero Frizzi 1990, 54–59.

93. Gerhard 1972, 286. They were: Achiutla; Amoltepec; Atoyaquillo; Cenzontepec; Yucuañe; Mitlantongo; Mixtepec; Yodocono; Tamazola; Tamazulapa; Teozacualco; Teposcolula; Texupa; Tezoatlan; Tilantongo; Tlaxiaco; Tuctla; Yolotepec.

94. Spores 1967, 107. Spores found no evidence of significant movement by the end of the sixteenth century; congregations did not begin until 1590 and were largely ineffective, though there were some earlier congregation attempts that have not been documented. Even in central Mexico, where the Spanish presence was most pronounced, congregation did not achieve the anticipated results (see Gibson 1964, 283–84; Martin 1985, 28; Haskett 1991a, 13).

95. On the relocation of Texupa, see Borah and Cook 1979.

96. Gerhard 1972, 298.

97. For a more detailed discussion and comparison of the effects of congregaciones in the Toluca Valley in central Mexico, see Wood 1984, 24–64, 364–74. Wood found that most of the structures remained intact, even after the final congregation of 1598–1606.

98. See Lockhart 1992, 45.

99. Spores called the Mixtec community a "loosely nucleated entity" and affirmed that there was an increased concentration of settlement in the center as a result of new alignment after the conquest (1967, 90–96).

100. Compare Lockhart 1992, 19, for Nahua organization.

101. See Wood 1984, 3–5, and Horn 1997, 30–31, for Toluca and Coyoacan, respectively.

102. Haskett 1991a, 9–10.

103. See Schroeder 1991 and Lockhart 1992 for a discussion of the tlayacatl altepetl.

104. Horn 1997, 22.

105. Spores 1967, 93.

106. Spores 1984, 167.

107. Spores 1967, 90–96.

108. Spores 1967, 93. This statement predates his intensive archaeological excavations of the Nochixtlan Valley (see Spores 1983d, 1984).

109. An archaeological survey of the Valley of Nochixtlan, of which Yanhuitlan occupies the northwestern corner, showed that the sociopolitical and demographic concentration that had been centered in Yucuita in the Ramos period (ca. 200 B.C. to A.D. 300) and Yucuñudahui in the Las Flores period (ca. A.D. 300–1000) shifted to Yanhuitlan in the Natividad period (ca. A.D. 1000–1520). Yanhuitlan, Nochixtlan, Etlatongo, Chachoapa, Soyaltepec, Jaltepec, and Tiltepec were all sizable sites located within five to twenty kilometers from one another, which probably subjected other smaller sites in the valley. The capital settlements of these kingdoms were located adjacent to the modern and colonial settlements. Spores noted that, despite the rise to dominance of Yanhuitlan, monumental architecture never reached the height of the earlier classic period and that, in fact, material evidence of urban development underwent a marked decline in this period. Ancient centers such as Yucuñudahui and Yucuita continued to serve as ceremonial centers (see Spores 1983d, 1984).

110. Spores 1983d, 246–48 (see map on 246); 1984, 48–57 (see map on 50–51).

111. Excavated and unexcavated sites suggest that Ayuxi (Ayusi) was probably the ancient royal residence of the capital before removal to the valley floor. Populous centers such as Ayuxi contained a core of elite palaces built of stone, surrounded by subsidiary structures. Spores observed that the second type of site was the "dependency, rancho, or sujeto-like settlement found by the dozens throughout the valley." He also pointed out that the site of the palace built during the early colonial period for don Gabriel de Guzmán may overlie a prehispanic site (1983d, 247; 1983c, 255–60). Further evidence of a lack of center or urban concentration comes from Lind's study of house structures in Coixtlahuaca, Chachoapa, and Yucuita. Lind divided the areas into categories of "rural" and "urban" and yet found no differences in the structures. He concluded that "the urban elite occupied houses which were virtually identical to the houses of the rural gentry" (1979, 69). This evidence suggests that the urban-rural dichotomy does not apply to settlement patterns of the Mixteca.

112. Spores 1967, 100.

113. Spores concluded that Yanhuitlan may have consisted of or controlled as many as fifteen to twenty-five settlements or clusters, some contiguous and others located as far as ten kilometers or more from the capital—this was essentially the colonial scenario (1983b, 236). Well aware of the complexity of this situation, Spores proposed a number of questions regarding settlement patterns, the interrelation of entities, their boundaries and territories, and political and socioeconomic relations among the various units.

114. AJT-CR, 1:52. Two other barrios have been noted for Coixtlahuaca: Totosaha (ibid., 1:85) and Cuxaga—a Chocho name (AJT-C, 4:440).

115. *Codex Sierra*, p. 13.

116. AGEO-AM, 8:26. Likewise, in 1578, don Gaspar de Guzmán was identified as someone from the "barrio and sujeto of Santiago of the pueblo of Santa Cruz Mitlantongo." AJT-C, 1:30.

117. Gibson 1964, 53–57; Spores 1967, 90–109; Gerhard 1972.

118. See Lockhart 1992, 46, for the Nahuas.

119. The term *dzini ñuu* appears in the *Vocabulario* as "cabecera del pueblo" but *daha ñuu* appears under "aldea" (Alvarado, ff. 40, 15v). It is possible that *daha ñuu* could be compared to the term that Haskett found for sujeto in Cuernavaca—*calmaitl*. As an alternative to the definition as tribute, *daha* could signify (depending on tone) "hand," like the Nahuatl *maitl*. For Cuernavaca, see Haskett 1991a, 10.

120. AJT-CR, 6:705.

121. AJT-C, 5:535. This was translated as the "cabecera de Santo Domingo Yanhuitlan," glossing over the yuhuitayu.

122. Ibid., 6:592.

123. Ibid., 10:873. The first phrase was translated later as "su patria y cabesera de Tlaxiaco."

124. Schroeder 1991, 137–39.

125. AJT-C, 1:190.

126. Ibid., 1:216; AJT-CR, 2:265; AJT-CR, 3:271.

127. Gerhard 1972, 299. These sujetos were: Yucuita; Isquisuchitlan; Chiyo; Maxcaltepec; Yucuñana; Coyotepec; and Suchitepec. Almoloyas, Sinaxtla, and Tecomatlan attempted to break away a few decades later.

128. AGN-T, 985:2; AGN-C, 516:2; AGI-ESC, 162C. See Spores 1967, 138.

129. AGN-INQ, 37:10, f. 231.

130. See also Spores 1967, 134–35, for a different interpretation. Ulterior motives notwithstanding, the inquisitorial investigation invited hostile witnesses to accuse Yanhuitlan of idolatrous acts and human sacrifices, discussed in chapter 8. As in Spanish society, denouncing one's enemy to the Inquisition was a common strategy of attack.

131. AJT-C, 1:95.

132. Ibid., 4:467.

133. Alvarado, f. 40.

134. AJT-CR, 1:40.

135. AGI-ESC, 162C. The extant expediente is numbered from f. 26 to f. 535.

136. These names were based on the Mesoamerican calendar: "matlactl çe miquiztli" is Nahuatl for 11-Death (*matlactli once* is 11), and "nahui caltzin" is the reverential form of 4-House. The following chapter discusses naming patterns based on the calendar.

137. AGI-ESC, 162C, ff. 499–505.

138. This scenario is analagous to Horn's observations that the residents of Tacubaya preferred to attend mass in Mexico City, rather than go to the church in Coyoacan, because they resented their inferior status in the new system (Horn 1997, 82). Clearly, the preconquest significance of paying tribute to one's local temple (and deity) applied to Christian worship, as well.

139. AGI-ESC, 162C, f. 521v. This is a position that Spores has considered, suggesting that "disenfranchised" lords such as don Diego lost their ruling identity and became simply members of the nobility (1967, 140).

140. AGI-ESC, 162C, ff. 527–29.

141. AGN-T, 24:6, f. 13v.

142. AGI-ESC, 162C, f. 41. Four hundred is a good round number in the indigenous vigesimal system.

143. AJT-C, 2:215, original decree in Mixtec; ibid., 2:218, complaint from cacique.

144. Compare Lockhart 1992, 57, for the Nahuas.

145. Pastor 1987, 111–12.

146. AJT-C, 18:1578.

147. This measurement was based on Spanish attempts in 1567 to confine damages caused by *ganado* (cattle) by establishing limits of five hundred varas between estancias and the outer edge of nearby communities, modified in 1695 to six hundred varas measured from the church. A vara was a length of about thirty-three inches. See Taylor 1972, 68–69, and Romero Frizzi 1990, 87.

148. See Gibson 1964, 285; Wood 1984, 183–90, 195–237; Lockhart 1992, 56.

149. In central Mexico, in the 1730s, a distinction was made between the cabecera and outlying units, in which the latter were called "barrios" instead of "sujetos," and their inhabitants belonged to the cabecera, just as in the original indigenous concept of the all-embracing altepetl. See Lockhart 1992, 52–53.

150. AJT-C, 6:578.

151. Gerhard 1972, 296.

152. AJT-C, 1:95.

153. Ibid., 7:762.

154. Pastor 1987, 176 and n. 25.

155. Ibid., 412–23.

156. See Horn 1997, 23–38, for the pursuit of cabecera status in colonial Coyoacan.

157. For comparable patterns among the Nahuas, see Lockhart 1992, 20, 58.

158. See Cook and Borah 1968, 49, for a discussion of how late colonial changes have affected existing settlement patterns in the Mixteca.

CHAPTER 5 — SOCIAL RELATIONS

1. See Spores 1967, 9–10, and 1976, 207–20.

2. In the Nahua region, for example, extant native-language records were written as early as two decades after the arrival of the Spaniards. Cuernavaca-region censuses constitute the earliest known Nahuatl documentary corpus and reveal practices and social categories that were not condoned by Spaniards, including polygyny. See Lockhart 1992, 110, for a discussion of why early colonial native-language sources are relevant for an understanding of preconquest social categories.

3. *Yya* is related to *yy*, a term associated with honored, sacred, precious, and delicate things.

4. Herrera 1947, 6:318 (dec. III, cap. XII).

5. Alvarado, f. 115. The entry is "generoso de buen linaje." Another entry is *tohondaa*, or "true toho."

6. Ibid., f. 124.

7. AGN-T, 59:2. Yucucuihi was called Tlazultepec by Spaniards.

8. AJT-CR, 1:16. Ñundecu was called Achiutla by Spaniards.

9. AGN-T, 637:1, ff. 65–73. The elders are discussed below.

10. Ibid., 245:2. *Yuhua* was another term for "father" in the Mixteca Baja that has not been attested in the Alta, where *dzutu* was the common term. Nahuas possessed a similar metaphor for ancestors based on "our mother and father," *in tonantzin in totatzin.*

11. AJT-C, 6:568.

12. In fact, the Ñudzahui nobility of Texupa in the *Codex Sierra* was referred to in Nahuatl as *tlatoque pipiltin*, the equivalent of yya toho. See *Codex Sierra*, p. 28, for example. In both Mixtec and Nahuatl, the categories were applied to women by adding the modifier *dzehe* and *cihua*, respectively.

13. Lockhart 1992, 138–39.

14. AJT-C, 7:804.

15. AGN-T, 571:1.

16. AJT-C, 5:506.

17. MFHL, roll #0671267, unnumbered pages. This undated document was written sometime in the second half of the seventeenth century.

18. Lockhart 1992, 102–3. This was especially true after the conquest, when secondary marriages were prohibited by Christianity.

19. Spanish sources such as Herrera and the *Relaciones geográficas* give the impression that lords in ruling centers appointed nobles to lead subordinate satellite units. This centralized, autocratic scheme does not correspond with the more complex sociopolitical arrangement that is presented in this work, especially in chapters 4 and 6. For comparison with the Nahua situation, see Lockhart 1992, 103–4, in response to Zorita's observation. It was thought that tlatoque named and appointed nobles to subordinate positions, but this seems to contradict or simplify the principle of the *teccalli* as a lineage. Likewise, eligibility for leadership positions in ñuu would seem to favor hereditary arrangements over outright appointments, or at least a more flexible situation. The topic of hereditary rule receives fuller treatment in the next chapter.

20. Lockhart 1992, 96.

21. Alvarado, f. 257v.

22. On the importance of tniño or "tiñu" today, and its interpretation as a necessary burden, see Monaghan 1995, 167–89. Farriss makes a similar association of office with burden for the Maya of colonial Yucatan (1984, 345).

23. Alvarado, f. 40. Among the Nahuas, nobles who served on the cabildo did not pay tribute in kind, either. But in the late colonial period, everyone who did not hold an office had the same tribute obligation as an ordinary native person. See Lockhart 1992, 132. I suspect, but cannot say for certain, that this was also true for Ñudzahui officeholders.

24. Compare with the Nahuas of central Mexico, where much of the terminolgy of social differentiation fell into disuse by the mid-seventeenth century, despite the persistence of an upper group (Lockhart 1992, 117).

25. AJT-C, 6:568.

26. Ibid., 6:586; ibid., 9:758. Compare with the latest reference to a *tlatoani* as dynastic ruler among the Nahuas of central Mexico, in the year 1661. See Lockhart 1992, 132.

27. AJT-C, 7:689.

28. Ibid., 11:921.

29. Ibid., 18:1578.

30. AGN-T, 245:2, ff. 80–81, and Tierras, 779: 1. In the sixteenth century, Spaniards usually defined *yya* as "cacique" or "señor" and *toho* as "principal." The two were later equated by the expression *cacique y principal*. The interpretation of ñandahi (not the usage) as "naturales" in this example resembles how "macehualli" came to signify an indigenous person in Nahuatl (Lockhart 1992, 114–16).

31. AGN-C, 2302:3. Again, plural nouns are not overtly marked in the Ñudzahui language.

32. Alvarado, f. 142. *Tay ñuu* means someone from a ñuu or, by extension, any person on the face of the earth. Pastor considers *tay ñuu* an abbreviated form of *tay ñuhu* and thus makes an association with earth or land (*ñuhu*); however, *ñuu* and *ñuhu* are different words distinguished by a glottal stop and tone (Pastor 1987, 56–57). See Spores 1976, 207–20, and Jansen 1982, 59–60, 292–93, for a discussion of social categories.

33. Alvarado, f. 200v.

34. Ibid., f. 115. See "gente o gentio."

35. Molina [1571] 1977, f. 565v. It is likely that *macehualli* originally meant "human being" or "the people" in the plural and did not originally connote the pejorative meaning it sometimes possessed. Lockhart called this social category of ordinary people the norm from which others are distinguished (Lockhart 1992, 96 and n. 6).

36. Alvarado, f. 33v. See "baxo hombre de linaje." The actual entry reads "nandahi" and "taindah"—both typesetting errors. Two other entries under this listing include *cuite* (humble or simple) and *tai ñuucuite* (person from a simple ñuu?); the latter construction suggests a direct relation between sociopolitical entities and social terminology.

37. AJT-CR, 1:52.

38. AJT-C, 1:164.

39. AJT-CR, 6:675. This was translated as "todos los hijos del pueblo de Tiyacu." They called the lieutenant "yya tiniñente capita" [lord lieutenant captain], assigning him a lordly title modified by loanwords.

40. Lockhart 1992, 96, 115. The Nahua historian Chimalpahin often used *macehualtzitzintin* for "poor commoners."

41. AJT-C, 4:467.

42. AJT-CR, 4:450, f. 5. Because it is a Spanish-language record, Juan de Silva's words were translated as "macehual" and "principales." Compare with the use of the term *macehualli* among the Nahuas in Lockhart 1992, 96.

43. It is also associated with the pejorative "vellaco" (villain) in the *Vocabulario* (f. 201).

44. Alvarado, f. 189v. See also "esclavo, nacido en casa" on f. 101v.

45. AJT-C, 6:568.

46. AGN-T, 308:4, f. 146.

47. AJT-CR, 7:804.

48. AGN-T, 236:6.

49. Alvarado, f. 43.

50. AGN-T, 59:2. It is possible that she drew a distinction between ñayuqh (which I interpret as a Tlaxiaco-area variant) and ñadehi.

51. AJT-C, 7:654.

52. AJT-CR, 3:377; ibid., 1:18.

53. Ibid., 6:640. Antonio López of Almoloyas, for example, in 1694.

54. For a discussion of native women's work in colonial central Mexico and Oaxaca, see Sousa 1998, 175–251.

55. Alvarado, f. 195.

56. Ibid., f. 134. Likewise, "worker" (*labrador*) or "farmer" in the context of land is *tay situ* (one who cultivates), and "farmed land" (*labrada tierra*) is *ñuhu nisitu* (cultivated land) or *ytu nisitu* (cultivated field). The same terminology was associated with the verb *cavar*. Ibid., f. 46. The entries are "cavada tierra," *ñuhu nisitu;* "cavador," *tay situ;* and "cavar labrando," *yositundi.*

57. Ibid., f. 139 for *lodo* and f. 155 for *negro.*

58. Spores 1976, 210–13; 1984, 64.

59. Lockhart 1992, 96–97; *mayeque* has only been attested twice in Nahuatl documentation, and it is paired with *macehualtin* each time. Rather than being a distinct category, they were a type of macehualtin. See also Zorita 1941; Dyckerhoff 1976; and Hicks 1976.

60. AGN-T, 245:2, ff. 75–76. Doña Juana was cacica of Yolotepec, Cosoltepec, and Acaquisapa. Interestingly, she also referred to the ñandahi in terms of "all the uncles, aunts, fathers, mothers, commoners" [niy cutu dzito dzidzi yuhua dzihiyu ñadehi], reminiscent of how don Jorge de la Cruz Alvarado referred to "all the fathers, mothers and grandfathers, grandmothers toho" [taca yuhua dzihiyu sihi siy sitna toho] as a metaphor for his noble ancestors, as discussed above.

61. AGN-T, 85:2. Don Miguel was cacique of Tonalá.

62. Ibid., 779:1.

63. Ibid., 571:1. Don Gerónimo de Guzmán was cacique of San Bartolomé Coculco. The last part was translated as "mis hijos."

64. Ibid., 571:1, f. 73v. He wrote: "todos los indios y yndias con todas las tierras de cacicazgo."

65. Ibid., 657:2. This was don Rafael de San Miguel y Salazar. The phrase "taca ñadehi dahui ñuu tayu" was translated as "pobres naturales del pueblo," and "dzaya dzanayu" was translated as "mis indios maseguales." The latter was repeated on lines 50, 52, 56, 71, and 126 of the document.

66. Compare with *macehualli* in the possessed form among the Nahuas in Lockhart 1992, 96.

67. AGN-T, 571:1. Doña María was cacica of San Bartolomé Coculco. In this case, "ñanday" is a variation of ñandahi, and "ñatahui" is a "poor person" from *dahui,* "poor, humble."

68. Ibid., 245:2, ff. 80–81, and Tierras, 779:1. This was translated poorly as "todos mis prinsipales y naturales y todas las tierras."

69. Ibid., 571:1; *ta* (as in *tay*) substitutes *ña* in this case to impart the meaning of "ñadehy"; the term was defined as "terrazguero" in a subsequent translation.

70. Spores 1983d, 229–30.

71. AJT-C, 6:568.

72. The important part of this phrase is *nino,* which can mean "from time to time" or "periodically," modifying the verb *situ* and perhaps referring to some type of temporary arrangement.

73. Alvarado, f. 134–134v, under "labrar milpa para coger a medias." The Spanish terms *peon* and *jornalero,* "wage laborer," are defined as *tay ndayu,* "person of the land, mud" and *tay tatu,* "worker." Ibid., f. 165v. Another phrase, "to work land for the common good" (*labrar milpa para bien comun*), contains the verbs *situ* and *cata,* "to dig or sow," and *tniño,* "duty, work."

74. AGN-T, 400:1, cited in Spores 1967, 164.

75. AJT-C, 4:400.

76. Ibid., 8:726, ff. 1–2v.

77. Alvarado, f. 194v. "To have someone in place of a father or mother" is "yoquidza nisanu ñahandi," whereas *nisanu* is "elder."

78. AJT-CR, 6:667. Two dependents from Coixtlahuaca who ran afoul of the law in Tlaxiaco were then sold to an *obraje* (workshop for the production of cloth) for ten years.

79. Ibid., 5:582.

80. Ibid., 5:551. This is one of several cases that I have seen in which a dependent, in this case a woman, apparently derived her name from her sponsor's. She could not expect to adopt the surname Orozco, for reasons explained in the final section of this chapter, but she could adopt her patron saint's name.

81. Ibid., 2:215.

82. Ibid., 2:247. On married couples who routinely worked together in the Mixteca during the colonial period, see Sousa 1998, 303.

83. Carrasco 1976b, 27; Dyckerhoff 1976, 161; Lockhart 1992, 99.

84. Reyes, p. xii. See also the *Relaciones geográficas* report of Tilantongo in Acuña 1984, 2:232–33. Likewise, a marriage between the lordly establishments of Zaachila and Almoloyas moved a contingent of dependents into the Valley of Oaxaca, who formed the basis of a Ñudzahui settlement around Cuilapa. Acuña 1984, 2:178–81; 1984, 2:157–58.

85. AGN-T, 2692, 2:16.

86. AJT-CR, 3:275.

87. Spores 1976, 212. Spores acknowledged the complexity of the situation by considering the advantages of dependents who worked for wealthy lords.

88. Lockhart 1992, 98.

89. Compare this situation among the Nahuas of central Mexico, where change occurred earlier, especially in the western region. Ibid., 112–14.

90. Alvarado, f. 101v. Likewise, for the Nahuas, lower dependents were hardly distinguishable from slaves. See Lockhart 1992, 100.

91. Alvarado, f. 189. The Nahuatl *mayeque* meant "possessors of hands and arms" and was supposed to have referred to dependents in the service of the lord. The term comes close to the literal meaning of "daha saha." I have never seen this latter term used in a document, however. Judging by a few references in the native-language record, the word for a native slave was not applied to African slaves, who were simply called "black people" (*tay tnoo*).

92. AGN-INQ, 37:9.

93. The practice of selling slaves in the market, usually captives taken in warfare with other communities, has been documented for the Nahuas of central Mexico. See Lockhart 1992, 100.

94. See Borah 1983, 50.

95. AJT-C, 1:51.

96. AJT-CR, 1:89.

97. Burke 1992, 76.

98. On the use of the Spanish justice system by native individuals and communities in the early colonial period, see Borah 1983.

99. AGN-T, 400:1, f. 79. It is unclear how many people worked on Yanhuitlan's aniñe lands, which numbered 102 plots in 1580 (43 within the territorial limits of Yanhuitlan). A sketch in the *Codex Yanhuitlan*, drawn around 1550, suggests that 400 dependents served the aniñe (palace) of Yanhuitlan (see fig. 5.1). The image depicts a woman carrying a large grinding stone on her back, walking with a man who transports a bundle of corn to the place glyph of Yanhuitlan. Below them is the Mesoamerican symbol for 400. Tribute labor was normally organized by pairs of married couples who represented individual households. Alternatively, the glyph could refer to *encomienda* labor. See Jiménez Moreno and Mateos Higuera 1940, plate 12.

100. AGN-T, 985:2, f. 47; ibid., 400:1, f. 80v.

101. For a similar arrangement, see ibid., 34:1.

102. Ibid., 985:2, f. 62v.

103. On systems of reciprocity and redistribution, see Polanyi 1944. For contemporary gifting and mutual feeding arrangements in the Mixteca, see Monaghan 1995, 303.

104. Farriss 1984, 343–44. Farriss concluded that the feasts defined social boundaries by reinforcing ties among elites and differences between elites and macehuales.

105. AGN-T, 2692 (2):16. This case is recorded in Spanish.

106. The first five couples had ruled before the Spaniards' arrival, the sixth had ruled at the time of the conquest, and the penultimate couple had lived under colonial rule. Whereas the earliest ruling couple is depicted in a temple, seated on a reed mat, don Francisco and his wife are standing, and they have adopted full Spanish dress. Thus, if the genealogical component of the document demonstrates continuity of rule, it also reveals significant cultural change. See Smith and Parmenter 1991, 92–94, and Jansen 1994, 36–45, for a discussion of this pictorial record.

107. Gerhard 1972, 23.

108. AJT-CR, 1:107 and 1:122.

109. Ibid., 1:127; see also AJT-C, 1:155. A similar accusation was made in 1598 by nobles and commoners from Chicahuastla against their cacique, don Martín Fonseca Pimentel. See AJT-CR, 1:107; see also AJT-CR, 1:122.

110. AJT-C, 1:246. Unfortunately, this document is badly damaged and unreadable in parts.

111. Ibid., 1:216. See also AJT-CR, 2:265; AJT-CR, 3:271. As in the previous example, some of these conflicts were related to sociopolitical tensions, as discussed in chapter 4.

112. Taylor 1979, 113–51, and 136 for the reference to jail breaks.

113. AJT-C, 1:246.

114. AGN-I, 15 (1a): 89, ff. 63v–64.

115. AJT-CR, 3:362.

116. AJT-C, 1:157.

117. AGN-T, 2935:88, f. 2.

118. Ibid., 2935:79, ff. 162–163v. The sujetos were San Bartolomé Maninaltepec, Santa María Tlatlaltepec, and San Juan Teyta.

119. Ibid., 2935:79–80, ff. 164–167v.

120. AGN-I, 15 (1a): 89, ff. 63v–64.

121. Dahlgren 1954, 282–87, and Smith 1973a, 24–26. The vocabulary of day signs is written in the Teposcolula variant.

122. The earliest record is from 1530, when a tribute assessment for Teposcolula refers to the yya toniñe as "Nahui Olin," which is Nahuatl for the calendrical name 4-Movement and hence a translation of the Ñudzahui *Quichi*. The translation process that relied on Nahuas in the early colonial period affected the recording of personal names as well as place-names. AGI-C, 657, f. 767. It is also possible that every Nahua originally had a calendrical name. Other Nahua names were based on nicknames or physical attributes, and all types are attested as early as the Cuernavaca region censuses of the 1540s. See Lockhart 1992, 118.

123. The one exception to this rule that I have seen comes from an archaic false title, dated 1523 but produced in the 1690s, which introduces a don Diego Cortés Dzahui Yuchi (rain, flint). This personal name glyph has been attested in the codices. AGN-T, 236:6.

124. Lockhart 1992, 119.

125. Cline 1986, 118.

126. See Lockhart 1992, 122.

127. AGN-T, 59:2. Written in the year 1571.

128. AJT-C, 7:654. He was referred to in the document as Juan Añoti (Juan Tecomatlan), in reference to the ñuu from which he came.

129. AGN-T, 1226:3, f. 9.

130. Ibid., 571:1, ff. 79–81.

131. AJT-CR, 1: 52. The ñuu, called a "barrio" in the Spanish summary of the case, was San Gerónimo Paxtlahuaca. Later in the document, San Gerónimo is called an "estancia y barrio." Francisco is called in the Ñudzahui language "regidores" (revealing the lack of marked distinction in writing of singular and plural Spanish terms) but is known in the Spanish summary as a "tequitlato" (tribute collector). This discrepancy was part of the problem with Francisco; the people did not recognize him as a tribute collector but rather as a regidor who had abused his "chiño" (Yanhuitlan-area equivalent of tniño).

132. In this case, *na* is "eight," and *huidzu* (alternately spelled as "vidzu") is "ocelot."

133. AJT-C, 4:400.

134. Ibid., 3:287.

135. Ibid., 1:164, in the year 1602. The day sign "mañe" appears in the same form several times elsewhere, but I am not sure of its meaning. Its closest equivalent is cuañe, or "grass."

136. Ibid., 8:705.

137. AJT-CR, 2:236. A few names have been noted that bear only one recognizable element, perhaps indicating some divergence from the vocabulary. However, names written in Spanish-language sources tend to misrepresent the original name. For this reason, I have not included calendrical names from Spanish-language sources in these examples.

138. AJT-C, 6:658.

139. Reyes's *Arte* provides examples of formal and informal terms used to express gender, kinship, and age relations. For example, the term *yco* was a familiar designation used by women referring to other women of the same age or younger, which translates roughly as "girl." The term *dzuq* was used by women referring to men of the same age or younger, or "boy." The familiar term *dacu* was used by men in reference to other men of the same age or younger. Men speaking to or about women used *do* as a title; women used the title of *dzu* for men. Men speaking to other men used the formal title *ye* or the informal title *dzi*. Kinship terms also specified point of reference; for example, men called their brothers *ñani,* while women called them *cuhua.* Men called their sisters *cuhua,* and women called them *cuhui.* Thus, the term *cuhua* referred to a sibling of the opposite sex. Sibling terms were also applied to first and second cousins. See Reyes 1976, pp. 15–19, 86–88. I have come across many of these terms in the native-language record.

140. AJT-CR, 4:502. In Tamasulapa.

141. A point also made for the Nahuas by Lockhart (1992, 117). Some Nahua royal dynasties may have passed on names to succeeding generations. The Maya are the exception to this rule in that indigenous patronymics were kept in Yucatan throughout the colonial period (Restall 1997, 41–50).

142. AGN-T, 779:1.

143. For a discussion of similar naming patterns among the Nahuas, see Lockhart 1992, 123–30.

144. Ibid., 122.

145. AJT-C, 7:654; ibid., 6:658.

146. AJT-CR, 6:666.

147. Ibid., 1:113.

148. AGI-ESC, 162C.

149. AGI-ESC, 162C, ff. 497–516.

150. AJT-C, 1:91.

151. Ibid., 1:12.

152. Among Nahuas, the title *doña* was used less frequently than among Spaniards, presumably because noblewomen did not hold office or head a *teccalli* (lordly house or establishment) and thus could not acquire the title in their lifetime. Lockhart 1992, 125–26. Differing conceptions of royalty and succession may have created more doñas in the Mixteca.

153. AJT-CR, 3:362.

154. AJT-C, 6:635. I cannot translate Chocho calendrical names, but I am sure that they are not Mixtec, and they do contain elements in common with those in the preceding list of 102 Chocho names. The area around Coixtlahuaca, Tamasulapa, and Texupa was populated by both Ñudzahui and Chocho speakers.

155. BNAH, 777, ff. 3–4.

156. AJT-C, 10:838.

157. Ibid., 4:440; ibid., 10:813. One calls Coixtlahuaca Guichee and the other Nguichee. The latter is called a *xade*, the Chocho term for a sociopolitical entity (Rincón-Mautner 1994, 4). The loan-word *barrio* was used in 1695 to refer to the entity of Cuxaga instead of an indigenous equivalent.

158. AGN-T, 236:6.

CHAPTER 6 — YUHUITAYU

1. Alvarado, f. 8ov: "dignidad o señorío." Plural nouns are not marked in Mixtec. The *Vocabulario* also defines "maiestad" and "reynado" as simply *sa toniñe* (ff. 144v, 180v). A "real cosa" or "royal thing" is *sa si yya toniñe* or *sayotnaha sa yya toniñe,* or "that which belongs to the ruler(s)" (f. 178v). A "cetro real," or royal scepter, was called the *tatnu yya,* "lord's staff," or *tatnu toniñe,* "staff of the rulership" (f. 63). The act of transferring the señorío to another ruler ("traspasar a otro el señorío") was *yosicotaa ñahandi sa toniñe,* or "to bestow to someone the rulership" (f. 198). The *taa* in this verbal compound may refer to the act of writing.

2. Alvarado, ff. 63v, 174v. *Tayu* is often used as an abbreviated form of *yuhuitayu.* In addition, "king's court" is listed as *siña toniñe,* and the "viceroy" was referred to as *yya ñoho siña toniñe,* or the "lord who guards the royal court" (ff. 55v, 202v).

3. For a discussion of the Nahua tlatocayotl, see Schroeder 1991 and Lockhart 1992.

4. Alvarado, f. 188v.

5. In one case *yya canu* is actually used to refer to two native alcaldes of the cabildo, who were probably not considered caciques. AJT-CR, 1:151.

6. Schroeder 1991, 174. For example, the term *huey tlatoani* was used occasionally by Chimalpahin to describe rulers of Tenochtitlan or rulers from distant parts of the world.

7. AJT-C, 7:654.

8. Ibid., 2:243.

9. AGN-T, 637:1, ff. 65–73.

10. AJT-C, 6:568, f. 15.

11. AGN-T, 657:2. Typically, *ñe* was written as *y* in the Baja.

12. AGN-C, 2302:3. In the Baja, the *ñe* of the Mixteca Alta was written as *y* in syllable-final position; the first-person plural possessive pronoun was *-yu,* not *-ndo,* as in Teposcolula.

13. *Tecpan* means "place of the lords(s)" in Nahuatl. For *aniñe,* the prefix *a-* usually refers to a place or "place within," and *to-* is a prefix associated with the nobility, or *toho;* the term *niñe* conveys royalty and may be related to blood (*neñe*). One Mixtec origin legend speaks of the original lords who came from *añuhu,* or from "inside the earth." Several place names begin with the *a* prefix in the Mixteca, including Atoco (Nochixtlan), Añute (Xaltepec), Añuu (Zoyaltepec); Ayuu (Xuchitepetongo), and Ayusi.

14. On palace structures in central Mexico, see Kubler 1948 and Evans 1991, 63–92. For Nahua house structures, in general, see Lockhart 1992, 59–72. See the *Florentine Codex* (bk. 11) and the *Codex Mendoza* (f. 62) for Nahua representations of the tecpan.

15. AGN-T, 400:1 and 985:2.

16. AGN-INQ, 37:10, f. 195v. Spanish normally used *casas* in reference to a large structure.

17. I am especially grateful to Ronald Spores for introducing me to this building in Teposcolula. Barry Kiracofe's study of this structure shows how the Casa de la Cacica is aligned with the open chapel of Teposcolula, signifying a planned, spatial relationship between the Christian temple and the native palace. Apparently, the two structures were built around the same time. See Kiracofe 1995.

18. In the *Codex Nuttall,* see the two palaces on p. 41, for example.

19. See Evans 1991, 73, and Kiracofe 1995, 52–62, on the disk motif or frieze of royal palaces. See Kiracofe 1995, 76 and n. 37, and fig. 12, on how the motif contains distinct representations of flowers. The author has observed the disk motif on several structures in central Mexico, Morelos, and the Mixteca.

20. AGN-T, 24:6, ff. 29–40. This land is probably "ytu nocoyoo," whereby *ytu* means cultivable field.

21. Ibid., 24:6, ff. 37–40. The document was written in Spanish, but it relied on some Nahuatl vocabulary.

22. For other descriptions of tecpan possession, see ibid., 34:1 (Texupa, 1587); ibid., 985:2 (Yanhuitlan, 1591, 1629); ibid., 59:2 (Tlazultepec, 1597); ibid., 400:1 (Yanhuitlan, 1629).

23. Ibid., 400:1, f. 105.

24. On the role of ceremony in creating and sustaining "social memory," see Cohen 1985; Goody 1986, 1987; Connerton 1989; and Bremmer and Roodenburg 1991.

25. See Connerton 1989, 75, and Goody 1987, 81–82, 161–66. This combination unified the practices of incorporation and inscription. The performance aspect of "reading" codices, discussed in chapter 2, already united textual and nontextual practices.

26. The ceremonial seating of rulers in the Mixteca brings to mind Clifford Geertz's description of seating rituals and divine kingship in Bali. Seating ceremonies are part of the "state theatre" that Geertz described (1980, 102–16). In Bali, as in the Mixteca, the palace is a temple where the lord is seated. Divine power extended from the central seat of secular authority. The royal rituals enacted, in the form of pageant, the main themes of Balinese and Mixtec political ideology. The ritual ceremonies also asserted a hierarchy of prestige and power. Whereas a male authority of the *negara* (Indonesian town or state) dominated the Balinese seating ceremony, men and women of the yuhuitayu shared the seat of power.

27. AJT-C, 4:417, f. 16v.

28. Ibid., 4:417, f. 19.

29. The *Vocabulario* lists *ñañu* under *pedazo*, "piece" or "part" (Alvarado, f. 164). This is the only meaning I can find for *ñañu*, unless it is interpreted as *ñaña* or *ocelotl* (often called "jaguar"). Since she did not name the lands separately, it is possible that the lands were also called *ñuuñañu* or that the entire site of the palace and its attached lands were known by that name. See the discussion of named lands in chapter 7.

30. AGN-T, 59:2.

31. AGN-T, 34:1, f. 82.

32. AGN-I, 21:78, f. 84. This information comes from a Spanish-language record; hence, the spelling of the aniñe name is unusual. The "hill" element, *yucu*, is obvious, but the preceding part is unclear.

33. AJT-C, 8:724. The name Dzahuico means "rain cloud," "rain feast," or "feast of Dzahui" (the rain deity).

34. AGN-T, 245:2.

35. Ibid., 245:2, f. 85, lines 139–42.

36. The Nahua chronicler Chimalpahin implied that there was an ideal relationship of one altepetl, one ruler, and one palace. See Schroeder 1991, 139.

37. Carrasco 1976a, 21; Offner 1983, 132; Lockhart 1992, 104–5.

38. Lockhart 1992, 104, 506 n. 60.

39. Alvarado, ff. 161, 146. See also the word *tayu* for the entry "de dos en dos" (f. 68). I have not found the term *throne* in the *Vocabulario*. Jansen has translated this as "petate, throne" and by extension "cacicazgo" or "señorío" (1982, 59–60). I agree with his intepretation, though I am adding an emphasis on the metaphorical use of *tayu* as both "couple" and "seat."

40. The *Vocabulario* lists "palacio" as *aniñe, tayu* (Alvarado, f. 160v); by far the most frequently used word for the structure is *aniñe*. In the response to "palanciano" [*sic*] only the word *aniñe* is used. "Silla" is given as *tayu* (189v).

41. See Spores 1967, 131–54.

42. Smith concluded, after a detailed discussion on the significance of seated figures, that the marriage scene was a pictorial convention with no corollary in the language. See Smith 1973a, 31.

43. Ibid., 40. In the codices and other pictographic writings, a ñuu was represented by the step-fret frieze, also known as the greca or tablero motif. The conventional hill motif also referred to a settled place, often corresponding with an actual place-name that began with *yucu*. The Lienzo of Ocotepec uses both conventions to represent the ruling couple of Cuquila (Ñuucuiñe), seated on a ñuu platform, which is perched on a hill.

44. Smith suggested that this pose indicated that the couple was already married (1973a, 29). But if the yuhuitayu glyph does not simply record a marriage, there would be little need for such a convention. I have observed that when a couple is seated in such a manner, it is usually the local lord or lady (from the perspective of the artist) who is seated in front. Compare for example, the position of the man and woman in the *Codex Sierra* and the tribute record from Tecomaxtlahuaca. In this sense, both male and female represented the yuhuitayu together, seated on the same mat, but one was the principal representative of that particular ñuu.

45. Michael Kearney has brought to my attention the fact that many of these yuhui or petates were probably palm mats, given the tradition of weaving with palm in the Mixteca.

46. For central Mexico, see Dibble 1971, 324; for the Maya area, see Robicsek 1975.

47. Schroeder 1991, 180. Chimalpahin does not discuss the petlatl icpalli in specific relation to the Spanish word for throne, whereas *cipolli, xihuitzolli,* and *teuhctzontli* are often equated with Spanish *corona* (crown).

48. For examples of a seated male tlatoani from the Nahua area, see the *Codex Mendoza* and the *Florentine Codex,* among others. Since no preconquest Nahua codices have survived, comparisons of Nahua and Mixtec preconquest iconography may appear to be incongruous. However, Mixtec pictorial writings continued to feature men and women as seated couples throughout the sixteenth century and beyond. In contrast, hundreds of Nahua manuscripts from this period feature the lone male ruler. Moreover, the Nahua historians, including Chimalpahin, present a clear view of preconquest Nahua dynastic arrangements that do not feature women as equal partners in the tlatocayotl.

49. See Smith 1973a, 29–31; Caso 1977–79, 1: 30; Jansen 1982, 59; Smith and Parmenter 1991, 20; Jansen 1992, 25; Marcus 1992, 229–37; and Jansen 1994. Most scholars have interpreted the pairing of seated males and females as marriage or conference scenes.

50. Caso 1949. See the discussion on hereditary succession below.

51. See Troike 1982 for an interpretation of postures and gestures in the *Codex Bodley, Codex Selden,* and the *Codex Colombino-Becker.* In the light of Troike's hypothesis that gestures indicate forms of "request" and "acceptance," it is possible that local residence patterns or tribute arrangements were part of the agreements. The use of hands and arms in the *Codex Sierra* as references to tribute, based on *daha,* may have a bearing on interpretations of the hand signals. I think that the prominence of the index finger in these gestures is significant. The *Vocabulario* defines "dedo index" as *nuundaha yonahatnuni.* The first word refers to the finger, and the second word is a verb meaning "to signal a command, notice, agreement." "Tnuni" is a functional term related to *mandar* and similar verbs; "naha" means "to signal" or "to show." The verb *nahatnuni* is also listed under "dar señas a otro." Thus, the pointed finger signals a particular type of command or agreement. A second entry for the index finger is simply "second finger." See Alvarado, ff. 67v, 144v, 65v. The concept of "gestural vocabulary" is discussed in Connerton 1989.

52. Smith 1983c, 243–44.

53. The *Vocabulario* provides only *yuhui* for "petate" and indicates no stylistic variety; the term *tayutehe* is given for "assiento de espaldar," but it is a chair and not a mat. The *Vocabulario* distinguishes between *assiento,* "site, location," and *asiento,* "seat" (Alvarado, ff. 167, 28). Smith has attributed variation in the motif to regional or temporal differences, as well as particular idioms and ceremonial practices. It is likely, also, that differences in style are related to differences in structure, a possibility discussed below in relation to the Mixteca Baja.

54. AGN-T, 70:2, ff. 46–48. Acatlan is located approximately fifty kilometers northwest of Huaxuapa and Atoyac. Don Diego de Villagómez and doña Ana de Guzmán, together with other nobles, petitioned to protect lands belonging to doña Ana's patrimony as *cihuapilli* (Nahuatl term for "noblewoman"; translated at the time as "cacica and señora") of Acatlan. The translator from Acatlan spoke Mixtec, Nahuatl, and Spanish.

55. Smith and Parmenter 1991. The codex also depicts the genealogy of Chila; both are located in the Mixtec-speaking region of modern-day southern Puebla. The *Codex Dehesa,* produced in the central Puebla/western Veracruz area, is very similar in its style and content. Glosses on the *Codex Tulane* are in Mixtec, whereas glosses on the *Codex Dehesa* are in Nahuatl.

56. Each woman's knees are bent, with her legs folded and off to one side, feet back and hands folded; the Mixtec pose usually depicted women in full profile with their feet in front and hands outstretched. See Caso 1960, 14; Robertson 1966, 302; and Smith 1983b, 244. They sit on what appears to be either a simple blanket or the hem of their *huipilli* (Ñudzahui *dzico*). The *Codex Sánchez-Solís* also has a number of central Mexican motifs, and it is also from the Baja region of northern Oaxaca and southern Puebla (see Smith 1983b, 244).

57. Women appear in the codex forty-six times, while there are sixty-six males, a ratio that compares favorably with the appearance of women in Mixtec codices but not in central Mexican manuscripts. See Smith and Parmenter 1991, 7, 20, and app. A, on manuscripts from the Baja region.

58. According to Smith, the women's parents appear to the left of the royal couples and are depicted in typical Mixtec pose and clothes. Do the women represent the Ñudzahui half of the marriage alliance? Smith suggests that Mixtec communities began to initiate alliances in the Baja (from the Alta) in the early thirteenth century. Ibid., 46–60, inserts 9–14.

59. See the discussion in chapter 4 of its Mixtec equivalent, *yucunduta.*

60. Spores 1967, 155–72.

61. On the Lienzo of Nativitas, see Rincón-Mautner 1994, 1999.

62. Alvarado, f. 85; see entries under "echar" and specifically "echarse con muger."

63. Acuña 1984, 1:286, from the *Relaciones geográficas* report of Justlahuaca.

64. This scene resembles a Nahua version depicted in the *Codex Mendoza.* See Berdan and Anawalt 1992, f. 61.

65. Reyes, p. 76.

66. The *relaciones* of Zacatepec and Ytnuhuaya, for example, speak of prolonged wedding feasts.

67. See Monaghan 1987 and 1990b, 567, on modern Mixtec associations of pulque with sexual fluids and sacrificial offering with sex. See also King 1988, 208–10, on sexual metaphors involving the mat and milpa.

68. For example, many Nahua rulers inherited the tlatocayotl of altepetl on the grounds that their mothers were from that place. Reckoning by the female line was even more frequent after the conquest, with its disruptions, increased mortality from diseases, and the consequent difficulty in finding heirs. On dynastic inheritance patterns among the Nahuas, see Lockhart 1992, 102–4.

69. See Schroeder 1991, 174–80.

70. Caso 1949, 1960, 1966a. No doubt, Caso's views evolved from his work on the Mapa de Teozacualco in 1949 to his analysis of succession in Yanhuitlan in 1962 (later published in English in 1966). Dahlgren's contribution falls within these dates.

71. Dahlgren 1954, 149–51.

72. Spores 1967, 145. This observation was introduced in a section titled "Female Succession." See also ibid., 131–54; 1984, 68–72; and 1997, 185–98.

73. Cook and Borah 1968, 13. See also Borah and Cook 1979, discussed below in relation to the *Codex Sierra.*

74. Smith and Parmenter 1991, 20.

75. Spores 1967, 10–11.

76. See Taylor 1972, 45.

77. Spores 1967, 149.

78. In terms of Pedro Carrasco's classification of royal marriages, the yuhuityau would be characterized as interdynastic isogamy. The arrangements between dynasties were not necessarily long-term relationships, however. See Carrasco 1984, 55–56.

79. Spores has detailed the frequent occurrence of matrilocal residence patterns among caciques of the Mixteca Alta (1964, 26) and has concluded that ambilocal patterns were the norm (1967, 11). Many of the reports of the *Relaciones geográficas,* especially those from the Baja, suggest patrilocal patterns, however. I have observed ambilocal patterns for lords and commoners, but especially among the yya and toho. For representative examples of matrilocal patterns, see AJT-C, 6:638 (1579); AGN-T, 571:1 (1633); AJT-C, 7:654 (1573); AGN-T, 59:2 (1571).

80. For example, see the relaciones reports of Justlahuaca, Mixtepec, Ytnuhuaya (Ayusuchiquilazala), Zacatepec, and Puctla. See Acuña 1984, 1:286–320.

81. This was also the case in central Mexico. See Carrasco 1984 and Horn 1997.

82. According to Spores, the postclassic was not a period of high-level intercommunity conflict within the Nochixtlan Valley; conflict was apparently alleviated by numerous marital connections. Many of the larger settlement sites had already been moved from earlier defensive locations atop slopes and hilltops to positions on the valley floor by the time the Spaniards arrived. This was the case, for example, in Yanhuitlan, Coixtlahuaca, and Texupa. This observation explains in part why the Mixtecs were so vulnerable to the Mexica empire and submitted so swiftly to the Spanish contingent in the 1520s (Spores 1983d, 248).

83. Spores 1967, 139–41. This fact may explain why the map of Teozacualco depicts the most recent ruler, at the top of the lineage string, as an unmarried person. Don Francisco de Mendoza was the heir apparent of his father, don Felipe de Santiago, who is seated below him. Don Felipe ruled in Teozacualco in 1580. The son is part of a partial yuhuitayu that will be complete only when he marries and inherits the toniñe on his parents' deaths. The convention of representing a future ruler in an unmarried pose confirms the importance of marriage in sealing this arrangement.

84. For example, in 1695, doña Juana de Lara bequeathed San Bartolomé Maninaltepec (Yucuañi) to her nephew, don Pedro de Lara, cacique of Texupa. The bequest was later disputed, in part, on the grounds that she had never been recognized as cacica because she never married. AGN-T, 3689:3, f. 31v.

85. I use *patrimony* here in the gender-neutral sense of the term, in reference to the estate and titles inherited from one's ancestors.

86. Acuña 1984, 1: 286.

87. Ibid., 294. See also the relaciones of Putla and Ayusuchiquilazala, also in the Mixteca Baja.

88. Spores 1967, 147–53; also, Caso 1966a. It seems that inheritance patterns were extremely flexible and subject to local variation and pragmatic concerns.

89. Jack Goody has observed this tendency in societies in which women were eligible to inherit titles. See Goody 1966, 32.

90. Dahlgren's study of marriages in the codices demonstrated the frequency of parallel-cousin marriage. See Dahlgren 1954, 149–51; Spores 1967, 12–13.

91. AGN-T, 637:1, ff. 65–73. In 1622, don Felipe de Velasco sought dispensation for his son, don Diego de Velasco y Arellano, and doña Micaela de la Cueva, the daughter of his nephew.

92. The legendary 8-Deer, for example, expanded Tilantongo's influence in the Mixteca by taking multiple wives and by waging war with other ñuu.

93. See Caso 1966a, 313–35 and the genealogical diagram on 332–33, and Spores 1967, 134–39, 152–54. I have also consulted the original documentation in AGN-C, 516:2, ff. 1–49; AGN-T, 400:1; and AGN-T, 985:2, ff. 1–90.

94. Caso 1966a; Spores 1967, 131–54. The glyph for Yanhuitlan in the *Codex Bodley* (19-III) represents "yodzocahi" with a bed of *yodzo*, or feathers. Caso used the *Codex Bodley* to trace this genealogy to the eleventh century.

95. These names are based on the ancient calendar, employing honorific vocabulary for numbers and signs. Namahu is 8-Death; Cauaco is 1-Flower; Nuqh is 6-Movement; Cocuahu is 2-House. Doña María is also shown in the *Codex Bodley* (19).

96. Spores 1967, 152.

97. AGN-C, 516:2, f. 4v. This fact is confirmed in a separate case that details the succession of Tamazola and Chachoapa in the sixteenth century (AGN-T, 3343:12). See Spores 1967, 152–53.

98. AGN-C, 516:2, f. 47. The Spanish passage is: "doña María fue la señora de aqui de Yanhuitlan que fue la señora y cacica que mandó los tiempos pasados." Unfortunately, the original native-language testament does not exist. Portions of the original were translated for the legal proceedings.

99. Curiously, don Gabriel stipulated that her title would revert to his son, don Francisco, on her death, thus consolidating two patrimonies in one head and denying doña María the choice of an heir. In other words, she would serve the same role that don Domingo had served in Yanhuitlan until 1558, ruling but not bequeathing. But don Gabriel also stipulated that if his son should die without heirs, doña María would inherit don Francisco's title and patrimony and the situation would be reversed. This attempt at consolidation suggests that don Gabriel was willing to bend the rules to enrich his own lordly establishment at the expense of others (Achiutla and Teposcolula, for example).

100. The provisions of this marriage arrangement are outlined in AJT-C, 7:654.

101. AGN-T, 400:2, f. 105; Spores 1967, 136–38. Again, the original testament is not preserved. The document states that he did not have children with his legitimate wife.

102. In 1717, a faction from Tlaxiaco recalled that don Juan Manuel was don Francisco's illegitimate child. It claimed that he had married three times without producing a legitimate heir. Tlaxiaco had become involved in Yanhuitlan's affairs through the marriage of don Francisco to doña María de Saavedra in 1587. AJT-C, 7:654.

103. AGN-T, 400:1.

104. Ibid., 571:1.

105. See Smith 1979 and Jansen 1994, 193–214. The place might be called Ñuunaa or "Lugar Oscuro" based on a glyph in the related Fragmento de Nochistlan.

106. Smith and Parmenter 1991, 20. On the other hand, one Mixteca Baja manuscript, the *Codex Egerton* 2895, emphasizes female inheritors.

107. AGN-T, 571:1, f. 25v.

108. AGN-V, 272:3, ff. 452–508.

109. Similarly, in Chimalpahin's accounts the royal lineage of Culhuacan was the origin of the tlatocayotl of many other central Mexican polities (Schroeder 1991, 163).

110. For example, Tamazola and Chachuapa were combined as a patrimony through four generations in the sixteenth century. See AGN-T, 3343:12. In 1580, don Pedro de Velasco was cacique of Tamazola y Chachoapa. He inherited them from don Matias de Velasco and doña María Magdalena, who inherited them from don Diego de Velasco and doña María Cocuahu. Don Diego Velasco inherited them from his brother, don Diego Conquisi, who died without children.

111. Spores noted the use of this legal terminology in the Mixteca Alta (1967, 141).

112. AGN-T, 24:6.

113. Borah 1983, 46.

114. AGN-T, 24:6, f. 10v.

115. Ibid., 400:1, f. 139.

116. Ibid., f. 321.

117. Ibid., 760:1.

118. Ibid., 1202:1.

119. Ibid., 1285:1, f. 82.

120. Ibid., 1425:14.

121. See Spores 1997 for a discussion of the wealth and influence of Mixteca cacicas.

122. For a comparison with Spanish women of late colonial Mexico City, see Arrom 1985.

123. A pioneering, landmark study of the native cabildo is Gibson's work on Tlaxcala (1952) and the Valley of Mexico (1964). For studies of the cabildo based on Nahuatl-language records, see Wood 1984; Haskett 1991a; Schroeder 1991; Lockhart 1992; and Horn 1997. For Yucatan, see Farriss 1984 and Restall 1997. These studies reveal a broad pattern of Mesoamerican adaptation to Spanish-style municipal government.

124. Alvarado, f. 116; another entry is *tay yocuvui nuu*, which could mean "one who is in front" or "one who is the face, the eyes," perhaps in reference to leadership. The fact that the governor is usually portrayed as the first person seated among a group of nobles, as in the *Codex Sierra*, suggests an association between descriptive words and images. Another important entry for "governor" is discussed below in relation to the concept of tniño.

125. Ibid., f. 116.

126. Haskett 1985, 88.

127. For the Nahua region, see Lockhart 1992, 30.

128. The solution in the Nahua area involved the representation of various parts of the altepetl by rotation. For a comparison with Nahua tlatoani and governor, see Gibson 1964; Haskett 1991a; and Lockhart 1992. For the Maya *batab* and governor, see Roys 1972 and Restall 1997.

129. AGN-INQ, 37:5. The proceedings were recorded before the lords had adopted Spanish surnames.

130. AJT-C, 7:654; this document is a copy of the original, which was said to be badly damaged and was supposedly transcribed verbatim in 1659.

131. See Haskett 1991a, 47, for a similar pattern among the Nahuas of Cuernavaca; for central Mexico, where rotation among *tlatoque* was more common than consecutive reelection by the end of the sixteenth century, see Gibson 1964, 167–72, and Lockhart 1992, 32. For Yucatan, see Restall 1997, 62–63.

132. Haskett provides examples of support from friars in the elections of Cuernavaca, favoring factions and upholding certain caciques (1991a, 43). The results of annual elections were usually confirmed by ecclesiastics.

133. AJT-C, 1:90, 91, 112.

134. Ibid., 4:382; ibid., 5:595. His predecessor, don Diego de Mendoza, was also governor and cacique (AGN-T, 24:6).

135. See Spores 1967, 128, in response to Gibson 1952, 102. The case of don Francisco Pimentel y Guzmán, discussed below, is an excellent example of this practice.

136. AJT-C, 6:586.

137. Ibid., 4:467.

138. A survey of scattered records indicates that in the 1560s the governorship was separated from the position of cacique in Teposcolula and Tlaxiaco but not in Yanhuitlan, Tamasulapa, Justlahuaca, Nochixtlan, Etlatongo, Tecomaxtlahuaca, and Tlatlaltepec. Ibid., 1:4–90.

139. The second point has been acknowledged by Spores (1984, 167).

140. AGN-T, 400:1, f. 139.

141. Ibid., 59:2.

142. AGN-I, 2:339.

143. AGN-T, 34:1.

144. AJT-CR, 2:233. The document does not reveal whether his wife was from Yanhuitlan, but it is very likely that she was. Thus, don Francisco had a house in each of the two communities. See Sousa 1998, 307–8, for additional examples of men who served on the cabildos of their wives' communities in the colonial period.

145. AJT-C, 3:329; ibid., 4:400.

146. Ibid., 4:467.

147. Ibid., 1:95.

148. Ibid., 4:417.

149. Ibid., 1:90. At this time, don Francisco was yya toniñe of Tlaxiaco and Yanhuitlan.

150. See Gibson 1964, 167–72.

151. AJT-C, 4:417. This phrase was translated as "Lorenzo González, principal de la cabecera de San Juan." The translation equated *toho* with *principal* and *yuhuitayu* with *cabecera.*

152. Ibid., 4:440. At that time, it had one *regidor,* three *alguaciles ordinarios,* one *alguacil doctrina,* and three *saquiñahi* (*tequitlatos,* or tribute collectors). These offices are discussed below.

153. It is questionable whether San Juan could have rightfully claimed yuhuitayu status based on existing ties to royal lineage. As doña Lázara de Guzmán did not fail to mention, Lorenzo González could claim neither of the crucial titles associated with high status, the Spanish *don* or the Ñudzahui *yya.* Lorenzo was the type of local ruler who might call himself "governor and cacique" in the later period.

154. AGN-I, 1:49–51, ff. 19v–20. He also received one field of maize (250 *brazas* wide and long) and other certain privileges, including rights to labor for lands belonging to his cacicazgo. In return, he was to pay twenty pesos per year to those who sowed the lands.

155. Ibid., 1:2, f. 1v.

156. AGN-T, 34:1, f. 63v.

157. AGN-I, 1:160, ff. 59–59v.

158. Ibid., 6.2:212, f. 47v.

159. Gibson 1964, 187.

160. AGN-I, 1:157, f. 58.

161. Ibid., 1:152, f. 56.

162. Ibid., 1:53, f. 20v; ibid., 1:30, f. 12.

163. Ibid., 2:339.

164. Ibid., 2:1004.

165. As discussed in chapter 2, this is a Ñudzahui text written in Nahuatl.

166. In reference to Texupa, using the *Codex Sierra* as a source, Borah and Cook wrote: "In the middle of the sixteenth century the ruler was a woman, doña Catalina. Expenditures for provision of food and a modest measure of other support for her appear in the town documents. Her powers were greatly reduced by the institution of a new organization of government, derived from Spanish models." They also suggested that the first governor was the cacica's husband. Borah and Cook 1979, 419.

167. AGN-T, 34:1.

168. AGN-I, 1:53, f. 20v.

169. AGN-T, 34:1, f. 26v.

170. The situation in Texupa is complicated by the fact that the main settlement was moved from its original site after 1564 and was renamed Santiago Texupa. Thus, the name of Santa Catalina may have been dropped altogether. The presence of two aniñe on the map of Texupa, drawn for the *Relaciones geográficas,* indicates the maintenance of two lordly establishments. On Texupa in the sixteenth century, see Bailey 1972 and Borah and Cook 1979.

171. AGN-T, 34:1, ff. 3–3v.

172. See Borah 1983, 46, for a discussion of how the Spanish emphasis on patrilineal succession affected legal rulings.

173. The custom of males representing their communities' will to outsiders has been noted in several native North American nations. See Allen 1986, 18–20.

174. Spores 1967, 152. Consider the following example: in 1677, doña Beatriz Maldonado bequeathed her patrimony of Nopaltitlan to her son, don Miguel de Santiago y Velasco. She also fulfilled the bequest of her husband, don Raimundo de Santiago y Guzmán, who in 1676 had bequeathed his patrimony of Coculco (Ñucucu) and Chinanco (Tisacu) to the same don Miguel. Don Raimundo had inherited both his mother's and father's patrimonies through the premature death of his brother. Thus, don Miguel de Santiago y Velasco was invested with three separate patrimonies that had been consolidated within two generations. The last bequest favored this older son over two eligible sisters and a younger brother. A new yuhuitayu was created by the marriage of don Miguel to doña Pascuala de Rivera, cacica of Yucuhuehi (Caltepec), thereby uniting four ñuu. AGN-T, 571:1.

175. For the Nahua area, see Gibson 1964, 172–73; Haskett 1991a, 95–123; and Lockhart 1992, 38. For the Mixteca, see Spores 1984, 165–80, and Pastor 1987, 85, 96–99. Some of the transcriptions

and translations of native-language terminology in Pastor are incorrect. For Yucatan, see Restall 1997, 61–72.

176. It is important to recognize, however, that some terms for cabildo offices in the *Vocabulario* were outdated by its publication in 1593, if they had ever been used at all. Spanish loanwords were used to describe most offices from the earliest time of native-language documentation, at least two decades before the *Vocabulario* was printed. In fact, terms for cabildo positions were among the first loanwords to be incorporated into the native language. Nonetheless, the descriptions and circumlocutions of the early period are insightful for their conscious choice of equivalences.

177. Alvarado, ff. 174v, 166v. Actually, it is listed in the possessed form as *tniñondi*, or "my duty," the standard version of a possessed noun in the *Vocabulario*.

178. Ibid., f. 40. A native-language document, written in 1598, describes how the tribute collectors (*saquiñehe*) of the siña of Yuhuyucha delivered the fruits of their labor to the "huahi tniño" of Yanhuitlan. AJT-CR, 1:113.

179. Alvarado, f. 116.

180. AJT-CR, 6:705.

181. AGN-C, 1429:3, f. 52.

182. AJT-C, 6:586. The document is dated 1709.

183. Alvarado, f. 30. The same term was applied to *auditorio el lugar para oyr,* "the hearing place." Perhaps the emphasis on "hearing" refers to the group's role of hearing petitions and speeches.

184. Molina's entries for *teccalli* and *tecpan* suggest the same association. The former is glossed as "casa o audiencia real," and the latter is called "casa o palacio real." Molina [1571] 1977, ff. 92, 93. Haskett (1991a, 32) found a similar association in Cuernavaca.

185. AJT-C, 8:724, f. 2, line 27. A separate document refers to the "aniñe comonidad yuhuitayu san pedro san pablo yucundaa" [the community palace of the yuhuitayu of Saints Peter and Paul Teposcolula] (AJT-CR, 6:705, f. 8).

186. AJT-CR, 3:367. In 1629, members of the cabildo were eating on the roof of the palace when a fracas broke out below. The document states that a local friar climbed up on the roof to speak to the officials.

187. Regional variation in the timing of this process is related to the location of the cabecera. For example, the cabildo of Teozacualco was not established until 1563, when native officials from Teposcolula were on hand to facilitate the initial ceremony. AJT-C, 1:5.

188. *Codex Sierra,* pp. 19, 35, 61.

189. Haskett 1991a, 47, 124–32; Lockhart 1992, 30–40.

190. Alvarado, f. 179v. For comparison with Nahuas, see Haskett 1991a, 104–7, and Lockhart 1992, 38–39.

191. AJT-C, 4:467.

192. Lockhart 1992, 35–37 and n. 80.

193. The cedula stated that communities with fifty to eighty tributary households were to elect one alcalde and one regidor, while those with more than eighty households were to elect two of each officer. For the Mixteca, see Pastor 1987, 86–88; for Nahua Cuernavaca, see Haskett 1991a, 32–36.

194. Whereas the Spanish regidores represented dominant families without regard to jurisdictions, the preconquest high council of nobles and lords represented subunits of the ñuu. This difference may be reflected by the lack of any equivalent for the entry "regidor" in the *Vocabulario.*

195. AJT-CR, 6:705.

196. It is possible that some ñandahi were present or that the reference was a symbolic gesture to the representation of commoners by the electors. Another possibility, suggested by Haskett in reference to the "macehualtin" of Nahuatl-language election records, is that the electors referred to themselves in a reverential manner. See Haskett 1991a, 30–31.

197. For example, "taa nisano" are mentioned in an election record from Huaxuapa, 1674 (AGN-C, 1429:3, f. 51). Tay nisano may have been authorities from subunits, or they may have been former officials. In many ways, tay nisano resemble the Nahua *huehuetque.* The composition and function of this group are unclear among the Nahuas. See Haskett 1991a, 22, 142, and Lockhart 1992, 138–39.

198. Alvarado, f. 102, also *tay yonaitniño taa tutu.*

199. AJT-CR, 5:508.

200. See Lockhart 1992, 41, for references to this practice among Nahua scribes in Tlaxcala.

201. AJT-C, 10:806. Carrillo's testament of 1738 reflects his status as a well-to-do toho.

202. Alvarado, f. 16.

203. The "vara de justicia de alcalde" is *tatnu sinotasi tniño,* "staff for ordering the tniño," and the "vara de alguazil" is *tatnu sino quachi,* "staff for crime." Ibid., f. 220v.

204. Ibid., f. 15.

205. Ibid., f. 144v under "mandon como tlequitato [*sic*]." "Saquiñahi" often appears as *saquiñehe.* For Nahuas, see Lockhart 1992, 44. Nahuatl employed *calpixqui,* "steward," and *tequitlato,* "tribute speaker."

206. See Lockhart 1992, 48.

207. Actually, I have located only twelve election records written in the Ñudzahui language, dated from 1674 to 1714. The scarcity of election documents in the judicial record suggests that election disputes were not very common. On elections in Cuernavaca, see Haskett 1991a, 26–51; for central Mexico, see Lockhart 1992, 47–52; for Yucatan, see Restall 1997, 78–83.

208. AJT-CR, 6:705, f. 8.

209. A point made by Haskett for Cuernavaca; see Haskett 1991a, 36–41.

210. AGN-T, 400:1, ff. 139–320.

211. Ibid., f. 321.

212. Ibid., ff. 8–38, 188.

213. Ibid., f. 190.

214. Ibid., ff. 371v–372. The ruling was written and signed by the *oidor* don Francisco Antonio de Echeverría.

215. For a discussion of the uneven nature of this process in the Valley of Oaxaca and the Mixteca Alta, see Taylor 1972, 52–53, and Pastor 1987, 175.

216. As Spores has demonstrated, cacicas were among the wealthiest, most influential people in the region throughout much of the colonial period. See Spores 1997, 185–98.

217. See Pastor 1987, 307–14, and Monaghan 1997 on caciques and their estates in the nineteenth century.

CHAPTER 7 — LAND AND LIVELIHOOD

1. Lockhart 1992, 141.

2. Alvarado, f. 45.

3. This conclusion is confirmed by late postclassic archaeological evidence, which I do not consider in detail here. For a discussion of late postclasssic residential structures in the Mixteca, see Spores 1984, 49. See also Cook 1939 and Lind 1979.

4. The same can be said for the Nahua *calli.* Nahuatl ordinarily marks distinctions between singular and plural animate (but not inanimate) nouns. Ñudzahui marks neither plural animate nor inanimate nouns. See Lockhart 1992, 60.

5. Alvarado, f. 56v. Some have considered whether the Nahua *cihuacalli,* or "woman's house," referred to the cooking area of the calli. An equivalent term has not been attested in the Mixteca. See Calnek 1974, 45–46; Cline 1986, 100–101; and Lockhart 1992, 66.

6. AGN-T, 400:1, and 985:2.

7. AGN-INQ, 37:10.

8. AGN-T, 985:2, f. 75.

9. See the letter of March 7, 1630, reproduced in Jiménez Moreno and Mateos Higuera 1940, 49.

10. AGN-T, 24:6, ff. 3–55.

11. Witnesses from Teposcolula testified in 1639 that about a hundred men and women had gathered in the cacique's patio (AJT-CR, 4:447).

12. AGN-T, 85:2 and 245:2. "Huehi" and "aniy" are Mixteca Baja equivalents of the Teposcolula-area *huahi* and *aniñe.*

13. Ibid., 59:2. Nahuas associated a patio (*ithualli*) with a calli (house). See Lockhart 1992, 59–72, for a discussion of Nahua terminology surrounding the house complex, including the metaphorical doublet for a house *in quiahuatl, in ithualli* (the exit, the patio).

14. Spores 1967, 91; Lind 1979, 64.

15. See Sousa 1998, 94 n. 2, for a preliminary discussion of household structure in Oaxaca.

16. AJT-CR, 4:407.

17. Ibid., 3:319, 3:363. See also ibid., 4:421, 4:440. In Tamasulapa, in the year 1635, Esteban de Velasco had a huahi consisting of one room, a cooking room, and a patio. In 1679, Luis de Mora, a noble from Tamasulapa, had one *huahi yuu* (stone house) and one *huahi tiyacu,* translated as "jacal." (AJT-C, 6:635).

18. The reports of Ytnuhuaya, Puctla, and Nochixtlan for the *Relaciones geográficas* attest to this fact. See Acuña 1984, 1:301, 317, 370.

19. AJT-C, 13:1109.

20. Alvarado, f. 185v.

21. AJT-CR, 5:513.

22. The Spanish house also tended to be an enclosed structure organized around a patio, and sizable houses were often called "casas," but the building was more integrated by connecting doorways, rooms, and stairways. On this point, see Lockhart 1992, 64.

23. AJT-C, 9:758.

24. Acuña 1984, 2:236.

25. AJT-C, 10:838, ff. 14–15.

26. Like the Nahuas, the Mixtecs defined *familia* with words focusing on the house. The association of family with household was pronounced in much of the Mediterranean world, as well. For "familia, gente de mi casa" the *Vocabulario* employs words such as "ee huahindi" (one's house) but also refers to distinct kin-related terms such as *dahi, tnuhu, yaa,* and *nduhu*. See Alvarado, f. 109v.

27. This *huahi nama* resembles the Nahuatl term *tepancalli*, discussed in Lockhart 1992, 68.

28. AJT-CR, 1:42.

29. AJT-C, 4:417.

30. Ibid., 6:575; ibid., 2:243. The tendency to refer to the position of houses in terms of the cardinal directions was also typical among the Nahuas. See Lockhart 1992, 62. The terminology for "east" and "west" based on the sun's apparent emergence from and disappearance into the horizon is common in Mesoamerica.

31. Acuña 1984, 2:300.

32. In 1754, Sebastián Sánchez Hernández of Yanhuitlan owned two of these huahi tiyahua, as well as four other large huahi. The latter structures were valued at around forty pesos each, but the two smaller huahi were worth no more than ten pesos. AJT-C, 15:1232.

33. The aniñe was apparently built around the mid-sixteenth century, when the nearby church was being constructed. This building, called the "Casa de la Cacica," is discussed in chapter 6. See fig. 6.2.

34. As Lockhart noted for the Nahuas, it is unclear whether native houses in the colonial period adopted the Spanish layout of contiguous, intercommunicating rooms arranged around a patio. See Lockhart 1992, 71.

35. AJT-C, 2:243. "Huahi nino" was translated as *azotea*. This type of house may be similar to the Nahua *tlapancalli*, or "roof house," discussed in Cline 1986, 99, and Lockhart 1992, 67–68.

36. AJT-C, 8:705, ff. 12v–13. The Ñudzahui phrase was "qhmi huahe nanu sihi uni huahi candodzo tnaha nino coocha," translated in the Spanish as "quatro aposentos grandes que estan sobre estos a modo de corridor cassas de altos," neglecting to translate the "uni huahi" [three houses]. The "corridor" translation either refers to *coo* (ridge, snake) or is an elaboration of the original wording. In Teposcolula, Lucía Hernández Ñuquihui also owned a "huahy cadzo nino," translated as a "una casa del alto" (ibid, 3:287). The word *nino* means "tall."

37. For example, in 1661, don Francisco Pimentel y Guzmán was said to "walk around in the manner of a Spaniard, with a dagger and a sword" (AJT-CR, 5:500). A list of all musket owners in the jurisdiction of Teposcolula in 1598 revealed that at least sixteen native individuals (ten caciques and six nobles) and three communities possessed muskets (ibid., 1:108).

38. AGN-T, 985:2, ff. 26–28. See Spores 1967, 241–44, for a list of this cacique's inventory.

39. AJT-C, 7:654, f. 4.

40. The Nahua equivalents of *ñuhu* and *ytu* are *tlalli* and *milli*, respectively. In comparison, Yucatac Maya used no general term for land but rather referred to parcels of forest land called *kax* (Restall 1997, 208–9).

41. For a discussion of the Nahua callalli, see Lockhart 1992, 150. For Nahua land tenure in the colonial period in general, see Gibson 1964, 257–99; Cline 1984, 277–309, and 1986, 125–59; Harvey 1984, 83–102; Williams 1991, 187–208; Lockhart 1992, 141–76; and Horn 1997, 111–43.

42. The *Vocabulario* lists "antiguo lugar" as *chiyo yata*. Alvarado, f. 22.

43. For a discussion of patrimonial land among the Nahuas, see Lockhart 1992, 158–59, and Horn 1997, 124. For the Yucatec Maya, see Restall 1997, 208–10, for a description of *matan kax*, or "inherited land."

44. AJT-C, 6:575.

45. Ibid., 3:287. The variant spellings of *huahi* reflect orthographic variation and phonetic differences.

46. Ibid., 4:417.

47. AGN-T, 571:1. This case is from Nopaltitlan, in the Mixteca Baja. The words "ñoho" and "aniy" are phonetic and orthographic equivalents of the Teposcolula-area *ñuhu* and *aniñe*. In another case from the Baja, don Jorge de la Cruz Alvarado located his aniñe within a specific *dzini* ("barrio" in the Baja region) called Nuchiyo, which can be translated as "patrimonial land" or "patrimonial place." AGN-T, 245:2.

48. The holding of scattered lands was common in central Mexico and the Valley of Oaxaca. For the latter, see Taylor 1972, 77.

49. Most areas produced maize, beans, and squash, with yields subject to seasonal variation. Ridgetop communities exploited forests and soils for wood, minerals, and clay. Salt came from the Teposcolula Valley and the northern Baja; cotton and cacao were cultivated along the coast and Cañada. See Spores 1984, 80–84; Pastor 1987, 43–44; and Monaghan 1994, 143–87, for a discussion of ecological diversity and vertical integration in the Mixteca.

50. AJT-C, 7:689.

51. Ibid., 5:506, ff. 22–23.

52. Gibson reported that Spaniards referred to *chinampas* as "camellones" in the Valley of Mexico (1964, 320), probably in reference to the organization of these plots into long, narrow strips. See also Cline 1986, 132–35, on chinampas called camellones in Culhuacan.

53. For example, the testament of María López Siñuu of Yucucata used *yuhua* numerous times in reference to strips of named lands (AJT-C, 5:506, ff. 10–17v). However, the term *coo* was more common. The *Vocabulario* combined the two terms as *cooyuhua* under the entry "camellon de piedra" (Alvarado, f. 42v).

54. For evidence of Ñudzahui women guarding milpa in the colonial period, see Sousa 1998, 179.

55. AJT-C, 4:467, f. 40v.

56. Ibid., 5:506. In the Valley of Oaxaca, Taylor cited evidence for lands possessed by barrios and compared them to *calpollalli* in central Mexico. See Taylor 1972, 67, 72.

57. See Gibson 1964, 267–70; Lockhart 1992, 142–49; and Horn 1997, 115–16.

58. Of course, noble households with multiple landholdings relied on dependent laborers to sow their lands. The ability to validate and reallocate landholdings did not mean that local officials had the right to promote equal distribution of lands. See Williams 1991, 206, on this point, made for Nahua Tepetlaoztoc.

59. For tequitlalli among the Nahuas, see Lockhart 1992, 157, 161, 171–75.

60. See Gibson 1964, 258–59, and Taylor 1972, 68–73, on the functions of "common" lands in central Mexico and Oaxaca, respectively. In Yucatan, see Farriss 1984, 272–85, and Restall 1997, 206–11.

61. AJT-C, 6:578. A complex overlay of native and colonial terminologies is at work in this example. The use of the term *huahi tniño*, or "duty house," for the cabildo, or the place where the cabildo met, also called *audiencia* and *casa de la comunidad*, is discussed in chapter 6.

62. For example, a document from Coixtlahuaca refers to "ytu comunidad chiño" (the phonetic equivalent of "tniño" in the Yanhuitlan area) in 1596. AJT-CR, 1:52.

63. See Lockhart 1992, 24, 102–9. It should be noted, however, that Cline found few references to calpollalli in testaments from Culhuacan (1986, 147–49, and 1984, 286); the same can be said for Horn's findings on Coyoacan (1997, 116–17). See also Chance 1996 on the caciques of Tecali, Puebla.

64. Lockhart 1992, 174–75. The term *tecpantlalli*, the equivalent of *ñuhu aniñe*, fell out of use in the early seventeenth century. In Culhuacan and Coyoacan, the term hardly appears at all (Cline 1986, 145–46; Lockhart 1992, 163; Horn 1997, 121). For Cuernavaca, see Haskett 1991a, 72–73. In Yucatan, there was no equivalent.

65. See Taylor 1972 for native land tenure in the Valley of Oaxaca.

66. AJT-CR, 3:275. The siqui is called a "barrio" in this Spanish-language document. Taylor found similar examples of "terrasguerro communities" formed by Mixtec caciques in the Valley of Oaxaca. See Taylor 1972, 43.

67. AGN-T, 44:1. Perhaps the name is Nahuatl because the document was written in Spanish; some interpreters translated Ñudzahui names into Nahuatl-Spanish equivalents.

68. Another related but ambiguous term was *ñuhu yahui* (bought lands). The verb "to pay" or "to buy" was *tniñoyahui*, often reduced to *yahui*. However, *yahui* was also the written word for "maguey" (as well as "market"). Some people referred to *ytu yahui* when speaking about fields sown with maguey plants. Thus, the use of *ñuhu yahui* in testaments, with little other context, is difficult to translate as one type of land or the other.

69. AJT-C, 5:506.

70. Ibid., 4:400.

71. The names of deceased persons were referred to with a *ñu-* prefix, perhaps in reference to the fact that they were buried in the ground (ñuhu). Unlike the Nahuas, the Mixtecs customarily buried their dead in preconquest times.

72. Horn noted that testators in Coyoacan indicated when they had inherited purchased land (1997, 123). In Culhuacan, Cline noted that testators sometimes indicated when they had sold land (1984, 292). Aside from these minor variations, the Nahua and Ñudzahui categories are similar in all regards.

73. See Lockhart 1992, 153–55, for a discussion of tlalcohualli among the Nahuas. The appearance of this Nahua term in the earliest postconquest documents, when cloth was a currency of exchange, indicates its preconquest origins. It is unknown whether commoners possessed this type of land before the conquest. Houses were also bought and sold freely in the colonial period. See also Restall 1997, 209, for a description of *man kax,* or "bought forest," among the Yucatec Maya.

74. For references to "saints' lands" among the Nahuas, see Gibson 1964, 129–30, and Lockhart 1992, 168–69. Gibson called these cofradías "unofficial." Among the Maya, see Farriss 1984, 179–80, 270, on cofradía estates and Restall 1997, 210, on saints' lands.

75. AJT-C, 20:1684.

76. Ibid., 8:705.

77. See Lockhart 1992, 148–49, for a comparison of Nahua and Spanish modes of land tenure.

78. For Nahua terminology referring to different types of land, see ibid., 139–202. Yucatec Maya land tenure categories seem to have distinguished mainly between inherited (patrimonial) and purchased lands. See Restall 1997, 206–11.

79. AGN-T, 245:2. Nahuatl equivalents are *tepetlalli* and *amilli.*

80. Alvarado, f. 139 for "lodo" and f. 155 for "negro." This type of land may be comparable to the Nahua *atoctli,* a type of fertile, alluvial soil. See Gibson 1964, 300.

81. Spores has demonstrated that the tendency toward occupation and full utilization of flat alluvial lands and slopes had begun long before the postclassic period. See Spores 1983d.

82. The *Vocabulario* uses "hill land," or *yucu ñuhu,* and other terms associated with *yucu,* "hill," to define the Spanish word *desierto,* "desert." See Alvarado, f. 75. As eroded, mainly uncultivable soil, hill land must have come close to the meaning of desert soil for Ñudzahui speakers who contributed to the *Vocabulario.* In fact, stylized hills were often depicted in the codices with small bumps to indicate a hard, stony surface, as a stone was depicted. In Nahuatl, these are quasi-phonetic symbols, representing the *tetl* (stone) sign, reinforcing the *te-* in *tepetl,* "hill." Likewise, *yuu* means stone in Mixtec and reinforces the *yu-* in *yucu.*

83. AGN-T, 245:2, ff. 77–79. The *Vocabulario* gives "ñuhundoyo" as *tierra de regadío.* See Alvarado, f. 195v.

84. BNAH, 777, ff. 3–4.

85. AJT-C, 7:654. He used the phrase "ytu alahuerta ñuhu." The interpretation of *alahuerta* as a discrete loan noun is discussed in chapter 3.

86. Perhaps this subtle distinction explains why the term was borrowed so readily, especially by the late seventeenth century, when a close native equivalent existed. See Lockhart 1992, 68–69, for a discussion of the solar among Nahuas in central Mexico. For Culhuacan, Cline noted that *solar* was adopted very early (1986, 135–36). In Yucatan, *solar* was the operative term for all lands not considered *kax,* "forest," in the colonial period. See Restall 1997, 206–9.

87. AJT-C, 7:689, f. 32v.

88. Ibid., 4:417.

89. For Nahua land measurements, see Cline 1986, 129–31; Lockhart 1992, 144–46, 166–67; and Horn 1997, 129–32.

90. A vara was 33 inches, and a Spanish braza was about 2 varas in length, or approximately 1.7 meters. Specifically, a "yunta" refers to the number of yuntas or yokes of oxen necessary to plow a tract of land in a day.

91. For example, see Cline 1986, 126, for the tradition of naming lands and locating plots relative to neighboring fields in Culhuacan.

92. AGN-T, 24:6, f. 41.

93. AGN-I, 32:157, ff. 151v–152. The meanings of the two names are entirely different.

94. A case from Texupa illustrates this phenomenon. Of the four documents presented in the case, one land title and a testament (dated 1587 and 1680, respectively) were written in Chocho; the

same folder also contained a land transfer in Nahuatl (dated 1551) with a Mixtec land transfer written on the back (dated 1579). The Nahuatl document did not assign a name to the land, whereas the
Mixtec and Chocho records did. AJT-C, 6:638.

95. AGN-T, 1226:3, ff. 3–4v.

96. AJT-C, 7:689, ff. 14–15v.

97. His attention to the cardinal directions represents a typical Mesoamerican concern. For a
discussion of the use of cardinal directions in land description among the Nahuas and Yucatec Maya,
respectively, see Lockhart 1992, 169, and Restall 1997, 189–93.

98. AGN-T, 400:1, f. 56.

99. AJT-C, 13:1109, f. 20.

100. See Spores 1969, 1984.

101. Taylor found ample evidence for use of the plow in the Valley of Oaxaca by the mid-
seventeenth century (1972, 81).

102. See Pastor 1987, 139–40, for the growing of wheat by cabeceras in the early period.

103. See Borah 1951.

104. AGN-T, 24:6, ff. 29–40. For the discussion of a similar response of Nahuas to European
ceremonies, see Lockhart 1992, 169–70.

105. AGN-I, 6.2:176, f. 41.

106. Taylor 1972, 78.

107. For central Mexico, see Harvey 1984, 87, and Cline 1986, 88.

108. AGN-T, 59:2.

109. AGN-C, 516:1. Ronald Spores calculated that don Domingo de Guzmán was guaranteed by
viceregal decree in 1548 the harvest from about six hundred acres of lands in Yanhuitlan. This was
only a part of his landholdings, however. See Spores 1967, 162. See also AGN-T, 400:1, for a list of
lands belonging to the cacicazgo in 1591.

110. Gibson indicated that *tlatoque* (Nahua rulers) possessed lands in other altepetl in the early
colonial period but that Spaniards rapidly reduced these extended patrimonies to local proportions
(Gibson 1964, 263–64). Horn noted that tlatoque in Coyoacan possessed lands scattered throughout
the tlaxilacalli of the altepetl but that they did not claim possessions outside Coyoacan (Horn 1997,
116).

111. AGN-T, 245:2, ff. 75–76.

112. Taylor 1972, 57; AGN-HJ, 118. The document is dated 1717.

113. Taylor attributed the expansion of caciques' lands after the conquest to the acquisition of
unoccupied lands. See Taylor 1972, 44.

114. For the region of Huexotzinco, Dyckerhoff and Prem found that as much as 69 percent of
the people were considered "terrazgueros" in the census of 1560 (1976, 160). The figure is much
lower elsewhere, however. Carrasco found figures of less than 20 percent of the total population for
Cuernavaca (1976a, 104).

115. AJT-C, 2:263.

116. To assess lords' landholdings, I have used eighteen native-language testaments and two
Spanish-language records. In each case, yya and yya dzehe were easily recognizable as dons and
doñas, caciques and cacicas.

117. AJT-C, 8:705.

118. Ibid., 13:1109.

119. Ibid., 1:33. See also Taylor 1972, 42, for the services received by *principales* in the Valley of
Oaxaca.

120. See Sousa 1998, 303, for several examples of commoners who worked for nobles. The following section on tribute and trade provides additional examples.

121. Even though coo and yuhua were apparently more marginal lands than ñuhu chiyo and
ytu, I have counted them together here because of the ambiguity in terminology. Namely, it is commonplace to see terms such as *coo ñuhu, coo ytu, sichi ytu*, and even *yuhua ytu ñuhu*. Not knowing the
qualitative or quantitative differences between these designations and their combined forms, I have
respected the testator's references to individual pieces of land. Most but not all of the separate tracts
are named. When a person referred to multiple coo that were grouped together in a certain named
place, I have counted them as only one tract.

122. Compare with Stephanie Wood's findings on Nahua Toluca, where women certainly owned
land, but less than men (1997, 172). Horn found that noblewomen possessed less land than their male
counterparts (1997, 137). However, whereas no woman owned more than nine plots of land in

Toluca, there were yya dzehe in the Mixteca who owned as many as sixty tracts of land, and even toho dzehe who possessed as many as thirteen plots. See also Cline 1984, 303, on Nahua Culhuacan, where evidence suggests that variations in estate size were not determined by gender but that women generally controlled less land than men.

123. These figures are comparable to Rebecca Horn's findings for Coyoacan, where Nahua commoners possessed one house and two or three pieces of land in the 1550s. See Horn 1997, 132.

124. The measurement of lands by "yuntas" (see above) was fairly common by the eighteenth century. Most people referred to plots of land that were only a few yuntas in size.

125. AJT-C, 7:689, ff. 7–8.

126. Ibid., 4:400, f. 3–3v.

127. Ibid., 14:1124. These are the types of writings one would not expect to find in a judicial dispute over land, mainly because these poor people had no land to claim or defend. In fact, the documents were filed in the judicial archive for an unusual reason. When Juan Francisco was accused of having forged a land sale record in 1776, allegedly signed by a former notary of San Francisco Chinduhua named Pedro de San Pablo, the alcalde mayor ordered local authorities to produce official documents written by the deceased notary in order to compare the signature on the land sale in question with the notary's verified signature. The testaments of Pascuala and Nicolás, written in 1730 and 1737, respectively, were used for the comparison. But the documents were not related to the case in any other way. The fact that landless commoners are uncommon in my collection of wills, derived mainly from judicial archives, indicates the bias toward propertied people in the judicial record. On the other hand, as we will see below, several testaments recognize landless dependents, who were the type of commoners least likely to be represented in the written record.

128. Ibid., 7:686, ff. 12–13. In this case, the *dz* of the Teposcolula area was pronounced as *d* in Yanhuitlan, especially in the late colonial period, so that *dzaya* is written as "daya" and *nidza-* is written as "nida-." It could be that people such as Nicolás were illegitimate children of nobles, but the use of *dzaya* may be more symbolic than literal. A term for poor commoners, *dzaya dzana*, discussed in chapter 5, combines the word for child with "orphan." In Culhuacan, Cline observed that orphaned nieces and nephews were likely candidates to serve in households (1986, 72).

129. AJT-C, 8:705.

130. Taylor 1972, 67–68; see also Pastor 1987, 144–46.

131. For the Valley of Mexico, see Gibson 1964, 268–82.

132. This discussion is based on the analysis of 125 native-language testaments, written on behalf of yya, toho, and ñandahi from the Mixteca Alta and Baja. In comparison, on inheritance among the Nahuas, see Lockhart 1992, 90–93. On the Nahuas of Culhuacan, see Cline 1984, 294–302, and 1986, 77–85. For Mexico City, see Kellogg 1995, 125–29, 142–58. For Yucatan, see Farriss 1984, 134–36, 169–71, and Restall 1997, 110–20.

133. This was also true among the Nahuas. For example, see Cline 1986, 90–94.

134. But as Lockhart noted for the Nahuas, affinal and collateral kin might be included in bequests, even though lineal descendants were preferred heirs and "the primarily intended ultimate beneficiaries." See Lockhart 1992, 93. According to Cline, the preferred order of heirs in Culhuacan was children and grandchildren; spouse; siblings; nieces and nephews; and stepchildren (1984, 296).

135. Cline observed that the preference for lineal rather than lateral bequests in Culhuacan conformed with general Spanish inheritance patterns. See Cline 1986, 84. Sons-in-law and daughters-in-law were often mentioned in testaments because they stood to gain from bequests made to lineal kin.

136. For example, in 1581, a woman from Achiutla named Catalina instructed her husband, Juan Delgado, to divide her property among their children when they came of age (AJT-CR, 1:25). For the Nahuas, Lockhart concluded that men were more likely to make bequests to their wives with their children in mind than vice versa (1992, 92). See also Cline 1986, 79–82. I have not found evidence suggesting that husbands had automatic claims on their wives' estates (Cline 1984, 296).

137. Compare with Cline 1984, 295, and Kellogg 1995, 143–44.

138. Taylor 1972, 44.

139. AJT-C, 8:705.

140. Ibid., 4:400. A subsequent translation of the document rendered this part simply as "por no tener hijos herederos."

141. This pattern contrasts with Wood's findings in Toluca, where only women bequeathed cooking and weaving items (1997, 176), and with Restall's findings for Yucatan (1997, 110). Some Ñudzahui

testators and testatrixes bequeathed movable goods according to the gender of their intended heirs, but most did not.

142. AJT-C, 7:686, ff. 12–13.

143. See Cline 1986, 138–39, and Wood 1997, 176, for the importance of magueys in Nahua wills.

144. AJT-C, 7:686, ff. 10–11.

145. Ibid., 8:726, ff. 1–2v.

146. Ibid., ff. 7–8.

147. Ibid., ff. 15–16v.

148. Ibid., 4:417, f. 16–16v.

149. Ibid., ff. 18–19v.

150. Lockhart 1992, 72–73. Restall observed a type of "joint inheritance" among the Yucatec Maya that resolved the problem of excessive division of lands (1997, 110–12). See also Farriss 1984, 132–36. The association between residency and inheritance in the Yucatec system resembles Mixtec patterns; however, bequests of lands generally did not extend beyond intrahousehold heirs in the Mixteca. Cline also recognized in some wills from Culhuacan an association between residency and inheritance but could draw no firm conclusions because of a lack of data on residence patterns of heirs (1986, 78).

151. Lockhart concluded that the system was so flexible that inheritance ultimately benefited certain individuals (1992, 93). Restall concluded that inheritance patterns in Yucatan benefited certain groups, emphasizing the larger kin group (*chibal*) rather than the household (1997, 120). Here I emphasize household members as the chief beneficiaries of Ñudzahui inheritance customs.

152. Lockhart suggested this possibility of confirmation in these terms: "it must have been possible in many cases to proceed as before." See Lockhart 1992, 91.

153. This pattern has been observed for the Nahuas in Culhuacan (Cline 1984, 303) and Toluca (Wood 1997, 169–72).

154. For residence patterns among the Nahuas, see Carrasco 1976a, 50–52; Harvey 1986a, 283; and Cline 1993, 62–69. For the Mixteca Alta (and the Sierra Zapoteca) and a discussion of the gendered significance of residence patterns, see Sousa 1998, 63–68.

155. This possibility may explain Cline's observation that women controlled less land than men in colonial Culhuacan and that fewer women owned patrimonial lands (1984, 303). It could also explain why men were more likely to make testaments in this period (judging by surviving records), since they were more likely to represent a household's landholdings.

156. AJT-C, 20:1684.

157. As Sousa observed, "marriage served to integrate households rather than to isolate individuals." Sousa 1998, 66–67.

158. Similarly, Charlton found that rented lands in Otumba were generally of a low quality (1991, 243).

159. Romero Frizzi 1990, 135–39.

160. Ibid., 188–92. See apps. 3 and 4 (pp. 543–94) for a list of leases by caciques and communities in the colonial period. See also Pastor 1987, 172, for a cumulative estimate of rented lands in the Mixteca Alta for this period. Haskett also found that land rentals were common in Nahua Cuernavaca in the late seventeenth and early eighteenth centuries (Haskett 1991a, 73–76, 105–6, 183–85). Lockhart observed that Nahua lessors were generally members of the upper social groups (1992, 181).

161. AJT-C, 3:365; ibid., 6:641; ibid., 6:642; ibid., 7:665; ibid., 7:688; ibid., 11:958; AGEO-AM, 24:1. See also Romero Frizzi 1990, 201, 565–608. Since lands are named or described relative to a given place-name and not measured, it is not possible to determine the size or quality of the land.

162. Romero Frizzi 1990, 193, 554, 581. For example, in 1661, don Francisco Pimentel y Guzmán leased lands in San Andrés, a sujeto of Teposcolula, and shared the profit of ten pesos with the community. In 1713, don Agustín Carlos shared sixty-two pesos from leased lands with three bordering communities. Romero Frizzi interpreted this phenomenon as an indication of the blurred distinction between cacicazgo and community lands. Perhaps this agreement represented a compromise between contested rights to ñuhu aniñe and ñuhu ñuu. Both compromises involved tracts of land located outside the caciques' immediate spheres of influence, where their claims were most vulnerable.

163. One hundred pesos was a considerable sum of money for indigenous people in this region. By comparison, the ñuu of Yolomecatl spent a total sum of 111 pesos in 1704 for its feasts and miscellaneous events.

164. Romero Frizzi 1990, 199.

165. See app. 5 in ibid., 595–608.

166. Spores 1984, 126; Romero Frizzi 1990, 219 and n. 152. Spores indicated that the production of unrefined *panela* in the Tlaxiaco area increased dramatically after 1715 but that the industry was most successful in the Mixteca Baja and coastal region.

167. See Taylor 1972, 74, for similar findings for the Valley of Oaxaca, especially in the seventeenth century.

168. AJT-C, 4:400

169. Ibid., 4:486. Fray Juan Reynoso testified in 1745 that don Francisco's son, don Agustín Carlos Pimentel y Guzmán, was prone to manipulate his titles to land, often selling plots of land that were not his to sell (AGN-T, 34:2, ff. 8–9).

170. See Taylor 1972, 46, for the observation that some nobles or *principales* owned large estates in the Valley of Oaxaca.

171. AJT-C, 8:705.

172. Ibid., 7:689. With the help of his sons and the neighboring community of San Juan Ytnoyaya, Domingo de Celís also bought a tract of "ñuhu mersed" for the sum of 420 pesos. Possession of this land was based on a royal license to use unoccupied land for a specific purpose, such as raising livestock. His emphatic statement that his own "comonidad" had contributed nothing to its purchase seems to indicate some tension in this matter.

173. Ibid., 3:287.

174. Taylor 1972, 44, 73.

175. AGN-T, 637:1, f. 74v.

176. AJT-CR, 4:492.

177. Pastor and Romero Frizzi have documented a continued preference among Spaniards in the Mixteca for leasing rather than buying lands, even by the end of the colonial period. At the same time, Pastor noted a tendency for merchants to invest in complementary activities and to acquire properties in the second half of the eighteenth century, especially in certain agricultural and commercial zones of the Mixteca. Romero Frizzi observed that in the sixteenth century some Spaniards who had received grants for estancias sold the land to caciques and communities, speculating in the purchase and resale of lands in order to invest money in interregional trade. See Pastor 1987, 230–33, 290–92; Romero Frizzi 1990, 137–39, 188, 196, 324, 353.

178. Horn 1997, 166–209. See also Gibson 1964, 272–99, for the Valley of Mexico; Cline 1984, 302, for Culhuacan; and Prem 1984, 205–28, for the Valley of Atlixco, Puebla.

179. See Taylor 1972.

180. See Spores 1984, 133–34, and Pastor 1987, 82–83.

181. AGN-T, 34:1, f. 82.

182. Ibid., 34:1, f. 77. The field was called "Yodzoninoo."

183. Romero Frizzi 1990, 195–96; Harvey 1984, 88, 95.

184. AJT-C, 4:488.

185. Ibid., 10:838.

186. AJT-CR, 5:513. The legal language of land sales represented a convergence of Spanish procedures, native concerns, and colonial conditions. Mixtecs who sold land often spoke of their need to avoid poverty or to pay the tribute with proceeds from the payment. These were often formulaic statements designed to justify the sale to authorities. On the other hand, many sellers probably did not exaggerate their state of need.

187. See Lockhart 1992, 176, for a comparable situation among the Nahuas.

188. For the Mixteca Alta, see Spores 1984, 209–25. For the Valley of Oaxaca, see Taylor 1972, 83–84. Pictorial writings demonstrate the existence of conflict before the Spanish invasion. Spores demonstrates that many of these disputes have persisted to the present.

189. For example, in the 1740s, three communities contested the claims of a cacica to lands in the area of Tehuacan, which she had rented to Spaniards and Jesuits. AGN-T, 1202:1, ff. 108–13.

190. AJT-C, 1:163. For the dangers of renting lands to Spaniards, see Gibson 1964, 274, 288; Spores 1984, 221; Haskett 1991a, 186; and Lockhart 1992, 182.

191. For example, if Sebastián Sánchez Hernández of Yanhuitlan possessed a title for each of his forty-three tracts of land in 1754, he would have paid 860 pesos, or nearly a third of the total value of his estate. AJT-C, 15:1232.

192. See Romero Frizzi 1990, 96–97, for several examples of intercommunity conflicts caused by livestock. Typical of many grievances, five communities protested in 1684 that cows from an estancia owned by the cacica of Juquila, doña Isabel Clara de Velasco, were trampling their fields and eating their maize. AGN-I, 28:148, ff. 131v–132.

193. AGN-M, 5, f. 271.

194. Taylor 1972, 68–69; Romero Frizzi 1990, 87.

195. AGN-T, 657:1.

196. Ibid., 657:1, f. 68.

197. AJT-C, 6:638.

198. AGN-T, 1202:1, ff. 108–13.

199. Gibson observed the contested nature of cacicazgo holdings in the Valley of Mexico in disputes between caciques and communities (1964, 259–60, 266).

200. Gibson made a similar observation for the Valley of Mexico (ibid., 163, 298).

201. In the thirty years before 1700, Pastor counted six legal disputes between caciques and communities in the Mixteca; but from 1700 to 1740, he counted twenty-nine disputes. During the 1740s, twenty-two caciques in the Mixteca were embroiled in legal cases involving their cacicazgos (Pastor 1987, 172–75). Romero Frizzi found that the number of land leases for the period from 1675 to 1725 increased by more than 300 percent in comparison with the preceding fifty-year period (Romero Frizzi 1990, 188–230).

202. Taylor 1972, 52–66; Pastor 1987, 170–73; Romero Frizzi 1990, 210–12.

203. For example, don Severiano Esquivel and doña Teresa Andrade de San Miguel y Mendoza accused the community of Comatlan of leasing some of their cacicazgo lands to a Spaniard of Teposcolula in 1752. The cabildo of Comatlan contradicted the caciques and retained possession of the lands. AGN-T, 760:1.

204. Ibid., 400:1, ff. 264–384.

205. Taylor 1972, 53–54. Of the cases cited by Taylor, the earliest is 1663, but the vast majority are from the eighteenth century. The timing of this process in the Valley of Oaxaca is comparable to the Mixteca. See also Gibson 1964, 163, 298, for the Valley of Mexico.

206. For a discussion of the uneven nature of this process in the Valley of Oaxaca and the Mixteca Alta, see Taylor 1972, 52–53, and Pastor 1987, 175.

207. AGN-T, 876:1.

208. Ibid., 1285:1. However, in 1807, the two caciques lost a prolonged legal battle to the community of San Miguel Tixaa, mainly because the cacica did not possess sufficient titles to support her claims.

209. See Pastor 1987, 511–13. For a discussion of cacicazgos in the postindependence period, see Monaghan 1997.

210. Jiménez Moreno and Mateos Higuera 1940, lámina xix and p. 61. The images confirm the coerced nature of this labor demand. In the first of three scenes, an armed Spaniard stands over a native man who kneels before a stream, panning for gold. The Spaniard raises a club in his right hand as if to beat the man, while his left hand grips a sheathed sword. The following scene to the right depicts a humble native man, dressed in a loincloth and cloak, handing a bowl of mineral deposits to the Spaniard. A third scene below depicts an armed, bearded Spaniard commanding a woman to pan for gold. I interpret the Spaniard's pointed finger in the bottom frame as a command signal, based on stylized writing conventions. This rare, surviving image of Spanish abuse in the early period is comparable to a scene in the *Codex Kingsborough* (f. 214).

211. Jiménez Moreno and Mateos Higuera 1940, 16. Other goods included quantities of cacao, food, wood, the harvest of one field of wheat, and ten native servants.

212. Gold and silver mining continued sporadically in the Mixteca Alta and in Silacayoapan in the Baja. Spores observed that, despite repeated registrations of mines throughout the late sixteenth and early seventeenth centuries, the mines yielded few profits. See Spores 1984, 126.

213. Romero Frizzi 1990, 50.

214. Hamnett 1971, 9–10. Cochineal production did not reach its peak, however, until the 1760s and 1770s. Hamnett demonstrated that the most prized *alcaldías mayores* (administrative jurisdictions) of New Spain in 1718 were in areas of high cochineal production, mainly in Oaxaca. The alcaldía of Teposcolula, in the heart of the Mixteca Alta region, ranked very high on the list.

215. On the growing of wheat by Nahuas in the Valley of Mexico, see Gibson 1964, 322.

216. Borah 1943, 39–44.

217. Ibid., 15–16; Romero Frizzi 1990, 72–73. Some of the most populous centers of the Mixteca escheated in the 1530s. See Romero Frizzi 1990, 47–61, for a discussion of encomiendas in the Mixteca.

218. Only the last four years record both expenditures and income. See Borah and Cook 1979, 424–28; Romero Frizzi 1990, 116–22.

219. Romero Frizzi 1990, 119, 122. Gibson estimated that native governments in the Valley of Mexico spent three-quarters or more of their income on church and fiesta supplies in the seventeenth and eighteenth centuries. See Gibson 1964, 187, 215.

220. The role of fiestas in the civil-religious hierarchy is a topic of considerable debate in ethnographic literature on the Mesoamerican community; the main contention is whether fiestas contribute to the leveling of social differences or, on the contrary, create and reinforce social hierarchy within communities. On the redistributive mechanisms of contemporary fiestas, see Carrasco 1963; Chance and Taylor 1985; and Monaghan 1990b and 1995.

221. AGN-T, 400:1. Spores 1967, 171, 242; Spores 1984, 125; Haskett 1991a, 165–68.

222. Romero Frizzi 1990, 117.

223. AGN-G, 2:546, f. 110v.

224. AGN-T, 2696:21; AGN-C, 400:1.

225. Of the 70 grants, cabeceras acquired 26, sujetos acquired 18, and the nobility possessed 26. Romero Frizzi 1990, 89–91. After 1597, licenses were necessary to own more than 300 head. Pastor counted 26 mercedes obtained by caciques from 1567 to 1597 and 57 mercedes by communities from 1563 to 1598. See Pastor 1987, 83, 93, 140. It is estimated that more than 100,000 head of sheep and goats were introduced into the region by indigenous owners during the period 1560–1620.

226. Pastor 1987, 142.

227. Gibson observed the same pattern for the Valley of Mexico (1964, 212–14).

228. See Romero Frizzi 1990, 205–8; for Spanish involvement in raising livestock, see also 323–54.

229. Borah 1943, 85–101.

230. Borah 1949; Pastor 1987, 149–51; Romero Frizzi 1990, 173.

231. See Borah 1943.

232. Spores 1984, 155; for the Teposcolula contract, see AJT-C, 1:79 (unnumbered protocolos).

233. AJT-C, 3:366. "Uagy" is an orthographic variant of *huahi*.

234. Ibid., 3:295.

235. Ibid., 2:263. The document is dated 1627.

236. Ibid., 1:90, protocolos. Generally, payments were made in April, August, and December.

237. See Pastor 1987, 102, n. 122, and 153–59; see also Romero Frizzi 1990, 147–50.

238. See Haskett 1991b for use of repartimiento labor for mining in Taxco.

239. AJT-C, 2:215.

240. Ibid., 2:218.

241. For an assessment of the impact of tribute burden and repartimiento on native communities in central Mexico, see Gibson 1964, 217–19, and Horn 1987, 91–92, 100. For the Mixteca, see Pastor 1987, 102, 153–59, and Romero Frizzi 1990, 246–48. See also Hamnett 1971, 3–14, for late colonial Oaxaca. For an alternative view emphasizing the noncoercive nature of repartimiento arrangements in late colonial Oaxaca, see Baskes 1996.

242. For the introduction of money among the Nahuas, see Gibson 1964, 357–58, and Lockhart 1992, 177–80.

243. AJT-CR, 1: sin número.

244. See Gibson 1964, 348–49, for a discussion of cacao commerce. The value of some indigenous goods and tribute items from southern Mesoamerica, such as quetzal feathers and jade, declined after the conquest.

245. Romero Frizzi 1990, 103 and n. 61; see Lockhart 1992, 177–80, for a comparison with the Nahuas.

246. AGN-T, 400:1, ff. 56–57. A long list of Spanish-style goods among his material possessions suggests that he may have accumulated some of the debts by buying from Spanish merchants. In fact, he owed 113 pesos to a Spaniard who owned a store under the arcades (*portales*) in the center of the community, 120 pesos to a native merchant named Diego García, and 300 pesos to various merchants (*mercaderes*) of Yanhuitlan. He mentions an additional 540 pesos in his inventory that should be paid by the community (300 to the encomendero and 240 for a delegation sent to Spain). Spores (1967, 170) came up with a slightly different calculation—635 pesos of debts and 560 pesos of credit.

247. See Cline 1986, 91–92, for a discussion of native moneylenders in Culhuacan.

248. AJT-C, 1:29. All the people to whom he owed money possessed native calendrical surnames, indicating their relatively humble status.

249. Ibid., 2:243.

250. Ibid., 12:1029.

251. Ornamental goods (feathers, jade, gold, and turquoise), beverages (cacao and pulque), dyes (cochineal), and nonagricultural food items (fish, fowl, and venison) rounded out the tribute items.

252. *Codex Mendoza*, ff. 42v–43r. Berdan and Anawalt 1992. Similarly, processed and raw cotton was the most significant tribute item given by Cuauhnahuac (Cuernavaca) to the Triple Alliance (Haskett 1991a, 18–19).

253. See Anawalt 1981, 95–146, for a study of Mixtec clothing in the codices.

254. AJT-C, 10:838. The term *tnu ydza* is confirmed in the *Vocabulario* as "telar" and is paired with *yutnu cono* (Alvarado, f. 193v). Some women possessed multiple weaving instruments. For example, Lucía de la Anunciación of Teposcolula possessed about a dozen *dzitu tnuquaa,* or "weaving sticks," in 1623. The term *dzitu tnuquaa* is repeated four times in the document, defined as "palos de tejer." She bequeathed these tools of her trade to both men and women. See AJT-C, 4:400.

255. AGN-I, 3:524, f. 122v.

256. AJT-C, 7:654. For pictorial representation of cloth given as gifts for a royal wedding, see p. 7 of the *Codex Selden,* reproduced in Anawalt 1981, 134, fig. 47. The importance of the giving of clothing for marriage is also evident in Sahagún (Anderson and Dibble 1950–82, bk. 2, pp. 240–41).

257. AGN-I, 3:279, f. 65.

258. AGI-C, 657, f. 767.

259. Spores 1967, 161, from AGN-T, 400:1.

260. AGN-T, 2692(2):16.

261. Alvarado, ff. 104, 193v, 124v–125.

262. For much of the colonial period, annual royal tribute was set at one peso and one-half fanega of maize per household, beginning around 1558 (Gibson 1964, 202, and Spores 1984, 130). But as Gibson noted, this figure does not take into account additional payments made to the community, and the fact is that tribute payments varied considerably among communities and often exceeded this minimal figure. See Gibson 1964, 196–209, for a detailed discussion of tribute asessment in New Spain.

263. For the Nahua area, see Lockhart 1992, 198. For the Maya area, see Farriss 1984 and Patch 1993.

264. Acuña 1984, 2:291. A document from 1578, around the time of the *Relaciones geográficas,* confirms that noble women sold clothing in the marketplace of Coixtlahuaca in exchange for pesos. AJT-CR, 1:23.

265. Acuña 1984, 2:248; ibid., 1:370.

266. AJT-CR, 1:52.

267. Gibson 1964, 197–202.

268. Acuña 1984, 2:296.

269. See Pastor 1987, 153–59, and Romero Frizzi 1990, 148–50, for a discussion of repartimiento involving cloth production. The record contains numerous examples involving Spaniards and alcaldes mayores who distributed reals in return for cotton, silk, and cochineal. For a discussion of this system in Yucatan, see Farriss 1984.

270. AJT-C, 1:157. One pound was distributed to every four tributaries, and one of every four tributaries was obligated to provide a chicken.

271. Ibid., 6:568. A record of community accounts indicates that many women were fined for not fulfilling this obligation.

272. AJT-CR, 6:644, f. 68v. For another example of women weaving cloth for the festival of a patron saint, see the case of Juana Mendoza in Sousa 1997, 209.

273. AJT-CR, 6:644, f. 64v.

274. See Cook and Borah 1968; Villanueva 1985.

275. See Sousa 1998, 228–30, for a discussion of the importance of native women's labor in social discourse and its defense against abuses.

276. AJT-C, 1:157. One pound of cotton was distributed to every four tributaries. The estancias were San Juan, Santa Catalina, and Santo Domingo. The group managed to win a settlement of 101 pesos from the nobles.

277. Hamnett 1971, 14–17; Pastor 1987, 153–59; Romero Frizzi 1990, 107, 147, 173. For central Mexico, see Gibson 1964, 92–95, and Villanueva 1985, 27–32. For the Maya area, see Farriss 1984, 43–79, 83–85, and Patch 1993, 81–92.

278. AGN-T, 2935:79, ff. 162–163v, 166–167v; ibid., 2935:80, ff. 164–165; ibid., 2935:88, f. 2; AGN-I, 15 (1a):89, ff. 63v–64. The communities included Yanhuitlan, Teposcolula, Soyaltepec, Coixtlahuaca, Achiutla, Maninaltepec, Tlatlaltepec, Teyta, Chalcatongo, Iscatlan, Yolotepec, Atlat-

lahuca, Atoyaque, Tlaxiaco, Cuquila, Chicahuastla, and Ocotepec. See also Sousa 1998, 209, for examples of Spanish and native officials who forced women to spin and weave in the Mixteca Alta. Sousa has also observed the participation of men in the spinning of cotton, indicating that the gendered division of labor was potentially flexible.

279. AJT-CR, 1:7.

280. AJT-C, 3:287.

281. For example, see the *Primeros memoriales* (Sahagún 1997, 225–26).

282. In many pueblos where women weave today, one's skill, age, and social status condition the types of materials used and the complexity of the woven object. Many designs and patterns are invested with specific meaning and require skilled labor; some huipiles take more than a year to weave.

283. Compare this great sum, for example, with the possessions of Yucatecan women (Restall 1997, 133) or Nahua women from sixteenth-century Culhuacan (Cline 1986, 91–94).

284. AJT-CR, 1:25.

285. This case is presented in Spores 1984, 116.

286. AJT-CR, 2:198.

287. Villanueva 1985, 34.

288. AJT-C, 15:1232. Romero Frizzi has documented the steady flow of European textiles into the Mixteca, which accounted for three-quarters of European products sold in the region by the early eighteenth century (1990, 314–16). Most of this trade consisted of cheap cloth from northern Europe (Flanders, Holland, France, and England).

289. AJT-C, 12:1029.

290. For the Nahua area, compare with Cline 1986, 112–14, and Lockhart 1992, 198.

291. The *Vocabulario* lists *tay cuica* for "mercader" and *tay dzata, tai yosai* for "merchante" (Alvarado, f. 149). I use this term in the most general sense, as it is unattested in the native-language record; long-distance traders were more likely called *toho* in reference to their high status.

292. AGN-I, 6.2:176, f. 41.

293. This road is now part of the Pan American highway, passing through Tamasulapa, Texupa, Yanhuitlan, Nochixtlan, and many other former cabeceras (see map 1). For a discussion of preconquest and colonial interregional trade routes in Mesoamerica, see Gibson 1964, 361, and Hassig 1985, 171–77.

294. AGN-M, 6:441–42.

295. See Gibson 1964, 359, and Romero Frizzi 1990, 105 and n. 66. See also Hassig 1985, 240, on the opposition of alcaldes mayores to the expansion of native traders.

296. Robinson Herrera cites several examples of trade between the Mixteca and Guatemala in his study of sixteenth-century Santiago de Guatemala. See Herrera 1997, 59–60. In fact, a group of Ñudzahui immigrants had settled in Guatemala after the Spanish conquest of the region. In 1564, a Mixtec contingent joined several groups from central Mexico and Oaxaca (from Tenochtitlan, Tlaxcala, Cholula, and the Zapoteca) to petition for land in the area of Santiago de Guatemala. These "conquistadores" had served as Spanish "allies" in the 1520s. AGI Justicia 291, f. 3v.

297. AJT-C, 1:161 bis. He made his testament in Nahuatl in a place called San Pedro and San Pablo Xiquipilan; this document is a good example of peripheral Nahuatl written by a non-Nahua speaker.

298. Ibid., 2:188.

299. In her bequest, she first separated her late husband's property (mules, wax, and woven goods) and disposed of it according to his wishes. Then she divided her property among an uncle, two daughters and two sons, her mother, a sister-in-law, her *compadre,* and her executor. Catalina bequeathed most of her money to her mother. She gave some "dancing feathers" and most of the mules to her two male sons, whereas she bequeathed her woven goods and most of the wax to her daughters and mother.

300. This "neenoria sera" [memoria de sera] or "wax inventory" includes a mound ("marqueta") of wax that weighs seven arrobas and thirteen pounds; another mound of six arrobas and twenty-four pounds; another mound of seven arrobas and eighteen pounds; another of seven arrobas and twenty-two pounds; and another twenty-one arrobas of wax that was added later by the executor. The value of all this wax can be approximated. In Texupa, one arroba of candles sold for twenty-five pesos in 1559 and 1560, though these were finished products (*Codex Sierra,* p. 24). In the same year as Catalina's testament, Miguel Jiménez sold an arroba of unfinished wax in Yanhuitlan for twenty-seven pesos (AJT-C, 2:243). Among Catalina's various debtors, Juan López owed twenty-three pesos on an

arroba of wax. From this information, I estimate that a pound of wax cost about one peso, and an arroba was worth about twenty-five pesos. In fact, this was the price of wax in a document from Yanhuitlan in 1677 (AJT-CR, 6:644). For a relevant discussion of apiculture in colonial Yucatan, see Farriss 1984, 179–80, 185, and Restall 1997, 126, 129, 186.

301. AJT-C, 1:161. For additional examples of trade and travel to the Isthmus of Tehuantepec and Guatemala, see ibid., 3:303 (Yanhuitlan, 1641); ibid., 1:159 (Teposcolula, 1603).

302. See also Romero Frizzi 1990, 108, for a discussion of the Yanhuitlan-Guatemala connection.

303. For comparable examples of noble traders in Nahua society, see Berdan 1982, 31–35; Cline 1986, 95–96; and Haskett 1991a, 167. The chronicler Antonio de Herrera, writing in the sixteenth century, associated Mixtec lesser nobles with "mercaderes." See Herrera 1934–57, 6:320 (dec. III, cap. XII).

304. Haskett considered the same possibility in his work on the Cuernavaca jurisdiction. He suggested, as a result of nobles' involvement in long-distance trade, that the pochteca may have had close ties to rulers (Haskett 1991a, 166–67). Gibson observed that pochteca disappeared relatively quickly after the conquest but that native merchants from Mexico, Tlaxcala, and Cholula continued to travel to the south and that a "genuine class of native muleteers" existed by the latter part of the sixteenth century (1964, 358–59). See Lockhart 1992, 191–92, for their occasional appearance in Nahuatl-language records; see also Berdan 1982, 176, and Hassig 1985, 113–26, for an overview of the pochteca from Mexico.

305. See Hassig 1985, 28–40, 187–92, 205–7, on the use of tlamemes in trade before and after the conquest and the official prohibition of using human carriers (but subsequent continuance) under Spanish law.

306. On the use of mules by native traders, see Hassig 1985, 200, 218, and Lockhart 1992, 192–97.

307. See Lockhart 1992, 194, for pochteca in central Mexico who possessed moderate to extensive landholdings.

308. See Cline 1986, 93–96, and Lockhart 1992, 195–97, for a comparison with Nahua men and women involved in trade. Haskett observed a few elite women in Cuernavaca who managed enterprises of their own (Haskett 1991a, 178). Nahua sources suggest that some noblewomen oversaw local and long-distance trading and sometimes served as administrative officials in local markets (Sahagún 1950–82, bk. 9: 12–16, 30–31; Villanueva 1985, 21). See Sousa 1998 for a discussion of women's work in Nahua, Mixtec, and Zapotec communities.

309. AJT-C, 2:179.

310. Ibid., 1:159.

311. See Lockhart 1992, 197, for a similar observation concerning the Nahuas.

312. See Gibson 1964, 359, and Haskett 1991a, 167 and n. 26, for references to this law among the Nahuas. See Romero Frizzi 1990, 105 and n. 66 for the Mixteca.

313. Romero Frizzi 1990, 104–8, nn. 71 and 72.

314. Ibid., 150, 185, nn. 79 and 80, and 108 n. 71. All evidence indicates that the Mixteca maintained much closer commercial and cultural ties with Puebla than with Oaxaca in the first half of the colonial period.

315. Ibid., 293, 461–62. The merchant was Miguel Sánchez de Tovar, who dealt mainly in indigenous products.

316. See Borah 1951 for a discussion of depopulation and economic depression in New Spain. For a qualification of this depression, see Hassig 1985, 259–61.

317. The number was reduced from about thirty-six in 1600 to sixteen in 1650. Romero Frizzi 1990, 174–87. Hassig points to the rising costs of transportation as a decisive factor in the decline of trade in this period (1985, 259–61).

318. Romero Frizzi 1990, 187.

319. Ibid., 185–86. Lockhart also observed the local nature of Nahua traders' activities in central Mexico after 1600 (1992, 194–95). See also Gibson 1962, 358–59. In Yucatan, Farriss noted the dominance of Spaniards in long-distance trade shortly after their arrival (1984, 152–53).

320. AJT-C, 3:303. See Spores 1984, 136, for an example of a Spanish merchant in Yanhuitlan who contracted a Puebla pack-train owner to deliver goods from Veracruz in 1587. In this case, however, all the goods were Spanish.

321. Romero Frizzi 1990, 457.

322. Based on app. 1 in ibid., 468–69.

323. Pastor 1987, 290–92.

324. Micaela Martín de Abrego, a vecina of Teposcolula and resident of the coastal ñuu of Jamiltepec, was another mestiza who profited from the cotton trade. In 1729, her estate was worth about nineteen hundred pesos. From app. 1 in Romero Frizzi 1990, 454, 461.

325. I have calculated this amount from a sample of eighteen testaments in app. 1 in ibid., 445–77. Of the forty-one inventories included in the appendix, I omitted people who specialized exclusively or primarily in ganado, as well as ten traders who died before 1650. Including those ten, the average assets of traders from the period between 1597 and 1724 amounted to 4,975 pesos. Many of the mercaderes and *dueños de recua* (pack-train owners) also invested in ganado, the value of which is included in the calculation of total assets. I did not include money invested in dowries. Finally, the average assets of forty-one Spaniards and mestizos living in the Mixteca from 1590 to 1724 were 3,943 pesos.

326. Silvestre Antonio de Siessa, a native of Cádiz and resident of Teposcolula, owed 10,883 pesos in 1718. Bartolomé Delgado, a petty trader who resided in Yanhuitlan, was worth only 25 pesos when he died in 1607. See app. 1 in ibid., 448, 445.

327. AJT-CR, 3:366. Gibson observed that zacate was one of the few indigenous products sold directly by natives to Spaniards in the marketplace during the early period (Gibson 1964, 354.)

328. Gibson 1964, 352; Lockhart 1992, 185.

329. See Pohl and Stiver 1997.

330. AGN-G, 1:355, f. 81. See Hassig 1985, 231–37, on the scheduling of local markets in central Mexico.

331. See Hassig 1985, 237–41, on the regulation of markets in the sixteenth century.

332. AGN-G, 1:637, f. 136v, and ibid., 2:49, f. 11. As Hassig noted, natives bought licenses to avoid harassment from Spanish officials (1985, 241).

333. AGN-G, 2:1266.

334. AJT-C, 1:102. Of the 104 people, only about a quarter had Spanish surnames, and a third of those had double Spanish-native names. None bore the title *don* or *doña*, and only 25 men could sign their name. There were 11 women in the group.

335. AGN-I, 3:540, f. 127. The tax was estimated at 2 percent of the value of the goods sold.

336. Ibid., 5:429, f. 116. The petitioners had typical noble surnames: Juan Gómez, Augustín García, Catalina López, Juana López, María García, Tomás López, Juana López, Catalina López, Lucas Hernández, Lucía Hernández, Tomás Pérez, and Luis Velásquez. See Cline 1986, 103, for references to *tochomitl*, or rabbit fur, as a luxury textile in sixteenth-century Culhuacan.

337. For example, see AGN-I, 5:660, f. 181v, and ibid., 10: 239, f. 135.

338. Lockhart 1992, 176; see also Gibson 1964, 354–56, on markets in early colonial central Mexico. The absence of Ñudzahui-language documentation on the marketplace is probably due to the cabildo's lack of involvement in market activities. The same may be said for central Mexico, though a few outstanding Nahuatl-language sources exist for the mid-sixteenth century. These sources on markets become increasingly scarce by the late sixteenth century, however, reflecting a strong Spanish presence in this arena of activity. See Lockhart 1992, 190–91.

339. AJT-C, 2:243. The two other huahi were called a "sala" and a "cocina" in the translation. See Haskett 1991a, 170, for shopkeeping among Nahua nobles in the Cuernavaca jurisdiction.

340. Pastor 1987, 290.

341. AJT-C, 12:1029. Unfortunately, a lack of any supporting documentation obscures the nature of his work and the origin of his goods. It is likely that the legal records to which the document belongs were filed separately, removed, or lost. See Spores 1984, 136, for an example of a well-stocked Spanish store in 1740.

342. AJT-C, 15:1232. Again, this lengthy testament and inventory contains no supporting documentation or translation.

CHAPTER 8 — SACRED RELATIONS

1. Taylor 1996, 62.

2. In New Spain, the episcopal or apostolic Inquisition, under the direction of the bishop and then the archbishop, had jurisdiction over native idolatries until 1571. In 1544, the visitor general of New Spain, don Francisco Tello de Sandoval, initiated the investigation in Yanhuitlan. The surviving record can be found in AGN-INQ, 37:5, 7–11. See Spores 1967, 25–27, and Greenleaf 1969, 76–79,

for brief descriptions of this case. Jiménez Moreno and Mateos Higuera have transcribed excerpts from the case (1940, 37–49). For a recent study of the trial, see Sepúlveda y Herrera 1999.

3. AGN-INQ, 37:6. Berlin provided a partial transcription of the fifty-five-page document with no analysis (1947, 35–38).

4. On the use of Inquisition sources, see Ginzburg 1982, xvii–xxvi; Ginzburg 1992, xvii–xix; and especially Ginzburg 1986, 156–64. For colonial Mexico and Peru, see Greenleaf 1969 and 1991; Gruzinski 1989, 3–5; and Mills 1997, 5–7. See also MacCormack 1991, 3–14, on the relevance of colonial sources in general for Andean religion.

5. Even these statements must be read with caution and tested against other statements and sources. See Greenleaf 1991, 264–65, and Mills 1997, 45, on using the testimony of native witnesses as historical evidence.

6. William Christian used the same types of questionnaires for his study of popular Christianity in sixteenth-century Spain. In the *Relaciones geográficas* for Castile, the relevant questions were numbers 51 and 52. See Christian 1981.

7. García [1607] 1981, libro v, cap. iv, pp. 137–38.

8. The distinction between "Culebra de Leon" and "Culebra de Tigre" ignores the fact that there were neither lions nor tigers in Mesoamerica. Perhaps one refers to the ocelot (often called jaguar) and the other to a puma. Or perhaps they both refer to an "ocelot serpent" and the distinction is arbitrary.

9. See Furst 1978, 13–60; Jansen 1982, 131–37; and Anders, Jansen, and Pérez Jiménez 1992b, 77–84, for interpretations of the *Codex Vindobonensis* in terms of the Cuilapan origin legend. Here I summarize and elaborate on their contributions (and those of their predecessors, Alfonso Caso and Karl Nowotny), focusing on the sacred couple and the gendered aspects of the legend.

10. The *Codex Vindobonensis Mexicanus I* was sent to Europe in the early colonial period. The codex is now owned by the Nationalbibliothek in Vienna. When the screenfold is fully extended, it measures 13.5 meters. Each of the fifty-two "pages" varies in height from 215 to 225 millimeters. At some point, a European owner of the manuscript numbered the pages on the obverse side from left to right with Arabic numerals. However, the side is read from right to left, so that page 52 is the first. The reverse side consists of thirteen painted pages, which were numbered with Roman numerals.

11. Jansen associates the skyband with García's reference to the place where the two deities took their seats, the "lugar donde estaba el cielo" [place of the sky], near Apoala. See Jansen 1982, 121.

12. Furst interprets the skeletal jaw, and skeletal features in general, as a symbol of regeneration and fertility, not death. See Furst 1978, 22–23, 55–56.

13. García [1607] 1981, libro v, cap. iv, p. 138. The names written by García are not conventional calendrical names. A calendrical name would be 9-Wind; the serpent and caves may refer to additional personal names. Two "yaha yahui" figures accompany 9-Wind in *Vindobonensis*, 48. These two flying figures, one in the costume of a fire serpent and the other dressed as an eagle, are sacrificers and magical specialists. See Furst 1978, 106; Jansen 1982, 148–51; and Pohl 1994a, 43–44.

14. For a discussion of 9-Wind and Quetzalcoatl, see Nicholson 1978.

15. *Vindobonensis*, obverse 48, 47.

16. Ibid., obverse 37. See Furst 1978, 132–36, and Jansen 1982, 99–110. Pérez and Jansen have found that people from the Apoala Valley continue to recite legends related to the tree birth ceremony.

17. These two nude figures are the same pair who were created by the 1-Deer couple in the beginning of the codex (obverse 2). Their appearance may symbolize progeny. They appear one more time in the codex, immediately following the (second) marriage scene involving 5-Wind and 9-Alligator on obverse 34, discussed below.

18. Furst suggested that this tree-woman may represent 9-Reed, a female deity who plays a prominent role in preceding scenes (1978, 136–37). She observed that "the birth tree of the noble lineages embodies male as well as female characteristics." The left side of the split tree contains white rings with inner red circles and the right side contains arrows. Furst 1978, 134–37.

19. The act of writing is also shown on obverse 48, when 9-Wind descends from the sky. Furst intepreted the tree birth scene in terms of paper making (ibid., 136). One of the men, 7-Rain, is the Mixtec variant of Xipe Totec, the flayed skin deity.

20. Ibid., 140–41; Jansen 1982, 90–91; Anders, Jansen, and Pérez 1992b, 120–21. It should be noted that personages, plants, animals, stones, and strange creatures descend from this couple, as if they gave birth to life in its many forms.

21. Reyes, prologue. Reyes called them "yya sandizo sanai" [lords who carry, who bring] and "yya nisaindidzo huidzo sahu" [lords who brought the laws]. I interpret the first "ndizo" as *ndidzo*, "to carry

or bring." See Jansen 1982, 218–19. Jansen associates this act of bringing the laws with the fire ceremony and the inauguration of dynasties, two prominent activities on the obverse side of *Vindobonensis*,
after the birth scenes at Apoala.

22. Reyes stated that the place was also called "yuta tnuhu," or "river of the lineages." This play
on words, involving *tnoho* and *tnuhu*, expanded the symbolic associations of the site. The term *tay ñuhu*
means "earth people" or "sacred people"; *ña ñuhu* is the same. *Tay* usually refers to men, especially
when paired with *ña*, which refers to women. The couplet reinforces gender parallelism. I interpret
the *n* of "nuhu" as *ñ*.

23. It is thought that the conquest of these figures from the earth is associated with the "War of
the Stone People" in the *Codex Bodley* and *Codex Nuttall*, 3, 20. In these scenes, male and female warriors fight figures whose bodies resemble stylized stones. The defeat of the "stone people" represented
the establishment of a new postclassic political order. These scenes do not occur in *Vindobonensis*, however. See Jansen 1982, 349–50, and Pohl 1994a.

24. Burgoa 1989a, 1:274. Burgoa dismissed the legend as an "illusory dream."

25. The reverse side of this screenfold manuscript treats the dynasty of Tilantongo since the tenth
century, the beginning of the postclassic period, focusing on the story of the legendary ruler, 8-Deer.

26. Furst 1978, 109.

27. Spanish sources referred to some images made from "green stones" or emeralds. There is
a light-colored green stone that is indigenous to Oaxaca. "Green stone" may have also referred to
turquoise. The Nahuatl *xihuitl* or *teoxihuitl* referred to turquoise, which was also called green stone.
Spaniards also confused jade with emeralds.

28. AGN-INQ, 37:7, f. 200. Cultural groups in the northern Mixteca Alta such as the Chochos,
Ixcatecs, and Cuicatecs shared many cultural traits with the Mixtecs. In the Chocho-Mixtec area, some
communities included both ethnic groups. Ixcatlan is located about fifteen miles from the Chocho-
Mixtec settlement of Coixtlahuaca and about twenty-five miles from Yanhuitlan.

29. Ibid., 37:5, f. 107–107v.

30. Acuña 1984, 1:84. The two stone images were kept inside a cave near Coatlan. Their names
in Zapotec were Beneleba and Jonaji, defined by the relación as 7-Rabbit and 3-Deer.

31. AGN-INQ, 37:6, ff. 149v, 151, 152.

32. Acuña 1984, 1:227–30. In 1579, two elders informed the writers of the relación, through an
interpreter, in front of the governor and alcaldes of the community. One elder, named Alonso, was
purported to be one hundred years old; the other was an octogenarian named Juan Acatl.

33. This scene reminds me of the term *tayu quacu*, "seat of the images," given in response to the
entry "altar of the demons" in the *Vocabulario*. *Tayu* could also be interpreted as "couple" or "pair,"
depending on tone. Alvarado, f. 17v.

34. Acuña 1984, 1:231.

35. AGN-INQ, 37:5, f. 118.

36. Alvarado, f. 129. On the term *cuacu*, see Jansen 1982, 284 and 478 n. 70.

37. Acuña 1984, 1:284.

38. Acuña 1984–85, 2:36–37. According to the relación, they performed heart sacrifice before
this cuacu.

39. AGN-INQ, 37:7, f. 204.

40. See Pohl 1994a, 23–30, on the significance of bundles in Mixtec religion.

41. Acuña 1984, 2:232–33.

42. Ibid., 1:239–40. This female image was the only deity mentioned in the relación.

43. AGN-INQ, 37:7, ff. 196–97.

44. Ibid., 37:6, f. 151.

45. Bundles in the *Codex Nuttall*, for example, can be found on pp. 8, 9, 15, 16, 17, 18, 19, 21,
22, 25, 42, 52, and 89.

46. See Jansen 1982, 318–25, and Pohl 1994a, 23–30, on the four basic types of bundles. In
Nuttall 15 and 42, for example, the head of the ñuhu is visible.

47. AGN-INQ, 37:5, ff. 105–6.

48. Burgoa 1989a, 1:332. According to Hernández, people made pilgrimages to the site to make
sacrifices.

49. Acuña 1984, 1:313–14; ibid., 1:293. Given the presence of this Toyna in the Baja, perhaps
the reference to "their" deity in the description of the Yanhuitlan image refers to a deity associated
with another region or ethnic group.

50. Acuña 1984–85, 2:44. The relación defined *toyna xiñuho* as "mono de agüeros" ("omen monkey").

51. AGN-INQ, 37:7, f. 200.

52. Ibid., 37:5, f. 116v.

53. Ibid., 37:5, f. 107–107v. This image was also referred to as "sicuyuy" (ibid., 37:8, f. 220v).

54. Ibid., 37:7, f. 192v. The names could be calendrical: "xio" could be *siyo* (10- or 13-Serpent), and "xique" could be *sique* (10- or 13-Lizard). See also Jansen 1982, 285–86.

55. AGN-INQ, 37:5, f. 107–107v. A native noble from Etlatongo said that certain households and communities were designated to pay tribute to certain images. The native priest named Xaco said that he relied on the lords of Yanhuitlan to provide the necessary sacrificial items, including slaves. Ibid., 37:7, f. 203v.

56. Ibid., 37:6, f. 152.

57. Ibid., f. 149v.

58. See Spores 1967, 24, for a discussion of funerary practices, based especially on Herrera.

59. AGN-INQ, 37:7, f. 197. The testimony comes from don Francisco, a noble of Etlatongo, who used the words "cara de *xihuitl*." Xihuitl is the Nahuatl word for turquoise.

60. Ibid., 37:5, f. 108. In similar fashion, a deceased lord is depicted in one of the *Codex Yanhuitlan* fragments with a stone in his mouth.

61. Mortuary or mummy bundles were usually stored or buried inside a house, cave, or decorated tomb. In the codices, mortuary or mummy bundles resemble sacred bundles. In central Mexico, where Nahuas cremated their dead, funerary bundles contained ashes.

62. Burgoa 1989a, 1:339–41.

63. On the relationship between divine ñuhu and historical yya in the codices, see Furst 1978, 10, and Jansen 1982, 288.

64. For example, many yya impersonated Dzahui, the rain deity. They often incorporated Dzahui's name into their own secondary "personal" name. On the relation between yya and ñuhu, see also Jansen 1982, 281–94, 324–25.

65. Jansen 1982, 285–86, and Pohl 1994a.

66. See Dahlgren 1954, 213, for a list of deities in the Mixteca, derived from the *Relaciones geográficas* and the Inquisition trial from Yanhuitlan. See also the discussion of *dioses* on 211–18.

67. Burgoa 1989a, 1:276–77.

68. Acuña 1984, 1:284. In Yanhuitlan, one was associated with merchants (Xitondodzo) and another with agricultural concerns (Dzahui). It is possible that this information from the *Relaciones* reflects Christian influence, considering the saints' association with particular trades.

69. Alvarado, f. 129.

70. On the Nahua Tlalocs, see Klein 1980, 155–204. Klein has noted that Tlaloc often appears as an ancestor deity. She and John Pohl have observed that, in three Mixtec codices (*Nuttall, Vindobonensis,* and *Bodley*), Dzahui appears in the beginning as an ancient deity (Klein 1980, 173).

71. AGN-INQ, 37:5, ff. 106v–107. Likewise, Tlaloc was associated with curing (see Klein 1980, 185).

72. For example, Fray Bernardo de Santa María acknowledged that the sacrifices were performed in response to drought and hunger. AGN-INQ, 37:10, f. 316.

73. Ibid., 37:7, ff. 196–97. This testimony came from don Francisco, a noble from Etlatongo, who said that he painted himself "like a tiger" (i.e., ocelot). The chronicler Antonio de Herrera commented on the Mixtec tendency for priests to smear their bodies with the resin of burned rubber until they were "as black as Ethiopians." See Herrera 1934–57, 6:323–24 (dec. III, cap. XIII). The codices contain numerous examples of priests, whose bodies are painted black.

74. AGN-INQ, 37:7, f. 195v.

75. Ibid., ff. 203–4.

76. Ibid., f. 200.

77. Ibid., ff. 198–99.

78. See for example, Sullivan 1997, 55–56, 78, 201, 248.

79. *Codex Magliabechiano,* 17, 22, 32. These include the feasts to Xilomaniztli, Eçalcoaliztli, and Atemuztle.

80. Other deities associated with Tlaloc, such as Opochtli and Tepictoton, had similar characteristics. See Sahagún 1950–82, bk. 1:7, 37, 47–49.

81. See Dahlgren 1954, 223–28.

82. Alvarado, f. 38, under "bolar por arte en bolador." The verb *sico* is associated with other symbolic acts, such as transforming, twisting, and turning around.

83. AGN-INQ, 37:5, f. 110v.

84. Acuña 1984, 1:313–14.

85. Burgoa 1989b, 478–81. See Klein 1980, 174, on Tlaloc's association with mountain caves and the underworld.

86. Tlaloc was often paired with the old earth goddess, Ilamatecuhtli-Cihuacoatl, who mothered his sons. See Klein 1980, 196. Alavez cites a manuscript by Manuel Martínez Gracida, written in 1905, that describes the female Dzahui as wearing a huipil and footwear, like the personage in the *Codex Yanhuitlan* fragment. Alavez Chávez 1997, 167.

87. On the continued presence of Dzahui in the Mixteca, see Jansen 1982, 186–92, 225–27; Monaghan 1995; and Alavez Chávez 1997, 165–78.

88. Alvarado, f. 185v. I interpret "naha" as *ñaha*, which is "person." The word *niñe* is associated with *toniñe*, "rule" and *aniñe*, the "site of rule" (palace). The word *niñe* may also be associated with *neñe*, "blood."

89. Ibid., f. 185v. The term *saque* is defined as "anoint," among other things, in Arana Osnaya and Swadesh (1965, 118). But I have not found the term in the *Vocabulario;* the Spanish entry *ungir* does not refer to "saque," and the verb *untar* is not listed.

90. The relación compares "Qhyosayo" with the Nahuatl *teotl,* or "god," and compares *tay saque* with the Nahuatl "totazi" or *totatzin,* "our precious fathers." However, *tay saque* does not refer to the Ñudzahui word for *dzutu,* "father," and the Mixtec equivalent for *teotl* is clearly *ñuhu.*

91. Burgoa 1989a, 1:276–78, and 1989b, 210.

92. AGN-INQ, 37:6, ff. 143–44.

93. See also Dahlgren's discussion of priests, based especially on the *Relaciones geográficas* and excerpts from the Yanhuitlan trial (1954, 240–50).

94. AGN-INQ, 37:7, ff. 203–4.

95. Ibid., 37:5, f. 119v, and 37:7, f. 200.

96. Ibid., f. 197.

97. Ibid., f. 203.

98. Acuña 1984, 1:293.

99. Ibid., 284.

100. AGN-INQ, 37:11, ff. 346–55.

101. Acuña 1984, 2:232–33.

102. AGN-INQ, 37:7, ff. 197, 201–2.

103. Ibid., 37:5, f. 119v. A slave of don Francisco named Domingo, who came from Etlatongo, also testified about the "india hechizera" named Xigua (f. 198v). Her powers were described as the ability to *adivinar.* Catalina called Xigua a slave; one witness said that don Francisco had married Xigua in the church in order to mock the holy sacrament of matrimony (f. 203). Sometimes the beans she cast were defined as "tanpuales" by the interpreters, in reference to the Nahuatl term *tlapohualli,* or "counters." According to the witnesses, Xigua died before the trial began. See Alvarado, f. 9v, for a number of terms associated with divining.

104. AGN-INQ, 37:6, f. 147.

105. For nahualism, see López Austin 1988, 1:305. On nahualism and magic in the Mixteca, see Dahlgren 1954, 251–55, and Jansen 1982, 312–17.

106. Alvarado, f. 38v. See "bruxo que engaña en dezir que se buelve leon." Acts of descending, impersonating, and shape shifting are commonplace in the codices.

107. Ibid., f. 122v. See "hechizero, embaidor que dezia se bolvia en tigre."

108. Ibid., f. 122v. See "hechizero, otro embaidor que por los ayres bolava."

109. See Pohl 1994a, 42–57, and Jansen 1982, 148–51.

110. Alvarado, f. 122v.

111. Ibid., f. 129. See "ydolatrar."

112. Ibid., f. 185v.

113. AGN-INQ, 37:5, ff. 105–6, and 37:7, f. 188.

114. Ibid., 37:5, f. 118.

115. Ibid., f. 106. This testimony comes from the cacique of Etlatongo.

116. *Codex Vindobonensis,* obverse 24–25; see Furst 1978, 201–3.

117. AGN-INQ, 37:5, f. 119.

118. Pohl has observed that Nahuas in the Tlaxcala-Puebla region emphasized both movable and fixed feasts in their writings, whereas Mixtec writings placed a greater emphasis on movable feasts. Deities with names based on the 260-day divinatory calendar suggest a moveable feast system. See Pohl 1997.

119. Pohl has recognized a number of calendrical dates associated with deities in the *Codex Zouche-Nuttall,* which he calls "personified feast dates." The dates could have also marked a ritual foundation ceremony associated with a sacred ancestor. If sacred ancestors were considered ñuhu, perhaps the dates marked their birthdays. See ibid., 40. Bárbro Dahlgren thought that the images possessed both personal and calendrical names, as did lords (1954, 212). The chronicler Herrera stated that lords' birthdays, not deaths, were commemorated (quoted in Spores 1967, 24).

120. The noun *birth* in the honorific register is *yotuvuinanaya,* literally "the lord shows his/her face." Unwrapped images revealed their faces in ceremonies that commemorated their birth dates. In 1573, don Felipe Saavedra used the expression "the lord's face appeared" in reference to the number of years since the birth of Jesus Christ.

121. AGN-INQ, 37:9, f. 276v. Caltzin, as he was known in the documentation, died around 1539.

122. Ibid., 37:7, ff. 202–3. The word *tuta* could be interpreted as "duta" or *nduta,* "water." *Tuta* means "atole." This testimony came from Diego of Etlatongo.

123. Ibid., 37:5, f. 108v.

124. Burgoa 1989a, 1:341–43.

125. AGN-INQ, 37:7, ff. 197, 201–2.

126. The priest named Xaco said that two boys were sacrificed in the middle of a cultivated field on a hill, near the border of Yanhuitlan. Ibid., 37:10, f. 321v.

127. Ibid., 37:6, f. 150. The male slave was named "Vyçil" and the female slave was named "Malinal."

128. Ibid., 37:5, f. 119v.

129. See Ginzburg 1982, xxiv, for the distinction between "collective mentality" and "cultural beliefs."

130. AGN-INQ, 37:10, f. 320v.

131. Ibid., f. 335v.

132. Ibid., 37:6, f. 140v.

133. Ibid., f. 152.

134. Acuña 1984, 1:84.

135. AGN-INQ, 37: 6, f. 128v. One witness claimed that it was the cacique of Tiltepec (f. 139v), and another witness stated that it was the cacique of Otelotepec (f. 141v).

136. AGN-INQ, 37:6, f. 144v. Diego de Albino, a noble from Tututepec, heard this story from don Alonso, the cacique of Nopala. Pedro de Olmos heard a similar story from the cacique of Istepec (f. 140v).

137. Ibid., ff. 149v–150.

138. Ibid., ff. 129, 136v, 139, 142v, 143v. The witnesses were Pedro de Olmos, Bartolomé Sánchez, Agustín de San Francisco, and Diego Albino.

139. Ibid., f. 143v.

140. The native priest was Caco of Coscatepec. He said that they ate parts of two men whom they had sacrificed. Ibid., 37:11, f. 337v. Other native witnesses who spoke of ritual cannibalism included don Cristóbal, a noble of Nochixtlan (f. 116), Domingo, a native of Etlatongo (f. 323), and Juan, a slave from Etlatongo (f. 327). The last three could be considered hostile witnesses against Yanhuitlan.

141. Ibid., 37:7, f. 185, and 37:9, ff. 273–274v.

142. Ibid., 37:6, f. 137v.

143. See Dahlgren on this question (1954, 231–33).

144. For example, in the *Codex Vindobonensis,* maize field ritual sacrifices involve the offering of hearts (obverse 15). See Furst 1978, 198–99.

145. AGN-INQ, 37:10, f. 337v.

146. Ibid., 37:7, ff. 198–99; exp. 8, f. 223; exp. 10, ff. 327, 328v, 339.

147. Ibid., 37:6, 143v. A slave of don Francisco testified that he performed autosacrifice on his tongue and on his private parts "so that it would not show" (f. 117).

148. See the *Codex Nuttall* (obverse 15 and 25) for examples of priests letting blood from their ears; in the second example, the priest bleeds onto a sacred bundle. See Jansen 1982, 165–71, on ear perforation in the codices. See also Furst 1978, 174–75.

149. AGN-INQ, 37:7, f. 187v.

150. Ibid., f. 185v.

151. Ibid., f. 184v. This seed pyramid sounds like the miniature "amaranth mountains" of the Nahua Tepilhuitl festival. Nobles in the *Primeros memoriales* recalled how, during the feast of Tepilhuitl, they fashioned figures of mountains from amaranth seed dough in their houses. See Sullivan 1997, 63–64. In his confession, don Domingo said that the seed pyramid was actually a straw container filled with a stack of tamales and a grilled quail. The feathers were intended for "mitotes" or dances. He received the food and feathers as gifts from a feast, he claimed. AGN-INQ, 37:9, f. 279–279v.

152. See Burgoa 1989a, vol. 1, and 1989b and Dávila Padilla 1955. All the early monasteries were abandoned temporarily in accordance with a papal bull.

153. Greenleaf 1969, 75–77.

154. Gómez de Maraver presented Tello de Sandoval with evidence of idolatries in the Yanhuitlan area, including human sacrifice. In 1544, Gómez de Maraver wrote a letter to the crown in which he criticized Indians as lazy and unworthy people. He supported the encomienda and advocated the enslavement of rebellious Indians. See Jiménez Moreno and Mateos Higuera 1940, 26 and n. 27.

155. AGN-INQ, 37:5, f. 104. Don Francisco testified that the cajetillas were given to him by some "Mexicanos" or Nahuas who had been in the area, as offerings of food. Ibid., 37:8, f. 226v.

156. Ibid., 37:7, f. 191.

157. Ibid., 37:8, ff. 212–215v.

158. Ibid., 37:7, f. 205v.

159. On the general Dominican conflict with encomenderos in the 1540s, see Hanke 1949, 81.

160. Apparently, Yanhuitlan was converted to a *corregimiento* from 1531 to 1536 before being reassigned to Francisco de las Casas as an encomienda in 1537. After his death and the trial, half the encomienda reverted to crown control in 1548. See Jiménez Moreno and Mateos Higuera 1940, 13–14, and Romero Frizzi 1990, 47–61.

161. AGN-INQ, 37:7, f. 200v.

162. Ibid., 37:6, f. 144.

163. Burgoa 1989a, 1:341.

164. See Ricard [1933] 1966, 239–63, on ecclesiastical "dissensions"; on native responses to ecclesiastical conflicts in the Valley of Mexico, see Gibson 1964, 110.

165. AGN-INQ, 37:5, f. 109. This testimony came from a translator who had allegedly conveyed this message to the encomendero.

166. On native collaboration in the spiritual conquest, see Ricard [1933] 1966, 273, and Gruzinski 1993, 59–60.

167. AGN-INQ, 37:8, f. 231. See chapter 4 of this work and Spores 1984, 209–10, on Yanhuitlan's conflicts with its neighbors.

168. AGN-INQ, 37:9, f. 287.

169. Ibid., 37: 8, f. 252.

170. Coatlan is located in a multilingual area, between Zapotec Miahuatlan and Mixtec Tututepec. Since it was closely connected to the Mexica empire, many nobles in this area had Nahuatl names and spoke Nahuatl. The case of 1544–47 indicates that it maintained close relations with several Ñudzahui communities, including Yanhuitlan, Tlaxiaco, Teposcolula, Tilantongo, Achiutla, Xaltepec, and Tututepec. Interpreters in this case spoke Nahuatl, Mixtec, and Zapotec. Witnesses in the case referred to the Mexican (Nahua) and Mixtec pueblos around Coatlan.

171. Gerhard 1972, 188–89.

172. Some Spaniards owned native slaves who were captured in "just wars." The document does not indicate the origin of this slave. Spaniards probably took slaves in the military campaigns of the 1530s.

173. Many witnesses in this trial came from Tututepec. According to the relación of 1580, Coatlan had been engaged in a state of intermittent warfare with Tututepec. Acuña 1984, 1:84.

174. AGN-INQ, 37:7, f. 195 and exp. 9, f. 266. This expression, translated from Mixtec to Spanish, makes the common association of *yni*, "heart," with volition and spirit. The phrase "to be of two hearts" [cuhui uhui yni] was used in the *Doctrina,* discussed below.

175. See Bhabha 1994, 85–92, on ambivalence in colonial discourse.

176. A point made by Ricard [1933] 1966, 274; Farriss 1984, 293; and Lockhart 1992, 203.

177. AGN-INQ, 37:8, f. 212.

178. Ibid., 37:7, f. 206. Francisco de Villegas, a resident of Antequera, claimed that the people of Yanhuitlan would not attend mass if they were not forced to do so.

179. AGN-INQ, 37:7, f. 184v.

180. Ibid., f. 185–185v. The name "estumeca" appears to be derived from the Nahuatl *oztomecatl,* a type of long-distance merchant.

181. Gerhard 1972, 23.

182. AGN-INQ, 37:7, ff. 202–3. This witness was Diego of Etlatongo, a slave of don Juan, the governor of Yanhuitlan.

183. Ibid., f. 198v. This witness was Domingo from Etlatongo, a former slave of don Francisco, the cacique of Yanhuitlan.

184. Ibid., f. 197.

185. Ricard referred to Inquisition records from the late 1530s as evidence of outright resistance ([1933] 1966, 270–73). But he distinguished between "indifference and ignorance" and organized hostility to Christianity. To Ricard, backsliding after baptism was due more to weakness and confusion than systematic resistance. Native neophytes unconsciously "mingled Christian elements with the practices and beliefs of their old religion" (267–69). However, the trial in Yanhuitlan suggests that ambivalence and resistance were conscious and overlapping, rather than distinct, responses to the spiritual conquest.

186. Ibid., ff. 201v–202.

187. Ibid., f. 193v. They did this because they were sinners, he surmised, and because they were jealous that Nochixtlan had such a beautiful church and altarpiece.

188. Ibid., f. 196. He said: "haciendo burla de ellos echandoles sus verguenzas de fuera y diciendoles pues sois christianos."

189. Ibid., 37:5, f. 121. If this statement was true, it suggests that don Domingo attempted to incorporate Christian rites into his propitiatory practices. On the nature of mockery and mimicry in colonial discourse, see Bhabha 1994, 86.

190. AGN-INQ, 37:5, f. 118. Don Juan, the cacique of Molcaxtepec, made this accusation.

191. Ibid., 37:8, f. 229v. A Spaniard testified that women who lived with don Francisco were also whipped and punished for adultery (exp. 7, f. 186).

192. Ibid., 37:7, f. 186. According to Delgado, don Francisco said that he hoped God ("nuestro Señor") would crush the men who took part in the destruction. This testimony suggests that the church was not built on top of the old structures but rather beside them, on the site of the church patio. Apparently, a provisional church was built before the old temple was completely destroyed. This earlier structure was not the church that stands in Yanhuitlan today. The construction of the larger church did not begin until after the trial.

193. Ibid., 37:5, f. 118v.

194. Ibid., 37:7, f. 186v.

195. Ibid., 37:5, f. 118.

196. Ibid., 37:7, ff. 198–99.

197. Ibid., f. 189.

198. Ibid., 37:5, f. 116v.

199. AGN-INQ, 37:6, f. 142. Agustín testified in Nahuatl.

200. Ibid., f. 144. Albino attributed much of his information to don Alonso, the cacique of Mistepec, who allegedly heard don Hernando's defiant words.

201. Ibid., f. 144–144v.

202. Ibid., f. 140. This was the same term employed by nobles of Yanhuitlan for Christians.

203. Ibid., f. 128v.

204. Ibid., ff. 129, 137, 140v–141.

205. Ibid., f. 136–136v. He called him a "cuylono ciguata." The term *cuylono* refers to sexual intercourse between men, derived from the Nahuatl *cuilonyotl,* based on the verb *cui,* "to take" (Molina 1977, 26v). "Cuilono" sounds like a Spanish version of *cuiloni,* literally "one who is taken." Perhaps "ciguata" (woman), derived from the Nahuatl *cihuatl,* refers to his role as the taken one, or perhaps it is simply an insult. Elsewhere in this case, Sánchez was called a "ciguata" when he tried to reprehend a native man who had hidden an image along the road. In addition, don Hernando was alleged to have called native Christians "ciguatas" and other insulting names, including "gallinas." The Nahuatl terms were probably Hispanized when they were translated and transcribed in the record.

206. AGN-INQ, 37:10, f. 341. See also Greenleaf 1969, 79. In December 1546, don Domingo was released on bail for two thousand pesos. The bail was paid by the encomendero, Francisco de las Casas.

207. AGN-INQ, 37:10, f. 330–330v. One of the inquisitors, Alonso de Aldana, was paid two gold *ducados* per day (ibid., 37:9, ff. 301v–302).

208. Ibid., 37:6, f. 148.

209. Ibid., 37:10, f. 335v.

210. Ibid., f. 337.

211. Ibid., ff. 346–47.

212. Richard Greenleaf suspected that the encomendero may have exerted pressure on the inquisitorial proceedings by vouching for the lords of Yanhuitlan. Greenleaf 1969, 79.

213. Romero Frizzi 1990, 58.

214. AGN-T, 400:1, f. 70.

215. Sahagún 1950–82, bk. 6:67–78.

216. On don Gabriel's status under Spanish rule, see Spores 1967, 177–81. Compare with Gibson 1952, 40, for Tlaxcala.

217. AGN-T, 220. The land called "Yuchadichaqh" measured 700 × 190 × 650 × 275 *varas*. In the document, he declared three times that none of his descendants should dispute the capellanía. Jiménez Moreno and Mateos Higuera 1940, 34.

218. Spores 1967, 180. When he passed through Yanhuitlan in 1630, Bernabe Cobo commented that "the house of the cacique is of the same workmanship as that of the church." See Jiménez Moreno and Mateos Higuera 1940, 49.

219. *Contemptus Mundi* was written by fray Diego de Estella (1524–78) in Spanish and was translated into several languages, including Latin, Italian, and English. I have read parts of a 1584 English edition, owned by the Huntington Library. The original Spanish edition used the Latin title, so it is likely that don Gabriel possessed a copy in the Castilian language.

220. See Jiménez Moreno and Mateos Higuera 1940, 34–36, and Spores 1967, 178–80. The original testament is in AGN-T, 400:1, ff. 55–60v.

221. AGN-T, 985:2, ff. 14v–23. See Spores 1967, 241–44, for a translation of the inventory of don Gabriel's goods into English.

222. In the Mixteca Baja, Chila was founded in 1535, abandoned after 1538, and formally "accepted" in 1556 along with Tonalá. Cuilapa was founded around 1556; Achiutla and Tamasulapa in 1557; Tecomaxtlahuaca about 1558, becoming independent of Tonalá; Mixtepec around 1558, becoming independent of Tlaxiaco. Other late foundations include Texupa in 1570, Huajuapan in the early 1570s, Nochixtlan in 1566, and Juxtlahuaca in the 1570s.

223. Dávila Padilla [1596] 1955, 64.

224. On the enterprising activities of the church in native communities, see Gibson 1964, 126–27; Spores 1984, 159–62.

225. See Lockhart 1992, 210–18, for a discussion of the Nahua "church people." For Yucatan, see Farriss 1984, 335.

226. I have seen one clear but brief reference to a female fiscal. When Juan Ramírez, a merchant from Yanhuitlan, recorded his dealings in a book of accounts, he entered his client's *oficio*, or occupation, after his or her name. He made the following entry on July 27, 1756: "I received five fanegas of maize from Pablo de la Cruz, the stone cutter, who sold it with his wife Theresa, the fiscal. They received ten tomines for each fanega, for a total of six pesos, two reales" [yosainju hoho fanegas nuni si Pablo de la Cruz, cantero, niquidicocha sihi ñaha dehecha Theresa, fiscal, yca nisaicha usi tomine ee, ee fanegas, yca 6 pesos 2 reales]. There is no mistaking the clear handwriting; nothing more is said about this couple, however. AJT-C, 12:1029, f. 23v.

227. The participation of women in sacred and political ceremonies in the codices suggests that this separation and exclusion did not conform to preconquest organization. The one exception of women in the church is nuns, a vocation for which indigenous women were not eligible. In any case, there were no nunneries in the Mixteca.

228. Alvarado, f. 111.

229. Ibid., f. 116.

230. Ibid., f. 185v.

231. Nahuatl employed a similar construction for playing the organ, based on the verb "to beat," the organ being considered a kind of drum. See Lockhart 1992, 282, for comparison with Nahuas.

232. See Romero Frizzi 1990, 112–20, on the types of objects purchased on behalf of local churches in the Mixteca. See also Ricard [1933] 1966, 148–49, and Farriss 1984, 262–65, on the cajas.

233. AJT-C, 1:91, f. 15; ibid., 1:14; ibid., 1:79. See also Spores 1984, 155. In Tamasulapa, Concha also received the services of two males and one female each week.

234. Pastor 1987, 247–48. Rudolfo Pastor counted more than two hundred cofradías in the Mixteca in the early eighteenth century. On cofradías in the Nahua area, see Gibson 1964, 127–32. and Lockhart 1992, 218–29; for Yucatan, see Farriss 1984, 265–70.

235. For example, in 1587, a cofradía in Achiutla was involved in the cacao trade (AJT-CR, 1:42). Numerous sources document the involvement of cofradías in herding and agriculture.

236. Despite the presence of cofradías in the Mixteca, the strength of corporate organization at the level of the ñuu and siqui precluded the dominant roles played by cofradías in other parts of Mesoamerica, especially in Yucatan. On the relative strength of the cofradía in Mexico, Oaxaca, and Yucatan, see Farriss 1984; Chance and Taylor 1985; Pastor 1987, 255–59; and Lockhart 1992, 219 and nn. 65 and 66. See Gibson 1964, 132, on the relationship between the rise of cofradías and the decline of corporate entities.

237. AGN-G, 2:188, f. 38.

238. From the letter of March 7, 1630, transcribed by Jiménez Moreno and Mateos Higuera 1940, 49.

239. The term is analogous to the Nahua *teocalli*. *Huahi ñuhu* could also be interpreted as "house of the deity" or "house of deities," since plurals were not marked in writing.

240. AGN-INQ, 37:5, f. 118, and 37:7, ff. 201v–202.

241. Ibid., 37:8, f. 252.

242. Jiménez Moreno and Mateos Higuera 1940, 65–66, plates 18 and 20.

243. Curiously, the church of Teposcolula is also perched on the place glyph of Yanhuitlan. Alphabetic glosses distinguish the two churches.

244. It is likely that this church was an earlier, intermediate structure with a thatch roof. The *Relaciones geográficas* reported that some structures had thatch roofs in 1580, such as the churches of Puctla and Zacatepec. Acuña 1984, 2:317, 323. See the *Codex Nuttall* and *Codex Vindobonensis*, among other preconquest-style codices, for depictions of temples.

245. Most preconquest-style pictorial writings drew no clear distinction between palaces and temples, depicting them in much the same manner. The temple was simply the palace of a ñuhu.

246. There are multiple churches in this lienzo. See Smith 1973a, 283, 293, for additional scenes of churches and seated rulers in the lienzo. The Lienzo of Ocotepec is another outstanding example of how artists juxtaposed the community's church with its temple and ruling couple. See Caso 1966b, 131–37, and Smith 1973a, 336–37.

247. AGN-T, 3556:6, f. 175. Mapoteca # 2463.

248. Ibid., 876: 1, f. 122. Mapoteca #867. See Smith 1973a, 167–68, for commentary on this map.

249. AGI-ESC, 165c, ff. 26, 67.

250. AJT-CR, 3:275 and 3:283.

251. For a discussion of how the church represented political autonomy among the Nahuas and how church construction represented political realities and aspirations, see Lockhart 1992, 209–10.

252. See MacCormack 1991 for a discussion of how the European imagination influenced Spaniards' vision of religion in the Andes.

253. García Icazbalceta 1954, 211–16; Jiménez Moreno 1962, 33; Burgoa 1989a, 1:332–48, p. 340 specifically.

254. Burgoa 1989a, 1:331.

255. See Mignolo 1995, 69–82, for a discussion of the colonizing use of writing and the book among proselytizing religions. See also Goody 1987, 5.

256. Hernández 1568, f. 62v.

257. In the *Arte*, Reyes explains the use of *yyacaa* as an example of "demostrativos," translated as "veis aqui" (p. 69). The *Vocabulario* defines *figura* and associated terms as *taniño* (f. 110v), approximating the meaning of "illustration" or "representation." The term was used with both painting (*tacu*) and writing (*taa*). *Taniño* is also associated with *mapa*, "taniño nee cutu ñuu ñayehui," literally "illustration of the entire world" (f. 146). *Ychi* is a common word for "path" or "road," and *andehui* is "sky" (and by extension "heaven"). This illustration appears in a 1567 edition of the *Doctrina*, owned by the Huntington Library.

258. Hernández 1568, f. 199v. This passage contains a few inconsistencies. For example, the convention of marking rearticulated vowels with an *h* is first observed and then not observed. The term *huaha* ("good" or "well") follows the verb "naa" twice; the second time, however, it is spelled "uaa." Then, the negative marker *hua* used with verbs is spelled "va," based on the character for *u*. And in the phrase "dehe tna quehui," *tnaha* has been abbreviated from the dictionary form to "tna" (Alvarado, f. 189). I have interpreted the verb "naa" as *nai,* "to guard" or "to keep." This verb was frequently used in relation to the commandments; the *Vocabulario* lists "naihuaha" (future: "conay") for "guardar mandamientos." I have seen this verb in testaments written as "naa" and "nahi." Another related verb is "to follow the commandments of God," listed as "ndaa huidzo dzaha nDios" (future: "condaa"). See Alvarado, ff. 117v and 187v, for this terminology. Either one of these two verbs fits the meaning of the passage; in contrast, the verb "naa" does not make sense. Literally, the phrase "hua cuhui cotondo nanaya" means "we will not be able to look upon the lord's face."

259. Reyes, p. 78.

260. Alvarado, f. 84. *Dudzu* (words) and *sahu* (laws) were also common terms used in this context. The *Doctrina* refers to the written "dudzu Prophetas" (Hernández 1568, f. 61v, for example).

261. AGN-T, 59:2, f. 48v.

262. See Eire 1995, 36, for a summary of the standard format of sixteenth-century Spanish testaments and Lockhart 1992, 468–74, for a model testament in Nahuatl, published by fray Alonso de Molina in 1569.

263. See Eire 1995 for a discussion of the religious preamble as a source for popular conceptions of Christianity in sixteenth-century Madrid. For Mesoamerica, Cline 1986, 13–34, considers expressions of Christian piety among Nahuas from early colonial Culhuacan, and Lockhart 1992, 251–56, examines doctrinal statements in Nahua testaments.

264. In his examination of fray Alonso de Molina's model Nahuatl testament of 1569, Lockhart (1992, 470) observed that this component of the preamble, also typical in most Nahuatl wills, was missing from the model.

265. In reference to statements of faith in Spanish wills from sixteenth-century Madrid, Carlos Eire observed that this was the part of the will least likely to exhibit individual expression because of pressures to conform to Christian doctrine. See Eire 1995, 79.

266. Alvarado, f. 81. The *Vocabulario* qualifies "ñuhu" with "ñuhu toniñe." The use of *ñuhu* was comparable to the Nahua *teotl.*

267. AGN-T, 59:2; spelled "yuhuiteyu" in Tlazultepec (Yucucuihi).

268. Hernández 1567, ff. 118, 52, for example.

269. AJT-C, 18:1578; spelled "yuhuichayu" in Tonaltepec (Yucundii). In some modern Mixtec-language religious texts, the term has been reduced to its simplest form, "andehui."

270. See Christian 1981, 158, in reference to local religion in sixteenth-century Spain.

271. Hernández 1567, f. 13v, and 1568, f. 192v.

272. Compare with Eire 1995, 68–72, for Spain.

273. Hernández 1567, f. 52v. This image comes from the 1567 edition of the *Doctrina,* owned by the Huntington Library. It is not contained in the Huntington's 1568 edition, however. Apparently, someone attempted to deface the illustration with a pen.

274. See the repeated examples of these gestures on pp. 40–41 of the *Codex Nuttall,* for example.

275. The representation of a crowd by depicting the outline of multiple, overlapping heads was a European convention employed in the *Codex Yanhuitlan.* See the illustration of a group of people assembled before the aniñe in figure 6.1, for example.

276. It is difficult to determine whether other illustrations in the *Doctrina* were done by native artists. David Szewczyk has suggested to me that the typesetting and art were probably done in Mexico City. If so, perhaps a group of Mixtecs accompanied Hernández to Mexico City to participate in the project. I am grateful for the comments of Louise Burkhart, David Szewczyk, and Daniel Slive on the topic of native involvement in the production of religious art.

277. AGN-T, 637:1, ff. 74–79. The term *hitoho* is the phonetic equivalent of stoho, "high lord," in the Achiutla area.

278. AJT-C, 7:689: f. 16.

279. Ibid., 4:417.

280. Likewise, in Nahuatl, Luis Laso de la Vega's *Huei tlamahuiçoltica* of 1649 refers to the Virgin of Guadalupe as *cihuapilli,* "noble woman," and *tlatoani,* "ruler." See Sousa, Poole, and Lockhart 1998.

281. Hernández 1567, f. 15.

282. AJT-C, 8:726, f. 1.

283. Ibid., 8:726. This document was written in 1726.

284. Ibid., 7:689, f. 14. This document was written in 1717.

285. Hernández 1568, f. 192v.

286. Ibid., f. 183.

287. AJT-C, 8:726, f. 1. *Dzehe* is "mother," and *mani* is "precious." In Nahuatl *totlaçonantzin,* "our precious mother," was used in reference to the Virgin Mary. The Nahuatl *tlaço* is the equivalent of the Nudzahui *mani.* See Sousa, Poole, and Lockhart 1998, 40–41, for a discussion of Nahua descriptions of the Virgin and other ecclesiastical terminology. See also Burkhart 1989, 39–44, and Lockhart 1992, 252–54.

288. See Lockhart 1992, 252–53.

289. Hernández 1568, f. 192v. In the Ave María, she is called "yya yy ñuhu" (f. 15), and in the Credo she is known as "yya nee ñuhu" (f. 14v).

290. Alvarado, f. 97v. See "entera cosa." For the term "yy" (also seen as "ij" or "iy") see "sancta cosa" and "sancta y sagrada" on f. 187. The term *yya* is apparently related to this term.

291. See Burkhart 1989, 153–56, and Sousa, Poole, and Lockhart 1998, 39–40.

292. See Alvarado, f. 83v. The term *ñaha nee yoco* refers to the hymen. The term *yoco* is listed in Arana Osnaya and Swadesh 1965, 135, as *membrana virginal.*

293. For a discussion of possible associations of the Virgin of Guadalupe with Tonantzin, see Taylor 1987 and 1996; Lockhart 1992; Poole 1995; and Sousa, Poole, and Lockhart 1998.

294. On popular devotion to the Virgin Mary in sixteenth-century Spain, see Christian 1981, 21.

295. Eire 1995, 69–71.

296. AJT-C, 7:689, f. 14.

297. Alvarado, f. 187. See three entries under "sanctos los que esta en el cielo."

298. AJT-C, 6:568, ff. 11v, 13, 14v.

299. Alvarado, f. 21. Alternatively, this could be "lords without bodies," since *yequecoño* "bones, flesh," was the standard term for "body." The two negative markers (*ña*) seem to emphasize the two components separately, however.

300. Ibid., f. 33v. The *Doctrina* gives it as "jha çonduta," which is much the same (Hernández 1567, f. 135v).

301. AJT-C, 6:568.

302. Hernández 1567, f. 140v.

303. One example can be found in the testament of doña Beatriz Maldonado, written in 1677, AGN-T, 571:1. See also AJT-C, 6:568.

304. The Ñudzahui responses are comparable to Nahua descriptions of the same acts. In Nahuatl, one of the earliest and most widespread verbal neologisms was the descriptive term for baptism, *quaatequia* (to throw water on someone's head), similar to other descriptive terms for religious rites. In addition, Nahuas used the expression "to see mass" (with the verb *itta*). Lockhart has noted that words with definite preconquest antecedents—such as marriage—seem to differ in this respect (e.g., *namictia*), focusing on abstract characteristics rather than visible acts. For comparison with the Nahuas, see Lockhart 1992, 270.

305. In Hernández 1567, f. 7, a typical passage reads: "çahua niniytahui sancto sacramento dutamani hitohoyo, nani baptismo, nicuhui christianoyo" [when you lords received the holy sacrament of the precious water, called baptism, you became Christians].

306. AGN-T, 637:1, ff. 66–73. I have punctuated this passage to conform to the translation, for the reader's sake, even though the original contains no punctuation.

307. Alvarado, f. 69. See also "demonio tener."

308. Burkhart 1989, 40–42.

309. Hernández 1567, f. 53.

310. Ibid.

311. See Sousa n.d. on indigenous references to the devil in colonial trial records from Mexico.

312. Alvarado, f. 69. The term *cuina* refers to a thief (f. 183v). See also Arana Osnaya and Swadesh 1965, 75, for its association with "engañar." The term "ymagen del diablo" was also associated with ñuhu, as in "naa ñuhu" or "image of the ñuhu" (Alvarado, f. 130v).

313. AJT-CR, 1:35.

314. Literally, "the devils tricked my heart." Since the arbitrary pluralization of loan nouns was common, "diablos" could signify the devil; on the other hand, it could refer to multiple devils, as in "demonios."

315. Alvarado, f. 132. The *Vocabulario* lists "ynfierno, lugar de dañados" as "andaya añuhu, añuhu naa, añuhu dahui."

316. Hernández 1567, f. 53.

317. Alvarado, f. 21v. The phrase is similar to the Nahua use of *-yolia*, from *-yollo*, "heart." See Lockhart 1992, 253.

318. *Quachi* has a broad meaning as "error," "defect," and "crime," but *quachi canu* (great crime) was applied to mortal sins and serious crimes such as homicide. In addition, the use of *quidzacuachi*, "to commit a sin," was common.

319. Burkhart observed that the Nahua version was too broad and "has a range of meanings alien to Christianity; the concepts overlap but are not synonyms." Sin had moral implications, while tlatlacolli referred simply to something that had gone wrong. For example, burning a tortilla or spilling a drink was considered a tlatlacolli. See Burkhart 1989, 28–34.

320. See Monaghan 1995, 103, for a discussion of the many "kuachi" that might offend the many ñuhu in modern-day Santiago Nuyoo.

321. Hernández 1567, f. 95v.

322. See Burkhart 1989, 60–66, for the metaphor of the road in Nahua ecclesiastical publications.

323. Hernández 1568, f. 168.

324. Ibid., f. 170.

325. Ibid., f. 168.

326. On the use of *neyolmelahualiztli* in Nahua confessions, see Burkhart 1989, 181–82. See Alvarado, f. 50, for related terminology. These two verbs (*quidzandaa, quidzacuite*) are also found in the opening formula of many testaments.

327. Alvarado, f. 122. The entry "hazer traycion el marido a la muger" is defined as *yodzacahanuuñahandi*. See also f. 85: "echar en verguença a alguno," given as *yodzacahandinuuta*. The word for "shame" is *caha*.

328. This was also true for the Nahuatl term *pinahuiztli*. Burkhart observed that sin did not carry a sense of shame in Nahuatl. See Burkhart 1989, 31–33.

329. On Nahua-Christian terminology in church-sponsored texts, see Burkhart 1989 and Sell 1993.

330. For a discussion of syncretism and religious change, see Taylor 1996, 53–62. In Yucatan, Nancy Farriss cites the idolatry trials of the 1560s as evidence of the crisis and conflict that preceded the "creative synthesis" of future generations, and the "gap between the Maya's public acceptance of Christianity and their private activities" (1984, 291, 318). Christian and Maya beliefs and practices were expressed at different levels. Louise Burkhart explored the ideological gap between Christian moral precepts and Nahua ideology (1989, 10, 184–93). For Farriss and Burkhart, the native-Christian synthesis represented cultural survival and creation more than substitution and loss.

331. In some cases, people pledged money on behalf of the testator when he or she was too poor to give anything. It is unclear whether individuals were obligated to meet a quota of pledges or whether the giving was motivated by piety or pride. I have seen two examples, cited in chapter 7, in which the testators went through the motions of giving money to the saints but had nothing to give. Sometimes, people gave more than they could afford, leaving their heirs with the debt.

332. As in the will of Tomás Hernández (AJT-C, 3:295). It was also called a "copa."

333. See Farriss 1984, 331, for a discussion of "feeding the saints" in Yucatan.

334. AGT-C, 4:417. The word *tay* means "person." Because the plural form of *tay* is unmarked, I interpret "tay ñudzahui" as Ñudzahui people.

335. Most cofradías were devoted to a particular named saint or image. In this case, cofradías were organized, at least to some extent, by ethnicity

336. AJT-C, 4:419.

337. Ibid., 8:726. Literally, "yia castilla" means "Castilian lord(s)." Rodríguez possessed ten Christian lienzos and images in all.

338. Ibid., 8:726. Literally, "box for the souls of Castilian lords."

339. For saints among the Nahuas, see Lockhart 1992, 235–25; among the Yucatec Maya, see Farriss 1984.

340. As reported by the Nahua historian Chimalpahin, cited in Lockhart 1992, 220.

341. AJT-C, 6:605, f. 2. The title *mayordomo* was usually reserved for stewards of cofradías. Its use in reference to the community and not a cofradía indicates the lack of differentiation between the cofradía and other organizations, including the church and cabildo. See Lockhart 1992, 223–24 and n. 66, for comparisons with the Nahuas.

342. Santiago Yolomecatl, known as Yniyoho Yuchiquaa to Ñudzahui speakers, represents a typical *sujeto de doctrina* or *iglesia de visita* in many respects. See Gibson 1964, 120; Haskett 1991a, 71, and Lockhart 1992, 206–7, for a discussion of this type of church in central Mexico.

343. When they did not send offerings, native officials in the cabecera reminded them of their obligations. In 1704, the officials received a letter from the cacique and governor of Teposcolula, inquiring why they had not sent an offering that year. In response, the officials of Yolomecatl immediately sent a peso to the yya toniñe of Teposcolula. AJT-C, 6:568, f. 15 of Ñudzahui-language text.

344. Christian 1981, 46–47.

345. AJT-C, 6:568, f. 16v of Ñudzahui-language text.

346. Christian 1981, 89, 121. According to Christian, the major Marian shrine in Aragon was devoted to Pilar.

347. See Jansen 1982, 186–92, 225–27; Monaghan 1995, 104–17; and Alavez Chávez 1997, 165–78.

348. See Monaghan 1995, 106–11. Monaghan found that people of Santiago Nuyoo speak of the universe in gendered terms: the earth is associated with female deities and the sky with male deities, and rain symbolizes the life-giving sexual exchange between the two.

349. AJT-CR, 6:644, f. 65.

350. Ibid., 6:568, f. 11 of Ñudzahui-language text.

351. See Ruíz de Alarcón 1984, 87–89, 216–17, 265.

352. AJT-C, 2:263. Use of the term *naa* for image and lienzo is comparable to the use of *ixiptlatl* in Nahuatl and *imagen* in Spanish. See Alvarado, f. 130v, for eleven entries under "ymagen," all relying on *naa*. The *Vocabulario* defines "lienço" literally as "dzoo cuisi" (white cloth) without referring to images.

353. AJT-C, 15:1232. Sebastián wrote his will in the 1750s.

354. Ibid., 2:188. On the Nahua *santocalli*, see Lockhart 1992, 66, 237.

355. Herrera 1947, 6:324 (dec. III, cap. XIII).

356. Sousa 1998, 74; AJT-CR, 5:544, f. 5.

357. For a discussion of the saints as ceremonial or formal owners of a household's land among the Nahuas, see Lockhart 1992, 239–42.

358. AJT-C, 10:873.

359. Ibid., 8:705, f. 33.

360. Ibid., 20:1684.

361. Ibid., 9:758.

362. Ibid., 6:568, f. 3v. This document is dated 1705.

363. See Gibson 1964, 130–31, on lands belonging to the images of saints.

364. Farriss 1984, 265–66. The case of Ayusi's image, discussed above, confirms this observation. The document concerning Ayusi does not mention a cofradía, even though its activities and offices resembled those of a confraternity. In this case, at least, the siña subsumed the role of a cofradía in its organizational and corporate capacity.

365. AJT-C, 6:568, f. 14 of Ñudzahui-language text. Ganado was a major source of income for cofradías and communities in the Mixteca.

366. See Farriss 1984, 320–21, for a discussion of the personification of saints in colonial Yucatan. Of course, one could make similar observations about local devotions of saints in sixteenth-century Spain. See Christian 1981.

367. Lockhart 1992, 243.

368. Alvarado, f. 201v, and Hernández 1568, f. 121. See the list of feast days in Hernández 1568, f. 200, for use of *quehui*.

369. In 1561, for example, they spent seventy pesos for Saint Catherine's feast and an average of forty pesos for each of the others. They spent thirty-two pesos on cotton, which was distributed to women who wove cloaks and other gifts for the feast.

370. In Yolomecatl, the community gave gifts of food and cloth to local priests on the days of their patron saints. For example, fray Juan Fernández was honored on the "feast of our lord Saint John the Baptist, the ñuhu" [huico stohondo San Jaun Bauptista si ñuhu]. The "si" possessive pronoun

refers to "ñuhu" as a possessor, presumably of the feast. They did the same for fray Sebastián López and fray Josef Cedeño. AJT-C, 6:568, ff. 11, 13, 14v of Ñudzahui-language text.

371. *Codex Sierra*, p. 22. In 1558, for example, they celebrated the feast days of Santa Catalina, Corpus Christi, Santiago, San Pedro y San Pablo, María de la Asunción, Pascua de Natividad, Pascua Flórida, Pascua Espíritu Santo, Todos Santos, San Juan, and San Cristóbal.

372. See Dúran 1971, 442, and Nutini 1988, 86–89.

373. Hugo Nutini (1988) has demonstrated the native roots of the Todos Santos complex and its continued celebration in contemporary Tlaxcala. Farriss observed that All Saints' Day is a major feast among the Yucatec Maya (Farriss 1984, 111, 123).

374. AGN-INQ, 37:7, ff. 202–3. This testimony came from Diego of Etlatongo, a slave. The word *tuta* is the calendrical name for water. According to Nutini 1988, 67–72, who drew on the work of Pedro Carrasco and Alfonso Caso, this period corresponded with the fourteenth month of the Nahua calendar (Quecholli), a time of harvest and the high point of the cult of the dead.

375. AJT-C, 5:506. This document is from Santa Magdalena Yucucata. *Tucu* means "all."

376. Often, the Spanish translation of this couplet reduced it to "santos." On the use of *santo* and *santa* in Nahua writings, see Lockhart 1992, 238–39. Similarly, a testament of 1642 referred to Christians in parallel male and female terms as "taca xptianos xptianas" (AJT-C, 4:467, f. 42).

377. AJT-C, 4:412. "Uico" is a variant spelling of *huico*.

378. Ibid., 7:686. Food and votive offerings are familiar characteristics of Day of the Dead ceremonies.

379. The *Vocabulario* distinguishes between dance ("yaa sitasaha") and ancient dance ("yaa yata, yaa sanaha"). See Alvarado, f. 32. See also Romero Frizzi 1990, 120, on dances and fiestas in the Mixteca.

380. AJT-CR, 1:36, f. 2v.

381. Ibid., 6:644, especially f. 67–67v.

382. AJT-C, 6:578, f. 26.

383. Ibid., 6:568, f. 14v.

384. For example, in 1597, the feast of the patron saint of San Miguel, a sujeto of Teposcolula, featured an organized mitote. People came from nearby communities to attend the feast, watch the dances, and drink pulque (AJT-CR, 1:103). In 1606, Gonzalo Sánchez, a young man from a sujeto of Yanhuitlan named Santa Magdalena, was proud to have danced in the festival of Santa Catalina (Ibid., 2:226).

385. Ricard [1933] 1966, 269.

386. For the use of feathers in indigenous Christian ceremony, see the decree of the Tlaxcalan cabildo of April 28, 1550, in Lockhart, Berdan and Anderson 1986, 70. See also Ricard [1933] 1966, 185–86, for the use of feathers in native Christian ceremonies.

387. *Codex Sierra*, p. 44. The manuscript depicts six bunches of long, green feathers. For the same amount of money, the community bought two horses, which were luxury items by native standards. See Romero Frizzi 1990, 113, on the value of feathers in Mixtec ceremonies.

388. AJT-C, 6:578. The phrase used was "petaca njay sita sitasaha yyo 4 njay yodzo cuij," employing the loanword *petaca*, which suggests that it contained some leather piece. Green feathers are "yodzo cuij," and "sitasaha" is "to dance."

389. Ibid., Anexo 1:18.

390. Ibid., 2:188. *Tnumi* is another common word for small feathers. See Alvarado, f. 168v.

391. AJT-C, 6:568. They spent sixty-nine pesos on food. I have not included some expenses in which the cost of the food, among other items, was not specified.

392. See Taylor 1979, 57–63, 68–69. Taylor observed that pulque was a replacement for potable water in the dry season, lending a pragmatic explanation for its consumption and questioning the exaggerated, posterior accounts of its strict prohibition in preconquest times.

393. Gibson 1964, 124, 214–15; for Yucatan, see Farriss 1984, 324–33.

394. Borah and Cook 1979, 425–28. Ronald Spores counted the value at roughly two-thirds the total. See Spores 1984, 154, 174–76. Although some pages are missing from the account book, it provides a representative sample for the period as a whole.

395. Romero Frizzi 1990, 119–21.

396. AJT-C, 6:568. The amount spent was 62 of 111 pesos.

397. For example, in 1561, Texupa spent 281 pesos for a taffeta vestment for its priest. *Codex Sierra*, p. 37.

398. AJT-C, 6:578, f. 26–26v. The community spent 465 of a total of 542 reals on religious activities. In pesos, the total amount spent was 67 pesos, 6 reals; nonreligious expenses cost about 9 pesos,

5 reals. See also Spores 1984, 154, for a reference to this case. His assessment of the tribute figures differs slightly from mine, but we draw the same conclusion. Spores also calculated the expenditures of San Pedro Tidaa from 1755 to 1763 (pp. 176–79).

399. AJT-CR, 6:644, f. 63. The nine barrios were Ticoo, Yuuyucha, Ayuçi, Caayuqu, Danaa, Tindee, Yuchacoyo, Yuchayoo, and Ñucaa.

400. *Tequios* is the Spanish word, derived from the Nahuatl *tequitl*, for communal duties. But the term *duayaqua* contains references to neither tribute ("chiño" or "daha") nor the church ("huehe ñuhu"). In the reverential lexicon, the verb *nduhuaya* refers to the act of dancing (Reyes, p. 75). It is possible that "duaya" is an orthographic version of "duhuaya." I do not understand the final "qua," however. Unfortunately, only a translation of the original Nudzahui-language document is included in the case. A transcription error may account for the unusual appearance of this word.

401. AJT-CR, 6:644, f. 68v.

402. On the redistributive aspects of the feast system, see Pastor 1987, 346–47, and Romero Frizzi 1990, 110–11, for the Mixteca, and Farriss 1984, 342–47, for Yucatan.

403. AJT-C, 6:568. The fines amounted to 140 reals (18 pesos). It is unclear, however, whether the community was forced to provide food for priests when members failed to meet this requirement. If so, the record did not indicate such an expense.

404. AJT-CR, 1:57.

405. AJT-C, 6:568, f. 2v of Ñudzahui-language text. A woman named Melchora de Santiago led the group of women.

406. AJT-CR, 2:233. For example, in 1606, a couple from Tocaçahuala came to watch the public spectacle after attending the market in Teposcolula. They sought out don Francisco de Mendoza, cacique of Tocaçahuala and alcalde of Yanhuitlan, who took part in the ceremony.

407. On processions in central Mexico, see Ricard [1933] 1966, 179; in Chiapas, see Megged 1996, 70–75; in Spain, see Christian 1981.

408. See the local, political implications of saints in Santiago Nuyoo, discussed in Monaghan 1995, 307–34.

409. See Andrews and Hassig 1984.

410. Burgoa 1989a, 1:288–89. Appropriately, Burgoa's discussion of the calendar is followed by a description of the native pictorial writing system.

411. Alvarado, f. 162 under "partera." The midwife is called "ñaha say dzaya" [woman who receives or takes hold of a child]; "ñaha sitna yya" [the grandmother of a child]; and "ñaha tatna say dzaya" [woman healer who receives a child]. This last definition associates a midwife with a curer (see f. 60).

412. For examples of curers, see Spores 1984, 150–52.

413. AJT-C, 7:654.

414. Hernández 1568, f. 161.

415. Hernández 1567, ff. 157v–158.

416. Monaghan 1995, 107–9. In Santiago Nuyoo, caves are considered "rain houses" where the "ñu'un savi" ("ñuhu dzavui," or "rain deities") live. For similar beliefs among the Nahuas of Veracruz, see Sandstrom 1991.

417. AJT-CR, 4:492. Spores also discusses this case (1984, 152).

418. AJT-CR, 6:689.

419. The document referred to them as *navajas de vidrio*. The *Relaciones* referred to obsidian *navajas* that priests used to bleed their tongues and ears. See the relación of Mixtepec, for example (Acuña 1984, 1:293–5).

420. Gibson 1964, 134. Gibson concluded that while the Nahuas were drawn to the most overt forms of Christianity after the conquest, they did not understand many basic Christian concepts, they never entirely abandoned their polytheistic views, and they managed to maintain many elements of the old religious system, often in "syncretic compromise" with Christian doctrine (1964, 100–101, 134–35). In his assessment of continuity and change, Gibson rejected the notion advanced by George Kubler (1948) and Robert Ricard (1966) that Christianity replaced native beliefs and practices. I might qualify the "preconquest survivals" to which Gibson refers by reiterating that nothing remains unchanged and by adding that non-Christian practices are not persecuted as they were in the colonial period. See Taylor 1996, 47–73, for a discussion of local religion in colonial Mexico that draws on the ethnographic literature.

421. See Jansen 1982 and Monaghan 1995. It is possible, too, that some Christian introductions have faded away since the colonial period. The incorporation of Christian concepts was not a fixed, one-way process. On the other hand, given the weak presence of the church in a place such as Nuyoo

during the colonial period, I do not believe that Christian introductions ever displaced the core of native beliefs and practices that Monaghan has documented in his ethnography.

422. Monaghan 1995, 101–2.

CHAPTER 9 — ETHNICITY

1. See Barth 1969, 9–14. Most sociological and anthropological studies on ethnicity since the appearance of Barth's seminal work of 1969 have relied on his basic premises as a starting point, especially his emphasis on self-ascription, interethnic interaction, and boundary maintenance. For recent, relevant works on the topic of ethnic identity, including critiques of Barth, see Rex 1986; Tonkin, McDonald, and Chapman 1989; Nash 1989; and Banks 1996.

2. Similarly, the term *indio* rarely, if ever, appears in sources written in Nahuatl and Maya. See Lockhart 1991, 8, for the Nahuas and Restall 1997, 13, for the Maya.

3. In general, references to native ethnic identity in Spanish sources are inconsistent and unreliable. For this reason, Jansen and Chance have commented on the difficulty of addressing issues of ethnic identity through the use of colonial sources. See Jansen 1982, 244; Chance 1989, 9; and Jansen 1992, 20.

4. See Pohl 1994a, 145. I thank John Pohl for bringing this legend to my attention.

5. Byland and Pohl 1994, 143–45.

6. Jansen 1982; Monaghan 1995; Alavez Chávez 1997.

7. See Jansen 1982, 226–28, and n. 490.

8. Ibid., 2:527, fig. 8, from the *Codex Selden* (19-III), depiction of 8-Movement; 2:528, fig. 13, from the Lienzo of Zacatepec, depiction of 11-Jaguar, taken from Smith 1973a, 270. *Codex Bodley* (27-II), depiction of 10-Lizard. Jansen 1992, 24, from the *Codex Selden*, 3135 (6-II). For the Lienzo of Zacatepec, see also Smith 1973a, figs. 89, 90, 91, 95 on pp. 268–70, 274.

9. The writing of the name is subject to many regional phonetic differences, as discussed in chapters 1 and 3. See Josserand 1983, 449, on variants of the term she calls "Ñu-Sawi."

10. Reyes, prologue.

11. Ibid., 74.

12. See Jansen 1982, chap. 4, for a discussion of the significance of the four directions in Mesoamerican iconography.

13. See Smith 1973a, 177.

14. Yucuñudahui was the largest late classic site (Las Flores phase, ca. A.D. 300–1000) in the Valley of Nochixtlan. The first distinct appearance of the "A-O" Ñudzahui year sign has been uncovered in a cave from this area, around the time when Mixtec and Cuicatec are thought to have split and a unique language and iconographic style emerged, diverging from the older Zapotec style of the region. Whether this site lent its name as a cultural center to the region and its people is unknown. See contribution by Spores (esp. pp. 155–58, 207, 246–48) in Flannery and Marcus 1983; and Marcus 1992, 121.

15. Alvarado, f. 151v. Again, this could be interpreted as all Ñudzahui ñuu.

16. Literally *dzini* is "head"; "ñuu nino" is a third definition that is obscure. Ibid., f. 151v.

17. Other terms include "ñuu qua ñuhu," "ñuu ditandaa," "ñudzavui nino." Their meanings are unclear. Why *Nuniñe* is not listed is puzzling, for it seems to be the most widely accepted term for the area today. Ibid., f. 151v. See Jansen 1982, 226, for an interpretation of these terms.

18. Hernández 1567, 91–91v. The Huntington Library in San Marino, California, owns two well-preserved and substantially complete copies (1567, 1568) of these rare imprints.

19. Hernández 1568, 97.

20. Ibid., 15v.

21. Hernández 1567, unnumbered endpapers that would constitute ff. 190–194v. A typical instruction is: "When the father says 'sanctus' we say these words in Latin: 'sanctus, sanctus, sanctus deus sabaath pleni sunt celi et terra gloria tua hossana in excelsis benedictus que benit in nomine tua hossana in excelsis' . . . in Ñudzahui we also say 'the glory and the kingdom of heaven'" [Quehui yocachi dzutu sanctus cachindo ndudzu latin yaha sanctus sanctus sanctus deus sabaath pleni sunt celi et terra gloria tua ossana yn excelsis benedictus que benit in nomine tua ossana yn excelsus . . . ndudzu ñudzahui tucu cachindo yuvichayu andehui gloria]. I thank Stafford Poole for his help with the Latin transcription.

22. AJT-CR, 5:581, f. 1v, line 6.

23. Hernández 1567, f. 3v; 1568, ff. 66, 67.

24. Hernández 1567, f. 63.

25. Ibid., f. 8.

26. Ibid., f. 19.

27. Ibid., f. 63.

28. AJT-C, 5:535, f. 8, line 5.

29. Ibid., 8:724, f. 2, line 27.

30. On the relationship between class, status, and ethnicity, see Rex 1986, 12–13.

31. AJT-C, 6:592, unnumbered foja, line 3.

32. AJT-CR, 5:581, f. 1, line 3.

33. AJT-C, 7:689, f. 16, line 18. This term *ñayehui,* or "people," is found in the expression for "world," *ñuu ñayehui,* the "place of people" or simply "ñuu and people."

34. Ibid., f. 21.

35. AJT-C, 4:417, f. 16v, lines 8–9. There are many references in other documents from Teposcolula to saints and images associated with Spaniards, especially in the almsgiving of testaments.

36. AJT-C, 4:417, f. 18v.

37. Hernández 1567, 157v–58; 1568, 161. See the discussion in chapter 8 on the religious ramifications of these references. Again, *quehui* was the word for feast used in the *Doctrina.*

38. Alvarado, f. 161. Also listed is "papel blanco" (*tutu* or *tutu cuisi*) and "papel en que escrivían los Indios antiguos" (*ñee tutu* and *dzoo nee ñuhu*).

39. This is also typical in central Mexico, as with the "quauhnahuacayotl" or Cuernavaca-style cloaks. See Lockhart 1992, 177.

40. AJT-C, 4:488, f. 1, lines 27, 30. The first was translated as "calzones de manta"; *dzama* is defined as *paño, pañuelo,* or *ropa.* The second was translated as "una camissa con sus mangas" but literally means "a shirt that has arms," consisting of *dzunu,* "vestidura"; *ndaha,* "arms"; and *tnaha,* "to possess."

41. Ibid., 15:1232. References to Nudzahui items are located on f. 3, line 25; f. 7v, lines 3, 4, 5, 6, 7; f. 11, lines 3, 4, 18; f. 11v, line 11; f. 14, line 14; f. 15, line 17; f. 16, lines 10, 19; f. 19, line 12. Typical of late colonial Yanhuitlan orthography, *dz* was consistently written as *d* in the text.

42. AJT-CR, 3:271. This document was written in 1612.

43. AJT-C, 6:568, ff. 12, 14. This document was written in 1705. Another document from Yucucata (1625), the testament of María López, mentions a "tiñoo ñudzahui." Ibid., 5:506, f. 16.

44. For example, Juan sold "one bunch of Ñudzahui soap herbs" [ee ñono nama ñuudahui] to a noblewoman named Dolores. AJT-C, 12:1029, f. 3, lines 11–12. The relación of Xicayan, in discussing various types of goods sold in the marketplace, mentions a type of root called *nama* that was used to wash clothes. *Nama* is the same as the Nahuatl *amolli,* which has come into Spanish as *amole.* See Acuña 1984, 2:311.

45. AJT-C, 4:400, f. 2, mentioned three times.

46. See Barth 1969, 37, on the effect of cultural change on perceptions of cultural difference and the maintenance of ethnic identity.

47. Barth 1969, 14–15.

48. AJT-C, 3:287.

49. AJT-CR, 6:675, f. 4.

50. AJT-C, 6:568; Oaxaca was called Ñunduhua, and Puebla was Yutendiyoho.

51. Ibid., 2:263.

52. Jansen 1982, 228. Jansen proposed that *Ñundaa* was the general term for the region. Today, Mixtecan-language speakers on the coast refer to themselves as "Ñu Sawi."

53. Paddock 1966; Moser 1977.

54. See Josserand 1983, 98–117, 462–46.

55. There is one hint of a Baja identity, however indirect, gleaned from a review of barrio names in Teposcolula. A barrio called "siqui ñuniñe" in Teposcolula could be an ethnic barrio containing residents from the Baja region. An arrangement of barrios by ethnicity was not uncommon in this area. AJT-C, 4:400.

56. Molina [1571]1977, p. iii, f. 162 (second numeration).

57. Ibid., 63v. The full entry reads "cosa que suena bien, assi como campana etc. o hombre ladino." The term *ladino* in this period usually referred to a native person who could speak Spanish. Related terms do not convey ethnic meaning: "nauatlato" is defined as "faraute o interprete" [translator], and "to have the occupation of an interpreter" [tener oficio de faraute] is the response for *nauatlatoa,* "to

speak Nahuatl." The emphasis on pleasant sound may explain why Sahagún's informants in book 10 of the *Florentine Codex* tended to characterize other groups that did not speak their language as speakers of "barbarous tongues." Mannheim has noted similar traits of "linguistic ethnocentricism" among Andean speakers (1991, 78–79).

58. In comparison, in the Andean area, a general and misconstrued reference to "valley speech" is the origin of the word *Quechua* for the language of southern Peru. See Mannheim 1991, 5–9.

59. See Sell 1993 for a discussion of the use of *Nahua* in church-sponsored texts. The term is frequently attested in many of the church-sponsored publications compiled by Anunciación, Molina, Laso de la Vega, Chimalpahin, and Sahagún.

60. Lockhart 1992, 115.

61. Ibid., 114. Similarly, a Ñudzahui-language document from Yanhuitlan referred to a native as "chay ñuhu yaha" [person from this land]; the accompanying Spanish translation interpreted it as simply "Indio." AJT-CR, 5:610.

62. Lockhart 1992, 115. The term *timacehualtin* was also used for groups of people in religious processions (who were probably not commoners) and also for non-Nahuas, when talking about Ñudzahui migrants in Mexico City. Lockhart also notes that the term *timacehualtin* does appear as a reference to ethnicity as early as the 1560s, in the annals of Tenochtitlan.

63. The term has not been attested in any Mixtec-language documentation; it does appear on rare occasion in Nahuatl. Even when it does appear, its use involved non-Nahuas and the translation of a Spanish document into Nahuatl. See Lockhart 1992, 115.

64. Alvarado, f. 142.

65. AJT-C, 3:353. This document was written and translated in 1656.

66. AJT-CR, 3:271; Gerhard 1972, 168.

67. AJT-C, 1:161, f. 4.

68. AGN-C, 2302:3, f. 11.

69. See Anderson, Berdan and Lockhart 1976.

70. See Restall 1997, 13–15.

71. Consider, for example, this description of the term *Maya* in an essay on Maya ethnicity: "a placename taken by the Spanish for the Yucatec people and generalized by anthropologists for all of the speakers of the related family of languages grouped as Mayan." Nash 1989, 92.

72. Restall 1997, 16.

73. Barth 1969, 9.

74. Mexico is still called "Ñucoyo" in many parts of the Mixteca, according to field research in Atlatlahuca ("ñucohyó"), Coatzospan ("ñúkohsho"), and Diuxi-Tilantongo ("ñúkóyo"). See Alexander 1980; Small 1988; and Kuiper and Oram 1991, respectively.

75. Reyes, 12, 50, 92.

76. Alvarado, f. 149v.

77. Jansen observed that Nahuas are represented in the codices with painted dark circles around their eyes or blackened faces (Jansen 1992, 27). Pohl has interpreted this identifying characteristic as an association with the legendary leader Camaxtli-Mixcoatl, a Chichimec leader from the seven caves of Chicomoztoc who killed Itzpapolotl, burned her body, and smeared the ashes on his face as a sign of conquest (Pohl 1996, 145, and Byland and Pohl 1994, 142–46). See also Smith 1973a, 209, for a discussion of this term. The only appearance of *saminuu* in the native-language record comes from San Juan Chapultepec's *título primordial* of the 1690s, which is an unusual source. However, this document consistently employs "ñuu coyo" as the term for Nahuas, even when it is clear that this group consisted of people from different central Mexican altepetl.

78. Mexico glyph on pp. 15, 18, 22, 33, 38, 41, 47, 59 of *Codex Sierra*. León identified this (p. 31) as a Popoloca glyph for Mexico City, but it is undoubtedly a literal translation of "ñuu coyo." See also Alvarado, f. 128, under "iunco."

79. *Codex Sierra*, p. 12.

80. Ibid., pp. 12, 27, 30.

81. AJT-C, 2:218; Lockhart 1992, 116, 220.

82. Gibson 1964, 373, 376, 391.

83. Kirchhoff, Odena Güemes, and Reyes García 1976.

84. Smith 1973a; Caso 1977–79; Parmenter 1982; Rincón-Mautner 1994.

85. Reyes, prologue.

86. AJT-CR, 1:85, f. 12.

87. The Chocho-language testament of María de Santiago refers to a Ñudzahui barrio in Coixt-lahuaca as late as 1669 (AJT-C, 4:440). If Ñudzahui nobles dominated the upper offices of the cabildo in Tamasulapa and Texupa, Chocho nobles represented their own ethnic constituencies. For example, Tamasulapa had a Ñudzahui cacique and governor and an alcalde in 1686, but there were several Chocho *tequitlatos* (native tribute collectors). A violent incident in 1686 suggests some conflict between these two groups. Don Flugencio de Santiago, the Ñudzahui cacique and governor of Tamasulapa, witnessed an attack by several Chocho tequitlatos on an alcalde; they stole his staff, burned his house down, and incited a riot. Neither the cacique nor the alcalde knew what had motivated the attackers because they could not understand Chocho, the language spoken by the assailants (AJT-CR, 5:595). In Coixtlahuaca, on the other hand, Nahuatl- and Chocho-language sources indicate that Chochos were clearly the majority.

88. *Nguichee* or *Inguinche* apparently conveys the same meaning as *Yodzocoo* (Smith 1973a, 65). For the identification of *xade* as a fundamental unit of sociopolitical organization among the Cho-chos, see Rincón-Mautner 1994, 4, and 1999.

89. AJT-CR, 1:41, f. 3.

90. AJT-C, 6:592.

91. Lockhart 1992, 115.

92. Ibid., 115.

93. AJT-C, 2:243, f. 2. Similarly, a yya named don Diego de Velasco referred to his female African slave in Tiquehui (Tamasulapa) as a "ña tnuu" [black woman] in 1627. Ibid., 2:263.

94. AJT-CR, 4:399.

95. Ibid., 6:684.

96. Taylor 1972, 22.

97. Ibid., 23.

98. AGN-HJ, 307:6.

99. Taylor 1972, 23.

100. AGN-HJ, 285 (2):8, no. 98.

101. Chance 1976, 611.

102. Ibid., 620.

103. AGN-T, 236:6. William Taylor and John Chance also used the false titles as sources for infor-mation on Mexicapa and Chapultepec (Taylor 1972, 40–41, 115, and Chance 1978, 32, 83). Wood-row Borah also referred to the document to illustrate how Spaniards created native towns in the early period (Borah 1982, 269).

104. Primordial titles exist in Nahuatl, Zapotec, Mixtec, Yucatec Maya, Chontal, Quiche, Cakchiquel, and perhaps other Mesoamerican languages. For recent research on the titles genre, see Lockhart 1982; Wood 1984, 1989, 1991; Borah 1991, 209–21; Lockhart 1991, chap. 3; Lockhart 1992, 410–18; Terraciano and Sousa 1992; and Gruzinski 1993, 98–145. For discussions of "chronicles" in the Maya region, see Scholes and Roys [1948] 1968; Brinton 1969; Carmack 1973; Hanks 1987; Hill 1991; and Restall 1998.

105. This term appears repeatedly throughout the text, and toward the end it is occasionally writ-ten as "mexicanos," with the last three letters, *nos*, crossed out, as if the author or someone realized that this was not a term used in earlier times.

106. See Sousa and Terraciano n.d. for a full transcription and translation of the two titles.

107. AGN-T, 236:6, f. 4–4v. The language of the title is characteristic of the valley variant. In 1593, Reyes wrote that "la lengua de Cuilapa" contained many influences from the Yanhuitlan area and from the Mixteca Baja, owing to migration and marriage alliances (Reyes, p. vii). These charac-teristics include the following: [t] and [tn] are pronounced as [ch] so that *tayu* in the Teposcolula area is "chayu" in the valley, and *huitna* is "huicha." In addition, the *ai* or *ay* of Teposcolula was written as *ee* in the valley, so that *tay* appears as "chee." Spanish loanwords include: "siyudad" (*ciudad*); "españole"; "vario"; "titulo"; "mapa"; "pesso"; and "pena".

108. For a synthetic account of these events, see Spores 1965, 964–67.

109. Lockhart 1992, 417. For central Mexico, he has found that a "broader ethnic awareness or solidarity is no more to be found in the titles than anywhere else."

110. In this sense, the Nahuatl title represents a departure from the altepetl-centered central Mex-ican titles. Mexicapan's articulation of a broad Nahua identity is probably a consequence of its inter-action with various ethnic groups in the Valley of Oaxaca. Stephanie Wood has also cited evidence of an indigenous identity that did not compromise an immediate identification with the altepetl in titles

from multiethnic or non-Nahua communities in Toluca, involving the Matlatzinca, Mexica, and Otomí. See Wood 1984, 332, 336, 343; see also Wood 1991.

111. See Barth 1969, 33, and Banks 1996, 34, on strategies associated with the "instrumentalist" position.

112. Spores 1984, 106–8. See also Gerhard 1972, 296.

113. AJT-CR, 3:275.

114. Romero Frizzi 1990, 358.

115. Ibid., 177, 187.

116. In the sixteenth century, slaves were sold for prices ranging from 280 to 550 pesos, depending on a slave's age and degree of fluency in Spanish. The Dominican order was active in buying and selling African slaves in the Mixteca.

117. See app. 1 in Romero Frizzi 1990, 445–77.

118. AJT-C, 1:251. Most slaves were unmarried, however.

119. Unfortunately, the vast majority of archival documents on slaves that I have seen are simple bills of sale that reveal little about the people being sold. See Spores 1984, 117–18, for a discussion of slaves in the Mixteca. For references to slaves in the sixteenth century, see AJT, 1:68, 84, 120, 130, 136, 160.

120. AGN-I, 6.2:236, f. 52.

121. Ibid., 173, f. 40v.

122. AGN-G, 2:80, f. 18v.

123. AGN-I, 6.2:244; AGN-G, 2:78–79, f. 18.

124. AGN-I, 4:934, f. 242.

125. AGN-T, 2595:155, f. 308v.

126. Ibid., 2984:69, ff. 163–64.

127. Additional cases against Spaniards and other outsiders include, among others, AGN-I, 2:18 (Coixtlahuaca, 1582); ibid., 6.1:220 (several communities); ibid., 6.2:1085 (Teposcolula, 1596); ibid., 10.2:109 (Yanhuitlan, 1640); ibid., 15:89 (Teposcolula, 1648); ibid., 16:90 (Teposcolula, 1651); ibid., 21:47 (Yanhuitlan, 1658).

128. AJT-CR, 3:316. This case ended without a verdict.

129. See Taylor 1979, 81–83, for a discussion of "fighting words" or insults in criminal records.

130. AJT-CR, 1:48.

131. Ibid., 1:106.

132. AGN-I, 6.2:1085, f. 295v.

133. For example, Nicolás de Santiago, a mestizo blacksmith born in Tlaxiaco, married Juana Pascuala, a native woman of Tlaxiaco who knew some Spanish. Their relationship was considered a good one by neighbors, but it came to a tragic end one night in 1642. Juana was home alone, reclining on a *petate*. Around midnight, the mulatto slave of doña Catalina de Nava, a Spanish resident of Tlaxiaco, knocked on the door because he wanted a light for his cigar. Juana let him in and locked the door. Then her husband came home. Before opening the locked door, Juana informed her husband: "do not be offended, but that mulatto has entered to smoke a cigar." Nicolás was so offended that he attacked and mortally wounded Juana with a butcher's knife. AJT-CR, 4:468.

134. Ibid., 2:195.

135. Ibid., 3:314.

136. Ibid., 5:581. See Terraciano 1998 for a transcription and translation of this note and an analysis of the case.

CHAPTER 10 — CONCLUSIONS

1. The amount of extant documentation from the Baja is quite limited in comparison with the collection from the Alta. No other equivalent term has been observed in the Baja. One thing is certain: people from the Baja did not call themselves "Mixtecs" in this period. The coastal region is entirely unrepresented in the native-language corpus, and people from the Alta referred to them as *tay ñundevui*. However, many Mixtecan-language speakers from the coastal region call themselves "nu sawi" today.

2. John Chance has begun to work in the Baja area, a natural extension of his study of southern Puebla. In the Mixteca Alta, future works might test and extend local findings by applying a microhistorical approach to a particular community or valley. Carlos Rincón-Mautner is working on such a project for the Coixtlahuaca basin. Bas van Doesburg is focusing on the Tamasulapa area. Chocholanguage records exist for both areas. For studies that focus on a community in the sixteenth century, see Borah and Cook 1979 on Texupa, and Spores 1967 on Yanhuitlan.

3. Ibid., 24. For Cuauhtinchan, see Reyes García 1977, 121–22. Reyes found that *teccalli* in Cuauhtinchan was used in much the same way as Chimalpahin used *tlayacatl*. The multiple teccalli in Tlaxcala were lineages to which all the nobles of Tlaxcala belonged; each was headed by a *teuctli*, with its own lands and its dependents. For the Nahua case of Chalco, based on the writings of Chimalpahin, see Schroeder 1991, 209–10. Complex or composite altepetl consisted of a number of constituent altepetl, which Chimalpahin called "tlayacatl," which were in turn divided into constituent tlaxilacalli. The composite altepetl lacked a single dynastic ruler with full authority over the whole. John Chance's recent work on the Nahua noble house of Santiago Tecalli in the Puebla-Tlaxcala Valley sheds new light on the teccalli. See Chance 1996, 1998, 2000.

4. Lockhart 1992, 1.

5. Restall 1997, 25, 29, 312–13. Restall's conclusion that the cah and altepetl were similar in structure (p. 312) is qualified by his findings that the cah lacked any subdivisions comparable to the calpolli (p. 313). On the same topic, Lockhart noted "the difference in structure between its [Yucatan's] sociopolitical units and the central Mexican altepetl." See Lockhart 1992, 219, 539 n. 64. The Maya *chibal* (patronym) system represented a form of internal organization, but it differed considerably from the calpolli or siqui.

6. Farriss noted little difference between elite residences and those of commoners, and little socioeconomic differentiation in general. See Farriss 1984, 167, 178. She did observe, however, a system of labor called *cuch* that was linked to *uayeb* rites and associated with the *cargo* or *tequio*. See ibid., 47–48, 184–85, 345–48. However, unlike the frequent appearance of the term *tniño* in Ñudzahui-language records, the term *cuch* is apparently absent from the Yucatec Maya-language record, as presented by Restall 1997.

7. Lockhart 1992, 436–42.

8. Jansen has come to a similar conclusion based on his work with the codices (1982, 240–44).

9. The conventional explanation is that Yucatan was conquered by groups from central Mexico and adopted the term. And yet it was the only category of social differentiation borrowed. In reality, the category "commoner" does not seem very well pronounced in the Maya record. See Restall 1997, 92, on the Maya "macehual."

10. See Rounds 1982, 75–78; Schroeder 1991, 174–80; and Lockhart 1992, 18–19.

11. See Schroeder 1991, 174–80.

12. Spores 1997, 185–97.

13. The marginalization of women by European colonizers corresponds with conclusions drawn for many North American native groups. For example, the Seneca system of sachems, who were appointed and removed by clan mothers, was eclipsed after the Quaker arrival by elected officials called "chiefs," who represented the group to outsiders. Women were increasingly marginalized as the Seneca nation came into greater contact with Anglo-American society in the nineteenth-century (Rothenberg 1980, 81). Similar research suggests that women rulers among the Iroquois, Cherokee, Narragansett, and various Algonkian cultures were ignored, altered, and thwarted by Anglo institutions and customs (Allen 1986, 30–42).

14. For example, Susan Kellogg (1995) has presented evidence of gender parallelism among the Mexica before and immediately after the conquest. Robert Haskett (1997, 145–63) has identified a widowed cacica who played a vital role in the politics of Tepoztlan in the early eighteenth century.

15. See Silverblatt 1987 for a discussion of parallel gender systems in the Andean region and the prominence of coyas or "queens."

16. Joan Scott questioned whether there have been "genuinely egalitarian concepts of gender in terms of which political systems were projected or built" (1988).

17. Goody referred to systems in which the "entitlement of valuables is easily generalized to land or to office" (1976, 13).

18. See the essays in Schroeder, Wood, and Haskett 1997, and Kellogg 1995, for the study of indigenous women. Regarding the use of judicial records to assess gender-rooted conflict, it is important to remember that the colonial record preserves cases that were violent enough to involve the Spanish alcalde mayor and other male officials and thus were recorded in writing. Many more incidences of contested gender rights did not result in aggravated assault or homicide and were heard by men and women within native households and communities, rather than at the level of Spanish authorities. In any case, we must use different types of evidence and a full range of criteria to assess gender relations within colonial indigenous societies. See Taylor 1979 and especially Stern 1995 for a discussion of violence against women in late colonial Mexico. See Sousa 1998 for her use of criminal records and other sources for the study of indigenous social and gender relations in colonial Oaxaca

and central Mexico. See also Terraciano 1998 on attitudes toward adultery and homicide in Yanhuitlan at the end of the seventeenth century.

19. Zapotec was written in both the Sierra Zapoteca and the Valley of Oaxaca. Nancy Farriss is collaborating with Juana Vásquez and María de los Ángeles Romero Frizzi in the translation and use of Zapotec-language records from the Villa Alta area of the Sierra. Michel Oudijk is working with lienzos and Zapotec-language documents from the early colonial period. See Oudijk 2000. Pamela Munro, Lisa Sousa, and I are working with a group of students in the departments of Linguistics and History at the University of California, Los Angeles, on the translation and analysis of Zapotec-language documents from the Valley of Oaxaca. Bas van Doesburg and Michael Swanton are working with hundreds of Chocho-language records.

20. For a discussion of social change among native peoples who came into sudden and violent contact with Europeans that emphasizes the radical nature of change, even when indigenous cultural systems are employed to understand externally imposed events, see Sahlins 1985, 136–56.

21. Lockhart 1992.

22. This pattern resembles a scenario proposed by Lockhart (1992, 448) for the Andean region.

23. Romero Frizzi 1990.

24. AJT-C, 4:417.

25. AJT-CR, 5:581.

26. Ibid., 2:195.

27. Ibid., 1:106.

28. Ibid., 3:314.

29. For population figures for the Mixteca Alta, see Cook and Borah 1968; Gerhard 1972, 296; and Spores 1984, 106–8.

30. Sahagún 1950–82, bk. 6:67–78.

31. On the collaboration of caciques with colonial officials in colonial Peru, see Stern 1982.

32. Hernández 1568, f. 161 of a copy owned by the Huntington Library.

33. A recent study of a modern Zapotecan language has identified several words that incorporate a reduced form of *Castilla* to the extent that the word is no longer recognized as a loanword by native speakers. This is true for a number of loan nouns. This example illustrates how new terms for introductions were fully incorporated into the language. See Munro and Lopez 1999, 364.

34. AGN-I, 5:698, f. 190.

35. Ibid., 101:1, f. 36.

36. Acuña 1984, 1:85.

37. Ibid., 2:144.

38. Ibid., 240.

39. Gibson 1964, 403–9.

40. Farriss 1984, 389–95. Similarly, Matthew Restall concludes that the cah rejected undesirable Spanish influences throughout the colonial period until the nineteenth century (1997, 312–18).

41. Taylor 1979, 114.

42. For studies of the Mixteca in the nineteenth century, see Berry 1981, Pastor 1987, and Monaghan 1997.

43. AGN-T, 400:1, f. 189v.

44. Cook and Borah 1968, 49.

45. Monaghan 1995, 167–89.

BIBLIOGRAPHY

Acuña, René. 1984. *Relaciones geográficas del siglo XVI: Antequera*. 2 vols. Mexico City: Universidad Nacional Autónoma de México.

———. 1984–85. *Relaciones geográficas del siglo XVI: Tlaxcala*. 2 vols. Mexico City: Universidad Nacional Autónoma de México.

Aguirre Beltrán, Gonzalo. 1967. *Regiones de refugio: El desarollo de la comunidad y el proceso dominical en mestizoamerica*. Mexico City: Instituto Nacional Indígenista.

———. 1979. *Regions of Refuge*. Washington: Society for Applied Anthropology.

Alavez Chávez, Raúl. 1997. *Ñayiu xindeku nuu ndaa vico nu'u: Los habitantes del lugar de las nubes*. Mexico City: Centro de Investigaciones y Estudios Superiores en Antropología Social and Instituto Oaxaqueño de las Culturas.

Alexander, Ruth Mary. 1980. *Gramática Mixteca de Atlatláhuca*. Serie de Gramáticas de Lenguas Indígenas de México, 2. Mexico City: Instituto Lingüístico de Verano.

———. 1988. "A Syntactic Sketch of Ocotepec Mixtec." In *Studies in the Syntax of the Mixtecan Languages*, ed. C. Henry Bradley and Barbara E. Hollenbach, 1:151–304. Dallas: Summer Institute of Linguistics (Arlington) and the University of Texas at Arlington.

Allen, Paula Gunn. 1986. *The Sacred Hoop: Recovering the Feminine in American Indian Traditions*. Boston: Beacon Press.

Altman, Ida, and James Lockhart, eds. 1976. *Provinces of Early Mexico: Variants of Spanish American Regional Evolution*. Los Angeles: UCLA Latin American Center Publications.

Alvarado, fray Francisco de. [1593]1962. *Vocabulario en lengua mixteca*. Edited by Wigberto Jiménez Moreno. Mexico City: Instituto Nacional de Antropología e Historia.

Anawalt, Patricia. 1981. *Indian Clothing before Cortés: Mesoamerican Costumes from the Codices*. Norman: University of Oklahoma Press.

Anders, Ferdinand, and Maarten Jansen. 1996. *Libro de la vida: Texto explicativo del llamado Códice Magliabechiano*. Vienna: Akademische Druck und Verlagsanstalt, and Mexico City: Fondo de Cultura Económica.

Anders, Ferdinand, Maarten Jansen, and Gabina Aurora Pérez Jiménez. 1992a. *Crónica mixteca: El rey 8 venado, garra de jaguar, y la dinastía de Teozacualco-Zaachila: Libro explicativo del llamado Códice Zouche-Nuttall*. Vienna: Akademische Druck und Verlagsanstalt; Madrid: Sociedad Estatal Quinto Centenario; and Mexico City: Fondo de Cultura Económica.

———. 1992b. *Origen e historia de los reyes mixtecos: Libro explicativo del llamado Códice Vindobonensis*. Vienna: Akademische Druck und Verlagsanstalt; Madrid: Sociedad Estatal Quinto Centenario; and Mexico City: Fondo de Cultura Económica.

Anderson, Arthur J. O., Frances Berdan, and James Lockhart, eds. 1976. *Beyond the Codices: The Nahua View of Colonial Mexico*. UCLA Latin American Studies. Berkeley and Los Angeles: University of California Press.

Anderson, Arthur J. O., and Charles E. Dibble, trans. 1950–82. *Florentine Codex: General History of Things of New Spain.* 13 parts. Salt Lake City: University of Utah Press, and Santa Fe: School of American Research.

Andrews, J. Richard, and Ross Hassig, eds. 1984. See Ruiz de Alarcón, Hernando.

Arana Osnaya, Evangelina. 1960. "El idioma de los señores de Teposcolula." *Anales del Instituto Nacional de Antropología e Historia* 13: 217–30.

Arana Osnaya, Evangelina, and Mauricio Swadesh. 1965. *Los elementos del mixteco antiguo.* Mexico City: Instituto Nacional Indigenista e Instituto Nacional de Antropología e Historia.

Archivo General de la Nación. 1982. *Documentos mexicanos: Cacchiqueles, mayas, mixtecos y nauas.* 2 tomos. Serie guías y católogos, 72. Mexico City: Talleres Gráficos de la Nación.

Arrom, Silvia Marina. 1985. *The Women of Mexico City, 1790–1857.* Stanford: Stanford University Press.

Bailey, Joyce W. 1972. "Map of Texupa (Oaxaca, 1579): A Study of Form and Meaning." *Art Bulletin* 54: 452–79.

Banks, Marcus. 1996. *Ethnicity: Anthropological Constructions.* London: Routledge.

Barabas, Alicia, and Miguel Bartolomé, eds. 1986. *Etnicidad y pluralismo cultural: La dinámica étnica en Oaxaca.* Mexico City: Instituto Nacional de Antropología e Historia.

Barth, Frederik. 1969. *Ethnic Groups and Boundaries: The Social Organization of Cultural Difference.* London: George Allen and Unwin.

Bartlett, Robert. 1993. *The Making of Europe: Conquest, Colonization, and Cultural Change, 930–1350.* London: Penguin.

Baskes, Jeremy. 1996. "Coerced or Voluntary? The 'Repartimiento' and Market Participation of Peasants in Late Colonial Oaxaca." *Journal of Latin American Studies* 28 (1): 1–28.

Bauman, Richard. 1977. *Verbal Art as Performance.* Prospect Heights, Ill.: Waveland Press.

Benson, Elizabeth, ed. 1973. *Mesoamerican Writing Systems.* Washington, D.C.: Dumbarton Oaks.

Berdan, Frances F. 1982. *The Aztecs of Central Mexico: An Imperial Society.* New York: Holt, Rinehart, and Winston.

Berdan, Frances F., and Patricia Rieff Anawalt, eds. 1992. *The Codex Mendoza.* 4 vols. Berkeley and Los Angeles: University of California Press.

Berlin, Heinrich. 1947. *Fragmentos desconocidos del Códice de Yanhuitlán y otras investigaciones mixtecas.* Mexico City: Antigua Librería Robredo de José Porrua e Hijos.

Berry, Charles. 1981. *The Reform in Oaxaca, 1856–76: A Microhistory of the Liberal Revolution.* Lincoln: University of Nebraska Press.

Bhabha, Homi. 1984. "Of Mimicry and Man: The Ambivalence of Colonial Discourse." *October 28* (Spring): 125–33.

———. 1992. "Double Visions." *Artforum International* 30 (5): 85–89.

———. 1994. *The Location of Culture.* London: Routledge.

Boone, Elizabeth. 1983. *The Codex Magliabechiano and the Lost Prototype of the Magliabechiano Group.* Berkeley and Los Angeles: University of California Press.

———. 2000. *Stories in Red and Black: Pictorial Histories of the Aztecs and Mixtecs.* Austin: University of Texas Press.

Boone, Elizabeth, and Walter Mignolo, eds. 1994. *Writing without Words: Alternative Literacies in Mesoamerica and the Andes.* Durham, N.C.: Duke University Press.

Borah, Woodrow. 1943. *Silk Raising in Colonial Mexico.* Ibero-Americana, 20. Berkeley and Los Angeles: University of California Press.

———. 1949. "Tithe Collection in the Bishopric of Oaxaca, 1601–1867." *Hispanic American Historical Review* 29 (November): 498–517.

———. 1951. *New Spain's Century of Depression.* Berkeley and Los Angeles: University of California Press.

———. 1983. *Justice by Insurance: The General Indian Court of Colonial Mexico.* Berkeley and Los Angeles: University of California Press.

———. 1984. "Some Problems of Sources." In *Explorations in Ethnohistory: Indians of Central Mexico in the Sixteenth Century,* ed. H. R. Harvey and Hanns J. Prem, 23–39. Albuquerque: University of New Mexico Press.

———. 1991. "Yet Another Look at the Techialoyan Codices." In *Land and Politics in the Valley of Mexico: A Two Thousand Year Perspective,* ed. H. R. Harvey, 209–22. Albuquerque: University of New Mexico Press.

Borah, Woodrow, and S. F. Cook. 1960. *The Population of Central Mexico, 1531–1570.* Ibero-Americana, 43. Berkeley and Los Angeles: University of California Press.

―――. 1979. "A Case History of the Transition from the Precolonial to the Colonial Period in Mexico: Santiago Texupa." In *Social Fabric and Spatial Structure in Colonial Latin America*, ed. David J. Robinson, 409–32. Published for Department of Geography, Syracuse University. Ann Arbor: University Microfilms.

Bos, Anne. 1998. *The Demise of the Caciques of Atlacomulco, Mexico, 1598–1821: A Reconstruction.* Leiden, Netherlands: Research School CNWS.

Bradley, C. Henry. 1970. *A Linguistic Sketch of Jicaltepec Mixtec.* Summer Institute of Linguistics Publications in Linguistics and Related Fields, 25. Norman: Summer Institute of Linguistics of the University of Oklahoma.

Bradley, C. Henry, and Barbara E. Hollenbach, eds. 1988–92. *Studies in the Syntax of Mixtecan Languages.* 4 vols. Dallas: Summer Institute of Linguistics and the University of Texas at Arlington.

Bremmer, Jan, and Herman Roodenburg, eds. 1991. *A Cultural History of Gesture: From Antiquity to the Present Day.* Cambridge: Polity Press.

Brewer, Forrest, and Jean G. Brewer. 1971. *Vocabulario mexicano de Tetelcingo, Morelos.* 2d ed. Mexico City: Instituto de Lingüístico de Verano.

Bricker, Victoria. 1981. *The Indian Christ, the Indian King: The Historical Substrate of Maya Myth and Ritual.* Austin: University of Texas Press.

Brinton, Daniel Garrison. 1969. *Ancient Nahuatl Poetry, Containing the Nahuatl Text of XXVII Ancient Nahuatl Poems.* With a translation, introduction, notes and vocabulary. New York: AMS Press.

Brown, Betty Ann. 1983. "Seen but Not Heard: Women in Aztec Ritual—The Sahagún Texts." In *Text and Image in Pre-Columbian Art*, ed. Janet C. Berlo, 119–53. Oxford: B.A.R. Press.

Brumfiel, Elizabeth M. 1991. "Weaving and Cooking: Women's Production in Aztec Mexico." In *Engendering Archaeology: Women and Prehistory*, ed. Joan M. Gero and Margaret W. Conkey, 224–51. Oxford: Blackwell.

Bryson, Norman, Michael Ann Holly, and Keith Moxey, eds. 1991. *Visual Theory: Painting and Interpretation.* Cambridge: Polity Press.

Burgoa, fray Francisco de. 1989a. *Geográfica descripción.* 2 vols. Mexico City: Editorial Porrúa.

―――. 1989b. *Palestra historial de virtudes y ejemplares apostólicos.* Mexico City: Editorial Porrúa.

Burke, Peter. 1992. *History and Social Theory.* Ithaca: Cornell University Press.

Burkhart, Louise. 1989. *The Slippery Earth: Nahua-Christian Moral Dialogue in Sixteenth-Century Mexico.* Tucson: University of Arizona Press.

―――. 1996. *Holy Wednesday: A Nahua Drama from Early Colonial Mexico.* Philadelphia: University of Pennsylvania Press.

Butterworth, Douglas. 1975. *Tilantongo: Comunidad mixteca en transición.* Mexico City: Instituto Nacional Indígenista.

Byland, Bruce, and John Pohl. 1994. *In the Realm of 8 Deer: The Archaeology of the Mixtec Codices.* Norman: University of Oklahoma Press.

Calnek, Edward, ed. 1974. *Ensayos sobre el desarollo urbano de México.* Mexico City: Secretaría de Educación Pública.

Carmack, Robert. 1973. *Quichean Civilization: The Ethnohistoric, Ethnographic, and Archaeological Sources.* Berkeley: University of California Press.

Carmagnani, Marcello. 1988. *El regreso de los dioses: El proceso de reconstitución de la identidad étnica en Oaxaca, siglos XVII y XVIII.* Mexico City: Fondo de Cultura Económica.

Carrasco, Pedro. 1963. "The Civil-Religious Hierarchy in Mesoamerica: Pre-Spanish Background and Colonial Development." *American Anthropologist* 63: 483–7.

―――. 1964. "Family Structure of Sixteenth-Century Tepoztlan." In *Process and Pattern in Culture: Essays in Honor of Julian H. Steward*, ed. Robert A. Manners, 185–210. Chicago: Aldine Publishing Co.

―――. 1971. "Social Organization of Ancient Mexico." In *Handbook of Middle American Indians*, gen. ed., Robert Wauchope; vol. 10, *Archaeology of Northern Mesoamerica*, ed. Gordon F. Ekholm and Ignacio Bernal, pt. 1: 349–75. Austin: University of Texas Press.

―――. 1976a. "The Joint Family in Ancient Mexico: The Case of Molotla." In *Essays on Mexican Kinship*, ed. Hugo G. Nutini, Pedro Carrasco, and James M. Taggart, 45–64. Pittsburgh: University of Pittsburgh Press.

―――. 1976b. "Los linajes nobles del Mexico antiguo." In *Estratificación social en la Mesoamérica prehispánica*, ed. Pedro Carrasco and Johanna Broda, 19–36. Mexico City: Centro de Investigaciones Superiores, Instituto Nacional de Antropología e Historia.

———. 1984. "Royal Marriages in Ancient Mexico." In *Explorations in Ethnohistory: Indians of Central Mexico in the Sixteenth Century*, ed. H. R. Harvey and Hanns J. Prem, 41–81. Albuquerque: University of New Mexico Press.

Carrasco, Pedro, and Johanna Broda, eds. 1976. *Estratificación social en la Mesoamérica prehispánica*. Mexico City: Centro de Investigaciones Superiores, Instituto Nacional de Antropología e Historia.

Caso, Alfonso. 1949. "El mapa de Teozacualco." *Cuadernos Americanos*, Año VIII, 5:145–81.

———. 1950. "Explicación del reverso del Codex Vindobonensis." *Memoria del Colegio Nacional* 5 (5): 9–46.

———. 1960. *Interpretación de Códice Bodley 2858*. Mexico City: Sociedad Mexicana de Antropología.

———. 1965. "Mixtec Writing and Calendar." In *Handbook of Middle American Indians*, gen. ed., Robert Wauchope; vol. 3, *Archaeology of Southern Mesoamerica*, pt. 2, ed. Gordon R. Willey, 948–61. Austin: University of Texas Press.

———. 1966a. "The Lords of Yanhuitlan." In *Ancient Oaxaca: Discoveries in Mexican Archaeology and History*, ed. John Paddock, 313–35. Stanford: Stanford University Press.

———. 1966b. "Mapa de Santo Tomás Ocotepeque, Oaxaca." In *Summa antropológia en homenaje a Roberto J. Weitlaner*, 131–37. Mexico City: Instituto Nacional de Antropología e Historia.

———. 1977–79. *Reyes y reinos de la Mixteca*. 2 vols. Mexico City: Fondo de Cultura Económica.

Chance, John K. 1976. "The Urban Indian in Colonial Oaxaca." *American Ethnologist* 3 (4): 603–32.

———. 1978. *Race and Class in Colonial Oaxaca*. Stanford: Stanford University Press.

———. 1986. "Colonial Ethnohistory of Oaxaca." In *Supplement to the Handbook of Middle American Indians*, gen. ed., Victoria R. Bricker; vol. 4, *Epigraphy*, ed. Ronald Spores, 165–89. Austin: University of Texas Press.

———. 1989. *Conquest of the Sierra: Spaniards and Indians in Colonial Oaxaca*. Norman: University of Oklahoma Press.

———. 1994. "Indian Elites in Late Colonial Mesoamerica." In *Caciques and Their People: A Volume in Honor of Ronald Spores*, ed. Joyce Marcus and Judith Francis Zeitlin, 45–65. Anthropological Papers, no. 89. Ann Arbor: Museum of Anthropology, University of Michigan.

———. 1996. "The Caciques of Tecali: Class and Ethnic Identity in Late Colonial Mexico." *Hispanic American Historical Review* 76 (3): 475–502.

———. 1997. "The Mixtec Nobility under Colonial Rule." In *Códices, Caciques, and Comunidades*, ed. Maarten Jansen and Luis Reyes García, 161–78. Netherlands: Asociación de Historiadores Latinoamericanistas Europeos.

———. 1998. "La hacienda de los Santiago en Tecali, Puebla: Un cacicazgo Nahua colonial, 1520–1750." *Historia Mexicana* 47 (4): 689–734.

———. 2000. "The Noble House in Colonial Puebla, Mexico: Descent, Inheritance, and the Nahua Tradition." *American Anthropologist* 102 (3): 485–502.

Chance, John K., and William B. Taylor. 1977. "Estate and Class in a Colonial City: Oaxaca in 1792." *Comparative Studies in History* 19 (4): 454–87.

———. 1985. "Cofradías and Cargos: An Historical Perspective on the Mesoamerican Civil-Religious Hierarchy." *American Ethnologist* 12 (1): 1–26.

Charlton, Thomas H. 1991. "Land Tenure and Agricultural Production in the Otumba Region, 1785–1803." In *Land and Politics in the Valley of Mexico: A Two Thousand Year Perspective*, ed. H.R. Harvey, 223–263. Albuquerque: University of New Mexico Press.

Christian, William. 1981. *Local Religion in Sixteenth-Century Spain*. Princeton: Princeton University Press.

Clifford, James, and Marcus George. 1986. *Writing Culture: The Poetics and Politics of Ethnography*. Berkeley and Los Angeles: University of California Press.

Cline, Howard F. 1972a. "A Census of the Relaciones Geográficas, 1579–1612." In *Handbook of Middle American Indians*, gen. ed., Robert Wauchope; vol. 12, *Guide to Ethnohistorical Sources*, pt. 1, ed. Howard F. Cline, 324–69. Austin: University of Texas Press.

———. 1972b. "The Relaciones Geográficas of the Spanish Indies, 1577–1648." In *Handbook of Middle American Indians*, gen. ed., Robert Wauchope; vol. 12, *Guide to Ethnohistorical Sources*, pt. 1, ed. Howard F. Cline, 183–242. Austin: University of Texas Press.

Cline, S. L. 1984. "Land Tenure and Land Inheritance in Late Sixteenth-Century Culhuacan." In *Explorations in Ethnohistory: Indians of Central Mexico in the Sixteenth Century*, ed. H. R. Harvey and Hanns J. Prem, 277–309. Albuquerque: University of New Mexico Press.

———. 1986. *Colonial Culhuacan, 1580–1600: A Social History of an Aztec Town*. Albuquerque: University of New Mexico Press.

———, ed. 1993. *The Book of Tributes: Early Sixteenth-Century Nahuatl Censuses from Morelos.* Nahuatl Studies Series 4. Los Angeles: UCLA Latin American Studies Center Publications.

Cline, S. L., and Miguel León-Portilla, eds. 1984. *The Testaments of Culhuacan.* Nahuatl Studies Series 1. Los Angeles: UCLA Latin American Center.

Codex Bodley 2858. 1960. Mexico City: Sociedad Mexicana de Antropología.

Codex Edgerton and Becker II. See Jansen 1994.

Codex Kingsborough. See *Códice de Tepetlaoztoc.*

Codex Magliabechiano. See Boone 1983; Anders and Jansen 1996.

Codex Mendoza. See Berdan and Anawalt 1992.

Codex Nuttall. See Anders, Jansen, and Pérez Jiménez 1992a.

Codex Selden 3135. 1964. Mexico City: Sociedad Mexicana de Antropología.

Codex Sierra. See León 1933.

Codex Vindobonensis Mexicanus I. See Anders, Jansen, and Pérez Jiménez 1992b.

Codex Yanhuitlan. See Jiménez Moreno and Mateos Higuera 1940.

Códice de Tepetlaoztoc (Códice Kingsborough), Estado de México. 1994. Edición facsimilar con un estudio de Perla Valle. Toluca: El Colegio Mexiquense.

Códice de Yanhuitlan. 1994. Edición en facsimile, con un estudio preliminar por María Teresa Sepúlveda y Herrera. Mexico City: Instituto Nacional de Antropología e Historia y Benemérita Universidad Autónoma de Puebla.

Cohen, A. P. 1985. *The Symbolic Construction of Community.* London: Tavistock Publications.

Collier, George A., Renato I. Rosaldo, and John D. Wirth, eds. 1982. *The Inca and Aztec States, 1400–1800: Anthropology and History.* New York: Academic Press.

Connerton, Paul. 1989. *How Societies Remember.* Cambridge: Cambridge University Press.

Cook, S. F. 1939. "Dwelling Construction in the Mixteca." *México antiguo* 4: 375–86.

Cook, S. F., and Woodrow Borah. 1968. *The Population of the Mixteca Alta, 1520–1960.* Ibero-Americana, 50. Berkeley and Los Angeles: University of California Press.

Cope, Douglas. 1994. *The Limits of Racial Domination: Plebeian Society in Colonial Mexico City, 1660–1720.* Madison: Univeristy of Wisconsin Press.

Covarrubias, Miguel. 1957. *Indian Art of Mexico and Central America.* New York: Knopf.

Dahlgren, Bárbro. 1954. *La Mixteca: Su cultura e historia prehispánicas.* Mexico City: Universidad Nacional Autónoma de México.

Dakin, Karen. 1981. "The Characteristics of a Nahuatl Lingua Franca." *Texas Linguistics Forum* 18: 55–67.

Daly, John P. 1973. *A Generative Syntax of Peñoles Mixtec.* Publications in Linguistics and Related Fields, 42. Norman: Summer Institute of Linguistics of the University of Oklahoma.

Dávila Padilla, Agustín. [1596] 1955. *Historia de la fundacion y discurso de la provincia de santiago de mexico de la orden de predicadores.* Mexico City: Editorial Academia Literaria.

Dibble, Charles. 1971. "Writing in Central Mexico." In *Handbook of Middle American Indians,* gen. ed., Robert Wauchope; vol. 10, *Archaeology of Northern Mesoamerica,* pt. 1., ed. Gordon F. Ekholm and Ignacio Bernal, 322–32. Austin: University of Texas Press.

Diringer, David. 1962. *Writing.* London: Thames and Hudson.

Dúran, Diego. 1971. *Book of the Gods and Rites and the Ancient Calendar.* Translated and edited by Fernando Horcasitas and Doris Heyden. Norman: University of Oklahoma Press.

Dyckerhoff, Ursula. 1976. "Aspectos generales y regionales de la estratificación social (en Huexotzinco)." In *Estratificación social en la Mesoamérica prehispánica,* ed. Pedro Carrasco and Johanna Broda, 157–77. Mexico City: Centro de Investigaciones Superiores, Instituto Nacional de Antropología e Historia.

———. 1979. "Forged Village Documents from Huejotzingo and Calpan." *Actas of the International Congress of Americanists* 42 (7): 51–63.

Dyckerhoff, Ursula and Hanns J. Prem. 1976. "La estratificación social en Huexotzinco." In *Estratificación social en la Mesoamérica prehispánica,* ed. Pedro Carrasco and Johanna Broda, 157–80. Mexico City: Centro de Investigaciones Superiores, Instituto Nacional de Antropología e Historia.

Dyk, Anne. 1951. *Vocabulario de la lengua mixteca de San Miguel el Grande, Oaxaca.* Mexico City: Instituto Lingüístico de Verano.

———. 1959. *Mixteco Texts.* Norman: Summer Institute of Linguistics of the University of Oklahoma.

Dyk, Anne, and Betty Stoudt. 1965. *Vocabulario mixteco de San Miguel el Grande.* Mexico City: Instituto Lingüístico de Verano.

Eire, Carlos. 1995. *From Madrid to Purgatory: The Art and Craft of Dying in Sixteenth-Century Spain.* Cambridge: Cambridge University Press.

Evans, Susan T. 1991. "Architecture and Authority in an Aztec Village: Form and Function of the Tecpan." In *Land and Politics in the Valley of Mexico*, ed. H. R. Harvey, 63–92. Albuquerque: University of New Mexico Press.

Farago, Claire, ed. 1996. *Reframing the Renaissance: Visual Culture in Europe and Latin America, 1450–1650.* New Haven: Yale University Press.

Farris, Edwin R. 1992. "A Syntactic Sketch of Yosondúa Mixtec." In *Studies in the Syntax of Mixtecan Languages*, ed. C. Henry Bradley and Barbara E. Hollenbach, 4:1–171. Dallas: Summer Institute of Linguistics (Arlington) and the University of Texas at Arlington.

Farriss, Nancy M. 1984. *Maya Society under Colonial Rule: The Collective Enterprise of Survival.* Princeton: Princeton University Press.

Fentress, James, and Chris Wickham. 1992. *Social Memory.* Oxford: Blackwell.

Flannery, Kent V., and Joyce Marcus, eds. 1983. *The Cloud People: Divergent Evolution of the Zapotec and Mixtec Civilizations.* New York: Academic Press.

Florentine Codex. See Sahagún 1950–82.

Furst, Jill. 1978. *Codex Vindobonensis Mexicanus I: A Commentary.* Albany: State University of New York at Albany, Institute for Mesoamerican Studies.

Galarza, Joaquín. 1979. *Estudios de escritura indígena tradicional azteca-náhuatl.* Mexico City: Archivo General de la Nación.

García, fray Gregorio. [1607] 1981. *Origen de los indios de el Nuevo Mundo e Indias Occidentales.* Mexico City: Fondo de Cultura Económica.

García Icazbalceta, Joaquín. 1954. *Bibliografía mexicana del siglo XVI: Catálogo razonado de libros impresos en México de 1539 a 1600.* Mexico City: Fondo de Cultura Económica.

Garibay, Angel María. 1971. *Historia de literatura náhuatl.* 2 vols. Mexico City: Editorial Porrúa.

Geertz, Clifford. 1973. *The Interpretation of Cultures.* New York: Basic Books.

———. 1980. *Negara: The Theatre State in Nineteenth-Century Bali.* Princeton: Princeton University Press.

———. 1983. *Local Knowledge: Further Essays in Interpretive Anthropology.* New York: Basic Books.

Gelb, I. J. 1963. *A Study of Writing.* 2d ed. Chicago: University of Chicago Press.

Gerhard, Peter. 1972. *A Guide to the Historical Geography of New Spain.* Cambridge: Cambridge University Press.

Gibson, Charles. 1952. *Tlaxcala in the Sixteenth Century.* New Haven: Yale University Press.

———. 1964. *The Aztecs under Spanish Rule: A History of the Indians of the Valley of Mexico, 1519–1810.* Stanford: Stanford University Press.

———. 1975. "Survey of Middle American Prose Manuscripts in the Native Historical Tradition." In *Handbook of Middle American Indians*, gen. ed., Robert Wauchope; vol. 14, *Guide to Ethnohistorical Sources*, pt. 3, ed. Howard F. Cline et al., 311–21. Austin: University of Texas Press.

Gillespie, Susan. 1989. *The Aztec Kings: The Construction of Rulership in Mexica History.* Tucson: University of Arizona Press.

Ginés de Sepúlveda, Juan. 1941. *Tratado sobre las justas causas de la guerra contra los indios*, con una advertencia de Marcelino Méndez y Pelayo, y un estudio por Manuel García-Pelayo. Mexico City: Fondo de Cultura Económica.

Ginzburg, Carlo. 1982. *The Cheese and the Worms: The Cosmos of a Sixteenth-Century Miller.* Translated by John and Anne Tedeschi. New York: Penguin Books.

———. 1986. *Clues, Myths, and the Historical Method.* Translated by John and Anne Tedeschi. Baltimore: Johns Hopkins University Press.

———. 1992. *The Night Battles: Witchcraft and Agrarian Cults in the Sixteenth and Seventeenth Centuries.* Translated by John and Anne Tedeschi. Baltimore: Johns Hopkins University Press.

Glass, John B. 1975a. "A Catalog of Falsified Middle American Pictorial Manuscripts." In *Handbook of Middle American Indians*, gen. ed., Robert Wauchope; vol. 14, *Guide to Ethnohistorical Sources*, pt. 3, ed. Howard F. Cline et al., 297–310. Austin: University of Texas Press.

———. 1975b. "A Survey of Native Middle American Pictorial Manuscripts." In *Handbook of Middle American Indians*, gen. ed., Robert Wauchope; vol. 14, *Guide to Ethnohistorical Sources*, pt. 3, ed. Howard F. Cline et al., 3–80. Austin: University of Texas Press.

Glass, John B., and Donald Robertson. 1975. "A Census of Native American Pictorial Manuscripts." In *Handbook of Middle American Indians*, gen. ed., Robert Wauchope; vol. 14, *Guide to Ethnohistorical Sources*, pt. 3, ed. Howard F. Cline et al., 81–252. Austin: University of Texas Press.

Glave Testino, Luis Miguel. 1989. *Trajinantes: Caminos indígenas en la sociedad colonial, siglos XVI–XVII.* Lima, Peru: Instituto de Apoyo Agrario.

Goody, Jack, ed. 1966. *Succession to High Office.* Cambridge: Department of Archaeology and Anthropology, Cambridge University Press.

———. 1976. *Inheritance, Property, and Women: Some Comparative Considerations.* In *Family and Inheritance: Rural Society in Western Europe, 1200–1800,* ed. Jack Goody, Joan Thirsk, and E.P. Thompson, 10–36. Cambridge: Cambridge University Press.

———. 1986. *The Logic of Writing and the Organization of Society.* Cambridge: Cambridge University Press.

———. 1987. *The Interface between the Written and the Oral.* Cambridge: Cambridge University Press.

———. 1997. *Representations and Contradictions: Ambivalence toward Images, Theatre, Fiction, Relics, and Sexuality.* Oxford: Blackwell.

Goody, Jack, Joan Thirsk, and E. P. Thompson, eds. 1976. *Family and Inheritance: Rural Society in Western Europe, 1200–1800.* Cambridge: Cambridge University Press.

Greenleaf, Richard E. 1969. *The Mexican Inquisition of the Sixteenth Century.* Albuquerque: University of New Mexico Press.

———. 1991. "Historiography of the Mexican Inquisition: Evolution of Interpretations and Methodologies." In *Cultural Encounters: The Impact of the Inquisition and Spain and the New World,* ed. Elizabeth Perry and Anne J. Cruz, 248–76. Berkeley and Los Angeles: University of California Press.

Gruzinski, Serge. 1987. "Colonial Indian Maps in Sixteenth-Century Mexico: An Essay in Mixed Cartography." *RES: Anthropology and Aesthetics* 13: 46–61.

———. 1989. *Man-Gods in the Mexican Highlands: Indian Power and Colonial Society, 1520–1800.* Stanford: Stanford University Press.

———. 1993. *The Conquest of Mexico: The Incorporation of Indian Societies into the Western World, 16th–18th Centuries.* Translated by Eileen Corrigan. Cambridge: Polity Press.

Guaman Poma de Ayala, don Felipe. [1615] 1980. *El primer nueva coronica y buen gobierno.* Edited by John V. Murra and Rolena Adorno. Translation and analysis of Quechua by George L. Urioste. Mexico City: Siglo Veintiuno.

Guha, Ranajit. 1988. "The Prose of Counter-Insurgency." In *Selected Subaltern Studies,* ed. Ranajit Guha and Gayatri Chakravorty Spivak, 45–88. Oxford: Oxford University Press.

Hamnett, Brian R. 1971. *Politics and Trade in Southern Mexico, 1750–1821.* Cambridge: Cambridge University Press.

Hanke, Lewis. 1949. *The Spanish Struggle for Justice in the Conquest of America.* Philadelphia: University of Pennsylvania Press.

Hanks, William. 1987. "Discourse Genres in a Theory of Practice." *American Ethnologist* 14 (4): 668–92.

Harvey, H.R. 1984. "Aspects of Land Tenure in Ancient Mexico." In *Explorations in Ethnohistory: Indians of Central Mexico in the Sixteenth Century,* eds. H.R. Harvey and Hanns J. Prem, 83–102. Albuquerque: University of New Mexico Press.

———. 1986a. "Household and Family Structure in Early Colonial Tepetlaoztoc: An Analysis of the Códice de Santa María Asunción." *Estudios de Cultura Nahuatl* 18: 275–94.

———. 1986b. "Techialoyan Codices: Seventeenth-Century Indian Land Titles in Central Mexico." In *Supplement to the Handbook of Middle American Indians,* gen. ed., Victoria R. Bricker; vol. 4, *Epigraphy,* ed. Ronald Spores, 153–64. Austin: University of Texas Press.

———, ed. 1991. *Land and Politics in the Valley of Mexico: A Two Thousand Year Perspective.* Albuquerque: University of New Mexico Press.

Harvey, H. R., and Hanns J. Prem, eds. 1984. *Explorations in Ethnohistory: Indians of Central Mexico in the Sixteenth Century.* Albuquerque: University of New Mexico Press.

Haskett, Robert S. 1985. "A Social History of Indian Town Government in the Colonial Cuernavaca Jurisdiction, Mexico." Ph.D. diss., Department of History, University of California, Los Angeles.

———. 1987. "Indian Town Government in Colonial Cuernavaca." *Hispanic American Historical Review* 67: 203–31.

———. 1991a. *Indigenous Rulers: An Ethnohistory of Town Government in Colonial Cuernavaca.* Albuquerque: University of New Mexico Press.

———. 1991b. "Our Suffering with the Taxco Tribute: Involuntary Mine Labor and Indigenous Society in Central New Spain." *Hispanic American Historical Review* 71 (3): 447–75.

———. 1996. "Paper Shields: The Ideology of Coats of Arms in Colonial Mexican Primordial Titles." *Ethnohistory* 43 (1): 99–126.

————. 1997. "Activist or Adulteress? The Life and Struggle of Doña Josefa María of Tepoztlan." In *Indian Women of Early Mexico,* ed. Susan Schroeder, Stephanie Wood, and Robert Haskett, 145–63. Norman: University of Oklahoma Press.

Hassig, Ross. 1985. *Trade, Tribute, and Transportation: The Sixteenth-Century Political Economy of the Valley of Mexico.* Norman: University of Oklahoma Press.

Hermann Lejarazu, Manuel Alvaro. 1994. "Glifos toponímicos en los codices mixtecos (region del Valle de Nochixtlan)." Thesis, Universidad Nacional Autónoma de México.

Hernández, fray Benito. 1567, 1568. *Doctrina en lengua misteca.* Mexico City: Pedro Ocharte.

Herrera, Robinson. 1997. "The People of Santiago: Early Colonial Guatemala, 1538–1587." Ph.D. diss. Department of History, University of California, Los Angeles.

Herrera y Tordesillas, Antonio de. 1934–57. *Historia general de los hechos de los castellanos en las islas y tierra firme del mar océano.* 17 vols. Madrid: Tipografía de Archives, Academia de la Historia.

Hicks, Frederick. 1976. "Mayeque y calpuleque en el sistema de clases del México antiguo." In *Estratificación social en la Mesoamérica prehispánica,* ed. Pedro Carrasco and Johanna Broda, 67–87. Mexico City: Centro de Investigaciones Superiores, Instituto Nacional de Antropología e Historia.

————. 1984. "Rotational Labor and Urban Development in Prehispanic Tetzcoco." In *Explorations in Ethnohistory: Indians of Central Mexico in the Sixteenth Century,* ed. H. R. Harvey and Hanns J. Prem, 147–74. Albuquerque: University of New Mexico Press.

Hill, Jane H., and Kenneth C. Hill. 1986. *Speaking Mexicano: Dynamics of Syncretic Language in Central Mexico.* Tucson: University of Arizona Press.

Hill, Robert M. 1987. *The Pirir Papers and Other Colonial Period Cakchiquel-Maya Testamentos.* Vanderbilt University Publications in Anthropology, no. 37. Nashville: Vanderbilt University.

————. 1991. *Colonial Cakchiquels: Highland Maya Adaptations to Spanish Rule, 1600–1700.* Orlando: Harcourt Brace Jovanovich.

Hill, Robert M., and John Monaghan. 1987. *Continuities in Highland Maya Social Organization: Ethnohistory in Sacapulas, Guatemala.* With a foreword by Victoria Bricker. Philadelphia: University of Pennsylvania Press.

Hills, Robert A. 1990. "A Syntactic Sketch of Ayutla Mixtec." In *Studies in the Syntax of the Mixtecan Languages,* ed. C. Henry Bradley and Barbara E. Hollenbach, 2: 1–260. Dallas: Summer Institute of Linguistics and the University of Texas at Arlington.

Horn, Rebecca. 1997. *Postconquest Coyoacan: Nahua-Spanish Relations in Central Mexico, 1519–1650.* Stanford: Stanford University Press.

Jameson, Frederic. 1988. "Cognitive Mapping." In *Marxism and the Interpretation of Culture,* ed. Cary Nelson and Lawrence Grossberg, 347–57. Chicago: University of Illinois Press.

Jansen, Maarten E.R.G.N. 1982. *Huisi Tacu: Estudio interprativo de un libro mixteco antiguo: Codex Vindobonensis Mexicanus I.* 2 vols. Amsterdam: Centrum voor Studie en Documentatie van Latijns Amerika.

————. 1985. "Las lenguas divinas del México precolonial." *Boletín de estudios latinoamericanos y del caribe* 38:3–14.

————. 1992. "Mixtec Pictography: Conventions and Contents." In *Supplement to the Handbook of Middle American Indians,* gen. ed., Victoria R. Bricker; vol. 5, *Epigraphy,* ed. Victoria R. Bricker, 20–33. Austin: University of Texas Press.

————. 1994. *La Gran Familia de los reyes mixtecos: Libro explicativo de los códices llamados Egerton y Becker II.* Vienna: Akademische Druckund Verlagsanstalt; Madrid: Sociedad Estatal Quinto Centenario; and Mexico City: Fondo de Cultura Económica.

————. 1997. "Símbolos de poder en el México antiguo." *Anales del Museo de América,* 5: 73–102.

————. 1998. "El 'Rosario' de Taix y la literatura mixteca." *Acervos: Boletin de los archivos y bibliotecas de Oaxaca* 2 (April–September): 24–32.

Jansen, Maarten, and Reyes García, Luis, eds. 1997. *Códices, Caciques, and Comunidades.* Cuadernos de Historia Latinoamerica, no. 5. Netherlands: Asociación de Historiadores Latinoamericanistas Europeos.

Jiménez Moreno, Wigberto, ed. 1962. *Vocabulario en lengua Mixteca por fray Francisco de Alvarado.* Reproducción facsimilar con un estudio de Wigberto Jiménez Moreno. Mexico City: Instituto Nacional Indigenista e Instituto Nacional de Antropología e Historia.

Jiménez Moreno, Wigberto, and Salvador Mateos Higuera, eds. 1940. *Códice de Yanhuitlán.* Edición en facsimile con un estudio preliminar. Mexico City: Instituto Nacional de Antropología e Historia, Museo Nacional.

Johnson, Audrey F. 1988. "A Syntactic Sketch of Jamiltepec Mixtec." In *Studies in the Syntax of the Mixtecan Languages,* ed. C. Henry Bradley and Barbara Hollenbach, 1: 11–150. Dallas: Summer Institute of Linguistics and the University of Texas at Arlington.

Josserand, J. Kathryn. 1983. "Mixtec Dialect History: Proto-Mixtec and Modern Mixtec Text." Ph.D. diss., Department of Anthropology, Tulane University.

Josserand, J. Kathryn, Maarten Jansen, and María de los Ángeles Romero Frizzi. 1984. "Mixtec Dialectology: Inferences from Linguistics and Ethnohistory." In *Essays in Otomanguean Culture History,* ed. Kathryn Josserand, Marcus Winter, and Nicholas Hopkins, 141–63. Vanderbilt University Publications in Anthropology, no. 31. Nashville: Vanderbilt University.

Josserand, J. Kathryn, Marcus Winter, and Nicholas Hopkins, eds. 1984. *Essays in Otomanguean Culture History.* Vanderbilt University Publications in Anthropology, no. 31. Nashville: Vanderbilt University.

Kanter, Deborah Ellen. 1995. "Native Female Land Tenure and Its Decline in Mexico, 1750–1900." *Ethnohistory* 42 (4): 607–16.

Karttunen, Frances. 1982. "Nahuatl Literacy." In *The Inca and Aztec States,* ed. George A. Collier, Renato I. Rosaldo, and John D. Wirth, 395–417. New York: Academic Press.

———. 1983. *An Analytical Dictionary of Nahuatl.* Austin: University of Texas Press.

———. 1985. *Nahuatl and Maya in Contact with Spanish.* Texas Linguistic Forum, 26. Austin: Department of Linguistics, University of Texas.

Karttunen, Frances, and James Lockhart. 1976. *Nahuatl in the Middle Years: Language Contact Phenomena in Texts of the Colonial Period.* University of California Publications in Linguistics, 85. Berkeley and Los Angeles: University of California Press.

———. 1978. "Textos en náhuatl del siglo XVIII: Un documento de Amecameca, 1746." *Estudios de Cultura Náhuatl* 13:153–75.

———. 1980. "La estructura de la poesía náhuatl vista por sus variantes." *Estudios de Cultura Náhuatl* 14: 15–65.

———, eds. 1987. *The Art of Nahuatl Speech: The Bancroft Dialogues.* Los Angeles: UCLA Latin American Center Publications.

Kellogg, Susan. 1995. *Law and the Transformation of Aztec Culture, 1500–1700.* Norman: University of Oklahoma Press.

———. 1997. "From Parallel and Equivalent to Separate but Unequal: Tenochca Mexica Women, 1500–1700." In *Indian Women of Early Mexico,* ed. Susan Schroeder, Stephanie Wood, and Robert Haskett, 123–243. Norman: University of Oklahoma Press.

Kellogg, Susan, and Matthew Restall, eds. 1998. *Dead Giveaways: Indigenous Testaments of Colonial Mesoamerica and the Andes.* Salt Lake City: University of Utah Press.

Key, Harold, and Mary Ritchie de Key. 1953. *Vocabulario mejicano de la Sierra de Zacapoaxtla, Puebla.* Mexico City: Instituto Lingüístico de Verano.

Kicza, John Edward. 1983. *Colonial Entrepreneurs, Families, and Business in Bourbon Mexico City.* Albuquerque: University of New Mexico Press.

King, Mark. 1988. "Mixtec Political Ideology: Historical Metaphors and the Poetics of Political Symbolism." Ph.D. diss., Department of Anthropology, University of Michigan.

———. 1990. "Poetics and Metaphor in Mixtec Writing." *Ancient Mesoamerica* 1: 141–51.

———. 1994. "Hearing the Echoes of Verbal Art in Mixtec Writing." In *Writing without Words: Alternative Literacies in Mesoamerica and the Andes,* ed. Elizabeth Boone and Walter Mignolo, 102–36. Durham, N.C.: Duke University Press.

Kiracofe, James B. 1995. "Architectural Fusion and Indigenous Ideology in Early Colonial Teposcolula: The Casa de la Cacica: A Building at the Edge of Oblivion." *Anales de Instituto de Investigaciones Estéticas* 66: 45–84.

Kirchhoff, Paul, Lina Odena Güemes, and Luis Reyes García, eds. 1976. *Historia Tolteca Chichimeca.* Mexico City: Instituto Nacional de Antropología e Historia.

Klein, Cecelia. 1980. "Who Was Tlaloc?" *Journal of Latin American Lore* 6 (2): 155–204.

Kubler, George. 1948. "Mexican Architecture of the Sixteenth Century." 2 vols. New Haven: Yale University Press.

———. 1962. *The Art and Architecture of Ancient America.* Baltimore: Penguin Books.

Kuiper, Albertha, and William R. Merrifield. 1975. "Diuxi Mixtec Verbs of Motion and Arrival." *International Journal of American Linguistics* 41 (1): 32–45.

Kuiper, Albertha, and Joy Oram. 1991. "A Syntactic Sketch of Diuxi-Tilantongo Mixtec." In *Studies in the Syntax of the Mixtecan Languages,* ed. C. Henry Bradley and Barbara E. Hollenbach, 3: 179–408. Dallas: Summer Institute of Linguistics and the University of Texas at Arlington.

Lastra, Yolanda. 1986a. "Centro vs. periferia." In *Las áreas dialectales del náhuatl moderno,* 84–87. Mexico City: Universidad Nacional Autónoma de México.

————. 1986b. "¿Hay áreas dialectales?" In *Las áreas dialectales del náhuatl moderno,* 189–233. Mexico City: Universidad Nacional Autónoma de México.

Le Goff, Jacques. 1992. *History and Memory.* Translated by Steven Rendall and Elizabeth Claman. New York: Columbia University Press.

León, Nicolás, ed. 1933. *Códice Sierra: Traducción al español de su texto náhuatl y explicación de sus pinturas jeroglíficas.* Mexico City: Museo Nacional de Antropología.

————. 1992. *The Aztec Image of Self and Society: An Introduction to Nahua Culture.* Edited by J. Jorge Klor de Alva. Salt Lake City: University of Utah Press.

Leibsohn, Dana. 1994. "Primers for Memory: Cartographic Histories and Nahua Identity." In *Writing without Words: Alternative Literacies in Mesoamerica and the Andes,* ed. Elizabeth Hill Boone and Walter D. Mignolo, 161–87. Durham and London: Duke University Press.

————. 1996. "Colony and Cartography: Shifting Signs on Indigenous Maps of New Spain." In *Reframing the Renaissance: Visual Culture in Europe and Latin America, 1450–1650,* ed. Claire Farago, 264–81. New Haven: Yale University Press.

León-Portilla, Miguel. 1969. *Pre-Columbian Literatures of Mexico.* Norman: University of Oklahoma Press.

Lind, Michael. 1979. *Postclassic and Early Colonial Mixtec Houses in the Nochixtlan Valley, Oaxaca.* Vanderbilt University Publications in Anthropology, no. 23. Nashville: Vanderbilt University.

Lockhart, James. 1968. *Spanish Peru, 1532–1560: A Colonial Society.* Madison: University of Wisconsin Press.

————. 1981. "Toward Assessing the Phoneticity of Older Nahuatl Texts." *Texas Linguistics Forum* 18: 151–69.

————. 1982. "Views of Corporate Self and History in Some Valley of Mexico Towns: Late Seventeenth and Eighteenth Centuries." In *The Inca and Aztec States, 1400–1800,* ed. George A. Collier, Renato I. Rosaldo, and John D. Wirth, 367–93. New York: Academic Press.

————. 1991. *Nahuas and Spaniards: Postconquest Central Mexican History and Philology.* Stanford and Los Angeles: Stanford University Press and UCLA Latin American Center Publications.

————. 1992. *The Nahuas after the Conquest: A Social and Cultural History of the Indians of Central Mexico, Sixteenth through Eighteenth Centuries.* Stanford: Stanford University Press.

————. 1998. "Three Experiences of Culture Contact: Nahua, Maya, and Quechua." In *Native Traditions in the Postconquest World,* ed. Elizabeth Hill Boone and Tom Cummins, 31–53. Washington, D.C.: Dumbarton Oaks Research Library and Collection.

————. 1999. *Of Things of the Indies: Essays Old and New in Early Latin American History.* Stanford: Stanford University Press.

Lockhart, James, Frances Berdan, and Arthur Anderson. 1986. *The Tlaxcalan Actas: A Compendium of the Records of the Cabildo of Tlaxcala (1545–1627).* Salt Lake City: University of Utah Press.

Lockhart, James, and Stuart B. Schwartz. 1983. *Early Latin America: A History of Colonial Spanish America and Brazil.* Cambridge Latin American Series, 46. Cambridge: Cambridge University Press.

Longacre, Robert E. 1961. "Swadesh's Macro-Mixtecan Hypothesis." *International Journal of American Linguistics* 27 (1): 9–29.

López Austin, Alfredo. 1988. *The Human Body and Ideology: Concepts of the Ancient Nahua.* 2 Vols. Translated by Thelma Ortiz de Montellano and Bernard Ortiz de Montellano. Salt Lake City: University of Utah Press.

MacCormack, Sabine. 1991. *Religion in the Andes: Vision and Imagination in Early Colonial Peru.* Stanford: Stanford University Press.

MacLeod, Murdo J., and Robert Wasserstrom, eds. 1983. *Spaniards and Indians in Southeastern Mesoamerica: Essays on the History of Ethnic Relations.* Lincoln: University of Nebraska Press.

Mannheim, Bruce. 1991. *The Language of the Inka since the European Invasion.* Austin: University of Texas Press.

Marcus, Joyce. 1992. *Mesoamerican Writing Systems: Propaganda, Myth, and History in Four Ancient Civilizations.* Princeton: Princeton University Press.

Marcus, Joyce, and Judith Francis Zeitlin, eds. 1994. *Caciques and Their People: A Volume in Honor of Ronald Spores.* Anthropological Papers, no. 89. Ann Arbor: Museum of Anthropology, University of Michigan.

Martin, Cheryl. 1985. *Rural Society in Colonial Morelos.* Albuquerque: University of New Mexico Press.

McCafferty, Sharisse D., and Geoffrey G. McCafferty. 1991. "Spinning and Weaving as Gender Identity in Post-Classic Mexico." In *Textile Traditions of Mesoamerica and the Andes: An Anthology,* ed. Margot Schevill, Janet Berlo, and Edward B. Dwyer, 19–44. New York: Garland Publishing.

Megged, Amos. 1996. *Exporting the Catholic Reformation: Local Religion in Early-Colonial Mexico.* Leiden: E. J. Brill.

Merrifield, William R., and Betty J. Stoudt. 1967. "Molinos Mixtec Clause Structure." *Linguistics* 32: 58–78.

Mignolo, Walter. 1995. *The Darker Side of the Renaissance: Literacy, Territoriality, and Colonization.* Ann Arbor: University of Michigan Press.

Miller, Arthur G. 1991. "Transformations of Time and Space: Oaxaca, Mexico, circa 1500–1700." In *Images of Memory: On Remembering and Representation,* ed. Susanne Küchler and Walter Melion, 141–75. Washington: Smithsonian Institution Press.

Miller, Mary, and Karl Taube. 1993. *The Gods and Symbols of Ancient Mexico and the Maya: An Illustrated Dictionary of Mesoamerican Religion.* London: Thames and Hudson.

Mills, Kenneth. 1997. *Idolatry and Its Enemies: Colonial Andean Religion and Extirpation, 1640–1750.* Princeton: Princeton University Press.

Mitchell, W. J. T. 1986. *Iconology: Image, Text, and Ideology.* Chicago: University of Chicago.

———.1994. *Picture Theory: Essays on Verbal and Visual Representation.* Chicago: University of Chicago.

Molina, Alonso de. [1571] 1977. *Vocabulario en lengua castellana y mexicana y mexicana y castellana.* Mexico City: Editorial Porrúa.

Monaghan, John. 1987. "'We Are People Who Eat Tortillas': Household and Community in the Mixteca." Ph.D. diss., Department of Anthropology, University of Pennsylvania.

———. 1990a. "Performance and the Structure of the Mixtec Codices." *Ancient Mesoamerica* 1: 133–40.

———. 1990b. "Reciprocity, Redistribution, and the Transaction of Value in the Mesoamerican Fiesta." *American Ethnologist* 17 (4): 758–774.

———. 1990c. "Sacrifice, Death, and the Origins of Agriculture in the Codex Vienna." *American Antiquity* 55 (3): 559–69.

———. 1994. "Irrigation and Ecological Complementarity in Mixtec Cacicazgos." In *Caciques and Their People,* ed. Joyce Marcus and Francis Zeitlin, 143–61. Ann Arbor: Museum of Anthropology, University of Michigan.

———. 1995. *The Covenants of Earth and Rain: Exchange, Sacrifice, and Revelation in Mixtec Sociality.* Norman: University of Oklahoma Press.

———. 1997. "Mixtec Caciques in the Nineteenth and Twentieth Centuries." In *Códices, Caciques, and Comunidades,* ed. Maarten Jansen and Luis Reyes García, 265–81. Netherlands: Asociación de Historiadores Latinoamericanistas Europeos.

Moser, Christopher. 1977. *Ñuiñe Writing and Iconography of the Mixteca Baja.* Vanderbilt University Publications in Anthropology, no. 19. Nashville: Vanderbilt University.

Mullen, Robert James. 1975. *Dominican Architecture in Sixteenth-Century Oaxaca.* Tempe: Center for Latin American Studies, Arizona State University.

Mundy, Barbara E. 1996. *The Mapping of New Spain: Indigenous Cartography and the Maps of the Relaciones Geográficas.* Chicago: University of Chicago Press.

Munro, Pamela, and Felipe Lopez. 1999. *Di'csyonaary X:tèè'n Dìì'zh Sah Sann Lu'uc* (San Lucas Quiaviní Zapotec Dictionary/Diccionario Zapoteco de San Lucas Quiaviní). Los Angeles: UCLA Chicano Studies Research Center.

Nash, June. 1978. "The Aztecs and the Ideology of Male Dominance." *Signs: Journal of Women in Culture and Society* 4 (2): 349–62.

———. 1980. "Aztec Women: The Transition from Status to Class in Empire and Colony." In *Women and Colonization: Anthropological Perspectives,* ed. Mona Etienne and Eleanor Leacock, 134–47. New York: Praeger Publishers.

Nash, Manning. 1989. *The Cauldron of Ethnicity in the Modern World.* Chicago: University of Chicago Press.

Nebrija, Antonio de. 1926. *Gramática de la lengua castellana.* Edited by I. González Llubera. London: Oxford University Press.

Nelson, Cary, and Grossberg, Lawrence, eds. 1988. *Marxism and the Interpretation of Culture.* Chicago: University of Illinois Press.

Nicholson, H. B. 1960. "The Mixteca-Puebla Concept in Mesoamerican Archaeology: A Re-examination." In *Men and Cultures: Selected Papers from the Fifth International Congress of Anthropological and Ethnological Sciences,* ed. Anthony F. Wallace, 612–17. Philadelphia: University of Pennsylvania Press.

———. 1961. "The Use of the Term 'Mixtec' in Mesoamerican Archaeology." *American Antiquity* 26 (3): 431–33.

————. 1966. "The Problem of the Provenience of the Members of the 'Codex Borgia Group': A Summary." In *Summa antropología en homenaje a Roberto J. Weitlaner*, 145–58. Mexico City: Instituto Nacional de Antropología e Historia.

————. 1973. "Phoneticism in the Central Mexican Writing System." In *Mesoamerican Writing Systems*, ed. Elizabeth P. Benson, 1–46. Washington, D.C.: Dumbarton Oaks.

————. 1978. "The Deity 9 Wind 'Ehecatl-Quetzalcoatl' in the Mixteca Pictorials." *Journal of Latin American Lore* 4 (1): 61–92.

Nutini, Hugo. 1988. *Todos Santos in Rural Tlaxcala: A Syncretic, Expressive, and Symbolic Analysis of the Cult of the Dead*. Princeton: Princeton University Press.

Nutini, Hugo G., Pedro Carrasco, and James M. Taggart, eds. 1976. *Essays on Mexican Kinship*. Pittsburgh: University of Pittsburgh Press.

Nuttall, Zelia. 1903. *The Book of the Life of the Ancient Mexicans Containing an Account of Their Rites and Superstitions*. [*Codex Magliabechiano*]. Reproduced in facsimile with introduction, translation, and commentary. Berkeley and Los Angeles: University of California Press.

Offner, Jerome. 1983. *Law and Politics in Aztec Texcoco*. Cambridge: Cambridge University Press.

Olmos, fray Andrés de. 1990. *Tratado de hechicerías y sortilegios*. Con introducción por Georges Baudot. Mexico City: Universidad Nacional Autónoma de México.

Oudijk, Michel. 2000. Historiography of the Benizaa: The Postclassic and Early Colonial Periods (1000–1600 A.D.). Leiden: CNWS Publications.

Paddock, John, ed. 1966. *Ancient Oaxaca: Discoveries in Mexican Archaeology and History*. Stanford: Stanford University Press.

Parmenter, Ross. 1982. *Four Lienzos from the Coixtlahuaca Valley*. Washington, D.C.: Dumbarton Oaks, Trustees for Harvard University.

Parodi, Claudia. 1995. *Orígines del español americano*. Vol. 1. *Reconstrucción de la pronunciación*. Mexico City: Universidad Nacional Autónoma de México.

Pastor, Rodolfo. 1987. *Campesinos y reformas: La mixteca, 1700–1856*. Mexico City: El Colegio de México.

Patch, Robert W. 1993. *Maya and Spaniard in Yucatan, 1648–1812*. Stanford: Stanford University Press.

Peñafiel, Antonio. 1900. *Lienzo de Zacatepec*. Mexico City: Oficina Tipográfica de la Secretarias de Fomento.

Pensinger, Brenda J. 1974. *Diccionario Mixteco del Este de Jamiltepec, pueblo de Chayuco*. Mexico City: Instituto Lingüístico de Verano.

Perry, Mary Elizabeth, and Anne J. Cruz, eds. 1991. *Cultural Encounters: The Impact of the Inquisition in Spain and the New World*. Berkeley and Los Angeles: University of California Press.

Peterson, Jeanette Favrot. 1993. *The Paradise Garden Murals of Malinalco: Utopia and Empire in Sixteenth-Century Mexico*. Austin: University of Texas Press.

Pike, Kenneth L. 1944. "Analysis of a Mixteco Text." *International Journal of American Linguistics* 10: 113–38.

————. 1945a. "Mock Spanish of a Mixteco Indian." *International Journal of American Linguistics* 11: 219–24.

————. 1945b. "Tone Puns in Mixteco." *International Journal of American Linguistics* 11: 129–39.

————. 1946. "Another Mixteco Tone Pun." *International Journal of American Linguistics* 12: 22–24.

————. 1947a. *Phonemics: A Technique for Reducing Languages to Writing*. Ann Arbor: University of Michigan Press.

————. 1947b. "A Text Involving Inadequate Spanish of Mixteco Indians." *International Journal of American Linguistics* 13: 251–57.

————. 1949. "A Problem in Morphology-Syntax Division." *Acta Linguistica* 5: 125–38.

————. 1975. *On Describing Languages*. Publications in Tagmemics, 2. Brussels: Peter DeRidder Press.

Pike, Kenneth L., and Evelyn G. Pike. 1982. *Grammatical Analysis*. Summer Institute of Linguistics Publications, 53. Arlington: Summer Institute of Linguistics and the University of Texas at Arlington.

Pohl, John M. D. 1984. "The Earth Lords: Politics and Symbolism of the Mixtec Codices." Ph.D. diss., Department of Archaeology, University of California, Los Angeles.

————. 1994a. "Mexican Codices, Maps, and Lienzos as Social Contracts." In *Writing without Words: Alternative Literacies in Mesoamerica and the Andes*, ed. Elizabeth Boone and Walter Mignolo, 137–60. Durham: Duke University Press.

————. 1994b. *The Politics of Symbolism in the Mixtec Codices*. Vanderbilt University Publications in Anthropology, no 46. Nashville: Vanderbilt University.

————. 1994c. "Weaving and Gift Exchange in the Mixtec Codices." In *Cloth and Curing: Continuity and Change in Oaxaca*, ed. Grace Johnson and Douglas Sharon, 3–13. San Diego: San Diego Museum of Man.

————. 1994d. "Notebook for the Mixtec Pictographic Writing Workshop at Texas: Codex Zouche-Nuttall." Unpublished manuscript.

————. 1995. "Notebook for the Mixtec Pictographic Writing Workshop at Texas: Codex Vindobonensis." Unpublished manuscript.

————. 1996. "Notebook for the Mixtec Pictographic Writing Workshop at Texas: Codex Bodley." Unpublished manuscript.

————. 1997. "Notebook for the Aztec-Mixtec Pictographic Writing Workshop at Texas: Codex Borgia." Unpublished manuscript.

————. 1998. "Themes of Drunkenness, Violence, and Factionalism in Tlaxcalan Altar Paintings." *RES: Anthropology and Aesthetics* 33:184–207.

————. 1999. "The Lintel Paintings of Mitla and the Function of the Mitla Palaces." In *Mesoamerican Architecture as a Cultural Symbol*, ed. Jeff Karl Kowalski, 177–97. New York: Oxford University Press.

Pohl, John M. D., and Bruce E. Byland. 1996. "The Identification of the Xipe Bundle—Red and White Bundle Place Sign in the Mixtec Codices." *Journal of Latin American Lore* 19: 3–29.

Pohl, John M. D., and Laura R. Stiver. 1997. "Religion, Economy, and Factionalism in Mixtec Boundary Zones." In *Códices y documentos sobre México: Segundo simposio,* ed. Salvador Rueda Smithers, Constanza Vega Sosa, and Rodrigo Martínez Baracs, 1: 205–32. Mexico City: Instituto Nacional de Antropología e Historia.

Polanyi, Karl. 1944. *The Great Transformation.* New York: Farrar and Rinehart.

Poole, Stafford. 1995. *Our Lady of Guadalupe: The Origins and Sources of a Mexican National Symbol, 1571–1797.* Tucson: University of Arizona Press.

Prem, Hanns J. 1984. "Early Spanish Colonization and Indians in the Valley of Atlixco." In *Explorations in Ethnohistory: Indians of Central Mexico in the Sixteenth Century,* eds. H.R. Harvey and Hanns J. Prem, 205–228. Albuquerque: University of New Mexico Press.

Quiñones Keber, Eloise, ed. 1995. *Codex Telleriano-Remensis: Ritual, Divination, and History in a Pictorial Aztec Manuscript.* Facsimile with commentary by Eloise Quiñones Keber and foreword by Emmanuel Le Roy Ladurie. Austin: University of Texas Press.

Ramírez, Susan Elizabeth. 1996. *The World Upside Down: Cross Cultural Contact and Conflict in Sixteenth-Century Peru.* Stanford: Stanford University Press.

Ravicz, Robert S. 1965. *Organización social de los mixtecos.* Colección de Antropología Social, 5. Mexico City: Instituto Nacional Indígenista.

Redfield, Robert 1941. *The Folk Culture of Yucatan.* Chicago: University of Chicago Press.

————. 1960. *The Little Community and Peasant Society and Culture.* Chicago: University of Chicago Press.

Restall, Matthew. 1995. *Life and Death in a Maya Community: The Ixil Testaments of the 1760s.* Lancaster, Calif.: Labyrinthos Press.

————. 1997. *The Maya World: Yucatec Culture and Society, 1550–1850.* Stanford: Stanford University Press.

————. 1998. *Maya Conquistador.* Boston: Beacon Press.

Rex, John. 1986. *Race and Ethnicity.* Philadelphia: Open University Press.

Reyes, fray Antonio de los. [1593] 1976. *Arte en lengua mixteca.* Vanderbilt University Publications in Anthropology, no. 14. Nashville: Vanderbilt University.

Reyes García, Luis. 1977. *Cuauhtinchan del siglo XII al XVI: Formación y desarrollo histórico de un señorío prehispánico.* Wiesbaden: Franz Steiner Verlag.

Ricard, Robert. [1933] 1966. *The Spiritual Conquest of Mexico: An Essay on the Apostolate and the Evangelizing Methods of the Mendicant Orders in New Spain, 1523–72.* Translated by Lesley Byrd Simpson. Berkeley and Los Angeles: University of California Press.

Rincón-Mautner, Carlos. 1994. "A Reconstruction of the History of San Miguel Tulancingo, Coixtlahuaca, Mexico, from Indigenous Painted Sources." *Texas Notes on Precolumbian Art, Writing, and Culture* 64 (February): 1–18.

————. 1995. "The Ñuiñe Codex from the Colossal Natural Bridge on the Ndaxagua: An Early Pictographic Text from the Coixtlahuaca Basin." *Institute of Maya Studies Journal* 1 (2): 39–66.

————. 1996a. "The 1580 Plan Topographique de Santa Maria Ixcatlan, Oaxaca: A Description and Summary." *Latin American Indian Literatures Journal* 12 (1): 43–66.

————. 1996b. "The Notes and Sketch of Lienzo Seler I or Mapa de Santa Maria Ixcatlan, Oaxaca, Mexico: A Description and Commentary." *Latin American Indian Literatures Journal* 12 (2): 146–77.

————. 1999. "Man and the Environment in the Coixtlahuaca Basin of Northwestern Oaxaca, Mexico: Two Thousand Years of Historical Ecology." Ph.D. diss., Department of Geography, University of Texas at Austin.

Robertson, Donald. 1959. *Mexican Manuscript Painting of the Early Colonial Period: The Metropolitan Schools.* New Haven: Yale University Press.

———. 1966. "The Mixtec Religious Manuscripts." In *Ancient Oaxaca,* ed. John Paddock, 298–312. Stanford: Stanford University Press.

———. 1972. "The Pinturas (Maps) of the Relaciones Geográficas, with a Catalog." In *Handbook of Middle American Indians,* gen. ed., Robert Wauchope; vol. 12, *Guide to Ethnohistorical Sources,* pt. 1, ed. Howard F. Cline, 243–78. Austin: University of Texas Press.

———. 1975. "Techialoyan Manuscripts and Paintings with a Catalog." In *Handbook of Middle American Indians,* gen. ed., Robert Wauchope; vol. 14, *Guide to Ethnohistorical Sources,* pt. 3, ed. Howard F. Cline et al., 253–80. Austin: University of Texas Press.

Robicsek, Francis. 1975. *A Study in Maya Art and History: The Mat Symbol.* New York: Museum of the American Indian Heye Foundation.

Romero Frizzi, María de los Ángeles, ed. 1986. *Lecturas históricas de Oaxaca: epoca colonial.* Mexico City: Instituto Nacional de Antropología e Historia.

———. 1990. *Economía y vida de los españoles en la Mixteca Alta: 1519–1720.* Mexico City: Instituto Nacional de Antropología e Historia.

———. 1996. *El sol y la cruz: Los pueblos indios de Oaxaca colonial.* Mexico City: Centro de Investigaciones y Estudios Superiores en Antropología Social.

Romero Frizzi, María de los Ángeles, and Ronald Spores. 1976. *Indice del Archivo Juzgado de Teposcolula, Oaxaca: Epoca Colonial.* Instituto Nacional de Antropología e Historia, Dirección de Centros Regionales, Cuadernos de los Centros, 32. Oaxaca: Centro Regional de Oaxaca.

Romney, A. Kimball, and Romaine Romney. 1966. *The Mixtecans of Juxtlahuaca, Mexico.* Six Cultures Series, 4. New York: Wiley & Sons.

Rothenberg, Diane. 1980. "The Mothers of the Nation: Seneca Resistance to Quaker Intervention." In *Women and Colonization: Anthropological Perspectives,* ed. Mona Etienne and Eleanor Leacock, 63–87. New York: Praeger Publishers.

Rounds, J. 1982. "Dynastic Succession and the Centralization of Power in Tenochtitlan." In *The Inca and Aztec States, 1400–1800,* eds. George A. Collier et al., 63–89. New York: Academic Press.

Roys, Ralph L., ed. and trans. 1933. *The Book of Chilam Balam of Chumayel.* Washington, D.C.: Carnegie Institution of Washington.

———. 1939. *The Titles of Ebtun.* Washington, D.C.: Carnegie Institution of Washington.

———. 1972. *The Indian Background of Colonial Yucatan.* Norman: University of Oklahoma Press.

Ruiz de Alarcón, Hernando. 1984. *Treatise on the Heathen Superstitions That Today Live among the Indians Native to This New Spain, 1629.* Translated and edited by J. Richard Andrews and Ross Hassig. Norman: University of Oklahoma Press.

Sabean, David Warren. 1990. *Property, Production, and Family in Neckarhausen, 1700–1870.* Cambridge: Cambridge University Press.

Sahagún, fray Bernardino de. 1950–82. *The Florentine Codex: General History of the Things of New Spain.* Translated by Arthur J. O. Anderson and Charles E. Dibble. 13 pts. Salt Lake City and Santa Fe: University of Utah Press and School of American Research.

———. 1997. *The Primeros memoriales.* Paleography of Nahuatl Text and English translation by Thelma Sullivan. Completed and revised, with additions, by H. B. Nicholson, Arthur J. O. Anderson, Charles E. Dibble, Eloise Quiñones Keber, and Wayne Ruwet. Norman: University of Oklahoma Press.

Sahlins, Marshall. 1985. *Islands of History.* Chicago: University of Chicago Press.

Sandstrom, Alan. 1991. *Corn Is Our Blood: Culture and Ethnic Identity in a Contemporary Aztec Indian Village.* Norman: University of Oklahoma Press.

Scholes, France V., and Ralph L. Roys. [1948] 1968. *The Maya Chontal Indians of Acalan-Tixchel.* Norman: University of Oklahoma Press.

Schroeder, Susan. 1991. *Chimalpahin and the Kingdoms of Chalco.* Tucson: University of Arizona Press.

Schroeder, Susan, Stephanie Wood and Robert Haskett, eds. 1997. *Indian Women in Early Mexico.* Norman: University of Oklahoma Press.

Scott, Joan W. 1985. "Gender: A Useful Category of Historical Analysis." In *Gender and the Politics of History,* ed. Joan W. Scott, 28–50. New York: Columbia University Press.

———. 1988. *Gender and the Politics of History.* New York: Columbia University Press.

Seler, Eduard. 1904. "Wall Paintings at Mitla." *Smithsonian Institute, Bureau of American Ethnology Bulletin* 28: 243–324.

Sell, Barry D. 1993. "Friars, Nahuas, and Books: Language and Expression in Colonial Nahuatl Publications." Ph.D. diss., Department of History, University of California, Los Angeles.

Sepúlveda y Herrera, María Teresa. 1999. *Procesos por idolatría al cacique, gobernadores y sacerdotes de Yanhuitlan, 1544–1546.* Mexico City: Instituto Nacional de Antropología e Historia.

Shields, Jäna K. 1988. "A Syntactic Sketch of Silacayoapan Mixtec." In *Studies in the Syntax of the Mixtecan Languages,* ed. C. Henry Bradley and Barbara E. Hollenbach, 1: 305–449. Dallas: Summer Institute of Linguistics and the University of Texas at Arlington.

Shoemaker, Nancy. 1991. "The Rise or Fall of Iroquois Women." *Journal of Women's History* 2 (Winter): 39–57.

———, ed. 1995. *Negotiators of Change: Historical Perspectives on Native American Women.* New York: Routledge.

Silverblatt, Irene. 1987. *Moon, Sun, and Witches: Gender Ideologies and Class in Inca and Colonial Peru.* Princeton: Princeton University Press.

Simeón, Rémi. 1988. *Diccionario de la lengua náhuatl o mexicana.* Translated from French by Josefina Oliva de Coll. Mexico City: Siglo Veintiuno Editores.

Small, Priscilla C. 1988. "A Syntactic Sketch of Coatzospan Mixtec." In *Studies in the Syntax of the Mixtecan Languages,* ed. C. Henry Bradley and Barbara E. Hollenbach, 2: 261–479. Dallas: Summer Institute of Linguistics and the University of Texas at Arlington.

Smith, Mary Elizabeth. 1963. "The Codex Columbino: A Document of the South Coast of Oaxaca." *Tlalocan* 4 (3): 276–88.

———. 1966. "Las glosas del Códice Columbino/The Glosses of Codex Columbino." In *Interpretación del Códice Columbino/Interpretation of the Codex Columbino.* Mexico City: Sociedad Mexicana de Antropología.

———. 1973a. *Picture Writing from Ancient Southern Mexico: Mixtec Place Signs and Maps.* Norman: University of Oklahoma Press.

———. 1973b. "The Relationship between Mixtec Manuscript Painting and the Mixtec Language: A Study of Some Personal Names in the Codices Muro and Sánchez Solís." In *Mesoamerican Writing Systems,* ed. Elizabeth P. Benson, 47–98. Washington, D.C.: Dumbarton Oaks.

———. 1979. "Codex Becker II: A Manuscript from the Mixteca Baja." *Archiv für Völkerkunde,* 33:29–43.

———. 1983a. "Codex Selden: A Manuscript from the Valley of Nochixtlan?" In *The Cloud People,* ed. Kent V. Flannery and Joyce Marcus, 248–55. New York: Academic Press.

———. 1983b. "The Earliest Mixtec Dynastic Records." In *The Cloud People,* ed. Kent V. Flannery and Joyce Marcus, 213. New York: Academic Press.

———. 1983c. "The Mixtec Writing System." In *The Cloud People,* ed. Kent V. Flannery and Joyce Marcus, 238–45. New York: Academic Press.

———. 1983d. "Regional Points of View in the Mixtec Codices." In *The Cloud People,* ed. Kent V. Flannery and Joyce Marcus, 260–66. New York: Academic Press.

Smith, Mary Elizabeth, and Ross Parmenter, eds. 1991. *Codex Tulane.* New Orleans: Middle American Research Institute, Tulane University.

Smith, Raymond T. 1996. *The Matrifocal Family: Power, Pluralism, and Politics.* New York: Routledge.

Sousa, Lisa. 1997. "Women and Crime in Colonial Oaxaca: Evidence of Complementary Gender Roles in Mixtec and Zapotec Societies." In *Indian Women of Early Mexico,* ed. Susan Schroeder, Stephanie Wood, and Robert Haskett, 199–214. Norman: University of Oklahoma Press.

———. 1998. "Women in Native Societies and Cultures of Colonial Mexico." Ph.D. diss., Department of History, University of California, Los Angeles.

———. n.d. "The Devil and Deviance in Native Criminal Narratives from Early Mexico." *Americas.*

Sousa, Lisa, Stafford Poole, C. M., and James Lockhart, eds. 1998. *The Story of Guadalupe: Luis Laso de la Vega's Huei tlamahuiçoltica of 1649.* Nahuatl Studies Series, 5. Stanford and Los Angeles: Stanford University Press and UCLA Latin American Center Publications.

Sousa, Lisa, and Kevin Terraciano. n.d. "The 'Original Conquest' of Oaxaca: Nahua and Mixtec Accounts of the Spanish Conquest." *Ethnohistory.*

Spivak, Gayatri Chakravorty. 1988. "Can the Subaltern Speak?" In *Marxism and the Interpretation of Culture,* ed. C. Nelson and L. Grossberg, 271–313. London: Basingstoke.

Spores, Ronald. 1964. "The Genealogy of Tlazultepec: A Sixteenth-Century Mixtec Manuscript." *Southwestern Journal of Anthropology* 20 (1): 15–31.

———. 1965. "The Zapotec and Mixtec at Spanish Contact." In *Handbook of Middle American Indians,* gen. ed., Robert Wauchope; vol. 3, *Archaeology of Southern Mesoamerica,* pt. 2, ed. Gordon R. Willey, 962–87. Austin: University of Texas Press.

———. 1967. *Mixtec Kings and Their People.* Norman: University of Oklahoma Press.

———. 1969. "Settlement, Farming, Technology, and Environment in the Nochixtlan Valley." *Science* 166: 557–69.

———. 1976. "La estratificación social en la antigua sociedad mixteca." In *Estratificación social en la Mesoamérica prehispánica,* ed. Pedro Carrasco and Johanna Broda, 207–20. Mexico City: Centro de Investigaciones Superiores, Instituto Nacional de Antropología e Historia.

———. 1983a. "The Mixteca Alta at the End of Las Flores." In *The Cloud People,* ed. Kent V. Flannery and Joyce Marcus, 207. New York: Academic Press.

———. 1983b. "The Origin and Evolution of the Mixtec System of Social Stratification." In *The Cloud People,* ed. Kent V. Flannery and Joyce Marcus, 227–38. New York: Academic Press.

———. 1983c. "Postclassic Mixtec Kingdoms: Ethnohistoric and Archaeological Evidence." In *The Cloud People,* ed. Kent V. Flannery and Joyce Marcus, 255–60. New York: Academic Press.

———. 1983d. "Postclassic Settlement Patterns in the Nochixtlán Valley." In *The Cloud People,* ed. Kent V. Flannery and Joyce Marcus, 246–48. New York: Academic Press.

———. 1983e. "Yucuñudahui." In *The Cloud People,* ed. Kent V. Flannery and Joyce Marcus, 155–58. New York: Academic Press.

———. 1984. *The Mixtecs in Ancient and Colonial Times.* Norman: University of Oklahoma Press.

———. 1997. "Mixteca Cacicas." In *Indian Women of Early Mexico,* ed. Susan Schroeder, Stephanie Wood, and Robert Haskett, 185–97. Norman: University of Oklahoma Press.

Spores, Ronald, and Kent V. Flannery. 1983. "Sixteenth-Century Kinship and Social Organization." In *The Cloud People,* ed. Kent V. Flannery and Joyce Marcus, 339–42. New York: Academic Press.

Spores, Ronald, and Ross Hassig. 1984. *Five Centuries of Law and Politics in Central Mexico.* Vanderbilt University Publications in Anthropology, no. 30. Nashville: Vanderbilt University.

Spores, Ronald, and Miguel Saldaña. 1975. *Documentos para la historia del estado de Oaxaca: Indice del Ramo del Archivo General de la Nación, México.* Vanderbilt University Publications in Anthropology, no. 13. Nashville: Vanderbilt University.

Stern, Steve J. 1982. *Peru's Indian Peoples and the Challenge of the Spanish Conquest: Huamanga to 1640.* Madison: University of Wisconsin Press.

———. 1995. *The Secret History of Gender: Women, Men, and Power in Late Colonial Mexico.* Chapel Hill: University of North Carolina Press.

Sullivan, Thelma. 1997. *Primeros Memoriales by Fray Bernardino de Sahagún: Paleography of Nahuatl Text and English Translation.* Completed and revised, with additions, by H. B. Nicholson, Arthur J. O. Anderson, Charles E. Dibble, Eloise Quiñones Keber, and Wayne Ruwet. Norman: University of Oklahoma Press in cooperation with the Patrimonio Nacional and the Real Academia de la Historia, Madrid.

Swanton, Michael, and Bas van Doesburg. 1996. "Some Observations on the Lost Lienzo de Santa Maria Ixcatlan (Lienzo Seler I)." *Baessler-Archiv* 44: 359–77.

Sweet, David G., and Gary B. Nash, eds. 1981. *Struggle and Survival in Colonial America.* Berkeley and Los Angeles: University of California Press.

Taylor, William B. 1972. *Landlord and Peasant in Colonial Oaxaca.* Stanford: Stanford University Press.

———. 1979. *Drinking, Homicide, and Rebellion in Colonial Mexican Villages.* Stanford: Stanford University Press.

———. 1987. "The Virgin of Guadalupe in New Spain: An Inquiry into the Social History of Marian Devotion." *American Ethnologist: The Journal of the American Ethnological Society* 14:1.

———. 1996. *Magistrates of the Sacred: Priests and Parishioners in Eighteenth-Century Mexico.* Stanford: Stanford University Press.

Taylor, William B., and Franklin Pease, eds. 1994. *Violence, Resistance, and Survival in the Americas: Native Americans and the Legacy of Conquest.* Washington, D.C.: Smithsonian Institution Press.

Terraciano, Kevin. 1994. "Ñudzahui History: Mixtec Writing and Culture in Colonial Oaxaca." Ph.D. diss., Department of History, University of California, Los Angeles.

———. 1998. "Crime and Culture in Colonial Mexico: The Case of the Mixtec Murder Note." *Ethnohistory* 45 (4): 709–45.

———. 2000. "The Colonial Mixtec Community." *Hispanic American Historical Review* 80 (1): 1–42.

Terraciano, Kevin, and Matthew Restall. 1992. "Indigenous Writing and Literacy in Colonial Mexico." *UCLA Historical Journal* 12: 8–28.

Terraciano, Kevin, and Lisa Sousa. 1992. "The 'Original Conquest' of Oaxaca: Mixtec and Nahua History and Myth." *UCLA Historical Journal* 12: 29–90.

Thompson, Philip C. 1978. "Tekanto in the Eighteenth Century." Ph.D. diss., Department of Anthropology, Tulane University.

Tonkin, Elizabeth, Maryon McDonald, and Malcolm Chapman, eds. 1989. *History and Ethnicity*. London: Routledge.

Troike, Nancy. 1978. "Fundamental Changes in the Interpretation of the Mixtec Codices." *American Antiquity* 43: 553–68.

———. 1982. "The Interpretation of Postures and Gestures in the Mixtec Codices." In *The Art and Iconography of Late Post-Classic Central Mexico,* ed. Elizabeth Boone, 175–206. Washington, D.C.: Dumbarton Oaks.

Vaillant, George C. 1944. *The Aztecs of Mexico: Origin, Rise, and Fall of the Aztec Nation*. Garden City, N.Y.: Doubleday, Doran.

Van Doesburg, G. Bas. 1996. "La herencia del Señor Tico: Fundación y desintegración de un cacicazgo cuicateco." Ph.D. diss., University of Leiden.

Villanueva, Margaret A. 1985. "From Calpixqui to Corregidor: Appropriation of Women's Cotton Textile Production in Early Colonial Mexico." *Latin American Perspectives* 44 (1): 17–40.

Watanabe, John. 1992. *Maya Saints and Souls in a Changing World*. Austin: University of Texas Press.

Williams, Barbara J. 1991. "The Lands and Political Organization of a Rural Tlaxilacalli in Tepetlaoztoc, c. A.D. 1540." In *Land and Politics in the Valley of Mexico: A Two Thousand Year Perspective,* ed. H.R. Harvey, 187–208. Albuquerque: University of New Mexico Press.

Wolf, Eric. 1957. "Closed Corporate Peasant Communities in Mesoamerica and Central Java." *Southwestern Journal of Anthropology* 13 (1): 1–18.

———. 1962. *Sons of the Shaking Earth*. Chicago: University of Chicago Press.

Wood, Stephanie. 1984. "Corporate Adjustments in Colonial Mexican Indian Towns: Toluca Region, 1550–1810." Ph.D. diss., Department of History, University of California, Los Angeles.

———. 1989. "Don Diego García de Mendoza Moctezuma: A Techialoyan Mastermind?" *Estudios de Cultura Nahuatl* 19: 245–68.

———. 1991. "The Cosmic Conquest: Late Colonial Views of the Sword and Cross in Central Mexican Títulos." *Ethnohistory* 38 (2): 176–95.

———. 1997. "Matters of Life at Death: Nahuatl Testaments of Rural Women, 1589–1801." In *Indian Women of Early Mexico,* ed. Susan Schroeder, Staphanie Wood, and Robert Haskett, 165–82. Norman: University of Oklahoma Press.

Young, Robert. 1995. *Colonial Desire: Hybridity in Theory, Culture, and Race*. London: Routledge.

Zorita, Doctor Alonso de. 1941. *Breve y sumaria relación de los señores . . . de la Nueva España*. In *Nueva colección de documentos para la historia de México,* ed. Joaquin García Icazbalceta. Mexico City: Editorial Chávez Hayhoe.

Zylstra, Carol F. 1991. "A Syntactic Sketch of Alacatlatzala Mixtec." In *Studies in the Syntax of the Mixtecan Languages,* ed. C. Henry Bradley and Barbara E. Hollenbach, 3: 1–177. Dallas: Summer Institute of Linguistics and the University of Texas Arlington.

INDEX

Page numbers followed by f and t refer to figures and tables, respectively. References to notes are cited as page number followed by n and note number.

Abrego, fray Gerónimo de, 267

Acaquisapa, community terminology in, 105

Acatlan (Yucuyuchi): cultural mixing in, 167; languages spoken in, 47t

Achiutla (Ñundecu): civil unrest in, 294; as colonial center, 119; commissioning of art, 236; languages spoken in, 47t, 71; nonindigenous residents of, 340; religion in, 264; tribute in, 240, 241

Acuña, Cristóbal de (mestizo of Yolotepec), 340

Africans: native opinion of, 340; in Ñudzahui language, 334; as slaves, 225, 227, 236, 238, 250, 272, 339–40, 358

Agriculture: crops, 212, 225, 234, 235, 445n49; division of labor in, 203; and land tenure system, 204; and livestock, 235 (see also Livestock); methods and productivity, 198, 209, 212; and population loss, 211–12, 224, 234, 235, 362–63; and Spanish market, 226; and trade, 234. See also Maguey; Maize; Wheat

Aguilar, Felipe de (resident Spaniard of Yanhuitlan), 340

Agustín, don Juan (cacique of Huaxuapa), 56, 114, 115, 141, 154, 209

Albino, Diego de (noble of Tututepec), 268, 281

Alcaldes: role of, 192–93; salary of, 185

Alcaldes mayores: appropriation of goods by, 241; role of, 413n122; and trade, 246

Alonso, don (cacique of Mistepec), 263, 281

Alphabetic writing in Nahuatl language: earliest examples of, 429n2; introduction of, 82, 88, 405n2; and literacy, 415n162

Alphabetic writing in Ñudzahui language, 48–54, 49f, 53f; contemporary revival attempts, 365; corpus, 346; correspondence, 53–54; criminal records, 51; and decline of pictorial writing, 57–63; introduction of, 15, 48, 54–56, 322, 357, 405n2; and literacy, 54–56; records and notarial documents, 48–52, 49f; wills, 50–51

Altepetl, 24, 103, 105, 205, 208, 329, 348, 349, 350

Alvarado, as name, 154

Alvarado, fray Francisco de, 8, 68, 69–70, 69–71, 75, 76, 77, 82–83

Alvarado, Pedro de, 2

Ambivalence: in early colonial writings, 27, 38; toward Christianity, 278–79; as general indigenous response to colonial rule, 361

Amoltepec (Yucunama): disease in, 362; etymology of name, 24; exposure to European influence, 31; map of, 24, 26f, 287–89

Andean region, gender relations in, 353; comparisons with, 478n22; caciques of, 478n31

Anders, Ferdinand, 7

Anderson, Arthur J. O., 7

Andrada, Agustín de (regidor of Ayusi), 385, 393

Andrada, doña Mariana de (noble of Tlaxiaco), 341

Andrada, Fernando de (cacique of Tamasulapa), 45, 183–84

Andrada y Montezuma, don Fernando (noble of Tlaxiaco), 340–41

Andrés, Francisco (of Cochoapa), 181

Angels, native conceptions of, 302

Ángeles, doña Manuela de los (cacica of Igualapa), 184

497

Made in the USA
Middletown, DE
20 January 2020